American Presidents

Fourth Edition

American Presidents

Fourth Edition

Volume 1
The American Presidency
George Washington—Woodrow Wilson

Editor, First Edition
Frank N. Magill

Editors, Third Edition
Robert P. Watson
Florida Atlantic University

Richard Yon
University of Florida

Editor, Fourth Edition
Robert P. Watson
Lynn University

SALEM PRESS
A Division of EBSCO Information Services, Inc.
Ipswich, Massachusetts

GREY HOUSE PUBLISHING

Publisher's Cataloging-In-Publication Data
(Prepared by The Donohue Group, Inc.)

American presidents. — Fourth edition / editor, Robert P. Watson, Lynn University.

  2 volumes : illustrations, maps ; cm

  "Editor, First Edition, Frank N. Magill ; editors, Third Edition, Robert P. Watson,
    Florida Atlantic University [and] Richard Yon, University of Florida."
  Includes bibliographical references and index.
  Contents: Volume 1. The American Presidency, George Washington–Woodrow Wilson
    — volume 2. Warren G. Harding–Barack Obama, Index.
  ISBN: 978-1-61925-940-9 (set)
  ISBN: 978-1-68217-081-6 (v.1)
  ISBN: 978-1-68217-082-3 (v.2)

  1. Presidents — United States — Biography. 2. Presidents — United States — History.
    3. United States — Politics and government. I. Watson, Robert P., 1962-

E176.1 .A6563 2015
973.09/9 B

First Printing
Printed in the United States of America

Contents

Volume 1

Alphabetical List

Publisher's Note

In the two and a quarter centuries since its inception, the U.S. presidency has survived controversy, scandal, resignation, civil war, and assassination. Every individual who has assumed the title of president has left a mark, for good or ill, on American history. *American Presidents* examines the strengths and weaknesses, the successes and failures of each chief executive.

Designed as a companion to Salem's *American First Ladies, Third Edition* (2015), *American Presidents, Fourth Edition* is an illustrated two-volume reference work that presents essays on the life and politics of each U.S. president, in chronological order, from George Washington to Barack Obama. In describing the personal and political events surrounding each president, it offers readers a comprehensive view of U.S. history. An "Alphabetical List of Presidents" at the beginning of Volume 1 also helps readers find a particular entry. Volume 1 opens with an informative Introduction by Editor Robert P. Watson, which examines the office of president, its duties, and the characteristics of its holders. It is followed by an essay "The American Presidency: An Overview," which provides a chronology of the presidency by administration.

New to This Edition

The *Fourth Edition* of *American Presidents* builds significantly on the value of the previous one, published in 2006:

- Barack Obama added
- Recent presidents revisited and updated
- Every essay reviewed for accuracy and currency
- Bibliography updated to include the latest scholarship
- All appendices revisited and updated
- Dozens of new photographs and illustrations
- New online access

Essay Organization

Each essay begins with ready reference information: name; administration number and years (*e.g.* "7th President, 1829-1837"); birth and death dates and locations; political party; vice presidents; and cabinet members by department. The text that follows offers a comprehensive portrait of the life and times of the president, from birth through political rise, election, term of office, defeat or retirement, and death. Topical subheadings help guide readers through the material. The legacy of each administration is measured against the yardstick of U.S. history, and the evolution of the office and the country can be traced clearly. Every essay ends with a current, annotated bibliography and is signed by the author.

Every entry features boxed sidebars on First Ladies and vice presidents. Other sidebars reproduce primary documents — such as Thomas Jefferson's *Declaration of Independence*, the *Monroe Doctrine*, and Abraham Lincoln's *Emancipation Proclamation* — and many entries offer excerpts from famous presidential speeches and other notable quotations, adding valuable historical context. More than two hundred photographs complement the text.

Appendices

A dozen appendices at the end of Volume 2 provide vital reference information in an accessible format. The U.S. Constitution is reprinted to provide the full context of the duties and limitations of the office of president. "The Law of Presidential Succession" outlines procedures following a president's death or removal. A "Time Line" chronicles important events by administration. "Presidential Election Returns, 1789-2012" includes all major candidates, with their political parties and tallies for both electoral and popular votes. Three different lists name the vice presidents, cabinet members, and First Ladies for every administration. Another appendix provides information about the location and holdings of presidential libraries. "Executive Departments and Offices" includes descriptions and contact information, and "Museums, Historic Sites, and Websites" provides visitor information for places that are on display or open to the public and lists Web sites of interest to presidential scholars and the general public alike. A "Glossary" of political terms, programs, and campaign slogans offers concise definitions. Finally, the general "Bibliography" lists books about the presidency, campaigns and elections, First Ladies and presidential families, presidential quotations, the White House, and each president to hold office. The comprehensive subject index allows easy access to the wealth of information found in these essays.

Acknowledgments

Salem Press thanks the scholars who contributed essays and appendices to *American Presidents*; their names and affiliations are listed in the front matter to Volume 1. We also thank Professor Robert P. Watson of Lynn University, Editor of this and previous editions, and Professor Richard Yon of the University of Florida, Editor of previous editions.

Introduction

The Pageantry of the Presidency

To many people, the presidency is the most visible part of the U.S. government, especially internationally, where the president is both the public face of the United States and the country's official representative abroad. While this has, to a degree, always been the case—George Washington was, after all, known as "the Father of His Country"—the intensive coverage by the media in recent years has only further increased the office's visibility and importance.

Stories about the president are found on the front page of the nation's newspapers and lead the evening news broadcast. The White House press corps treats the public to the most mundane and private details about the First Family: Ronald Reagan liked jelly beans; George and Barbara Bush's dog was named Millie; Bill Clinton's daughter, Chelsea, graduated from Stanford; and Gerald Ford apparently had a tendency to trip or fall at the most public and inopportune times. In short, the centrality of the presidency in the American political system is beyond question.

To scholars and students alike, the presidency is also an important academic field of study in both political science and U.S. history. Yet, ironically, it is one of the least understood and least studied components of American government. Although scores of good biographies exist on presidents throughout history, the formal study of the institution is a relatively recent scholarly endeavor.

One of the challenges in studying the presidency is that, as of 2015, only forty-three men had held the office. (Barack Obama was the forty-third man to hold the office, but he was the forty-fourth president because Grover Cleveland served two nonconsecutive terms as the twenty-second and twenty-fourth president.) Among the few who have occupied the office, there has been much variation in their approach to the presidency as well as in their experiences in office and the skill with which they discharged their duties. This fact makes it difficult to draw conclusions about the nature of the institution based on so few examples.

At the same time, however, the office has seen little diversity and variation in the types of individuals elected. For instance, as of this writing all the presidents have been male. The United States has yet to elect a female president, even though a few dozen nations around the world have been led by women in the modern era. This list includes some of the United States' closest allies, such as Canada, Great Britain, and Israel. Women have pursued the American presidency beginning with Victoria Woodhull in 1872, but none has come close to winning. When Geraldine Ferraro was selected by Walter Mondale to join the Democratic ticket in 1984, she became the first female vice presidential nominee of a major political party in history.

Likewise, all the presidents have been white except Barack Obama. Only a handful of other African-Americans have even campaigned for the office—Jesse Jackson, Alan Keyes, Al Sharpton—and until the 2016 presidential campaign, no major campaign had been launched by an Hispanic, Asian, or other ethnic candidate. The 2016 campaign, however, saw two prominent Latinos—Marco Rubio and Ted Cruz, both Cuban-American—in the race. Every president has come from northern European ancestry, and the United States has yet to elect a president from southern or eastern European lineage. The only exception is Barack Obama, whose father was from Africa. All but five of the presidents have been of British descent (English, Irish, Welsh, Scottish): Both Roosevelts and Martin Van Buren were Dutch, Herbert Hoover was Swiss, and Dwight Eisenhower was German. Nonetheless, it must be said that in an increasingly pluralistic society, it is not a matter of *if*, but rather *when*, the country elects its first female president.

Many presidents also shared a common occupation and educational experience. The field of law is the most represented occupation of presidents before their political careers, with only a few exceptions. Several presidents had military experience, and a few—George Washington, Andrew Jackson, William Henry Harrison, Zachary Taylor, Ulysses Grant, Dwight Eisenhower—were generals or career officers. Washington, Thomas Jefferson, and others such as Jimmy Carter earned their living by farming, while Woodrow Wilson was a professor and university president and Ronald Reagan was an actor. Most presidents were well educated, graduating from prestigious private colleges. Both George H. W. and George W. Bush as well as William Howard Taft graduated from Yale, while both Franklin and Teddy Roosevelt as well as John F. Kennedy and Barack Obama were Harvard graduates. But there are a few exceptions. The last president to not have a college degree was Harry Truman, and both George Washington and Abraham Lincoln received very little in the way of a formal education.

There are other similarities among the presidents worth noting. All but one of the commanders in chief were Protestant Christians (John F. Kennedy was Roman Catholic), and the lion's share of them were "mainline" denominations such as Episcopalian or Presbyterian. All but one president was married, the exception being lifelong bachelor James Buchanan, although Grover Cleveland married when he was already president. The only divorced president was Ronald Reagan, who had been married to actress Jane Wyman before his wedding to Nancy Davis, who would serve as First Lady.

Few presidents came from west of the Mississippi River, and many states have yet to produce a president. The earliest presidents hailed from Virginia and Massachusetts, and Ohio and New York have also produced several presidents. Physically, many of the presidents have been taller than average in height, and most have had blue or gray eyes.

So what does all this mean? The presidents are, in many ways, from a rather narrow cross section of American society, and this fact suggests something about the prevailing political preferences of the American public. Also, the United States has been served by some great presidents, men of distinction who left deep footprints on the office and nation. Among them are such presidents as Abraham Lincoln, Franklin Roosevelt, George Washington, Thomas Jefferson, Harry Truman, Teddy Roosevelt, and Andrew Jackson, all leaders rated by scholars as among the best to serve. So too have there been presidents who struggled with the challenges of the office. The experiences of Warren Harding, James Buchanan, Franklin Pierce, and Andrew Johnson were such that the office and the nation were fundamentally weaker after their presidencies than when they were inaugurated.

Founding

Another challenge that presidents have faced is crafting their approach to the office. Article II of the Constitution, which discusses the chief executive, is among the shortest, most vague components of the founding document. From its inception, the presidency was configured as a weak office with few formal powers. And this was not by accident but by design.

The political arrangement that governed the newly declared states during the revolutionary struggle did not take long to prove ineffectual. The Continental Congress was often unable to provide the political or financial support that General George Washington needed to wage war. Under the Articles of Confederation after independence, the lack of an executive branch, coupled with weak governorships, precluded the new nation from adequately addressing such pressing problems as the war, debt, trade, squabbles among states and between the central government and the state governments, the need for a uniform currency, and continued threats from abroad. Indeed, by 1786 it had become clear to many of the leaders of the new nation that change was necessary in order for the grand experiment in popular democracy to work. As such, on September 11, 1786, delegates from the states met in Annapolis, Maryland, to discuss various problems facing the government, most notably commerce and trade.

Many in attendance—most prominently Alexander Hamilton and James Madison—maintained that the problems facing the young government were such that a convention to revisit the design of the Articles was necessary. The convention in question (the Constitutional Convention) commenced in May of 1787 in Philadelphia, and the task of revising the Articles quickly gave way to the more ambitious project of drafting an entirely new system of government.

One of the issues generating the most debate among the Framers of the Constitution was the nature of the executive office. During the long summer of debate at Philadelphia's Constitution Hall, momentum gradually gathered for establishing an executive, increasing national powers, and creating a blended (federal) system whereby the task of governing would be shared by the federal and state gov-

ernments. The questions surrounding the executive included whether it should be assumed by one person or a council, whether it would be selected by the legislature or by some other means, what the length of the executive's term should be as well as whether to limit the number of terms that any person could serve, and how much power to grant to the executive. Hamilton and his Federalist supporters favored a stronger executive, citing the obvious problems created by the ineffectual Articles of Confederation. Yet, the antifederalists remained firm in their concern over a strong executive and preference for a weaker office. In the "Great Compromise" between the large and small states and among the Framers, the Federalists ultimately succeeded in designing an office to be held by one person who would serve for four years and without term limits. However, it was a constitutionally weak office by design.

The views of the Framers regarding the issues of an executive and the amount of power to grant him were to a large measure the result of two factors—the experience of the colonies as British subjects and the writings of European political philosophers. Regarding the former, Britain's King George III and most of the appointed governors had abused their powers and showed little concern for the general welfare of the colonials. As the first calls for an expanded role in governing were heard from the colonists, Britain unwisely responded by levying new taxes on popular goods and expanding the presence of soldiers in the colonies. This action led to the so-called Boston Tea Party and only further inflamed the fledgling movement for political rights and self-determination.

The Framers had justifiable concerns about tyranny by an executive. Accordingly, they devoted considerable attention to making sure that the executive's powers were neither excessive nor unchecked. The result was the creation of a weak executive in the formal sense, one whose powers were balanced with those of other branches of government. As such, the president had "limited powers," "divided powers," and "checked powers." For instance, the president is able to veto legislation, but the veto can be overridden by a two-thirds majority of both houses of Congress. The president has the power to appoint federal officers, but judicial, ambassadorial, and senior administrative appointees must be confirmed by the Senate. And, the president can make treaties, but they too are subject to Senate approval by a two-thirds concurrence. Although the language in Article II is often ambiguous, the phrase "The executive Power shall be vested in a President of the United States of America" has been used to establish many of the powers and general authority that the president now enjoys and needs in order to manage the executive branch of the national government.

Article II of the Constitution is purposely vague and brief, raising more questions than it provides answers. Debate over the nature and extent of the presidential powers listed in Article II depend on one's view of the Constitution. Indeed, for well over two hundred years presidents, members of Congress, the courts, and the public have wrestled with the matter of what the president can and cannot do. It is interesting to note that many of the situations defining the office historically are not based in constitutional decrees but rather were the result of precedents set by George Washington. So imposing was the first president's standing that his legacy continues to define the office that he helped forge with every action and inaction.

The language in the Constitution discussing the requirements for the office provides one of the few specific details about the presidency. Presidents must be thirty-five years of age, native-born citizens of the United States, and residents of the country for a period of fourteen consecutive years prior to taking the oath of office.

A Growing, Dynamic Office

The presidency is a dynamic institution. Although the presidency is rooted in the Constitution and many of the traditions and customs of the institution are carried over from president to president, it is at the same time certainly not the office today that was occupied by George Washington. Washington oversaw five federal agencies: the departments of war, state, and treasury (which was conceived as a congressional department); the attorney general; and the post office. He also managed a small staff and few federal employees, and he administered a budget of roughly $250,000. Today, the president's staff numbers in the thousands, the federal government's budget has long surpassed the trillion-dollar mark, the federal workforce numbers in the millions, and fifteen federal cabinet departments and scores of other agencies report to the chief executive.

In the words of the late presidential scholar Edward S. Corwin, the Constitution produces an "invitation to struggle." The balance of powers among the three branches creates an environment where conflict and compromise are inevitable results of the task of governing. The fact that the president must share power with Congress has meant that presidents have relied on their personalities to enhance their otherwise limited powers or to respond to crises of the day in a way that expands their powers.

A good example was Franklin D. Roosevelt, whose charisma and the momentous events of the Great Depression and World War II created an opportunity for him to win four presidential elections and fundamentally change the nature of the office. More recently, George W. Bush sought to expand presidential war powers through the use of military tribunals, the Patriot Act (which, among other things, expanded government's surveillance and arrest powers), and the detention of "enemy combatants" in order to fight the war on terrorism and did so within the backdrop of national security.

The personality of individual presidents

and factors such as national security and crises have contributed to the evolving role and power of the office. Recent presidents have recognized that real power in the office is neither formal nor constitutional in origin. Executive powers are too limited, divided, and checked by constitutional design. Rather, their power and ability to govern stem from influence, which is the by-product of their character, political skills, and ability to lead through their bully pulpit. In the words of the noted presidential scholar Richard Neustadt, the president must use the "power to persuade" in order to govern.

Many have even commented that charisma is a necessary ingredient for success in the White House, and polling has suggested that presidential character plays a role in the minds of voters. Clearly, much of the success enjoyed by Washington, Lincoln, and both Roosevelts, for example, can be attributed to the strength of character and attractiveness of their personalities. By the same measure, other presidents—most notably Richard Nixon—were plagued by shortcomings in their character.

The size, roles, and scope of the federal government have ballooned since 1789, when Washington was inaugurated. They have grown dramatically since 1933, when Franklin D. Roosevelt expanded in a revolutionary manner the function of government in order to address the Great Depression. Arguably, the first fundamental shift in and growth of the role and scope of the presidency occurred under FDR and is frequently referred to as the starting point for the "modern presidency," with the period from Washington leading up to the inauguration of the thirty-second president in 1933 known as the "traditional presidency."

Roosevelt entered the office with the government unable to respond to the high unemployment rate, widespread failure of businesses, and collapse of the banking and financial systems that had paralyzed the nation. With assistance from the Brownlow Commission, the organization of federal agencies was revamped. Through his record four terms in office, Roosevelt managed the economy, created Social Security and other social supports for citizens falling through the cracks of society, provided electricity to rural areas, and put the jobless to work on large public infrastructure projects. By the time of his death in 1945, the presidency's power had been greatly increased and its centrality in American life was established.

As the times have changed, so has the presidency. Factors such as the central role that the United States has played in international affairs since World War II and the growing technological and economic complexity of the country have contributed to the evolving nature of the office. One such development was the advent of the mass media, which began some years earlier at the turn of the century.

The presence of mass circulation newspapers, radio, television, and more recently satellite technology, cable television, the Internet, and twenty-four-hour news coverage have revolutionized the presidency. The effective use of the radio by FDR, for instance, allowed him to speak to the nation and, in so doing, bypass the usual legislative process and White House press corps. By taking his message directly to the people, FDR established an intimate rapport between the president and the public, one that would further strengthen the presidency and last to the present time. Presidents are now able to make direct appeals to the public, using the media to build support for themselves and their policy agenda. Coined by presidency scholar Samuel Kernell, this strategy of "going public" enables presidents to bypass Congress to a degree and move their proposals forward. Television would further add to the intimacy and connectedness of president and voters.

By the 1960's and 1970's, presidential power was seen as excessive and problematic. In the words of historian Arthur Schlesinger, Jr., an overextended, so-called imperial presidency emerged. Commentators have suggested that this phenomenon contributed to the Vietnam War, the Watergate scandal, and other negative actions by presidents. Gerald Ford and Jimmy Carter entered the presidency in the mid- and late 1970's attempting to heal the nation, return the office to a sense of normalcy, and renew respect for the institution.

But their efforts were apparently not enough. Starting in the 1960's, public frustration with, and even hostility toward, the office grew. The growing cynicism of the public coincided with increasing animosity between Congress and the president, antagonistic relations between the White House and the press corps, and divided government—whereby the presidency was in the hands of one party and Congress was controlled by the other party—which seemed to become the norm and resulted in policy gridlock. Not only were individual presidents challenged by these conditions, but public opinion polls revealed that public faith in the institution itself was eroding as well.

In the past few decades, the presidency has suffered from major foreign policy crises seemingly beyond the control of the sitting president, a series of foreign policy and political missteps, and scandals that were magnified by an adversarial press and an already weakened office: Watergate in the 1970's, Iran-Contra in the 1980's, the Monica Lewinsky scandal in the 1990's, the war in Iraq and the poor federal response to Hurricane Katrina's devastation in the first decade of the new century. Barack Obama faced an extraordinary array of international challenges including upheaval in Egypt, Libya, Syria, and Yemen, threats from China, Russia, and North Korea, and massive refugee movements from Central America and in the Middle East, and the effects of the crippling economic downturn just prior to his presidency.

Media commentators were quick to focus on Ronald Reagan's disconnected (even absent) style, George H. W. Bush's inability to connect with the public and articulate a vision for the country, Bill Clinton's lack of personal integrity, and George W. Bush's suspect intellectual abilities and arrogance to the point that these issues became defining traits of their presidencies and further eroded public confidence in the office.

Accordingly, the United States finds itself today in a position whereby some scholars and commentators note the near ungovernability of the office. Yet, it must be said that such problems are not new, and similar criticisms were directed at many of the presidents serving in the mid- and late nineteenth century. Others have noted some fundamental limitations inherent in the political system facing presidents. For instance, presidential scholar Michael Genovese has identified a "variety of built-in roadblocks" which make it difficult for presidents to lead, including a cynical public, the difficulty of making good on campaign promises, conflicting expectations of presidents, a hostile media, and the inherent constitutional weakness of the office.

Roles and Duties

The Constitution loosely discusses the fundamental duties of a president. Five basic roles can be traced to and are derived from the Constitution. The first is "chief of state." The United States (unlike Great Britain, for instance) does not have a monarch or separate head of state. As such, both executive and ceremonial roles are merged into one office, whereby the president functions as the symbolic head of state, visiting other nations, receiving dignitaries, and presiding over ceremonies and national events.

The Constitution is clear about the president's role as "Commander in Chief of the Army and Navy of the United States, and of the Militia of the several states, when called into the actual Service of the United States," although considerable debate remains over the role of the president and Congress in declaring a war and the extent of war powers.

A third role is that of "chief executive." The president is the head of the executive branch and oversees the numerous departments, agencies, and bureaus that compose the federal government. In this capacity, the president can appoint and remove federal administrative officers and can grant pardons and reprieves (a postponement of the execution of a court sentence).

The president also has the power to veto legislation, making him the "chief legislator." As such, the president fulfills an important component in the legislative process. While Congress is the legislative branch, the president often influences the legislative agenda through the State of the Union address and the development of the federal budget.

Finally, the president functions as "chief diplomat," making treaties, appointing the country's ambassadors, and recognizing nations. In this capacity, the president has come to dominate U.S. foreign policy.

As the nation and office have changed, so too have some of the basic roles and duties of the president. The president now functions as "party chief." Even though the United States is said to have a weak party system — or perhaps because of it — presidents are looked to by their political parties for leadership. The president often selects the national party chair, recruits candidates for office, and establishes the party's policy platform.

In the words of Franklin Roosevelt, the presidency is "preeminently a place for moral leadership." Acting as something of a "preacher in chief," the president appeals to what Abraham Lincoln called "the better angels of our nature" and is expected to set a moral example for the nation. Lincoln led by moral courage, and his shadow continues to loom large over the office.

Lastly, through the power of their personality and use of the media, presidents have a bully pulpit from which to speak to the country. In so doing, many presidents have served both symbolically and practically as advocates for U.S. products, culture, and achievements, boosting and promoting the United States at home and abroad. The president is expected to invigorate the national spirit in times of crisis and to champion all things American in the capacity of what can be described as a "cheerleader in chief." Certainly FDR's famous "fireside chats" — his radio addresses to a nation struggling through the Great Depression — soothed anxieties, calmed fears, and lifted hopes, as did George W. Bush's words — bullhorn in hand — from atop the rubble of the World Trade Center in New York City a few days after the tragic terrorist attacks on September 11, 2001.

Washington's Legacy

George Washington served as the country's first president from private mansions in New York City and later Philadelphia while the new nation's capital buildings and executive mansion were being constructed. Paralleling the institution that it houses, the White House has endured times of tragedy (it was burned by the British in 1814 during the War of 1812), has experienced great growth (it was enlarged under Theodore Roosevelt and other presidents), and has changed in response to the times (it was gutted and rebuilt under Harry Truman).

Washington, who played a prominent role in the building's planning and construction, did not live to see it completed, dying in December of 1799 almost one year before the mansion opened its doors to President John Adams. Washington and Adams would scarcely recognize the building — or the office — today.

At the dawn of the twenty-first century, few would doubt the centrality of the presidency in the American political system or world affairs. Although the presidency would be unrecognizable to Washington, his fingerprints remain on the office. The American president has emerged as a symbol of the nation internationally, the focal point of media coverage, and the most influential actor in the American drama.

Robert P. Watson, Consulting Editor

Contributors

Jeffrey S. Ashley
Eastern Illinois University

Wayne R. Austerman
*Staff Historian
USAF Space Command,
    Peterson AFB*

Jean Baker
Goucher College

Barbara C. Beattie
Independent Scholar

Robert A. Becker
Louisiana State University

Michael Les Benedict
Ohio State University

Kevin J. Bochynski
Independent Scholar

Mimi Lynette Bogard
National First Ladies' Library

Susan Roth Breitzer
University of Iowa

Mark T. Carleton
Louisiana State University

Robert Dewhirst
*Northwest Missouri State
    University*

Daniel Feller
Assistant Editor, The Papers
    of Andrew Jackson
University of Tennessee

James E. Fickle
Memphis State University

Robert Flatley
Kutztown University

Gaines M. Foster
Louisiana State University

Raymond Frey
Centenary College

William E. Gienapp
University of Wyoming

Sheldon Goldfarb
University of British Columbia

Lewis L. Gould
University of Texas at Austin

Hugh Davis Graham
*University of Maryland,
    Baltimore County*

Myra G. Gutin
Rider University

Ellis W. Hawley
University of Iowa

Sarah M. Hilbert
Independent Scholar

Joan Hoff-Wilson
Indiana University

Robert W. Johannsen
University of Illinois

Burton I. Kaufman
Kansas State University

Joyce P. Kaufman
Whittier College

Ralph Ketcham
Syracuse University

Richard S. Kirkendall
Iowa State University

Richard N. Kottman
Iowa State University

Richard B. Latner
*Newcomb College, Tulane
    University*

Bryan Le Beau
Creighton University

Anne C. Loveland
Louisiana State University

Richard Lowitt
Iowa State University

Robert McColley
*University of Illinois at
Urbana-Champaign*

Donald R. McCoy
University of Kansas

Robert S. McElvaine
Millsaps College

Dale C. Mayer
*Herbert Hoover Presidential
Library*

Daniel P. Murphy
Hanover College

David Murphy
American University

Burl Noggle
Louisiana State University

Allan Peskin
Cleveland State University

Barbara Bennett Peterson
*University of Hawaii, East-
West Center
Oregon State University*

Mary Jane Child Queen
National First Ladies' Library

George C. Rable
Anderson College

Randy Roberts
Sam Houston State University

Charles Royster
Louisiana State University

Robert A. Rutland
Editor in Chief, Papers of
James Madison
University of Virginia

Craig Schermer
National First Ladies' Library

Terry L. Seip
*University of Southern
California*

Dean M. Shapiro
University of New Orleans

R. Baird Shuman
*University of Illinois at
Urbana-Champaign*

Elizabeth Lorelei Thacker-
Estrada
Independent Scholar

Ann Toplovich
*Executive Director, Tennessee
Historical Society*

Gil Troy
McGill University

Robert P. Watson
Lynn University

Twyla R. Wells
Independent Scholar

William C. Widenor
*University of Illinois at
Urbana-Champaign*

Major L. Wilson
Memphis State University

Michael Witkoski
Independent Scholar

Lisa A. Wroble
Independent Scholar

Richard Yon
University of Florida

The American Presidency

An Overview

It was a formidable task to found the United States. Revolution and domestic turbulence gave way only slowly to an ordered and stable republic. From May 25 through September 17, 1787, fifty-five delegates met in Philadelphia to draft a constitution for a new nation. They had a number of difficult problems to resolve, most of them connected with the extent and distribution of powers in the federal government. A central concern was the office of chief executive: How much power was the president to have? What would be the relationship of the executive to the legislative and judicial branches? Perhaps most significant and far-reaching of all, how was the president to be chosen? The method on which the Founding Fathers finally agreed has served the nation for more than two hundred years, and the presidents elected by that method reflect the development of the United States.

The possibility of having the president elected by direct vote of the people was rejected. The delegates believed that popular elections would be an incentive to demagoguery on the part of potential candidates and factions among the electorate. In addition, the new nation was spread across the breadth of the continent, with travel slow and difficult; under such circumstances, it would be impossible to conduct a nationwide popular election that would not be subject to fraud or open to dispute.

A second possibility was to select the president by means of the various state legislatures, but again, practical difficulties were prohibitive. Would there be an electoral convention every four years? If the state legislatures convened in their separate capitals, how could they agree upon a candidate both known and accepted by a majority?

There was strong support for having the president elected by Congress, which was—at least in theory—the direct representative body of the people. This would give the general population the opportunity to participate in the election process yet would reduce the chance for emotionalism and mob rule. At the same time, this method would mean that the president was selected by the men with whom he would work most closely in governing the nation. Election by Congress, argued its supporters, would give the choice to the most qualified, most knowledgeable, and most concerned segment of the nation.

These very points were the ones raised by opponents to congressional elections. A president selected by the legislature would be dependent upon its members, seeking their favor before the decision and rewarding his supporters after it. As James Madison pointed out, there was agreement that the three branches of the national government would be independent and equal, their powers separate and distinct. If Congress elected the president, then inevitably the legislative and executive powers would be mingled.

The Electoral College

The convention turned to a compromise plan, one which allowed the people to retain a role in presidential elections but which built safeguards around the choice. The method was to have a group of electors, chosen by each state, to cast the actual votes for president. These electors were to be chosen in a manner deter-

1

mined by the individual legislatures. Each state was entitled to a number of electors equal to its representation in Congress. Once the electors were chosen, they would vote for president, and the person with the majority of votes from this electoral college would be named to office. The person with the second highest total would be vice president. Should no candidate receive a majority for president, then the House of Representatives, voting by states, would make the decision. In this way, the convention attempted to reconcile the varying interests of the small and large states.

This method was defended in *The Federalist* (number 68), probably by Alexander Hamilton, as having four points to recommend it. First, it did give the people a choice in selecting the president, even if this choice was indirect. Second, it reduced the possibility of corruption and bribery. Third, it removed the president from those persons who had put him into office, thus making favoritism and faction less likely. Finally, it ensured a capable, rather than merely popular, chief executive: "Talents for low intrigue, and the little arts of popularity, may alone suffice to elevate a man to the first honours of a single state; but it will require other talents, and a different kind of merit, to establish him in the esteem and confidence of the whole union."

Since the ratification of the Constitution, the electoral college has undergone several changes, some modifications the result of formal amendments, others from state legislative actions, and some from the evolutionary development of the American political system. In the election of 1796, for example, John Adams received the highest number of votes, and so was elected president; Thomas Jefferson, as the second-place candidate, assumed the office of vice president. Yet Adams and Jefferson were the leaders of rival parties; clearly such a situation was unacceptable. In succeeding elections party loyalty and discipline resolved this type of dilemma.

Party loyalty created its own difficulty in 1800, when all Republican (modern Democratic) electors cast their ballots for Jefferson and Aaron Burr. Their intention had been to elect Jefferson president and Burr vice president, but the ballots were not so marked, since the Constitution had no provision for the separate election of the vice president. The tie was decided by the House of Representatives after thirty-six ballots, and the troublesome issue was resolved by the Twelfth Amendment to the Constitution.

As the years passed, the states made changes in the manner in which electors were chosen. By 1836, all states but South Carolina had adopted some variety of the "general ticket" system, which gave the winner of a state's popular vote all of the state's electoral votes. This method continues to be used in modern elections.

There have been several criticisms of the electoral college: that it is outdated, that it is unnecessary, and that it can lead to the election of presidents who win enough large states to gain an electoral vote majority but who fall behind in the national popular vote. There have been elections in which the candidate who took a majority in the electoral college did not also have a majority of the popular vote: James K. Polk, Abraham Lincoln, Woodrow Wilson, and George W. Bush are four examples. Because this phenomenon is more likely to occur when third parties are involved (or, in the case of Lincoln, four contenders), it could be argued that the electoral vote system provides for a more objective measure of decisiveness than a simple count of the popular vote.

In any case, and with only relatively minor adjustments, the electoral college has remained intact for more than two centuries. Its presence has helped to shape the unique pattern and process of American presidential elections.

Washington and the Men of the Revolution

The first five presidents of the United States were of such distinction and accomplishment that they left a legacy of respect for the presidency which involves far more than its immense powers and responsibilities. From Washington through Monroe, these presidents set standards by which succeeding generations have measured chief executives. One of the aims of the Constitutional Convention had been to fashion a government that could remain beyond party politics and the dangers of faction; however, even the generation that had won the Revolution could not submerge the party instinct, which emerged during the first term of the first president.

Not that Washington approved of these forces; on the contrary, he consistently sought to forestall the dangers of faction. While he favored the views of Alexander Hamilton and the rapidly forming Federalist Party, Washington retained in his cabinet Thomas Jefferson and others of the emerging Democratic Republican (modern Democratic) Party. In politics as in war, Washington reached for coalition. His selection as president had been unanimous precisely because of that. Throughout the long and often difficult debate over the Constitution, all sides had tacitly agreed on one point: The first chief executive would be George Washington; there was simply no other figure so universally accepted, so completely trusted. Washington's shaping of the presidency began even before the position was created, and long before he assumed it; his impact was achieved not only through his own actions but through the collective belief and desires of his countrymen as well.

Although these beliefs and desires could find common ground in the person of Washington, their competing natures could not be reconciled within the office of the presidency. Party politics and personal rivalry were rapidly and permanently established. Within a few years of the establishment of the new republic, Federalists and Republicans were fighting for local and national offices, drawing up competing agendas, and carrying their battles into the very councils of the president. Washington, fifty-seven and in poor health when he first assumed office in 1789, had originally intended to serve but one term; the increasingly bitter struggle between Hamilton and Jefferson forced him to change his plans, for he recognized his unique position in keeping the new government stable. Once Washington was gone, the rivalries could not be stilled. Washington was the only presi-

dent elected by unanimous vote of the electoral college; in 1796, his successor, John Adams, only narrowly defeated Thomas Jefferson, 71 to 68. The brief national honeymoon was over.

Adams had an outstanding career in public service before becoming president; it did not save him from political attacks. In some ways, Adams drew these upon himself; he was a brilliant but prickly individual, strong in his belief in freedom but suspicious of too much liberty. Adams and the Federalist Party were mistaken in moving against the tide of Republican and Democratic sentiment: the Alien and Sedition Acts, for example, were a prime political blunder. Jefferson and the Democratic Republicans instead built a broad-based party reaching from the local to the national level, a solid structure that has made the modern Democratic Party the oldest continuous political party in the world. Its power was felt as early as the election of 1800, when Jefferson exploited a split between Adams and Hamilton to take the White House. Jefferson's reelection four years later was a landslide and marked the beginning of the end for the Federalists.

It is with Jefferson that one can truly gauge the caliber of the nation's early leaders. Washington, even to his contemporaries, was almost more than human, the embodiment of the national ideal. Jefferson, on the other hand, was clearly a man, but a man of extraordinary talent and diversity: statesman, legislator, naturalist, educator, politician, artist, architect, philosopher. He excelled in all these roles, and in that he was unique; he was not unique, however, among his contemporaries, in assaying these various pursuits. A striking difference between the earliest presidents and those who followed is precisely this: From Washington to Monroe, the men were well rounded and experienced in many fields, and the presidency was but one form of their public service.

For Jefferson, Madison, or Monroe, the most pressing issue, that of slavery, was still held in abeyance. Madison's administration was deeply troubled by the unpopular and largely unsuccessful War of 1812, but the sectional dis-

3

sension which led New England to talk of secession was seemingly forgotten with the election of James Monroe in 1816 and his reelection in 1820 with only one dissenting electoral college vote; the one vote against was cast so that no man might match Washington.

Yet, a look at Monroe's election reveals that the lingering days of revolutionary America were ending. The northern members of the Democratic Party were tired of domination by the Old Dominion. In the meetings of the party's congressional caucus, which then selected the nominee, there was a move to pick a candidate other than Monroe; it failed, but the caucus's lockhold on presidential nominations was seriously questioned. By the election of 1824, the power of the caucus to nominate would be severely weakened; by 1828, its choice would be ignored; and by 1832, the Democratic Party would hold its first national convention.

The Rise of Political Parties and the Coming of the Civil War

The selection of presidents from Monroe to Lincoln was determined by two factors: the rise of political parties and heightening tensions over slavery, which politicians sought to defuse by a series of increasingly desperate compromises. As political parties grew more dominant and professional and as conventions became the method of nominating candidates, there was a tendency to select the nominee most likely to win the election. The practical effect of this was that the least objectional man available was chosen, which frequently meant that the candidate not only had taken few controversial stands but also would be a weak president. Although the intent was to reduce tensions between North and South by avoiding the issue of slavery, the actual result was an escalation of the nation's drift toward conflict. In a sense— and with two notable exceptions—the elections from 1824 to 1860 represented the politics of presidential weakness.

The election of 1824 was a watershed in American political history. The Federalist Party had fallen apart, but the Democrats were in disarray: That year, they could not agree on a candidate, and four men waged a vicious campaign for the presidency. John Quincy Adams, son of former president John Adams and himself a distinguished public servant, was perhaps the most experienced and accomplished. His opponents included Henry Clay and other notables, but the most famous was Andrew Jackson, hero of the Battle of New Orleans. Jackson was the first people's candidate, a man who owed his support not to family or political connections but to his widespread popularity, especially in the South and the West.

This distinguished group promptly entered into a campaign in which personal attacks supplanted debate over public issues, and, when it was over, no one held a majority of electoral or popular votes, although Jackson had run ahead of the rest. The decision was left to the House of Representatives, which chose Adams; Henry Clay was named secretary of state. Jackson's supporters were quick to denounce this "corrupt bargain" and made it the main focus of the election of 1828. By then, Jacksonian forces had taken control of the Democratic Party and formed a majority in Congress. Having established firm discipline over the party organization, the Jackson Democrats conducted the first modern-style campaign, using popular election techniques such as songs, cartoons, symbols (hickory trees in honor of "Old Hickory," Jackson's nickname), mass meetings, and parades. The result was a 178-83 victory in the electoral college for Jackson; a trend had been set for American presidential campaigns.

Jackson was one of the two strong presidents between Monroe and Lincoln; he demonstrated this strength most notably in the stand he took with South Carolina in the nullification crisis of 1832. Had later presidents proved as firm, the drift to civil war might have been prevented, but few of the presidents who followed had Jackson's toughness. Martin Van Buren, his chosen successor, was a genius at party politics but hardly an inspiring national leader.

A new party, the Whigs, followed the lead of the Democrats by building their local base in preparation for an assault on the White House in 1840. They had a good issue—the economic crisis of 1837—and a popular candidate in William Henry Harrison, hero of the Indian wars, who stumped the country, making numerous appearances, and won the election.

Two traditional themes have determined American presidential elections: economic conditions at home and dangers abroad. In 1840, the Whigs had economics on their side; in 1844, the Democrats returned to power over the issue of annexing Texas. The Democrats favored annexation; the Whigs were opposed. In its stand, each party followed the sentiment of the region where its strength lay: Democrats, the South, which wanted new land for slave states; Whigs, the North, which opposed the spread of the slavery system.

Two particular aspects of the 1844 election made it notable. The Democrats nominated James K. Polk, the first "dark horse" candidate. Polk had a distinguished career, including Speaker of the House, but in 1844 he was only hoping for the vice presidential nod. When the Democrats could not choose one of their frontrunners, he was the convention's compromise choice. The second aspect was the impact of a third party. Harrison had died shortly after assuming office, but the Whigs had not nominated his successor, John Tyler, choosing Henry Clay instead. Tyler formed a new party to support his independent candidacy, and his efforts may have cost Clay enough votes to swing the electoral count in favor of Polk. Ever since, this spoiler effect has been the traditional role of third parties in American presidential politics.

Polk was the second strong president between Monroe and Lincoln, and he successfully conducted the Mexican War, adding enormous territory to the nation. Although the Whigs had been unenthusiastic about the war, they used it to win the White House in 1848, nominating General Zachary Taylor. It was neither the first nor the last time that success in combat would pave the way to the presidency. With a popular figure leading the ticket, the Whigs were able to dodge the increasingly divisive issue of slavery.

The Democrats, on the other hand, were deeply split by the problem, and their division ensured the election of Taylor.

In the election of 1852, both Whigs and Democrats mirrored the nation, as they tried to find one more compromise to hold the sections together, while in each party increasingly strong factions pressed for an ultimate resolution. Seeking to restrain their firebrands, both parties nominated middle-of-the-road candidates. After fifty-three ballots, the Whigs selected Winfield Scott, another Mexican War general, while the Democrats went with Franklin Pierce of New Hampshire, chosen on the forty-ninth ballot. Pierce was a "doughface," a Northerner who sympathized with the South; he owed his victory to strong support in the South and residual Democratic strength in the North. This was the last election in which the fiction of compromise could be maintained.

The year 1856 was the first time an elected president was denied renomination by his party. Pierce had proven unable to reconcile the two sections of the Democratic Party, much less the nation, so the Democrats turned to James Buchanan, who had served in the House, in the Senate, and as secretary of state. In spite of his impressive record, Buchanan was a weak and indecisive man. His opponent was no Whig, but the first nominee of the new Republican Party, John Charles Frémont.

For a new party, the Republicans made an outstanding effort; significantly, they presented a more coherent political philosophy than the Democrats, especially on the issue of slavery. While the Republicans were by no means total abolitionists, they were unified in their opposition to slavery, particularly its spread into new territories. By contrast, the Democratic Party was unable to confront, much less resolve, the issue. By 1860, the party had exhausted its moral and political reserve; like the nation, the Democrats had finally run out of compromises and evasions over slavery.

The Democrats met that year in Charleston, South Carolina. Their strongest candidate was Stephen A. Douglas, best known for his re-

5

cent series of debates with Abraham Lincoln. Southern Democrats feared that he was not sufficiently committed to the protection and expansion of slavery; they deadlocked the convention. The Democrats left Charleston without a candidate and by the end of the summer had divided into three factions, each with its own nominee. This split virtually assured the election of the Republican candidate.

Before the Republican convention, it was generally thought that the nominee would be William H. Seward, the nationally known party leader. Seward, however, had liabilities: Some Republicans feared that he would be too soft on slavery, while others, recalling Seward's speech calling war between the sections an "irrepressible conflict," worried that his candidacy would wreck their chances in the vital border states. The Republicans who met in Chicago realized that they could nominate the next president, if they chose the right candidate. They chose Abraham Lincoln.

Abraham Lincoln

The election of 1860 was a four-man race that split along sectional as well as party lines. The Democrats divided into Northern and Southern branches, with Stephen Douglas heading the Northern faction and John C. Breckinridge as the nominee of the Southern Democrats. In addition, a hasty coalition named the Constitutional Union Party was formed, with John Bell as its candidate. Basically, these three candidates were competing for the same voters, with only Stephen Douglas having much opportunity to make inroads on Lincoln's potential strength.

The election revealed how deeply split the nation was. Bell carried the border states of Kentucky, Tennessee, and Virginia, while Breckinridge won the rest of the slave states. Douglas polled large numbers nationwide, but his totals were scattered, so that he carried only Missouri. As for Lincoln, he won all of the Northern and Western free states, with the exception of New Jersey, and there he took four of the eleven electoral votes. This gave Lincoln 180 electoral votes, a majority, although his popular vote total was less than 40 percent of all ballots cast. Lincoln had carried no Southern state and had hardly registered any votes in the region, since the Republicans were identified and feared as the vehicle of the abolitionists.

Although Lincoln made no attempt to hide his opposition to slavery and particularly its spread into new territories, he had certainly not campaigned on a platform of immediate abolition. The South, however, had virtually made the election a referendum on the continued existence of the Union, and the terms were quite simple: The election of Lincoln was unacceptable and would be regarded as cause for secession. In a sense, this was the final installment in a pattern of political blackmail in which the South had engaged for several generations. Feeling threatened and beleaguered, the South had convinced itself that any compromise on the slavery question would be fatal to its economic and social institutions. For years the rest of the country had acceded to this, preferring to retain the Union, imperfect as it was. The rise of the Republican Party had changed that, and Lincoln's election was a call for redefinition of the compact of the Union. Whether this could have been accomplished peacefully is a moot point, for the Southern states precipitated the war by secession.

As Lincoln's election in 1860 was a referendum on the Union, his reelection campaign in 1864 was a vote upon conduct of the war. After three years of struggle, the casualty lists were long, Union victories had not proved decisive, and there was a strong movement toward peace, through either compromise with the South or acceptance of an independent Confederacy. The Democrats had become known as the peace party, and it was widely believed that their nominee—General George B. McClellan, former commander in chief of the Union armies—would reach some accommodation with the South if elected. Lincoln's chances were linked with success on the battlefield and the will of the North to continue the struggle.

The fall of Atlanta in September was a signal of victory and reinforced Northern desire to see the conflict to a successful conclusion. Lincoln's resounding triumph, 212 electoral votes to 21, indicated that popular sentiment was in accord with the president's determination to preserve the Union, despite the costs and regardless of the burdens.

Lincoln, like Franklin D. Roosevelt, stands beyond the considerations of conventional politics. Both men took office at times when the nation seemed to have reached the end of its tether, and the American experiment was in danger of coming to an ignominious, perhaps violent, end. Yet both tapped resources that other, less visionary politicians had abandoned, and so preserved the nation.

The Aftermath of War

Following the Civil War, it might have seemed that the future of the Democratic Party was bleak; indeed, the Republicans won five of the next seven presidential elections. Yet only one was a decisive victory, and with the shifting of only a few thousand popular votes, the Democrats might have swept six out of the seven.

In 1868, the Republicans seemed to have the perfect candidate in Ulysses S. Grant. By contrast, the Democrats had no war hero, nor could they point to an unquestionable role in the conflict; they turned to party leader Horatio Seymour, hoping that he could ensure the votes of his native New York, a rich electoral prize. In the campaign the Republicans first waved the "bloody shirt," recalling the suffering of the Civil War in order to associate the Democrats with the rebellion. Instead of the landslide that the Republicans had expected, however, the election was close, proving the surprising resilience of the Democratic Party.

By 1872, the corruption of the Grant administration was so excessive that an entire wing of the party, the Liberal Republicans, bolted to join with the Democrats in nominating newspaper editor Horace Greeley. The regular Republicans renominated Grant; to repudiate a sitting president would mean admitting that the charges of their opponents were correct, the spoils of office had grown too tempting, and black votes from

the Southern states under Reconstruction could be depended upon to provide the margin of victory.

By 1876, moderate Republicans welcomed the tradition against a third term as a method to force the choice of a candidate less tainted than Grant. Reformers and traditional party members deadlocked the convention, which turned to Rutherford B. Hayes, a third-term but otherwise obscure Ohio governor. During this period, such struggles for control of the Republican Party were frequent; they ended with a compromise candidate, reformers defused, and the money and big business powers securely in control of the party.

The Democrats chose Samuel J. Tilden, another New Yorker. Once again, the strength of the Democratic organization and the popular revulsion with the corruption of Grant's two terms were clear: The popular vote was solidly in Tilden's favor, and the outcome in the electoral college hinged on the contested votes from three Southern states, Louisiana, Florida, and South Carolina. If the Republicans lost any of these states, they lost the White House; only if they carried all three could Hayes win by a single electoral vote. The scene was set for a deal and a deal was made, revolving around the removal of federal troops from the South. A special election commission was formed to decide the disputed votes; it had eight Republicans and seven Democrats, and every vote was strictly along party lines. On March 2, 1877, only two days before inauguration, Hayes was finally declared president. It was during his term that the last federal troops were withdrawn from the South.

In 1880, control of the Republican Party was again an issue, and when reformers and hardliners had exhausted themselves after thirty-six ballots, Congressman James A. Garfield of Ohio was chosen. In many respects, Garfield was a typical Republican candidate of the period: A Civil War general with respectable service in state and congressional politics, he stressed that he had risen from a poor family, at one time working as a barge driver on midwestern canals. This was the keynote in Garfield's campaign biography, *From Canal Boy to President*, written by that relentless chronicler of American opportunity, Horatio Alger. This election institutionalized the myth of humble beginnings for the presidential candidate. William Henry Harrison had made great play with his log cabin birthplace in 1840, and Lincoln's tenure as a rail-splitter had quickly entered election folklore; after Garfield, it became nearly essential that a candidate claim the supposedly ennobling experience of poverty in his youth as a prerequisite to the Oval Office. Such a view is in contrast to the backgrounds of earlier presidents, such as Washington, the Adamses, and the Virginians, who were established and well connected and who valued family traditions as much as individual initiative. American elections were moving toward a more populist and democratic system—at least on the surface, since the childhoods and characters of Garfield's backers and financial supporters went unrecounted in any campaign biography.

The Democrats selected Winfield Scott Hancock, whose war record more than matched his opponent's: Garfield had served honorably, but Hancock had played a decisive role at the Battle of Gettysburg. At the same time, the removal of federal troops had created the "Solid South," which would be a Democratic stronghold; the Republicans won not a single Southern state in 1880, nor would they until well into the twentieth century. The Democrats thus had an excellent opportunity, and out of some 9.2 million votes cast, Hancock came within 8,000 ballots of winning. His loss was largely attributable to a recurring situation in the American political system: a third party.

In American politics, third parties have tended to arise out of intense but short-lived dissatisfaction with a particular situation and the perceived failure of the two existing major parties to deal with it. Third parties are able to capitalize on voter frustration, but only for a relatively short period of time. They lack the organization and discipline needed for a sustained effort. In this sense, third parties are agents for political protest rather than political power, and

in the national arena their effect has always been to deny the presidency to someone else rather than win it for their own candidates. Ironically, they frequently ensure the defeat of the candidate more attuned to their particular views. This was certainly the case in 1880, when the Greenback Party was active. Formed in opposition to the restrictive monetary policies of the Republicans, which had led to economic hardships for the middle and lower classes, the Greenbacks drew away voters who would otherwise have gone Democratic. Enough defected to make the difference in the electoral votes in key states to allow Garfield to win.

The campaign of 1884 was a study in contrasts. The Republicans chose James G. Blaine, the "Plumed Knight." Although a leader in the Senate and the party, Blaine was mistrusted by many, especially for his more questionable financial dealings. His opponent was Grover Cleveland, who had begun his political career as a sheriff in New York State and had gone on to become the honest, hardworking mayor of Buffalo and then governor of New York. Cleveland's honesty was almost painful and might have wrecked another man's political career; against Blaine, it was the Democrats' greatest asset.

The contest between the urbane, polished senator and the bluff, forthright governor was focused on two issues, economics and personal character. Economically, the two parties followed their traditional platforms, with the Republicans favoring big business and special interests and the Democrats championing the small businessman, farmers, and the middle and lower classes. There was nothing new in this, and it has remained a constant party division even into contemporary elections. In 1884 the main issue was character. Blaine and his strategists sought to defuse mistrust over his character by attacks on Cleveland, making special use of the fact that the Democratic nominee, while a young man, might have fathered an illegitimate child. "Ma, Ma, where's my pa?" was the chant the Republicans used to keep the matter before the public. When Cleveland's managers asked what to say about the incident, Cleveland's reply was characteristic: "Whatever you do, tell the truth." Responding to such personal integrity, the voters gave Cleveland victory in November.

Four years out of power sharpened the appetites of the special interests that controlled the Republican Party. In 1888, their nominee was Benjamin Harrison, another Civil War general popular with veterans. Labor unrest offered the Republicans the opportunity to campaign against "anarchy." Seldom were the economic divisions between the two parties more clearly drawn, and in 1888 the configuration favored the Grand Old Party. Four years later, the same candidates and the same issues put Cleveland back in the White House. The difference was that the country had moved into a new era, leaving behind elections determined by memory of the Civil War and entering a period of new economic and social forces.

The Modern Presidency Begins

With the presidency of William McKinley, American politics moved into the modern era. There had been professional politicians before McKinley—indeed, one of the strengths of the Democratic Party was its core of officeholders—and there had been organizations dedicated to the cause of a single candidate—again, the Democrats had done it first, as far back as Andrew Jackson—but there had never been politicians and organizations such as those that placed McKinley in the White House in 1896. What made the difference was not McKinley's public service but his friendship with Marcus A. Hanna, an Ohio businessman. The two formed a potent combination: McKinley had popular charm and presence, and Hanna brought enormous financial resources and business connections. Together they fashioned strategies that made McKinley the inevitable nominee of the 1896 Republican convention.

By contrast, the Democrats selected their candidate because of circumstance, oratory, and the genius of the moment. The central issue of the campaign was economics, specifically hard currency, backed by gold, versus soft

money, backed by silver. The Republicans followed the lead of big business and opted for gold: Hard currency kept down inflation and raised profits. It also brought high unemployment and difficulties for small business, farmers, and the working class—the natural constituency of the Democrats. The Democratic convention found its nominee when William Jennings Bryan delivered his famous "cross of gold" speech, and the resulting election pitted an impassioned but outmaneuvered Democratic crusade against a coolly organized and well-financed Republican onslaught.

The Democrats had ensured that they would continue to move in a more populist and progressive fashion. Although this led to defeat in 1896, it proved to be the course that would bring the Democrats to power during times when they would shape modern America. By contrast, the Republicans and big business further strengthened their ties, believing that only their union and hold on power brought national prosperity, but this philosophy was being undermined by growing popular resentment at the excesses of industry and capital. The strength of the progressive movement during the last decade of the century caused a shift in Republican strategy, as the link between the party and big business was masked, but not broken, especially during the presidency and election campaign of Theodore Roosevelt.

Roosevelt, who had come to the White House upon the assassination of McKinley, had a reputation as a progressive, a reformer who was prepared to support legislation that would put restraints upon the more high-handed actions of large corporations. This orientation was more image than substance, however, and during his election campaign of 1904, Roosevelt moved quickly to compromise his "progressive" views with Republican conservatives and their allies among the business community.

Roosevelt had ruled out another term in 1908, so his handpicked successor, William Howard Taft, was the Republican nominee. After Taft's election, it was not long before Roosevelt had broken with him and was busy seeking

9

a third term. Publicly, the rift was caused by Taft's failure to follow in the progressive line; actually, the cause was Roosevelt's desire to return to power, and his recognition that 1912 was an excellent year for a progressive candidate.

Roosevelt was counting on the threat of a progressive split from the Republican Party if Taft were renominated, but Roosevelt had underestimated Taft's abilities, which proved quite formidable: Taft became the first sitting president to take part in the new primary process, and he did well enough to win renomination on the first ballot. Enraged, Roosevelt and his supporters bolted to form the Progressive Party, known to its friends as the Bull Moose Party and to more detached observers as the Moosevelt Party.

The split gave victory to the Democratic candidate, Thomas Woodrow Wilson, a scholar, author, and former president of Princeton University. He had come to politics relatively late, but once in office, as governor of New Jersey, Wilson became the nation's chief exponent of modern progressive thought; he was an intellectual rather an emotional leader, but it was clear that the voters responded to his integrity and vision.

A Democratic majority in Congress allowed Wilson to put into place the key elements of his "New Freedom," a distillation of major populist and liberal ideals. The thrust of these reforms was blunted by the outbreak of World War I and the eventual involvement of the United States in the conflict. Having campaigned on a peace platform in 1916 ("He kept us out of war" was the Democratic slogan), Wilson considered the war a calamity, but he saw in the Allied victory an unparalleled opportunity to fashion a better world, guided by international cooperation secured through the League of Nations.

Fearful of further foreign entanglements, Republicans and conservative Democrats rejected the League, and controversy over it formed a large part of the 1920 campaign. The Republicans linked rejection with an even greater desire of the American people to return to "normalcy." The Republicans tapped this sentiment in their candidate, and after eight years of a high-minded and demanding professor, the American voter got Warren G. Harding.

Harding won by more than seven million votes, but his administration was the most corrupt since Grant's. The knowledge that cabinet officers had prostituted public trust for personal profit should have been an unbeatable issue for the Democrats in 1924, but the death of Harding removed much of the focus of the scandal, while the Republican nominee, Vice President Calvin Coolidge, was a walking, barely talking example of Yankee rectitude. Economic prosperity continued at an unprecedentedly high rate; little wonder that voters responded to the Republican slogan "Keep cool with Coolidge."

There is a tendency in the Democratic Party to move toward the populist, more liberal viewpoint and widen its base to include more of the electorate. This is especially true in defeat, and the party illustrated this tendency in 1928, when its members chose Al Smith of New York as the Democratic presidential nominee. Smith represented the urban voters, with their emigrant backgrounds, and his nomination was a signal that the Democrats sought to be an inclusive party. Smith represented change; Herbert Hoover, the Republican, was the embodiment of the status quo. Hoover's victory relied on the contrast between these two but was mainly based on good economic times — and those times were about to end, and end badly.

Franklin D. Roosevelt

Shortly after Franklin D. Roosevelt was elected president in 1932, a friend told him, "If you succeed, you will be the greatest president this country has ever had." Roosevelt replied, "And if I fail, I shall be its last."

When Roosevelt took office, the nation was in the midst of what has become known as the Great Depression: One-quarter of the workforce was unemployed; banks had failed throughout the country, wiping out the life savings of hundreds of thousands; breadlines and soup kitchens ministered to thousands of urban poor; and farm families were forced from their homes. In Washington, D.C., fifteen thousand work veterans camped on the banks of the Anacostia River, petitioning Congress for their bonus pay from World War I. President Hoover had the veterans dispersed and their camp destroyed by the Army. Across the nation there was real fear that the United States was sliding into revolution.

This was the situation when the Democrats convened in Chicago. The prime candidate was Roosevelt, then governor of New York. Roosevelt had already won recognition as the leader of the progressive wing of the party, and his efforts in New York to provide relief for victims of the Depression stood in stark contrast to the deadening inaction of the Hoover administration. Roosevelt was nominated on the fourth ballot. In a break with conventional protocol, he flew to Chicago to accept the nomination in person; it was the first indication of the dramatic, innovative nature of the coming presidency. Projecting energy and optimism, Roosevelt won handily, building an electoral college advantage over Hoover of 472 to 59.

Roosevelt's first term was a whirlwind of activity: Starting with the Hundred Days, FDR and the Democratic Congress pushed through a wide variety of measures, programs, and legislation called the New Deal. Some of these worked well; others were less effective; some, such as the National Recovery Act, were declared unconstitutional. While these activities did not end the Depression—it took the economic impetus of World War II to accomplish that—they did blunt its worst effects. Even more important, Roosevelt gave the country hope.

The country resoundingly approved FDR's efforts in 1936, when he was reelected in the largest landslide to that time: He carried every state except Maine and Vermont, and the Democrats increased their hold on Congress. One of the most enduring political legacies of Roosevelt's first term was the powerful coalition that he forged among old and new elements of the Democratic Party. The farmers in the West and South were won by federal programs supporting agriculture; blacks deserted the Republicans to join with the party that offered them equal economic opportunities in the new relief programs;

ethnics, urban voters, and Roman Catholics were also recipients of attention from the Roosevelt administration, after long years of neglect by the Republicans. Finally, organized labor, then just coming into its own, became a keystone in the Democratic edifice. This combination of forces not only allowed FDR to continue the programs of the New Deal but also established the American political landscape for a generation.

During Roosevelt's second term, focus shifted from domestic issues to the growing threat of war. As Adolf Hitler moved to rearm Germany and expand in Europe, Roosevelt pressed for increased buildup of American might, and support for Great Britain. While these actions raised the ire of isolationists, they were applauded by a majority of Americans, including the 1940 Republican nominee, Wendell Willkie.

Willkie had taken the Republican nomination in an unexpected, grassroots campaign. A businessman, a liberal, and an internationalist, Willkie had few disagreements with Roosevelt or his efforts to aid Great Britain. The major issue in the campaign was the fact that Roosevelt was running for a third term; since Washington, there had been an unspoken prohibition against this, and the change troubled many, even some of FDR's strong supporters. Roosevelt's margin of victory shrank to five million votes, but he still carried the electoral college by a large majority, and the Democrats remained in control of the House and Senate.

War came to America in 1941, and Roosevelt turned from the New Deal to matters of strategy. During the conflict he was, in a literal as well as constitutional sense, the commander in chief of American forces, and the broad scope of American strategy, including the "Europe first" emphasis, was Roosevelt's. By 1944, the United States and its allies were on the verge of victory, and Roosevelt was nominated for a fourth term; he was reelected by his smallest margin, defeating Republican nominee Thomas Dewey by less than three million votes. Four months after his inauguration, Roosevelt was dead, a victim of a cerebral hemorrhage.

Roosevelt was a richly contradictory man: born to wealth, he became the champion of the poor and the needy; crippled by polio, he was tempered and deepened by his affliction; attacked by some as a dictator, he was among the most popular and democratic of presidents. His twelve years in office changed the presidency and the nation more than any other presidency since Lincoln's.

The Contemporary Presidency

Post-World War II presidential elections have gone through two phases: a transition period under Harry S. Truman and Dwight D. Eisenhower, and the subsequent rise of a new phenomenon in American politics, the permanent candidate. This second development was closely and perhaps inevitably linked with the spread of modern media, in particular television, which has transformed elections, the style in which they are conducted, and the candidates they favor.

Truman was vice president in 1944 largely through domestic political considerations. A product of the rough school of Missouri Democratic politics, Truman was generally regarded as honest and competent, but he was not believed to have any extraordinary qualities, especially when compared to Franklin D. Roosevelt. Hence, he surprised many by the statesmanlike manner in which he filled the office. The decision to use atomic weapons to end the war with Japan, his firm stance with the Soviets, and his sponsorship of the Marshall Plan to rebuild Europe were major accomplishments. Indispensable as these are to Truman's presidency, his place in American political history is ensured by his dramatic reelection.

By 1948, Truman and the Democrats had fallen alarmingly low in the polls. Many Americans seemed ready for a change; the Democrats had been in office since 1932, and the country had weathered the most serious depression and greatest war in its history. Truman, by his connection with the Roosevelt presidency, suffered both by being linked to Roosevelt's failings and by comparison to FDR's successes. More than

that, he seemed determined to continue the policies of change and innovation begun by the New Deal, leading in areas where even FDR had hardly entered, most notably civil rights.

In 1948, as in 1860, the Democratic Party split over the fundamental issue of blacks in American society. In 1860, the Southern Democrats had fought to preserve slavery; in 1948, they battled to continue segregation. The difference was that Truman and enough of the national Democrats refused to back away from their moral commitment, even when J. Strom Thurmond of South Carolina led disaffected Southerners into the short-lived Dixiecrat Party (officially known as the States' Rights Party). Standing firm on the civil rights plank was a courageous decision for Truman; he was facing a difficult election, and the votes of the traditionally Democratic South could easily be the deciding factor, especially since he had already alienated the more liberal wing of the party. Henry Wallace, whom Truman had replaced as vice president, had yoked various elements to form yet another progressive party, that perennial vehicle of American populist aspirations. Wallace would draw away many liberal voters; Thurmond would capture the Deep South; the national Democrats were in disarray, and Truman's own popularity was sinking— no wonder the Republicans sensed victory.

They renominated Thomas Dewey, who conducted a campaign that was basically a prelude to his inauguration. Truman took his cause directly to the American people. In a time before the electronic media brought the candidate into millions of living rooms, Truman literally crossed the country in person, conducting a whistle-stop campaign during which he lambasted the Republicans and richly earned his slogan, "Give 'em hell, Harry." His victory in November was a triumph of personal, traditional politics, with his popular vote total matching his rivals' combined strengths and his electoral vote count easily leading theirs.

The personal victory of Truman was repeated, but for different reasons, in the back-to-back triumphs of Dwight D. (Ike) Eisenhower.

The popular hero of World War II, Eisenhower had been courted by both parties, but when it became apparent that his inclinations led him to the Republicans, there ensued yet another round in the struggle for control of the Grand Old Party. The true believers were lined up behind Senator Robert A. Taft of Ohio, but the pragmatic professionals recognized that Taft would probably lose the election, whereas Eisenhower would almost certainly win. In the end, a potentially fatal convention battle was avoided and the Taft loyalists, while bitter, rallied behind Ike as the nominee.

Against a popular and victorious war hero, the Democrats probably had slight chance of retaining the White House; still, they nominated their best-qualified candidate: Adlai Stevenson, the governor of Illinois. Stevenson was brilliant, humorous, and eloquent, and has been described as "the best president the United States never had." He had no chance against Eisenhower, either in 1952 or when the two were rematched in 1956. The personal popularity of Eisenhower, the peace and prosperity which settled over the nation, and the simple desire to enjoy that peace were far more potent factors than any campaign issues devised by either party.

By 1960, the nation was on the threshold of a new style in presidential politics. There were several reasons for this shift: Eisenhower's personal popularity could not be transferred; even as president, he could not carry a majority in Congress, prompting one wit to remark, "There are no coattails on an Eisenhower jacket." There was also a consensus that it was time for America to get moving again; after all, it was the second half of the twentieth century. In addition, television had transformed the political process: It made elections faster, longer, and more calculated.

The candidate who exemplified this change was John F. Kennedy, and in a sense, he was the first of the permanent candidates, having decided in 1956 to run for the 1960 presidential nomination. There had been lengthy and well-devised campaigns before, but none conducted with the skill, tenacity, or flair of Kennedy's. Young, attractive, intelligent, and well financed, Kennedy edged out his party rivals who attacked him on traditional lines: that he was too young, that he lacked a record in the Senate, that he was a Catholic and could not carry the South or West. By accepting the challenge and making himself the focus of the campaign, Kennedy simply made most of these attacks irrelevant. In a similar fashion, the election itself, which pitted Kennedy against Vice President Richard M. Nixon, revolved around competing images.

Nixon was certainly no stranger to the politics of image; he had retained his spot on the 1952 Republican ticket with his famous Checkers speech, portraying himself as an honest man unfairly attacked. Nixon's problem, however, was that his talent for imagery was purely negative; he could not match Kennedy's optimistic visions and instead evoked the supposedly inevitable ruin that would follow a Democratic victory. It was a typical Nixon tactic and would work for him in 1968 and in 1972, when his opponents gave him enough substance to make his charges creditable. It failed in 1960, when the American voters narrowly preferred the politics of optimism and Kennedy's New Frontier.

The key point in Kennedy's victory was the style of his campaign. Although issues would change, the essential method was fixed: The successful candidate would establish an appealing image within a short period of time, mixing a shrewd combination of voters' perceptions and actual substance. The vehicle for the message was television, which presented short messages on the same theme, endlessly repeated. In a sense, the candidate became the image.

The first full-fledged example was in 1964. Lyndon Johnson had assumed the presidency after Kennedy's assassination and had replaced the New Frontier with the Great Society, an ambitious mélange of social, economic, and civil rights programs designed to rival the New Deal of Franklin D. Roosevelt. Johnson could rightly claim the image of a social progressive, a president of consensus. His rival, Barry Goldwater, was leader of the far-right wing of the Republican Party, which had taken control of the party after yet another internecine struggle. Aided by Goldwater's intemperate statements, Johnson and the Democrats had little difficulty in portraying the Republican as a dangerous, warlike individual who would reverse progress in civil rights and wreck Social Security. The result was a landslide for Johnson and what appeared to be a period of Democratic ascendancy. Yet, within four years, Johnson was practically driven from the White House and Richard Nixon had been elected president.

Once again, a campaign of images had been waged. The Democrats, badly split over the war in Vietnam, had seen their Chicago convention turn into a battle between delegates, demonstrators, and the police; worse, the entire country had seen it too, on their television sets. When Hubert Humphrey emerged as the nominee, his campaign was flawed by this burning image and the pain of an unsuccessful, apparently endless war in Southeast Asia. Nixon—the "new Nixon"—fashioned a persona that was presidential: He had a plan to end the war, he declared, but he could not reveal it. In a close decision, the American voters preferred vague Republican potential to the Democratic record.

Four years later, Nixon repeated the campaign of image, this time even more successfully, since it is fairly easy to appear presidential when one is actually the president. Unfortunately for Nixon and the Republicans, the image of a president ending wars and establishing peaceful relations with Communist China was replaced by that of a president engaging in third-rate burglaries and covering up crimes. So deep was the revulsion with Watergate across the country that the next successful candidate, Jimmy Carter, won in large part because he ran as an outsider, the candidate *not* from Washington, D.C.

Carter's theme and image were good ones, and he rode them to victory in 1976 against the hapless Gerald R. Ford, but in 1980 these very weapons were turned against Carter by a much more skillful player, Ronald Reagan. In a way, Reagan was the epitome of the post-FDR presidential candidate. He had enough background in government to demonstrate competence, but not so much as to be seen as merely another professional politician. He was skilled and at ease before the cameras, and he appeared to believe, even if he did not fully understand, what he said. Finally, he was adept at discerning what image the American people seemed to desire and presenting it to them. This is a talent all successful politicians have possessed, but few have shown Reagan's mastery in demonstrating it so consistently and to such a vast audience. Not since Franklin D. Roosevelt has the country felt so close to one man.

Ronald Reagan and His Legacy

After surviving an assassination attempt early in his first term, Reagan first challenged organized labor by firing striking air traffic controllers who had followed their union off their jobs to protest working conditions. Despite the difficulties which followed, Reagan persisted and inflicted a severe blow on the American labor community. He then moved to dismantle much of the traditional machinery of government. His most ambitious, and far-reaching, goals were a series of drastic, across-the-board tax cuts and a rapid increase in military spending. The two combined to produce a spiraling federal deficit that, in a few years, moved the United States from the world's largest creditor nation to its greatest debtor. At the same time, however, the arms buildup forced the Soviet Union to increase its own military spending, eventually wrecking the Soviet economy.

The United States was spared a similar fate by its innate economic strength, but the growing deficit plagued Reagan's second term, causing turmoil on the stock market. Still, the president and his allies in Congress pledged to "stay the course" in their belief that the unfettered free market system would ultimately be vindicated. Even if minor problems were encountered, they argued, government properly had no major role to play in correcting them. Although Reagan often evoked the name of Franklin Delano Roosevelt, his two terms were largely dedicated to undoing much of the heritage of the New Deal. However, it was a legacy not to be undone, as Reagan gradually learned and which his vice president and successor discovered.

Elected in 1988 to continue the Reagan Revolution, George Herbert Walker Bush had boldly pledged, "Read my lips: No new taxes." However, after only one month in office he had to propose a plan to bail out the threatened savings and loan industry by raising taxes. Bush agreed to tax increases in 1990, which further incited the anger of Reagan loyalists. Bush also faced an increasingly stagnant economy, crippled by continued deficits. The bright spot for the Bush presidency was the brief Persian Gulf War, which united a coalition of European and Middle Eastern states against the aggression of Iraq under its leader, Saddam Hussein. However, even this victory paled as Americans realized that Hussein, although defeated, remained in power and a threat to U.S. interests in the area.

By 1992, the American electorate was restive, even rebellious. Bush found himself under scornful attack from the right wing of the Republican Party, challenged by wealthy independent candidate Ross Perot, and facing in Bill Clinton a Democratic candidate who had claimed the vital center ground of American politics. As Bush's reelection campaign foundered, he grew more shrill, trying to discredit Clinton's character and questioning his patriotism. Intensely partisan rhetoric had returned to the presidential election process; soon, it would spread to all aspects of national government.

After Clinton's election with a minority of the popular vote in 1992, Republicans set out to undo his victory. The proposed Clinton health care reforms drew the fire of the insurance and health care industries and eventually died. Meanwhile, congressional opponents demanded investigation of alleged Clinton offenses in what became known as "Whitewater," an old and tangled real estate development project in Arkansas. When Republicans gained control of the House and Senate in 1994 (the first time they had done so in forty years), their attacks on the president increased, finally resulting in the

appointment of Independent Prosecutor Kenneth Starr, who used all means available to secure the president's impeachment. Despite, or perhaps because of, Clinton's easy reelection in 1996, the partisan attacks continued.

However, for many Americans clearly the partisanship had gone too far. In the 1998 congressional elections, the Republicans tried to make Clinton's impeachment the centerpiece of their campaigns. The result was a serious defeat that almost cost them their majority in the House and caused the resignation of their belligerent and abrasive Speaker, Newt Gingrich. Undeterred, Starr and House Republicans pushed on, finally bringing about President Clinton's impeachment on two counts, of perjury and obstruction of justice, on December 19, 1998. Ironically, the impeachment drama reached its end on February 12, 1999, just before President's Day weekend, when the Senate, sitting as a jury, found William Jefferson Clinton "not guilty" on both counts. Despite Republican control of the Senate, the House's impeachment articles could not even muster a simple majority. It seemed to many observers that the politics of partisanship had reached its inevitable conclusion. The country had simply had enough.

George W. Bush came into office in 2001 with the shadow of the 2000 presidential election still looming large. That election, between Bush and then-Vice President Al Gore, was one of the closest and most bitterly contested in American history, marred by allegations of poorly designed ballots, disenfranchisement of black voters, and conflict of interest by election officials—all in Florida. Gore won the popular vote, but Bush prevailed in the electoral college, although only after recounts in Florida gave him the edge by the slimmest of margins and the U.S. Supreme Court rendered a controversial split decision supporting the election results.

Bush's first one hundred days were rather unremarkable, and his administration worked to move beyond the lingering effect of the divisive election. However, all this changed on September 11, 2001, when terrorists hijacked and crashed four commercial aircraft into the tow-ers of New York's World Trade Center, the Pentagon, and a field in rural Pennsylvania. In the wake of the tragedy, Bush's approval ratings skyrocketed to the high eighties and even the low nineties, and the president enjoyed widespread support for his war efforts against the terrorist group al-Qaeda and the Taliban regime in Afghanistan and, later, against Saddam Hussein and his Baathist regime in Iraq.

As a war president, Bush achieved popularity that translated into impressive victories for his political party in the midterm elections of 2002 as well as support for his political agenda of tax cuts; a variety of faith-based initiatives and "family values," market-based solutions to public problems; and a general weakening of environmental and civil rights protections. Bush's popularity produced several legislative victories, and he did not have to veto a single bill. The president survived another tight race to win reelection in 2004.

However, Bush's agenda bogged down during his second term as support for the war in Iraq declined with evidence that the president's arguments for invading Iraq—the country's possession of weapons of mass destruction, efforts to buy weapons-grade materials from Niger, and links to terror groups and the September 11 attacks—were false. Relatedly, daily American casualties in Iraq, no announced plan for securing the peace or reconstructing the war-ravaged nation, the presence of a strong insurgency, and ongoing international opposition to the war further harmed the president's agenda in Iraq.

On the home front, the divisiveness over the war took a toll on Bush's domestic agenda as well. Most notably, the president was forced to back off his plan to privatize Social Security. During the first year of Bush's second term, skyrocketing gasoline prices and health care costs, further setbacks in the war in Iraq, ethical scandals among some of Bush's closest allies, and the failure of the administration to respond promptly to communities destroyed by Hurricane Katrina, the worst natural disaster in the nation's history, eroded the president's approval ratings.

Barack Obama came to power in 2009 amid the worst economic collapse since the Great Depression. The Stock Market was in free-fall, countless major financial institutions were teetering on the brink of collapse, major automobile manufacturers were bankrupt, unemployment escalated to over 10 percent, and the budget deficit soared to well over one trillion dollars. Over strong opposition by Republicans, Obama was able to broker a deal to organize rescue programs for major banks and the U.S. auto industry and promote a massive economic stimulus plan that included targeted federal spending, federal investments, and tax relief.

In what will surely be one of Obama's lasting legacies, under his management the economy enjoyed a difficult but steady recovery beginning in 2010 and running through his second term in office. Unemployment levels dropped dramatically to pre-recession levels, the budget deficit was cut by two-thirds, American auto manufacturers and financial institutions recovered and posted healthy annual profits, and the stock market soared to record highs.

Domestically, the president presided over a number of accomplishments including funding for stem cell research, streamlining student loans, conserving record acres of sensitive lands, and progress on the civil rights front. For example, "Don't Ask, Don't Tell," which prohibited gays from openly serving in the military, was repealed in 2010. In 2015, the president proudly proclaimed the Supreme Court's marriage equality ruling "a victory for America." However, the president encountered opposition from Republicans in Congress in his efforts to pass gun control laws. Obama repeatedly noted that one of the most frustrating experiences of his presidency was having to address the nation many times after mass shootings and yet have his calls for gun control ignored.

Arguably Obama's most significant domestic policy achievement was the passage of the Patient Protection and Affordable Care Act of 2010, also known as "Obamacare." The president was able to greatly expand health care coverage, but was unable to achieve universal coverage as he had hoped. The measure endured a protracted battle in Congress, lawsuits that went before the Supreme Court, and countless calls by Republicans in Congress to repeal the act. Obamacare suffered a major set-back when, during the roll-out of the massive program, the online system for registering people for coverage failed to work properly. Nevertheless, millions of uninsured Americans received health care and millions more were able to expand existing care and lower the cost of the coverage. The plan remained very controversial throughout the president's two terms in office.

In foreign affairs, the president made good on a campaign promise to end combat operations in the long conflicts in Afghanistan and Iraq, developing a phased withdrawal of troops over his terms in office. The drawdown was controversial and was made more difficult by a number of international crises, including aggressive actions by Russian president Vladimir Putin in Ukraine, the Crimean Peninsula, and Syria. The collapse of regimes in the Middle East, worsening of age-old sectarian and religious violence, and rise of the so-called Islamic State brought both security threats and refugee crises in Yemen, Syria, Libya, and other countries. Obama's critics blamed him for not being "stronger" in his response to these crises but the president pointed to the killing of Osama bin Laden, the erosion of al-Qaeda's strength, and the effective drone strikes that killed many terrorists leaders as successes.

The president faced a difficult reelection in 2012, but managed to defeat former Massachusetts governor Mitt Romney to capture a second term. However, his party suffered devastating defeats in both the 2010 and 2014 midterm elections, which resulted in a Republican takeover of Congress. The backdrop for these elections was a decline in civility in politics and a bitter partisanship that produced gridlock in Congress and derailed several of the president's priorities.

The election of Barack Obama in 2008 as the nation's first African-American president was a groundbreaking moment in American politics.

The experiences of Clinton, Bush, Obama, and other recent presidents reveal the challenges of presidential leadership: Great threats, in the form of terrorist attacks or natural disasters, may arise without warning, and the country will demand a response from the White House. At the dawn of the twenty-first century, the American presidency remains somehow the same, yet changed. The office retains immense power and prestige, despite ethical lapses of several recent presidents and despite the ongoing struggle between the political parties and the executive and legislative branches of government. Yet, the presidency is increasingly seen as "the people's office."

Michael Witkoski; updated by Robert P. Watson

George Washington

1st President, 1789-1797

Born: February 22, 1732
    Bridges Creek, Westmoreland
     County, Virginia
Died: December 14, 1799
    Mount Vernon, Virginia

Political Party: Federalist
Vice President: John Adams

Cabinet Members
Secretary of State: Thomas Jefferson, Edmund
    Randolph, Timothy Pickering
Secretary of the Treasury: Alexander Hamilton,
    Oliver Wolcott, Jr.
Secretary of War: Henry Knox, Timothy
    Pickering, James McHenry
Attorney General: Edmund Randolph, William
    Bradford, Charles Lee

George Washington stands unique among presidents of the United States in the near unanimity with which politically influential Americans agreed that he should be elected. No other president has enjoyed a comparable degree of public confidence upon entering the office, and few if any other presidents have had equal scope for defining the chief executive's place in the federal government and the nation's life. The symbolic prestige attached to the presidency comes not only from its constitutionally defined powers but also from the implicit expectation that each new incumbent may achieve some of the unifying popular respect commanded by Washington.

The Character of a Leader: Ambition and Self-Control

Rather than deriving this respect from his posi-

tion as president, Washington brought to the office the esteem he had won personally by virtue of his character and career. Little in Washington's youth gave promise of the exceptional stature he later attained; yet, beginning in those early years, he developed the circumspection and reliability that became integral to his public career. Washington was born February 22, 1732, in Westmoreland County in the northern neck of Virginia, near the Potomac River. His mother, Mary Ball Washington, was the second wife of Augustine Washington. Augustine's grandfather John had emigrated from

Portrait of George Washington. *(Whitehouse.gov)*

England to Virginia in 1657-1658. George was eleven years old when his father died. Augustine's adult son by an earlier marriage, Lawrence Washington, filled some of the role of a father for George until Lawrence died in 1752. First by lease and then by ownership, Lawrence's estate, Mount Vernon, became George's property and his preferred home for the rest of his life.

Washington grew to adulthood in an agricultural, slaveholding society that combined the stability of a self-perpetuating gentry leadership with the volatility of expanding settlement, immigration, and natural population increase. Through Lawrence's marriage to the daughter of Colonel William Fairfax, George came into contact with the comparatively cosmopolitan proprietary family, including Thomas Lord Fairfax, whose holdings included much of north-ernmost Virginia as far west as the Shenandoah Valley. The prospective value of this land lay in peopling it with tenants or buyers. Washington worked with a Fairfax surveying team in the Shenandoah Valley in 1748 and was appointed Culpeper County surveyor in 1749. Like other surveyors, the eighteen-year-old acquired land on his own account, in addition to inheriting Ferry Farm, which had belonged to his father. Washington was a home-taught and self-taught youth; he did not attend college. His reading tended toward history, biography, novels, and practical works on agriculture and the military. The ambition that Thomas Jefferson, James Madison, and John Adams manifested through intellectual self-development George Washington sought to realize in the world of plantation and military affairs.

In 1753 and 1754, as a major and then a lieu-

The First Lady
Martha Washington

Martha Washington remains one of the most admired women in U.S. history. She was born on June 2, 1731, in New Kent County, Virginia. Her father, John Dandridge, was a county clerk and owned a successful 500-acre plantation in the eastern Tidewater region of the colony. Martha's mother, Frances Jones, was descended from a line of well-respected English preachers and was born in the colony.

As a teenager in 1749, Martha Dandridge married Daniel Parke Custis, who was twenty years her senior and son of one of the colony's wealthiest and foremost families. The two had four children: Daniel, born in 1751; Frances, born in 1753; John, born in 1754; and Martha, born in 1755. Tragically, the first two children died in infancy and, in 1757, Martha Custis would find herself widowed.

The following year, George Washington entered Martha's life, and the two were married on January 6, 1759, at the Custis family home, which was known as the White House. The Washington marriage was childless, but in marrying Martha, George Washington gained two adopted children, one of Virginia's largest plantations, two mansions, and an attractive bank account in London. Most important, he also gained what the obituary pages would eventually call "a worthy partner."

Martha's status as heroine of the early Republic is without dispute. However, although she described herself as "an old-fashioned Virginia housekeeper," there was much more to Martha Washington. "Lady Washington," as she was affectionately known to the troops of the American Revolution, was arguably the young nation's most admired woman and foremost hostess. The role she played helping her husband and war-weary soldiers while in camp each winter of the Revolutionary War and in forging the official duties of the president's wife define her legacy.

Martha Washington died on May 22, 1802, at Mount Vernon, two years after her husband.

Robert P. Watson

Washington and his family at home, by Currier & Ives. *(Library of Congress)*

tenant colonel in the Virginia militia, Washington became conspicuous in his activities as Governor Robert Dinwiddie's emissary to the chiefs of the Six Nations and to the French who were constructing a chain of forts from Lake Erie to the Ohio River. Washington's first skirmish with the French late in May, 1754, is often described as the beginning of the Seven Years' War. His military career during the war, although it attracted attention and won respect, was linked to several reverses: In July, 1754, he surrendered his command to a much larger French force from Fort Duquesne; in the summer of 1755 he served as an aide-de-camp with General Edward Braddock's expedition against Fort Duquesne, which ended in ambush and rout; as colonel and commander in chief of Virginia militia, he spent two frustrating years trying to protect the Shenandoah Valley and

western Virginia with about three hundred men and inadequate supplies. Moreover, in 1755 and 1757 Washington stood for election to the Virginia House of Burgesses and was twice defeated. At the same time, he unsuccessfully sought a regular commission in the Royal Army.

After cooperating with the last expedition against Fort Duquesne in 1758, which ended in French withdrawal and the establishment of Fort Pitt at the forks of the Ohio, Washington returned to civil life. He won election to the House of Burgesses in 1758. In January, 1759, he married Martha Dandridge Custis, a wealthy widow, and settled with her and her children at Mount Vernon. For fifteen years he enjoyed the life of a family man, planter, colonial legislator, and justice of the peace; and yet, to decorate his home, Washington ordered portrait busts of Alexander the Great, Julius Caesar, Charles XII of Sweden, Frederick II of Prussia, Prince Eugene, and the duke of Marlborough — all famous commanders. When his London agent could not get them, Washington declined to accept busts of poets and philosophers as substitutes. His own appearance was imposing: He was 6 feet, 3 inches tall and weighed 209 pounds. His shoulders were narrow, but his arms, hands, legs, and feet were large. He had great strength yet was graceful in posture and movement. He was an excellent dancer and an expert horseman. His large head had a prominent nose and a firm mouth. His eyes were gray-blue, and in his forties he began to use spectacles to read.

By the time that Washington attained national stature as commander in chief of the Continental Army in 1775, the character that buttressed his popular standing was well formed. As a young man, he was emotional, effusive, audacious, and ambitious. These traits remained with him throughout his life, but he schooled himself to keep these manifestations of his passionate nature under rigorous control. He had purposefully chosen a life of outward stability and inward disappointment. He gained the rewards of equanimity at the cost of curbing his strongest inclinations. The cost was high. Washington often said that he would not relive his life if given the chance.

As Revolutionary War commander and as president, Washington won an unequaled public respect for integrity and reliability. He maintained this public, ideal character while remaining privately aware of the gap between his studied moderation of demeanor and his emotional preference for bold risks, high honors, impulsive attachments, and strong aversions. Without ever losing the enthusiastic temperament of his youth, he subjected it to the control of his will, so that his public expression of his deepest anxieties or strongest joys remained temperate. Only rarely — as in his occasional angry rages or in his effusive friendship with the marquis de Lafayette — did the young Wash-

ington and the inner Washington appear to others without being moderated by the mature, public Washington. After he became a general, he was asked whether he really had written the often-quoted lines from his report of his first skirmish with the French in 1754 — "I heard the bullets whistle, and, believe me, there is something charming in the sound." Washington replied, "If I said so, it was when I was young."

Having worked so hard to build it, Washington set a very high value on his reputation. He distinguished his personal honor from the popular opinion of him: Praise did not make him overweening, nor did censure paralyze him, but he tended to believe that anyone who attacked his conduct or reputation thereby impugned his honor. Knowing that his public character was his own creation, maintained at the cost of great effort, he resented suggestions that it had flaws. At the same time, possessing a private distance from his public posture, he could see mistakes he had made and correct them, even when he did not want to admit them. Two of the most intimate views of Washington may provide the best brief summary of his character. Gilbert Stuart, who painted portraits of the public Washington, saw the private Washington clearly: "All his features were indicative of the most ungovernable passions, and had he been born in the forests . . . he would have been the fiercest man among the savage tribes." Lafayette, who knew the private Washington better than most, described the reliability of the public Washington: "Had he been a common soldier, he would have been the bravest in the ranks; had he been an obscure citizen, all his neighbors would have respected him."

The American Revolution: Commander in Chief

By the time that Americans' resistance to the British government's measures to levy colonial taxes and to tighten imperial administration had become armed conflict, George Washington was one of the most important Virginia politicians. On May 27, 1774, he joined the extralegal meeting of burgesses in the Raleigh Tavern in Williamsburg, after the royal governor had dissolved the House; and he was one of Virginia's delegates to the First and Second Continental Congresses in 1774 and 1775. He was not a theorist or propagandist of the political thought by which Americans explained their effort to win independence and to establish a republican form of government. Nevertheless, he understood the intellectual bases, as well as the moral vision, on which the American Revolution was undertaken. His wartime addresses to his soldiers went beyond the appeals to discipline and professional pride characteristic of the British commanders' orders to include brief summaries of the significance of civil liberties, self-government, and the prospect for America's greatness. He concluded in 1789 that the "sacred fire of liberty and the destiny of the re-

publican model of government" depended "on the experiment intrusted to the hands of the American people." There were more learned, more philosophically profound, more articulate explicators of the American Revolution than Washington. His standing owed most to the personal reliability that had impressed Virginians before the war and that became integral to American victory.

The Continental Congress appointed Washington to command the American forces on June 15, 1775. The importance of unity among sections while most of the fighting was being done by New Englanders made a military veteran from the most populous colony especially appropriate. He remained commander in chief throughout the war, resigning his commission on December 23, 1783, in a ceremony before Congress. His conduct during these eight years established his unique national fame, which led to his election as the first president of the United

Washington Crossing the Delaware, an engraving by F. O. Freeman from the painting by E. Leutze. *(Library of Congress)*

The Vice President
John Adams

John Adams was born on October 30, 1735, in Braintree, Massachusetts. At the age of sixteen, Adams enrolled in Harvard College, where he earned a bachelor of arts degree in 1755. Choosing law as his profession, he was admitted to the bar after completing an apprenticeship. On October 25, 1764, Adams married Abigail Smith, with whom he had five children. The eldest son, John Quincy Adams, would later follow in his father's footsteps to become the sixth president of the United States.

Adams began his career as a politician and diplomat while serving as a delegate from Massachusetts in the Continental Congress in 1774. As one of the signers of the Declaration of Independence, Adams was entrusted with the mission of seeking aid from France and Holland for the new fledgling republic as well as the negotiation of a peace treaty with Great Britain. In 1785, he was appointed as the American minister to the Court of St. James. Upon arriving home from Great Britain, Adams was elected vice president and was sworn into office on June 3, 1789. Adams referred to the vice presidency as "the most insignificant office that ever the invention of man contrived or his imagination conceived." He would be elevated to the nation's highest office in 1796. However, in the contentious election of 1800, Adams lost his second bid for the presidency to his onetime friend and political adversary, Thomas Jefferson.

Adams, now retired, returned to his home in Massachusetts, where he worked the land and began writing his autobiography. He died at the age of ninety on July 4, 1826. Ironically, he and Jefferson died on the same day — the fiftieth anniversary of the signing of the Declaration of Independence.

Robert P. Watson and Richard Yon

States. Three elements of Washington's wartime service underlay his success and the public esteem that he won: his unselfishness, his persevering constancy, and his restraint with power. The tableaux that Americans repeatedly celebrated were Washington's declining to accept a salary as commander in chief, Washington's holding the army together at Trenton or Valley Forge or at other crucial times, and — above all — Washington's resigning his commission. These seemed to exemplify the civic-mindedness that should characterize the citizens of a republic, guaranteeing the new nation's survival.

As commander in chief, Washington aspired to be a victorious general who commanded a veteran regular army. He resorted to short-term soldiers, militia auxiliaries, and cautious Fabian strategy from necessity rather than preference. Although he achieved some critical victories — especially the Battle of Trenton (December 26, 1776) and the capture of Lord Cornwallis's army at Yorktown (October 18, 1781) — his main accomplishment was the painstaking diligence with which he labored on what he called "minutious details" in the interest of supply, discipline, recruitment, and popular support of the war effort — all of which were in jeopardy during the war. The army's wartime difficulties, symbolized by the hardship of the winter at Valley Forge, Pennsylvania (1777-1778), but prevalent at many other times as well, Washington attributed to the deficiencies of the decentralized, state-oriented government under the Continental Congress and the Articles of Confederation ratified in 1781.

Although Washington grew convinced that the United States needed a stronger central government, he remained scrupulously deferential to civil authorities while he was a general. When a few officers, early in 1783, suggested that the army should defy Congress and refuse to disband until provision had been made for back pay and officers' pensions, Washington called a meeting of officers in camp at Newburgh, New York, to quell any attempt to use the army to influence Congress. Perhaps the most widely praised single act of Washington's life was his resignation. Most of the soldiers had already disbanded; Washington, far from contemplating a dictatorship, felt eager to return to private life. Nevertheless, his voluntary surrender of command — in contrast with generals since antiquity who had seized supreme power — stood for his contemporaries as proof that independence had been won without subversion of the political principles of the American Revolution. Here was confirmation that public-spirited citizens could wield power without being corrupted, that self-government could survive. The celebration of Washington's trustworthiness during and after the American Revolution did not glorify only one personality but also made a public character a basis for national unity.

The Drafting of the Constitution

The almost universal respect that Washington enjoyed after the war made him a pivotal figure in the establishment of the government created by the Constitution of 1787. Among Americans critical of the weakness of the Confederation government, the prospect of Washington as chief executive of a new government promised more effective central authority. Americans who were suspicious of the powers granted to the new federal government by the Constitution could not convincingly portray him as a potential dictator. The new institutions, like republicanism itself, were experimental, and Washington brought a proven record to a tentative

undertaking.

Washington's reluctance was sincere as he wrote in April, 1789: "My movements to the chair of Government will be accompanied by feelings not unlike those of a culprit who is going to the place of his execution." He correctly anticipated that he stood a better chance of partly losing the "good name" he already possessed than of adding luster to it. He preferred private life to public power, yet he had taken an active part in the interstate political mobilization on behalf of a stronger federal government and had presided over the Philadelphia Convention of 1787 in which the Constitution was drafted. He supported ratification of the Constitution by the states and accepted the presidency because he believed that the weakness of the Confederation endangered American liberty and independence. The Continental Congress

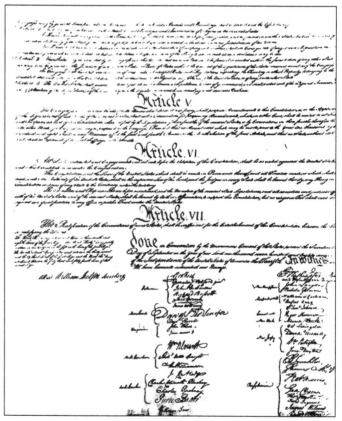

A page from the original copy of the U.S. Constitution. *(NARA)*

lacked the power to tax or to coerce. States' neglect denied Congress revenue. The opposition or absence of delegates from a few states could prevent major legislation, and the opposition of any one state could prevent Congress from expanding its powers. Hence, the central government could not pay its foreign or domestic debts; nor could it amass sufficient power to protect the expanding Western settlements from British forts or American Indian resistance. It lacked the power to retaliate against discriminatory foreign trade regulations by European nations and to compel trade reciprocity. A state government confronted with unrest—such as that of Massachusetts when farmers in 1786 closed courts to protest heavy taxation—could not rely on a national government to maintain order. As Washington and other supporters of strong central government understood history, the prospect of anarchy was an even greater threat to republics than the danger of dictatorship. In fact, weak government would give way to mob rule, ending in tyranny. Washington entered the presidency keenly aware of the fragility of American unity and of the suspicion with which the conduct of the new government would be watched. Yet these centrifugal forces were the very influences that helped convince him to lend his influence to greater political centralization.

Establishing the Presidency

When Washington took the oath of office as president in New York City on April 30, 1789, two states—North Carolina and Rhode Island—had not yet ratified the Constitution. Furthermore, large numbers of Americans in such important states as Virginia, New York, and Pennsylvania had opposed adoption of the new form of government, thinking its powers too great. Political alignments within the states were highly complex and diverse. Some states, such as New York, Rhode Island, and New Jersey, had two-party divisions of long standing. In Pennsylvania, the state constitution of 1776

divided political allegiances between its supporters and its critics. In most states, even those as different as Georgia and New Hampshire, political coalitions shifted according to personal, familial, and patronage loyalties. Small wonder that Washington, preparing to appoint federal officials, feared that a "single disgust excited in a particular State, on this account, might perhaps raise a flame of opposition that could not easily, if ever, be extinguished."

One of the first measures of the new government, designed to allay some of the concern provoked by its powers, was Congress's adoption, on September 25, 1789, of twelve amendments to the Constitution, of which ten were eventually ratified by three-fourths of the state legislatures. These amendments were an explicit recognition of rights reserved by the people, not to be violated by the United States government. They included prohibition of a national religious establishment and of federal abridgment of free speech, freedom of the press, peaceable petition and assembly, and the right to bear arms in the common defense. Other amendments prohibited arbitrary quartering of soldiers in private homes and regulated the procedures for the arrest and trial of persons accused of crime. The ninth amendment provided that other rights, not specified in this list, remained intact; and the tenth amendment read: "The powers not delegated to the United States by the Constitution, nor prohibited by it to the States, are reserved to the States respectively, or to the people." The ratification of these amendments—the Bill of Rights—was completed on December 15, 1791. Meanwhile, North Carolina had ratified the Constitution and joined the federal government on November 29, 1789. Rhode Island, under pressure from internal threats of secession, did so on May 29, 1790.

Despite the fact that Americans considered their country to be "the rational empire of human liberty and equality, founded upon the natural rights of mankind and sovereignty of the people," the first federal officeholders, including President Washington, devoted much attention to rituals of official behavior and to the mystique of precedent. The Federalists, as supporters of the Constitution called themselves, commanded a large majority in both houses of Congress. There were only three or four Antifederalist senators and no more than thirteen Antifederalist representatives. Some Federalists, especially in the Senate and above all Vice President John Adams, believed that the government needed not only the rational consent of its citizens but also the emotional attachment inspired by awe at its magnificence. Thus, senators proposed to exalt Washington with a quasi-monarchical title, such as "His Excellency" — the form of address often used while he was commander of the army — or "His Elective Highness." Washington himself addressed Congress in person and received con-

gressional delegations with replies, as did the British monarch. He rode in state in a carriage with uniformed outriders; he did not accept invitations or return visits. All these proposals and practices excited comment, especially criticism from the more egalitarian-minded. The House of Representatives refused to adopt a special title for the president, and all holders of the office have since been addressed simply as "Mister President." The controversy was comparatively minor; yet, it first raised one of the fundamental issues of Washington's presidency and of early national period politics: a conflict between the attempt to establish a government that could command obedience and the fear that the American Revolution would be subverted by monarchical institutions.

George Washington probably overestimated the potential long-term significance of the precedents that he set, ceremonial or substantive. Thomas Jefferson, as president, abandoned Washington's social rules; Andrew Jackson abandoned Washington's practice of vetoing bills only when he deemed them unconstitutional. Washington's fundamental accomplishment was to inaugurate an executive office with strong — and potentially much stronger — authority among a people whose political life in part had long consisted of resistance to centralized executive power. Subject to the Senate's role in ratifying treaties and confirming nominees to office, the president conducted foreign relations; appointed diplomats, federal judges, and other federal officials; and commanded the nation's military forces, including state militias called into federal service. He held office for four years at a time when most state gubernatorial terms were one year or two, and there was no restriction on reelection of the president. He could prevent by veto the enactment of legislation

The inauguration of Washington. *(Library of Congress)*

that did not command a two-thirds majority in the House and the Senate.

Early in the first administration, Representative James Madison complained to Secretary of State Thomas Jefferson that Washington's followers "had wound up the ceremonials of the government to a pitch of stateliness which nothing but his personal character could have supported, and which no character after him could ever maintain." At the same time that Madison identified a drawback to Washington's distinctive position, he acknowledged its impact. The difficulties in fighting, recruiting, supplying, and financing the Revolutionary War effort had dramatized the deficiencies of state and continental governments with weak executives. No person embodied the impulse to constitutional change so emphatically as Washington. The "pitch of stateliness" supported by his "personal character" combined augmentation of power with the expectation that it would not be abused.

One of the clearest examples of Washington's personal importance as a nationalizing influence was his travel throughout the United States during his first years in office. In April, 1789, he traveled from Mount Vernon to New York to assume the presidency. In the autumn and winter of 1789-1790, he toured New England, crisscrossing Massachusetts and Connecticut and going as far north as Portsmouth, New Hampshire. In the spring of 1791, he completed an ambitious circuit of the Southern states that covered both the tidewater and the piedmont regions of Virginia, North Carolina, South Carolina, and Georgia. These progressions were an almost unending series of ceremonial addresses, parades, formal greetings, fetes, and honors. Officials welcomed him, choirs serenaded him, girls strewed flowers in his path, tavern keepers played host to his entourage, and volunteer companies of horsemen escorted him. After having passed through some of the areas where opposition to the Constitution had

Excerpt from George Washington's first inaugural address, April 30, 1789:

Among the vicissitudes incident to life no event could have filled me with greater anxieties than that of which the notification was transmitted by your order, and received on the fourteenth day of the present month. On the one hand, I was summoned by my country, whose voice I can never hear but with veneration and love, from a retreat which I had chosen with the fondest predilection, and, in my flattering hopes, with an immutable decision, as the asylum of my declining years — a retreat which was rendered every day more necessary as well as more dear to me by the addition of habit to inclination, and of frequent interruptions in my health to the gradual waste committed on it by time. On the other hand, the magnitude and difficulty of the trust to which the voice of my country called me, being sufficient to awaken in the wisest and most experienced of her citizens a distrustful scrutiny into his qualifications, could not but overwhelm with despondence, one, who inheriting inferior endowments from nature and unpracticed in the duties of civil administration, ought to be peculiarly conscious of his own deficiencies. In this conflict of emotions all I dare aver, is, that it has been my faithful study to collect my duty from a just appreciation of every circumstance by which it might be affected. All I dare hope, is, that if, in executing this task, I have been too much swayed by a grateful remembrance of former instances, or by an affectionate sensibility to this transcendent proof of the confidence of my fellow-citizens, and have thence too little consulted my incapacity as well as disinclination for the weighty and untried cares before me, my error will be palliated by the motives which misled me, and its consequences be judged by my country with some share of the partiality in which they originated.

been strongest, Washington summarized the main lesson of his tour: "Tranquility reigns among the people, with that disposition towards the general government which is likely to preserve it. They begin to feel the good effects of equal laws and equal protection."

In establishing his administration, Washington neither foresaw nor desired the development of national political parties. Parties, or factions, because they were self-serving and self-perpetuating, were thought to be inimical to the public-spiritedness on which republican institutions were based. The balanced powers of the branches of government were designed to impede any attempt to unite control of the federal authority under one group. The electoral college, in theory, confided the selection of the president and vice president to a few of the best-informed and most judicious citizens. A nonparty ideal of government seemed to prevail at the opening of the Washington administration.

With James Madison, a central figure in the Constitutional Convention, as an especially prominent leader, the Congress in 1789 enacted legislation to establish the federal judiciary and the executive departments—not yet customarily called a "cabinet"—of State, Treasury, and War. The attorney general was legal counsel to the executive and not the administrator of a department. The Judiciary Act of 1789 established a Supreme Court, two circuit courts, and thirteen district courts but left the state courts with original jurisdiction over most cases arising under the federal Constitution, laws, or treaties. The Supreme Court was given appellate jurisdiction over cases in which state courts decided against a claim of federal right. This established the principle of federal judicial review of state legislation. Cases not falling under federal jurisdiction, however, could not be appealed beyond the state court systems. Washington appointed firm Federalists to the Supreme Court, with an eye to even geographical distribution and with John Jay of New York

as chief justice. As secretary of state, Washington chose Thomas Jefferson, who had been minister to France since 1784. Edmund Randolph became attorney general. The secretary of war, Henry Knox, and the secretary of the treasury, Alexander Hamilton, were men whom Washington had measured during their service in the Continental Army.

Economic Policies: Hamilton's Guiding Vision

Secretary Hamilton took the initiative in defining a domestic legislative program for the administration. An intelligent, ambitious, hard-working man, Hamilton had a vision of governmental policy that encompassed a design for the future of the United States as a populous, industrially productive, powerful, centralized nation. In September, 1780, at a low point of the American effort in the War of Independence, Hamilton—then an aide-de-camp to Washington—had outlined the kinds of measures that he brought to fruition ten years later: executive authority in the hands of departmental administrators, more rigorous federal taxation, and a federally chartered bank that could loan money to the government and attract, through the prospect of profits, the support of rich men for the government. As secretary of the treasury, Hamilton submitted to Congress in 1790 three reports on provision for the support of the public credit. These contained his plan for funding the national debt, which consisted of approximately $11.7 million owed to Dutch bankers and to the governments of France and Spain, plus $40 million in securities held by foreign investors and by Americans. The Confederation government had been paying interest on the Dutch debt only by contracting additional loans and had allowed interest payments on the rest of the debt to fall into arrears, to a total of about $13 million. Hamilton proposed to convert the unpaid back interest to principal and to fund the total principal by an issue of interest-bearing securities, to the interest on which and to the redemption of which the government would permanently pledge part of its revenue.

The proposal not only was confined to the debt that had been contracted by the Continental Congress but also provided for the assumption by the federal government of the war debts owed by the states, which would add $25 million to the new national debt. In imitation of the British system by which Sir Robert Walpole had established his government's credit, the goal of the funding plan was not to retire the debt completely but to establish confidence that interest on government securities would be paid and that they could be sold or redeemed at or near their face value. When this situation prevailed, government securities could serve as collateral for private loans that expanded the credit available for business ventures.

Hamilton further proposed that Congress charter a Bank of the United States with a capital of $10 million, one-fifth of which would be subscribed by the government, the rest by private investors. One of the bank's functions would be to make short-term loans to the government. The income of the Treasury, primarily from import duties, fluctuated seasonally, whereas to maintain the value of its securities, the Treasury needed a reliable, consistent source of cash. The bank's loans would serve this purpose. The government would deposit its money in the bank, which could also make its own private loans and issue bank notes that citizens could tender to the government at face value for the payment of taxes and other obligations. The notes of the Bank of the United States would be the principal currency in circulation.

Hamilton's conception of the government's responsibilities went beyond the management of its debts and finances. He sought, especially in his Report on Manufactures — submitted in December, 1791 — to use federal power to shape the American economy. He wanted the United States to achieve the complex, internally balanced, self-sufficient economy toward which European nations were striving. Fearing that America's traditional trading partners would increasingly rely on their own and their colonies' resources and exclude American agricultural exports from their markets, Hamilton urged that the United States imitate this closed mercantilist system by developing the nation's industrial capacity to meet its domestic demand for manufactured goods, thereby diminishing dependence on Europe. His report proposed protective tariffs on some foreign manufactured goods, bounties for new American industries, and awards and premiums for improvements in productivity and quality. Such incentives would persuade capitalists that they could make greater profits from domestic manufacturing than from the traditional investments in shipping American agricultural products to Europe and selling European manufactures in America.

Not coincidentally, the features of Hamilton's proposals interlocked to foster one another. Holders of the public debt who stood to profit from the plan would lend their support to the federal government; the assumption of state debts would induce public creditors to look to the nation and not to the state for maintenance of the value of their holdings; relieved of their Revolutionary War debt, states would have less justification for levying taxes of their own, whereas the federal government would have more reason to assert its powers through taxation; such federal taxes could promote the growth of manufacturing by raising the cost of competing imports; an excise tax on liquor would not only raise revenue from large-scale distillers but would also establish the federal government's direct authority over backcountry independent distillers and backcountry opponents of federal power; a stable federal revenue would secure the confidence of investors in the public credit — they could then devote some of their profits and some of the credit newly available through the Bank of the United States to investment in manufacturing; the de-

A portrait of Alexander Hamilton. *(Library of Congress)*

velopment of an integrated economy of agricultural suppliers, American manufacturers, and American consumers would promote the consolidation of the Union through ties of commerce; thus the United States could, by national policy, hasten the day of its becoming a great power.

Although Hamilton had an almost visionary enthusiasm for his conception of national greatness and did not seek to profit personally from the implementation of his program, the grand design, like the earlier system of Walpole, had as its motive power the pursuit of self-interest. If Hamilton were correct, the United States could enhance its international security, its domestic prosperity, its cultural unity, and its political stability by exploiting the selfishness of private advantage for the ends of national policy. In fact, Hamilton believed, the nation could achieve these goals in no other way.

President Washington took no hand in the

drafting of Hamilton's program. Although Washington managed his own business affairs astutely and amassed a fortune through a lifetime of land transactions, he was not expert in the complexities of public finance. His support for Hamilton's policies, however, was crucial to their enactment by Congress. Hamilton said that Washington "consulted much, resolved slowly, resolved surely." In August, 1790, after prolonged debate and by a narrow margin, most of Hamilton's proposals were enacted, followed by the legislation for the Bank of the United States in February, 1791.

Opposition to Hamilton's Program:
Origins of the National Party System

Although almost everyone agreed that provision for the public debt was essential, Hamilton's plan excited strong, widespread opposition, which contributed to a lasting political division among the supporters of the Constitution. Some of the bases for opposition were highly specific. James Madison and his followers protested that most of the original holders of the public debt—people who had provided loans, goods, and services for the winning of independence, receiving the Continental government's paper money, loan office certificates, or promissory notes—had subsequently sold their claims to speculators for a fraction of the face value. Hamilton's plan would confer large profits on the monied men who now held the claims, while neglecting the patriots who had done most for the American Revolution. Madison proposed to divide the government's repayment between the original and the ultimate creditors. Although congressmen joined Madison in commiserating with victimized widows, orphans, and veterans—denouncing greedy speculators—his alternative was too complex and entailed too much expense to attract much support in Congress.

The assumption of state debts aroused the opposition of congressmen from states that had contracted small debts or had paid off most of their debt since the war. Such states disliked the idea of now having to share in the cost of funding the debts of their less conscientious neighbors. To win support, the proponents of assumption had to add to the legislation federal grants to those states that would benefit least from assumption as well as special advantages for Virginia. Southerners, especially Virginians, were concerned by the fact that more than 80 percent of the holders of the national debt were Northerners and that most of the state debts were also in the North. Hamilton's system would increase the disparity of wealth and power in favor of the North. Hamilton obtained the additional votes needed to enact the funding and assumption plan by supporting the establishment of the national capital on the Potomac River in Maryland and Virginia, to take effect after a ten-year residence in Philadelphia.

Other bases of the resistance in Congress were broader concerns of principle, which became more urgent after Hamilton presented his plan for a national bank. To justify the demand for American independence, some proponents of the American Revolution had argued that British liberty was being undermined by the manufacturing economy and the politics based on self-seeking (or, as Americans said, corruption) that Hamilton now proposed to import to the United States. Urban concentrations of population, great disparities in wealth, the dependent status of wage workers, a powerful central bank whose resources lessened the reliance of the executive on the voters and their representatives, discriminatory taxes that used the government's power for the benefit of a few at the expense of the many—all these tendencies that made the British Empire seem a threat to liberty would systematically subvert a republican form of government in the United States. Far from sharing Hamilton's fear that a solely agricultural America would be at the mercy of Europe, his critics, especially Thomas Jefferson, contended that America's crops and raw materials were the foundation of the more industrialized nations' well-being. This fact made the United States more stable and secure than its trading partners. Moreover, Americans' buying the bulk of their manufactured goods from Europe left the evils of industrial society far away. Americans could aspire to perpetuate the independent-minded, public-spirited citizenry essential for the survival of self-government exactly because Americans remained self-sufficient farmers free from the economic and political engines admired by Hamilton.

Although Hamilton won enactment of his program, it became, with the divergent opinions on America's foreign relations, the source of a basic division leading to competing political mobilization in rival parties, called Federalist and Republican (or Democratic Republican). Political organizations, including long-standing two-party competition, were already well known in state politics, and many of these factions, or parties, were soon aligned in the new national party system. The Federalist and Republican parties, however, originated in Congress and among leading politicians. These men then encouraged a more general public alarm over governmental policy, which could best be influenced by systematic political cooperation. James Madison and Alexander Hamilton had collaborated in winning public ratification of the Constitution, and Hamilton had consulted Madison as he prepared his reports. Madison, however, became the parliamentary leader of opposition to Hamilton's system in the House of Representatives. Secretary of State Thomas Jefferson, who did not take office until March, 1790, soon became the central figure in the nascent party, though not publicly its spokesperson. In the cabinet, Attorney General Edmund Randolph was an ally. In the Senate, the adept political organizer from New York, Aaron Burr, could be used, if not trusted. In the House of Representatives, the anti-Hamilton (or, by the time of Jefferson's resignation in December, 1793, the antiadministration) group was strongest, approaching a majority on some issues.

Hamilton could count on a strong majority in the Senate, led by such able men as Oliver Ellsworth of Connecticut, Robert Morris of Pennsylvania, and Rufus King of New York. Representatives Fisher Ames and Theodore Sedgwick of Massachusetts and William Loughton Smith of South Carolina led pro-Hamilton members of the House, who controlled that body. Secretary of War Henry Knox allied with Hamilton in the cabinet.

For factions in the capital to become parties with national support, organized in even rudimentary networks, the concerns of the cabinet and Congress would have to become the concerns of influential men throughout the country and of voters who could change the composition of the House and, indirectly, the Senate, whose members were elected by state legislatures. One of the principal means of disseminating and intensifying these concerns was the partisan press, especially in Philadelphia after that city became the capital in 1790. The *Gazette of the United States*, edited by John Fenno, became the leading advocate of Hamilton's measures. Fenno dramatized and personalized his arguments by extravagant praise of Hamilton. To his critics, this was cause for alarm. George Washington was the most conspicuous example of the intimate connection between receiving fulsome adulation and possessing political power. Jefferson and Madison feared that the *Gazette of the United States* was exalting Hamilton similarly in order to make him the wielder of power that would overawe republican institutions. In 1791, to present the necessary warnings and to refute Fenno's support of the Hamiltonian program, Jefferson and Madison induced the poet and journalist Philip Freneau to undertake the editorship of a new paper, the *National Gazette*. In it, Freneau denounced Hamilton's conspiratorial designs and praised Jefferson for fidelity to the principles of the American Revolution. In practice, both editors were agents of the factions for which they spoke. They were responsible for organizing, clarifying, and exaggerating the opinions that would form one of the bases of party loyalty. Fenno's operations were supported partly by printing contracts from the Treasury Department and loans from Hamilton. Freneau received a clerkship in the State Department, which gave him an income with plenty of free time for his editorial labors. Hamilton wrote many of the attacks on Jefferson, published under pseudonyms, whereas Attorney General Randolph wrote defenses of Jefferson. As Hamilton's financial program and other issues attracted more widespread opposition and support, an avowedly partisan press developed in other cities, discussing not only local concerns but also the controversies originating in the capital.

George Washington felt strong concern about the increasingly bitter divisions within his administration. Both Jefferson and Hamilton offered to resign, but the president hoped for a nonparty government that would help attach the public to the Constitution. He wanted to keep Jefferson in office, but he refused to believe that Hamilton or any significant number of Americans were guilty of conspiring to introduce monarchy. Washington had accepted the presidency with sincere reluctance. Part of his reluctance came from the thought that, although his personal popularity might lend dignity to the government, political controversy might undermine the popular esteem for him. To his distress, he saw this happening, as criticism of Hamilton and of monarchists widened to touch the president himself. Washington set great store by the reputation of respect for republican institutions that he had established during the Revolutionary War. In 1789, he feared that accepting the presidency might look like ambition — reneging on the promise implied in his resignation of his commission — and he hoped to minimize any such suspicion by serving only one term. In 1792, at his request, Madison wrote a draft of a farewell address, with which Washington hoped to close his presidential term fittingly, but the growing political divisions, along with crises in the economy and in American dealings with Britain and France, made Washington's continuance in office for a second term seem imperative to Hamilton, Jefferson, Madison, and many others. Even as Washington won reelection, however, the inchoate Republican Party gathered fifty electoral votes for Governor George Clinton of New York—as well as four for Jefferson and one for Burr—in an unsuccessful attempt to defeat the reelection of John Adams as vice president.

Having accepted a second term despite his own reluctance, Washington was keenly sensitive to accusations that he was arrogating power to himself and betraying his image as a civic-minded Cincinnatus who served only as long as the public needed him. When a newspaper called him a king and depicted him on a guillotine in 1793, Washington lost his temper in a cabinet meeting, which Jefferson recorded:

> The President was much inflamed, got into one of those passions when he cannot command himself, ran on much on the personal abuse which had been bestowed on him, defied any man on earth to produce one single act of his since he had been in the government which was not done on the purest motives, that he had never repented but once the having slipped the moment of resigning his office, and that was every moment since, that *by god* he had rather be in his grave than in his present situation. That he had rather be on his farm than to be made *emperor of the world* and yet that they were charging him with wanting to be a king. That that *rascal Freneau* sent him three of his papers every day, as if he thought he would become the distributor of his papers, that he could see in this nothing but an impudent design to insult him. He ended in this high tone.

During his second term, Washington, though still deploring parties and aspiring to preserve his position as a figure of national unity, became increasingly a partisan, Federalist president.

The debate over Hamilton's program and the ensuing partisan rhetoric revealed that Americans had a source of political unity and authority at the national level other than respect for Washington: the Constitution. Despite the widespread opposition to its ratification, the document soon became an object of veneration and the appeal of last resort on controversial questions. Few men remained Antifederalists, and the developing parties of the 1790's had few significant continuities with the factions of the 1780's. The Constitution, almost everyone in political life agreed, defined the way to preserve an ever-vulnerable republican system of government. Contrary to the partisans' charges, Hamilton and the Federalists did not want to introduce monarchical tyranny; nor did Jefferson and the Republicans want to sabotage American unity and independence with anarchy or French revolutionary radicalism. In their deep disagreement, however, the two groups were appealing to a common source of authority for their claim to be patriots. They were constructing sharply divergent interpretations of the Constitution's ambiguous provisions.

For Hamilton, the main threat to American republicanism came not from the prospect of a tyrannical central government but from a weak federal government's inability to maintain its unity, solvency, and national independence. Thus, when Madison, Jefferson, and Randolph tried to persuade Washington to veto the bill establishing the Bank of the United States, on the grounds that the Constitution gave the federal government no such power, Hamilton disagreed. His defense of the constitutionality of the bank appealed to the last clause of Article I, Section 8 of the Constitution, which authorizes Congress to make laws that are "necessary and proper" for executing the powers vested in the government. In Hamilton's interpretation, which convinced Washington to sign the legislation, "necessary" meant not only essential for but also useful in or conducive to the execution of the government's duties. Since a bank would aid in collecting taxes, regulating trade, and providing defense—all of which the Constitution authorized—it was constitutional. This broad construction of the document's wording implied that the Constitution authorized an unlimited array of means whose use it did not specifically prohibit.

For Jefferson and the Republicans—at least until they took control of the federal government in 1801—the greatest threat to the republic was the use of what Jefferson called "props" for the government other than the freely given consent of the people. Such props would include officials' conspicuous military reputations, social and political rituals in imitation of European monarchies, concentrations of financial power aided by governmental policy, or displays of force through the taxing power, the judiciary, and other federal authorities. The Constitution, Republicans agreed, restricted the scope for abuses by confining the federal government to an essential minimum, keeping the remainder of governmental power at the state level, where it could be more closely supervised by the electorate.

The text of the Constitution could plausibly be construed along either of these lines. Its claim to delineate a dual sovereignty divided between federal and state governments and constituencies was theoretically ingenious and politically expedient but practically ambiguous. This ambiguity enabled the Constitution to function as a shared symbol of nationality and of successful self-government among people who deeply mistrusted one another's loyalty.

Despite their familiarity with state political factions, Americans were not accustomed to regarding as patriots those with whom they differed on fundamental questions of political principle, particularly when their opponents began to organize. Differences on immediate issues were quickly traced back to the basic issue of the American Revolution: the survival of liberty. Yet when differences were cast in these terms, it was difficult to credit opponents with patriotic intentions or republican sentiments. Instead, it seemed self-evident that a faction

that was pursuing dangerous measures must be a conspiracy—at best, to serve the self-interest of its members; at worst, to subvert the American Revolution. The Federalists and the Republicans tended to see themselves not as conscientious rivals over questions of official policy but as combatants, each party claiming to be the rescuer of American independence from internal enemies of the republic. This antiparty outlook and this apocalyptic interpretation of partisans' motives remained influential in political discourse long after parties were no longer new in national politics.

Westward Expansion: Settlers and Speculators

Americans of the nineteenth and twentieth centuries have often portrayed the economy and society of late eighteenth century America as comparatively stable, traditional, almost decorous; yet, to people of the time, the country seemed volatile, potentially explosive. Even without massive immigration—though the importation of slaves continued legally until 1808—the population was almost doubling every twenty years. Both the growth of population and the economic ambitions of Americans focused attention on the lands west of the Appalachian mountain chain. Anticipating the rapid extension of settlement between the Appalachians and the Mississippi River, many American investors, including George Washington, speculated in Western lands. They acquired claims to vast holdings, which they hoped to sell at a profit to other investors, even before actual migration began on a large scale. Opponents of Hamilton's funding and assumption measures contended that the national debt could be retired without recourse to Hamilton's federal "engine" simply by selling parcels of the public domain to speculators and settlers—so sure were the migration and the resulting revenue. Under the influence of bribes given to state legislators, the state of Georgia sold sixteen million acres to three Yazoo land companies for

$200,000—a vast tract of Georgia's western lands in present-day Alabama and Mississippi. Robert Morris and his associates John Nicholson and James Greenleaf formed the North American Land Company, amassing claims to six million acres that they expected to resell at a large profit. Investors in the Potomac Company planned, with the help of a canal around the falls of the Potomac and a canal connecting the Ohio River network with the upper Potomac, to funnel much of the trade of the expanding West, from the Great Lakes to Tennessee, past the new national capital.

The vision and optimism of the speculators ran too far ahead of the actual settlements and purchases on which their hope for profits was ultimately based. Their market was soon impaired by the rising value of American government securities, which could be advantageously pledged in payment for land while they were depreciated but which became more expensive and less useful to speculators as the securities approached face value. Also, the outbreak of war in Europe in 1792 offered European capitalists more attractive returns on loans to belligerent powers than on purchases of American forests. Significantly, at the peak of speculative land values in the early 1790's, Washington, who had played this kind of game for thirty-five years and who needed money, was prudently selling some of his holdings while other men were still buying extensively. In 1795, the bottom began to drop out of the inflated market in Western lands. During the next fifteen years, a wide array of speculators found themselves insolvent. Several, including Robert Morris, went to prison at the suit of their creditors.

Indian Affairs: Benign Policies, Brutal Realities

Although the migration to Ohio, Kentucky, and Tennessee was well under way during Washington's administration, the intensive settlement that would eventually match the speculators' vision depended on more than population growth. The West already had a population—the diverse American Indian peoples, most of whom regarded the westward movement of whites with alarm. Their leaders, especially Joseph Brant of the Mohawk and Alexander McGillivray of the Creek, hoped to confine white settlement within the narrowest possible limits, primarily near the major rivers. Great Britain and Spain, whose empires bordered the United States, also wanted to restrict American expansion. The British continued to occupy forts on territory ceded to the United States in 1783, acting as if Ohio were still British, and the Spanish in the Southwest encouraged American Indians to confederate and whites to separate politically from the United States.

Washington, like many of his successors, announced a policy of equitable dealings and peaceful relations with Native Americans. In 1791, he concluded a treaty confirming Indian title to most of the land granted by Georgia to the Yazoo land companies. He urged Congress to define legal means for the transfer of land from Indians to white settlers, for the supervision of trade with Indians, and for the prevention of white settlers' attacks on Indians. Leaving out the question of the later governmental violations of treaties concluded during the Washington administration, this policy confronted immediate difficulties. First, the goal of most American Indians was not regional coexistence with whites under federal supervision but exclusion of whites from their ancestral lands. Second, the policy of coexistence was repeatedly violated by whites who settled on native lands. As one American officer reported, "The people of Kentucky will carry on private expeditions against the Indians and kill them whenever they meet them, and I do not believe that there is a jury in all Kentucky will punish a man for it." Third, the British and the Spanish encouraged American Indians to fight and provided them with arms and ammunition.

Early in 1790, attempting to exclude white

35

settlers from the region north and west of the Ohio River, a group of Indians attacked, defeating Josiah Harmar's army at the Maumee River. In the autumn of 1791, General Arthur St. Clair, governor of the Northwest Territory, took the field with an ill-trained army. He fell into an ambush on November 4, 1791, with more than nine hundred of his men killed or wounded. White settlers in Ohio withdrew to Cincinnati and Marietta. President Washington privately received the news of St. Clair's defeat while guests were dining with him. His courteous, formal demeanor remained unchanged until the guests had left and Mrs. Washington had retired. Then, alone with his secretary, Tobias Lear, Washington's emotions mounted into a rage as he said, "It's all over—St. Clair's defeated—routed;—the officers nearly all killed, the men by wholesale; the rout complete—too shocking to think of—and a SURPRISE into the bargain!" Remembering his parting words to St. Clair in Philadelphia, Washington now spoke in a torrent, throwing his hands up several times, his body shaking:

> Yes, HERE on this very spot, I took leave of him; I wished him success and honor; you have your instructions, I said, from the Secretary of War, I had a strict eye to them, and will add but one word—BEWARE OF A SURPRISE. I repeat it, BEWARE OF A SURPRISE—you know how the Indians fight us. He went off with that, as my last solemn warning thrown into his ears. And yet!! to suffer that army to be cut to pieces, hack'd, butchered, tomahawk'd, by a SURPRISE—the very thing I guarded him against!! O God, O God, he's worse than a murderer! how can he answer it to his country;—the blood of the slain is upon him—the curse of widows and orphans—the curse of Heaven!

St. Clair's defeat prompted the creation of the first congressional investigating committee, which reviewed the pertinent documents and blamed the outcome on army contractors who had failed to supply proper equipment. The government's Indian policy continued to entertain the prospect of a settlement by treaty until chiefs of the Six Nations, encouraged by the British, made clear in January, 1793, their insistence on an Ohio River boundary. Thereafter, despite some further negotiations, the administration concentrated on defeating resistance. Between 1790 and 1796, the Indian wars accounted for almost five-sixths of the federal government's operating expenses, eventually consuming a total of $5 million. To command in the West, Washington chose General Anthony Wayne, who reached Ohio in 1793. He carefully developed a trained, disciplined force, consisting of two thousand U.S. Army soldiers and more than fifteen hundred Kentucky militiamen. In June, 1794, supported by British construction of Fort Miami on the Maumee River, two thousand American Indians gathered there. Wayne began the march against them in August and met a force of thirteen hundred at Fallen Timbers, where he won a decisive victory on August 20, followed by the devastation of American Indian towns and crops. The British were discredited in Indians' eyes by their refusal to fight the Americans, with whom they were officially at peace. Within a year, Wayne used his new power to dictate the Treaty of Greenville, removing all American Indians from the area that later became the state of Ohio, for which the United States paid $10,000.

Foreign Affairs: Internal Debate over Policies Toward France

The most difficult, divisive problem that confronted the Washington administration was the conduct of America's foreign relations. For its security, as well as its pride in being a republic, the new nation needed to demonstrate that it was not a temporary aberration. Markets abroad were essential to the prosperity of its maritime carrying trade, its commercial farmers, and its producers of raw materials. The nation owed money to European creditors; Britons who had made loans to Americans before the Revolutionary War still demanded payment. The eighteenth century had seen a series of European wars, which had extended to the overseas empires—wars that reached an unprecedented scale began during Washington's presidency. More so than many of its citizens desired, the United States was touched by events in other countries.

The greatest series of such events was the French Revolution. A sequence of bloody changes in the leadership of France, its transformation into a republic, and its war with other European powers forced the Washington administration to make choices, both internationally and among American politicians who differed in their reactions to these developments. Although the early phases of the French Revolution attracted extensive sympathy in the United States, by 1793 the rise of the Jacobins, the Reign of Terror, and the expanding war on behalf of atheistic republican revolution alarmed many Americans without destroying the pro-French sympathies of others. More than thirty local political groups, partly imitating the Jacobin clubs, formed into Democratic societies and Republican societies, which were among the first community political organizations in the United States emphasizing national and international concerns.

Washington and the members of his cabinet agreed that the United States should stay out of the war that France had declared against Britain, Holland, and Spain in January, 1793. Hamilton and Jefferson disagreed, however, on how this should be effected. Hamilton and many other Federalists were appalled at the revolutionary violence in France and at the Frenchmen's assertion that they were the vanguard of similar revolutions throughout the world. In a private letter in May, 1793, Washington, discreetly omitting the name of the country, wrote that France's affairs "seem to me to be in the highest paroxysm of disorder . . . because those in whose hands the G[overnmen]t is entrusted are ready to tear each other to pieces, and will,

more than probably prove the worst foes the Country has." Hamilton argued early in April, 1793, that the Constitution authorized the president to proclaim neutrality and to enforce the policy against any Americans who might try to aid France. He wanted the United States to refrain from diplomatic relations with the revolutionary regime, giving France no grounds to invoke American aid under the terms of the 1778 treaty of mutual defense.

Jefferson did not want the United States to go to war, but he argued that since the Constitution gave to Congress the power to declare war, only Congress could declare neutrality. He wanted to delay a declaration of neutrality in the hope that the belligerent powers would grant more favorable terms of trade to Americans in order to keep the United States out of the war. Despite such calculations for American advantage, he believed that the survival of republicanism in France was essential for the security of republican government in the United States and for the future prospects of liberty elsewhere. In January, 1793, Jefferson expressed his regret that the executions in France had extended beyond "enemies" of the people to include friends of liberty, but he said of the French Revolution, "Rather than it should have failed, I would have seen half the earth desolated." On March 12, 1793, Jefferson instructed the American minister in Paris to recognize the National Assembly as the government of France.

Washington accepted Jefferson's recommendation that the United States recognize the new regime, but he accepted Hamilton's interpretation of the president's authority to proclaim neutrality. In his April 22, 1793, proclamation he omitted the word "neutrality" but declared a policy of "conduct friendly and impartial toward the belligerent powers." Republicans, including James Madison writing under a pseudonym, denounced the proclamation as an unconstitutional aggrandizement of the executive and a betrayal of Americans' moral obligations to their fellow republicans in France.

Madison argued that "every nation has a right to abolish an old government and establish a new one. This principle . . . is the only lawful tenure by which the United States hold their existence as a nation."

The divisions among Americans over the French Revolution and the European war grew more intense as a result of the activities of Edmond Genet, the first minister to the United States from republican France. Genet, a Girondist, was politically out of favor at home by the time he reached America, as the Jacobins were replacing and liquidating the Girondists; but to many Americans, including Jefferson, he was an attractive representative of the fight for republicanism in France, with which they sympathized. On April 8, 1793, Genet landed at Charleston, South Carolina, where he received an enthusiastic welcome and began a month-long trip to Philadelphia. In Charleston and at stops along his route, Genet made arrangements with American supporters for raising armies to liberate Louisiana and Florida from Spain, as well as Canada from Britain. These grandiose plans came to nothing, but they showed Genet's intention to secure Americans' aid in France's wars, contrary to the policy of neutrality. The effusive public demonstrations of solidarity convinced Genet that his policy enjoyed more support than did Washington's. Jefferson, who asserted that 99 percent of Americans approved of the French Revolution, told Genet about the divisions within the cabinet and looked the other way when the French agent André Michaux sought to organize attacks on Louisiana and Canada.

Genet, in violation of Washington's proclamation, commissioned twelve privateering vessels to raid British shipping. Eighty British merchant ships were brought into American ports; they were condemned and sold—not by American admiralty courts, but by French consuls, for whom Genet claimed extraterritorial status. In July, 1793, Washington asked the Supreme Court to rule on the constitutionality of Genet's actions. The Court declined to do so. It asserted its equal status as a branch of government by refusing to act as counsel to the executive branch, confining itself to decisions in litigation. In 1794, in the case *Genet v. Sloop Betsy*, the Court ruled that Genet's consular courts were illegal and that any condemnation of prizes of war should take place in United States district courts, acting as admiralty courts. By August, 1793, Washington was ready to take action against Genet's operations. He prohibited the organizing of military units in America by belligerents. He forbade the privateers commissioned by Genet to enter American ports. The United States, however, had no navy and no army on its coast adequate to enforce these rules. Genet believed that he had sufficient popular support to defy Washington. He threatened to appeal "over Washington's head" to the pro-French sentiment of the American public. This threat was his undoing. Jefferson disassociated himself from Genet, and the government requested that France recall the minister. Since the Jacobins probably would have executed Genet, he was not forced to go home but was allowed to live in the United States as a private citizen.

Although Genet could not overthrow Washington, the controversy over his brief but excited tenure as minister clarified the deep division among Americans in their attitudes toward France. Washington could no longer aspire to preside over a people united in praise of him or over a nonparty government. In December, 1793, Jefferson resigned as secretary of state, to be succeeded by Edmund Randolph. Washington, during his second term, became decisively aligned with the developing Federalist Party, as his policies aroused more vigorous denunciation by Republicans.

Relations with Britain: Threats of War

The European wars did not give the United States the position of commercial advantage that Jefferson had imagined. On the contrary, the ports and the navies of the two main belligerents, France and England, both plundered the American merchant marine. Each stood to gain from trade with neutrals, but each also stood to gain from interrupting its enemy's neutral trade. France, beginning in 1793, confiscated cargoes in its ports. In June, Britain proclaimed a naval blockade of France, which became the basis for seizure of American cargoes headed there. In the autumn, when Britain undertook the conquest of the French West Indies, the government ordered the seizure of all ships trading with those islands — principally American — and kept its order secret until the concentration of ships for seizure was greatest.

Jefferson and the Republicans were troubled by the fact that 75 percent of American imports came from the British Empire and that most American exports went to Britain, even if the goods were subsequently reexported to the Continent. Such a pattern of trade might make the United States dependent on British policy and susceptible to the monarchical influence of Britain's reactionary policies, the Republicans feared. They hoped to establish a more extensive trade with France — indeed, to force American trade into French channels in order to destroy the influence over American politics arising from commercial ties with Great Britain.

Jefferson and the Republicans imagined that they could use the weapon of American trade against Britain without fear of British military action against the United States. The Republicans opposed expenditures for an American military establishment on the scale that Federalists favored. In response to raids on American commerce by Algerian corsairs, Madison recommended that the United States hire the Portuguese navy to do the fighting. Washington, though he and the Federalists deprecated war with Britain, believed that the British might attack America as an ally of France. Moreover, the British seemed to be encouraging the activities of the Barbary pirates to drive American shipping out of the Mediterranean. In February,

1794, Congress authorized the construction of six frigates but also, during the same year, voted bribes to the dey of Algiers for the protection of American vessels.

Few people in government doubted, in the early months of 1794, that the United States and Britain would soon be at war. Hamilton and some Federalist senators believed, however, that the United States could persuade the British that America did not intend to wage covert war under the pretense of neutrality. To this end, these men urged Washington to send a special minister to Britain, charged with concluding a treaty that would avoid war and would settle such points of controversy as the continued presence of one thousand British troops on United States territory and the terms of American trade with Britain and the British West Indies. The Republicans, clinging to Jefferson's belief in commercial coercion of Britain, passed a bill in the House of Representatives prohibiting American trade with Britain. The bill lost in the Senate only by the casting vote of Vice President Adams. The ensuing compromise, an embargo keeping American ships in port, was lifted when it proved detrimental to the trade of the Southern states. Washington decided to send a minister plenipotentiary to Britain and chose Chief Justice John Jay. Hamilton, whose attachment to Britain matched that of Jefferson to France, drafted Jay's instructions. Jay was to secure British withdrawal from the American West, reparations for British seizures of American merchant vessels, compensation for the slaves that the British army had removed from the Southern states during the Revolutionary War, and a commercial treaty defining the Americans' trading rights with the British Empire.

Jay wanted a treaty and not war with Britain. He did not go to London to issue ultimatums. Even if he had wanted to hold out the threatening possibility that the United States might join with neutral European nations to enforce trading rights, he could not have done so because

Hamilton, on his own initiative, had already assured the British minister in Philadelphia that the United States would not join the Armed Neutrality. Hamilton and Jay hoped to get the best results by a friendly approach. The British were primarily concerned with preventing any American friendship with France and keeping Anglo-American trade open to offset British merchant marine losses, crop failures, and falling government revenues. Nevertheless, they were disposed to make few concessions to the United States at the expense of British interests, as wartime mercantilist policy defined those interests.

Jay secured very little beyond maintaining peace with Britain. The British agreed to remove their troops from American territory by June, 1796, and allowed Americans to trade with India. American vessels of 70 tons or less could trade with the British West Indies but could not take molasses, sugar, coffee, cocoa, or cotton to ports other than American ones. Since a small, single-masted sloop might measure nearly 400 tons, this was a very limited concession. Other subjects of dispute—compensation for British spoliation of American commerce, British creditors' claims against American debtors, the location of the northwest international border—were referred to arbitration by joint commissions. Jay, who opposed slavery, did not even ask for compensation to slaveowners whose slaves had been freed by the British army. To secure these terms, Jay made a number of substantial concessions to Britain. He abandoned the American claim that neutrals had the right to trade freely with all belligerents, and he acquiesced in the British restrictions on neutral trade, including limitations on such commodities as naval stores and food. The treaty conceded Britain most-favored-nation status in American ports, thereby precluding American taxes and other legislation directed specifically against the British. The United States also conceded that it could not sequester money owed by Americans to Britons for private debts. Finally, the treaty guaranteed that American ports would

General George Washington Reviewing the Western Army at Fort Cumberland the 18th of October 1794. (Library of Congress)

not be open to the navies or the privateers of enemies of Britain; nor would prize vessels any longer be condemned in American ports.

The Federalists still had a commanding majority in the Senate; and, after removing from the treaty a prohibition on American export of cotton and the objectionable article on the West Indies trade, they were able to muster the two-thirds vote to ratify the treaty on June 24, 1795. Although the Senate undertook to deliberate in secret, Senator Stevens Thomson Mason of Virginia, an opponent of ratification, leaked a copy of the treaty, the terms of which were soon widely publicized. Jay's terms attracted bitter denunciation from Republicans: Mass meetings deplored the betrayal of American rights and national dignity, and antitreaty petitions received many signatures. Workers in the port cities north of Baltimore were especially conspicuous in the protests organized by Republicans. The treaty was overwhelmingly unpopular among the political leaders of the Southern states.

Washington came near to leaving the treaty unsigned. He was especially provoked by learning, late in June, that the British had begun to seize American vessels carrying foodstuffs to France. In July, however, the British minister disclosed to the American government captured dispatches from the French minister in Philadelphia to his superiors. These convinced Washington that his secretary of state, Edmund Randolph, had sought bribes from the French. Washington decided to sign the treaty in order to assert that American policy was not subject to corrupt French influences. He feared that pro-French and anti-British sympathies among American politicians had already grown so great that only a treaty with Britain could forestall the degradation of the United States into a satellite of France. He required Randolph to execute the ratification before he revealed the captured documents to the secretary. When Randolph saw that his explanations did not convince Washington, he immediately re-

signed. Not until after the treaty went into effect did the British rescind the order for the seizure of American vessels.

Republicans decided to resist the implementation of the treaty in the House of Representatives by refusing to enact the legislation needed to carry its provisions into effect. They held the first congressional party caucus in order to mobilize their majority. Although this meeting did not produce consensus, it was an important innovation in disseminating a party policy and in seeking organized support. In March, 1796, the House called on the president to submit the documents pertaining to the negotiation of the treaty. This action implied that treaties need not be considered effective until the House approved them by its implementing legislation. Washington refused the request and asserted that the Jay Treaty was now the supreme law of the land. He cited as evidence of the House's error in its constitutional stance the fact that the Constitutional Convention had voted down a proposal to give the House a role in treaty making. In rebuttal to Washington, Madison argued what became the prevailing view of constitutional interpretation: that the specific opinions of the framers of the Constitution were not binding on subsequent interpretations of it. The House endorsed Madison's argument by a majority that included some Federalists.

To counteract the Republicans' defiance and to solidify Federalists' loyalty to the administration, Hamilton—who had been succeeded as secretary of the treasury by Oliver Wolcott, Jr., on January 31, 1795, but who remained an influential party leader—set out to stimulate and dramatize protreaty public opinion. With the support of businessmen who wanted increased trade and closer ties with England, public meetings and petitions voiced support for Washington and the treaty. At the end of April, 1796, the supporters of the treaty narrowly won a vote in the House in favor of implementing it. The aftermath fulfilled the expectations of those interested in American commerce. Exports to the

British Empire increased 300 percent within five years. In the same period, exports of American cotton rose from six million pounds to twenty million pounds. The rapid extension of this staple crop underlay the growth of a slave labor society in the southern states. In 1796, British troops withdrew from the American Northwest, and the arbitration commissions in later years eventually settled the remaining issues.

The domestic agitation over the Jay Treaty promoted the coordination of party activities both in Congress and among the electorate, though the percentage of eligible citizens who voted remained small. Divisions over economic interests, the French Revolution, presidential power, sectional grievances, and competing visions of America's future came increasingly to be expressed through a partisan system. The Republicans enhanced the sophistication of their appeals to "the people" — that is, to many citizens whom the Federalists had not originally expected to have weight in matters of national policy. Newspapers, pamphlets, mass meetings, parades, local committees, and other techniques helped to expand the politically active population. The Federalists, though ultimately with less success, used similar methods on their own behalf.

Conspicuous in the denunciation of the Jay Treaty was bitter public abuse of President Washington. The Republican press charged him with affecting "the seclusion of a monk and the supercilious distance of a tyrant." He was called a "usurper" who was guilty of "political degeneracy" and who harbored "dark schemes of ambition." According to a writer in the *Philadelphia Aurora*, Washington had fought in the Revolutionary War only for power and personal glory. Another accused him of military incompetence. He was even charged — correctly, as it turned out — with drawing his salary as president in advance. This meant, his critic said, that Washington intended to extract more than his allotted $25,000 per year from the Treasury — and he should therefore be impeached. Early in Washington's second term, Jefferson had noticed that the president was "extremely affected by the attacks made and kept up on him in the public papers. I think he feels those things more than any person I ever met with." Politically, Washington's reaction to the criticism was to ally himself more fully with the Federalists. After the resignation of Randolph, the cabinet had only Federalists in it: Wolcott as secretary of the treasury, Timothy Pickering as secretary of state, James McHenry as secretary of war, and Charles Lee as attorney general. All these men, as well as Washington, continued to be influenced by the advice of Hamilton, now an attorney in New York.

The Whiskey Rebellion and the Western Lands

The Washington administration confronted a domestic challenge to federal authority during the summer of 1794, while Hamilton was still in the cabinet. The secretary of the treasury took advantage of the occasion to dramatize his conception of the federal government's power. The challenge consisted of violent resistance in four western counties of Pennsylvania to the collection of the federal excise tax on whiskey. Private distilling of whiskey was common in the West, partly because it made corn crops a more readily exchangeable and transportable commodity. The federal tax struck many Westerners exactly as Hamilton intended it should — as a direct assertion of their subordination to the federal government. Many western Pennsylvanians decided to resist. They threatened excise officers, robbed the mails, stopped federal judicial proceedings, and seized United States soldiers who were guarding the home of an excise inspector. A general meeting threatened an attack on Pittsburgh.

Washington initially sent federal commissioners to the disturbed area; they were authorized to negotiate a peaceful settlement. Any federal use of force would have to rely on state militias called into federal service. Fearing more widespread defiance, the administration soon decided to use force. An army of thirteen thousand militiamen from Pennsylvania, New Jersey, Maryland, and Virginia was mobilized under the command of Governor Henry Lee of Virginia. Contrary to the Westerners' threats, the federal units met no resistance. Some leaders of the resistance fled, and the followers remained quiet when the army arrived. About twenty men were arrested, of whom two were later convicted and subsequently pardoned by Washington.

The president agreed with Governor Lee and other Federalists that the Pennsylvania unrest did not arise from reluctance to pay taxes. It had been incited, Washington and his supporters charged, by the Democratic and Republican societies and by the inflammatory speeches of Republicans in Congress, who denounced the policies of the Washington administration. Madison, Jefferson, and their supporters protested that the administration was using its role as executor of the law to discredit conscientious critics by unjustly linking them with lawbreakers in western Pennsylvania. These Republican complaints had merit. Hamilton had acted provocatively in the spring of 1794 by proceeding with prosecutions of delinquent distillers in distant federal courts after the law had been revised to allow remote cases to be tried in the closest state courts. When Hamilton explained that he was accompanying the militia in Pennsylvania because Governor Lee "might miss the policy of the case," it is likely that he was referring to this opportunity to demonstrate federal power — an opportunity he had orchestrated. Ultimately, Hamilton's eagerness to use federal force and Washington's denunciation of Republican provocateurs backfired, as fellow Federalist Fisher Ames recognized. Ames said, "A regular government, by overcoming an unsuccessful insurrection, becomes stronger; but elective rulers can scarcely ever employ the force of a democracy without turning the moral force, or the power of public opinion, against the government." Washington's partisan interpretation of the Whiskey Rebellion helped establish him, in the eyes of the Republicans, as a thoroughgoing Federalist — a view that the Jay Treaty confirmed.

The volatility of western Pennsylvania exemplified a source of concern that had troubled American politicians since the Revolutionary War — the political cohesion of such a large, diverse country. The controversies over Hamilton's financial program and the Jay Treaty disclosed severe sectional divisions between Northern and Southern states. The expansion of trans-Appalachian settlement raised the threat of separatism and unrest among Western settlers. The Federalists preferred that the Western lands be settled gradually and comparatively stably. To this end, the Land Act of 1796 required that federal land be surveyed before purchase and settlement, that it not be sold for less than two dollars an acre, and that purchasers not receive extended credit. The effect of these provisions was to confine purchasing of federal land primarily to land corporations.

The Mississippi River was the obvious natural channel for the exports of the West, but its southernmost banks were under the control of Spain, the possessor of Louisiana. For Mississippi River trade to be feasible, Americans would have to be allowed to navigate the river through Spanish territory and to deposit their products temporarily near the mouth of the river while the goods awaited export. At the invitation of Manuel de Godoy of Spain, Washington sent Thomas Pinckney to Madrid in May, 1795, to negotiate a treaty on this matter as well as on the questions of the border between the United States and the Spanish colony of Florida and the role of the Spanish in stimulating Indian resistance in adjacent American territory.

French military successes against Spain meant that Spain would have to make territorial concessions to France from its empire. These would include returning Louisiana to France. In doing so, Spain could still undermine the security of France's imperial position by weakening the defensibility of Louisiana. Thus Pinckney found Godoy ready to offer the United States generous terms. In the Treaty of San Lorenzo, October 27, 1795, Spain granted the privilege of navigation of the Mississippi and the privilege of deposit, recognized America's claim to the thirty-first parallel as the border of Florida, and promised not to incite American Indians against the United States. Godoy evaded compliance with these terms until 1798 but left them as an encumbrance on French control of Louisiana thereafter.

Washington's Farewell Address: Three Lessons for the Young Nation

At the height of the scheming and political agitation in the presidential campaign of 1796—which turned on the choice of presidential electors and the attempts to influence the electoral college—Washington published his farewell address. In addition to declining to be considered for reelection, Washington sought to impress upon his fellow citizens three lessons that he considered crucial for the survival of the United States: The Union must be maintained by quelling sectional animosities; political parties threaten liberty by subordinating the people to factional leaders; and American interests are best served by avoiding intense attachments or intense aversions to other nations. Lacking the erudition and intellectual virtuosity of Hamilton or Jefferson, Washington also avoided the self-righteous dogmatism and immoderate enthusiasms to which the two younger men were susceptible. Washington asserted that the interests of the United States militated against exclusive attachment to one great power, even if that nation seemed to be the vanguard of liberty or the bulwark of civilization. Conversely, obsessive hostility toward any country clouded the pursuit of American interests by the preoccupation with the object of hatred.

Although most of the farewell address spoke in abstract terms—the president did boast of Pinckney's treaty and stressed the need to uphold the public credit—a reader could easily see that the address was in many respects a defense of Washington's policies as president as well as a condemnation of the behavior of his critics. Madison, who had helped with a draft in 1792, believed with other Republicans that the address was purely partisan and pro-British. Washington may have seen some vindication in the election of Vice President John Adams as his successor, but the circumstances were not very edifying, considered in the light of Washington's admonitions. Newspaper polemics reached new levels of personal abuse, whereas partisans, not content with denouncing their enemies, betrayed their allies, too. Jefferson's supporters mistrusted their own vice presidential candidate, Aaron Burr. Since electoral votes were cast for individuals, without specifying the office, Hamilton hoped to manipulate the Federalist electoral votes so that Thomas Pinckney rather than Adams would emerge as president. New England Federalists were as determined to check Pinckney as Virginia Republicans were to check Burr. In the outcome of the double crosses, Adams was narrowly elected president, and his Republican opponent, Jefferson, received the second largest vote and became vice president. Although the party organizations were obviously rudimentary, the election luridly demonstrated how little weight Washington's farewell advice carried in practice; nor did posterity heed his counsel on sectional antagonism or on foreign relations.

Washington did not expect his advice to prevail. He wrote that he hoped only that in the future the memory of his words might "recur to moderate the fury of party spirit, to warn against the mischiefs of foreign intrigue, to guard against the imposture of pretended patriotism." At the time of his retirement, there were many grounds for satisfaction. The governmental institutions had survived changes in officials, partisans had not destroyed the government, and states had not left the Union. Indeed, Vermont, Kentucky, and Tennessee had joined it as new states. Nevertheless, Washington's address had a note of detachment, even pessimism, in it. He was eager to retire to Mount Vernon, to take with him intact his personal honor and his public reputation—leaving his fellow citizens and their posterity to endure the consequences of the illusions he vainly warned them against. He said of his warnings, "I dare not hope they will make the strong and lasting impression I could wish—that they will control the usual current of the passions or prevent our nation from running the course which has hitherto marked the destiny of nations." To Washington and his contemporaries, the course that nations had always run ended in the loss of their liberty and independence. The United States had a destiny no different from that of other countries; but he knew that, when it came, no one would be able to say that it was the fault of George Washington.

In 1799, resisting any hint that he should again be a presidential candidate, Washington wrote, "A mind that has been constantly on the stretch since the year 1753, with but short intervals and little relaxation, requires rest and composure." In retirement, he still had many visitors, took an active interest in the crises of the Adams administration, and accepted the nominal command of the special army established during the quasi-war with France. He censured the Virginia Resolutions against the Alien and Sedition Acts, urged Patrick Henry to come out of retirement as a Federalist candidate in Virginia, and rejoiced in the election of Federalist Virginians John Marshall and Henry Lee to the House of Representatives in 1798. Yet, despite the increasingly partisan role of Washington as an aegis for the Federalist Party—even including many eulogies of him in 1800—he remained an evocative symbol of American nationality. This stature grew even more conspicuous in the nineteenth century, after the alarms of the early national period had faded. The memory of

Washington's unique strength of character and his providential achievements in the founding of the nation seemed to posterity to give promise that the United States enjoyed God's special favor. The historian George Bancroft wrote of him in 1858, "Combining the centripetal and the centrifugal forces in their utmost strength and in perfect relations, with creative grandeur of instinct he held ruin in check, and renewed and perfected the institutions of his country. Finding the colonies disconnected and dependent, he left them such a united and well ordered commonwealth as no visionary had believed to be possible."

Washington died as he had lived—practicing self-control, attending to details. In the early hours of December 14, 1799, he developed a severe inflammation of the throat, with labored breathing and much pain. During the day, he submitted quietly to a battery of medical treatments, including bleedings, blisters, and emetics, but he believed from the first attack that the disease was fatal. Finally, he said to his doctors, "I feel myself going. I thank you for your attention. You had better not take any more trouble with me; but let me go off quietly; I cannot last long." To his secretary, Tobias Lear, he said, "I am just going. Have me decently buried and do not let my body be put into the vault in less than two days after I am dead." When Lear did not reply, Washington asked, "Do you understand me?" Lear answered, "Yes, sir." Then Washington said, " 'Tis well." His last action, a few minutes later, was to take his own pulse as it fell.

Washington's Definitive Example: The Centrality of the Presidency

Like many subsequent presidents, Washington left office less popular and less influential than he entered it. Unlike other presidents, whom Americans have expected to be partisan, Washington lost some of his acclaim simply by developing a political affiliation. Compared, however, with the bitter experiences of his immediate successors—Adams, Jefferson, and

Excerpts from George Washington's farewell address, September 19, 1796:

The impressions, with which I first undertook the arduous trust, were explained on the proper occasion. In the discharge of this trust, I will only say, that I have, with good intentions, contributed towards the Organization and Administration of the government, the best exertions of which a very fallible judgment was capable. Not unconscious, in the outset, of the inferiority of my qualifications, experience in my own eyes, perhaps still more in the eyes of others, has strengthened the motives to diffidence of myself; and every day the increasing weight of years admonishes me more and more, that the shade of retirement is as necessary to me as it will be welcome. Satisfied that if any circumstances have given peculiar value to my services, they were temporary, I have the consolation to believe, that while choice and prudence invite me to quit the political scene, patriotism does not forbid it. . . .

Citizens by birth or choice, of a common country, that country has a right to concentrate your affections. The name of AMERICAN, which belongs to you, in your national capacity, must always exalt the just pride of Patriotism, more than any appellation derived from local discriminations. With slight shades of difference, you have the same Religion, Manners, Habits, and political Principles. You have in a common cause fought and triumphed together. The independence and liberty you possess are the work of joint councils, and joint efforts; of common dangers, sufferings and successes. . . .

Though in reviewing the incidents of my Administration, I am unconscious of intentional error, I am nevertheless too sensible of my defects not to think it probable that I may have committed many errors. Whatever they may be I fervently beseech the Almighty to avert or mitigate the evils to which they may tend. I shall also carry with me the hope that my Country will never cease to view them with indulgence; and that after forty-five years of my life dedicated to its Service, with an upright zeal, the faults of incompetent abilities will be consigned to oblivion, as myself must soon be to the Mansions of rest. Relying on its kindness in this as in other things, and actuated by that fervent love toward it, which is so natural to a Man, who views in it the native soil of himself and his progenitors for several Generations; I anticipate with pleasing expectation that retreat, in which I promise myself to realize, without alloy, the sweet enjoyment of partaking, in the midst of my fellow Citizens, the benign influence of good Laws under a free Government, the ever favourite object of my heart, and the happy reward, as I trust, of our mutual cares, labours, and dangers.

Madison—Washington's presidency left him comparatively unscathed. The basic concern of the first president was to vindicate the proposition that republican institutions could function and survive. The specific tasks they faced seem much less complicated than those of many later presidents. The additional difficulty of the earliest chief executives was the uncertainty of maintaining the existence of the United States. In this undertaking no American could have inaugurated—or rather created—the office of president to such dramatic effect as did George Washington. His use of his personal reputation to promote his policies of public credit, expanding commerce, international neutrality, and the extension of westward settlement largely succeeded. Later presidents, pursuing different policies or facing concerns unimagined by Washington, would continue to emulate his use of the presidency. Hardly anyone could imagine a republican America pursuing any course of policy without a president of the United States taking the initiative. In that presumption of the centrality of the office lies Washington's most lasting governmental legacy.

Charles Royster

Suggested Readings

Brookhiser, Richard. *Founding Father: Rediscovering George Washington*. New York: Free Press, 1996. Recounts Washington's heroic deeds in a quarter-century of public life and reflects upon his legacy.

Clark, Harrison. *All Cloudless Glory: The Life of George Washington*. 2 vols. Washington, D.C.: Regnery, 1995. Clark draws on primary sources, including letters, photographs, diaries, and official documents, to present a thorough account of Washington's life.

Cunliffe, Marcus. *George Washington: Man and Monument*. 1958. Rev. ed. New York: New American Library, 1982. An accessible one-volume study of Washington's life.

Ellis, Joseph J. *His Excellency: George Washington*. New York: Alfred A. Knopf, 2004. Using primary documents about Washington that were cataloged in the late twentieth century, Ellis re-creates the cultural and political context into which Washington emerged as a war hero and leader and offers fresh insights into his personality.

Flexner, James Thomas. *Washington: The Indispensable Man*. New York: New American Library, 1984. This abridged volume combines four volumes of work about Washington that were published between 1965 and 1972 and serves as a good biography of the president.

Freeman, Douglas Southall. *George Washington: A Biography*. 7 vols. New York: Scribner, 1948-1957. A thorough examination of Washington's life that includes chapters titled "Young Washington," "Leader of the Revolution," and "Patriot and President."

Hirschfeld, Fritz. *George Washington and Slavery: A Documentary Portrayal*. Columbia: University of Missouri Press, 1997. Chronicles the evolution of Washington's attitudes toward slavery as both a statesman and a slave owner.

Johnson, Paul. *George Washington: The Founding Father*. New York: HarperCollins, 2005. Part of the Eminent Lives series, this volume serves as a compact biography of Washington that will appeal to lay readers and scholars.

Lewis, Thomas A. *For King and Country: The Maturing of George Washington, 1748-1760*. New York: HarperCollins, 1993. Lewis places Washington within the context of the emerging American culture, noting that the tension between the aristocratic East Coast and the adventurous movement to the West changed the character of Washington and helped him achieve his early goals.

McCoy, Drew R. *The Elusive Republic: Political Economy in Jeffersonian America*. New York: Norton, 1980. Examines the policy debates among political leaders during Washington's political career.

Miller, John C. *The Federalist Era, 1789-1801*. 1960. Reprint. Prospect Heights, Ill.: Waveland Press, 1998. Provides a valuable analysis of Washington's administration within the context of the Federalist period.

Randall, Willard S. *George Washington: A Life*. New York: Henry Holt, 1997. In a single-volume biography that details Washington's private and public lives, Randall pays close attention to Washington's position as a young lawyer on the frontier, his tenure as Virginia's ineffectual war governor, and his ambassadorship to France.

Smith, Richard N. *Patriarch: George Washington and the New American Nation*. Boston: Houghton Mifflin, 1993. Examines the statecraft of Washington as president over a fractious new republic.

Wills, Garry. *Cincinnatus: George Washington and the Enlightenment*. Garden City, N.Y.: Doubleday, 1984. Examines American intellectual life during the Enlightenment and Washington's role within it.

John Adams

2d President, 1797-1801

Born: October 30, 1735
    Braintree, Massachusetts
Died: July 4, 1826
    Quincy, Massachusetts

Political Party: Federalist
Vice President: Thomas Jefferson

Cabinet Members

Secretary of State: Timothy Pickering, John Marshall
Secretary of the Treasury: Oliver Wolcott, Jr., Samuel Dexter
Secretary of War: James McHenry, Samuel Dexter
Secretary of the Navy: Benjamin Stoddert
Attorney General: Charles Lee

On September 19, 1796, President George Washington published his farewell address and revealed to the nation what he had decided privately months earlier, that he would retire from public life at the end of his second term. The news disappointed staunch Federalists, who hoped Washington would run again and thus avoid even the possibility that Thomas Jefferson might become president. It also delighted their opponents, who, not having to counter Washington's immense popularity, might be able to elect Jefferson president. Finally, it relieved Vice President John Adams, who wanted badly to be the Federalist candidate but who had, along with everyone else, to wait nervously until September to be certain Washington intended to retire after all.

Adams did not so much win the Federalist nomination in 1796 as inherit it. He had served Washington loyally as vice president for eight years, presiding quietly over the Senate, dutifully breaking tie votes in favor of Federalist economic and foreign policies when necessary (Adams broke twenty such ties, more than any other vice president in history). With the exception of Washington, no Federalist still active in national affairs rivaled his reputation with the public as an early and steady advocate of independence. No one still active, Federalist or otherwise, could bring with him to the presidency the long and successful experience in government and diplomacy and the reputation as a legislator, essayist,

Portrait of John Adams. *(Whitehouse.gov)*

and speaker that Adams could. If he was not loved by the people at large as was Washington, he was at least genuinely and widely respected for his service to the American Revolution and the republic. In the minds of many Americans, and certainly in his own mind, Adams was Washington's heir apparent.

Lawyer, Revolutionary, Diplomat

Adams was born in 1735 to a middle-class farming family in Braintree (now Quincy), Massachusetts. His parents expected him to enter the ministry. He was graduated from Harvard in 1755 and taught school briefly in Worcester while he convinced himself that he would be far happier and much more successful disputing law before juries than dispensing piety from a pulpit. In 1758, he was admitted to the bar in Massachusetts and began practicing law in Braintree.

Public-spirited and ambitious, Adams soon began writing essays for the Boston newspapers and was already established in a minor way as a public spokesperson when the Stamp Act crisis vaulted him into politics and prominence. Resolutions denouncing the stamp tax that he prepared for the Braintree town meeting were well received and circulated throughout the colony. Soon after, he joined James Otis in Boston to challenge the constitutionality of the Stamp Act in court, and he found himself being drawn into popular politics in the capital and into the nascent political party forming around Otis, Samuel Adams, John Hancock, and others. In 1768, Adams moved to Boston, and by the end of the decade his growing reputation as an opponent of British taxation and tyranny won for him election to the Massachusetts General Court.

Ill health forced his withdrawal from office for a while, but the Tea Act crisis brought him back into public view. In 1774, Massachusetts sent him to the First Continental Congress, where he urged a strong stand against British policy and opposed reconciliation on anything but colonial terms. Back in Massachusetts, he wrote a series of essays under the pseudonym of "Novanglus" refuting the Tory essays of Loyalist Daniel Leonard. The Novanglus essays circulated widely and began to build for Adams a national reputation in a nation not yet quite born. He returned to the congress after the war began, and in the spring of 1776, he was appointed to a committee to prepare a declaration of independence. Though Adams had little to do with drafting the declaration, he had much to do with wrestling Jefferson's text through an excited but nervous and often balky congress. In Jefferson's opinion, Adams was the declaration's "ablest advocate and defender" in the congress.

Adams began his diplomatic career in February, 1778, when the Continental Congress dispatched him to Paris to replace the discredited Silas Deane as a member of the American diplomatic team seeking French aid against Britain. For the next ten years, with only one brief hiatus during which he helped write Massachusetts's revolutionary constitution, Adams represented the republic abroad at Paris, Amsterdam, The Hague, and London on a variety of diplomatic missions: seeking recognition for the new nation, raising money, negotiating treaties of trade and alliance, and, most challenging of all, helping draft the Treaty of Paris, which finally brought the War of Independence, if not the American Revolution, to a formal close. In Paris, he acquired a healthy skepticism about French diplomats and a thorough dislike of Benjamin Franklin. Between 1785 and 1788, he served in London as the first United States minister to Britain. During his last two years abroad, he wrote *A Defense of the Constitutions of the United States of America*, which argued that bicameral (as opposed to unicameral) legislatures; the sharp separation of legislative, executive, and judicial functions in government; and a powerful executive with an absolute veto were all crucial elements of good constitutions. "The people's rights and liberties," he con-

The First Lady
Abigail Adams

Abigail Adams was the wife of America's second president, John Adams, and the mother of the sixth president, John Quincy Adams. She was born on November 22, 1744, in Weymouth, Massachusetts.

Consistent with practices of the day, Abigail received no formal education, but she enjoyed her father's substantial library and the informal tutoring of educated relatives and friends.

Abigail married the young attorney, John Adams, on October 25, 1764, and they established their home in his hometown of Braintree. The couple had five children.

In August of 1774, John departed for Congress in Philadelphia, the first of his several prolonged absences from his family. Although she regretted his absence and dreaded the prospect of war, Abigail supported the position that her husband and others were taking. With the actual coming of independence, Abigail urged her husband to consider the role of women in the new republic. She argued that educated and enlightened wives and mothers would be important instruments for the inculcation of those virtues essential for the survival of the new republic.

In the fall of 1783, following the restoration of peace, Congress asked Adams to join John Jay and Benjamin Franklin in negotiating a commercial treaty with Britain. This time, Abigail joined him, and together they spent a year in Paris and three years in London, which deepened her republican sensibilities and commitment to the better education of American women.

The Adams family returned home in 1788. In 1789, John was elected vice president of the United States. For most of her husband's second term in office as vice president, illness forced her to remain in Braintree.

In 1796, John Adams was elected to the presidency, and Abigail became First Lady. It was a tumultuous four years, during which her husband became embroiled in highly contentious international and domestic political controversies. Abigail was criticized for her partisanship and for the influence she allegedly had over the president. Her greatest satisfaction came from her private role as confidante of, and counselor to, her husband.

Abigail accepted the election results of 1800, and the defeat of her husband, with resignation. They returned to Braintree, now called Quincy, where they lived comfortably in retirement but not with great wealth. Chronic illness plagued Abigail her for most of her remaining years, and she died of typhus fever on October 28, 1818. She was buried in the First Church in Quincy.

Bryan Le Beau

tended, could "never be preserved without a strong executive," for "if the executive power, or any considerable part of it, is left in the hands. . . of . . . a democratical assembly, it will corrupt the legislature as rust corrupts iron, or as arsenic poisons the human body." Such ideas would not be popular in America, he told Jefferson in 1787 (accurately, as it turned out), but he intended to publish his opinion anyway, "however unpopular it might be."

Adams returned home in 1788 and the following year won the vice presidency. It was not a particularly gratifying victory, since he received only 34 of the 69 electoral votes cast, and it placed him in a job he described halfway through his tenure as "the most insignificant office that ever the invention of man contrived or his imagination conceived." By 1796, then, Adams was determined either to move on to the presidency or, failing that, to retire to his law practice, his farm, and his family in Quincy.

The Campaign of 1796: No Electoral Mandate

The presidential campaign of 1796 was, by modern standards, a curious one. Both candidates thought it demeaning and unseemly to plead for votes, so neither campaigned. In Adams's opinion, and Jefferson's too, public men should be called to office by an unsolicited electorate, very much as a minister was called to his pulpit by a congregation—a relaxed approach to presidential politics that would not survive Adams's presidency. Still, a campaign did take place in 1796, carried out mostly by newspaper essayists, editors, and political pamphleteers. Also, the election was expected to answer important questions. For example, what kind of government had the Philadelphia Convention of 1787 created? Or, put a little differently, where, precisely, was the limit of federal power with respect to the states? With England and France again at war, where did the best interests of the United States lie: as an ally of the revolutionary French Republic or as an ally in all but name of Great Britain? Did they lie somewhere in between?

Jefferson and his backers believed that Adams, Alexander Hamilton, and the Federalists had already perverted the Constitution and increased the powers of the central government at the expense of the states to a dangerous degree during Washington's two terms. Should Adams win, they warned, this assault on the Constitution and on the liberties of all Americans would doubtless continue. Adams, Republican essayists insisted, was a monarchist at heart who would reestablish in America the principles of monarchial government if he could. He was therefore unfit to govern a free people, and for proof they pointed to *A Defense of the Constitutions*.

From Adams's point of view, the creation of an effective national government with its powers properly distributed among its branches, and the imposition of order on licentious state governments prone to truckle to the whim of popular majorities, had been two important

Abigail Adams. *(Library of Congress)*

purposes of the Constitution. Two-thirds of the states, he thought, had constitutions so defective that they were, "as sure as there is a Heaven and an Earth," bound to produce "disorder and confusion." For Adams, Jefferson's election promised not liberty but licentiousness, not an ordered and orderly republic but the chaos and injustice inevitably born of weak government.

The two men differed as well over foreign affairs. Jefferson looked upon the War of Independence as the beginning of a revolution that would secure for Americans new liberties. He considered the American Revolution the first stage of an international movement that would topple monarchy throughout Europe as well as in America. Thus Jefferson and his Democratic Republicans welcomed the French Revolution and insisted that both America's revolutionary principles and its self-interest demanded close ties with France.

Adams and most Federalists, in contrast, looked on the War of Independence as the end

The Vice President
Thomas Jefferson

Thomas Jefferson was born on April 23, 1743, at Shadwell Plantation in Virginia. His father, Peter Jefferson, was a member of the Virginia House of Burgesses, and his mother, Jane Randolph, came from a highly influential family of British ancestry. Jefferson pursued his studies at William and Mary College and graduated in 1762, whereupon he studied law for five years under the supervision of George Wythe and was admitted to the bar in 1767.

On January 1, 1772, Jefferson married a widow, Martha Wayles Skelton, and together they had six children. Devastated and heartbroken by his wife's untimely death in 1782 at the age of thirty-three, Jefferson would never remarry. From 1768 until 1775, he served as a member of the Virginia House of Burgesses, and later he was chosen as a delegate from Virginia to the Continental Congress. Author of the Declaration of Independence, wartime governor of Virginia, and diplomatic representative of the United States to France, Jefferson was instrumental in laying the foundation for the new democracy. George Washington appointed him as the nation's first secretary of state, and after serving in the position for one term, Jefferson resigned and returned to his beloved home, Monticello.

His retirement would be short-lived, for in 1796, Jefferson became a candidate for president running against his political foe, John Adams. Unable to garner enough votes to beat Adams and win the presidency, Jefferson was relegated to the vice presidency, and the two men ended up representing two very different political factions that were emerging as the young nation's first political parties. Nonetheless, in four short years, he would succeed in besting Adams by winning the presidency in 1800.

Jefferson served two terms as president and subsequently retired from political life and returned to Monticello, where he was instrumental in the founding of the University of Virginia. Severely in debt and nearly bankrupt, he died on the fiftieth anniversary of the Declaration of Independence on July 4, 1826.

Robert P. Watson and Richard Yon

of a revolution that had been fought, not so much to establish new liberties, as to preserve traditional ones. He thought of the Constitution as a means of securing these familiar liberties by returning order and authority to American national government. Neither America's principles nor its self-interest, then, dictated an alliance with the architects of the Reign of Terror in France or their successors. If forced to choose between embracing the tricolor or the Union Jack (and unlike arch-Federalists such as Timothy Pickering and Alexander Hamilton, Adams did not believe that the nation *had* to choose one or the other), he would have preferred the British, whose balanced constitutional system (the recent perversions of George III and his henchmen aside) Adams rather admired. A Jefferson presidency, he feared, would draw the nation into a disastrous war with England and weaken the republic, perhaps fatally.

In the end, the clumsy maneuverings of Hamilton probably had as much to do with the outcome of the election as the often-hysterical debates conducted in the press. Even before Washington's farewell address, Hamilton hoped to find a way to prevent Adams's election without ensuring Jefferson's. Adams was far too independent to work comfortably and closely with a man of Hamilton's arrogance and ambition. Hamilton eventually plotted to have Adams's vice presidential running mate, Thomas Pinckney of South Carolina, elected president, thus consigning Adams again to the limbo of the vice presidency. Since each elector cast two ballots, the scheme involved convincing a few Federalist electors to vote for Pinckney but not Adams. Presuming the Federalists won the election, Pinckney would have a few votes more than Adams and so would be president. He would, it was expected, accept with little protest Hamilton's advice on domestic and foreign affairs.

Inevitably, word of Hamilton's plot reached Adams. Angry about "treacherous friends" in his own party, he told his wife in December, 1796, that he was "not enough of an Englishman nor little enough of a Frenchman for some who would be very willing that Pinckney should come in chief." He predicted, however, that "they will be disappointed."

He was right. New England's eighteen Federalist electors, annoyed that Hamilton intended to steal the election from one of their own, voted solidly for Adams but gave no votes to Pinckney. South Carolina's eight electors voted for Pinckney but then cast all of their second-ballot votes for Jefferson. When the ballots were counted, Adams stood highest with 71 electoral votes, only two of which came from states south of the Potomac River. Jefferson stood second with 68 and so became vice president. Pinckney finished third with 59, and Jefferson's running mate, Aaron Burr of New York, polled only 30. Adams was president by three votes, a margin he found humiliating. Neither the Democratic Republicans nor his own pride would let him forget over the next four years just how narrow his victory had been. Unlike Washington, who had received every electoral vote in 1789, Adams was just barely president. He could hardly claim or even pretend, as Washington could, that he was president of all the people.

Adams as President: Under the Shadow of France

John Adams took the oath of office on Saturday, March 4, 1797. The new president was not a physically impressive man as he rose to deliver his inaugural address. Short and overweight, his hands occasionally trembling as the result of one of the vague illnesses that plagued him all of his life, he spoke with a lisp that made his words sometimes hard to follow. He praised Washington's policies and promised to continue them, and he tried to allay Republican-inspired fears that he might, by fiat presumably, alter the Constitution. He had, he insisted, no thought of making any changes in it "but such as the people themselves" might think necessary, and those only by amendment in the proper way. He hoped to "maintain peace . . . with all nations" and "neutrality . . . among the belligerent powers of Europe," and he professed (somewhat dishonestly) "esteem for the French nation" and (more truthfully) a determination to preserve Franco-American friendship by every reasonable means in his power, a pledge arch-Federalists thought uncomfortably Republican in tone. As the inauguration ended, a tired and relieved Washington told Adams, "Ay! I am fairly out, and you fairly in! See which of us will be happiest."

Adams began his term by trying to unite the nation and his own party behind his presidency. He offered a critical diplomatic mission to France to Thomas Jefferson, hoping to impress the French and to preempt Republican criticism of his foreign policy, but Jefferson refused the appointment. To foster unity in his own party, Adams kept Washington's cabinet officers: Timothy Pickering as secretary of state, James McHenry as secretary of war, Oliver Wolcott, Jr., as secretary of the treasury, and Charles Lee as attorney general. It was not, on the whole, a distinguished group. McHenry, for example, had been appointed only after a half dozen men declined to serve and Washington despaired of finding anyone more talented who would accept. Worse, most of the members owed their appointments and their influence in the party to Hamilton. McHenry and Pickering (and Wolcott more often than not) seemed determined to undermine the president's policies in order to implement Hamilton's in their place. McHenry went so far as to pass President Adams's queries to him on to Hamilton, who prepared replies that McHenry then passed back to the president as his own. At the head of a divided nation, a divided party, and a divided administration, Adams faced his first test as president.

Rarely in American history has a president been as completely preoccupied with a single issue throughout his term as Adams was with Franco-American relations. From his first day in office, the subject monopolized his time and destroyed his hopes for bipartisan support. It poisoned his already troubled relations with important leaders in his own party and crippled his attempts to earn the trust of his Republican opponents. Denounced throughout much of his term by the Jeffersonian left as a warmongering lackey of monarchist Federalists, and condemned by the Hamiltonian right as a cowardly panderer to American Jacobins, Adams followed his own independent policy, guided by his sense of integrity and his intuitive understanding of public opinion and the national interest. For four years no one, least of all Adams, knew whether his stubborn moderation in dealing with the French would succeed. In the end, when it did, Adams considered the result—enduring peace with France—the proudest achievement of his public life.

Even before Adams took office, it was clear that France and the United States were dangerously close to open war. Angered by President Washington's declaration of American neutrality (which helped England and hurt France), by the Jay Treaty (which did the same), and by Washington's recall of James Monroe as American envoy in Paris, the French reacted by ordering Monroe's replacement, Federalist Charles Cotesworth Pinckney, out of the country. Shocked again by Jefferson's defeat in 1797, the French began to treat the United States in many ways as an enemy state. French naval vessels and privateers began to capture American ships and confiscate cargoes bound to or from English ports, especially in the West Indies. Americans serving in the British navy—even those who had been forced to serve against their will—were declared pirates subject to execution on capture. As more and more American cargoes were seized, many on meager pretexts, the two nations began to drift into war.

Adams called Congress into special session in May, 1797, to deal with the crisis. His opening message warned France "and the world" that Americans were "not a degraded people, humiliated under a colonial spirit of fear and a sense of inferiority," fated to be "the miserable instruments of foreign influence." He recommended some limited military preparations in case war came and, equally important in Adams's view, to establish American credibility overseas. After all, on the day he took office, the regular army numbered less than three thousand men, and it had its hands full on the frontier. The navy, politely so called, barely existed, boasting only a few light revenue cutters, though three substantial frigates were under construction. Congress agreed to build twelve new frigates, to put the militia on alert, to strengthen coastal fortifications, and to arm American merchants trading to the East Indies and the Mediterranean.

The XYZ Affair

Having begun to prepare for war, Adams also asked the Senate to sanction a special commission to France to preserve the peace if possible. He proposed sending John Marshall of Virginia and Charles Cotesworth Pinckney of South Carolina, both moderate Federalists very much in Adams's mold, and (over the shrill protests of Timothy Pickering and the brooding suspicions of other high Federalists) anti-Federalist

Elbridge Gerry of Massachusetts. The Senate somewhat reluctantly agreed. Congress adjourned in mid-July, and the president and nation settled back to await the outcome. Everything depended on the commissioners' reception in France.

Early in March, 1798, Adams learned that not only had the ruling Directory of France refused to receive the commissioners officially but also that Talleyrand, the foreign minister, had demanded a bribe of 50,000 pounds sterling and a substantial loan for France as his price for merely beginning negotiations.

Talleyrand did not yet know (though he was about to learn) that whereas diplomacy in Europe might customarily be conducted by gentlemen in the privacy of their chambers, diplomacy in a popular republic could be conducted very differently. In the United States, the most sensitive diplomatic communications might even appear in the press and be hotly debated in

the finest townhouses and the rawest frontier taverns if there were votes to be won as a result. Talleyrand also did not understand (though he was about to learn this, too) that new nations tend to be extraordinarily sensitive about their national honor and downright starchy about insults to the flag—and the United States in 1798 was still a very new nation.

After Secretary of State Pickering replaced the names of the French agents who carried Talleyrand's demands to the American commissioners with the letters *X*, *Y*, and *Z*, Adams sent the commission's dispatches to Congress. The Senate ordered them published in April, 1798, and the nation exploded with anger. Their publication, wrote Charles Francis Adams, "was like the falling of a spark into a powder magazine." Even some Republicans now denounced France and applauded Charles Cotesworth Pinckney's reply to the insulting demand for money: "No! No! Not a sixpence!" Adams, who normally

Excerpt from John Adams's address to Congress regarding the XYZ affair, May 16, 1797:

It is impossible to conceal from ourselves or the world what has been before observed, that endeavors have been employed to foster and establish a division between the government and people of the United States. To investigate the causes which have encouraged this attempt is not necessary; but to repel, by decided and united councils, insinuations so derogatory to the honor and aggressions so dangerous to the Constitution, union, and even independence of the nation is an indispensable duty.

It must not be permitted to be doubted whether the people of the United States will support the government established by their voluntary consent and appointed by their free choice, or whether, by surrendering themselves to the direction of foreign and domestic factions, in opposition to their own government, they will forfeit the honorable station they have hitherto maintained.

For myself, having never been indifferent to what concerned the interests of my country, devoted the best part of my life to obtain and support its independence, and constantly witnessed the patriotism, fidelity, and perseverance of my fellow citizens on the most trying occasions, it is not for me to hesitate or abandon a cause in which my heart has been so long engaged.

Convinced that the conduct of the government has been just and impartial to foreign nations, that those internal regulations which have been established by law for the preservation of peace are in their nature proper, and that they have been fairly executed, nothing will ever be done by me to impair the national engagements, to innovate upon principles which have been so deliberately and uprightly established, or to surrender in any manner the rights of the government. To enable me to maintain this declaration I rely, under God, with entire confidence on the firm and enlightened support of the national legislature and upon the virtue and patriotism of my fellow citizens.

walked the streets of Philadelphia without the public much noticing or caring, suddenly drew cheering crowds when he attended the theater or appeared in public. "Adams and Liberty" became a popular slogan, and overnight public opinion turned on France and rallied behind the president and the party that had long been suspicious of the French Revolution and that had warned that a French alliance was not in America's interest. The XYZ affair, as it came to be called, carried Adams and the Federalists to heights of popularity neither would ever know again. Almost as angry as the people he led, Adams promised Congress that he would "never send another minister to France without assurances that he will be received, respected and honored as the representative of a great, free, powerful and independent people."

The Half-War with France

Protecting American commerce from French attack was the first priority. To that end, Adams asked Congress to create a department of the navy, to buy or build another twenty warships as soon as possible, to permit merchant ships to arm against French attack, and to abrogate all existing treaties with France. He also wanted the navy and American privateers authorized to prey on armed French ships (but not on unarmed vessels).

Many Federalists in Congress and out, such as Fisher Ames and Stephen Higginson, almost eager for a grand patriotic war, were pleasantly surprised by Adams's strong words. They assumed that he now saw the justice, the utility, and the inevitability of the war they were certain must come.

They could not have been more wrong. What Adams wanted was to force France to negotiate with the United States yet again, but this time on equal terms. The key to his plan was a fighting navy strong enough along the Atlantic coast and in the West Indies to neutralize French pressure on American commerce and to make the price of French belligerence at sea

high enough that Talleyrand would seek a diplomatic end to the conflict. The Federalist majority in Congress, however, looked on the XYZ affair, the public rage it fostered, and the full war they expected to follow as a heaven-sent opportunity to destroy their Jeffersonian opponents by branding them traitors and as a chance to rid the country (as one of them put it) of "democrats, mobocrats and all other kinds of rats." Hamilton's allies in Congress and the cabinet pushed through a program of military preparation that went well beyond Adams's carefully measured response to French provocations. Congress approved raising an army of ten thousand men and enlisting another fifty thousand in a provisional army that could be quickly mustered into service following a declaration of war or a French invasion. Without consulting the president, the Federalist majority adopted a new series of taxes on houses, land, and slaves to pay for it all.

Adams had not asked for a large army to fight a declared war; he wanted a strong navy to prevent one. Yet he dared not veto the army bill. National unity, or at least the appearance of it, was crucial to Adams's plan. With the nation already engaged in an undeclared war with France at sea, he could not permit the angry brawl between the president and Congress that a veto would trigger.

Adams's lukewarm enthusiasm for the new army soon grew cooler. Many Federalists who were dissatisfied with Adams's leadership saw the army as a way to raise their preferred leader, Alexander Hamilton, to military glory and possibly to the presidency. Washington had converted success on the battlefield into a presidency. Perhaps Hamilton could too. Washington was the only possible man for commander in chief of the new army. Even Adams saw that, and he promptly offered him the post. The aging general, one of the few prominent Federalists who understood that Adams's goal was to establish peace rather than to promote a war and who thoroughly approved, accepted on two conditions. Happily retired at Mount Vernon, he did not want to take command in the field unless dire national emergency (presumably a French invasion of the South aimed at raising a slave rebellion) made his presence with the army absolutely essential. Also, he insisted he be allowed to name his own subordinate officers. "If I am looked at as the Commander in Chief, I must be allowed to chuse such as will be agreeable to me," he wrote to Secretary of War McHenry.

Washington, however, who had been privately lobbied by Hamilton and his supporters, including (unknown to Adams) Secretary McHenry, eventually insisted that Hamilton become his second in command and therefore, in effect, field commander of the army. He threatened to resign if he did not get his way. By now, Adams despised Hamilton. He is, he wrote to Abigail Adams in January, 1797, "a proud Spirited, conceited, aspiring Mortal always pretending to Morality, with as debauched Morals as old Franklin." As president, however, Adams had little choice. Washington's resignation would divide the nation and turn a good part of the public against the administration. Angrily ("You crammed him down my throat," Adams complained later), he consented to Hamilton as the army's ranking major general.

The Alien and Sedition Acts

In the meantime, Congress laid plans to suppress enemy aliens and French sympathizers in America, to shield the government from divisive criticism during the war that was doubtless only months away, and to restrict the growth of the Republican Party. The Sedition Act of July, 1798, made libelous or false statements about public officials of the United States, or any statement fostering sedition or contempt for the government, federal crimes punishable by fine and imprisonment. Republicans denounced the law and warned that Federalists thought virtually all dissent seditious and all criticism treasonable. In the hands of partisan judges and prosecutors, they predicted, the law would be used to suppress the kind of public debate over men and measures that was essential in a free republic. Some of their fears were borne out as the editors of important Republican newspapers were prosecuted under the Sedition Act and several were jailed. Yet no Federalist editor went to prison for printing charges about Vice President Jefferson (presumably shielded from criticism by the law too) that were as false and malicious as any leveled at Adams.

The acts moved Jefferson and James Madison to introduce resolutions into the Virginia and Kentucky legislatures, arguing that the Constitution was, properly understood, a compact among sovereign states that were competent to judge for themselves whether federal laws were or were not constitutional. Jefferson went further, claiming that states could nullify federal laws they deemed unconstitutional.

The president had not asked for the Sedition Act, but he had no real objection to it either. For a public man, he was remarkably thin-skinned, and he would recall for years the pain and humiliation newspaper attacks on him produced. In his anger, he found it difficult to distinguish between partisan attacks on his integrity and seditious attacks on the presidency and the nation. "The profligate spirit of falsehood and malignity" in the press, he told the people of Boston at the time, threatened "the Union of the States, their Constitution of Government, and the moral character of the nation."

New alien laws, passed in the same session of Congress, gave Adams the power to expel enemy aliens during wartime and dangerous aliens in peacetime and increased the time an immigrant had to live in the United States before becoming a citizen from five years to fourteen. There is no need, said Harrison Gray Otis, summing up Federalist thought on the matter during an earlier debate over naturalization, "to invite hordes of wild Irishmen, nor the turbulent and disorderly of all parts of the world, to come here with a view to disturb our tranquility," especially, he might have added, when those Irishmen and their like voted Republican with alarming consistency once they became citizens.

The summer and fall following Congress's adjournment in 1798 was the worst time of Adams's presidency. His wife, Abigail, fell sick, and Adams, afraid she was dying, stayed with her in Quincy and conducted such affairs of state as he could by mail. In early October, he had to humble himself and agree to have Hamilton command the army under Washington. His plan to make the army acceptable to voters of all parties by appointing some prominent Republicans to high positions in it failed when Washington and Congress combined to thwart him. Congressional Federalists argued that Jacobins and Republicans (synonymous terms in their opinion) could not be trusted to lead troops against their French friends — or against American rioters and rebels if it came to that. Of Washington's refusal to accept Republicans as staff officers, a still-bitter Adams wrote years later, "I was only Viceroy under Washington and he was only Viceroy under Hamilton." As the officer corps filled up with Federalists — and there were a lot of them, so many that eventually the new army had one commissioned officer for every seven men — the army began to resemble not so much a national force as a Federalist one.

Since Adams was in no particular hurry to enlist men for Hamilton to command, he delayed serious recruiting until 1799, well after the passions and inflamed patriotism of the XYZ affair had cooled. In 1798, the ostensible reason for creating the army (fear of a French invasion) had disappeared altogether when Lord Nelson's fleet defeated the French at the Battle of the Nile. Adams thought there was "no more prospect of seeing a French army here than there is in Heaven." As the possibility (it had never been a probability) of invasion receded month by month, more and more voters began to agree.

Hamilton, however, hoped to use the army for more than simply repelling invaders and helping the British destroy the French Revolution, attractive though the idea was. He also dreamed of launching, in alliance with Britain, an invasion of Spanish America and of attaching Florida and Louisiana to the United States. When this scheme was presented to Adams (by third parties), he replied that the United States did not happen to be at war with Spain just then, so it was improper for the president even to receive such a proposal, much less act on it. Hamilton also thought it likely that the army would have to suppress insurrection in states such as Virginia, known to be teeming with unrepentant Jeffersonians who might take up arms to resist the Alien and Sedition Acts and the collection of federal taxes.

Adams thought Hamilton's immediate fears groundless, but he did not entirely dismiss the possibility of serious dissent. The large standing army, commanded exclusively by Federalists, and the resulting high taxes that Hamilton thought essential to preserve "domestic tranquility," Adams believed would be very likely to destroy it. If people are forced to pay for "a great army . . . without an enemy to fight," Adams told McHenry in October, 1798, there was no telling what might happen. The public, he warned Theodore Sedgwick early the next year, had so far "submitted with more patience than any people ever did to the burden of taxes, which has been liberally laid on, but their patience will not last always!" Americans had, after all, an uncomfortable amount of practical experience in subverting governments and overturning constitutions; they had done it twice in the last twenty-five years, once by convention and once by rebellion. When Jefferson and others argued in 1798 that laws clearly repugnant to the Constitution were not laws at all, and that they might be nullified by the states, they were speaking the language of revolution, the same language that had justified colonial resistance to the Stamp Act and the Intolerable Acts and had finally laid the groundwork for independence. Few who had lived throughout the American Revolution could have missed the resemblance.

By the end of 1798, protests over high federal taxes were increasing and petitions demanding relief were reaching Congress and the president. In Northampton County, Pennsylvania, three militant tax protesters were jailed for refusing to pay. A local auctioneer named John Fries then led a mob that captured a federal marshal and forced him to release the jailed men. Hamilton seemed almost happy at the news: Perhaps at long last his army would have someone to fight and a rebellion to suppress. President Adams, calling on the rioters to disperse, sent the army in to restore order. The troops, however, found order already restored and no one to fight. Fries and two others were promptly arrested, tried, and convicted of treason. When they were sentenced to hang, they appealed to Adams for pardons, which he granted against the unanimous advice of his cabinet. Breaking three men out of jail, Adams reasoned, hardly amounted to treason. Also, hanging Americans for protesting taxes that Adams himself thought high and ill advised seemed neither just nor politic. Besides, when dealing with dissent, Adams preferred, if he could, to remove its causes rather than to treat its consequences. Events at home and abroad soon made it possible for him to do just that.

Peace Negotiations with France

By the summer of 1798, it was clear to Talleyrand that his attempt to obtain money from the American envoys and France's attempt to bludgeon the United States into a friendlier foreign policy not only had failed but also had driven the United States close to open alliance with England. The English were already accepting American vessels into their convoys and offering to lend the United States cannon to help fortify its coast. The last thing France needed in 1798 was another declared enemy. Talleyrand began to signal his desire to reopen negotiations. American ships being held in France were released. French privateers in the West Indies were reined in, and French courts there were ordered to stop condoning on the thinnest of grounds the seizure of American cargoes. Some of the most notorious judges involved were recalled to France.

In July, Talleyrand let Elbridge Gerry, the only American envoy still in France, know that any new negotiator Adams might wish to send to Paris would be respectfully received. He even claimed that the demand for a bribe had been instigated by underlings without his knowledge or approval—a lie John Adams found it as convenient to pretend to believe as Talleyrand found it prudent to tell.

In October, 1798, Gerry returned to the United States and reported to Adams Talleyrand's eagerness to negotiate. At the same time, letters from William Vans Murray, American minister to The Hague, came in reporting the same. Shortly thereafter, Adams told his cabinet that although he was still thinking about a declaration of war, he was also considering sending a new peace commissioner to France.

By February, 1799, the president had made up his mind to try negotiations again. Talleyrand's messages had much to do with his decision, but so did conditions at home. Anger over the Alien and Sedition Acts and the army taxes was on the rise and might get out of hand, and public opinion was beginning to turn against England. The English, too, were seizing American ships, and English admiralty court judges in the West Indies were condemning American cargoes just as enthusiastically as their French counterparts. Republican papers sarcastically recounted these "evidences of British amity." In February, 1799, the *Philadelphia Aurora* reported that in the last six months of the previous year, England had seized $280,000 worth of American goods, $20,000 *more* than France. Also, only the English stopped American ships routinely and hauled off able-bodied seamen to serve in the British navy, claiming that they were British nationals. Some doubtless were; others were not. Then, in November, 1798, HMS *Carnatic* stopped the American warship *Baltimore* en route to the West Indies and removed five crewmen as suspected British deserters. This act was a violation of American sovereignty (and honor, Republican papers happily pointed out) so raw that even Secretary of State Pickering, England's strongest advocate in Adams's cabinet, had to protest. By early 1799, then, to a growing number of Americans it was by no means as clear as it had been that the English were friends and the French enemies.

On February 18, Adams regained control over foreign policy, which had been slipping by inches out of his hands and into the war Federalists' hands since the XYZ affair. At the same time, although he certainly did not intend to do so, he destroyed what remained of Federalist Party unity and probably his own chance for reelection. Without consulting his cabinet, he sent the Senate a brief message, which Vice President Jefferson, then presiding, read: "Always disposed and ready to embrace every plausible appearance of probability of preserving or restoring tranquility, I nominate William Vans Murray, our minister resident at The Hague, to be minister plenipotentiary of the United States to the French Republic."

The Senate was stunned. Astonished Republicans were puzzled, since they were still convinced that Adams lusted after a war. Federalist senators, expecting war and believing it necessary, were outraged. When the House of Representatives heard the news, wrote one eyewitness to the scene, "the majority acted as if struck by a thunderbolt."

High Federalists thought the proposal madness, but moderate Federalists rallied to Adams. John Marshall liked the idea, as did Benjamin Stoddert (secretary of the navy and the only cabinet member not left over from the Washington administration), Charles Lee, and Henry Knox. Most important of all, Washington, to whom Adams wrote explaining what he had done and why, approved—or at least he

did not publicly disapprove. Nothing, however, could be done without Senate consent, and militant Federalists there were determined to block new negotiations. Adams unbent far enough to add two more men acceptable to the Senate to the peace commission, but he hinted that if the Senate refused to consent to *any* commissioners, he might resign, leaving Thomas Jefferson as president. The Senate promptly approved a three-man peace commission.

Rumors that the peace might be saved turned into a growing hope that it would be and then into popular insistence that it must be. Adams, however, would not be rushed. Just as public bawling about avenging the nation's honor after the XYZ affair could not impel him to declare war, so now he would not be driven to conclude a peace "that will not be just or very honorable" by, as he put it, a "babyish and womanly blubbering for peace." "There is not much sincerity in this cant about peace," he told Washington. "Those who snivel for it now were hot for war against Britain a few months ago, and would be now if they saw a chance. In elective governments, peace or war are alike embraced by parties, when they think they can employ either for electioneering purposes." Presidents must lead, Adams believed, not follow either popular whim or party preference. Their function under the Constitution was to hold to the course they thought best to prevent the republic from changing direction with every shift in the public mood. The House of Representatives should reflect popular views, but all presidents should—and this president *would*—stand above all that.

Adams delayed sending the commission overseas for eight months, until he received "direct and unequivocal assurances" from the French government that it would be properly dealt with and, not incidentally, until several more American warships had been launched, increasing the nation's strength on the seas and its credibility at the bargaining table. At last, in November, 1799, the peace commission sailed for France. Months of intrigue by Hamilton, Pickering, and others to get Adams to change his mind, to stop the peace and save the war *somehow*, had failed. Adams held to his decision. They never forgave him for it.

The Campaign of 1800: Republican Slurs and Federalist Infighting

In May, 1800, a Federalist congressional caucus nominated Adams for reelection and Charles Cotesworth Pinckney for vice president. A Republican caucus chose Jefferson and Aaron Burr. There followed eight months of brutal campaigning. Federalist writers and clerics denounced Jefferson as an atheist, a libertine, and a Jacobin whose election would trigger an epidemic of rape, riot, and infanticide across the land. Republicans countered that Adams was a monarchist, an aristocrat, and an enemy to the Constitution. It was rumored in Republican circles that he had intended to reestablish aristocracy in America by marrying one of his children to one of George III's, and that he had planned to become King John I of North America. Only Washington's threat to kill him if he tried it, the rumor went, had saved the republic. Other reports had Adams sending Pinckney to Europe to procure four mistresses, two for himself and two for the president. (If true, Adams quipped, "Pinckney has kept them all for himself and cheated me out of my two.")

Jefferson presented himself in the election as the defender of states' rights against overweening federal power, as the protector of civil liberties against the authors of the Alien and Sedition Acts, and as the advocate of fiscal responsibility against the profligate spending of tax-happy Federalists. Adams found these issues hard to handle. He knew by now that the Sedition Act had been a mistake, but his party had passed it, and had recently refused to repeal it, and he had signed it into law. He opposed a larger army and high taxes, but his party had championed both, and he had signed the resulting laws. He could not deny that federal spending during his term had nearly

doubled or that taxes had soared, and he *did* think federal law and government were, and ought to be, superior to state law and government.

Adams, however, distanced himself from the more militant Federalists. It was obvious by election time that he wanted to avoid a declared war with France and to end the undeclared war at sea. Also, the Federalist majority in Congress, uneasily eyeing the coming election, had voted to begin reducing the army early in 1800. All that helped, but the nation did not learn that Adams's peace commission had reached an accommodation with France until the last days of the campaign, after nearly all the electors had already been chosen.

Finally, Adams had to fend off not only Jefferson but also a powerful segment of his own party. In May, he asked Secretaries McHenry and Pickering for their resignations on grounds of gross disloyalty to the president. When Pickering refused, Adams fired him. Hamilton and his allies understandably looked on another term for Adams as a disaster almost as great as a Jefferson presidency. They asked Washington to run again, and when he refused, they tried to arrange the election of Pinckney. Hamilton wrote a venomous pamphlet, intended only for influential Federalists and electors, denouncing Adams as unfit to govern. Republican editors got hold of a copy, printed it, and gleefully wondered aloud when Hamilton would be indicted under the Sedition Act.

Yet, with all his problems, Adams made a fight of the election and came close to winning. Much of the party's old leadership abandoned him, but the rank and file did not. The pivotal state was South Carolina, Pinckney's home state and the only Southern state with a vigorous Federalist tradition, but Republican campaign managers so skillfully distributed promises of federal patronage to the state legislature (which chose South Carolina's electors) that its eight votes went to Jefferson.

By December, Adams, who had just moved

An engraving of President Adams made by Amos Doolittle in 1799. Adams is surrounded by the coats of arms of the sixteen states in the Union at that time, and the eagle holds a banner with the motto Millions for Our Defence, Not a Cent for Tribute, a reference to the XYZ affair. *(Library of Congress)*

Bitter and exhausted, like Washington before him, Adams longed to be free of the incessant, vicious, partisan wrangling that seemed to him now virtually part of the presidency. Yet he wanted badly to be reelected as a vindication of his first term and a public endorsement of his judgment, integrity, and character. He blamed Hamilton for his defeat and humiliation as well as the end of Federalist rule.

As Congress wrestled over whom to declare president, Jefferson or Burr, and as it prepared for the inauguration to follow, Adams carried out his final duties as president—signing a new judiciary act and appointing John Marshall as chief justice of the United States were the two most important. Then, at four in the morning on inauguration day, he boarded a public stagecoach heading north. Somewhere near Baltimore, as Jefferson took his oath of office in the Capitol, Adams's public career ended.

He retreated to Quincy, to farm and read (at last there was time enough), to write occasionally about history or law, and to correspond with friends. Not for thirteen years did his pain, humiliation, and anger fade enough to permit him to write again to his old enemy and older friend, Jefferson. As the years passed and the nation changed around him, he remained proud of his presidency and convinced that it had been a success. He would be happy, he said in later years, if his gravestone bore only this: "Here lies John Adams, who took upon himself the responsibility of the peace with France in the year 1800." He died on July 4, 1826.

the government to the still-uncompleted Capitol at Washington, D.C., knew he had lost. When the electoral votes were tallied, Jefferson and Burr each had 73 (thus they tied for the presidency), whereas Adams had 65; Pinckney, 64; and John Jay, 1. Four years earlier, thirteen different men had received electoral votes. By 1800, the two national political parties so dominated presidential politics that no one but candidates they endorsed received any votes. (The lone vote for Jay was deliberate, cast so that Adams and Pinckney would not tie for the presidency if the party won.)

Adams in Retrospect: "A Self-Made Aristocrat"

Throughout his public life, Adams displayed an almost cynical understanding of how and why men and governments do what they do. "I have long been settled in my opinion," he told Jefferson in 1787, "that neither Philosophy, nor Religion, nor Morality, nor Wisdom, nor Interest, will ever govern nations or parties against their Vanity, their Pride, their Resentment or Revenge, or their Avarice or Ambition. Nothing but Force and Power and Strength can restrain them." As the foundation for the foreign policy of an infant republic in a world of monarchies, Adams's ideas had much to recommend them. As the foundation for policy and governance in a popular republic, they left much to be desired. His continued belief in them explains to some extent why as president he had more success in dealing with foreign adversaries than with his fellow countrymen.

He was, wrote historian Gilbert Chinard, "a self-made aristocrat." As such, he never completely understood the democratic strain in the American Revolution, and he never accepted fully its implications. As time and generations passed, the author of *A Defense of the Constitutions* seemed more and more alien to the increasingly democratic and populist mainstream of American thought, until in the minds of Americans Adams's memory was all but completely overshadowed by Washington and eclipsed by Jefferson.

Robert A. Becker

Suggested Readings

Adams, Charles Francis, ed. *The Works of John Adams*. 10 vols. Boston: Little, Brown, 1850-1856. Adams's grandson used John Adams's diary entries, personal notes, and correspondence, among other sources, to highlight his grandfather's career and personality.

Brown, Ralph A. *The Presidency of John Adams*. Lawrence: University Press of Kansas, 1975. Provides good historical context of the Adams presidency.

Cappon, Lester J., ed. *The Adams-Jefferson Letters*. 2 vols. 1959. Reprint. Chapel Hill: University of North Carolina Press, 1987. Provides insight into the relationship between Adams; his wife, Abigail; and Thomas Jefferson.

Ellis, Joseph J. *Passionate Sage: The Character and Legacy of John Adams*. 1993. Rev. ed. New York: Norton, 2001. A perceptive study that focuses on Adams in retirement and examines his achievements and irascible personality.

Ferling, John. *John Adams: A Bibliography*. Westport, Conn.: Greenwood Press, 1994. Provides a comprehensive listing of primary and secondary sources on the life and presidency of Adams.

Grant, James. *John Adams: Party of One*. New York: Farrar, Straus and Giroux, 2005. A one-volume biography of Adams.

Kurtz, Stephen G. *The Presidency of John Adams: The Collapse of Federalism, 1795-1800*. Philadelphia: University of Pennsylvania Press, 1957. A good biography of Adams and the historical context of his career.

McCullough, David. *John Adams*. New York: Simon & Schuster, 2002. An epic account of Adams's life, including minute details of daily life, his relationship with Thomas Jefferson, and his presidency.

Smith, Page. *John Adams*. 2 vols. Garden City, N.Y.: Doubleday, 1962. A thorough biography of Adams.

Thompson, C. Bradley. *John Adams and the Spirit of Liberty*. Lawrence: University Press of Kansas, 1998. Provides an analysis of Adams's political and constitutional philosophy.

Thomas Jefferson

3d President, 1801-1809

Born: April 13, 1743
  Shadwell, Goochland (now
    Albemarle) County, Virginia
Died: July 4, 1826
  Monticello, Albemarle County,
    Virginia

Political Party: Democratic Republican
Vice Presidents: Aaron Burr, George
  Clinton

Cabinet Members
Secretary of State: James Madison
Secretary of the Treasury: Samuel Dexter,
  Albert Gallatin
Secretary of War: Henry Dearborn
Secretary of the Navy: Benjamin Stoddert,
  Robert Smith
Attorney General: Levi Lincoln, John
  Breckinridge, Caesar Rodney

The third president of the United States was the first to gain office by successfully challenging an incumbent. The orderly transfer of authority from John Adams to Thomas Jefferson was a novel success for the new American constitutional system. Jefferson was the only president to be followed by two trusted and loyal friends, James Madison and James Monroe. This "Virginia dynasty," lasting a full six presidential terms, remains unique in American history.

When Jefferson took office, the United States had more than five million inhabitants and extended from the Atlantic to the Mississippi and from the Great Lakes to the northern boundary of Florida. When Jefferson retired, the population had grown beyond eight million people, and American territory extended to the crest of the Rocky Mountains; indeed, the United States now pretended to have some claim to the Oregon Country on the Pacific Ocean. While Jefferson was president, Robert Fulton, with the backing of Jefferson's political friend Robert Livingston of New York, succeeded in introducing steam navigation on the Hudson River. Eli Whitney, having failed to realize a fortune on his celebrated cotton gin, nevertheless pros-

Portrait of Thomas Jefferson. *(Whitehouse.gov)*

pered with a contract from Jefferson's War Department for manufacturing rifles with interchangeable parts in Springfield, Massachusetts. Native talent was continually being augmented by gifted immigrants, such as the radical British scientists Joseph Priestley and Thomas Cooper and the gifted architect Benjamin Latrobe, who helped design the public buildings of the new city of Washington, D.C.

A Child of the Enlightenment

With most developments in American society, Jefferson was happily and deeply sympathetic. An optimistic child of the Enlightenment, he especially valued education, scientific inquiry, mechanical invention, and voluntary organizations for the improvement of humankind. He believed that government should not tax people to do these things for them but rather should

---

The First Ladies
Martha Jefferson and Patsy Jefferson Randolph

When Thomas Jefferson came courting, Martha Wayles Skelton at twenty-two was already a widow, an heiress, and a mother whose firstborn son would die in early childhood. Perhaps a mutual love of music cemented the romance. Jefferson played the violin, and one of the furnishings he ordered for the home that he was building at Monticello was a "forte-piano" for his bride.

Like many of the early First Ladies, Martha was born—on October 19, 1748—to a family of wealthy Virginia planters. Her first marriage in 1765 to Bathurst Skelton (1744-1768) resulted in one son, John (1767-1771).

Following the death of her husband and child, she married the future president on January 1, 1772, at the bride's plantation home, The Forest, near Williamsburg. They had six children: Martha "Patsy" Washington (1772-1836), Jane Randolph (1774-1775), an unnamed son (born and died 1777), Mary Wayles (1778-1804), Lucy Elizabeth (1780-1781), and a second Lucy Elizabeth (1782-1785).

The physical strain of frequent pregnancies weakened Martha so gravely that her husband curtailed his political activities to stay near her. He served in Virginia's House of Delegates and as governor, but he refused an appointment by the Continental Congress as a commissioner to France. Just after New Year's Day, 1781, a British invasion forced Martha to flee the capital in Richmond with a newborn baby girl, who then died in April. In June, the family barely escaped an enemy raid on Monticello.

Martha bore another daughter the following May and never regained full strength. She died on September 6, 1782, a month before what would have been her thirty-fourth birthday.

When Jefferson became president in 1801, he had been a widower for nineteen years. It was Patsy—now Mrs. Thomas Mann Randolph, Jr.—who appeared as the lady of the President's House (later called the White House) in the winter of 1802-1803, when she spent seven weeks there. She was there again in 1805-1806 and gave birth to a son who became the first child born in the executive mansion and was named for James Madison.

Patsy became her father's comforter and close adviser, perhaps the single most important personal factor that stabilized him during his presidency. After his term was over, she and her husband retired to their Edgehill estate, and then to Monticello. She was with her father when he died in 1826. Eventually, debts and Randolph's death in 1829 forced the family to sell both estates. Patsy died on October 10, 1836, and is buried with her parents at Monticello.

Dean M. Shapiro

Monticello, Jefferson's home. *(Library of Congress)*

create a climate in which such good things would be done at the people's initiative. Jefferson's maxim, "That government is best which governs least," was therefore not intended to encourage radical individualism but rather to encourage the widest and fullest possible participation in society.

Like many of the democratic heroes of the United States, Jefferson started life in the first rank of society. His father, Peter Jefferson, had worked hard and effectively to build an estate of nearly ten thousand acres around Albemarle County, which he had helped create. Peter was married to Jane Randolph, whose many-branched family was as wealthy and powerful as any in Virginia. He flourished as a tobacco planter, surveyor, militia officer, and justice of the peace. Thomas was born April 13, 1743, into a world not of dignified leisure but

of bustling, wilderness-clearing, slave-trading, Indian-fighting activity. Among his father's associates were men who already yearned for the virgin lands of the Ohio Valley. Westward expansion, something closely associated with Jefferson until he retired from the presidency, was a family inheritance.

Educated in the local schools of two Anglican clergymen until he was seventeen, Jefferson rode down to the provincial capital of Williamsburg in 1760 to complete his liberal education and learn the law at the College of William and Mary. Such was his precocity that he soon found himself a regular guest at the table of the acting governor, Francis Fauquier. There, too, were Jefferson's favorite teachers, Dr. William Small from Edinburgh and the kindly and erudite lawyer George Wythe. Before he was twenty-one, Jefferson was accustomed to seeing the world through the eyes of learned, active, and powerful men.

Peter Jefferson had died in 1757, when Thomas was fourteen, and from then on Thomas took little interest in his family but much in his studies and in his friends. After six years of study in Williamsburg, he settled into the life of planter and lawyer and was reasonably successful at both occupations. In 1769, he won election to the House of Burgesses, where he quickly joined the majority there defending colonial rights against the supposed incursions of ministerial authority from England. In 1772, he married a wealthy widow, Martha Wayles Skelton, by most accounts an attractive and intelligent woman as well as a fine musician. She died only ten years later, in 1782, leaving Jefferson with three young daughters: Martha, Mary, and Lucy (who died three years later). Several other children had been stillborn or died in infancy.

A National Leader: From the House of Burgesses to the White House

Marriage added greatly to Jefferson's responsibilities, and so did the growing crisis between England and its American colonies. The young burgess from Albemarle became familiar to radicals throughout the colonies through his fiery pamphlet of 1774, *A Summary View of the Rights of British America*. The next year, he attended the Continental Congress in Philadelphia, where his draft of "Causes for Taking Up Arms" was too strong for most of the other delegates but where his literary talents were fully recognized. This led to his appointment to the committee that drafted the Declaration of Independence. Though Congress made a few changes in it (which seemed much more significant to Jefferson than to most subsequent readers), the document remains an example of Jefferson's remarkable style, both for the force and felicity of its general philosophical statements and for the almost reckless élan with which the crimes of George III are cataloged.

Though established as a national leader, Jefferson left the Continental Congress in September, 1776, preferring to be closer to his wife and children. For three years, he worked tirelessly in the Virginia legislature, collecting all the laws of the colonial era and, with Wythe and Edmund Pendleton, forging a new legal code appropriate to a liberal planter's republic. He then served as governor for two terms, from 1779 to 1781, a period which unfortunately coincided with a sustained British invasion of the state. Jefferson was as helpless to prevent the marches and raids of Lord Cornwallis's army as other Southern governors had been. Still, some Virginia politicians tried for a time to blame Jefferson for the inability of the militia to turn the British away. Later, Generals George Washington and Comte de Rochambeau, not Jefferson, received the credit for finally defeating the British army in Virginia.

Retired from office with some feeling of relief, Jefferson wrote the only book he ever published in his lifetime, *Notes on the State of Virginia*, a work about the geography, products, and social and political life of eighteenth century Virginia.

The death of his wife left Jefferson temporarily despondent and aimless. Also, perhaps, it made him willing to serve away from home again. The year 1783 found him once again in the Continental Congress, where he was chiefly responsible for the new nation's system of weights and measures. As chair of a committee on Western lands, he also drafted an elaborate ordinance for the development of Western territories into eventual statehood. His draft included the provision that after a few years, no more slaves could be introduced into the West, a provision that failed to secure the needed support of nine states in the Congress. Before Congress finally acted to create the Northwest Territory, Jefferson had departed for Paris, initially to help John Adams and Benjamin Franklin with commercial negotiations and then, in 1785, to replace the aging and homesick Franklin as

United States minister to France.

In Paris, Jefferson tried hard to strengthen commercial relations between France and the United States, but the feebleness of the Congress under the Articles of Confederation and the increasing ineffectiveness of the government of Louis XVI made such changes impossible. From a personal point of view, however, this was a very satisfying period. Jefferson's five years in Europe introduced him fully to the best minds, architecture, wines, and amenities of France. He was a close observer and, to a degree, even an unofficial adviser in the first stage of the French Revolution.

Back in the United States at the beginning of

An 1866 engraving of the drafting of the Declaration of Independence, with (left to right) Benjamin Franklin, Jefferson, John Adams, Robert R. Livingston, and Roger Sherman. *(Library of Congress)*

1790, he accepted President Washington's invitation to become secretary of state. Within a year, however, he had begun to organize opposition to Alexander Hamilton, who as secretary of the treasury functioned as a sort of prime minister under Washington. Since Washington usually supported Hamilton, Jefferson eventually found his position untenable. At the end of 1793, he resigned after completing a report on American trade that indicted the British for unfair trading practices and urged closer ties with the chief ally of the United States, France. Jefferson then enjoyed three years of retirement in which he especially concentrated on building his mansion at Monticello. He still kept up a full political correspondence and became John Adams's chief rival for the presidency in the election of 1796. The Constitution as originally adopted did not anticipate the existence of political parties. Members of the electoral college voted for two candidates for president. The one receiving the greatest number of votes, if a majority, became president, and the one with the next highest number, vice president. Under this system, in 1796 John Adams, a Federalist, was chosen president and Jefferson, a Democratic Republican, was elected vice president. While conscientiously presiding over the Senate during the next four years, Jefferson kept his political activities well concealed. They included writing Kentucky Resolutions of 1798, which asserted the right of the states to nullify acts of Congress—in this case, the Alien and Sedition Acts, which were intended to silence or remove from the country critics of the Federalist Party.

The election of 1800, in which Jefferson challenged the incumbent Adams, took place in a heated partisan atmosphere. Jefferson and the Re-

The Declaration of Independence

In CONGRESS, July 4, 1776.

The unanimous Declaration of the thirteen united States of America,

When in the Course of human events it becomes necessary for one people to dissolve the political bands which have connected them with another and to assume among the powers of the earth, the separate and equal station to which the Laws of Nature and of Nature's God entitle them, a decent respect to the opinions of mankind requires that they should declare the causes which impel them to the separation.

We hold these truths to be self-evident, that all men are created equal, that they are endowed by their Creator with certain unalienable Rights, that among these are Life, Liberty and the pursuit of Happiness — That to secure these rights, Governments are instituted among Men, deriving their just powers from the consent of the governed, — That whenever any Form of Government becomes destructive of these ends, it is the Right of the People to alter or to abolish it, and to institute new Government, laying its foundation on such principles and organizing its powers in such form, as to them shall seem most likely to effect their Safety and Happiness. Prudence, indeed, will dictate that Governments long established should not be changed for light and transient causes; and accordingly all experience hath shewn that mankind are more disposed to suffer, while evils are sufferable than to right themselves by abolishing the forms to which they are accustomed. But when a long train of abuses and usurpations, pursuing invariably the same Object evinces a design to reduce them under absolute Despotism, it is their right, it is their duty, to throw off such Government, and to provide new Guards for their future security. — Such has been the patient sufferance of these Colonies; and such is now the necessity which constrains them to alter their former Systems of Government. The history of the present King of Great Britain is a history of repeated injuries and usurpations, all having in direct object the establishment of an absolute Tyranny over these States. To prove this, let Facts be submitted to a candid world.

He has refuted his Assent to Laws, the most wholesome and necessary for the public good.

He has forbidden his Governors to pass Laws of immediate and pressing importance, unless suspended in their operation till his Assent should be obtained; and when so suspended, he has utterly neglected to attend to them.

He has refused to pass other Laws for the accommodation of large districts of people, unless those people would relinquish the right of Representation in the Legislature, a right inestimable to them and formidable to tyrants only.

He has called together legislative bodies at places unusual, uncomfortable, and distant from the depository of their Public Records, for the sole purpose of fatiguing them into compliance with his measures.

He has dissolved Representative Houses repeatedly, for opposing with manly firmness his invasions on the rights of the people.

He has refused for a long time, after such dissolutions, to cause others to be elected, whereby the Legislative Powers, incapable of Annihilation, have returned to the People at large for their exercise; the State remaining in the mean time exposed to all the dangers of invasion from without, and convulsions within.

He has endeavoured to prevent the population of these States; for that purpose obstructing the Laws for Naturalization of Foreigners; refusing to pass others to encourage their migrations hither, and raising the conditions of new Appropriations of Lands.

He has obstructed the Administration of Justice by refusing his Assent to Laws for establishing Judiciary Powers.

He has made Judges dependent on his Will alone for the tenure of their offices, and the amount and payment of their salaries.

He has erected a multitude of New Offices, and sent hither swarms of Officers to harass our people and eat out their substance.

He has kept among us, in times of peace, Standing Armies without the Consent of our legislatures.

He has affected to render the Military independent of and superior to the Civil Power.

He has combined with others to subject us to a jurisdiction foreign to our constitution, and unacknowledged by our laws; giving his Assent to their Acts of pretended Legislation: — For quartering large bodies of armed troops among us: — For protecting them, by a mock Trial from punishment for any Murders which they should commit on the Inhabitants of these States: — For cutting off our Trade with all parts of the world: — For imposing Taxes on us without our Consent: — For depriving us in many cases, of the benefit of Trial by Jury: — For transporting us beyond Seas to be tried for pretended offences: — For abolishing the free System of English Laws in a neighbouring Province, establishing therein an Arbitrary government, and enlarging its Boundaries so as to render it at once an example and fit instrument for introducing the same absolute rule into these Colonies: — For taking away our Charters, abolishing our most valuable Laws and altering fundamentally the Forms of our Governments: — For suspending our own Legislatures, and declaring themselves invested with power to legislate for us in all cases whatsoever.

He has abdicated Government here, by declaring us out of his Protection and waging War against us.

He has plundered our seas, ravaged our Coasts, burnt our towns, and destroyed the lives of our people.

He is at this time transporting large Armies of foreign Mercenaries to compleat the works of death, desolation, and tyranny, already begun with circumstances of Cruelty & Perfidy scarcely paralleled in the most barbarous ages, and totally unworthy the Head of a civilized nation.

He has constrained our fellow Citizens taken Captive on the high Seas to bear Arms against their Country, to become the executioners of their friends and Brethren, or to fall themselves by their Hands.

He has excited domestic insurrections amongst us, and has endeavoured to bring on the inhabitants of our frontiers, the merciless Indian Savages whose known rule of warfare, is an undistinguished destruction of all ages, sexes and conditions.

In every stage of these Oppressions We have Petitioned for Redress in the most humble terms: Our repeated Petitions have been answered only by repeated injury. A Prince, whose character is thus marked by every act which may define a Tyrant, is unfit to be the ruler of a free people.

Nor have We been wanting in attentions to our British brethren. We have warned them from time to time of attempts by their legislature to extend an unwarrantable jurisdiction over us. We have reminded them of the circumstances of our emigration and settlement here. We have appealed to their native justice and magnanimity, and we have conjured them by the ties of our common kindred to disavow these usurpations, which would inevitably interrupt our connections and correspondence. They too have been deaf to the voice of justice and of consanguinity. We must, therefore, acquiesce in the necessity, which denounces our Separation, and hold them, as we hold the rest of mankind, Enemies in War, in Peace Friends.

We, therefore, the Representatives of the United States of America, in General Congress, Assembled, appealing to the Supreme Judge of the world for the rectitude of our intentions, do, in the

Name, and by Authority of the good People of these Colonies, solemnly publish and declare, That these United Colonies are, and of Right ought to be Free and Independent States, that they are Absolved from all Allegiance to the British Crown, and that all political connection between them and the State of Great Britain, is and ought to be totally dissolved; and that as Free and Independent States, they have full Power to levy War, conclude Peace, contract Alliances, establish Commerce, and to do all other Acts and Things which Independent States may of right do.

And for the support of this Declaration, with a firm reliance on the protection of Divine Providence, we mutually pledge to each other our Lives, our Fortunes and our sacred Honor.

publicans campaigned against Adams and the Federalists by portraying them as threats to the very notion of republican liberty. They had suppressed freedom, taxed heavily, and created a dangerous military establishment, the Republicans charged. The people responded with wide support for Jefferson and his vice presidential candidate, Aaron Burr, but again the voting in the electoral college produced an unintended result. The electors still did not distinguish between candidates for president and vice president and cast the same number of votes for Burr as they did for Jefferson. The Constitution dictated that the election was to be decided in the lame duck House of Representatives that had been elected in 1798. Many Federalist members in the House thought Burr the lesser evil and a man with whom they could work and cast their votes for him. After many ballots prolonged a stalemate well into February, 1801, a group of border state Federalists withdrew their support from Burr, and Jefferson was finally elected. Two years later, Congress, led by Republicans fearful of a repetition of the dangerous confusion of 1800, passed and the states quickly ratified the Twelfth Amendment to the Constitution, which provided for separate balloting for president and vice president.

The new president was close to his fifty-eighth birthday, but he still stood erect and lean, well over 6 feet tall, with red hair and a ruddy complexion. Always wise in his diet and drink and conscientious in taking exercise, Jefferson enjoyed exceptionally good health until his very last years. He had broken his right wrist in France and never quite recovered complete control of his right hand, but its effect on his violin playing was worse than on his writing. Otherwise, his only physical problem was an occasional severe migraine, which had a way of striking and prostrating him at times when he could scarcely afford to leave his work. Indeed, Jefferson was so industrious that the headaches may have been the way his system forced him to rest from time to time.

A Federalist Legacy of Peace and Prosperity

As John Adams's successor, Jefferson began his first term with several important assets. The United States was at peace with all the major powers, revenues exceeded expenditures, and trade was at an all-time high. So, too, were personal incomes. A good case can be made for saying that Jefferson inherited a strong and prosperous nation because the policies he had systematically opposed had nevertheless served the nation very well. In any case, Jefferson began his term in a conciliatory and generous mood. He came to his inauguration on March 4, 1801, dressed in homespun, as George Washington had done twelve years earlier. Although he owned a handsome carriage, he chose to ride to the Capitol on horseback, emphasizing the fact that he was an ordinary citizen whom his fellow citizens had elected chief magistrate. "We are all Republicans, we are all Federalists," he asserted; the previous quarrels had represented mere differences of opinion and not fundamental differences of principle.

Repeating ideas on foreign policy that had appeared in Washington's farewell address, he called for friendship with all foreign nations, "entangling alliances" with none. Disarming critics who charged that he would sell out to the French, Jefferson promised that he would not restore the Alliance of 1778. Furthermore, he was determined to continue the nation's profitable trade with England. He urged a harmony of interests in the republic, though he did assert the primacy of agriculture by describing commerce as "her handmaiden."

Jefferson enjoyed the advantage of having two devoted, loyal, and highly intelligent friends serve in his administration through its full eight years: James Madison as secretary of state and Albert Gallatin of Pennsylvania as secretary of the treasury. His other appointees

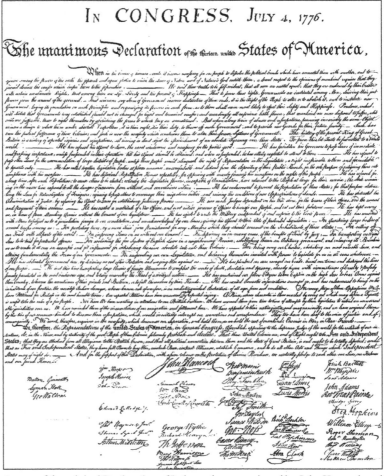

A copy of the original Declaration of Independence, as signed by John Hancock and the other delegates. *(NARA)*

were reasonably able and represented unavoidable political considerations. Thus his secretary of war, Henry Dearborn, came from the Maine district of Massachusetts and his attorney general, Levi Lincoln, came from Worcester, Massachusetts. Robert Smith, secretary of the navy, was from Maryland. Most of these men, and especially the trio of Jefferson, Gallatin, and Madison, were extremely attentive to the important details of administration.

Jefferson grasped instinctively that he was both chief administrator for the government and head of its majority party; he performed the latter role shrewdly and with masterful informality. Abandoning the formal levees held ev-

ery week when Congress was in session by his predecessors — they were excessively monarchical for Jefferson's taste — the president entertained congressmen and members of the small diplomatic community in a series of dinner parties. Even there he abandoned protocol, letting each guest scramble for his seat at the table. Still, these were hardly potluck affairs; Jefferson had a fine French chef and a cellar of excellent wines. He had no taste for public oratory but a splendid gift for conversation. In the give-and-take around the president's dinner table, Jefferson quite pleasantly did most of the giving, and his ideas unfailingly filtered into the two chambers of Congress.

Reducing the Government's Reach: The Judiciary Act of 1802

With such promising men and methods at his disposal, Jefferson was, at the outset of his administration, still chiefly concerned with reducing, not expanding, the sphere of government. Economy and retrenchment were his paramount goals, and they required that something be done about the Judiciary Act of 1801. After losing the election of 1800, in an effort to retain control of the judicial branch, the Federalist lame ducks in Congress passed a bill greatly expanding the number of judgeships in the federal system. Besides its partisan purpose, the law wisely anticipated the future growth of the nation and the increasing need for federal courts. It also relieved the justices of the Supreme Court from riding circuit, and as these justices were likely to be men of advanced years, this change was both prudent and merciful. Just before leaving office, Adams appointed loyal Federalists to the new judgeships. The federal judiciary had thus become, as John Randolph of Virginia quipped, "a graveyard for decayed politicians."

With Jefferson's encouragement, the new Congress passed the Judiciary Act of 1802, which essentially repealed the act of 1801 and abolished all the new posts. Secretary of State James Madison further struck at the opposition by declining to deliver a number of certificates of appointment to office that Adams had made out the last night of his presidency and left for his successors to deliver. One of these made William Marbury a justice of the peace for the District of Columbia. Upon failing to obtain his commission, Marbury sued, asking the Supreme Court to issue a writ of mandamus ordering Madison to deliver it. In the celebrated case of *Marbury v. Madison*, the Court found that, although Marbury was entitled to have his commission, the Court could not force Madison to deliver it, for the section of the Judiciary Act of 1789 that empowered the Supreme Court to issue writs of mandamus under its original juris-diction was unconstitutional. Although Jefferson and Madison were naturally pleased that Madison did not have to deliver to Marbury his commission, they found very unpalatable the Supreme Court's asserting the right of judicial review — that of nullifying an act of Congress on the ground that it violated the Constitution.

Besides the Judiciary Act of 1802, the Seventh Congress, Jefferson's first, passed other measures that pleased a majority of Americans. With the end of Adams's Half-War with France in 1800, the Federalists had reduced the army and navy, but the Republicans cut them further. Also, with trade flourishing and customs receipts mounting, they declared that internal taxes were no longer needed and eliminated all of them, including a very controversial one on distilled liquor. The income from land sales alone permitted the government to meet all of its current expenses and to reduce the national debt significantly as well. It had as a further source of funds the income from the sale of its stock in the Bank of the United States. Even though Jefferson had argued against the constitutionality of the bank when it was chartered in 1791, the institution flourished and expanded during his presidency, and it saved the Treasury considerable sums by transferring funds from one part of the country to another at no charge.

War with the Barbary Pirates: To the Shores of Tripoli

There was one small exception to the general pattern of reduced federal activity under Jefferson's presidency. In 1801, the pasha of Tripoli declared war on the United States by the customary device of having his agents chop down the flagpole in front of the U.S. legation. Such a declaration meant that warships of Tripoli would attack American merchant shipping in the Mediterranean, taking ships and cargoes as prizes and holding their crews for ransom. For several years, the Federalist administrations had paid subsidies and ransoms to three other

Stephen Decatur fights the Barbary pirates of Tripoli. *(Library of Congress)*

North African potentates to protect American shipping and rescue its sailors. Now Tripoli was, in effect, demanding a generous payment. In the 1780's, Jefferson had advocated development of a powerful American navy, in no small part to relieve the United States of the necessity of paying blackmail to the piratical princes of the Barbary Coast. Without seeking authorization from Congress, President Jefferson dispatched a small fleet to the Mediterranean to protect American ships and, if necessary, attack the Tripolitans. Like his predecessors, Washington and Adams, Jefferson tended to disregard the clear prescription of the Constitution that the president make foreign policy with the advice and consent of the Senate. The war with Tripoli went badly until 1805, when, as a result of a combination of American naval pressure and diplomatic skill, the pasha was induced to sign a peace treaty, although the United States

was required to pay $60,000 for the release of American prisoners.

Peaceful Expansion: The Louisiana Purchase

Jefferson presided over an era of peaceful growth in the Western territories of the United States. He eased out the old Federalist governor of the Ohio Territory, Arthur St. Clair, who had made many enemies by his indifferent administration and by his opposition to the admission of Ohio to statehood. Following his removal, Ohio became a state in 1803, adding strength to the Republican majorities in Congress. Meanwhile, Congress had authorized a government for the Indiana Territory, and Jefferson appointed William Henry Harrison, son of a former governor of Virginia, to be its governor.

About the same time, a series of events occurred that led to the greatest achievement of

A map of the United States in 1819 showing the Louisiana Purchase. *(Library of Congress)*

Jefferson's presidency and to the single largest addition to American territory, the Louisiana Purchase. In 1763, Bourbon France had reluctantly transferred Louisiana to Spain as compensation for its loss of Florida. A succession of French ministries in the 1780's and 1790's pondered various schemes for reoccupying Louisiana but found none practical. By 1800, however, the king of Spain considered the area a burden rather than an asset. Its only purpose for him was to protect Mexico by offering a buffer against the notoriously expansionist English and Americans. By the secret Treaty of San Ildefonso (1800), Spain retroceded Louisiana to France, which promised in another document that the territory would not be alienated to a third power.

In 1802, news of the retrocession reached Jefferson, followed by the more alarming news that the Spanish governor had used the transfer as an excuse to close the Mississippi to American commerce. Worse still, Jefferson learned

that Napoleon Bonaparte had sent a great fleet and army under General Charles Leclerc to reconquer the former French colony of Haiti, which had been the world's foremost producer of sugar before rebellious blacks succeeded in overturning their former masters. After he had reestablished French rule and slavery in Haiti, Leclerc was instructed to occupy Louisiana.

Jefferson responded by alerting his Western military commanders to the possibility of war with France in the Mississippi Valley. He also set in motion a plan he had first conceived as a member of the Articles of Confederation Congress in 1783: an expedition of expert observers and mapmakers to explore the uncharted trans-Mississippi West. This expedition, to be led by two veteran frontiersmen, Meriwether Lewis of Virginia, Jefferson's private secretary, and William Clark of Kentucky, when first projected by the president was intended as a reconnoitering of foreign and potentially enemy territory. At about the same time, Jefferson advised his representative in Paris, Robert Livingston, to inform Napoleon that the United States could not tolerate France's control of access to the Gulf of Mexico through the Mississippi River. The United States could accept moribund Spain's control of Louisiana and the mouth of the Mississippi, at least for a time, but with the French at New Orleans, the United States would be forced to seek a firm alliance with Great Britain and then attack Louisiana as soon as the next European war started. Livingston added, however, that the United States was prepared to buy New Orleans from France and thereby remove the major cause of future strife.

Livingston's threats would have been wasted on Napoleon had his campaign in Haiti succeeded, but it failed: The blacks, partly armed by British and American traders, fought ably, and Leclerc's men suffered dreadfully from tropical diseases. Though the French general succeeded by treachery in capturing the black

leader, Toussaint-Louverture, other leaders arose and eventually drove out the French.

Having lost one army in Egypt and another in the West Indies, Napoleon decided to pursue his ambition closer to home. He determined to concentrate his efforts on the defeat of Great Britain, the perennial and formidable enemy of France. Without a single French soldier to defend it, Louisiana was no longer of any value to him, but he badly needed money. He therefore offered to sell the whole territory to the United States for $15 million, then a considerable sum of money. James Monroe, sent by Jefferson to help with negotiations, joined Livingston in accepting the emperor's offer. President Jefferson and Congress ratified their agreement and voted money for the purchase as quickly as possible. Recalling his belief in a strict construction of the Constitution and noticing that the document nowhere authorized the executive to purchase territory from foreign governments, Jefferson had at first suggested to his cabinet that it

---

Thomas Jefferson's message to Congress regarding the Louisiana Purchase, January 16, 1804:

To the Senate and House of Representatives of the United States:

In execution of the act of the present session of Congress for taking possession of Louisiana, as ceded to us by France, and for the temporary government thereof, Governor Claiborne, of the Mississippi Territory, and General Wilkinson were appointed commissioners to receive possession. They proceeded with such regular troops as had been assembled at Fort Adams from the nearest posts and with some militia of the Mississippi Territory to New Orleans. To be prepared for anything unexpected which might arise out of the transaction, a respectable body of militia was ordered to be in readiness in the States of Ohio, Kentucky, and Tennessee, and a part of those of Tennessee was moved on to the Natchez. No occasion, however, arose for their services. Our commissioners, on their arrival at New Orleans, found the Province already delivered by the commissioners of Spain to that of France, who delivered it over to them on the 20th day of December, as appears by their declaratory act accompanying this. Governor Claiborne, being duly invested with the powers heretofore exercised by the governor and intendant of Louisiana, assumed the government on the same day, and for the maintenance of law and order immediately issued the proclamation and address now communicated.

On this important acquisition, so favorable to the immediate interests of our Western citizens, so auspicious to the peace and security of the nation in general, which adds to our country territories so extensive and fertile and to our citizens new brethren to partake of the blessings of freedom and self-government, I offer to Congress and our country my sincere congratulations.

might be wise to propose an amendment specifically granting that power. Madison, however, pointed out that amendments, like laws, could not operate *ex post facto*. To propose an amendment would be virtually to admit that the purchase had been unconstitutional. Thus the Jeffersonians became self-conscious broad constructionists.

The Louisiana Purchase was enormously popular in the United States, but a remnant of Federalists, led by Timothy Pickering of Massachusetts, opposed the purchase bitterly, and with a degree of merit often overlooked. The territory, opponents pointed out, was not Napoleon's to sell. Why pay $15 million to an international swindler for stolen goods? If the United States had any right to Louisiana at all, it would have been better simply to occupy it and defy the French tyrant. Furthermore, the people who actually lived in Louisiana had not been consulted, and therefore the United States had no right to annex them unless they were willing to be annexed, according to the principle of the right of self-government so central in the Republican creed. In fact, Congress had, on Jefferson's advice, set up a special military government for Louisiana, which, though it treated the inhabitants fairly enough, allowed migrants from the older United States to move in and take control. Slavery was confirmed, which pleased the creole planters, but the African slave trade stopped, which angered some of them. Louisiana thus became another market for the surplus slaves of the upper South and especially valuable for Virginia, the largest and most populous of the slave-selling states.

Pickering now wrote a number of private letters proposing that the states without slavery explore the possibility of joining with Canada and the maritimes in a new and free confederation. None of his friends thought such a scheme feasible, including the strong-minded George Cabot of Massachusetts, the most influential member of the so-called Essex Junto. From that time to this, however, rumors have abounded of

a New England secessionist conspiracy, waxing and waning from the time of Pickering's letters of 1804 down to the Hartford Convention of 1814.

Signs of Disunion: The Burr-Hamilton Duel and the Impeachment Trial of Samuel Chase

Many Federalists, though opposed to disunion, were again willing in 1804 to unite with Aaron Burr in the hope of regaining political power. Burr, when he realized that he would be replaced as Jefferson's candidate for vice president, sought that year to be elected governor of New York as a base from which to run for president. During his campaign, Alexander Hamilton, horrified at the proposed alliance between Federalists and Burrites, privately spread his opinion that Burr was a man of talent but no scruples. Burr subsequently lost the race for governor, although less because of Hamilton's comments than because of the strong tide in favor of Burr's former Republican allies that year. Nevertheless, Hamilton's remarks had found their way into print, which led Burr to challenge Hamilton to a duel in which he shot and mortally wounded Hamilton. Although his political career had come to an end, Burr completed his term as vice president.

With Burr no longer a viable candidate, the Federalists never found a serious challenger for the presidency in 1804. Some tried to gather votes for Charles Cotesworth Pinckney of South Carolina, but he had neither a program nor a network of supporters required for an effective campaign. Moreover, Jefferson had become extremely popular. Frugality in government, peace with foreign powers, general prosperity, and especially the Louisiana Purchase all served to heighten Jefferson's appeal. Even former president and Federalist John Adams allowed it to be known that he favored the Virginian's election. Only Connecticut, Delaware, and two electors from Maryland gave their votes to Pinckney; Jefferson carried the rest of New England and even his rival's home state of South Carolina.

During the period between the election and Jefferson's second inauguration, the Republicans proceeded with the impeachment trial of Federalist Samuel Chase, an associate justice of the Supreme Court. It was, in fact, with this trial that Jefferson's fortunes as president began to change. Earlier the Federalists had been quite helpless to prevent the Senate's removal of John Pickering, a United States district court judge in New Hampshire, for that old Federalist was mentally incompetent and should have resigned. Since he was unwilling to do so,

neither the Constitution nor the Judiciary Act prescribed a legal method of his removal.

Impeachment is limited to cases involving high crimes and misdemeanors, yet the House drew up a bill of impeachment for Pickering and the Senate mustered more than the needed two-thirds vote in 1804. Pickering was unable to appear in his own defense, nor did he send anyone to appear for him. Once again, the Jeffersonians were proving far less scrupulous about the letter of the Constitution than they had been when out of power. The impeachment of Samuel Chase, however, was quite a different matter from that of Pickering. Although Chase had

The Vice President
Aaron Burr

The United States' third vice president was born on February 6, 1756, in Newark, New Jersey. Orphaned at the age of four, he was raised by relatives in Pennsylvania and Massachusetts. Burr enrolled in Princeton in 1769 and was graduated at the age of sixteen with high honors.

By May of 1776, he had joined the rebellion against Britain and was under the command of General George Washington. At the age of twenty-two, he was promoted to the rank of lieutenant colonel and later to colonel. Forced to resign due to poor health in 1779, Burr began studying law. By 1781, he had passed the bar and had set up a law practice in Albany with a colleague from his days in the army. On July 2, 1782, he married Theodosia Prevost, and within six years his political career was well underway. By 1792, Burr had served as attorney general of New York, United States senator, and justice on the New York State Supreme Court.

Chosen as a candidate for vice president in 1800, he tied Thomas Jefferson for the presidency and, under the electoral college, the election was decided by the House of Representatives in Jefferson's favor. Unhappy in the vice presidency, Burr announced his candidacy for New York governor in 1803, and to his dismay, he lost the election partly as a result of opposition from Alexander Hamilton. As a result of the animosity that existed between the two men, Burr challenged Hamilton to a duel in Weehawken, New Jersey, in 1804, which ended with the death of Hamilton. Escaping charges of murder and disappointed with his failing political career, he went West and conspired with General James Wilkinson to seize the land that fell within the Louisiana Territory by force in order to establish an independent nation with Burr as its emperor.

Burr was tried for treason for his unsuccessful scheme but was acquitted by Chief Justice Marshall, to the great dismay of Jefferson. After his acquittal, he spent four years trying to garner support from European nations to aid him in his plan to establish an independent nation. Leaving Europe with little success, Burr returned to New York, where he opened a law office. In 1834, he suffered a stroke; he died two years later on September 14, 1836, in Staten Island, New York, at the age of eighty-one.

Robert P. Watson and Richard Yon

The duel between Alexander Hamilton (left) and Aaron Burr. *(Library of Congress)*

been an intensely partisan Federalist, accustomed to insulting Republicans from the bench, he had not lost his reason and was quite able to defend himself in a legal proceeding. A team of outstanding lawyers joined in his defense. With Burr presiding and John Randolph leading the prosecution for the House of Representatives, Chase received a fair and full trial before the United States Senate. Had he been found guilty and removed from office, the subsequent history of the United States might have been quite different, for after removing one partisan judge, Congress might more easily have removed others. The Senate, however, would not supply the needed two-thirds vote on a single one of the charges against Chase. One reason was a continuing respect for the independence of the judiciary. Chase had clearly been guilty of bad manners, arbitrary conduct, poor taste, and partisan harangues in his courtroom. Yet none of these

was in violation of federal statutes, and the Constitution makes no provision for removing unpleasant or even bungling judges. Chase had perhaps disgraced the bench, but he was no criminal.

Jefferson's Second Term: Optimistic Beginnings, Unforeseen Difficulties

If Jefferson felt any personal disappointment over Chase's acquittal, no trace of it appeared in his buoyant second inaugural address. He congratulated his countrymen on the success of pure Republicanism. "The suppression of unnecessary offices, of useless establishments and expenses, enabled us to discontinue our internal taxes," he declared. Then, warming to his theme of frugality, he continued, "It may be the pleasure and pride of an American to ask, what farmer, what mechanic, what laborer, ever sees a tax-gatherer of the United States?" Yet, thanks to good management, the day would soon dawn when all the debts of the federal government would be retired and the Treasury would enjoy a surplus. Would it not then be timely, "by a just repartition among the states, and a corresponding amendment of the constitution," to spend such surpluses on the improvement of "rivers, canals, roads, arts, manufactures, education, and other great objects within each state." Turning toward Native Americans, Jefferson declared that he had regarded them "with the commiseration their history inspires." He would continue his policy of introducing the domestic and agricultural arts of the United States among them and, like his predecessors and successors, would work to assimilate American Indians into the large and growing U.S. society. The address also contained a brief affir-

mation that the federal government should not meddle in religious institutions, and a rather surprising claim that, though a forbearance against libel and falsehood had been in itself a good thing, allowing truth to drive out error, nevertheless, "no inference is here intended, that the laws, provided by the State against false and defamatory publications, should not be enforced; he who has time, renders a service to public morals and public tranquility, in reforming these abuses by the salutary coercions of the law." The address ended with an appeal to the American people to sustain good government and with a dignified appeal to "that Being in whose hands we are, who led our forefathers, as Israel of old, from their native land, and planted them in a country flowing with the necessaries and comforts of life."

The Vice President
George Clinton

George Clinton was born on July 26, 1739, in Ulster County, New York. After serving as a seaman on a privateer vessel during the French and Indian War, Clinton was named clerk of the Court of Common Pleas in Ulster County. His new position required familiarity with the law; therefore, Clinton studied under William Smith in New York and, by 1764, he was admitted to the New York bar. Four years later, Clinton would be elected as a member of the New York Assembly, where he was an outspoken opponent of British taxation of the colonies. On February 7, 1770, he married Cornelia Tappen, and they had four children together.

By 1775, Clinton was serving as a delegate to the Second Continental Congress and was named brigadier general of the New York State militia. Elected as the first provincial governor of New York in 1777, he remained governor for eighteen years and witnessed the birth of a new nation. Initially opposed to the ratification of the Constitution because of its emphasis on national power, he authored seven letters under the pen name "Cato" in which he pleaded for states' rights. As governor of New York, Clinton was instrumental in establishing free public education for all citizens and advancing higher education, which led to the establishment of New York State University.

In 1793, he retired from politics and enjoyed a life of leisure with his wife in Poughkeepsie, New York. However, with the death of his wife in 1800, his friends and family urged him to reenter politics. Clinton was elected vice president in 1804, serving under Thomas Jefferson, with whom he had a good relationship. Clinton had hoped to be the presidential nominee in 1808, but James Madison was nominated instead and Clinton served as his vice president. By the end of Madison's first term in office, Clinton's health was failing, and he subsequently died in office of pneumonia in Washington, D.C., on April 20, 1812.

Robert P. Watson and Richard Yon

Jefferson's second term would end on a far more somber and uncertain note than his first term, but one can hardly blame him for his optimism on March 4, 1805. Indeed, the prosperity of the United States would continue until Jefferson himself curtailed it in 1808. A major source of American prosperity throughout the years from 1793 to 1812 was the neutral carrying trade during the French Revolution and Napoleonic Wars, which, for all its risks and inconveniences, expanded American opportunities for foreign enterprise—and attracted foreign capital to the United States—far more than was possible when all of Europe was at peace. A European peace did hold from 1801 until early 1803, and the trade of the United States declined somewhat as a result, but with the resumption of the European war, foreign trade again grew and in 1804 actually flourished under a most unusual condition: None of the belligerents placed any serious obstacles in the way of American involvement in the carrying trade. When the warring powers later undertook to prevent the United States from contributing significantly to their enemies' prosperity by trading with them, Jefferson and Madison tried to defend what had been the status quo of 1804, but this proved impossible.

Unaware of the difficulties into which European events must soon plunge him, Jefferson in 1805 pressed for further national triumphs. The Lewis and Clark expedition, launched in the spring of 1804, carried the American flag over the Rockies to the mouth of the Columbia River in 1805. Although failing to find the waterways that Jefferson hoped would link the upper Missouri to the Pacific, the expedition convinced Jefferson and his successors that the United States should span the continent. Before the return of Lewis and Clark, Zebulon M. Pike led an unsuccessful search for the source of the Mississippi River. In 1806-1807, he conducted a second expedition into the Spanish Southwest and brought back important information about that area. East of the Mississippi, Jefferson turned his attention to East and West Florida. They

The Lewis and Clark expedition. *(Library of Congress)*

Excerpts from Thomas Jefferson's letter to Meriwether Lewis regarding the Lewis and Clark expedition, June 20, 1803:

Instruments for ascertaining, by celestial observations, the geography of the country through which you will pass, have already been provided. Light articles for barter and presents among the Indians, arms for your attendants, say from ten to twelve men, boats, tents, and other traveling apparatus, with ammunition, medicine, surgical instruments and provisions, you will have prepared....

The object of your mission is to explore the Missouri River, and such principal streams of it, as, by its course and communication with the waters of the Pacific Ocean, whether the Columbia, Oregan [*sic*], Colrado [*sic*], or any other river, may offer the most direct and practible water-communication across the continent, for the purposes of commerce. . . .

The commerce which may be carried on with the people inhabiting the line you will pursue, renders a knowledge of those people important. You will therefore endeavour to make yourself acquainted, as far as a diligent pursuit of your journey shall admit, with the names of the nations and their numbers;

The extent and limits of their possessions;

Their relations with other tribes or natins [*sic*];

Their language, traditions, monuments;

Their ordinary occupations in agriculture, fishing, hunting, war, arts, and the implements for these;

Their food, clothing, and domestic accommodations;

The diseases prevalent among them, and the remedies they use;

Moral and physical circumstances which distinguish them from the tribes we know;

Peculiarities in their laws, customs, and dispositions;

And articles of commerce they may need or furnish, and to what extent.

And, considering the interest which every nation has in extending and strengthening the authority of reason and justice among the people around them, it will be useful to acquire what knowledge you can of the state of morality, religion, and information amoung them; as it may better enable those who may endeavour to civilize and instruct them, to adapt their measures to the existing notions and practices of those on whom they are to operate.

Other objects worthy of notice will be;

The soil and face of the country, its growth and vegetable productions, especially those not of the United States;

The animals of the country generally, and expecially those not known in the United States;

The remains and accounts of any which may be deemed rare or extinct;

The mineral productions of every kind, but more particularly metals, lime-stone, pit-coal, and saltpetre; salines and mineral waters, noting the temperature of the last, and such circumstances as may indicate their character;

Volcanic appearances;

Climate, as characterized by the thermometer, by the proportion of rainy, cloudy, and clear days; by lightning, hail, snow, ice; by the access and recess of frost; by the winds prevailing at different seasons; the dates at which particular plants put forth, or lose their flower or leaf; times of appearance of particular birds, reptiles or insects.

pointed, in George Dangerfield's useful simile, like a pistol aimed at New Orleans and the gateway to the heartland of North America. He urged his diplomats in Europe to persuade Spain that further retention of the Floridas was both costly and futile. They were of no use to Spain and belonged naturally to the territories already owned by the United States. Finally, Jefferson allowed the commercial terms of Jay's treaty with England to expire, trusting that the increased size and strength of the United States would enable him to secure a new treaty considerably more favorable to United States interests.

At first, negotiations over Florida went badly. Jefferson asked Congress for a secret appropriation of $2 million for the purchase of Florida. He then sent a public message to Congress taking a hard line against Spain, threatened Spain through diplomatic channels, and quietly suggested to Napoleon that if Spain could be influenced to sell Florida, the money could wind up in Paris. Napoleon and his agent Talleyrand took the position that they could not help the United States at this time because Spain was unwilling to sell, yet they left the impression that something might be done later. The following year, 1806, Jefferson sponsored and Congress enacted a total embargo of American trade with the independent black nation of Haiti. This was partly to foster the goodwill of Napoleon, who still hoped to reconquer the former French colony, and partly in response to the racial attitudes of many congressmen. Even after currying favor with Napoleon, the Jefferson administration still did not acquire East or West Florida; the former was annexed only in 1810 and the latter in 1819.

Conflicts with Britain

The British, far from becoming more tractable during their new war with France, swiftly became more hostile to the United States than they had been at any time since 1783. The reason was the huge increase of American shipping after 1803. The British had encouraged American trade in the late 1790's because the United States was then engaged in an undeclared naval war with France and was in effect a British ally. In 1804, far from being at war with France, the United States was carrying a great deal of its shipping, as well as that of its reluctant ally, Spain. Bound by recent custom from attacking American merchant shipping, Britain saw more and more trade pass into American hands. Indeed, the demand for American shipping grew so rapidly that there were not enough ships and sailors to meet it. Foreign ships therefore transferred to American registry, and foreign sailors, including many Englishmen, took service on American ships.

By the summer of 1805, many Englishmen had come to resent the way the United States raked in profits while they bore the cost of protecting the Atlantic from the aggressive French emperor. Neutral rights were all very well; the American contribution to French prosperity was, however, profoundly unneutral.

Throughout the French Revolution and Napoleonic Wars, Britain had adhered to its unilaterally proclaimed Rule of 1756, which held that no trade normally prohibited in times of peace would be allowed — even in the hands of neutrals — in time of war. This rule was interpreted to mean that American vessels could not carry cargoes from the French West Indies to France since that trade had been proscribed before the war. Britain's Admiralty Court, however, modified this rule in 1800, when considering the case of an American merchant ship, *Polly*. If an American ship bought French colonial goods, carried them to the United States, and paid duties on them there, they might then reexport them to Europe, where the British would regard them as American goods and not subject to seizure under the Rule of 1756. This practice of the "broken voyage" was liable to fraud. American ships often sailed directly from the West Indies to Europe, pretending by means of forged papers to have completed a broken voyage via the United States.

In 1805, the British Admiralty Court in the case of the American merchant ship *Essex* rejected the broken voyage concept and reasserted the Rule of 1756 in its full vigor. British ships again claimed as prizes of war American vessels laden with French goods. Showing some discrimination, they seized only sixty American vessels, far fewer than they had in a similar crisis in 1793. Still, the use of British sea power to regulate American trade was galling, and no relief could be expected from Europe. In 1805, Horatio Nelson led his British fleet to a decisive victory over the combined fleets of France and Spain at the Battle of Trafalgar. Nelson died gloriously, and Napoleon remained from then until the end of his career a military threat only on land. Not since the days of Sir Francis Drake and Sir John Hawkins had Englishmen felt so superior, or acted so arrogantly, on the high seas. Now to prevent French goods sailing for Europe on American ships, they stationed their own warships just outside the major harbors of the United States, where they boldly stopped and searched American merchant vessels. Once at New York Harbor, an American ship refused to stop for a search by HMS *Leander*. *Leander* fired what was supposed to be a warning shot across the American ship's bow, but the shot struck and killed a sailor.

British commanders on the blockading ships looked for British sailors as well as French merchandise on American ships. Service in the British navy was hard, and the pay was poor. Many British tars had been drafted by a system little better than kidnapping. By the thousands they jumped ship and took berths on American merchant ships, where the service was easier and safer and the pay better. No matter how inhumanely they were recruited or treated, however, such men were deserters in time of war. England could not tolerate their loss, for if a few thousand desertions were winked at, the number would soon reach tens of thousands, and England's mighty fleet would stand unmanned.

To stop this drain on manpower, ships of the Royal Navy stopped and searched American vessels, seized any deserters who were discovered, punished them, and returned them to service. Shorthanded British captains, however, often took not only deserters from the Royal Navy but also American citizens of English birth and Englishmen who had not served in the navy and had taken out papers applying for United States citizenship. Occasionally, they even seized native-born Americans. Americans differed over whether the United States should tolerate British searching of its ships for deserters. Those Federalists who were most sympathetic to Britain's struggle against Napoleonic France were inclined to allow the indignity. A large minority would tolerate the Rule of 1756 in its application against the French tyrant, but few could stomach British blockades of American harbors. The guns of *Leander* had given the United States grounds for war.

Jefferson wanted war even less than did his few remaining Federalist opponents. He was no pacifist, as he had most recently proved in fighting Tripoli. In the present crisis, however, Jefferson was above all an opportunist. Even with a galling semiblockade, American shipping enjoyed in 1806 its most profitable year ever. Warfare would increase the costs of government, reduce revenue, and yield no certain advantage in return. Convinced of the proposition that free ships make free goods (and free sailors), Jefferson and Madison decided to negotiate. They sent William Pinkney, a moderate Federalist lawyer from Baltimore, to assist the regular minister to England, James Monroe. Madison drew up instructions, which were expertly reasoned but hopelessly one-sided, demanding all possible advantages for American trade while offering the British nothing but goodwill in exchange. Departing from these instructions, Monroe and Pinkney negotiated a treaty in which England, although explicitly recognizing the right of American ships to carry cargoes from the West Indies to Europe if they had first stopped and paid a tariff in an American port, conceded nothing material on the matter of impressment. When the treaty reached the United States early in 1807, Jefferson refused even to submit it to the Senate for its ratification. Had the Senate learned the full contents of the agreement, along with the explanations of Monroe and Pinkney, it might have accepted the treaty.

Not long after, on June 22, 1807, the only new frigate commissioned under President Jefferson, the USS *Chesapeake*, under the command of Commodore James Barron, was sailing down Chesapeake Bay on its maiden voyage when the British frigate *Leopard* insisted on searching the ship for deserters from the Royal Navy. Barron quite properly refused, but his ship was in such poor order and his crew so little trained that he could offer no resistance when *Leopard* opened fire. After sustaining three dead and eighteen wounded and firing one shot for the sake of honor, Barron surrendered. The *Leopard*'s officers then removed four sailors from the *Chesapeake* and departed. At Halifax, the British convicted and hanged one of these men. The other three, Americans who had volunteered to join the British navy, were also convicted but pardoned on the understanding that they would resume their service.

The British foreign secretary, George Canning, disavowed *Leopard*'s actions on the grounds that his government had never claimed the right to stop and search ships of the United States Navy. Canning also offered reparations for the dead and wounded. Even so, Jefferson might have had a declaration of war had he summoned Congress immediately and asked for one. The president, however, waited until October to summon Congress, while strengthening shore defenses, sending a number of stiff notes to the British government, and closing American ports to British warships. The latter move curtailed the warships' effectiveness markedly by forcing them to go either to Halifax or to Bermuda for supplies. Jefferson declined to accept the apologies and reparations offered by Canning unless Britain agreed to do much more. He wanted the government to punish

Admiral Berkeley, who had ordered the affront and had since been transferred to another part of the world, and to promise to desist from all forms of impressment. Canning refused to negotiate further until the ban on British warships had been lifted. The question of reparations for the *Chesapeake* dragged on until 1811; by the time it was settled, other aggravations had made it seem a negligible matter.

Commercial Warfare: The Ill-Conceived Embargo

In the closing months of 1807, the United States found itself pressed by both Britain and France in a wholly new and uncomfortable way. After the defeat of Trafalgar, Napoleon had conceived the plan of ruining the British by cutting off all their trade with the continent of Europe. In his infamous Berlin Decree of November 21, 1806, Napoleon declared the British Isles under a state of blockade, which he enforced by confiscating any ship found in European harbors carrying British goods. The British retaliated early in 1807 by extending their blockade to all European ports complying with the Berlin Decree. When Napoleon completed his "continental system" by bringing Russia into it, the British added Orders in Council, which declared that no nation might trade in Europe unless its ships first secured a license and paid duties in England. Napoleon's Milan Decree of December 17, 1808, then declared that any ships obeying the British orders would be confiscated.

Before the British and French had completed their measures for destroying each other's trade, Jefferson asked Congress to activate a limited Non-Importation Act first passed in 1806 but suspended during the Monroe-Pinkney negotiations. The act, aimed entirely at England, barred a number of importations that Americans could live without. Jefferson next persuaded Congress to adopt the Embargo Act, one of the most extraordinary acts in the history of American legislation. Not merely prohibiting trade with Britain and France, the Embargo Act required all American ships to stay at home and prevented the exportation of all American commodities. Although, in a way, a logical response to the de facto commercial warfare that the two greatest powers in the world had turned against the United States, unfortunately, it did more harm to America than it did to France and England. Hundreds of American ships sat idle and deteriorating in their harbors, the shipbuilding industry ceased, sailors were thrown out of work, New England fishermen lost their markets, and farmers lost outlets for their surplus grain, salt meat, and livestock. Tobacco and cotton planters, perennially short of cash, also suffered, but their commodities at least kept fairly well, and their chief capital — their slaves — continued to appreciate in value. Napoleon used the Embargo Act as an excuse to seize $10 million worth of American shipping.

As 1808 wore on, the act produced numerous complaints at home, but Congress supported the administration in a series of acts that served to make the ban more effective. It placed coastal shipping under strict controls and heavy bonds. It increased the size of the army and used small army detachments to patrol the long Canadian border where Americans were smuggling goods overland that they could not get out by sea. It also increased the "mosquito fleet" of gunboats, too small to challenge British warships but low in cost and useful for catching the small sailing craft that specialized in smuggling. After a trial of fourteen months, just before he retired from the presidency, Jefferson signed the act repealing the embargo. He also signed a new Non-Importation Act, which prohibited trade with France and Britain, but he promised to restore trade with whichever power withdrew its decrees against neutral shipping. Since the new act permitted trade with all other nations and allowed American ships to return to the high seas, prosperity began to return.

Jefferson's handling of the nation's relations with France and England not only had been strongly criticized by the Federalists but also had alienated some of the members of his own party. One of the most important was John Randolph of Virginia. Randolph had been a loyal Republican throughout the president's first administration, chairing the powerful House Committee of Ways and Means in the interests of retrenchment and economy. In the 1790's, Randolph had been an ardent supporter of the French Revolution, believing, with many other educated Americans, that its cause was that of human freedom. By 1806, however, the self-proclaimed emperor Napoleon Bonaparte ruled France by naked power and was launched on the conquest of Europe, whereas the British, however high-handed and selfish, were fighting for liberty. Randolph accordingly shifted his sympathies to Britain. He was highly displeased that Jefferson and Madison, although they detested Napoleon, were quite willing to cooperate with him if they could gain advantages for the United States by doing so.

Randolph, supported by a small faction of the Democratic Republican Party called "Quids," turned even more strongly against Jefferson over the so-called Yazoo land claims. In 1795, the Georgia legislature had sold to the Yazoo land companies several million acres of its western lands in an area later ceded by Georgia to the United States. The next legislature rescinded the sale on the ground that it had been made fraudulently. Jefferson arranged a compromise settlement of the matter that would have satisfied Georgia and the Yazoo investors, many of whom were Northern Republicans whose support he sought. Randolph blocked the necessary legislation in Congress, charging that Jefferson had abandoned the states' rights principles of his party and become in essence a Federalist. The Yazoo claims were not settled until after Jefferson left office.

Internal Opposition: The Burr Conspiracy
In the meantime, Jefferson became involved in an imbroglio with his former vice president,

Aaron Burr. Burr, thoroughly discredited because of his political machinations in New York and his killing of Alexander Hamilton in a duel, embarked on a scheme, the exact nature of which has never been clearly known. He visited the English minister to Washington, Anthony Merry, and proposed a plan for creating an independent Louisiana under British protection. Merry forwarded this proposal to his government with an enthusiastic endorsement; sager heads advised against plotting with Burr and soon recalled Merry to England. Meanwhile, Burr had been to see the Spanish minister with quite a different appeal. To forestall a planned invasion of Mexico, Burr proposed a *coup d'état* against Jefferson right in the District of Columbia. He would engage to organize this with the help of money from Spain. No money was forthcoming, but Burr went on seeing people and making daring proposals. In Washington, Philadelphia, and especially in the new towns of the trans-Appalachian West, Burr built up a network of committed friends, most of whom believed that he was planning an expedition against Mexico.

By the early months of 1806, Jefferson had heard from many Western correspondents warning him of Burr's activities. These Westerners cared nothing for the rights of Spain in Mexico, but they did fear a secession plot, centered in New Orleans, where many citizens still grumbled at the American annexation. Such fears were plausible: From the earliest days of the United States, there had been Americans of independent minds and great ambitions who had believed that the Mississippi Valley, including its great tributaries, the Ohio and Missouri, must someday be the seat of an empire quite independent from the Eastern states. Jefferson himself had contemplated such a separation with equanimity in the 1780's, but his views were now quite different.

In August, 1806, Burr concentrated a force of sixty to eighty armed men and ten boats on an island in the upper Ohio River. As the expedition descended first the Ohio and then the Mississippi, Jefferson sent word to his Western commanders that Burr was leading an illegal expedition and should be arrested. Evidently, Jefferson had become convinced that such action was necessary on receiving an urgent warning from his military authority at New Orleans, General James Wilkinson, who later became the government's most important witness at Burr's trial. Burr and Wilkinson had plotted together in Philadelphia and later in New Orleans. Wilkinson, as it was later learned, had been a well-paid spy for Spain at various times. He collected more Spanish gold by pretending to save Mexico from Burr's military invasion. He then posed as protector of the United States, claiming that he was saving Louisiana from the menacing Burr. Whatever Burr may actually have had in mind, he knew that it would not work with Wilkinson now against him and a warrant out for his arrest. He tried to reach sanctuary in Florida by traveling overland but was recognized, arrested, and sent to Richmond to stand trial for treason.

A grand jury, with John Randolph as foreman, found ample grounds for indicting Burr, and he came to trial in August, 1807. Jefferson's attorneys gathered an enormous amount of evidence, but much of it was contradictory. To this day, no one really knows exactly what Burr had in mind or even if he knew himself. The trial did reveal that Jefferson was something less than an absolute civil libertarian, for he had published the government's case against Burr in advance of the trial and prejudged him guilty. Ironically, the Republican Judiciary Act of 1802 established procedures by which Jefferson's political enemy, John Marshall, sitting as a circuit court judge, presided at Burr's treason trial. In instructing the jury, Marshall narrowly defined treason as an overt act against the United States observed by at least two witnesses, and the jury found that Burr's guilt had not been proved. In the course of the trial, Jefferson invoked executive privilege by declin-

Aaron Burr. *(Library of Congress)*

ing to answer Marshall's subpoena to appear as a witness. Jefferson, sorely disappointed at what he regarded as yet another instance of reckless Federalist obstruction to good government and believing Marshall's conduct on the bench to have been criminally wrong, sent the record of the trial to the House of Representatives, hinting that it might find grounds for the chief justice's impeachment. He also suggested amending the Constitution to make federal judges removable. Nothing came of these ideas.

Jefferson could at least take pleasure in the loyalty to the Union exhibited by almost all Westerners during Burr's scheming, arrest, and trial. Meanwhile, it was still possible to convict Burr for the lesser charge of violating the neutrality laws, which he had admitted doing while denying the charge of treason. Burr, however, jumped bail and fled to Europe, where he spent several years trying to sell chimerical schemes to the British and French governments. In 1813,

he returned quietly to New York, where he prospered modestly as a lawyer until his death in 1836.

As the time for the election of 1808 approached, Jefferson decided that he would not run for a third term. Despite the failure of his foreign policy and the unpleasantness of the Burr conspiracy, no widespread political reaction occurred against the president and his party. Although the Republicans failed to duplicate their sweep of 1804, they still easily elected their candidate, Jefferson's friend James Madison, with 122 electoral votes compared to only 47 for the Federalist candidate, Charles Cotesworth Pinckney. They also retained comfortable majorities in both houses of Congress. Only in New England did the Federalists reestablish strong party organizations and win control of state governments.

Following the precedent of Washington and John Adams, Jefferson retired completely from public life at the end of his presidency. Returning to his beloved Monticello, he spent the last seventeen years of his life in "philosophical serenity," but in great financial difficulty. He always answered queries from Madison and Monroe fully and cordially, but he made no effort to influence them. The chief fruits of his long and active retirement were a philosophical correspondence with his ancient friend and sometimes foe, John Adams, and the founding of the University of Virginia. Jefferson and Adams both died on July 4, 1826, as citizens throughout the United States were celebrating the fiftieth anniversary of American independence. Jefferson had planned a small and elegant monument to himself at Monticello. Its inscription identified him as author of the Declaration of Independence and the Virginia statute for religious freedom and as founder of the university.

Jefferson's Record as President
Significantly, Jefferson did not list any of the public offices he had held. This was in part mod-

esty, but it was also an expression of his lifelong fear of government's tendency to become too powerful and hence tyrannical. This fear, along with his urbane but retiring manner—he was never comfortable in public meetings—kept Jefferson from being one of the nation's most striking chief executives. The best and worst deeds of his administration—the Louisiana Purchase, the prosecution of Burr, and the enforcement of the Embargo Act—were all responses to major crises thrust on Jefferson and the nation. Otherwise, it was his wish that government should encourage constructive voluntary activity, and the years of his presidency were happily marked by the founding of new banks, the digging of canals, the laying of roads, the expansion of industries, the introduction of new inventions, the founding of schools, and the growth of population. Slavery, unfortunately, was spreading rather than declining, especially because of the acquisition of the sugar-growing province of Louisiana and the rapid spread of cotton as a major crop for export. Jefferson did sign, with satisfaction, an act that closed the international slave trade at the earliest moment the Constitution permitted, January 1, 1808.

Jefferson's style and methods were too subtle to be imitated, but he was a better president than the bare record suggests. Ideally, an American president must be the boss of a national political party, a ceremonial and ideological leader capable of reaffirming and adapting national values and ideals, and a tough-minded executive able to run the government and delegate authority to competent and honest subordinates. Very few presidents have done as well in each of these categories as Thomas Jefferson.

Robert McColley

Suggested Readings

Bernstein, R. B. *Thomas Jefferson*. New York: Oxford University Press, 2003. A brief and historically reliable account of Jefferson's life.

Boyd, Julian P., et al., eds. *Papers of Thomas Jefferson*. 31 vols. Princeton, N.J.: Princeton University Press, 1950-1997. Jefferson's own official documents and public notes are gathered in this multivolume work.

Cunningham, Noble E. *The Process of Government Under Thomas Jefferson*. Princeton, N.J.: Princeton University Press, 1978. Reveals how Jefferson's administration functioned.

Ellis, Joseph J. *American Sphinx: The Character of Thomas Jefferson*. New York: Knopf, 1997. Provides a balanced reassessment of the life, career, and character of Jefferson.

Gaustad, Edwin S. *Sworn on the Altar of God: A Religious Biography of Thomas Jefferson*. Grand Rapids, Mich.: W. B. Eerdmans, 1996. Examines Jefferson's dedication to the cause of religious liberty and the contradiction of his ownership of slaves.

Gordon-Reed, Annette. *Thomas Jefferson and Sally Hemings: An American Controversy*. 1996. Rev. ed. Charlottesville: University Press of Virginia, 2000. A thorough and evenhanded examination of the evidence that Jefferson had a long-term affair and fathered children with one of his slaves.

McCoy, Drew R. *The Elusive Republic: Political Economy in Jeffersonian America*. New York: Norton, 1980. An ideological study of Jefferson's foreign policy.

Malone, Dumas. *Jefferson and His Time*. 6 vols. Boston: Little, Brown, 1948. An older but still outstanding biography.

Randall, Willard S. *Thomas Jefferson: A Life*. New York: H. Holt, 1993. A comprehensive single-volume portrayal of Jefferson's public and private life that explores the contradictions between his life and ideals.

Risjord, Norman K. *Thomas Jefferson*. Madison, Wis.: Madison House, 1994. A brief biography which asserts that Jefferson's rhetoric was a matter of time and circumstance rather than absolute belief.

Simon, James F. *What Kind of Nation: Thomas Jefferson, John Marshall, and the Epic Struggle to Create a United States.* New York: Simon & Schuster, 2002. Details the struggle between Jefferson and Marshall, who was chief justice of the United States, in the ongoing battle over which branch of the government would dominate.

James Madison

4th President, 1809-1817

Born: March 16, 1751
    Port Conway, Virginia
Died: June 28, 1836
    Montpelier, Virginia

Political Party: Democratic Republican
Vice Presidents: George Clinton,
    Elbridge Gerry

Cabinet Members

Secretary of State: Robert Smith, James Monroe
Secretary of the Treasury: Albert Gallatin,
    George Campbell, Alexander J. Dallas,
    William H. Crawford
Secretary of War: William Eustis, John
    Armstrong, James Monroe, William H.
    Crawford
Secretary of the Navy: Paul Hamilton, William
    Jones, Benjamin Crowninshield
Attorney General: Caesar Rodney, William
    Pinkney, Richard Rush

No man ever came to the presidency with better credentials than James Madison. Most of his friends believed that Madison was among the most brilliant men in America. Indeed, Thomas Jefferson once spoke of him as "the greatest man in the world," by which he meant that his friend was second to none in his intellectual abilities. By the time he became president, his place as a great American statesman was already assured.

Madison was born on March 16, 1751, at Port Conway, Virginia, the home of his maternal grandparents, but he grew up at the Madison home in Orange County, Virginia. After preparatory training by tutors, he entered the College of New Jersey (Princeton) in 1769. He was grad-

uated two years later and remained for an additional year's study.

Madison first entered politics as a young delegate to the Virginia convention of 1776, which drafted the state constitution and declaration of rights. After serving as a member of the state assembly and governor's council, in 1780

Portrait of James Madison. *(Whitehouse.gov)*

he became a delegate to the Continental Congress. There he played a major role in creating the public domain out of the Western lands and worked to defeat Spain's efforts to close the Mississippi River to American commerce. Returning to Montpelier, his home in Virginia, at the end of the Revolutionary War, he was elected to the state house of delegates, where he helped complete the disestablishment of the Anglican Church. During the turmoil that followed the American Revolution when the upper classes felt threatened by uprisings of the discontented poor farmers and workers, such as Shays's Rebellion in Massachusetts, it was Madison who sought, more actively than any other American, to replace the inadequate Articles of Confederation with a constitution providing for a stronger central government. The federal convention of 1787 was in a real sense Madison's handiwork, from its seedling moments in a commercial conference of delegates from Maryland and Virginia in 1785 to the actual gathering of the constitutional framers two years later. On the convention floor he was an able debater, and his Virginia Plan, introduced at the outset, gave the delegates a working draft of a plan of government that with many changes eventually became the Constitution. Madison's journal of the proceedings not only made him the ultimate authority on the Constitution but also preserved a record for history. He also played a major role in the struggle to secure state ratification of the new Constitution, producing, along with John Jay and Alexander Hamilton, a superb body of essays interpreting and explaining the Constitution, published as *The Federalist*.

The Jefferson-Madison Philosophy

Madison served in the first four Congresses under the new Constitution, where he proposed the first ten amendments to the Constitution — the Bill of Rights — in 1791. He was also instrumental in forming the political faction that grew into the Democratic Republican Party, which opposed Alexander Hamilton's Federalist policies. Working with Jefferson, Madison was, in fact, the most visible public opponent of Hamilton's program of funding the public debt, creating a national bank, and expanding American armaments. In 1797, Madison retired from Congress and returned to Montpelier. At home, he kept abreast of political developments and, as coauthor with Jefferson of the Virginia and Kentucky Resolutions of 1798, which asserted the right of the states to nullify acts of Congress they considered to be unconstitutional, supplied a rallying point for the political opposition to Federalist programs.

When Jefferson became president in March, 1801, Madison, as expected, became secretary of state and served his chief for the next eight years as both a loyal party supporter and principal foreign policy adviser. The sorest trials faced by Jefferson and Madison grew out of the Anglo-French War that had begun in 1793. No problems were more vexing than those involving overseas trade. American maritime commerce had expanded rapidly, partly in response to the opening of lucrative wartime commodity markets. The British navy challenged this growth by impressing seamen from American ships on the ground that they were British citizens and by seizing ships bound for European ports under the control of France. Napoleon countered by seizing American vessels in the Caribbean or en route to British ports. The existence of hundreds of captured American vessels and thousands of impressed seamen testified to the weakness of the United States, if not its actual failure to have established itself as a true nation. No truly independent power could possibly accept such insults to its sovereignty.

Yet both Jefferson and his secretary of state acted with restraint when a declaration of war against either Britain or France would have been fully justified. On one hand, as dedicated republicans, they believed war was the worst evil that could befall a nation. Wars meant large armies and navies, huge expenditures, and the loss of life. Peace, on the other hand, allowed

The First Lady
Dolley Madison

Dorothea "Dolley" Payne Madison was born on May 20, 1768, in North Carolina, to a Quaker family. Dolley was intelligent and well-educated. In 1790, she married a Quaker lawyer named John Todd. She had a child, John Payne, in 1792 and gave birth to another son, William Temple, in 1793. Sadly, her husband and infant son both died of yellow fever that same year.

Dolley married James Madison on Sept 15, 1794. Because James was Episcopalian, Dolley was excommunicated by the Quakers. This gave her the freedom to express her outgoing personality by dressing fashionably, wearing colorful turbans, and taking snuff. She loved to entertain, and she often served as surrogate hostess for the widowed President Thomas Jefferson.

James Madison became president in 1809, and Dolley quickly epitomized the role of First Lady as social hostess. Her social prowess was a great asset to James, who was very reserved in public. She transformed the White House into a distinguished political focal point. Her famous Wednesday night drawing room soirees became a crucial venue for political and social connections. Dolley's skillful way of bringing together people of differing opinions allowed her to exercise her political acumen without overstepping her bounds as a woman of her time and proved valuable in garnishing support for James. Indeed, Dolley's beloved stature in the Washington milieu is said to have helped James achieve his reelection.

When the British were invading Washington during the War of 1812, Dolley bravely stayed in the White House until the last possible moment, overseeing the removal of documents and the noted portrait of George Washington by Gilbert Stuart.

When James's term ended in 1817, they retired to Montpelier, their Virginia estate. James died in 1836. Dolley sold Montpelier for financial reasons and returned to Washington, retaining her status in Washington society. She was even granted a lifetime seat on the floor of the House of Representatives. She died in 1849.

Barbara C. Beattie

government to maintain a low tax structure, even the retirement of the national debt and, for the most part, minimal interference in the life of the average citizen. In early agrarian times, American voters enthusiastically supported the Jefferson-Madison philosophy.

As Jefferson neared the end of his second term, he was urged by his supporters to stand for reelection but he declined, helping to set a two-term tradition that stood until Franklin D. Roosevelt successfully ran for a third term in 1940. Jefferson used his influence to secure the nomination by the Republican congressional caucus for his good friend and secretary of state, James Madison. The Federalist candidate in 1808 was Charles Cotesworth Pinckney of South Carolina. Madison defeated him easily, receiving 122 electoral votes to 47 for Pinckney. Six votes went to Vice President George Clinton, the candidate of a small number of disaffected eastern Republicans.

Madison as President: Inherited Conflicts

The new president was not physically impressive. Slender and only about 5 feet, 6 inches tall, he had a high forehead and a face so wrinkled by early middle age that he appeared to be much older. Madison, however, had considerable fame, and he brought great political experience to the presidential office. Moreover, when he assumed office on March 4, 1809, he inherited a popular and generally unified political party from Jefferson.

The administration had reduced federal expenditures and lowered taxes, which contributed to Jefferson's and his party's wide acceptance. Yet, beneath the surface, factions had begun to form in the Democratic Republican Party. For the most part, in his last months in office Jefferson ignored the problem and tried to avoid any issue that would create discord. He had not been able to escape every confrontation, however, especially one with dissident senators from his own party. One of his last official acts was the nomination of his former secretary, William Short, as minister to Russia. The Senate's 31-0 vote against confirming Short's appointment was not only the most mortifying event of Jefferson's final days as president but also a warning to his successor not to risk similar humiliation; the senators would not accept a continuation of Jefferson's policy of rewarding enemies and neglecting friends.

In choosing the members of his cabinet, consequently, Madison was circumspect. Although wishing to make the able, Swiss-born Albert Gallatin his secretary of state, Madison was intimidated by the threat of Senate rejection into retaining him as secretary of the treasury, the post he had held under Jefferson. Similarly, bowing to pressure from Senate Republicans who professed to be his friends, he offered the State Department post to Jefferson's navy secretary, Robert Smith, brother of Senator Samuel Smith of Maryland. A worse choice could hardly be imagined. Congressman John Randolph gave the nomination backhanded approval by remarking that Smith knew "how to spell," but he neglected to add that Smith did not know how to write a dispatch or state paper. The president himself had to write most of his diplomatic correspondence. Finally tiring of Smith's incompetence, in 1811 Madison dismissed him and named his old friend and fellow Virginian James Monroe secretary of state. Madison replaced Smith in the

Montpelier, Madison's home. *(Library of Congress)*

Navy Department with Paul Hamilton of South Carolina. For secretary of war he chose Dr. William Eustis of Massachusetts, and he kept Caesar Rodney as attorney general.

Anglo-American Discord: False Hopes for Resolution

The chief problem facing the new president was the continuing dispute with Britain and France over America's right as a neutral on the high seas. Just before he took office, Congress repealed Jefferson's Embargo Act, which had banned carrying foreign goods in American ships, and replaced it with a law—the Nonintercourse Act of 1809—that forbade all trade with England and France but permitted a resumption of commerce with either power if and when it ceased to violate American maritime rights. This new piece of legislation pleased neither the War Hawks (the Western and Southern congressmen who favored war with England and the annexation of Canada and the seizure of Florida from Spain) nor the New England commercial classes, who wanted peace and unrestricted commerce with all nations. The situation seemed to change, however, when David Erskine, the British minister in Washington, hinted to Secretary of State Smith that he had the power to revoke the detested Orders in Council, under the authority of which the Royal Navy attempted to halt American trade with French-controlled Europe. Erskine, who had married an American, was perhaps overly zealous in his efforts to achieve an Anglo-Amer-

---

The Vice President
Elbridge Gerry

Elbridge Gerry, a signer of the Declaration of Independence and the Articles of Confederation, was born on July 17, 1744, in Marblehead, Massachusetts. The only son in his family to attend college, he graduated from Harvard in 1762. After college, Gerry joined his father to work in the shipping business until he was appointed as town inspector with the responsibility of enforcing the prohibition against consuming imported tea from England.

In 1772, Gerry was elected as a representative to the General Court and went on to be a delegate at the First Continental Congress. Gerry was an ardent supporter of independence and adamantly opposed any semblances of an aristocracy and standing army or militia. At the age of forty, he married Ann Thompson, who was twenty years his junior, and they had ten children. As a delegate to the Constitutional Convention in 1787, Gerry remained opposed to a strong national government and lobbied for states' rights. Refusing to support the draft of the Constitution because of its weakening of states' rights and the excessive power granted to the national government, he later changed his position and endorsed it as a result of the addition of the Bill of Rights. In 1789, Gerry was elected to the United States House of Representatives to serve in its first session. In 1797, President John Adams asked him to join Charles Cotesworth Pinckney and John Marshall on a diplomatic mission to France to avert war. After returning to the United States, Gerry was elected governor of Massachusetts in 1810, whereby he approved a redistricting scheme to benefit his party and ensure their victories in subsequent elections. To the present day, this practice carries his name and is known as gerrymandering. Within two years, Gerry was selected as the vice presidential nominee to serve in the Madison administration; however, his tenure in office was be short-lived after he suffered a heart attack on November 23, 1814, en route to the Capitol to preside over the Senate.

Robert P. Watson and Richard Yon

ican accord, whereas Madison was too eager to believe that Great Britain was suddenly ready to do what justice required. The president was undoubtedly influenced by the need to unclog American ports of their stockpiles of grain and cotton in order to bolster the prices of these commodities and end the agricultural depression. Furthermore, with foreign commerce at a standstill, income from import duties, the chief source of revenue for the federal government, had almost stopped. Consequently, Madison welcomed Erskine's overtures and accepted his assurances that the Orders in Council would be revoked. In return, under the provisions of the Nonintercourse Act, Madison issued a proclamation declaring that Americans could resume trading with England. Madison's achievement was acclaimed across the nation: Even the Federalist newspapers in Boston gave the president credit. Tough-talking congressmen from the Southwest grew silent, scores of ships loaded cargoes destined for British ports, and for a few weeks Madison basked in glory.

Madison's glory proved short-lived, however. When the British foreign secretary, George Canning, learned of Erskine's action, he repudiated it and ordered Erskine home. Erskine's instructions had stipulated that British concessions were dependent on American agreement to the right of the Royal Navy to intercept American ships bearing raw materials and goods for France. As historian Henry Adams has noted, Canning probably realized that such a brazen affront to American sovereignty would eliminate all chance for an accord.

The Madisons were enjoying a summer vacation at Montpelier when an express rider from Washington, D.C., arrived with word of Canning's action. Madison was forced to issue a humiliating counterproclamation repudiating his earlier one and acknowledging that nothing had changed. Not only did Canning recall Erskine, but he also rubbed salt in the wound by appointing, as the next minister to Washington, Francis James Jackson, the devious diplomat who earlier, as minister to Denmark, had spoken of peace to the Danes a few hours before the British bombarded their capital.

From the time Madison learned of Canning's rejection of the Erskine agreement, one could convincingly argue, the United States was set on a course for war with England. In a matter of weeks, the winds of diplomacy had forced American ships back into port and whipped up a storm of public outrage against Britain. "The late conduct of the British ministry has capped the climax of atrocity towards this country," observed the *National Intelligencer*, a Washington newspaper published by Madison's friends.

After learning from Secretary Gallatin that the new British minister appeared to have "nothing to say of importance or pleasant," the president decided to delay his return to Washington for a while. When he finally arrived there in late September, he had an interview with Jackson that was painfully short. In a subsequent conversation with the secretary of state during which the nature of Jackson's instructions was discussed, a shouting match took place, ending with the exhaustion of American patience and Madison's refusal to have any further dealings with Jackson. His recall was sought early in January, 1810.

Testing the British and the French: Macon's Bill No. 2

War talk revived, although the military forces of the United States remained on a peacetime footing. Unwilling to accept the idea that a large military establishment gives strength to a nation's diplomacy, Madison adhered to the republican belief that in a time of crisis the militia could do America's fighting. Great Britain showed its contempt for American public opinion by leaving its ministry in Washington vacant after Jackson left. Meanwhile, Napoleon matched the British for arrogance by issuing the Rambouillet Decree in March, 1810, calling for the confiscation of all American ships in French-controlled ports that had violated the Nonintercourse Act. In doing so, the French emperor was ordering his navy to operate exactly as the British government had stipulated in its instructions to Erskine—but now France was going to seize the Yankee ships as prizes of war.

Madison, despite his generally antiwar disposition, was coming to believe that war was unavoidable. When, in 1810, the well-intentioned Pennsylvania Quaker George Logan prepared to undertake a private peace mission to England, Madison applauded Logan's motives but cautioned him, "Your anxiety that our Country may be kept out of the vortex of war, is honorable to your judgment as a Patriot, and to your feelings as a man. But the question may be decided for us, by actual hostilities agst. us or by proceedings leaving no choice but between absolute disgrace and resistance by force."

In the meantime, Gallatin worked with Nathaniel Macon, chair of the House Foreign Affairs Committee, to draft legislation that would open the sea lanes to American ships but close all ports in the United States to belligerent vessels. Gallatin's object was to revive trade and increase lagging customs income so sorely needed by the federal Treasury. Although Macon's first bill failed in the Senate, Macon's Bill No. 2 passed and became law in 1810. Disarmingly simple, it repealed the Nonintercourse Act and removed all restrictions on American commerce, but, holding "up the honor and character of this nation to the highest bidder," the law stated that if England would repeal its Orders in Council, the United States would reimpose nonintercourse with France, and if France would withdraw its obnoxious decrees, the United States would reimpose nonintercourse with England.

Although Madison believed that the American people approved of Congress's action and of his relatively passive role in the management of the nation's foreign affairs, the Federalists, at least, were highly critical of the president's performance. Samuel Taggart, congressman from Massachusetts, observed, "Jefferson by a system of intrigue and low cunning managed the party. Madison is a mere puppet or a cypher managed by some chiefs of the faction who are behind the curtain." The radical Republicans, noted Taggart, overlooked French provocations while castigating England. "Because France burns our ships, confiscates our property, and imprisons our seamen they want to fight Great Britain."

Madison considered Macon's Bill No. 2 to be a poor successor to earlier legislative efforts to protect American rights on the high seas. "The inconveniences of the Embargo, and non-intercourse, have been exchanged for the greater sacrifices as well as disgrace, resulting from a submission to the predatory systems of force," he wrote William Pinkney, the American minister to London. Madison knew that the new law favored Britain, implicitly acknowledging its control of the seas. "She has now a compleat interest in perpetuating the actual state of things, which gives her the full enjoyment of our trade and enables her to cut it off with every other part of the World," he told Pinkney. Napoleon, however, might "turn the tables on G. Britain" by announcing France's resumption of trade with the United States if the United States would renew nonintercourse with Great Britain, the president observed.

Madison proved to be a good prophet. On learning of the new American law, Napoleon instructed his foreign minister, the duke of Cadore, to write a letter to John Armstrong, the United States minister to France, stating that France was prepared to revoke its decrees effective November 1, 1810, and calling on the United States to issue a proclamation reopening trade with France alone unless the British revoked their Orders in Council. Madison was informed of the emperor's action while on a summer vacation in Virginia. A decent interval would be needed to discover whether Great Britain intended to follow suit, but meanwhile Madison felt relieved. Napoleon's actions, he said, "promise us at least an extrication from the dilemma of a mortifying peace, or a war with both the great belligerents." Even so, Madison's position remained precarious. If Napoleon was insincere and had to be denounced as a liar, England would have no reason to change its policy. The result would be disastrous for American commerce and agriculture, for it would create a de facto monopoly for the British.

Assuming that the revocation of the French decrees was genuine, on the day following the date on which they were set to expire, Madison issued a proclamation reinstituting nonintercourse with Great Britain under the terms of Macon's Bill No. 2. Napoleon, however, then issued new decrees against American shipping in French ports, decrees equally as damaging as the earlier ones. In his annual message to Congress, Madison had to acknowledge that France had acted in bad faith and, in effect, admitted that nobody in Washington knew the true situation in Europe.

Annexation of Florida

During this time, developments on the Southern frontier in that part of West Florida adjacent to the Mississippi River required a response from Madison. Following the purchase of Louisiana, Jefferson had quietly tried, without success, to purchase the region from Spain. In the fall of 1810, however, Americans in Baton Rouge revolted and asked to be annexed to the United States, and Madison quickly issued an executive order transferring all of West Florida to the Territory of Orleans, although the area east of the Pearl River was not effectively organized until 1812.

Federalists in Congress denounced the West Florida "invasion" as unconstitutional. Americans in the Southwest, on the other hand, were not satisfied because they wanted all of Florida. The territory still in Spanish hands was a refuge for runaway slaves and a base from which hostile American Indians mounted raids across the border. Besides, control of the rivers flowing

through Florida into the Gulf of Mexico would give the farmers in the region easy access to outside markets for their products. Responding to their wishes, in January, 1811, Madison sent a secret message to Congress asking for authority to order a temporary occupation of East Florida if the Spanish would agree to it, or in the event of "an apprehended occupancy therefore by any other foreign power." After demurring for a while, Congress gave Madison such authority.

Although Madison was mainly concerned with foreign affairs, important domestic problems arose that also claimed his attention. In 1811, the charter of the Bank of the United States would expire. As a congressman, Madison had strongly opposed Congress's chartering of the bank in 1791, claiming that its action was unconstitutional. As president, though, he recognized the government's need for the bank to carry on its business efficiently. Despite Secretary Gallatin's pleading, however, so much Southern rhetoric had been spent excoriating the bank that Senate Republicans from Virginia and Maryland felt obliged to lead a drive to kill the institution. The recharter bill was defeated by the tie-breaking vote of Vice President George Clinton. Finding himself powerless in the situation, Madison was forced to watch the bank's dismantling.

Meanwhile, dispatch ships arriving from Europe during the spring and summer of 1811 brought no news of change in British or French policy. The president ordered the American minister to London, William Pinkney, home without naming anyone to take his place. Nevertheless, shortly after, Augustus J. Foster appeared in Washington, D.C., as Jackson's replacement as British minister. The only important news he brought was that the Orders in Council would remain in force until Napoleon withdrew his decrees in a verifiable manner.

Although having nothing to say about the French decrees, the new French minister in Washington did inform Madison that the emperor would not interfere if the Americans

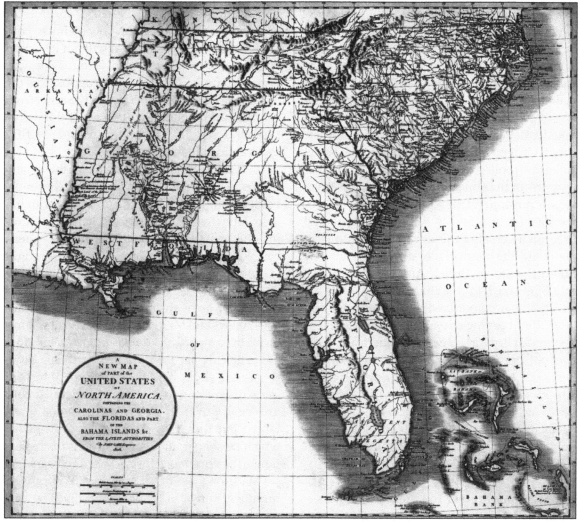

This 1806 map of the United States shows East and West Florida. *(Library of Congress)*

should seize the rest of Florida. Madison had already sent two American emissaries to East Florida with authority to take possession of the territory if conditions were favorable. By August, one of them, General George Mathews, a former governor of Georgia, reported that the area was ripe for plucking and that the price would be low—"two hundred stand of arms and fifty horsemen's swords," as he estimated. Still, Madison held back, apparently willing to recognize a fait accompli but not eager to order an invasion.

Acknowledging the urgency of the international situation, Madison moved the date for convening the forthcoming session of Congress forward thirty days. As the congressmen drifted into Washington, the British minister reported hearing talk of war, but he discounted it as more American hyperbole. Henry Clay, he noted, "talked to me of war as of a duel between two nations, which, when over, would probably leave them both better friends than they had ever been before." Another congressman, Robert R. Livingston, was far more blunt, warning Foster that he had only thirty days in which to pack and leave for home.

In his State of the Union message to the belligerent congressmen, Madison spoke with more confidence than he had in many months. Knowing that newspapers across the country would print his message in full, he wanted to make his case with the American people. The president reported that the British had been asked to match the French by withdrawing their hated Orders in Council but that the Royal Navy had replied by an even "more rigorous execution" of the obnoxious orders. British naval vessels hovered off the American coast in a provocative fashion, and an American frigate had fired on a vessel of the Royal Navy simply to maintain "the honor of the American flag." The existing state of British-American relations, said Madison, had "the character, as well as the effect, of war on our lawful commerce."

Without saying so explicitly, Madison suggested that Britain had pushed America as far as it could go. Yet the British minister so misperceived Madison's true feelings that he sent a message to London implying that the president was merely bluffing. Keep the Orders in Council, call the president's bluff, and the Republicans will lose the next election, counseled Foster.

Tippecanoe: Pretext for the War Hawks

Madison's message was being read at crossroads and in courtrooms across the land when a dramatic incident in the Indiana Territory helped build support for war. On November 7, 1811, General William Henry Harrison's troops beat back an American Indian attack near the confluence of the Wabash and Tippecanoe Rivers with heavy losses for the warriors led by The Prophet, brother of Chief Tecumseh. Frontier rumors connected the Shawnee leaders with British officials in Canada, leaving a conviction in the minds of most Americans that the attack had been inspired by red-coated Englishmen. While the young War Hawks in Congress rattled sabers for the folks back home, the secretary of state talked with the House Foreign Affairs Committee frankly about the prospects for peace. When he finished, one member concluded, "The present session will not be closed without *arrangement*, or an actual war with Great Britain." With only token opposition, the House approved bills increasing the army from six thousand men to an authorized thirty-five thousand regular troops supported by fifty thousand militiamen.

Before he would move to use these new troops, however, Madison waited for the return of the sailing vessel *Hornet*, which was bringing dispatches from the American chargé d'affaires in London. If they should reveal that the American government's recent actions had brought about no change in the British Orders in Council, Madison was ready to abandon all hope of peace. Still, in the spring of 1812, Republican antiwar views and Madison's indecisiveness combined to dampen the war fervor in Washington. Some angrily accused Madison of being more concerned about his reelection than about the issue of war or peace. As one Federalist congressman put it, "There is not a doubt entertained but the great pole star in the view of which he shapes all his measures, is his reelection to the presidency for the next four years."

Madison's attention was diverted from the imminent threat of war with England by disconcerting news of events in East Florida, where in March, 1812, General Mathews reported that with a tiny American expedition he had seized Fernandina, at the mouth of St. Mary's River in the northeast corner of Florida, and had forced the Spanish commandant's surrender. Mathews requested instructions on what to do next. Instead of praising his action, however, the State Department rebuked the general, and Madison described his action, in a letter to Jefferson, as having been taken "in the face of common sense, as well as his instructions." Madison rightly thought that the Florida invasion placed his administration "in the most distressing dilemma." His actions repudiated by the American authorities, Mathews was

The Battle of Tippecanoe. *(Library of Congress)*

forced to abandon his conquest while Madison turned his attention back to European affairs.

The government continued anxiously to await the return of the *Hornet* and news from England. Before its arrival, however, Madison learned that Spencer Perceval had the prince regent's support to become the new prime minister, which meant that no important change in British policy could be expected. "It appears that . . . they prefer war with us, to a repeal of their orders in Council," Madison wrote Jefferson. "We have nothing left therefore, but to make ready for it." When the *Hornet* finally arrived in late May, the dispatches it carried revealed that indeed nothing had changed. The Orders in Council remained in effect. Only a cancellation of those orders would have prevented war. Even though Madison believed "that war contains so much folly, as well as wickedness, that much is to be hoped from the progress of reason; and if any thing is to be hoped, everything ought to be tried," he now thought that all the peaceful options had been

tried, leaving war as the only way to protect the nation's rights and honor.

Congress, acting as if it knew what Madison intended to do, voted to extend a sixty-day embargo, designed to keep American ships at home in case a war started, to ninety days so that merchant vessels on the high seas might have time to reach an American port in safety. Members of the Republican Party in Congress had already caucused and voted unanimously to support the president for reelection. He thus felt assured that they would vote for a declaration of war should he request it. Presciently, on May 25, Jefferson wrote Madison, "Your declaration of war is expected with perfect calmness, and if those in the North [the antiwar New England Federalists] mean systematically to govern the majority it is as good a time for trying them as we can expect."

Madison, with the aid of Secretary of State Monroe, evidently worked on the president's war message to Congress for a week before he delivered it. The president wanted to present an unassailable argument, for he anticipated trouble from the New England Federalists and yearned for vindication in the forum of public opinion. His message was delivered to the clerk of the House of Representatives on June 1 and read at a secret session of Congress. Stripped of its rhetoric, the president's message declared that by virtue of Britain's actions in impressing American citizens into the Royal Navy, interfering with American trade, and inciting American Indians on the frontier, a state of war between the two countries already existed and Congress's duty was to recognize that fact officially. The House voted for the war resolution 79-49, but in the Senate the division appeared so close that votes had to be rounded up until the last minute. Although the antiwar Federalists stood firm, to the president's great relief the vote for war was 19-13. Madison signed one declaration of war on June 18. A few days later Augustus Foster, the British minister, called on Madison before departing for home. He subsequently recalled that in this last interview the president said he considered "that the war would be but nominal." Several months later, Washington learned that two days before the United States declared war, Viscount Castlereagh had relented and told Parliament that the Orders in Council were being repealed. Reports of the British turnaround made some members of the administration hesitate to support the declaration until Madison let it be known that it was too late to undo Congress's action. Henceforth, hot lead and cold steel would decide the matter.

War with Great Britain

As the fighting began in the War of 1812, earlier predictions that Canada would quickly fall to the American invaders and become a bargaining chip at the diplomatic tables proved to be exceedingly optimistic. General Henry Dearborn's army moved so slowly that his planned capture of Montreal turned into a fiasco. Even worse, General William Hull, after crossing the Detroit River into Upper Canada and advanc-

ing timidly toward Fort Malden, lost his nerve and withdrew to Detroit, where he surrendered to the British without firing a single shot. Hull was later court-martialed and sentenced to be shot, but because of his fine Revolutionary War record, Madison pardoned him. American attacks on Canada at the western end of Lake Ontario also failed when militiamen refused to cross the Niagara River into Canada. At first the Navy gave a good account of itself, winning a number of single-ship duels with British vessels, but the British preponderance of ships was so great that by the spring of 1813, the American Navy was bottled up in port and the British had blockaded the American coast.

In the presidential election in the fall of 1812, following these military failures, Madison was challenged by DeWitt Clinton of New York, an antiwar Republican running with Federalist support. Even though the Republicans put Elbridge Gerry of Massachusetts on the ticket with Madison, the president carried only one New England state and garnered fewer than half the electoral college votes of the Middle Atlantic states, but he swept the South and West and received a total of 128 electoral votes to 89 for Clinton. New England's antiwar votes and its leading newspapers' harsh criticism of his administration bewildered Madison: He could not conceive of citizens placing pecuniary interest above patriotism.

Madison Begins a Second Term: A Beleaguered America

In his inaugural address following his reelection, Madison restated the nation's war aim as the restoration of American independence, but by the winter of 1812-1813, only an extreme patriot could have claimed progress in that effort. The Canadian invasion had failed on all fronts, the Royal Navy had clamped a tight blockade on American ports, and America's ally France was mired in an invasion of Russia and could do nothing to ease British pressure on the United States. Gallatin scrounged for funds to pay for weapons, blankets, uniforms, and food for the armies. In the face of so many problems and battlefield defeats, Secretary of War Eustis left the cabinet. His replacement, John Armstrong, former minister to France, started off badly by choosing the ill-starred James Wilkinson to command another Canadian invasion. After a short skirmish at Chrysler's Farm, on the north side of the St. Lawrence River, Wilkinson retreated. Commodore Oliver Hazard Perry's victory on Lake Erie and William Henry Harrison's triumph at the Battle of the Thames River in upper Canada in October, 1813, helped restore flagging American morale. When the Russian czar offered to act as a mediator in peace talks, Madison accepted and appointed three commissioners, led by Secretary of the Treasury Gallatin, to meet with the British at a neutral site.

The fighting continued, however, and developments in Europe left the Americans in an even more precarious position. After his great victory at Dresden in August, 1813, Napoleon began the long retreat that ended with his surrender to the British at Waterloo. The peace that followed in Europe released fourteen British regiments for service in the American theater. Britain continued to fight even though it had abandoned the practices of impressment and blockade that had originally led to war. Now with the best army in the world, the British decided on a series of attacks in North America that would end the war once and for all.

Totally inexperienced in military matters and lacking an assertive character, Madison relied on his cabinet and a growing horde of generals to provide the leadership required to stop the British offensive. Unfortunately, problems plagued both the military effort and the cabinet itself. The American militia, despite all rhetoric, was no match for the well-trained British regulars. Furthermore, as England escalated its war effort, American commerce was swept from the seas, and customs receipts, the main source of federal revenue, declined dramatically. With Gallatin's departure on the peace mission to Eu-

rope, William Jones, who had replaced the incompetent Paul Hamilton as secretary of the navy, assumed the extra burden of running the Treasury Department, and under his leadership financial crises were solved by expedients that offered only short-term relief. In the War Department, Secretary Armstrong, harboring presidential ambitions, made his decisions with an eye toward the 1816 election and consequently became an increasing liability to the administration.

When the American peace mission reached Europe, it soon discovered, as Gallatin reported from London, that British public opinion favored a continuation of the war. "They thirst for a great revenge," he observed, "and the nation will not be satisfied without it." With the American oceangoing navy shrunk to a single ship of the line, the venerable *Constitution*, the British were free to navigate at will along the Atlantic coast. Raids on American ports brought prize money that the Royal Navy crews shared, leading British sea captains to cast covetous eyes on Baltimore, New Orleans, and other depots of American commodities that would bring high prices in Europe. Thus in the British strategic planning for 1814, a major objective was the Chesapeake Bay region, where an attack on Washington in retaliation for the burning of York (Toronto) in 1813 was planned to accompany a raid for plunder on Baltimore.

The British plan for 1814 also included a pincers movement, with the northern prong striking at Lake Champlain and the southernmost one directed at New Orleans. A courageous American defense at Plattsburgh, New York, thwarted the British army coming down from Canada, however, and logistical delays hampered the New Orleans expedition. Meanwhile, a combined British army-navy task force moved up Chesapeake Bay toward the capital and Baltimore. The sudden appearance of the British fleet in rendezvous off Tangier Island near the mouth of the Potomac River forced the president to seek counsel in preparing a hurried

Excerpt from James Madison's fourth State of the Union address regarding the War of 1812, November 4, 1812:

The situation of our country, fellow citizens, is not without its difficulties, though it abounds in animating considerations, of which the view here presented of our pecuniary resources is an example. With more than one nation we have serious and unsettled controversies, and with one, powerful in the means and habits of war, we are at war. The spirit and strength of the nation are nevertheless equal to the support of all its rights, and to carry it through all its trials. They can be met in that confidence.

Above all, we have the inestimable consolation of knowing that the war in which we are actually engaged is a war neither of ambition nor of vain glory; that it is waged not in violation of the rights of others, but in the maintenance of our own; that it was preceded by a patience without example under wrongs accumulating without end, and that it was finally not declared until every hope of averting it was extinguished by the transfer of the British scepter into new hands clinging to former councils, and until declarations were reiterated to the last hour, through the British envoy here, that the hostile edicts against our commercial rights and our maritime independence would not be revoked; nay, that they could not be revoked without violating the obligations of Great Britain to other powers, as well as to her own interests.

To have shrunk under such circumstances from manly resistance would have been a degradation blasting our best and proudest hopes; it would have struck us from the high rank where the virtuous struggles of our fathers had placed us, and have betrayed the magnificent legacy which we hold in trust for future generations. It would have acknowledged that on the element which forms three-fourths of the globe we inhabit, and where all independent nations have equal and common rights, the American people were not an independent people, but colonists and vassals.

It was at this moment and with such an alternative that war was chosen. The nation felt the necessity of it, and called for it. The appeal was accordingly made, in a just cause, to the Just and All-powerful Being who holds in His hand the chain of events and the destiny of nations.

It remains only that, faithful to ourselves, entangled in no connections with the views of other powers, and ever ready to accept peace from the hand of justice, we prosecute the war with united counsels and with the ample faculties of the nation until peace be so obtained.

defense of the capital. On July 2, he chose General William H. Winder to command a motley collection of regulars, marines, and gunboat crews totaling fewer than two thousand. On paper at least, some fifteen thousand militiamen were also armed and available for duty.

The British Take Washington: The Burning of the White House

The British commanders delayed their assault until August 18, but even with the extra time, General Winder had still done little to thwart their plans. Confusion and incompetence were the order of the day: Monroe took the field with a small band of dragoons, Armstrong proved utterly incapable of issuing a sensible order, and Winder became *hors de combat* after falling off his horse. The British landing party continued toward the capital, panic broke out in Washington, D.C., and Madison took off on horseback with some of his staff and cabinet members. In the ensuing melee, Dolley Madison made her famous flight to the suburbs with most of the White House silver, some prized velvet curtains, a small clock, and a huge portrait of Washington loaded on a wagon driven by a faithful black servant.

Winder returned to action, but the militia

were overwhelmed at Bladensburg, Maryland, and the meager defense forces disappeared. Unmolested, the British troops walked into a nearly deserted Washington, D.C., on August 24. During the next twenty-four hours, they managed to burn the White House, the Capitol, and several other public buildings, while the re-treating Americans destroyed the navy yard. From different vantage points, the president and his wife viewed the glowing sky. Their in-tended rendezvous at a plantation house near McLean, Virginia, thwarted by delays in the president's party, they were finally reunited at Falls Church, Virginia, the next day.

That same day, August 25, a freak tornado struck Washington, D.C., adding to the devas-tation wrought by the British. Finding little of value to plunder, the British troops returned to their ships that night. Only two days after the enemy's initial attack, Madison returned to Washington, D.C., though not to the blackened White House, which he never again occupied. The president instead took up quarters in a rela-tive's house on F Street and looked for a place to hold a cabinet meeting. William Wirt, a fellow Virginian who saw the president at this time, found the sight distressing. "He looks misera-bly shattered and woe-begone," noted Wirt. "In short, he looked heart-broken."

With the British fleet and troops still some-where below the city, Madison assembled his cabinet to decide on a course of action. When the president expressed to Secretary Armstrong his disappointment at the collapse of the capital's defenses, Armstrong took affront and soon re-signed amid rumors from Baltimore that Sena-tor Samuel Smith had taken charge of that city's defenses. Reports from Richmond, Philadel-phia, and elsewhere that the people's reaction to the news of the British attack on the capital was one of defiance rather than depression helped to restore the administration's morale. Only in certain parts of New England, it seemed, did the leading citizens think that Madison got the drubbing he deserved. Early in 1814, resolu-tions were already circulating at a number of town meetings calling for an end "to this hope-less war" and abandonment of a wartime em-bargo on trade. Madison tried to mollify the dis-sidents by convincing Congress on April 14 to repeal the embargo. Only half satisfied by this concession and goaded by the high Federalists, the Massachusetts legislature sent out a call for a general convention, to meet at Hartford, Con-necticut, in December for a discussion "by any or all of the other New England states upon our public grievances and concerns." To secede or not secede from the Union was, in the minds of some extreme Federalists, the main question.

The news was not all bad, however. Along with the information that Baltimore had re-pelled a British attack, Madison had learned of the beginning of negotiations between British and American diplomats in Ghent, Belgium. Castlereagh, who had turned down the czar's mediation offer, agreed to talk directly with the American envoys. On the other hand, the coun-try's financial condition remained precarious. The Treasury held large quantities of private banknotes, mostly from Southern institutions, which Northern bankers would not accept, and Boston financiers refused to buy Treasury notes unless they were heavily discounted. To keep the army paid and fed, as well as to prevent the bankruptcy of the federal government, would be no mean feat. Madison had to find some way to keep an army in the field in order to keep Eng-land at the negotiating table.

In September, 1814, with the smell of burnt furniture still in the air, the Madisons moved to John Taylor's Octagon House on New York Av-enue, not far from the ruins of the White House. While his wife worked at decorating the house and attempted to create a pleasant atmosphere there, the president sent Congress, reassembled in temporary quarters in the patents and post office building, a message full of foreboding. If "the negotiations on foot with Great Britain" should lead to something concrete, he stated, money would be needed to implement "a re-

The 1814 engraving by G. Thompson titled *The Taking of the City of Washington in America. (Library of Congress)*

turn of peace." In view of what had happened in the last month, however, intensive hostilities seemed more likely than peace. In either case, the nation's Treasury needed an immediate infusion of cash, for it held only $5 million at the start of the fiscal year in July. Failure to find "pecuniary supplies" and provide for an adequate military force, Madison warned, would threaten "our national existence." The full extent of the financial crisis was revealed later when Acting Treasury Secretary George W. Campbell explained that a shortfall of some $50 million could be expected during the coming year unless Congress found a way to raise the money. Congress decided that the Treasury Department needed a more resourceful head and suggested to the president Gallatin's friend Alexander J. Dallas for the post. Madison, accordingly, nominated Dallas on October 5, and the Senate confirmed the nomination the next day.

Despite the serious interference of the war with the nation's commerce, the government continued to derive a substantial part of its income from the tariff, especially after Congress raised the rates. Also, in spite of the aversion to such sources of taxation as "unrepublican," near the end of the war, some revenue was raised through an excise tax and a stamp duty. Congress also tried, with indifferent success, to levy a direct tax on the states, which it had no power to enforce. Two-thirds of the cost of the war was met by loans. As a result, by the end of the conflict, the national debt amounted to well over $100 million. Although the nation's financial situation was grim indeed, in his State of the Union message in December, 1814, Madison managed to note a ray of hope in the military situation to the south. General Andrew Jackson's Tennesseeans, he reported, had scored a victory over the Creek Indians at Horseshoe Bend, Alabama, which eliminated the possibility of a successful alliance between that tribe and the British. Almost as Madison's message was read, Jackson's forces repulsed a British attack on Mobile, which American forces had seized in 1813. In a matter of weeks, reports of a British expeditionary force in the West Indies, probably headed for New Orleans, brought Jackson to Madison's attention this time as the logical leader of the Southern port's defenses.

Meanwhile, the negotiations at Ghent, Madison learned early in October, were continuing, although the British were confident that they would prevail after Napoleon's downfall. They demanded the exclusion of American fishermen from British territorial waters, pressed for the cession of part of Maine to Canada, and urged the creation of an Indian barrier state in the West, south of the Great Lakes. British negotiators also sought some agreement on naval vessels on the Great Lakes, fixing the northern boundary of the United States at the source of the Mississippi, and an acknowledgment of the British right to use that river. Although some of these demands had the stamp of British arrogance, Madison seemed to be encouraged by the progress of the talks. In any event, he decided to make the British peace terms public. A storm of opposition arose from Republican newspaper editors, who screamed that the propositions called for abject surrender, while the party's patron saint at Monticello ticked off the demands one by one and concluded: "In other words...she reduces us to unconditional submission."

New England Separatists: The Hartford Convention

In New England, the November, 1814, elections seemed to indicate that a majority of voters there still favored a policy of appeasement toward England and whatever additional action the Hartford Convention, which was soon to convene, might endorse to restore the region's prosperity. Madison looked back at the actions of the New Englanders and saw a pattern of behavior very close to treason itself—smuggling to avoid the embargo, a refusal to send the state militia forces to fight when Canada was invaded, insults to recruiting officers, and niggardly support for the anemic federal Treasury. He hoped that these actions represented the views of only a minority of the people of the region.

Besides the official delegations from Massachusetts, Connecticut, and Rhode Island who gathered at Hartford in December were three informal representatives from New Hampshire and Vermont. The delegates decided to hold

A political cartoon of the Hartford Convention showing Massachusetts, Connecticut, and Rhode Island contemplating a leap into the arms of King George III. *(Library of Congress)*

their sessions behind locked doors. As Henry Adams has noted, this "excess of caution helped to give the convention an air of conspiracy." Although Madison decided against trying to interfere with the convention's deliberations, as a precaution he sent a loyal recruiting officer to Connecticut to observe the situation and instructed him to ask for aid from neighboring states if overt acts of treason should occur. Some of the extremists among the delegates, such as Timothy Pickering of Massachusetts, talked of preparing the way for "the separation of the northern section of the states" from the rest of the Union. More moderate Federalists, such as Harrison Gray Otis, whom Madison had known from their days together in Congress, played a moderating role and prevented any radical action. The convention proposed seven amendments to the Constitution intended to limit Republican influence and protect the interests of their section. After three weeks, the delegates adjourned but voted to meet again if the Congress did nothing to satisfy their grievances, in which event they would presumably recommend a more extreme course of action.

With the approach of Christmas, 1814, Madison appeared to have little to celebrate. Ghent and Hartford were ominously silent, while in Washington the president's party chieftains bickered over ways of carrying on the war in 1815. Not the least of Madison's worries came from rumors out of the South. Some of the duke of Wellington's Waterloo veterans, it was reported, were on board British vessels waiting for the winds to carry them to New Orleans. There the townspeople were at odds with General Andrew Jackson over his preparations for the city's defense. So dark were the American prospects that Timothy Pickering gloated, "From the moment the British possess New Orleans, the Union is severed."

Dramatic Reversals: Victory at New Orleans, a Peace Treaty at Ghent

The new year soon brought a dramatic change in Madison's and the nation's fortunes. First came the breathtaking reports brought by an express from the South: New Orleans was saved. Jackson's men had swept the British invaders from the field, inflicting twenty-six hundred casualties to a mere handful for the defenders. The manner in which the British retreated meant they would not try another attack. Church bells tolled their joyous refrain as well-wishers called at the president's house to offer congratulations. At the same time, a stagecoach from Hartford unloaded three delegates from the secret convention ready to hand the president their demands, but the delirium created by Jackson's victory left them no stomach for the business. In an ill humor, they trudged off to await a better opportunity.

Their opportunity never came, for ten days after the news of Jackson's victory at New Orleans a messenger arrived in Washington with the preliminary peace treaty from Ghent. The war was over, if the Senate ratified the treaty, and the nation had lost not an inch of territory or conceded a major right to the enemy. Unsolved matters of fishing rights off the coast of Canada and boundaries were left to the future arbitration of special commissions. Because the nadir of the American cause had been reached a few months earlier, this unexpected news appeared to be something of a miracle. Torchlight parades and banners extolling the president testified to his sudden popularity in every section of the country save one. Madison saw two of the Hartford delegates at a social gathering shortly after and was mildly amused by their obvious embarrassment. Suddenly, what New England thought or did was of little or no concern to the president.

The scenario for Madison's final years as president seemed to have come from the pen of a guardian angel. On February 18, 1815, he sent Congress a special message with his version of the war's origin and end. "The late war, although reluctantly declared by Congress, had become a necessary resort to assert the rights and independence of the nation," he declared. Ignoring the militia failures, the inept military leadership, and the constant search for dollars as he exulted in the outcome, Madison observed, "The Government has demonstrated the efficiency of its powers of defense, and . . . the nation can review its conduct without regret and without reproach."

In his eagerness for national unity, Madison even glossed over the wartime dissent of New England. No sign of vindictiveness was evident in his retrospective view of "Mr. Madison's War," as the high Federalists on Beacon Hill chose to call it. Madison must have read the public letter sent from a Boston meeting of Republicans with particular pleasure. It thanked him for "maintaining the honor of the American Flag against those who had arrogantly assumed the Sovereignty of the Ocean." Of all the accolades Madison received, however, none could have been more welcome than Jefferson's. "I sincerely congratulate you on the peace; and more especially on the éclat with which the war closed," Jefferson wrote. With peace restored, Jefferson hoped his old friend would push hard for a return to Republican principles, particularly in the field of foreign affairs, where Americans had so much to learn. "We cannot too distinctly detach ourselves from the European system, which is essentially belligerent," Jefferson advised, "nor too sedulously cultivate an American system, essentially pacific."

Never had the blessings of peace been so apparent to Madison as in the days that followed. The nation's mood was euphoric, and more than one observer realized that something fundamental had happened in America as a result of the war. With the peace and with the licking administered the British at the Battle of New Orleans, the young republic had proved something to itself. A sense of nationhood, which even Washington's administration had failed to nourish, began to flower. Returning to his adopted land after the diplomatic mission, Gallatin perceived the change. The people, he

observed, "are more American; they feel and act more like a nation."

One of the first manifestations of the surge in national pride was the Mediterranean expedition dispatched to attack the Barbary pirates of North Africa. The American warships devastated the pirate vessels. So thoroughly did they accomplish their task that the dey of Algiers sued for peace and promised to promptly free the American prisoners he was holding for ransom. Further action at Tunis and Tripoli brought a similar response, ending in a complete American triumph. Henceforth, the American flag was respected by the Barbary pirates, who had for decades contemptuously extracted an annual tribute from the United States Treasury.

The new nationalism that followed the war also found expression in domestic policy. Madison, in a sharp reversal of his earlier advocacy of states' rights and a federal government of strictly limited power, called for a strong military establishment, a uniform national currency, a tariff that would protect new American industries, a federally subsidized system of roads and canals, and a national university. The experiences of the war amply justified Madison's request for a stronger military establishment, and Congress responded by authorizing an army of ten thousand men and appropriating $8 million for the construction for fifteen new naval units. While emphasizing the basic financial soundness of the nation, the president conceded that some alternative to the inadequate state banks was needed to provide for a stable public credit and a uniform national currency and expressed a willingness to support a bill chartering a Second Bank of the United States.

When a bill creating such an institution with a twenty-year charter passed Congress, Madison promptly signed it into law. How much the political parties had reversed themselves was evident as Republicans pushed the bank bill forward while Federalists, who had pleaded for the First Bank of the United States in 1791, made an earnest but feeble effort to defeat it. When Congress passed another measure appropriating $1.5 million to pay for the bank's charter, and all future dividends on government-owned stock in the bank to create a permanent fund to support the construction of roads and canals, Madison vetoed it, but only on constitutional grounds. He believed that a constitutional amendment was required to enable Congress to exercise such power.

To protect new industries established just before and during the war from the competition of cheap foreign, and especially British, goods being dumped on the American market, Congress passed and Madison signed a protective tariff bill that maintained or increased the wartime duties.

Madison's proposal for a national university, which was to be repeated by John Quincy Adams when he became president, was ignored by Congress, as it would be in Adams's time.

Madison enjoyed his final year in office as Congress, under the leadership of Henry Clay and John C. Calhoun, worked through his legislative program. He spent a leisurely summer and fall at Montpelier, looking forward to the election of his successor. The Republican congressional caucus had selected his choice, Secretary of State James Monroe, as the party's candidate. The Federalist candidate was Rufus King of New York. His party badly weakened by its near-treasonous opposition to the war, King carried only three New England states with a total of 34 electoral votes to 183 for Monroe. The succession of presidents from Virginia — the "Virginia dynasty" — would continue.

Madison's last months in Washington, D.C., were marked by a civility and popularity he had rarely known during forty years of public service. A veritable procession of well-wishers called at the temporary presidential residence on Pennsylvania Avenue. In his valedictory State of the Union message in early December, 1816, Madison described the chief achievement of his eight years in office in a single sentence: "I have

the satisfaction to state, generally, that we remain in amity with foreign powers." All the travail of two wars with England, the quasi-war with France during the Adams administration, the battles with the Barbary pirates, and the long squabble with Spain over the Mississippi River and Florida was subsumed in Madison's terse announcement. America was at peace with the world. Taking the Constitution as the palladium of American liberty, Madison predicted the continuation of "a Government pursuing the public good as its sole object" and one "whose conduct within and without may bespeak the most noble of all ambitions — that of promoting peace on earth and good will to man."

John Adams was one of the two Americans who best understood Madison's feelings as he left the presidency. "Notwithstanding a thousand Faults and blunders," Adams wrote Jefferson, Madison's "administration has acquired more glory, and established more union, than all his three predecessors . . . put together." The former president's gracious remarks undoubtedly reached Montpelier, and for the next decade when Madison visited with Jefferson (who kept up a lively correspondence with Adams) there was a mingling of thoughts of self-congratulation among the three Founding Fathers. Only they understood all the difficulties a president faced, and only they knew how much America had needed the sense of nationhood it finally achieved in 1815.

Madison in Retirement

Madison's achievements of eight years in the presidency can be succinctly summarized as having given the nation a stronger loyalty to the idea of republican government and a full awareness of American nationhood. As the Madisons traveled homeward in 1817 only one problem remained as a stain on American independence: slavery. Up to 1817 Madison's energies had been devoted to preserving independence and the civil liberties it guaranteed to the American people. As a Virginian, a slaveholder, and a planter, it was beyond Madison's capability to shape a solution for the slavery issue that was beginning to crystallize. In his retirement, which lasted for another nineteen years, Madison worried more about political threats to the Union—nullification and later secession—than about the corrosive effects of slavery on the national character. Until his dying day, Madison never claimed that slavery was right—only that its abolition was beyond his power.

During the remainder of his life, Madison experienced his share of trials and triumphs. The dissolute conduct of his stepson, John Payne Todd, was a constant problem as Madison tried to shield the young man's shady character from public view. Madison once estimated that he had spent more than $20,000 trying to keep Todd out of jail or other scrapes. Family matters aside, Madison's health remained as fragile in retirement as during his active days. His medicine chest must have taken up a large part of his living quarters at Montpelier, where he alternately tended to his aged mother, watched as Dolley lost her good looks and comely figure, and wrote checks to cover Todd's indiscretions.

Despite a reduction in his standard of living (his salary of $25,000 annually while president had no equivalent in farming income later), in retirement Madison and his wife were still noted for their hospitality. Famous visitors and ordinary citizens who called at Montpelier always found a dining table loaded with a variety of meats, vegetables, sweetcakes, breads, cider, and wine. During his last years, the expenses outran income, and Madison was forced to sell some slaves—an experience common to many planters after the 1819 panic—which he excused by saying that the blacks were simply going from his plantation to that of a relative.

At Jefferson's urging, Madison became involved in the founding of the University of Virginia and served briefly as its rector. His remarkable friendship with Jefferson ended when black crepe shrouded Monticello in 1826.

Madison spent his last decade arranging personal papers, with an eye toward creating a legacy for the nation and for Dolley Madison, for he realized that the cash value of his notes of the federal convention alone would provide a financial cushion for his widow.

When Madison became ill in June, 1836, well-meaning friends and relatives suggested that drugs might prolong his life until the Fourth of July, so that he might expire on Independence Day, as had Adams, Jefferson, and Monroe. Madison dismissed the suggestion outright. He looked on July 4, 1776, as the beginning of a new era and saw no value in an artificial reminder of one of humankind's most glorious moments. He died on June 28, 1836.

Robert A. Rutland

Suggested Readings

Adams, Henry. *The Formative Years: A History of the United States During the Administrations of Jefferson and Madison.* 9 vols. 1889-1891. Reprint. New York: Viking Press, 1986. Although the tendency of this classic is to regard Madison as a failure as an administrator, there is much merit and sound information in this interpretive work.

Brant, Irving. *James Madison.* 6 vols. Indianapolis: Bobbs-Merrill, 1941-1961. An older biography that is nonetheless valuable for its originality and sympathetic treatment.

Cerami, Charles. *Young Patriots: The Remarkable Story of Madison, Hamilton, and the Crisis That Built the Constitution.* Naperville, Ill.: Sourcebooks, 2005. Celebrates Madison and Hamilton as the leaders of a group of young men who battled the old guard to construct a new national government.

Goldwin, Robert A. *From Parchment to Power: How James Madison Used the Bill of Rights to Save the Constitution.* Washington, D.C.: AEI Press, 1997. Details Madison's transformation from skeptic to advocate of a bill of rights.

Koch, Adrienne. *Jefferson and Madison: The Great Collaboration.* 1950. Reprint. Lanham,

Md.: University Press of America, 1986. A classic that details the relationship between Jefferson and Madison with great scholarship and affection.

_____. *Madison's "Advice to My Country."* Princeton, N.J.: Princeton University Press, 1966. Explores Madison's political philosophy.

McCoy, Drew R. *The Last of the Fathers: James Madison and the Republican Legacy.* Cambridge, England: Cambridge University Press, 1989. Explores the human side of critical political and cultural issues during tests to the survival of the republic.

Madison, James. *James Madison: Writings.* Edited by Jack N. Rakove. New York: Library of America, 1999. A comprehensive, one-volume collection of Madison's key writings.

Matthews, Richard K. *If Men Were Angels: James Madison and the Heartless Empire of Reason.* Lawrence: University Press of Kansas, 1995. Examines Madison's worldview, humanity, and vision of the future.

Miller, William L. *The Business of May Next: James Madison and the Founding.* Charlottesville: University Press of Virginia, 1992. Puts Madison in the context of the moral and intellectual foundations of the American nation.

Rakove, Jack N. *James Madison and the Creation of the American Republic.* 2d ed. New York: Longman, 2002. A good biography of Madison.

Stagg, J. C. A. *Mr. Madison's War: Politics, Diplomacy, and Warfare in the Early American Republic, 1783-1830.* Princeton, N.J.: Princeton University Press, 1983. Offers monumental research and a forthright view of Madison as a wartime president.

Wills, Gary. *James Madison.* Edited by Arthur M. Schlesinger. New York: Henry Holt, 2002. Wills, a Pulitzer Prize-winning historian, traces the role of Madison in the young American republic.

James Monroe

5th President, 1817-1825

Born: April 28, 1758
     Westmoreland County, Virginia
Died: July 4, 1831
     New York, New York

Political Party: Democratic Republican
Vice President: Daniel D. Tompkins

Cabinet Members
Secretary of State: John Quincy Adams
Secretary of the Treasury: William H. Crawford
Secretary of War: George Graham, John C.
    Calhoun
Secretary of the Navy: Benjamin
    Crowninshield, Smith Thompson, Samuel
    Southard
Attorney General: William Wirt

The day began auspiciously for a new administration and a new era. March 4, 1817, inauguration day for President James Monroe, dawned mild and radiant. Some five thousand to eight thousand citizens witnessed the simple yet impressive ceremony. It was held outdoors, on the steps of the so-called Brick Capitol, a temporary structure for Congress located on the present site of the Supreme Court. Everywhere there were signs of the steady progress that had been made since British troops left the nation's capital in fiery ruins. The newly renovated President's House, soon to be called the White House, would be ready for occupancy in six months, and the Capitol would be usable in December, 1819.

The Virginia Dynasty
The vision of the American republic rising from

the ashes of war formed an appropriate backdrop to Monroe's inauguration. The new president was the last of the generation of revolutionary heroes to head the nation, a member of what John Quincy Adams called a special "race of men." He was also the last of the three great members of the Virginia Republican dynasty to lead his country in the early years of the nineteenth century.

Born of Scottish and Welsh ancestry in Westmoreland County, Virginia, on April 28,

Portrait of James Monroe. *(Whitehouse.gov)*

113

1758, Monroe came from a family of modest estate. With the support of his mother's brother, however, an influential member of the Virginia ruling aristocracy, Monroe entered the College of William and Mary in 1774. In Williamsburg, he was swept up in revolutionary activity, joined the Third Virginia Infantry, and in the fall of 1776 was fighting with George Washington's army in New York. His military record was distinguished, and at the Battle of Trenton, he was severely wounded in a daring charge that succeeded in capturing the enemy's cannons.

Monroe emerged from the fighting with the rank of major, the esteem of General Washington, and the fixed ideal of serving the worldwide cause of liberty. He thoroughly identified the principles of the American Revolution with "free republican government," and he considered the success of America's republican experiment essential to the spread of liberty everywhere. He therefore turned to the study of law as preparatory to a career in politics. Significantly, his teacher and mentor was the wartime governor of Virginia, Thomas Jefferson, and thus began a lifelong association that brought social and intellectual, as well as political, rewards. It was also Jefferson who introduced Monroe to James Madison. Monroe's friendship with these men was occasionally strained, but it endured, and as president, he continued to solicit their advice.

Beginning in 1782 with his election to the Virginia House of Delegates, Monroe began a political career in which success and accomplishment were punctuated by periods of disappointment. He served as a delegate to the Continental Congress in 1783, where he sought to strengthen the Confederation government and to uphold the rights of the West to navigate the Mississippi River. Nationalism and expansionism would continue to be keynotes of his political thinking. He also attended the Virginia ratifying convention (he was a moderate opponent of the Constitution) and then, in 1790, was elected to the United States Senate.

A Precocious Diplomat

In 1794, Monroe, who was now identified with the Democratic Republican Party, was appointed by Washington as minister to France, but he was soon recalled by the president for being overly pro-French. The political tide was flowing in a Republican direction, however, and Monroe soon reentered public life, first as governor of Virginia in 1799 and, in 1803, as President Jefferson's special envoy to France to conclude the Louisiana Purchase agreement.

Monroe's triumph in France was not followed by further success as minister to England and envoy to Spain. When a treaty with England was not even submitted to the Senate for ratification, Monroe returned to the United States in late 1807, his political fortunes temporarily impaired. Yet the growing crisis with England again brought a need for his services, and after a short period as a state legislator and governor, he returned to national office as Madison's secretary of state. Monroe's experience and skill proved so valuable that during the War of 1812, he also took over the War Department when its previous occupant proved woefully incompetent.

By the time Madison's presidency drew to a close, Monroe's record of public service made him the Republicans' heir apparent. It came as little surprise that in March, 1816, the Republican congressional caucus nominated him. With the Federalist Party moribund, Monroe won an overwhelming presidential victory with 183 electoral votes against only 34 for his opponent, Rufus King.

The Virtues of Nonpartisanship

The president-elect was an impressive figure, both in height (he was about 6 feet tall) and bearing. His clothing resembled Revolutionary-period fashion, often a dark coat, knee-length pantaloons, and white-topped boots. His hair was cut short in front, powdered, and gathered in a queue behind. It was, however, his plain, honest, and virtuous character that most struck con-

The First Lady
Elizabeth Monroe

Elizabeth Kortright Monroe was born on June 30, 1768, in New York City to congressman Lawrence Kortright and Hannah Aspinwall Kortright. Like most women of high standing during her time, Elizabeth had some formal education. She was fluent in French and Latin, as well as in the traditional "social graces" for young women of her status—literature, music, dancing, and sewing.

Elizabeth married James Monroe of Virginia on February 16, 1786. After her father retired from Congress, they returned to Virginia, moving to Charlottesville to be near James's friend, Thomas Jefferson. They had three children: Eliza Kortright Monroe, James Spence Monroe, and Maria Hester Monroe.

After Monroe's election to the U.S. Senate in 1790, the Monroes relocated to the temporary capital city of Philadelphia. Elizabeth, however, spent much of her time in New York with her sisters and their families. Four years later, when Monroe was named U.S. minister to France, they relocated to Paris. There, the Monroes hosted American Revolutionary writer Thomas Paine in their Paris home after Monroe secured Paine's freedom from prison. He had been imprisoned by French revolutionaries for opposing the execution of King Louis XVI.

Elizabeth became First Lady on March 4, 1817, at the age of forty-eight. She served two four-year terms while her husband was president. To what extent Elizabeth was politically influential or expressed an opinion on the decisions faced by her husband—including his famous Monroe Doctrine—are not known. It was widely accepted that after her death, James burned all of their correspondence.

In remembering his wife, Monroe would later write that she had shared in all aspects of his public service career and was always motivated by the best interests of the United States. One letter, from her influential son-in-law George Hay, suggests that she was sought for her political savvy in response to at least one difficult situation involving the controversial Virginia congressman John Randolph.

A year after leaving the White House in 1825, Elizabeth suffered a seizure and collapsed near an open fireplace. She sustained severe burns and lived only three years after the accident. Upon her death, Monroe predicted that he would not live long. He died ten months later.

Dean M. Shapiro

temporaries. As Adams noted, Monroe did not possess brilliance, but rather "natural prudence and good sense, a tact, and a knowledge of men, which eminently fitted him for a successful politician." Somewhat slow and cautious in forming judgments, he was firm and energetic in upholding them. Others reached a conclusion more rapidly, another cabinet member observed, "but few with a certainty so unerring."

Monroe had his imperfections. Overly sensitive to criticism and given to brooding over alleged slights, he never won the kind of passionate devotion that some presidents have. Yet his modesty and warmth were major assets and account for his continued popularity in the midst of heated controversy.

The country that Monroe now headed was, under the beneficent sway of peace, undergoing a period of rapid change that would, in a few short years, make the world of his birth appear as quaint as Rip Van Winkle's phlegmatic Dutch community. Settlers poured into the West, advancing the frontier and adding six new states to the Union between 1812 and 1821.

Planters and farmers in the South rushed into more fertile lands, spreading slavery in their wake. In the North, particularly in New England, the pace of industrialization quickened as capital flowed into manufacturing. Meanwhile, a revolution in transportation was under way, primarily involving the construction of canals but also embracing steam navigation and river and road improvements. Jeffersonian agrarian ideals inevitably faded, but the national pride and prosperity that immediately followed the War of 1812 helped ease the strains of adjustment to these new conditions.

Monroe's political philosophy admirably suited this period of transition. He was not a Jeffersonian ideologue, but rather a pragmatic and moderate nationalist ready to adjust Republican limited government principles to the demands of commerce, communications, and manufacturing. A more doctrinaire president would most likely have added to, rather than muted, the difficulties of post-1815 America.

Monroe's inaugural address established the "liberal and mild tone" of his administration. Following Republican tradition, he celebrated the intelligence and virtue of the people, pledged "economy and fidelity" in government, and promised to discharge the national debt. Monroe also added new emphases to Republican doctrine. He endorsed the "systematic and fostering care" of manufacturing and spoke of the "high importance" of internal improvements, the construction of roads and canals, which he wanted to "bind the Union more closely together." Finally, he underlined the need for a large-scale program of fortifications and the improvement of the militia and navy.

Monroe's thinking about political parties and the presidential office constitutes one of the most fascinating aspects of his administration. More than any president except Washington, Monroe scorned political parties and acclaimed the virtues of nonpartisanship. He believed that political parties were neither necessary nor desirable in a free society. Indeed, he considered them a "curse" and thought government should be based instead on the people's "virtue."

Monroe recognized that the elimination of parties would have to take place gradually. In the meantime, he had no intention of reviving Federalism by appointing Federalists to office. For the present, the country needed to depend on its friends, Republicans, whose loyalty would be jeopardized if former enemies received political favor, but Monroe hoped that the effects of peace, the spirit of "moderation," and the absence of great political excitement would eventually bring an end to parties.

Monroe sought to place his administration on "national grounds," and his search for unity and harmony was most conspicuously demonstrated in his famous tour of the East and Northwest in the spring of 1817 and, two years later, of the South. Everywhere—from Baltimore to Portland, from Detroit to Pittsburgh—Americans hailed the new president with a burst of "national feeling" and demonstrations of respect for the Union and its "republican institutions." It was during his visit to Boston that the phrase "Era of Good Feelings" originated to become a label for the two terms of Monroe's presidency. The expression captured the patriotic hopes of its president that Americans would "all unite" to secure the success of self-government.

Monroe has generally been considered a weak president, content to drift with outside events and to follow the lead of Congress. Only in the realm of foreign policy has his more active contribution been acknowledged. This picture has some validity. He was, by temperament and circumstance, a less activist president than Jefferson or Andrew Jackson.

Yet Monroe was a surprisingly effective and able executive. His model was Washington, the disinterested, moral, and patriotic leader who was above class, party, or section. He was, therefore, not a passive president. Within the executive branch, he controlled the cabinet and the power of appointing officials. His frequent cabinet meetings—about 180 sessions in eight years—provided him with information and ideas and also enabled him to develop a consensus on policy. Monroe realized that in the absence of party loyalty, the agreement of powerful cabinet members more readily assured support for measures in Congress and the countryside. He also used his annual presidential message to help set the nation's political agenda, and he often exerted a strong behind-the-scenes influence on Congress when controversial matters were before it. Considering the political obstacles confronting him, Monroe was quite successful in shaping the course of events.

The cabinet Monroe selected was, according to a leading authority, "one of the strongest that any President had assembled." He appointed Massachusetts's brilliant and dour John Quincy Adams as secretary of state. After failing to find a prominent Westerner to accept the War Department, he eventually settled on the young and talented South Carolinian John C. Calhoun. For Treasury secretary, Monroe maintained continuity with the past by reappointing William H. Crawford of Georgia, a "giant of a man," popular and exceedingly ambitious. Rounding out the cabinet were Benjamin Crowninshield of Massachusetts as secretary of the navy, a holdover from the Madison administration, and William Wirt of Maryland, an accomplished lawyer and man of letters, as attorney general. The cabinet was unusually stable, the most notable turnover occurring in 1818, when Crowninshield resigned and was replaced by the New Yorker Smith Thompson.

Monroe paid a heavy price, however, for the excellence of his selections. Without the con-

---

The Vice President
Daniel D. Tompkins

Daniel Tompkins, the son of a New York politician, was born June 21, 1774, in Fox Meadows, New York (later known as Scarsdale). He attended Columbia College and graduated as valedictorian in May of 1795. Upon graduation, Tompkins was admitted to the New York bar in 1797 and subsequently began practicing law in New York City. He married Hannah Minthorne, and they had eight children.

In 1800, Tompkins was elected as an alderman in New York City and went on to a impressive legal career as commissioner of bankruptcy in federal court, counselor in the New York Supreme Court, representative in the New York State Assembly, and associate justice of the New York Supreme Court. By 1804, he was elected to the United State House of Representatives but quickly resigned in order to remain an associate justice. However, within three short years, Tompkins would be elected governor of New York. Elected to a second term in 1809, Governor Tompkins was instrumental in the defeat of the British in the War of 1812 by mobilizing and financing his troops to defend New York from invasion.

With the conclusion of the war, Tompkins was sworn in as vice president in 1817 and served in the Monroe administration in this capacity for two terms. Severely in debt from his personal support of the New York militia during the War of 1812 and in failing health, Tompkins died on June 11, 1825, in New York.

Robert P. Watson and Richard Yon

straint of party discipline, its leading members ambitiously jockeyed for position in the hope of succeeding Monroe. Monroe remained in charge of his administration, but the harmony of the first years gradually evaporated and with it a portion of his effectiveness in dealing with Congress.

Domestic Initiatives

With his cabinet in place, the new president grappled with the substantive issues of politics. Buoyed by the country's prosperity, Monroe recommended in 1817 the repeal of internal taxes, and Congress enthusiastically responded. Prosperity also enabled Monroe to reduce the public debt. Despite problems caused by a drop in revenue during his first term, the debt was progressively lowered and Monroe could happily report by the end of his first term that nearly $67 million had been paid. By his last year in office, further reductions permitted Monroe to entertain a "well-founded hope" that the entire debt would be discharged within a decade. His wish was realized during Jackson's presidency.

Reducing government burdens was not undertaken at the expense of national needs. In keeping with his long-standing concern for national defense, Monroe forwarded with "zeal and activity" the system of coastal fortifications begun in Madison's administration. Congress appropriated substantial sums throughout his first term, and in December, 1819, Monroe announced the virtual completion of a survey of coastal defense as well as "considerable progress" in the construction of fortifications. By 1820, some $650,000 had been spent on various projects.

The panic of 1819 and consequent political maneuvering temporarily reduced expenditures, but once the economy rebounded, Monroe successfully urged larger annual appropriations. He could be satisfied when he left office that the nation's defense was considerably stronger than in the period before the War of 1812.

Much more problematic was the establish-ment of an acceptable policy toward internal improvements. This issue aroused competing sectional and constitutional claims. For Monroe himself, the desirability of such projects clashed with traditional Jeffersonian scruples about excessive federal power and violations of states' rights. In his first annual message, Monroe seemed to rule out active federal participation by asserting that members of Congress "do not possess the right" to establish a system of internal improvements without a constitutional amendment. His sentiments provoked a House debate that provided much heat but little light on the subject. A combination of declining revenue, congressional opposition, and presidential caution effectively handcuffed internal improvements legislation during Monroe's first term.

During his second term, the issue again came to the fore in a way that gave Monroe an opportunity to present his full views on the subject. In April, 1822, Congress passed a bill authorizing the construction of tollgates and the collection of tolls to keep the Cumberland, or National, Road in repair. This impressive project had received the support of previous Republican presidents, and Monroe had approved bills for its extension westward toward the Mississippi River. He vetoed this bill on May 4, 1822, however, asserting that it unduly infringed on states' rights. Again denying Congress the power "to adopt and execute a system" of improvements, he now proclaimed that Congress had unlimited power to raise money and could "appropriate" it for "purposes of common defense and of general, not local, national, not State, benefit."

Monroe's compromise, which left the door open to federal assistance for national projects, satisfied neither extreme opponents nor proponents of internal improvements, but it managed to balance demands for better transportation with fears of excessive federal power and the dangers of opening the Treasury to competing sectional and local interests. In 1824, he signed both a bill subscribing to stock in the

Chesapeake and Delaware Canal Company and a general survey bill authorizing a comprehensive survey of routes for roads and canals of national importance. The lasting impression made by Monroe's formula became evident in 1830, when President Jackson referred to it as a precedent for his famous Maysville Road veto.

The Panic of 1819 and the Missouri Crisis

The favorable circumstances attending the start of Monroe's presidency were shattered by two major upheavals during his first term, the panic of 1819 and the Missouri crisis. The economic and sectional unrest unleashed by these events acted like a corrosive to national harmony and the one-party political system. The issues raised at this time would help shape the course of national politics for a generation, but their full impact would become evident only after Monroe left office.

The postwar economic boom proved short-lived, and by early 1819, the country was immersed in a full-scale depression. The price of land and agricultural commodities plunged; laborers were discharged; factories, businesses, and banks failed; and farms came under the sheriff's gavel. The South and West were especially hard hit. By 1821, the economy was recovering, and a period of economic expansion that would last into the 1830's marked the remainder of Monroe's presidency.

Monroe was concerned about the nation's "pecuniary embarrassments," but he tended to discount the panic's severity and to adopt a traditional moral posture that such setbacks served as "mild and instructive admonitions" for Americans to return to their republican habits of "simplicity and purity." The solution for economic ills lay with the people and Providence, not government.

In fact, however, the government did undertake various measures to improve conditions. The Second Bank of the United States, which had irresponsibly aggravated the boom-bust cycle from 1815 to 1819 by its restrictive financial policies and had mismanaged its affairs, was being called the "Monster" by angry citizens. Monroe, who considered a national bank essential for the country's stability and growth, helped the bank weather the storm. He forced the resignation of the bank's incompetent president, William Jones, and approved the appointment of Jones's successors, first Langdon Cheves and then, in 1823, Nicholas Biddle. Under their management, the bank was placed on a sound footing and became an increasingly useful instrument in the government's monetary and fiscal transactions.

The panic also made imperative an adjustment of the nation's land policy. Fueled in part by liberal credit terms, a tremendous speculative boom had preceded the depression. When land prices tumbled, land purchasers owed the federal government $22 million and faced the prospect of losing their lands. Congress first responded in 1820 by abolishing credit purchases and selling land for cash only. This reform reduced speculation, but made land purchases more difficult. Monroe came under considerable Western attack for signing this Land Act of 1820.

The president consequently recouped some favor from critics by recommending "a reasonable indulgence" to relieve land debtors. Congress soon approved a relief bill that allowed buyers to apply their previous payments to portions of their claims, relinquishing those portions for which they could not pay. The Relief Act of 1821 slashed the land debt in half and eliminated this issue as a national concern. Westerners, however, continued to agitate for cheaper land for the next decade.

Hard times also set off a wave of sentiment in favor of reducing expenditures. This movement gained momentum in 1821, then peaked and evaporated the following year. It was particularly unwelcome to Monroe because it severely undercut his efforts to strengthen the nation's defense. Congress reduced the army from ten thousand to fewer than six thousand

"The House That Jack Built" as a parody of the Panic of 1819. *(Library of Congress)*

men, cut naval appropriations, and slowed the fortifications program. Efforts to reduce civil salaries, however, ground to a halt when cuts were proposed in the salaries of members of Congress.

The economy drive had political overtones as the supporters of Henry Clay, Crawford, and Calhoun sought to turn the movement against their rivals, sometimes embarrassing Monroe as well. More than politics, however, was involved. Many people, especially in the South, encouraged retrenchment as part of a larger campaign to reassert limited government principles. These "Old Republicans" warned that Monroe's moderate nationalism dangerously swelled federal powers and jeopardized liberty and states' rights.

The panic of 1819 stimulated sectional and political disaffection with the course of national affairs. So, too, did the famous Missouri crisis that erupted suddenly in February, 1819, when representative James Tallmadge, Jr., of New York, introduced an amendment to a bill permitting Missouri to form a state government that would have gradually abolished slavery in the future state of Missouri.

Once raised, the slavery question flared into heated controversy that brought the possibility of violence and civil war. The House, where the North predominated, passed the restriction amendment in a sectional vote, but the Senate, where slave and free states were balanced, rejected it. Congress adjourned in March, 1819, without resolving Missouri's fate.

When the Sixteenth Congress convened the following December, Maine was applying for statehood and opponents of slavery restriction promptly announced that they would block Maine's admission until antislavery forces agreed to Missouri's admission with slavery. After considerable debate, a sufficient number of Northern representatives (called doughfaces) retreated and a compromise was adopted that, in effect, admitted Maine and Missouri, without restriction, to the Union. In addition, slavery was prohibited in all the Louisiana Purchase territory north of 36 degrees 30 minutes, the southern boundary of Missouri. By early March, 1820, the Missouri crisis was over.

Blinded to the genuine antislavery convictions involved in the restriction movement, Monroe believed that its leaders merely sought increased political power by rallying the non-slaveholding states against the South. Like many Jeffersonians, Monroe disliked slavery, but he was determined not to sign any bill that incorporated the principle that Congress could impose slavery restriction on a state, as distinct from a territory. He therefore drafted a veto message in case the restriction measure passed both houses of Congress.

Since Monroe "never doubted" Congress's power to regulate the territories, he supported the compromise. When the House approved the bill, he called his cabinet together to develop a consensus in support. The entire cabinet agreed that Congress could prohibit slavery in the territories, but there was considerable wrangling about whether that prohibition extended into statehood. Adams, who had strong antislavery convictions, ardently maintained against the rest of the cabinet that the restriction applied to future states. The impasse was finally resolved when the cabinet agreed to a vague and modest statement that the compromise was not unconstitutional. Monroe "readily assented" to this formulation, and on March 6, 1820, he signed the Missouri enabling bill.

Monroe was heartened by the "auspicious" resolution of the sectional contest, and he applauded the "patriotic devotion" of those who had put the nation's welfare above local interests. He considered the slavery issue as "laid asleep" but the Missouri crisis, in reality, boded ill for the future. Many Northerners were disappointed at the setback to the cause of freedom,

whereas the Old Republicans in the South condemned the acknowledgment of Congress's power over slavery in the territories and grew more vocal in their complaints against federal aggrandizement. In Monroe's own state of Virginia, there was powerful opposition to his renomination because he signed the compromise, a telling sign of the resurgence of sectionalism and the erosion of Republican Party unity in the wake of the Missouri dispute.

Foreign Affairs: Relations with Spain

Although domestic issues had dramatic consequences for the nation, Monroe's most striking achievements as president were in foreign affairs. His objectives were to preserve amicable relations with other nations, to protect and encourage American commercial operations, and to expand American boundaries. Perhaps most conspicuously, he wanted to make the United States a respected and recognized power in world affairs. "National honor is national property of the highest value," he lectured his countrymen.

Ironically, Anglo-American relations proved to be considerably smoother than before the War of 1812. Great Britain was now eager to cultivate American goodwill and the American marketplace. Monroe and Adams were therefore able to resolve some thorny issues.

In July, 1818, negotiations began to resolve fishing and boundary differences, which resulted in the Convention of 1818, Monroe's first treaty. The agreement compromised the complex fisheries issue by restoring American fishing liberties "for ever" to limited areas of British North America. The treaty extended the boundary line of 49 degrees between Canada and the United States westward from the Lake of the Woods to the Rocky Mountains, securing to the United States an area of the Midwest rich in farmland and natural resources. The Oregon Country was left open to both sides for ten years, neither side renouncing its claim. Finally, it left to arbitration the issue of compensation for slaves taken by British troops during the War of 1812 and renewed the commercial convention of 1815 for trade between the two countries. The Convention of 1818, Monroe declared, gave "great satisfaction" and firmed the rapprochement between Britain and the United States.

Relations with Spain were probably the most engrossing problem of Monroe's presidency. The disintegration of Spain's empire not only posed problems for the United States in dealing with the struggling Latin American independence movement but also gave opportunities for expanding American boundaries at Spain's expense. Astutely combining patience and boldness, Monroe capitalized on this situation to gain Florida, further establish American claims as a continental nation, and announce a special American role in the Western Hemisphere.

Americans were naturally sympathetic to the cause of Latin American independence, and this sentiment was seized on by Henry Clay, who eloquently demanded American recognition of the newly independent states. Monroe's position was delicate. He, too, favored the revolutionaries, but he warned that premature recognition might provoke the European powers to intervene against them. Instead, he adopted a policy of neutrality, but a neutrality that gave the rebels belligerent status. To Monroe, this gave them "all the advantages of a recognition, without any of its evils."

Withholding recognition also gave Monroe a lever to loosen Spain's hold on East Florida, an area he had long coveted, and to define the western boundary between Spain and the United States. Spain contended that the dividing line was the Mississippi River and that the Louisiana Purchase was invalid. Negotiations between the Spanish minister, Don Luis de Onís, and Adams initially proceeded slowly, but in December, 1817, they were given a new impetus when Monroe ordered General Andrew Jackson to put down Seminole border dis-

turbances and authorized him to pursue the Indians into Florida if necessary.

Jackson responded with his customary energy, and by June, 1818, he had routed the Seminoles, overwhelmed the Spanish posts of St. Marks and Pensacola, executed two British subjects for allegedly aiding American Indians, and engaged in a dispute with the governor of Georgia over the killing of some of his Indian allies. He was also ready, he informed the president, to take Cuba, if that were desired.

Whether Jackson had Monroe's permission to seize Florida is still in dispute. Jackson contended that Monroe had signaled his approval; Monroe categorically denied it. Although Monroe was probably right, it is also evident that the administration took no action to caution or restrain a general whose expansionary appetite was well known.

When word reached Washington, D.C., of Jackson's exploits, the whole cabinet, with the exception of Adams, favored disavowing him. Adams thought the general entirely justified and even argued at first against restoring the posts to Spain. Monroe, employing "candor and good humor" in these exciting deliberations, skillfully built a consensus around his own views. Out of respect for Congress's war power and to deny Spain an excuse for war, he would return Spanish posts and acknowledge that Jackson had exceeded his instructions. Yet in justice to Jackson and to turn the incident "to the best account of our country," he refused to repudiate or censure Jackson. Instead, he alleged that the misconduct of Spanish officials justified Jackson's actions.

Monroe's refusal to repudiate Jackson supplied the "pressure" for Spain to conclude a treaty. The Transcontinental Treaty of 1819 ceded Florida to the United States and defined the western and northern boundary between the countries by drawing a line to the Pacific at 42 degrees north latitude from the source of the Arkansas River, thereby granting to the United States Spain's claim to the Oregon Coun-

A map of the United States from December, 1820. *(Library of Congress)*

try. The United States agreed to assume up to $5 million of American claims against Spain and to yield its pretensions to Texas. Although ratification was delayed until February, 1821, the treaty was a major triumph for the administration. It not only acquired Florida, Monroe's primary objective, but also gained international recognition of the United States as a continental nation.

Final approval of the treaty, coupled with significant military victories by the revolutionary armies in Latin America in 1821, tipped Monroe toward the side of recognition. In March, 1822, he informed Congress that La Plata (Argentina), Colombia, Chile, Peru, and Mexico ought to be recognized as independent. Congress agreed, and the United States became the first nation outside Latin America to recog-

nize the new Latin American states.

A Second Term: The Monroe Doctrine

In March, 1821, Monroe was inaugurated for a second term. He humbly accepted his overwhelming reelection—only one electoral vote was cast against him—as a sign of national unity, not as a personal victory. He hoped that similar accord could be reached on all national questions. Like other presidents, however, he would find that his second term would present less cause for satisfaction than his first.

The course of affairs in Europe seemed to pose an increasingly serious threat of foreign intervention to restore Spain's former colonies. The autocratic rulers of Europe, organized as the Holy Alliance, helped oversee Europe's post-Napoleonic arrangements. Increasingly, they interpreted their charge as the suppression of revolutionary challenges to established regimes. In late 1822, after a revolution broke out in Spain, France was authorized by the Holy Alliance to restore the deposed Spanish monarch to the throne, and in April, 1823, French troops marched into Spain. That the Holy Allies, using the French navy, would next intervene in Latin America seemed a distinct possibility to Americans in the summer of 1823.

In reality, the chance of military intervention was remote, largely because Britain, with George Canning as foreign secretary, utterly opposed the use of force in Latin America. In August, 1823, Canning sought to bolster his anti-intervention stance by proposing to America's minister, Richard Rush, that the United States "go hand in hand with England" and issue a joint declaration on Latin American policy. This overture was forwarded to Washington, D.C., in early October.

Although initially inclined to meet the British proposal, Monroe favored rejecting Canning's offer by the time he convened his cabinet in early November, 1823, to deal with the European crisis. Adams vigorously supported this course. It was better for the United States to avow its principles independently, he argued, rather than "come in as a cock-boat in the wake of the British man-of-war." Adams recommended a systematic formulation of policy that would apply not only to the Holy Alliance but also to British pretensions in the Northwest and possibly Cuba, as well as to Russian claims on the Pacific Coast.

Adams advised the use of private diplomatic letters to Britain and Russia as the appropriate medium to convey American views. Monroe, however, desired to broadcast American ideals and principles to the world. Thus while the cabinet deliberated on the wording of the diplomatic correspondence, it also considered Monroe's draft on foreign policy for his annual message.

The Monroe Doctrine—the term itself was first applied in the 1850's—was announced in Monroe's message of December 2, 1823. Its crystallization of basic foreign policy tenets owed much to Adams, but its rhetoric and inspiration were indeed Monroe's. The document asserted

The Monroe Doctrine

This doctrine was announced during President James Monroe's message to Congress on December 2, 1823:

In the discussions to which this interest has given rise and in the arrangements by which they may terminate the occasion has been judged proper for asserting, as a principle in which the rights and interests of the United States are involved, that the American continents, by the free and independent condition which they have assumed and maintain, are henceforth not to be considered as subjects for future colonization by any European powers. . . . We owe it, therefore, to candor and to the amicable relations existing between the United States and those powers to declare that we should consider any attempt on their part to extend their system to any portion of this hemisphere as dangerous to our peace and safety. With the existing colonies or dependencies of any European power we have not interfered and shall not interfere. But with the Governments who have declared their independence and maintain it, and whose independence we have, on great consideration and on just principles, acknowledged, we could not view any interposition for the purpose of oppressing them, or controlling in any other manner their destiny, by any European power in any other light than as the manifestation of an unfriendly disposition toward the United States.

the principle of noncolonization (the concept was Adams's) that the American continents "are henceforth not to be considered as subjects for future colonization by any European powers." It also affirmed the principle of nonintervention, whereby the United States disclaimed any intent to interfere in the internal concerns of Europe and declared that any attempt by the European powers to extend their systems to this hemisphere was "dangerous to our peace and safety."

Although somewhat toned down from Monroe's original draft, which had seemed to Adams like a summons to arms against the Holy Alliance, the message was a high-minded expression of American nationalism. Issued before word reached Washington, D.C., that an agreement between Britain and France had entirely removed any threat of European intervention in Latin America, it courageously and independently avowed American aspirations in both North and South America.

An attempt at a display of America's diplomatic muscle on the long-standing West Indies trade issue, however, backfired. During Monroe's first term, Congress had passed retaliatory legislation against British restrictions on American trade in the West Indies. These Navigation Acts of 1818 and 1820 had indeed struck hard at West Indies prosperity, and Parliament, in 1822, yielded significant concessions by opening certain West Indies ports to American ships. Preference was still given, however, to British colonial trade. Monroe and Adams insisted that Britain do away with its system of imperial advantage and abandon intercolonial preferences. In March, 1823, Congress passed legislation granting President Monroe authority to

In this painting by Clyde Deland, Monroe (standing) discusses the policy known as the Monroe Doctrine with his cabinet, (left to right) John Quincy Adams, William H. Crawford, William Wirt, John C. Calhoun, Samuel Southard, and John McLean. *(Library of Congress)*

levy new discriminatory tariffs until Britain eliminated imperial preferences. Monroe quickly imposed the duties, the British retaliated, and by the close of his presidency, the West Indies trade remained restricted, a token of the administration's overzealous assertion of the principle of equal commercial opportunity.

Failure to Abolish the Slave Trade: The End of Republican Unity

Equally unsuccessful, though for different reasons, were efforts to reach an agreement to abolish the odious international slave trade. Great Britain, the foremost agent in the campaign against the trade, urged adoption of a proposal that would have granted a reciprocal right to search vessels and established tribunals to judge cases. Monroe and Adams both wanted to end the trade, Monroe calling it "an abominable practice," but they vividly recollected previous British violations of American shipping. They therefore rejected the proposal as "repugnant to the feelings of the nation and of dangerous tendency."

Instead, the United States acted unilaterally. In 1819, Congress provided for the use of armed vessels to patrol the African coast, sometimes in cooperation with British patrols, and the following year legislation declared the participation of American citizens in the trade piracy was punishable by death.

These measures proved ineffective, and continued British pressure and growing public outrage at the trade brought stronger demands for international cooperation. The administration therefore modified its previous stand. The United States would in effect permit the right of search by declaring the slave trade piracy — pirates were not protected by a flag — without conceding the general principle of freedom of the seas.

In March, 1824, a slave trade convention was concluded with Britain, which declared the African slave trade piracy, and authorized the search, seizure, and punishment of offenders. In the Senate, however, Crawford supporters and Southerners anxious about cooperating with British antislavery forces rallied in opposition. An "astonished" Monroe urged ratification, but its foes were sufficiently strong to add crippling amendments that led Britain to reject the convention. Not until 1862, after the South seceded, did the United States sign a treaty suppressing the slave trade.

The trouble over the slave trade treaty was indicative of the problems posed during Monroe's second term by the political scuffling associated with the breakup of the Democratic Republican Party into personal factions. Three of the five major presidential contenders were in Monroe's cabinet — Adams, Crawford, and Calhoun. The other two leading candidates were Clay and Jackson. Personal relations among cabinet members cooled, and an "embittered violent spirit" was often evident among their congressional followers. Monroe expressed "embarrassment and mortification" at the maneuvering of the candidates. He adopted a strict neutrality among them, but this only allowed the flames of factionalism to spread unchecked.

The end of Republican unity brought the demise of the congressional caucus. It met for the last time in February, 1824, when a small group of congressmen nominated Crawford. The other candidates disregarded the decision and condemned the caucus as undemocratic. The ensuing contest among Jackson, Adams, Crawford, and Clay — Calhoun dropped out to seek the vice presidency — ended without a majority selection. The decision went to the House of Representatives in February, 1825, where John Quincy Adams received the votes of a majority of states. When he chose Clay as his secretary of state and likely successor, the Jackson men cried "corrupt bargain" and organized an opposition that would, four years later, bring Old Hickory to the White House. The one-party system was dead, and the second American party system

An engraving depicting the horrors of the slave trade. Monroe supported strong legislation to punish those who participated in this practice. *(Library of Congress)*

was emerging.

In the midst of this feverish presidential activity, Monroe gained a modest triumph when, in May, 1824, he signed a tariff bill providing for increased protection for manufactures. He had continually recommended that Congress encourage manufacturing, which he considered essential to national security, unity, and prosperity. Congress at first agreed, and in 1818 raised duties on iron and textiles, but the panic of 1819 and the Missouri controversy sparked hostility to protection, particularly in the South. In the spring of 1820, a new bill failed in the Senate by one vote, as the South and Southwest showed stiff opposition.

Despite this setback, Monroe persisted. In early 1824, with the ardent protectionist Clay once again in the speaker's chair, Congress passed legislation providing additional support for iron, wool, hemp, cotton bagging, and textiles. Although the new rates were moderate, they were distinctly protective, and a howl of protests arose from the South. Southern spokespeople denounced the tariff as unjust and, even more ominously, as unconstitutional. The vote on passage resembled the sectional alignment over Missouri, an omen of the bitter tariff battles that lay ahead.

Expansion and Other Euphemisms: Indian Removal

Monroe's second term also marked an important turning point in Indian relations. Previous policy included a number of different and sometimes conflicting programs: efforts to encourage American Indians to adopt white ways, inducements to remove tribes to Western lands, and efforts to cede only portions of the Indian domain to land-hungry white frontiersmen. Under Monroe, the confusion of multiple programs continued, but his administration brought a new vigor in all areas, particularly to Indian removal.

Monroe's interest in expansion and concern

for national security led to the conclusion of a number of cession treaties, sometimes moving all or a portion of tribes westward. Treaties virtually cleared the old Northwest of American Indians and opened millions of acres of fertile land in the South. At the same time, Monroe urged a continuation of efforts to extend the "advantages of civilization" by encouraging education, religious training, and the individual ownership of land. Beginning in 1819, Congress appropriated $10,000 annually to this program, and by December, 1824, Monroe claimed that American Indians were making "steady" progress.

Despite Monroe's humanitarian intentions, it was increasingly evident that American Indian relations were reaching a crucial juncture. The problem was brought to a head by the state of Georgia, which stridently complained that the federal government had failed to live up to an 1802 agreement to extinguish the Indian title in the state. Both the Creek and Cherokee tribes stood fast against ceding any more land or moving westward, and when Monroe informed Georgia officials of this situation, the state's congressional delegation delivered a protest in March, 1824, demanding the eviction of American Indians and reproaching the government for encouraging them to stay. Monroe considered the protest an "insult," defended his efforts to gain cession treaties, but refused to consider the forcible removal of tribes as "unjust" and "revolting."

Nevertheless, the controversy with Georgia resulted in a new emphasis on removal as a means of saving the tribes and furthering their acculturation to white ways. In the last year of his presidency, Monroe called for the adoption of some "well-digested plan" of removal whereby civilization efforts could proceed "by degrees." He again rejected force, relying instead on such inducements as secure land and financial compensation to secure American Indian approval. Congress, however, failed to implement Monroe's recommendation before his

term expired. Monroe's struggle with the Indian problem ended on a sour note when, on the day before he left office, he submitted a treaty with the Georgia Creeks so fraudulently negotiated that President John Quincy Adams was compelled to withdraw it and negotiate another.

Despite the discord evident at the close of Monroe's administration, he, as well as the nation, regained a sense of the nationalistic euphoria that marked its beginning when the marquis de Lafayette returned to the United States in August, 1824, and undertook a nationwide tour that extended through and beyond the remainder of his term. The outpouring of affection for the "Guest of the Nation" recalled the great revolutionary cause of liberty and the "blessings" derived from it. With Monroe's active promotion, Congress granted Lafayette $200,000 and a township of land to alleviate his financial embarrassments.

Monroe's Presidency: Steadiness in a Period of Change

Monroe left office on March 4, 1825, in a period of rapid social change and of political and sectional conflict. Yet throughout his presidency, his personal character and presidential style conveyed a sense of dignity, unity, and national purpose that eased the country's transition into the more dynamic and complex world of the nineteenth century. As Adams later wrote in a fitting tribute, "By his mild and conciliatory policy . . . a large and valuable acquisition of territory was made; the foundations for national prosperity and greatness were laid; and . . . the American Union was advancing, with the vigor and stride of a giant, on its path to true glory and fame."

Monroe retired to his Oak Hill plantation, where he busied himself largely with farming and personal matters. He avoided partisan activity but did not entirely neglect politics. During the late 1820's, he condemned disunionist proceedings in the South and reiterated his support of internal improvements and protective tariffs. He also defended his record from misrepresentation, particularly on the issue of his ordering Jackson's invasion of Florida. Retirement did not erase a lifetime habit of public service, either. He was an active member of the Board of Visitors of the University of Virginia, and until ill health forced him to resign, he served as president of the Virginia constitutional convention of 1829-1830, characteristically working to effect a compromise between conservative planters and Western demands for a greater voice in government.

Monroe left the White House in serious financial distress, having accumulated over his public career a debt of about $75,000. Selling his Albemarle estate provided some relief, but he concentrated his efforts on gaining congressional reimbursement for his past public expenses. A portion of this bill was paid to him in 1826, but not until five years later did Congress, in response to public sympathy, appropriate another substantial sum, enabling Monroe to pay off most of his debt.

In the fall of 1830, after his wife's death, a distressed and enfeebled Monroe moved from Virginia to New York to live with his younger daughter and family. There, on July 4, 1831, he died. Throughout the country, Americans commemorated the passing of a leading figure of their revolutionary past.

Richard B. Latner

Suggested Readings

Ammon, Harry. *James Monroe: A Bibliography*. Westport, Conn.: Meckler, 1991. Provides a detailed listing of primary and secondary resources.

_____. *James Monroe: The Quest for National Identity*. New York: McGraw-Hill, 1971. An authoritative biography on Monroe.

Cunningham, Noble E. *The Presidency of James Monroe*. Lawrence: University Press of Kansas, 1996. A good, single-volume study in the University Press of Kansas series on American presidents.

Dangerfield, George. *The Era of Good Feelings*. 1952. Reprint. Chicago: I. R. Dee, 1989. Captures the details of the period of Monroe's presidency.

Ketcham, Ralph. *Presidents Above Party: The First American Presidency, 1789-1829*. Chapel Hill: University of North Carolina Press, 1984. Monroe's style of presidential leadership is explained deftly by Ketcham.

McCoy, Drew R. *The Elusive Republic: Political Economy in Jeffersonian America*. New York: Norton, 1980. Gives a provocative view of Republican Party doctrine during the Monroe era.

May, Ernest R. *The Making of the Monroe Doctrine*. 1975. Reprint. Cambridge, Mass.: Harvard University Press, 1992. Provides the domestic and diplomatic context for the Monroe Doctrine.

Monroe, James. *Political Writings of James Monroe*. Edited by James Lucier. Washington, D.C.: Regnery, 2001. Provides insight into Monroe's political ideology.

Moore, Glover. *The Missouri Controversy: 1819-1821*. 1937. Reprint. Gloucester, Mass.: P. Smith, 1967. Chronicles the sectional battle over Missouri.

Perkins, Dexter. *A History of the Monroe Doctrine*. Boston: Little, Brown, 1963. An older but still worthwhile examination of the catalysts behind the Monroe Doctrine and its long-standing impacts.

Preston, Daniel. *A Comprehensive Catalog of the Correspondence and Papers of James Monroe*. 2 vols. Westport, Conn.: Greenwood Press, 2001. Contains more than thirty-five thousand entries representing collections from nearly two hundred libraries in the United States and Great Britain.

White, Leonard D. *The Jeffersonians: A Study in Administrative History, 1801-1829*. New

York: Macmillan, 1951. Examines the contributions of Monroe's administration to the
Jeffersonian era.

John Quincy Adams

6th President, 1825-1829

Born: July 11, 1767
Braintree, Massachusetts
Died: February 23, 1848
Washington, D.C.

Political Party: National Republican
Vice President: John C. Calhoun

Cabinet Members
Secretary of State: Henry Clay
Secretary of the Treasury: Richard Rush
Secretary of War: James Barbour, Peter B.
Porter
Secretary of the Navy: Samuel Southard
Attorney General: William Wirt

No American, it can safely be said, ever entered the presidency better prepared to fill that office than John Quincy Adams. Born in 1767 in Braintree, Massachusetts, he was the son of two fervent revolutionary patriots, John and Abigail Smith Adams, whose ancestors had lived in New England for five generations or more. When John Quincy was seven years old, his father wrote Abigail of their duty to "Mould the Minds and Manners of our children. Let us teach them not only to do virtuously but to excel. To excel they must be taught to be steady, active, and industrious." Already drilled in these traits, John Quincy wrote at this time, in his earliest surviving letter, that he was working hard on his studies (emphasizing ancient history) and that he hoped to "grow a better boy." A year later, in an event he often recalled, he held his mother's hand as they stood on a hill near their farm and saw the fires of Charleston and heard the cannon of the Battle of Bunker Hill. Experiencing the battles of the Revolutionary War around Boston in 1775-1776 and reading his father's letters from Philadelphia about the tense struggle to declare independence, John Quincy Adams was literally a child of the American Revolution. He absorbed in his earliest memories the sense of destiny his parents shared about the new nation born when he was a precocious nine-year-old.

At age ten, he entered public service, in a way, by accompanying his father on a dangerous winter voyage to France. On the crossing, the ship was struck by lightning (killing four of

Portrait of John Quincy Adams. *(Whitehouse.gov)*

the crew), survived a hurricane, and fought off British vessels. Returning a few months later, John Quincy perfected his own French by teaching English to the new French minister to the United States and to his aide, François de Barbé-Marbois, who, twenty-five years later as Napoleon's foreign minister, would negotiate the sale of Louisiana to the United States. When his father was appointed a commissioner to negotiate peace with Great Britain, he again took John Quincy to Europe, this time as his private secretary. When their ship sprang a serious leak, John Quincy, with the other passengers, manned the pumps as the unseaworthy vessel barely reached the Spanish coast. A fascinating but grueling journey of two months across Spain and France finally returned them to Paris in February, 1780. After a year at school in Holland, at age fourteen he was appointed secretary to Francis Dana, American commissioner to the Russian court. John Quincy thus took two more long, eye-opening, and hazardous journeys across Europe, in between which he wrote and translated for Dana and pursued his own studies of history, science, and ancient languages. He spent three more years in Paris and London as his father helped negotiate the peace treaty of 1783 with Great Britain and then served as first American minister to the former mother country.

When, in 1785, at age eighteen, he returned to the United States to enter Harvard College, John Quincy Adams had already been five years in public employment, knew four or five modern languages, as well as Greek and Latin, and had shared in the most important diplomacy of the American Revolution. A bright, handsome, and serious youth, he never failed to impress the renowned American, French, Dutch, Russian, and British statesmen whom he met during his seven years abroad. His proud father declared him "a Son who is the greatest Traveller of his age, and without partiality, I think, as promising and manly a youth as in the whole world." Though the office was not yet

created, he had also served an ideal apprenticeship for being president of the United States.

After graduation from Harvard and a few years as law student and young barrister, Adams resumed his preoccupation with public affairs by engaging with his father in strenuous newspaper polemics over the French Revolution. President George Washington returned him to public service in 1794 by appointing him minister to Holland. His skill in negotiations there and in London and his brilliant reports to the American government on the wars and revolutions convulsing Europe earned for him Washington's praise as "the most valuable public character we have abroad." Before he returned to the United States in 1801, he served four years as American minister to Prussia, translated a long German poem into English, wrote letters warning of the ambitions of Napoleon Bonaparte (Adams called him "the Corsican ruffian"), and married Louisa Catherine Johnson, the daughter of a Maryland merchant then acting as American consul in London.

In eight years at home, John Quincy served briefly in the Massachusetts Senate and then for five years in the United States Senate, where he was an increasingly unorthodox Federalist. He approved of the Louisiana Purchase (1803), refused to take a pro-British stance as the Napoleonic Wars reached their climax, and increasingly aligned himself with the policies and views of Secretary of State James Madison. Adams's adherence to his own principles in supporting the Embargo Act (1807) at once earned for him the gratitude of the Jeffersonian Republican administration, the bitter hostility of the Federalists (who forced his resignation from the Senate), and—150 years later—a place in John F. Kennedy's *Profiles in Courage*. In 1806, he was made professor of rhetoric and oratory at Harvard (his lectures were soon published in two volumes), and three years later he argued the landmark *Fletcher v. Peck* case before the Supreme Court. These distinctions were enough to earn for him in 1810 an appointment from

The First Lady
Louisa Adams

The only American First Lady born outside the United States, Louisa Catherine Johnson was born on February 12, 1775, in London to a British mother, Catherine Nuth, and an American father, Joshua Johnson. Louisa's father was a successful tobacco importer who had moved from Maryland to England and would later be appointed U.S. consul to England. Her uncle was one of the signers of the Declaration of Independence. When she was three, her family moved to France, where she attended a convent school and an elite boarding school.

After a rocky courtship, she married John Quincy Adams on July 26, 1797. Four children followed: George, born in 1801; John, born in 1803; Charles, born in 1807; and Louisa, born in 1811. The couple seemed an odd match, with Adams being as demanding and aloof as his wife was warm and sensitive. The Adams family traveled throughout Europe on diplomatic assignment, and Louisa felt her husband showed more interest in his career than his family.

When John Adams was appointed minister to Russia, Louisa found the harsh winters unbearable and her loneliness and frail health were only made worse by the loss of her infant daughter. When Adams was appointed secretary of state in 1817, Louisa played an active role in her husband's career, distinguishing herself as a popular hostess and keen observer of politics. However, Adams's election as president in 1824 did little to improve the marriage, and the couple began to take separate vacations and barely spoke to one another. In fact, Louisa blamed her husband's critical demeanor for the apparent suicide in 1829 of their eldest son.

Louisa Adams was a prolific writer and poet, penning her memoirs, *Adventures of a Nobody*, a play titled *The Metropolitan Kaleidoscope*, and the travel log *Narrative of a Journey from St. Petersburg to Paris*. Like her famous mother-in-law, Louisa developed an interest in women's issues and politics and became an opponent to slavery and the government's Indian removal policies. She died on May 15, 1852, in Washington, D.C.

Robert P. Watson

President Madison to the Supreme Court, which the pressure of other tasks forced him to decline.

The proffered appointment reached him in St. Petersburg, where he was American minister to Russia in the final years of the Napoleonic era. He represented critical American interests there for four years as he and his young family endured the rigors of Russian winter and marveled, half in horror, at the dazzling court of the czar. From 1813 to 1815, he traveled about Northern Europe seeking a negotiated end of the War of 1812, an effort capped by Adams and other American commissioners when they signed the Treaty of Ghent, ending the war respectably if not triumphantly, on Christmas Eve, 1814. Adams concluded his long and brilliant career as a diplomat in Europe (he had lived there for more than twenty years between 1778 and 1817) by serving for two years as American minister to Great Britain, a post his father had held at the end of an earlier war with Britain and in which both Adamses stood staunchly for a dignified equality between mother country and former colony that would assure lasting peace between them.

John Quincy Adams was President James Monroe's widely approved choice to be secretary of state in the new administration. His service there, from 1817 to 1825, has rightfully earned for him standing as the premier secretary of state in American history. He guided negotiations with Great Britain that resolved the remaining disputes between the two countries and began an era of friendly relations between the two nations. Included in the settlement was a prohibition on armaments along the border with Canada that made it the longest (and longest-lasting) unfortified national boundary in the world. He also arranged for the purchase of Florida from Spain and negotiated a transcontinental treaty with that nation which established the boundary between Spanish and American possessions from the Gulf of Mexico to the Pacific Ocean. He adopted a posture of benevolent neutrality toward the independence movements in Spain's New World possessions and guided the joint British-American resistance to European efforts to thwart independence that resulted in the Monroe Doctrine in 1823. Adams was proud of these signal accomplishments in the State Department, regarding them as fulfilling the goals of the new nation he had seen form in the battles around Boston a half century earlier: equal standing in the family of nations, security within transcontinental boundaries, and sympathy for the national independence and republican aspirations of all the countries of the New World.

The Election of 1824: The Era of Sectionalism

Though Adams devoted his energies mainly to the large tasks of the State Department, he also was heavily engaged in the politics of the misnamed Era of Good Feelings. The Federalist Party had disappeared, and Monroe's elections as president were virtually unanimous but factions seethed within his National Republican Party (a faction of the Democratic Republican Party). The able members of his cabinet jockeyed for position to succeed Monroe. Secretaries William H. Crawford and John C. Calhoun had respectable aspirations for the presidency, as did House Speaker Henry Clay and the hero of New Orleans, General Andrew Jackson. Adams nevertheless regarded himself as

the legitimate heir apparent: The patriotic history of his family, his own long, brilliant public service, and his success in the usual stepping-stone position as secretary of state made him the obvious choice—or at least so he thought. During Monroe's second term, the politics of his succession increasingly dominated conversation and alignments in Washington, D.C. Adams still accepted the ideal of the antiparty presidency held by Monroe and his predecessors, yet he was intensely ambitious and did all he could "backstage" to further his interests. His detailed diary, kept faithfully during these years, is by far the fullest account available of the intense, increasingly bitter politicking.

The jockeying among potential candidates mirrored in many ways the changes and traumas of the years following the War of 1812. Though a burst of national pride and enthusiasm followed immediately on the conclusion of the war, during the Monroe administrations rancorous disputes accumulated. New manufacturing interests grew in New England and the mid-Atlantic states. Settlement of the West accelerated. Canals, turnpikes, and, soon, railroads increasingly connected the country and provided myriad sources of conflict. The Missouri Compromise controversy polarized slave and nonslave states. The power of the reenfranchised Second Bank of the United States heightened animosities in the nation's financial system. Perhaps most aggravating of all, a severe depression afflicted the nation as it sought to adjust to the post-Napoleonic era. Farm prices fell sharply as war-fueled demand for grains in Europe subsided; the price of flour, which was $15 per barrel in Baltimore in 1817, had fallen to less than $4 by 1821. Low-priced manufactured goods from Great Britain threatened to overwhelm fledgling American producers. As hardship spread, competition intensified, and bankruptcies threatened, the rancor within the political system grew apace.

As these animosities burgeoned, the old political parties, which might have contained and modulated them, largely ceased to function as effective national organizations. The Federalist Party had disappeared by 1824, and the Republican Party was so incoherent that only 68 of its 261 members in Congress participated in its presidential nominating caucus in February of 1824. The effect was to give free rein to the always-potent sectional divisions within the country, divisions reflected in the regional strengths of the leading presidential aspirants. Jackson and Clay had strength mainly in the West, Crawford and Calhoun principally in the South, and Adams's support was confined largely to New England and some of the mid-Atlantic states. This properly named "Era of Sectionalism" was especially unwelcome to Adams because his own earlier career and strong sense of national purpose led him to den-

igrate regional biases—although his opponents, and, indeed, much of the country, saw him as very much the Northeastern sectional candidate.

After this failure of the National Republican caucus to nominate a majority candidate, the aspirants set out to gain as much support in the states as possible. Calhoun soon dropped out to ensure his election as vice president. It appeared, too, that Clay and Crawford would lag well behind Jackson and Adams in both popular and electoral votes. When the returns were in, Adams was clearly behind Jackson in both tallies: He had 84 electoral votes to Jackson's 99 and only 114,000 popular votes to Jackson's 153,000 (in states where the electors were chosen by popular election). Nevertheless, the 41 electoral votes for Crawford and 37 for Clay threw the decision into the House of Represen-

The engraving *Lockport, Erie Canal* by W. Tombleson after the painting by W. H. Bartlett. Adams was a champion of federal funding for internal improvements such as canals. *(Library of Congress)*

135

tatives, where each state would have one vote for any of the three leading candidates. The final contest was between Jackson and Adams, and both maneuvered for support from Clayites and Crawfordites. The Jackson forces, with their clear pluralities in the popular and electoral votes, thought the contest was rightfully theirs. Adams's solid base of six New England states plus enough support elsewhere (much boosted by Clay's efforts to throw his strength to Adams), though, gave him the victory on the first ballot in the House of Representatives, thirteen states to seven for Jackson and four for Crawford.

Thus, despite his splendid preparation for the office and earnestly nationalistic outlook, John Quincy Adams entered the presidency on March 4, 1825, with distinctly minority backing, which was decidedly sectional as well. Furthermore, even before his inauguration, Jackson's backers charged that Adams and Clay had entered a "corrupt bargain" in which Clay supported Adams's election in the House of Representatives in exchange for a promise that he become secretary of state in the new administration. There probably was an agreement of sorts between the two men, but not one that either regarded as corrupt. They were generally aligned in their more nationalistic views, as opposed to the more states' rights stand of the other candidates, and each regarded the other as an able and distinguished public servant. Clay thought Adams infinitely more qualified to be president than Jackson, and Adams believed Clay would be an excellent secretary of state. Nevertheless, the charges of corrupt bargain persisted, and Jackson's supporters began immediately to oppose and thwart Adams in every way they could, looking ahead to the 1828 election. Adams entered the White House, then, with severe and debilitating political liabilities.

A National President, Above Party

Adams announced his energetic, nationalist, nonpartisan outlook and program in his inaugural address and in a remarkable first annual message to Congress. As he assumed office, Adams acknowledged to the American people that he was "less possessed of your confidence in advance than any of my predecessors," but he promised to make up for this with "intentions upright and pure, a heart devoted to the welfare of our country, and the unceasing application of all faculties allotted to me to her service." Then, on a note of self-delusion or wishful thinking, he assured his audience that ten years of good feelings had "assuaged the animosities of political contention and blended into harmony the discordant elements of public opinion." He condemned party rancor and regional biases in appealing to all Americans to unite behind a common program for the public good. He hinted at his approach to promoting it by endorsing federal support for internal improvements and other energetic uses of national power. The address approached pure fantasy as the president doggedly asserted his active, above-party idea of leadership and public purpose in a political landscape where sectional disputes, contentions over states' rights, and party factionalism blossomed on all sides.

Adams returned, in detail and lofty rhetoric, to his theme of broad national purposes in his first annual message in December, 1825. "Were we to slumber in indolence or fold up our arms and proclaim to the world that we are palsied by the will of our constituents," the earnest and Puritan-descended president intoned, "would it not be to cast away the bounties of Providence and doom ourselves to perpetual inferiority? . . . The great object of the institution of civil government," Adams asserted, echoing a theme he had found in Aristotle, Cicero, and other advocates of good government through the ages, "is the improvement of the condition of those who are parties to the social contract. . . . No government . . . can accomplish [its] lawful ends . . . but in proportion as it improves the condition of those over whom it is established." Within this conception Adams had little use for strict con-

---

Excerpt from John Quincy Adams's inaugural address, March 4, 1825:

Fellow-citizens, you are acquainted with the peculiar circumstances of the recent election, which have resulted in affording me the opportunity of addressing you at this time. You have heard the exposition of the principles which will direct me in the fulfillment of the high and solemn trust imposed upon me in this station. Less possessed of your confidence in advance than any of my predecessors, I am deeply conscious of the prospect that I shall stand more and oftener in need of your indulgence. Intentions upright and pure, a heart devoted to the welfare of our country, and the unceasing application of all the faculties allotted to me to her service are all the pledges that I can give for the faithful performance of the arduous duties I am to undertake. To the guidance of the legislative councils, to the assistance of the executive and subordinate departments, to the friendly cooperation of the respective State governments, to the candid and liberal support of the people so far as it may be deserved by honest industry and zeal, I shall look for whatever success may attend my public service; and knowing that *"except the Lord keep the city the watchman waketh but in vain,"* with fervent supplications for His favor, to His overruling providence I commit with humble but fearless confidence my own fate and the future destinies of my country.

---

structionist, states' rights, special interest dicta that denied deliberate, effective pursuit of the common national good.

In particular, the president recommended establishment of a national university and national naval academy to help train the wise and patriotic leadership he thought the country needed. He also advocated an extensive system of internal improvements (mostly canals and turnpikes, but railroads were also clearly in the offing) to be paid for out of increasing revenues from Western land sales and a continuing tariff on imports. He called, too, for the establishment of a uniform system of weights and measures and the improvement of the patent system, both to promote science and to encourage a spirit of enterprise and invention in the land. In a further effort to support science and spread its benefits to the nation and to the world, Adams advocated not only an extensive survey of the nation's own coasts, land, and resources but also American participation in worldwide efforts for "the common improvement of the species." "[Are] we not bound," the president asked, "to contribute our portion of energy and exertion to the common stock?" He urged American initiatives to explore the South Seas (partisan bickering largely thwarted attempts to launch an American expedition) and erection of an astronomical observatory, "light-houses of the skies," so the United States could make at least one such contribution to the advancement of knowledge to supplement the 130 observatories that had already been erected in Europe.

In general, Adams proved himself completely out of step with Congress and perhaps the nation as well. His proposals were greeted with scorn and derision, regarded as so many efforts to enlarge the national power under his control and to create a national elite that would neglect the common people and destroy the vitality of state and local governments. Senator Martin Van Buren complained of the "most ultra-latitudinarian doctrines" in Adams's message, and former President Thomas Jefferson condemned some of the proposals as unconstitutional (echoing disputes he had had with John Adams a quarter century or more earlier). With Congress dominated by an unruly collection of his political enemies and the mood of the country preoccupied with the release of its diverse sectional and individual energies, Adams had virtually no legislative success with his programs and found himself increasingly isolated, apparently living in a bygone age.

Adams sought to further his nationalistic, nonpartisan outlook through the design of his cabinet and in other appointments to office. He intended to retain as much as possible Monroe's cabinet, he said, to sustain a sense of continuity and national unity and to avoid implications that he would fill offices with his own friends and supporters. Samuel Southard agreed to remain as secretary of the navy, John McLean as postmaster general (not yet a full cabinet office), and William Wirt as attorney general. When the ailing William H. Crawford declined to stay as secretary of the treasury, Adams appointed an able and politically sympathetic Pennsylvanian, Richard Rush, to the office. This opened up the post of minister to Great Britain for a New Yorker, first offered to DeWitt Clinton, who declined, and then accepted by the aged Federalist Rufus King. Adams intended the War Department, vacated by Calhoun's election as vice president, for Andrew Jackson, but the general's contempt for the Adams administration precluded a formal nomination. Adams then gave the office to James Barbour, a Virginian and supporter of Crawford. The appointment of Clay to the State Department completed an able cabinet with a reasonable balance of men from the various sections of the country, which was, however, with the exception of Rush, filled with people friendly to other presidential aspirants. Nevertheless, owing to Adams's obvious intention to act in the national interest and his effectiveness as an administrator, and also to Clay's great personal affability, the cabinet functioned with harmony and good humor for most of its four-year existence.

Adams professed indifference to this political disarray because he was determined to exclude partisanship from the presidency. He was well aware, though, as his diary attests, that he was to face debilitating political quarrels in the years to come. In other appointments he renominated, as his predecessors had, "all

against whom there was no complaint." He refused, he said, to make "government a perpetual and intermitting scramble for office." Throughout his term of office, he removed only twelve incumbents from federal jobs, and those for gross incompetence. While his enemies intrigued around him and used appointments for blatantly political purposes, Adams adhered strictly to his above-party ideology. He presented a paradoxical picture of a president intent on ignoring, even to the point of apparent naïveté, party politics, while surrounded by some of the most avid, factious political warfare in American history. Thus unenviably positioned, he turned his attention to the day-to-day problems of his presidency. Bald, of average height, erect in bearing, somewhat stern visaged, with a rather long, sharp nose and tending toward the stoutness that characterized his family, Adams gave the impression of a man determined to do his duty as he saw it.

Foreign Affairs: Trade Agreements and the Collapse of Spain's New World Empire

Adams sought in his conduct of foreign relations (which he expected to be the dominant concern of his administration) to further the Jeffersonian goals of competitive world trade and access to foreign markets under terms favorable to American trading interests. This meant reciprocal trade agreements, giving the United States most-favored-nation status in peacetime and protection of neutral's rights on the high seas in time of war, all objectives of critical concern to the nation since its founding and which had been the substance of Adams's long diplomatic career. With Secretary of State Clay, he negotiated general commercial treaties that improved American relations with Britain, France, the Netherlands, Sweden, Austria, Portugal, Turkey, and Mexico. Though Adams and Clay accepted less-than-ideal terms in some of these treaties, in each case American interests were furthered and a precedent set for amicable trade relations likely in the future to be beneficial to each nation. Meanwhile, trade with the growing number of newly independent nations of Latin America, released at last from the constrictions of Spanish regulation, remained unsettled and often chaotic.

More troublesome were the administration's efforts to remove the longstanding burdens imposed on American trade with European colonies in the Western Hemisphere, especially with British possessions in the West Indies. Continued efforts by Britain to monopolize trade with its North American possessions and, it seemed as well, to sustain a century-long preference for its West Indian merchants and planters at the expense of mainland producers of food and lumber resulted in irritating and sometimes insulting strictures on United States trade. Patient efforts by Adams and Clay to protect American interests and at the same time open up profitable trade, however, became entangled in domestic politics. Pro-Jacksonians, based in the South and West, alleged that the rigidity of the New England-biased administration in defending American merchants led to neglect of the needs of staple exporters. Britain sought to take advantage of the dissension by framing its regulations to favor first one side and then the other, and then ridiculing American negotiators caught in the political cross fire. As a result, there was no satisfactory agreement, and the Adams administration was blamed for inaction. The problem found its long-range solution in the diminishing importance of United States trade with the British West Indies.

Looming beyond the diplomacy of commerce were the ideological and geopolitical implications of the near demise of Spain's New World empire. Using rhetoric echoing Thomas Paine and Jefferson, John Quincy Adams welcomed the end of Spanish tyranny in Latin America and hoped the newly independent nations would become both kindred republics and partners in the economic growth of the New World. "The natural rights of mankind, and the sovereignty of the people ... fundamental maxims which we from our cradle first proclaimed," Adams averred, should become the foundation of all the nations of the Americas, as "the will of kings" was expelled from the hemisphere. He shared as well, though, his father's reservations about whether the former Spanish colonies, untutored in any of the habits of self-government, would be able to establish stable republican institutions. Disputes among factions in the former colonies, incessant efforts by European powers to interfere for their advantage, and the difficulty of exercising any United States influence without also seeming to interfere or dominate complicated the fluid and volatile situation. The prospect that Spain might retain control of Cuba and Puerto Rico, the possessions of most strategic interest to the United States, added further complications. American efforts to encourage republican independence in Mexico, Central America, Colombia, and La Plata (Argentina) were inconclusive and left the Adams administration with more problems than resolutions. Yet, circumstances seemed to call for United States leadership.

The issue came to a head when, shortly after Adams became president, the United States received an invitation from Colombia and Mexico to attend an "assembly of Plenipotentiaries" of the newly independent Latin American states to be held in Panama. Britain and the Netherlands, who along with the United States had opposed the reactionary designs of the Holy Alliance to reestablish Spanish power in its former colonies, were also invited. Adams, with Clay's enthusiastic support, favored American attendance, though both were aware of many difficulties. Would the United States be drawn into the wars still going on between Spain and its former colonies or drawn into wars with European powers? Would American commercial interests be better protected by bilateral negotiations with the new nations than by an international congress with an unpredictable agenda? Most complicated of all, what about Cuba and Puerto Rico? The United States pre-

The signing of the Independence of Venezuela, one of several colonies to gain freedom from Spain during the Adams administration. *(Library of Congress)*

ferred continued (weak) Spanish control to British or French domination of the islands, to conquest of them by Colombia or Mexico, and most of all to a slave revolt that would plunge Cuba and Puerto Rico into the Haitian nightmare of bloodshed and black domination. Yet, strong sentiment existed in the United States for both independence (under white settler control) and annexation of the strategic islands.

All these possibilities were aired in Congress and the press when Adams appointed American commissioners to the Panama congress and requested funds for their mission. Political opponents denied the president's authority to respond to the invitation without consulting Congress, pictured the whole enterprise as another federal-presidential power grab, and insisted that it betrayed the already hallowed injunctions of Washington and Jefferson against "entangling alliances." South-

erners feared the Panama congress would act against slavery and encourage black revolt and tumult in the Caribbean. As a result, the approval of the American commissioners was so delayed that they missed the congress (one of them died en route of tropical fever), and all the world could see that political discord within the United States would prevent the country from taking any leadership role. The congress, in any case, failed to reconvene for its second session, so the whole idea of a Pan-American union died. Adams had a certain sympathy for the idea and wanted the United States to encourage republican self-government in Latin America, but his political weakness and the continuing volatility there prevented significant results. Altogether, Adams and Clay were unable to respond constructively to the opportunity opened by the demise of Spanish power in Latin America.

Domestic Policies: The "American System" and the "Tariff of Abominations"

Even more than in foreign affairs, political liabilities and ineptitude vitiated the domestic policies of the Adams administration. Both the president and his secretary of state sought to translate their belief in active guidance of national development by the federal government into what Clay called the "American System." Essentially, it entailed protective tariffs to encourage American industry, land and Indian policies designed to hasten settlement of the West and provide revenue for internal improvements, the enlargement of markets for Western grains and Southern cotton, federal support of internal improvements to bind the nation together for the benefit of all, and the strengthening of the national bank as a device for guiding the economy of the country. Adams liked especially the grand design of the American System: its encouragement of growth in all sections of the country, its planned use of the resources of the nation, and the important role it gave to the federal government in organizing and fostering the common welfare. To him, such a design fulfilled, in a deliberate and coherent way, the purposes of the American Revolution and what he often saw as "the hand of

The Vice President
John C. Calhoun

Born on March 18, 1782, John Calhoun was introduced to politics at a young age, as his father was a member of the South Carolina legislature. The untimely death of his father interrupted Calhoun's education and forced him to return to his family home to work the farm. However, Calhoun was urged by his older brothers to attend college, and he entered Yale, graduating in 1804.

After Yale, he studied law in Connecticut and returned to his home state of South Carolina to practice law in 1807. That same year, he was elected to the South Carolina General Assembly, where he would serve for three years. In 1810, he was elected to his first of three terms to the United States House of Representatives. Calhoun married the daughter of his cousin, Floride Calhoun, and had nine children. Six years later, President James Monroe nominated him as secretary of war, where he distinguished himself by creating military outposts in the Northwest Territory.

Although he was interested in running for president in 1824, he quickly withdrew his candidacy because of the realization that he could not win. Subsequently, John Quincy Adams asked him to be the vice presidential nominee in the election of 1824. As a result of differing political views, Adams would not ask Calhoun to remain on ticket in 1828. However, Andrew Jackson, in his second bid for the presidency, sought Calhoun for the national ticket as vice president. However, animosity between the two men quickly developed, and Vice President Calhoun resigned from office one year before his term ended in 1832.

That same year, he was elected to the United States Senate from South Carolina, although by 1843, he retired from politics in order to spend time with his ailing wife. His retirement would be quite short; on March 6, 1844, President John Tyler nominated him as secretary of state. As secretary of state, Calhoun negotiated the treaty to annex Texas. At the conclusion of his term in office, he was once again elected to the United States Senate. Predicting the divisiveness of the Civil War, Calhoun is quoted as saying "The dissolution of the union is the heaviest blow that can be struck at civilization and representative government." Shortly thereafter, on March 31, 1850, he died in Washington, and his funeral was held in the Senate Chamber.

Robert P. Watson and Richard Yon

Providence" in American history and his own ideas of the active, above-party role of the nation's leader.

During Adams's administration, he, Clay, and Secretary of the Treasury Richard Rush spoke eloquently about the American System and managed to push many measures for federal subsidy of canals, harbors, and roads through Congress. Support for them, though, arose more from local enthusiasm for particular projects than from any sense of national purpose. The administration also broadened the effectiveness of the National Bank, but again criticism of administration policies by various sectional interests foreshadowed crippling controversies to come. Adams continued policies of removal of Eastern Indians to new reservations in the West (more humanely than would be characteristic of later Jacksonian administrations) and of carefully controlled, revenue-producing sale of frontier lands. In both areas, however, Southerners and Westerners saw prejudice against their interests in favor of those of the Northeast and the middle states extending westward from Pennsylvania to Ohio and Kentucky.

Most troublesome of all was the question of protective tariffs. Adams repudiated the argument "that the Congress of the Union are impotent to restore the balance in favor of native industry destroyed by the statutes of another realm" and saw the advantages of fostering domestic manufactures, but he misjudged the degree of Western and Southern hostility. Jacksonians in Congress, moreover, saw an opportunity to manipulate the tariff issue in a way most damaging to the administration. In 1828, they maneuvered through Congress a tariff bill that gathered together various objectionable and contradictory features advocated by special interests—and then blamed the legislation on the administration, which had backed a revision of the tariff. The "Tariff of Abominations," as the act was called, became a rallying point of opposition to the administration and played a significant part in the campaign of 1828.

The Growing Strength of the Party System

The Adams presidency in its last years became increasingly engulfed in administrative tangles, quarrels within and between the armed forces, and, worst of all, the swirling political forces gathering around the popular but combative figure of Andrew Jackson that were determined to push Adams and all he stood for out of office. As the tariff legislation illustrated, proposals and alliances in Congress were calculated according to their likely effect on the next presidential election. Appointments to office were blocked or shifted in Congress according to their political colorations. Everywhere the burgeoning energies of the nation created new and often centrifugal forces and political alignments that thwarted or bypassed Adams's earnest, systematic efforts at orderly national development.

Adams was caught, as he perceived but could do nothing about, in one of the key transformations in American political history. He still sought, as the first five American presidents had done, to be a leader in the style of "civic republicanism" that harked back to the standards of good government, nonpartisan citizenship, and active pursuit of the public welfare he had learned from his study of Aristotle, Cicero, Plutarch, and other classical writers. Thus he regarded political parties as inherently corrupt because they were parts, or factions, of the whole. A president who celebrated, led, or even condoned parties was, ipso facto, not what a good national leader should be. Adams sought to sustain the apparent demise of the rival parties during Monroe's presidency and instead to include all political energy within a national republicanism that sought an inclusive public good.

Sectional and economic interests became more diverse, vociferous, and effective as access to politics broadened under the democratizing reforms (particularly within the states) of the 1820's, transforming the public life of the country into the vigorous, bewildering arena of "factions" that Madison had predicted, in *Federalist No. 10*, would be the fruit of freedom. Adams understood and accepted this in a way and did not oppose the enlargement of political participation, but he was deeply disturbed by the decline of active pursuit of the common good.

Jacksonian partisans, particularly Martin Van Buren, articulated and brought into existence a new, positive idea of political party. They saw political parties as manifestations of the needs and interests of the people of a free society. The job of the party and its leaders was to accept, enlarge, and fulfill the aspirations of the multitude of factions in the country and mold them into a political instrument (that is, party) that could gain national power. Instead of this goal being corrupt or partisan as Adams and his predecessors thought, to Van Buren it represented the triumph of democracy. The party would stand for certain principles and coordinate diverse interests, defining the public good in the only way suited to a free and pluralistic nation. The continuing competition between the parties would be "the life blood of democracy," providing policy alternatives to the citizens and a ceaseless criticism and honing of public needs.

Within this framework the president had the responsibility of leading and sustaining his political party as a necessary part of the machinery of a democratic society. It would be proper for a president to welcome the support of various interest groups, to campaign for office, to build party organization, to encourage party discipline in Congress, and even to use appointments to office to strengthen the party, all on the grounds that strong political parties were good for democracies. Van Buren declared that party disputes would "rouse the sluggish to exertion, give increased energy to the most active intellect, excite a salutary vigilance over public functionaries, and prevent that apathy which has proved the ruin of Republics."

The Election of 1828: Triumph of the Jacksonians

Under this new ideology of party, Van Buren and others organized the Jacksonian party, beginning before Adams's inauguration in 1825. Resting on solid Western and Southern opposition to Adams's alleged Northeastern bias, responsive to a wide diversity of interests, and gathering the forces of Calhoun, Crawford, Van Buren, and all the other anti-Adams politicians, the Democratic Party came into being around the objective of electing Andrew Jackson president in 1828. At the same time, it rejected not only John Quincy Adams but also all the older conceptions of good government and national purpose for which he stood. Calhoun and other pro-Jacksonians held "opposition" meetings even before Adams entered the White House. The Tennessee legislature nominated Jackson for the presidency in October, 1825, and Van Buren traveled about the country putting the party machinery together. Proadministration forces were active as well, especially Clay and his supporters, in seeking local support and fostering newspaper advocacy of Adams's programs. The president himself, however, held stiffly aloof from what he regarded as "politicking," which was beneath the dignity of his office, though he earnestly wanted to be reelected and did what he thought permissible behind the scenes to further his cause.

By mid-1828, the campaign became increasingly rancorous, and it was clear that the tide was running strongly for the Jacksonians. The pro-Adams press — operating without Adams's support, encouragement, or often even his approval — played up scandalous charges about Jackson's marriage, whereas the pro-Jackson press dredged up stories about Adams's alleged aristocratic airs and misuse of public funds on his missions abroad. One newspaper even charged that Adams had acted as "a pimp" in arranging for one of his servants, while he was in Russia, to be the czar's mistress. New England and some of the mid-Atlantic states remained faithful to Adams, but the Jacksonians successfully enlisted the burgeoning sectional and democratic energies of the country and benefited from the skillful party-building efforts of Van Buren and others. When the returns were in, Jackson had gained a 178 to 83 victory in the electoral college and had a 647,276 to 508,064 margin in the popular vote. The heroic general swept every state in the South and West (both he and his running mate, John C. Calhoun, were slave-owning planters) and even managed to win Pennsylvania and more than half the electoral votes of New York. The gloom and illness in the Adams administration as it prepared to leave office during the winter of 1828-1829 and the joyous, tumultuous celebrations of the Jacksonians as they inaugurated their leader in the White House on March 4, 1829, measured the decisive change that had taken place in the nation's political life.

Adams and the Presidency: An Uncompromising Vision of Good Government

To Adams, his defeat marked nothing less than the end of the noble aspirations of his first annual message that an active, above-party president and government might lead the nation in deliberate, coordinated pursuit of the public good. Five days after Jackson's inauguration, Adams wrote bitterly that the new administration would "be the day of small things. There will be neither lofty meditations, nor comprehensive foresight, nor magnanimous purpose." Henceforth, Adams complained a few years later, national development would depend on "the limping gait of State legislatures and private adventure, and the American Union is to

Englishman Robert Cruikshank shows his disapproval of American democracy in his depiction of a House of Representatives debate over the "gag rule" against discussing slavery. Adams fought the gag rule during his presidency and afterward, as a member of the House. *(Library of Congress)*

live from hand to mouth, and to cast away, instead of using for the improvement of its own condition, the bounties of Providence." Grand purposes and rational ideals, such as the planned development of national resources or the gradual abolition of slavery (a cause Adams fostered courageously during a unique and remarkable eighteen-year, postpresidential career in the House of Representatives), were to give way to what he regarded as the often shortsighted, selfish interests and designs of the increasingly diverse peoples and sections of the nation.

The John Quincy Adams presidency, then, somewhat like that of his father, ended in frustration and a sense of having lost a vital battle to new and, to the Adamses, unwelcome political forces. Though sometimes regarded as antidemocratic (so the Jeffersonians in 1800 and the Jacksonians in 1828 charged), the Adamses are more properly seen as upholding a different model, or style, of republican leadership. John Quincy Adams accepted earnestly the idea of government by consent. He hoped as well that inspired national leadership in the public interest, eschewing the divisive forces of faction and party, might enlist support among the people. This would sustain what Adams regarded as the vital principle of good (wise, virtuous) government even in a democratic era. He despised his Jacksonian opponents, not because they were democrats, but because they assumed that partisanship and the clash of sectional and economic interests would by themselves result in the common good. Yet, this new ideology of liberal, private enterprise, suited to the energies that would develop the frontier and absorb millions of immigrants, seemed the wave of the future, and it did in fact characterize American growth and public life in the century to come. In the years before his fatal stroke on the floor of the House of Representatives on February 23, 1848, Adams refused to approve the "new politics" of the nation. He continued to believe that his own presidency had been a worthy, though perhaps futile, effort in sustaining a more purposeful and virtuous public life in the nation he had seen born in the revolutionary battles and diplomacy of his youth.

Ralph Ketcham

Suggested Readings

Adams, John Quincy. *Memoirs of John Quincy Adams . . . 1795 to 1848.* Edited by Charles Francis Adams. 12 vols. 1874-1877. Reprint. New York: Praeger, 1970. The classic source for the life and presidency of Adams.

Bemis, Samuel F. *John Quincy Adams and the Foundations of American Foreign Policy.* 1949. Reprint. New York: Knopf, 1956. Serves as a biography of Adams against a backdrop of his achievements in foreign affairs.

_____. *John Quincy Adams and the Union.* New York: Knopf, 1956. Serves as a biography of Adams against a backdrop of his achievements in civil liberties and domestic programs.

Hargreaves, Mary. *The Presidency of John Quincy Adams.* Lawrence: University Press of Kansas, 1985. A detailed, scholarly account of Adams's presidency especially thorough in its recording of the economic and political context of the era.

Hecht, Marie B. *John Quincy Adams: A Personal History of an Independent Man.* New York: Macmillan, 1972. Gives a full account of his family life and is also very good on his career in the House of Representatives.

Howe, Daniel W. *The Political Culture of the American Whigs.* Chicago: University of Chicago Press, 1979. Surveys the ideas and practices of the party closest to Adams.

Lewis, James E. *John Quincy Adams: Policymaker for the Union.* Wilmington, Del.: SR Books, 2001. Examines Adams's presidency through the lens of his foreign policy achievements.

Nagel, Paul C. *John Quincy Adams: A Public Life, a Private Life.* New York: Alfred A. Knopf, 1997. A biography that draws on Adams's extensive diaries and explores his complex nature.

Parsons, Lynn H. *John Quincy Adams*. Madison, Wis.: Madison House, 1998. A concise biography that chronicles Adams's life from boyhood in 1778, when he accompanied his father to France on a diplomatic mission, to his last years.

_____. *John Quincy Adams: A Bibliography*. Westport, Conn.: Greenwood Press, 1993. Provides a detailed listing of primary and secondary resources.

Remini, Robert V. *John Quincy Adams*. New York: Time Books, 2002. A straightforward, accessible biography.

Andrew Jackson

7th President, 1829-1837

Born: March 15, 1767
    Waxhaw area, South Carolina
Died: June 8, 1845
    the Hermitage, near Nashville,
    Tennessee

Political Party: Democratic
Vice Presidents: John C. Calhoun, Martin
    Van Buren

Cabinet Members

Secretary of State: Martin Van Buren, Edward
    Livingston, Louis McLane, John Forsyth
Secretary of the Treasury: Samuel Ingham,
    Louis McLane, William John Duane,
    Roger B. Taney, Levi Woodbury
Secretary of War: John Henry Eaton, Lewis
    Cass, Benjamin Butler
Secretary of the Navy: John Branch, Levi
    Woodbury, Mahlon Dickerson
Attorney General: John M. Berrien, Roger
    Taney, Benjamin Butler
Postmaster General: William Barry, Amos
    Kendall

Andrew Jackson is one of the great mythic characters of American history. Acclaimed a hero for his military prowess, he became the dominant political figure of the half century between Thomas Jefferson and Abraham Lincoln. He was the first president elected from west of the Appalachians and the first to rise from humble origins to the White House. He became a symbol of the new opportunities open to the common people in nineteenth century society and of the triumph of the democratic principle in American politics. While serving as president, he fashioned his personal following into the Democratic Party, the longest surviving of all American political organizations. Jackson lent his name first to a movement, then to a party, and finally to an era in American history.

A Leader Formed on the Frontier

Jackson was born on March 15, 1767, in the Waxhaw settlement, a community of Scotch-Irish immigrants located along the North Carolina-South Carolina border. His father died just be-

Portrait of Andrew Jackson. *(Whitehouse.gov)*

147

Jackson—"The Brave Boy of the Waxhaws," by Currier & Ives. *(Library of Congress)*

fore Andrew's birth, and his mother and her three small boys moved in with her nearby relatives, the Crawfords. Growing up in the Crawford household, Andrew received a satisfactory elementary education and perhaps a smattering of higher learning. According to later remembrances, he was a tall, lanky, and high-spirited youth.

The Revolutionary War shattered Jackson's placid childhood and wiped out his remaining family. Fighting in the Carolina backcountry was particularly savage, a nightmare conflict of ambushes, massacres, and sudden skirmishes. The Jacksons devoted themselves wholeheartedly to the American Revolution. Andrew's oldest brother, Hugh, enlisted in a patriot regiment and died, apparently of heatstroke, on the battlefield. Too young for formal soldiering, Andrew and his brother Robert fought with American irregulars. In 1781, they were captured and contracted smallpox, of which Robert

died soon after their release. Shortly afterward, Jackson's mother also succumbed to disease contracted while trying to retrieve two nephews from a British prison ship.

Alone in the world at the war's end, a combat veteran at the age of fifteen, Jackson drifted for a time, taught school, then read law in North Carolina. Completing his studies in 1787, he soon accepted a friend's offer to serve as public prosecutor in the newly organized Mero District west of the mountains. The seat of the district was Nashville on the Cumberland River. Founded in 1780, it had a population of only five hundred but excellent prospects for growth, and it offered fine opportunities for an aspiring young lawyer of small education but already much experience of the world. In Nashville, Jackson rose rapidly. He was ambitious, energetic, shrewd, and an agreeable companion. He did not know much law, but neither did anybody else, and a frontier town that was awash in bad debts and disputed land titles provided plenty of business. Jackson built a large private practice to supplement his public duties, entered into trading ventures, and began to acquire slaves. He also ingratiated himself with the leaders of Nashville society and with Tennessee's leading politician, William Blount, who became governor when the district was set off as a federal territory in 1790.

Jackson solidified his rising status in Nashville by marrying Rachel Donelson Robards, daughter of the late John Donelson, one of the city's founders. The circumstances of the marriage caused much controversy during Jackson's presidential campaign many years later, for at the time of their union, Rachel's estranged first husband, Lewis Robards, had initiated but not yet completed his divorce proceedings against her. Frontier Nashville, however, saw nothing wrong in the marriage. To ensure its legality, Andrew and Rachel performed the ceremony again after Robards finalized his divorce.

The First Lady
Rachel Jackson

Rachel Donelson was born in frontier Virginia in 1767 to Rachel Stockley and John Donelson, a wealthy land speculator and politician. One of eleven children, Rachel received no formal education but was trained in the skills needed by a plantation mistress. When she was twelve, the family ventured with a large party of settlers into the wilds of Tennessee and Kentucky.

At seventeen, Rachel married Lewis Robards, a Revolutionary War captain from a wealthy Virginia family. By 1788, trouble arose in the marriage, and Rachel went to Nashville. There she met a boarder in her mother's home, Andrew Jackson, and in late 1789, the pair eloped to Natchez, then Spanish territory. Robards began legal proceedings in 1790, and in 1793, he was awarded a divorce based on Rachel's adultery and bigamy. In January, 1794, the Jacksons legally wed in Nashville, where they had lived as a married couple since mid-1790.

In the early American republic, women of the elite and middle classes who left their husbands — for whatever reason — lost all honor and social standing. Rachel Donelson's decision to elope with Jackson was an extraordinary act of courage — or desperation. Their unorthodox union would haunt the Jacksons for the remainder of their lives and would be a major flashpoint in Jackson's campaign for the presidency in the 1820's.

Rachel Jackson lived the majority of her life as a plantation mistress, caring for the Jacksons' farm and slaves during Andrew's many absences as a lawyer, judge, general, and politician. She wrote to a niece that Jackson spent less than a quarter of his days with her. Unable to have children, Rachel filled her life with caring for her adopted son Andrew Jackson, Jr. (he was also her nephew), at least seventeen wards, three Creek Indian orphans, and many kin.

Swept up in the great revival movement about 1800, Rachel became increasingly pious and often warned Jackson of the dangers of public acclaim. She regretted his decision to seek the presidency and deeply suffered from the public attacks on her as an "American Jezebel." She reluctantly agreed to join him in the White House after his election in November, 1828, assured by friends that she would be accepted by Washington society rather than shunned. However, she collapsed from a heart attack just days before their departure, dying on December 22, 1828. She was buried that Christmas Eve in the dress she had chosen for the inauguration. Jackson's White House thus opened in mourning, and he continued to fight for Rachel's reputation until the end of his life.

Ann Toplovich

Despite its haste, Andrew's marriage to Rachel was perhaps the happiest event of his life, for the union proved an enduring success. It brought Jackson into an extensive and influential Tennessee clan and provided countless in-laws to replace his own lost family. The couple's youthful ardor matured into a devotion that deepened as they grew older. Lengthy periods of separation, the loss of Rachel's girlish beauty, and her increasingly religious, sometimes hysterical temperament could not shake Jackson's affection for her. Not surprisingly, in view of his violently attenuated childhood, Jackson was a man of fierce and, at times, uncontrollable emotions. He carried a reputation as a hellion from some youthful escapades, and explosive quarrels surrounded him well into middle age, but his passions and inexhaustible energies never swayed him from his attachment to Rachel. Their mutual affection and utterly conventional domestic life furnished a needed emotional anchor throughout his turbulent military and political career.

Only one misfortune marred their marriage. Though Jackson loved children and desperately desired some of his own, the couple remained childless. Rachel's brothers and sisters obligingly provided a corps of nieces and nephews for the Jacksons to stand godparent to, and one, Andrew Jackson, Jr., son of Rachel's brother Severn, for them to adopt.

Jackson's adherence to Governor William Blount brought him rapid political preferment in the 1790's. Chosen a delegate in 1795 to Tennessee's state constitutional convention, he was then elected the state's first congressman and shortly promoted to senator. After a year, he resigned to take a job closer to home, as judge of Tennessee's superior court. Meanwhile, he was undertaking large-scale land speculations in partnership with John Overton. Still a very young man, Jackson seemed destined for greatness, but the next few years brought a series of setbacks that halted his meteoric rise and threatened to close out his political career.

The Blount faction fell from power at the turn of the century, and Jackson fell with it. Over his head in land speculations, Blount entered into a conspiracy to seize Spanish Florida and Louisiana for the British. The conspiracy came to light; Blount was expelled from the United States Senate in 1797 and died in 1800. Governor John Sevier, commanding a rival faction, replaced him as Tennessee's most powerful politician. Jackson and Sevier quarreled first in 1797, when Jackson was in Congress. The dispute was patched over, but it reopened in 1802, when Jackson challenged Sevier for election as major general in command of the Tennessee militia. Jackson won the post, but the aftermath brought the two men to a showdown in the streets of Knoxville, followed by preparations for a formal duel. No one was hurt, but his estrangement from the now-dominant Sevier faction shut Jackson off from further political advance in Tennessee. His subsequent angling for a federal appointment in Louisiana also came to nothing.

The Sevier feud inaugurated a series of quarrels, over matters both vital and trivial, between Jackson and a variety of Tennessee foes. The most notorious of these, in 1806, began with a minor misunderstanding over a horse race and ended with a duel in which Jackson shot young Charles Dickinson dead after taking Dickinson's own bullet in his chest. A coterie of close friends — most notably John Coffee, John Overton, and the Donelson clan — stood by Jackson (and sometimes fought in his behalf) through these troublous affairs, but they made for him many other enemies and earned for him a reputation as a bellicose and perhaps unstable man.

Financial reverses accompanied the collapse of Jackson's political prospects. In the course of his freewheeling speculations, Jackson had carelessly endorsed the notes of one David Allison of Philadelphia. The notes came due, Allison defaulted, and Jackson found himself hard pressed by creditors. He met his

The Hermitage, Jackson's home. *(Library of Congress)*

obligations, but only by unloading some of his holdings and exchanging his Hunter's Hill plantation for a less-developed property named the Hermitage. In subsequent years, Jackson recouped his losses by raising cotton at the Hermitage and breeding and racing horses. He also continued his ventures in trading and storekeeping, though without much success. The Allison episode, however, taught him prudence. Henceforth, he trusted no one in money matters and avoided debt at all hazards—lessons that he later labored in vain to impart to his spendthrift adopted son, Andrew, Jr.

In 1804, Jackson relinquished his judgeship, and for the rest of the decade he focused his ambition on military rather than political objects. Still holding his militia command, he yearned for the war that would bring honor, glory, and a vent for his relentless energy. He also had old scores to settle—with the British who had destroyed his family, with American Indians who had once terrorized Tennessee and still hovered over its western and southern borders, and with their aiders and abettors, the Spanish in Florida and Mexico. Jackson's thirst for action led him to befriend Aaron Burr when the latter came through Nashville in 1805, seeking recruits for his shadowy schemes of Southwestern conquest. Jackson cut loose from Burr in time to avoid implication in his alleged treason, but he was still eager for war against the Spanish. In the following years, Jackson busied himself with militia reorganization plans, and he volunteered himself and his troops for service at every hint of Indian trouble. He also watched with mounting indignation the government's inept efforts to win redress from Great Britain for violations of American neutral shipping privileges.

The War of 1812: The Making of a National Hero

In June of 1812, the United States at last declared war on Great Britain. Jackson immediately tendered his services, but the government had no use for him. In November, however, orders arrived for a Tennessee force to proceed to New Orleans, and Governor Willie Blount (William's half brother) designated Jackson to command. Jackson gathered two thousand volunteers and led them as far as Natchez, where he received a curt War Department order dismissing him and his troops. Fuming and raging at the government's imbecility, Jackson marched his command back to Nashville, where it dispersed. Throughout the summer of 1813, he awaited orders. In the interlude, he fell into another quarrel about nothing, this time with the Benton brothers, Jesse and Thomas Hart, the latter of whom had recently completed services as a colonel under Jackson's command. The affair terminated in a street brawl; Jackson took a bullet that nearly cost him his left arm.

In September, 1813, American Indian hostilities finally brought an end to Jackson's inactivity. Summoned to punish the Creeks for frontier massacres, he regathered his volunteer force and invaded the Creek homeland in northern Alabama. In a series of engagements culminating at Horseshoe Bend in March, 1814, Jackson annihilated the main hostile Creek force. In subsequent treaty negotiations, he exacted a huge cession of land—more than twenty million acres—from the vanquished tribe. The Creeks would never again be a formidable power.

Jackson's success in the Creek War made him a minor national hero; his defense of New Orleans was to make him an icon. In May, 1814, he was commissioned United States major general and given command of the Southern frontier. The British were planning an attack on New Orleans, the strategic gateway to the American interior. Jackson beat off a preliminary assault at Mobile Bay, then raided eastward to destroy the British base at Pensacola before returning to New Orleans. In December, a British seaborne invasion force made landfall and reached the Mississippi ten miles below the city. Jackson blocked their advance upriver. For two weeks, the British probed his position astride the Mississippi. Failing to find an exploitable weakness, on January 8, 1815, British general Sir Edward Pakenham ordered a direct frontal assault on Jackson's lines. The attack was a complete failure. Pakenham's men advanced over exposed and difficult terrain toward Jackson's fortified position and were mowed down by American artillery and rifle fire. The British suffered more than two thousand casualties, including Pakenham, dead on the field; Jackson's losses were thirteen killed, fifty-eight wounded and missing.

Almost simultaneously with the word of Jackson's incredible victory came news that British and American commissioners in Europe had signed a peace treaty two weeks earlier. Though unconnected, the two events fused in the public mind to make Jackson appear as the agent of deliverance from a mismanaged and nearly disastrous war. After a series of defeats and disappointments that sorely tried their patriotism and their patience with the government, Americans hailed Jackson and his frontier soldiers with unrestrained adoration. For a generation of patriots, Jackson became the symbol not only of American military prowess but also of the superior republican virtue that produced it.

Jackson had begun the War of 1812 as major general of Tennessee militia, amateur commander of an amateur force. He ended it as a regular major general, second highest ranking officer in the United States Army. After failures at trading, storekeeping, and land speculation, and a promising but stunted political career, he had at last found an occupation that matched his talents. Though no master strategist, Jackson for that time and place was a very good general. He lacked formal military training, but he knew the prerequisites for successful frontier warfare. His judgments were always decisive and his movements energetic. Most important, he understood the role of supply in waging wilderness campaigns and the necessity for discipline in leading half-trained, often insubordinate soldiers. He commanded the full confidence of his troops and the absolute loyalty of his subordinate officers.

Jackson stayed in the army when the war ended. Its main peacetime job was to protect the frontier against American Indians, a task that suited his tastes exactly. He had long believed that white settlers and "savage" Indian nations could not coexist in peace; and as the former represented a higher civilization, American Indians must abandon their nomadic habits and settle down as individuals in white society or remove westward beyond the advancing frontier. Jackson's dual position as army commander and treaty commissioner gave ample opportunity to implement those views, and in the years after the war, he extracted major cessions of land from the Chickasaw, Choctaw, and Cherokee.

In December, 1817, Jackson received orders to subdue the Seminoles, who were raiding across the border from Spanish Florida. Liberally interpreting his vague instructions, Jackson effected a lightning conquest of Florida itself, in the process capturing, trying, and summarily executing two British nationals whom he accused of encouraging the Seminoles. Jackson's invasion brought foreign protests and domestic calls for his court-martial or congressional censure, but he successfully rode out the storm. Spain soon ceded Florida to the United States, thereby accomplishing his ulterior object. Jackson defended himself by claiming that he had merely carried out the real but unstated desires of President James Monroe and Secretary of War John C. Calhoun. This was a defense of much merit but in later years, as the controversy continued to smolder, Jackson weakened

The Battle of New Orleans. *(Library of Congress)*

it by fashioning (with the help of compliant friends) a chain of evidence to show that Monroe had expressly authorized the campaign. Monroe denied it on his deathbed; whether Jackson believed his own concoction is difficult to say.

On the conclusion of the Florida cession treaty in 1821, Monroe offered the governorship of the new territory to Jackson. He accepted, but after presiding in stormy and controversial fashion over the installation of American authority there, he resigned and came home to Tennessee. There, his friends were beginning to promote him as a candidate for the presidency in 1824.

Presidential Aspirations

James Monroe, heir to Thomas Jefferson and James Madison in the Virginia presidential dynasty, was now in his second term, and he had no obvious successor. Three seasoned statesmen vied for the post: Secretary of State John Quincy Adams of Massachusetts, Treasury Secretary William Harris Crawford of Georgia, and Henry Clay of Kentucky, speaker of the House of Representatives. Jackson's own candidacy was first floated to serve the local purposes of his friends in Tennessee, but it quickly caught on elsewhere. In the absence of party opposition from the moribund Federalists, the machinery for fixing on a single Republican candidate had broken down, leaving a vacuum to be filled at the polls by personal popularity. The returns made it plain that Jackson's military heroics had a far greater hold on the public imagination than the civil attainments of Adams, Crawford, or Clay. Jackson was the only candidate whose strength transcended a regional base. He gathered a plurality of popular votes, carrying eleven states out of twenty-four, including Pennsylvania, New Jersey, and the Carolinas, along with the entire Southwest. No one received a majority of electoral votes, however, so the contest among Jackson, Adams, and Crawford was thrown into the House of Repre-

sentatives. There, speaker Clay announced his support for Adams, and his influence, together with a general suspicion of Jackson's unfitness for the presidency by both temperament and training, enabled Adams to win the requisite majority of states on the first ballot. He promptly appointed Clay secretary of state. Jackson cried that a "corrupt bargain" had swindled him out of the presidency and began planning for a rematch in 1828.

The four years of John Quincy Adams's presidency really constituted one long, increasingly acrimonious, and, in the end, one-sided presidential campaign. To Jackson's own tremendous popularity was added widespread outrage against the method of Adams's ascension to power. While Adams floundered in Washington, D.C., alienating key constituencies with indiscreet policy statements, Jackson drew around him a deft group of organizers and publicists to manage his campaign. They avoided discussion of issues and credentials and focused their propaganda on Jackson's mystique: his rise from humble origins, his heroism in war, his indomitable patriotism. As Jackson's candidacy gathered strength, powerful regional leaders swung to his side: Vice President John C. Calhoun of South Carolina, deserting the administration to accept the same post on Jackson's ticket; Martin Van Buren of New York, marshal of the former Crawford men; and Thomas Hart Benton, Jackson's former antagonist, now a senator from Missouri. In the end, the combination of a superior candidate and superior management produced a rout. In the 1828 election, Jackson carried the entire West and South, plus New York and Pennsylvania.

Hard on the news of this victory came personal sorrow. In its latter stages, the presidential campaign had turned ugly, as editors and pamphleteers mercilessly exposed the private lives of the candidates. Adams's publicists scrutinized the peculiar circumstances of Jackson's marriage, labeling him a wife stealer and Rachel a bigamist. As if in response to this torrent of abuse, Rachel withered and sickened. On December 22, she died at the Hermitage. For days, Jackson was inconsolable.

An Outsider in the White House

Jackson's victory in 1828 represented a radical break from tradition in the young republic. He was a genuine outsider in Washington, D.C., the first such to be elected president, and this fact was to color his perceptions and actions throughout his presidency. His election inspired trepidation among veteran politicians and bureaucrats, for he was, as Henry Clay warned, a "military chieftain" rather than an accomplished statesman. Jackson's predecessors in office had undergone extensive apprenticeships in national politics and diplomacy. Jackson had less formal education than any of them; he had acquired a little experience in Congress and almost none in public administration. Further, he had on occasion in his military career displayed an apparent contempt for civil authority. Though prominent men had attached themselves to his candidacy, his real political strength came from the mass of voters, who seemed not to care about his lack of traditional qualifications. Some established politicians admired Jackson; many feared him; few knew him well. They could only guess at what he might do in office.

Many doubted whether he could even survive his term. He was sixty-two, the oldest president to take office up to that time. Despite age and infirmity, Jackson's appearance was still striking: He carried his lean body erect, and his firm countenance and direct gaze won immediate respect, while his frank but dignified manners inspired admiration. He had, however, recently sustained a devastating blow in the death of his wife of thirty-seven years. He still carried bullets from Charles Dickinson and Jesse Benton in his chest and arm, and he suffered from persistent cough, wracking headaches, and debilitating digestive troubles.

His first task was to choose a cabinet. The chief place, the State Department, went to Martin Van Buren of New York, who had contributed vitally to Jackson's election and commanded the reigning political machine in the nation's largest state. The rest of Jackson's choices were weak and, to many of his supporters, alarming. Treasury secretary Samuel Ingham of Pennsylvania, Navy secretary John Branch of North Carolina, and Attorney General John M. Berrien of Georgia were politicians of modest reputation who brought no great strength to the administration. As all these men were practically strangers to Jackson, he saved the last post, the War Department, for a trusted confidential friend. The nod went to John Henry Eaton, a senator from Tennessee and Jackson's campaign biographer. Ironically, it was the appointment of Eaton—the safest one, in Jackson's mind—that eventually brought the whole cabinet down.

Reforming the Federal Bureaucracy: Jackson and the Spoils System

Having selected his cabinet, Jackson began a housecleaning at the second level of federal officeholders—the Washington bureau chiefs, land and customs officers, and federal marshals and attorneys. During the campaign, he had cried loudly for "reform," charging the Adams bureaucracy with fraud and with working to thwart his election. Now as president, Jackson implemented a policy of removals designed to eliminate the corruption, laxity, and arrogance that he associated with long individual tenure in office. Haste and naïveté in naming replacements did much to confuse Jackson's purpose. Under the guise of reform, many offices were doled out as reward for political services. Newspaper editors who had championed Jackson's cause came in for special favor. Jackson denied that he was injecting political criteria into the appointment process; yet he accepted an officeholder's support for Adams as evidence of unfitness, and in choosing replace-

The Vice President
Martin Van Buren

The son of a tavern owner, Martin Van Buren was born on December 5, 1782, in Kinderhook, New York. As a result of poor family finances, Van Buren was unable to receive a formal education beyond the rudimentary foundation offered in his small hometown. However, Van Buren was highly motivated, and he served as an apprentice to Francis Sylvester in order to study law. Upon completing the apprenticeship, he was admitted to the New York bar and began practicing law in New York City with William Van Ness.

In 1807, Van Buren returned to Kinderhook, where he married Hannah Hoes and they had four children. Elected to the New York State Senate in 1812, he became attorney general of the state in 1816. He took a brief reprieve from politics to be with his ailing wife and, upon her death in 1819, a mourning Van Buren immersed himself in politics once again. Winning a seat in the United States Senate in 1821, he served as chairman of the Judiciary Committee and the Finance Committee. After serving two terms as senator, Van Buren was elected governor of New York in 1828. However, he served only two months as governor, resigning to join President Jackson's cabinet as secretary of state.

With the resignation of John Calhoun as vice president, Van Buren was nominated for the position in the election of 1832. He proved to be a very loyal vice president. After the conclusion of Andrew Jackson's second term and with Jackson's endorsement, Van Buren won the Democratic nomination for president in 1836. However, Van Buren encountered difficult times in the nation's highest office, as the country experienced a harsh economic downturn that cost him his bid for reelection in 1840.

Van Buren returned to Kinderhook and in retirement traveled through the United States and Europe. Unable to keep out of politics, he unsuccessfully lobbied for the Democratic nomination for president in 1844. In 1848, he introduced himself as a candidate for president on the Free Soil Party, but he lost to Zachary Taylor. Suffering from circulatory problems and contracting pneumonia, Van Buren died at his home, Lindenwald, in Kinderhook on July 24, 1862.

ments he relied exclusively on recommendations from his own partisans, few of whom shared his own concern for honest and efficient administration.

Some of Jackson's early appointments were truly appalling. He made John Randolph of Virginia, the most undiplomatic man in the United States, minister to Russia, and he placed an alcoholic editor at the head of the General Land Office. He raised the postmaster generalship to cabinet rank and filled it with William Taylor Barry of Kentucky, a genial bungler who reduced the postal system to chaos. Several of Jackson's land office appointees defaulted for large sums. Most damaging to his administration's reputation—he ignored warnings from Van Buren and Ingham—was the appointment of an old comrade, Samuel Swartwout, as collector of the New York Customhouse, through which passed nearly half of the federal government's revenue. Swartwout absconded with more than $1 million in 1838.

Jackson is usually charged with bringing the "spoils system" into American politics. That was the result, though not his intent. He always claimed, and evidently believed, that he had introduced greater efficiency and economy into government. He had, indeed, broken the hold of a bureaucratic clique on federal offices and thrown them open to all comers. The result was a democratization of public service at a temporary sacrifice in efficiency and honesty, though

Jackson later found capable subordinates who instituted important administrative reforms. Jackson claimed the credit for returning the opportunity for office to the people at large, but he also deserved the responsibility for opening the way to manipulation of the federal bureaucracy for purely partisan purposes.

Indian Affairs: An Aggressive Policy

With his purge of the officeholders under way, Jackson bent his energies toward removing American Indians, particularly the powerful Southern tribes, beyond the frontier of white settlement. In its Indian relations, the federal government had hitherto continued the early practice of treating the tribes as though they were foreign nations, while reserving to itself the abstract right of ultimate sovereignty. As a frontier negotiator, Jackson had protested this anomaly, claiming that the treaty form clothed the tribes with the trappings of an independent sovereignty that they did not really possess. Nevertheless, the practice continued.

Jurisdictional conflict between the tribes and the government was avoided simply by inducing them to remove whenever white advances created a demand for their land and threatened their tribal integrity. Just as Jackson took office, the underlying issue was finally joined. The Cherokees, having acquired many of the attainments of white civilization, asserted sovereignty over their territory in Georgia and adjacent states and called on the federal government to defend them under treaty obligations. Georgia countered by formally extending its laws over all the state's Cherokee domain. Alabama and Mississippi followed by extending state jurisdiction over their Choctaw, Chickasaw, and Creek lands.

Faced with a direct contradiction between federal treaty stipulations and state sovereignty, Jackson came down unhesitatingly on the side of the latter. The government had no right to intercede on the Cherokees' behalf against Georgia, he announced; if the Indians wished to retain their tribal government and

---

Excerpt from Andrew Jackson's first State of the Union address, regarding the removal of American Indian tribes to lands west of the Mississippi, December 8, 1829:

I suggest for your consideration the propriety of setting apart an ample district west of the Mississippi, and without the limits of any State or Territory now formed, to be guaranteed to the Indian tribes as long as they shall occupy it, each tribe having a distinct control over the portion designated for its use. There they may be secured in the enjoyment of governments of their own choice, subject to no other control from the United States than such as may be necessary to preserve peace on the frontier and between the several tribes. There the benevolent may endeavor to teach them the arts of civilization, and, by promoting union and harmony among them, to raise up an interesting commonwealth, destined to perpetuate the race and to attest the humanity and justice of this Government.

This emigration should be voluntary, for it would be as cruel as unjust to compel the aborigines to abandon the graves of their fathers and seek a home in a distant land. But they should be distinctly informed that if they remain within the limits of the States they must be subject to their laws. In return for their obedience as individuals they will without doubt be protected in the enjoyment of those possessions which they have improved by their industry. But it seems to me visionary to suppose that in this state of things claims can be allowed on tracts of country on which they have neither dwelt nor made improvements, merely because they have seen them from the mountain or passed them in the chase. Submitting to the laws of the States, and receiving, like other citizens, protection in their persons and property, they will ere long become merged in the mass of our population.

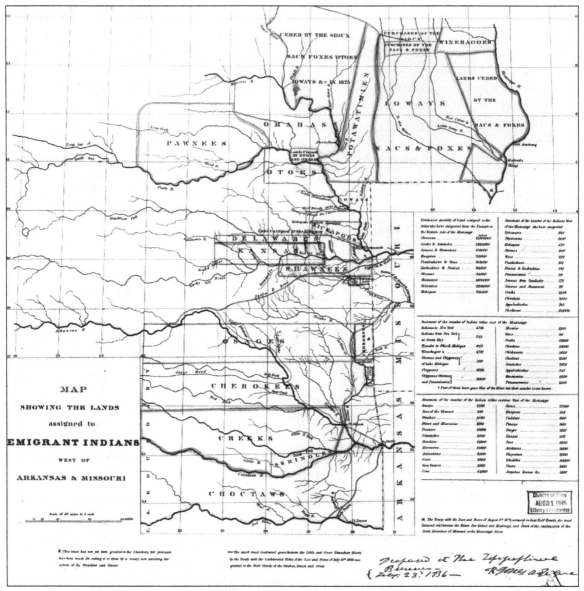

A map of the lands assigned to American Indian tribes in 1836. *(Library of Congress)*

landownership, they must remove outside the state. To facilitate the removal, Jackson induced Congress in May, 1830, to pass a bill empowering him to lay off new American Indian homelands west of the Mississippi, exchange them for current tribal holdings, purchase the Indians' capital improvements, and pay the costs of their westward transportation. With this authority, Jackson departed for Tennessee in June to conduct the initial negotiations in person.

To American Indians, Jackson presented a simple alternative: Submit to state authority or remove beyond the Mississippi. The Chickasaws met Jackson near Nashville and agreed to emigrate. The Choctaws followed in September, treating with Jackson's intimates John Henry Eaton and John Coffee. The Creeks and Cherokees refused to come in, preferring to seek judicial support for their treaty rights, but after holding out two more years, the Creeks capitulated in March, 1832.

Only the Cherokees resisted to the bitter end. In *Cherokee Nation v. Georgia* (1831) and *Worcester v. Georgia* (1832), the Supreme Court upheld the Cherokees' independence from state authority, but the decisions pointed out no practical course of resistance to Georgia's encroachments. Tacitly encouraged by Jackson, Georgia ignored the rulings. Still, the Cherokees, led by Chief John Ross, refused to remove. Jackson cultivated a minority faction within the tribe, and with this rump he negotiated a removal treaty in 1835. Under its authority, the resisting Cherokees were rounded up and removed by force after Jackson left office in the infamous Trail of Tears.

Meanwhile, dozens of similar treaties closed out the remaining pockets of American Indian settlement in other states and territories east of the Mississippi. A short military campaign on the upper Mississippi quelled resistance by Black Hawk's band of Sacs and Foxes in 1832, and in 1835, a long and bloody war to subdue the Seminoles in Florida began. Most of the tribes went without resistance.

Granted the coercion and sometimes trickery that produced them, most of the removal treaties were fair, even generous. Their execution was miserable. The treaties included elaborate provisions to ensure fair payment for American Indian lands and goods, safe transportation to the West and sustenance on arrival, and protection for the property of those individuals who chose to remain behind under state jurisdiction. These safeguards collapsed under pressure from corrupt contractors, unscrupulous traders, and white trespassers backed by state authorities. Federal officials' efforts to protect the tribes were further hamstrung by the Jackson administration's drive for economy and its desire to avoid confrontation with state governments. For this abysmal record, Jackson bore ultimate responsibility. Even under the

best of circumstances, the logistics of the gigantic removal operation would have taxed the federal government's limited resources. Jackson did not countenance its inadequacies, but he did little to prevent or correct them. Though usually a stickler for the precise performance of formal obligations, he allowed his administration to enter into engagements with American Indians that it was manifestly unprepared to fulfill. The precepts of Jackson's Indian policy differed little from those of his predecessors. Like previous presidents, he regarded American Indians as children and believed that only through an extended tutelage in quarantine from white society could they absorb civilization and thus escape ultimate extinction. Yet while his predecessors undertook to uproot the tribes only in response to pressing white demand for their land, Jackson anticipated that demand, and by his posture he did much to encourage it. He made removal of American Indians, a peripheral concern in previous administrations, a central priority of his own. Inevitably, his impatience to remove the tribes encouraged other men who desired the same end and were not scrupulous as to means.

Petticoat Politics and the Nullification Controversy

Meanwhile, Jackson's cabinet was embroiling him in difficulties. Shortly before the inauguration, John Henry Eaton, his secretary of war, had married Peggy O'Neale, the daughter of a Washington boardinghouse keeper. Peggy's previous husband, a naval purser, had committed suicide under suspicious circumstances only shortly before her marriage to Eaton. Scandalous rumors circulated about Peggy's sexual promiscuity, and Washington's formal society refused to accept her. Among those who collaborated in snubbing her were the wives of cabinet secretaries Ingham, Branch, and Berrien.

Jackson came charging to Peggy's defense. Believing her innocent, he divined a deeper plot to drive Eaton from his cabinet, isolate himself among strangers, and control his administration. At first, he blamed Henry Clay's partisans, but his suspicions soon fixed on his vice president, John C. Calhoun, whose wife, Floride, was among Peggy's persecutors. To cement Jackson's convictions, the old controversy over his Seminole campaign of 1818 suddenly flared up again. In the spring of 1830, Jackson learned that Calhoun, as secretary of war under Monroe, had privately advocated disciplining Jackson for exceeding his orders while publicly posturing as his defender. Jackson now accused Calhoun of treachery, initiating an angry correspondence that ended in the severance of social relations between the two chief officers of the government.

Secretary of State Van Buren, who had no wife to contend with, also sided with Peggy Eaton's defenders, and the controversy over her morals became the vehicle for a struggle for supremacy in the administration between him and Calhoun. Both men were aspirants to the presidential succession; further, they represented competing, though loosely defined, branches of the Jackson electoral coalition. Both opposed the nationalizing "American System" policy of a protective tariff and federal subsidies for road and canal construction (known as internal improvements) espoused by Henry Clay and embraced by the previous Adams administration, but their opposition rested on very different grounds.

Calhoun represented a group of politicians, in his home state of South Carolina and throughout the plantation South, whose opposition to the American System rested on essentially sectional motives. The central burden of their complaint was the protective tariff. They saw it as the culprit for all the South's economic ills, especially the stagnation in cotton prices, and as a humiliating reminder of their inferior and threatened position in the Union. An unheeding Congress had raised the tariff in 1824 and again in 1828 despite their an-

guished protests. As they saw it, the affront was not only to their pride and pocketbooks but also to their very way of life, for the emergence of a small but vocal northern antislavery movement had raised the specter of a strong central government controlled by a sectional antislavery majority. Though the Calhounites sought refuge in states' rights, they were not doctrinaire strict constructionists. They opposed internal improvement expenditures mainly because these created a demand for tariff revenues, and some of them defended the constitutionality of the federally chartered Bank of the United States.

Against the tariff menace, Calhoun had conceived of a procedural remedy. He and his radical cohorts considered the current tariff unconstitutional; although federal taxation of imports was clearly authorized by the Constitution, the underlying purpose — to foster American manufactures — in their opinion was not. Building on the Jeffersonian notion of a state's right to protect its own citizens from federal tyranny, Calhoun elucidated a process by which a state could formally nullify an unconstitutional federal law and prevent its enforcement. Though he had not yet publicly avowed his nullification doctrine, Calhoun was known as its author by 1830.

Van Buren's opposition to the American System came from a different quarter. He was not against a protective tariff; indeed, he had helped engineer the tariff of 1828 that so outraged the plantation South. Van Buren's political musings lay in the direction of resurrecting the old transsectional Jeffersonian Republican Party. To do so would require conciliation on the tariff, but the key in Van Buren's mind would be to return to Jeffersonian strict constructionism — in particular, to the party's traditional antagonism to federal internal improvements and a national bank.

Where Jackson stood on these questions no one yet knew. His electoral coalition had embraced not only all the American System's op-

John C. Calhoun. *(Library of Congress)*

ponents but also many of its staunch advocates in Pennsylvania and the Northwest. Jackson himself had ducked the tariff and internal improvement issues in the 1828 campaign, and his previous record was hard to read. He claimed allegiance to the old Republican Party and its strict constructionist doctrines. As a Westerner, a strident nationalist, and a military man, however, he had also in the past supported a protective tariff to make the United States industrially self-sufficient in wartime, along with internal improvements to strengthen the frontier and facilitate military movements.

Actually, Jackson's private views were quite close to Van Buren's. Like Van Buren, he accepted the constitutionality and, within limits, the wisdom of protective tariffs. He also nursed a deep animus against the Bank of the United States. Though in other areas he had once inclined toward constitutional latitudinarianism, the transgressions of the Monroe and Adams administrations convinced him of the urgent need to return the government to its original

simplicity and purity. That meant clamping the lid on mushrooming internal improvement expenditures and returning to strict economy in government. Jackson craved the honor of presiding over the extinction of the national debt, already much reduced by previous administrations from its high following the War of 1812.

Hence, as petticoat politics threw Jackson and Van Buren together, they found grounds of agreement that extended far beyond their common faith in Peggy Eaton's moral character. Though a cotton planter and slaveholder himself, Jackson decried Calhoun's brand of narrow sectionalist politics. Nullification he regarded as incipient treason, a prelude to disunion and civil war. At a political dinner in April, 1830, he pronounced his ban on it by staring at Calhoun and toasting, "Our federal Union: *It must be preserved.*"

Jackson's first move to clarify his policy came in May, 1830. When Congress convened the previous December, he had urged moderation on both the tariff and internal improvements, and on sectional conciliation in general. Ignoring his plea for restraint, the majority in Congress pushed through several major internal improvement subsidies, including three in the form of purchases in the stock of private road and canal companies. Jackson vetoed all three, singling out for an explanatory message the most politically vulnerable, a bill to subscribe $50,000 for construction of the Maysville Road in Henry Clay's home state of Kentucky. Van Buren helped write the veto message, which questioned the constitutionality of internal improvement subsidies and complained that they would exacerbate sectional tensions and postpone payment of the national debt. Southern antitariffites greeted the veto with apprehensive applause. They approved its tendency but suspected quite correctly that Jackson was not entirely in their camp. Indeed, his compromise proposal to distribute some federal funds directly to the states for their own use struck Calhoun and many Southerners as even more objectionable than direct federal internal improvement spending.

Calhoun's estrangement from Jackson deepened with the establishment of the *Washington Globe* in December, 1830, as the administration's newspaper office. A different paper, the *United States Telegraph*, had done excellent service as Jackson's campaign organ and had hitherto served as his official mouthpiece, but the *United States Telegraph*'s editor, Duff Green, was wholly devoted to Calhoun, and Jackson thought that his columns displayed too much sympathy with nullification and the Bank of the United States. To supplant him, Jackson brought in Francis Preston Blair of Kentucky. Closely associated with Blair in founding the *Washington Globe* was another Kentuckian, treasury auditor Amos Kendall. Blair and Kendall were not Van Buren's men, but like Van Buren, and unlike Green or Calhoun, they gave Jackson their complete loyalty and won his confidence in return. Together with a few other intimates—most notably Jackson's nephew and private secretary, Andrew Jackson Donelson, and his political manager, William B. Lewis—they formed a ring of confidential advisers who gave Jackson invaluable assistance in formulating his policies and presenting them to the public. Jackson's foes derisively dubbed them the Kitchen Cabinet.

A New Cabinet and a New Conception of Its Role

While Jackson drew closer to Van Buren, the Eaton controversy smoldered on. Jackson's own household split over Peggy's acceptability, and his niece, White House hostess Emily Donelson, was banished to Tennessee for refusing to call on her. Her husband, private secretary Donelson, was at one point reduced to communicating by letter with Jackson even while living with him at the White House. Finally, to avoid utter paralysis of the administration, Van Buren and Eaton offered to resign in the spring of 1831. Jackson seized the occasion to demand the resignations of the opposing secretaries, Ingham, Branch, and Berrien. In their place, he appointed an entirely new cabinet.

The consequences of this move were momentous. Van Buren remained in Jackson's confidence as chief counselor and expected running mate in 1832. Calhoun and his faction were formally cast out. After two years of distraction and division, the administration was now prepared to steer a direct and unimpeded course. No less important, Jackson had liberated himself from the cabinet intrigues that had ensnared his own and previous administrations. Henceforth, his official advisers would be men he chose to implement his own ideas, not factional emissaries planted there to influence him. The most successful of Jackson's later cabinet secretaries—Roger Taney, Lewis Cass, Levi Woodbury, and Amos Kendall—were workhorses who administered their departments efficiently, offered advice when asked, accepted direction when given, and stood clear of political intrigue. Those who could not harmonize with administration policy were expected to keep quiet, invited to resign, or, if necessary, simply dismissed. For the remainder of his tenure, Jackson dominated his administration as no president had before, and he pioneered for future generations the conception of the cabinet as a subordinate agent of the presidential will.

Jackson vs. the Bank of the United States

The cabinet reconstruction of 1831 cleared the way for Jackson's next major policy move—his assault on the Bank of the United States. The bank had received a twenty-year charter from Congress in 1816. It was a private corporation, created for public purposes. The government held one-fifth of its stock and one-fifth of the seats on its board of directors. The bank's notes were legal tender for debts due the United States, and its branches served as exclusive federal depositories in their respective cities. The charter obliged the bank to perform various services, including transferring and disbursing federal funds without charge; in return, the charter guaranteed that Congress would create no competing institution.

Since its creation, the bank had provided a national currency through its notes, and in other ways had made itself useful to the Treasury. Jackson, however, was one of many who had never become reconciled either to the bank's constitutionality or to its financial power. Over his cabinet's objections, Jackson announced his opposition to a recharter of the bank in his very first message to Congress, and he had since recommended replacing the existing bank with a wholly governmental agency.

The bank's charter was due to expire in 1836.

In January, 1832, its president, Nicholas Biddle, determined to apply for a recharter under the urging of Senators Daniel Webster of Massachusetts and Henry Clay of Kentucky, who were looking for an issue against Jackson in the pending presidential race. The recharter bill duly passed Congress, and on July 10, Jackson vetoed it.

The veto message, one of the most significant state papers in American history, was less an argument directed at Congress than a political manifesto to the American people. Jackson recited his constitutional objections to the bank and introduced some peculiar economic arguments against it, chiefly criticizing foreign own-

---

Excerpts from Andrew Jackson's bank veto message regarding the Bank of the United States, July 10, 1832:

A bank of the United States is in many respects convenient for the Government and useful to the people.... I sincerely regret that in the act before me [to renew the Bank of the United States] I can perceive none of those modifications of the bank charter which are necessary, in my opinion, to make it compatible with justice, with sound policy, or with the Constitution of our country.

The Bank of the United States enjoys an exclusive privilege of banking under the authority of the General Government.... The powers, privileges, and favors bestowed upon it in the original charter, by increasing the value of the stock far above its par value, operated as a gratuity of many millions to the stock-holders.

Every monopoly and all exclusive privileges are granted at the expense of the public, which ought to receive a fair equivalent. The many millions which this act proposes to bestow on the stockholders of the existing bank must come directly or indirectly out of the earnings of the American people. It is due to them, therefore, if their Government sell monopolies and exclusive privileges, that they should at least exact for them as much as they are worth in open market. . . .

But this act does not permit competition in the purchase of this monopoly. It seems to be predicated on the erroneous idea that the present stockholders have a prescriptive right not only to the favor but to the bounty of Government. It appears that more than a fourth part of the stock is held by foreigners and the residue is held by a few hundred of our own citizens, chiefly of the richest class. For their benefit does this act exclude the whole American people from competition in the purchase of this monopoly and dispose of it for many millions less than it is worth. This seems the less excusable because some of our citizens not now stockholders petitioned that the door of competition might be opened, and offered to take a charter on terms much more favorable to the Government and country. . . .

But this proposition, although made by men whose aggregate wealth is believed to be equal to all the private stock in the existing bank, has been set aside, and the bounty of our Government is proposed to be again bestowed on the few who have been fortunate enough to secure the stock and at this moment wield the power of the existing institution. I cannot perceive the justice or policy of this course.

---

ership of some of its stock. (On any rational grounds, foreign investment in the underdeveloped American economy was to be welcomed, not scorned.) The crux of the message, however, was its attack on the special privileges that accrued to the bank's stockholders from their official connection to the government. Jackson did not attack wealth as such — he issued no call for class warfare or redistribution of private assets — but he condemned the addition of public privilege to private advantages. He also set forth an alternative vision of the government as a neutral arbiter in the economy, neither assisting nor obstructing the accumulation of private fortune, intervening only where necessary to protect basic rights. Jackson's earlier congressional messages and the Maysville Road veto had intimated this fundamental theme; the bank veto stated it powerfully and definitively.

Historians have debated whether Jackson attuned his blast against the bank to the ears of Western farmers, Northeastern mechanics and laborers, or rising entrepreneurs. In fact, it was aimed at no particular class or section. Rather, it was an appeal to all of society's outsiders — to anyone who had to make his way without benefit of inherited fortune; to those who worked with their hands, owned no stock in corporations, and to whom no congressman hearkened; to those outside the commercial community that connected every city and town and that in Jackson's mind had controlled the country before his election. It was a convincing appeal because it was heartfelt. Though Jackson's own success qualified him for admission to the existing centers of political and economic power, he had never felt at home there. He had run for president in 1824 against the regular political establishment, and even in 1828, his candidacy had secured only the grudging approval of some of its members. Not a member of the bankers' circle himself, he felt the outsider's resentment against its manipulation of public power for private purposes. Hence it was with no sense of incongruity that Jackson, a well-to-do planter and slave-

holder, cast himself as the tribune of the people against the aristocracy of wealth and power.

Jackson and his opponents alike seized on the bank veto as the central issue of the 1832 presidential campaign. The American System supporters, under the name of National Republicans, nominated Henry Clay and savaged the veto for its display of economic ignorance, its demagogic appeal to the masses, and its obstruction of the people's will as expressed through their elected representatives in Congress. The campaign was complicated by the participation of two splinter groups: the anti-Masons in the Northeast, whom the National Republicans vainly tried to absorb, and the Southern antitariffites. After failing to substitute Philip Barbour of Virginia for Van Buren as vice presidential candidate, most of the latter supported the Jackson ticket, but South Carolina ominously refused its vote to any of the national candidates.

The election returns spelled a virtual repeat of 1828. Jackson again carried New York, Pennsylvania, and all the West and South, except South Carolina and Clay's home state of Kentucky. Whether the bank veto — or any other specific issue — cost or gained Jackson votes is uncertain. His foes traced their defeat solely to his untouchable personal popularity; Jackson himself read it as a popular ratification of his policies.

A Challenge from South Carolina: Resolving the Nullification Crisis

Jackson planned a further attack on the Bank of the United States, but before he could pursue it he faced a crisis in South Carolina. There, within days after the election, a state constitutional convention formally declared the tariff laws null and void and initiated steps to prevent the collection of customs duties within the state.

Nullification was a desperate move. A series of congressional ploys against the tariff in Jackson's first term had all failed, and South Carolinians no longer saw hope for relief from Washington, D.C. Congress had indeed reduced some duties earlier in the year, and with the national debt approaching extinction, Jackson now called for still further reduction. Even as it lowered some rates, however, the tariff of 1832 enshrined the protective principle, and a majority in Congress apparently regarded the issue as settled. South Carolinians felt themselves thrown back on their own resources.

To Jackson and to most Americans, including a majority of antitariffites outside South Carolina, nullification was an inadmissible recourse. Inclined by nature to personalize every dispute, Jackson traced South Carolina's action to Calhoun's corrupt ambition to rule at home if he could not rule in Washington, D.C. Still, Jackson also saw clearly the fundamental principle at stake. Calhoun claimed that nullification would actually save the Union, by providing a method short of state secession for resisting the federal government's unconstitutional excesses. To Jackson, this was nonsense. He was a strict constructionist, an advocate of limited government, and, to that extent, a states' rights advocate. The reserved rights of the states, however, did not in his opinion extend to defying legitimate federal authority. The tariff was an act of Congress duly and lawfully passed, and its constitutionality, though denied by South Carolina, had never been doubted by Congresses, presidents, or the Supreme Court. If a state could unilaterally repudiate federal laws and ban the collection of federal taxes, then the Union was no Union at all. To Jackson, nullification was tantamount to secession, and secession was treason.

Jackson was prepared to uphold federal authority in South Carolina at the point of a gun, but he preferred peaceful remedies or, if there were to be violence, that the state should strike the first blow. He quietly prepared for military action yet also pointed the way to accommodation. He again urged Congress to reduce the tariff, then followed with a proclamation warning South Carolinians to abjure their folly. In ringing phrases, the proclamation enunciated Jackson's conception of the United States as an indissoluble nation, not a mere league of sovereign states. Jackson followed up the proclamation by asking Congress for legislation to enforce the collection of customs duties over South Carolina's legal obstructions.

With Jackson applying pressure from all sides, the issue was successfully compromised. Congress passed a "force bill," giving Jackson the coercive powers he requested, but it simultaneously adopted a new tariff, which reduced duties to a uniform low rate over the next nine years. South Carolina accepted the new tariff and rescinded its ordinance of nullification. The adroit solution allowed all sides to claim victory, while Jackson basked in public acclaim throughout the North for his firmness in preserving the Union. What popularity he gained in the North, however, he lost in the South. The proclamation and the force bill angered Southern states' rights advocates. They gave credit for resolving the crisis, not to Jackson, but to Clay, who had introduced the compromise tariff bill, and to Calhoun, who had supported it.

Jackson's Second Term: The Bank War

The resolution of the nullification crisis in March, 1833, brought Jackson's first term to an end. His record thus far was one of signal success. He had survived the incapacitating Eaton affair and established control over his administration, set the removal of American Indians in train, won a resounding reelection over the opposition's best candidate, and maneuvered his man Van Buren into position to succeed him. More important, by circumscribing internal improvements and orchestrating the tariff settlement, he had finally got clear of the sectional wrangling that had paralyzed the Adams administration and threatened to rip apart the Union. He had presided over the extinction of the national debt and revitalized the old Jeffersonian doctrine of strict construction and limited government.

Yet, in Jackson's mind, his tack was only half

The Bank War—"Downfall of the Mother Bank." *(Library of Congress)*

finished. His victories thus far were merely personal and incomplete. He had yet to convert his own electoral mandate into an effective instrument of policy. Congress was uncooperative. Politicians of varying creeds were all too willing to attach themselves to his name, and Jackson had repeatedly endured the frustration of seeing men elected under his banner defy his most cherished recommendations. The Senate had rejected a string of important appointments, including even Van Buren himself for minister to Great Britain after the cabinet breakup of 1831. Congress's eagerness to spend and susceptibility to lobbying pressure had forced Jackson to employ vetoes as his chief instruments of policy.

Jackson never doubted that the American people were on his side. He expected popular vindication for everything that he did, and thus far his confidence had been justified. In the face

of his own resounding public support, Congress's ungovernability demanded explanation. By early 1833, Jackson had identified the culprit and had begun to see all of his myriad political antagonists as instruments of one central foe. The reconciliation of Clay and Calhoun, which he had anticipated long before, confirmed his suspicions; though directly opposed to each other on the sectional issues of Jackson's first term (with Jackson himself in the middle), they were both in his mind instruments of the concentrated economic and political power directed by that "hydra of corruption," the Bank of the United States.

News of the bank's activities since his veto of its recharter in 1832 outraged Jackson. The bank had been created and endowed with monopolistic privileges to serve the government's own needs, not those of its stockholders or directorate. As a creature of the government, the bank, therefore, in Jackson's eyes, had no right to an independent political character, no right to attempt to influence public policy even in defense of its own existence. Yet the bank had lavishly pamphleteered in its own defense (and implicitly against Jackson's reelection) in the 1832 campaign and had lent freely to congressmen and newspaper editors. Despite the election verdict of 1832, informants warned Jackson that bank president Nicholas Biddle still aimed to procure a recharter.

Jackson determined to draw the bank's fangs. The bank's enormous economic and political leverage stemmed largely from its role as the depository of federal funds. The government deposits augmented the bank's own capital and enabled it to restrain the lending of state banks by gathering and presenting their notes for redemption in specie. Jackson therefore fixed on withdrawing the deposits as the surest way to disarm the bank for the three years remaining under its original charter.

Removing the deposits was a maneuver that required some delicacy. Legal authority to do it lay with the treasury secretary, not the president, and the House of Representatives had only recently voted by 109 to 46 that the deposits were safe where they were. In the spring of 1833, Jackson carefully canvassed his cabinet and confidential advisers on removal; most of them opposed it, but he got the support and arguments that he needed from Attorney General Roger Taney. Jackson next dispatched Amos Kendall on a mission to recruit state banks to accept the federal deposits. On Kendall's return, Jackson announced to the cabinet his decision to begin depositing federal revenues with selected state banks, simultaneously drawing down the government's balances in the Bank of the United States.

Here, a sticking point appeared. Treasury Secretary William John Duane, who alone possessed legal authority to order the change, refused to do it. He also refused to resign, so Jackson dismissed him and put Taney in his place.

Taney duly issued the necessary order, and the drawdown, or removal, commenced on October 1. It was largely complete by the time Congress convened in early December.

The obstreperousness that Jackson had met from previous Congresses was nothing to the fury that he encountered in this one. A majority in Congress had supported the bank's recharter, but even many of its enemies there could not countenance Jackson's method of proceeding against it. Under the law, the secretary of the treasury, though an appointee of the president and member of his cabinet, was a distinct agent who, unlike other department heads, reported directly to Congress. Jackson's dismissal of Duane therefore looked like a bold stroke to draw all power over the federal purse into his own hands, and his hasty removal of the deposits seemed calculated to preempt action by Congress on a matter rightfully under its own authority. Moreover, Jackson appeared to be recklessly tampering with the nation's finances, removing control over the money supply from the responsible and lawfully sanctioned hands of the Bank of the United States to an untried, unregulated, and perhaps thoroughly irresponsible collection of state bankers. Jackson himself spoke of the arrangement with the state banks as an "experiment." Naturally, the removal forced the bank to curtail its widespread loans, and whereas Jackson and his allies accused it of exaggerating the contraction for political effect, the commercial community blamed the resulting distress on the president himself.

In the 1833-1834 congressional session, known as the "panic session," the deposit issue finally prompted Jackson's enemies to coalesce into a coherent political grouping. They called themselves Whigs, the name of British opponents of royal prerogative, to denote their opposition to Jackson's executive sway. Although political expediency obviously influenced the cooperation of men so different in principle as Clay and Calhoun, a genuine unity of outlook underlay the anti-Jackson coalition. The Whigs saw in Jackson the same danger that he saw in the bank—the threat of an unbridled centralized power, wielding sufficient money and influence to overawe or corrupt the opposition and ultimately to destroy the substance, if not the form, of republican government. It was true that Jackson claimed both popular mandate and constitutional sanction for his actions—but tyrants have ever spoken in the name of the people. Also, Jackson's assertions of presidential authority, though made familiar to the modern ear by later experience, sounded positively dangerous to men accustomed to legislative supremacy in government.

Fortunately for Jackson, his adversaries overplayed their hand. While denunciations raged in Congress, Biddle carried the bank's financial contraction beyond what was necessary, in an undisguised effort to force a recharter on Congress and the president. The maneuver served only to confirm Jackson's strictures against the bank's unwarranted power over the national economy. The House of Representatives refused to support either recharter or the restoration of the deposits, forcing the Whig majority in the Senate to wage battle on peripheral ground. The Senate rejected Jackson's nominations for the government seats on the bank's board of directors, rejected Taney as secretary of the treasury, and on March 28, 1834, adopted Clay's resolution that "the President, in the late Executive proceedings in relation to the public revenue, has assumed upon himself authority and power not conferred by the Constitution and laws, but in derogation of both."

To this unprecedented censure, Jackson returned a formal protest, complaining that the Senate had neither specified the grounds of his offense nor followed the constitutional process of impeachment. The Senate rejected the protest as an abridgment of its own freedom of expression. The Whigs, however, could do no more. The panic eased as the congressional session closed, and the bank, defeated, began preparations to wind up its affairs.

The Bank War aroused violent political passions on both sides. The future not only of the bank but also of the American system of government seemed to ride on the outcome. For Jackson, his struggle took on even religious significance; he saw himself serving "the Lord" against "the worshippers of the golden Calf." Partisans on both sides attributed the vilest motives to their adversaries. Biddle privately referred to the president and his advisers as "these miserable people," whereas Jackson raged against "reckless and corrupt" United States senators.

The right and wrong of the Bank War are difficult to sort out centuries later. The verdict depends more on one's point of view than on any dispute over facts. The bank's defenders, then and later, argued that its management had been prudent and responsible. The bank had regulated credit and the currency precisely as Congress had chartered it to do, and did it far more efficiently than any substitute Jackson was prepared to offer. To the Whigs, the president's wanton destruction of the one great stabilizing influence in the economy was thus unpardonably ignorant at best, criminally vicious at worst.

To Jackson, such arguments were essentially irrelevant. Useful or not, the bank was illegitimate: a private institution, unsanctioned by the Constitution, employing public funds and public power to serve the ends not of the government or the people but of its own wealthy, privileged stockholders. Jackson believed that the country could do without the bank, but his fundamental grievance against it was political, not economic.

Between these opposing views no real accommodation was possible. The bank's dual public and private functions provided endless ground for misunderstanding. If it expanded its loans, Jackson accused it of political bribery; if it contracted, of blackmail. The bank's dealings with congressmen and editors, damning evidence of corruption in Jackson's eyes, were from a less malign viewpoint simple and sound business transactions. Jackson demanded reports of the bank's transactions from the government directors, in fulfillment of their public office; to the rest of the directorate, the reports were violations of bankers' confidence that justified excluding the government directors from participation in the bank's deliberations and access to its books. In these circumstances, a true noninvolvement in politics, to which Biddle had originally adhered, proved impossible to maintain, and if the bank were not the partisan agency that Jackson claimed it to be at the beginning of the Bank War, it had certainly become so by its end.

Solidifying the Democratic Party

The Bank War furnished the opportunity Jackson and his advisers had long been seeking to shape his adherents into a unitary political organization. Opposition to the Bank of the United States became the first test for membership in the new Democratic Party, and as Jackson's own thinking on monetary policy progressed, that test was expanded to include opposition to any central bank, then to banking in general. Jackson himself by mid-1834 had come to advocate stripping banks of their monetary function entirely, and replacing their notes of small denomination with gold and silver coin as the medium of everyday exchange. Banks, said Jackson, were essentially swindling machines, whose obscure transactions and erratic currency fluctuations bilked the common man of the rightful fruit of his labor.

On the banking issue thus broadly defined, the Democrats went to the people. Theirs was, again, an appeal to the outsiders in society, to the simple producers—farmers, laborers, mechanics—who did not comprehend the mysteries of banking and finance and resented the commercial community's use of them to control the economy. It was a powerful appeal, for im-

provements in transportation were transforming the American economy, making it more stratified and specialized, more dependent on regional and national markets. Some Americans heralded the new complexity and the opportunities it created, but to others, it foretold the loss of control over their lives, the end of their economic independence and political freedom. To these men, Andrew Jackson stood forth as the champion of their liberties and of the old, simple, republican virtues. As Democrats carried his message to the state and local level, they broadened it to appeal to other outsiders as well, especially to ethnic and religious groups (most notably Irish Catholics) outside the native Protestant mainstream.

Simultaneously, Jackson's men conducted a purge of the party apparatus in the states. The chief instrument of the purge was a campaign to compel the Senate to expunge the censure of Jackson from its journal of proceedings. Thomas Hart Benton of Missouri made an expunging motion in the Senate, and resolutions supporting it were promptly introduced in state legislatures. Legislators and senators who opposed expunging were thrust out of the party. With this weapon, Jackson's lieutenants forced several senators from their seats and finally brought the rebellious Senate to heel. On January 16, 1837, Benton's motion passed the Senate, and the censure was formally expunged.

Foreign Policy

While the expunging campaign progressed, the administration suddenly found its attention diverted to foreign affairs. In dealing with overseas nations, Jackson had contented himself with negotiating trade openings and settling commercial damage claims, mostly left over from the Napoleonic Wars. In these routine endeavors, he had succeeded well. His agents had secured recognition of American claims against Denmark, Spain, France, and Naples, and they had concluded commercial treaties with Turkey, Austria, Russia, Siam (Thailand), Muscat

(Oman), Venezuela, and Chile. Jackson's repudiation of the Adams administration's negotiating position in order to win an agreement with Great Britain on the West Indian colonial trade in 1830 provoked partisan attack, but otherwise his overseas diplomacy was not controversial.

His attempt to collect American claims against France, however, brought the country to the brink of war. In an 1831 treaty, France had agreed to pay 25 million francs for Napoleonic depredations on American shipping. The first installment was due in February, 1833, but the French Chamber of Deputies refused to appropriate the funds. When another year went by without payment, Jackson lost patience and asked Congress to authorize reprisals should France stall any further. The insulted French then demanded explanation of this threat as a condition of payment. Jackson responded in effect that what he said to Congress was none of a foreign power's business. The impasse deepened throughout 1835; ministers were recalled and military preparations begun. Finally, under British urgings, the French decided to construe a conciliatory passage in a later message to Congress as sufficient explanation. France paid the debt, and the crisis, once resolved, left no repercussions.

The same could not be said of Jackson's dealings with Mexico. Jackson had craved Texas for the United States ever since his days as a Tennessee militia general, and he made its purchase from Mexico the first priority of his presidential diplomacy. Given the instability of Mexico's government and its suspicion of American designs, a Texas negotiation required extreme patience and discretion to have any hope of success. The agent Jackson chose, Anthony Butler of Kentucky, possessed neither of those qualities, and Jackson's own careless instructions encouraged Butler's clumsy dabbling in the diplomatic underworld of bribery and personal influence. Butler's machinations, combined with the flow of American settlers into Texas, served only to arouse Mexican apprehensions

that the United States was bent on fomenting a revolution there. In 1835, American emigrants in Texas did revolt successfully against Mexican authority. Jackson prudently declined to back the annexation of the new Texas republic to the United States, or even to recognize its independence from Mexico without prior congressional approval, but his earlier inept efforts to purchase the province had helped to sow the seeds of mutual distrust that erupted into war between the two countries a decade later.

The Rise of the Whigs

Jackson's primary concern as his administration drew toward its close was to ensure that his policies, and particularly his hard-money and antibanking campaign, would continue beyond his own retirement to the Hermitage. He had long before settled on Martin Van Buren as the man best qualified to carry on his work, and he now bent every effort to secure Van Buren's nomination and election to the presidency. It was a difficult battle, for Van Buren was as roundly distrusted as Jackson was loved and revered. Rivals resented Van Buren's closeness to the president, and Democrats and Whigs alike considered him an artful schemer and flatterer. Further, Jackson's own forthright stance on every prominent issue of his long administration, and his vigorous and unprecedented conduct of the executive office itself, had aroused opposition at one time or another in many quarters. Men who could not bear — or did not dare — to disagree directly with Jackson himself were quick to assign responsibility for their grievances to Van Buren. He had become, unwittingly, the universal scapegoat of the Jackson administration.

Given his initial unpopularity and the weight of accumulated complaints against him, Van Buren needed the full weight of Jackson's influence behind his candidacy. Jackson wrote letters, attended political functions (which he had shunned during his own campaign), threatened reprisals on dissenters, and oversaw the Democratic convention that nominated Van Buren in May, 1835. The Whigs, who lacked a central directing head and hence lagged behind the Democrats in party organization, capitalized on the diversity of disgruntlement with Van Buren by encouraging the candidacies of regional favorites. William Henry Harrison of Ohio emerged as their main candidate, but Daniel Webster of Massachusetts and Hugh Lawson White of Tennessee also received Whig backing. Tennessee deserted the Democrats for White, a former Jackson intimate who had gradually fallen out of his confidence. The defection mortified Jackson, and he poured out his bitterest denunciations against White and the Democratic apostates who backed his candidacy.

Van Buren won the election. Even without a national candidate against him, however, he garnered a bare majority of the popular vote, and the real message of the campaign was the rise of the Whigs and Jackson's failure to pass on his own personal popularity to his Democratic successors. The party Van Buren inherited was better disciplined and more clearly focused than the diffuse coalition that had swept Jackson into office eight years before, but it was also smaller. Henceforth, Whigs and Democrats would do battle on nearly equal terms.

A Debased Currency

While working to ensure the succession, Jackson also refined and extended his campaign for hard money. His destruction of the Bank of the United States had inadvertently encouraged the spread of bank currency, as state governments proceeded to fill the void by chartering new banks that issued notes without any central restraint. There was an eager demand for this capital, for a decade of general growth and prosperity had begun to culminate in a speculative land boom. Federal revenue from Western land sales, which had previously hung at $2 million to $3 million annually, leaped to $11 million in 1835 and to $24 million in 1836. Unwanted banknotes of dubious convertibility poured in, producing an embarrassing treasury surplus.

Jackson was appalled at this debasement of the currency, so contrary to his own intentions. He viewed the problem as essentially moral, tracing the profusion of banknotes not to impersonal economic forces but to the unrestrained spirit of speculation and avarice. He called again for the stricter regulation of banking and for the elimination of notes of small denomination, and in July, 1836, he directed the issuance of a specie circular, which required payment in coin for federal lands. In June, Congress did provide statutory regulation of the federal deposit banks and limited their issuance of notes, but, by the same act, disbursed the deposits among a much larger number of banks, then unloaded the treasury surplus by returning it to the state governments as a "deposit"—in form, a loan; in effect, a gift. These measures merely forced a shifting of balances among the banks. Even had they understood it to be necessary, neither Jackson nor Congress possessed the tools for the delicate and perhaps impossible task of easing down an overheated economy. As Jackson prepared to leave office, the nation's financial structure teetered on the edge of a deflationary collapse.

The Impact of Jackson's Presidency

Jackson's quiet departure from the White House in March, 1837, stood in sharp contrast to his tumultuous entrance eight years earlier. The administration's final weeks were calm, almost spiritless. Age and an accumulation of bodily ailments had finally caught up with Jackson; during his last congressional session, he was practically an invalid. Before retiring, however, he roused his strength for one more veto—of a bill overriding the specie circular—and for a farewell address, issued on the day of Martin Van Buren's inauguration as president.

The very act of delivering such an address bespoke Jackson's understanding of the extraordinary importance of his presidency. No chief executive since George Washington had departed office with a formal valedictory. Jackson began humbly, thanking the people for their confidence. In fatherly phrases, he admonished them to cherish the Union, avoid sectional divisions, and preserve the Constitution in its original purity.

Jackson's mood shifted sharply as he went on to discuss banking and currency. He condemned paper money as an engine of oppression in the hands of the bankers. In dark tones, he warned of a conspiracy of "the money power" to control the state and federal governments and subvert the liberties of the people.

In eight years, Jackson had fundamentally reordered the American political landscape. He entered the presidency at the end of a decade when the stresses and hardships of economic development had given rise to sectional conflict over the issues of the tariff and internal improvements. More than any politician of his day, Jackson stood above sectional feelings. Seeing that sectional antagonisms jeopardized the permanence of the Union, he sought with remarkable success to quiet the issues that prompted them. Though the ultimate sectional issue — slavery — began to intrude into politics during his term, the economic questions of the previous decade lost most of their divisive force under his conciliatory influence.

Jackson, however, substituted a new set of demons for the old. In the place of sectional opponents, he identified a new threat to the republic in the commercial oligarchy of bankers, speculators, and chartered corporations. Like many Americans, he was alarmed by the growing complexity and interdependency of the national economy. Interpreting it as a corrupt conspiracy rather than an economic process, he appealed in vivid language for the American people to redeem their traditional liberties and virtues from this alien power.

Jackson's attack on the money power set the tone for a generation of Democratic politicians. At the same time, his conduct of the presidency reshaped the structure of American politics. Elected president on a wave of popular enthusiasm, he had interposed his will against Congress, vetoing more bills than all of his predecessors put together. For justification, he appealed over the head of Congress directly to the mass of people, in the unshakable conviction that they would support him. Reversing a tradition in American politics, he claimed that he as president represented the people directly, whereas Congress represented only special interests. To make this claim effective, to transform his personal popularity into a workable instrument of policy, he and his advisers labored to shape his following into a political party. In thus forging a link between the highest and lowest levels of government, between the people and the president, Jackson elevated the importance of the presidential office and reduced the importance of Congress — especially the Senate — by bringing its members within reach of the party apparatus. At the same time, Jackson's bold measures and political innovations prompted his foes to coalesce into an opposing partisan organization. The Democratic Party was Jackson's child; the antebellum two-party system was his legacy.

Yet with all of his importance to the development of the American political system, Jackson's dominance of an era rested as much on his forceful personality as on his particular achievements. His character, which combined tremendous strengths with appalling weaknesses, inspired devotion from his friends, loathing from his enemies. Contemporaries disagreed violently in their assessment of Jackson, and historians have followed in their paths.

Concluding Perspectives: Jackson the Man

Jackson cut such a titanic figure that both admirers and detractors reckoned him an elemental force rather than a human being. Henry Clay likened him to a tropical tornado. Jackson's determination and willpower impressed friends and enemies alike. Intimates marveled at his fortitude. He suffered constant pain, and he often appeared so feeble that friends feared for his life; yet he met the demands of a brutal work and social schedule. He seemed to keep himself alive by sheer determination, an awesome domination of the will over the flesh. His moods, like the weather, were unpredictable. His violent rages were legendary, yet he could be perfectly cool when the occasion required. White House visitors wnho were expecting to see a growling monster were charmed by his courtly demeanor and pleasant conversation.

Jackson radiated a magnificent self-assurance. Both as a general and as a president, he never admitted the possibility of defeat and never suffered it. His faith in his own ability to master the task at hand, no matter how formidable, mesmerized his associates. He seemed to be without weakness and without fear. Jackson's confidence in himself was an important political asset. It enabled him to overawe his enemies, for few men could face him without blinking; and it drew to his side weaker men, less sure of themselves, who found their strength in him.

Yet Jackson upheld this tremendous strength of character only at great cost in flexibility. He was indeed indomitable, but not infallible; yet, like many of his admirers, he tended to confuse the two. Though he condemned flattery, he was an easy mark for it. He could not take criticism, and he was extraordinarily sensitive to imagined personal slights. He viewed himself entirely too seriously to enjoy or even permit a joke at his own expense; indeed, he seemed to find little humor in anything. Though he made many errors in his long career, he could not acknowledge them, even to himself. He never apologized and rarely explained. His self-righteousness, combined with a wholly unwarranted confidence in the accuracy of his own memory, trapped him in one pointless personal controversy after another, and when he was in the wrong he sometimes stooped to substitute bluster for truth.

Throughout his life, Jackson wore a pair of moral blinders. He saw his own path of duty marked clearly ahead and followed it rigorously, but no alternative perspectives or courses of action ever entered his field of vision. He simply believed that whatever he did was right. Hence, he never learned to accept political disagreement with the equanimity of a Henry Clay or Martin Van Buren. He took all opposition as a personal affront.

Trusting as much in the people's virtue as in his own, he ascribed every victory of an opposition candidate to fraud or deception. Jackson was neither gracious in adversity nor magnanimous in triumph. He railed bitterly after his own defeat in 1824 and Van Buren's in 1840, and he exulted at Whig president William Henry Harrison's sudden death after only one month in office.

Trapped inside his own clear but narrow view of the world, Jackson failed to see the contradictions in his own career, which critics wrongly attributed to conscious hypocrisy. He thought himself modest and humble, though he was neither. He repeated so often the myth that he had never sought public office that he apparently came to believe it, even though his whole career bespoke otherwise. Although outraged at violations of his own confidence, he willingly read others' private mail when it was shown to him. He excoriated the Adams administration for corruption and partisan manipulation of the patronage, failings that were much more evident in his own. Opposed to a strong central government, he greatly strengthened the presidency, its most concentrated locus of power.

The depth of Jackson's emotional engagement in his political career, his unremitting search for personal vindication and for victory over his foes, suggest a character controlled by some deeply seated animus. His enemies—and some later historians—appraised him as a driven, vengeful, self-obsessed man. Yet the traits they condemned were fused with others that inspired reverence and devotion from those who knew him well.

Jackson was a faithful husband and a loving and indulgent father. He lavished affection on the wife and children of his adopted son, Andrew, Jr., and he exhibited endless patience with Andrew's own serious failings. Curiously, Jackson found it much easier to forgive personal shortcomings than political transgressions, and from those who gave him their loyalty he could tolerate almost any fault. He had many wards — relatives and children of deceased comrades — and he gave freely of money for their education and advice to guide their careers. Examples of his private generosity and kindness are legion. Widows and orphans found him an easy touch. He demanded good treatment for his slaves and dismissed overseers who handled them too roughly.

Though he did not join the Presbyterian Church until very late in life, Jackson was a religious man. He cared little for doctrine, but he enjoyed hearing sermons and found consolation in the Bible and devotional literature. He coupled an unquestioning faith in his own destiny with a humble, almost fatalistic submission to the workings of Providence. A simple Christian charity was the centerpiece of his religious practice.

Jackson's mind was quick and forceful, but not subtle. His associates marveled at his ability to cut through to the heart of a difficult subject — which indeed he could do if the argument were reducible to a simple principle of direct action. More complex and sophisticated expositions eluded his comprehension; he dismissed them as trickery. Firm in his political convictions, he saw no need to explore them through systematic thought. With the great moral and intellectual dilemma of his era — the problem of slavery — he never concerned himself; he simply accepted the institution. Characteristically, he interpreted the rising abolitionist agitation as a political ploy to disrupt the Union and the Democratic Party, and on that ground he condemned it.

Jackson had few intellectual or cultural pursuits, though he liked to attend the theater, and few diversions other than horse racing, to which he was passionately devoted. He read mainly newspapers. He had acquired the gentleman planter's expensive tastes in food and wine, along with a sufficient veneer of higher learning to scatter classical allusions (sometimes misplaced) throughout his letters. Contemporaries attested his extraordinary abilities as a conversationalist, but they left little hint of what he talked about besides politics.

Jackson's writing lacked polish, but he had a gift for vigorous expression. He was best with maxims: "Our federal Union: it must be preserved" and "Ask nothing that is not right; submit to nothing that is wrong" were classics, and he repeated them often. With the help of Andrew Jackson Donelson, Jackson kept up a voluminous private correspondence. For aid in formal composition, he relied on Donelson, Van Buren, Kendall, and Blair, plus other advisers of the moment. The nullification proclamation was largely Edward Livingston's work; the farewell address, Roger Taney's. Most of Jackson's major presidential papers were group productions. They were always intended for the public eye, even when addressed to Congress. Measured against the florid standards of that era, Jackson's state papers were masterpieces of clarity and lucidity.

Throughout Jackson's presidency, he yearned for a quiet retirement at the Hermitage, but when the time for it came, he found that he could not let go of politics. Indeed, he was as unprepared as ever to lead the withdrawn life of a country gentleman. He yearned to see his policies carried through and what he called "my fame" upheld. In the financial panic that broke as Jackson left office, President Van Buren required guidance and fortitude. Jackson willingly supplied both. He demanded a complete divorce of the government from the banks and badgered Van Buren and Francis Preston Blair with advice, exhortations, and warnings. He summoned all of his failing energies in behalf of Van Buren's independent treasury plan and his reelection bid in 1840.

William Henry Harrison's defeat of Van Buren staggered Jackson, but he soon found cause for rejoicing in Harrison's death and his successor John Tyler's reversion to Democratic principles on banking and the tariff. To his great satisfaction, Jackson's influence was again required from Washington, D.C., this time in behalf of the annexation of Texas. Ever eager for Texas, Jackson enlisted avidly in the annexation cause and when Van Buren declared against it, he helped set in train the movement to jettison Van Buren in favor of Tennessean James K. Polk for the 1844 Democratic nomination. Before Jackson died, he reaped the final vindication of seeing his loyal disciple Polk installed in the presidency to carry on his work.

Honors and tributes enriched Jackson's retirement. He was the living apostle of democracy, and an endless parade of well-wishers journeyed to the Hermitage to do him homage. Jackson welcomed them all. Though he accepted public tributes with an air of diffident humility, he never tired of them, and in 1840, he dragged himself to New Orleans for an exhausting celebration of the twenty-fifth anniversary of his great military triumph.

Conscious of his historical importance and jealous of his reputation, Jackson occupied much of his spare time in arranging his papers and overseeing preparations for Amos Kendall's projected biography.

Financial worries darkened Jackson's final years. The luckless Andrew, Jr., conjured up debts without end and meeting them gradually drained away Jackson's assets.

In the end, despite his horror of indebtedness, the old chief was driven to borrowing large sums from the faithful Francis Preston Blair. Jackson died in comfort but with his once ample estate heavily encumbered by debt.

Gradually, the weight of age, illness, and worry bore down on Jackson. For years, his health had been precarious, yet he had recovered from the brink so many times that friends half seriously questioned his mortality. Jackson knew better. He had long anticipated death, and he faced it without fear.

In the spring of 1845, his condition worsened, and on June 8 he died, surrounded by family and friends. He was buried at the Hermitage, next to Rachel.

Daniel Feller

Suggested Readings

Cole, Donald B. *The Presidency of Andrew Jackson*. Lawrence: University Press of Kansas, 1993. A thorough, single-volume biography.

Hermitage, The. http://www.thehermitage .com/indexHome.htm. The Web site of the home of Jackson that serves as the primary museum of the president.

Marszalek, John F. *The Petticoat Affair: Manners, Mutiny, and Sex in Andrew Jackson's White House*. New York: Free Press, 1997. Examines Jackson's defense of Peggy Eaton and the results of the controversy on the Jackson administration.

Parton, James. *Life of Andrew Jackson*. 1860. Reprint. New York: Johnson Reprint, 1967. The earliest and biggest scholarly biography and still considered by some historians to be the best.

Remini, Robert V. *Andrew Jackson*. 1969. Reprint. New York: HarperPerennial, 1999. A biography from one of the preeminent historians on Jackson.

_____. *Andrew Jackson: A Bibliography*. Westport, Conn.: Meckler, 1991. Provides a comprehensive listing of primary and secondary sources on the life and presidency of Jackson.

_____. *Andrew Jackson and His Indian Wars*. New York: Viking, 2001. Provides an indepth analysis of Jackson's arguably most controversial act as president—the expulsion of American Indians from the eastern half of the country.

Schlesinger, Arthur. *The Age of Jackson*. Boston: Little, Brown, 1945. Although an older volume, it remains one of the most provocative and influential views of Jackson's historical significance.

Smith, Sam B., Harriet C. Owsley, and Harold D. Moser, eds. *The Papers of Andrew Jackson*. Knoxville: University of Kentucky Press, 1980-   . Began publication in 1980, has several volumes to date, and is projected to be an edition of fifteen volumes.

Wallace, Anthony F. C. *The Long Bitter Trail: Andrew Jackson and the Indians*. New York: Hill and Wang, 1993. Examines the racist attitudes within the Jackson administration that led to the Indian Removal Act.

Watson, Harry L. *"Andrew Jackson vs. Henry Clay": Democracy and Development in Antebellum America*. Boston: Bedford/St. Martin's, 1998. Details the conflict between Jackson and Clay and their differing views on the course of American political development.

Watson, Harry L., and Eric Foner. *Liberty and Power: The Politics of Jacksonian America*. New York: Hill and Wang, 1990. Surveys public life from 1816 to 1848 and shows how social, cultural, and economic factors interacted with politics.

Martin Van Buren

8th President, 1837-1841

Born: December 5, 1782
     Kinderhook, New York
Died: July 24, 1862
     Kinderhook, New York

Political Party: Democratic
Vice President: Richard M. Johnson

Cabinet Members

Secretary of State: John Forsyth
Secretary of the Treasury: Levi Woodbury
Secretary of War: Joel R. Poinsett
Secretary of the Navy: Mahlon Dickerson,
    James K. Paulding
Attorney General: Benjamin Butler, Felix
    Grundy, Henry D. Gilpin
Postmaster General: Amos Kendall, John M.
    Niles

On March 4, 1837, Martin Van Buren became the eighth president of the United States. It was a beautiful early spring day, and great numbers turned out for the occasion. Some lined the route from the White House to the Capitol to see Van Buren and the outgoing president ride by in an open carriage; many others gathered at the East Portico to witness the inaugural ceremonies. Yet a dramatic happening at the end of the ceremonies showed that the crowds belonged to the old president and not the new one: As the inaugural party returned to the carriage, Andrew Jackson was greeted with thunderous cheering and applause. "For once," Thomas Hart Benton later recalled, "the rising was eclipsed by the setting sun." Three days later, President Van Buren escorted Jackson to the rail station, where the old hero began the first leg of his journey back to the Hermitage. Only then, many felt, did the new presidency begin.

Or was it the "third term" of Jackson? Most observers supposed that Van Buren had become president through Jackson's influence and had bound himself to defend the heritage. His preelection pledge "to tread generally in the footsteps of President Jackson" was thus welcomed by Democrats and understood by Whigs in the same light, even though they would at times indulge the temptation to taunt Van Buren for a "footsteps administration." The

Portrait of Martin Van Buren. (*Whitehouse.gov*)

central domestic measure of his presidency, the independent Treasury, followed logically from the policy of his predecessor: Jackson's Bank War had separated the Treasury from the national bank; in response to the panic of 1837, Van Buren divorced Treasury operations from the state banks as well. To him also fell much of the burden for carrying out Jackson's policy of Indian removal. In other ways, however, Van Buren pursued a distinctly different course. More cautious than Jackson, he kept the peace at a time when problems with Mexico and Great Britain might have drawn a bolder spirit into war. With a keen awareness of the sectional tensions generated by abolitionism, he worked, in like manner, for sectional peace. After the stormy events of Jackson's administration, moreover, the new president sought to give the nation a period of repose. A review of Van Buren's earlier career shows that he had helped to shape the heritage he vowed as president to defend.

The Fox of Kinderhook

The long road Van Buren followed from Kinderhook, New York, to the White House also dramatized the remarkable achievements of a self-made man. He was born on December 5, 1782, into the household of Abraham and Hannah Van Buren, both of respectable if undistinguished Dutch stock. From his father, a somewhat improvident farmer and tavern keeper, the son received an amiable temper, robust health, and Republican politics, but not the means for a good education. Ending his formal schooling at fourteen, the young Van Buren read law for the next seven years and then began his own practice in Kinderhook. Once established in the law, he married a childhood playmate, Hannah Hoes, and began a family amounting to four sons before her untimely death in 1819. (Though there were later flirtations and the rumor of a union with Thomas Jefferson's granddaughter, he never remarried.) Meanwhile, a move to Hudson and then to Al-

bany marked growing success in his profession, earning for him a comfortable estate, the respect of his fellow lawyers, and consideration in the 1820's for appointment to the Supreme Court. In default of higher education, the law provided the basic discipline for his mind and served to deepen a conservative instinct to accept the existing arrangements of society. As a public official he was ever disposed, as in his law practice, to react to specific events rather than to shape them.

Politics, along with the law, engaged Van Buren from an early day and opened the pathway to power. Political talk in his father's tavern, revolving around the dramatic struggles in the 1790's between Federalists and Republicans, fired a lifelong passion. During the next two decades, he exhibited a sure instinct for the winning side among the warring factions in New York and reaped, as a reward, appointment as a county judge, election to the state senate, and the commission of attorney general. Attributing his success to the shady arts of management and intrigue, foes condemned him as a "politician by trade," a low-class upstart presuming to enter the political sphere once reserved for gentlemen. Close associates of Van Buren, by contrast, pointed to a keen knowledge of human nature that enabled him to penetrate the motives and foil the designs of his enemies. He possessed as well a remarkable capacity for self-control, a suavity of manners, and a smoothness of style that helped him conciliate friends and relate with good sportsmanship to opponents.

Personal appearance added to the force of his style and lent some measure of support to the image foes cast of him as a "red fox" or "little magician." Fashionably dressed, meticulously groomed, and endowed with grace of movement, he struck most observers as shorter than 5 feet, 6 inches, and this impression remained as obesity overtook him later on. Even more striking was his large round head, bald by the middle years and framed by thick sideburns of sandy

The First Ladies
Hannah Van Buren and
Angelica Singleton Van Buren

Hannah Hoes Van Buren was born on March 8, 1783, in Kinderhook, New York, to Johannes Dircksen Hoes (1753-1789) and Maria Quakenbush (1754-1852). Through both paternal and maternal lines, Hannah and Martin Van Buren were closely related, their ancestors all coming from the small, rural Dutch-speaking community of Kinderhook.

Little is known of Hannah prior to her marriage. Legend has it that she and Martin were sweethearts since childhood. They got married on February 21, 1807, soon after Martin established a law practice with his half brother. Hannah was twenty-four at the time.

The Van Burens had five sons and one daughter who was stillborn: Abraham (1807-1873), John (1810-1866), Martin, Jr. (1812-1855), Winfield Scott (born and died in 1814), and Smith Thompson (1817-1876).

A year after their marriage, Martin and Hannah Van Buren moved from Kinderhook to Hudson, New York, the Columbia County seat. Following his 1812 election to the state senate, the family moved to the state capital of Albany. Martin made many friends in political circles, and Hannah helped entertain them in the family home. She also became involved in local charities through her church.

Slow to recover from the birth of her fifth child in 1817, Hannah died of tuberculosis in Albany on February 5, 1819. She never lived to see her husband elected to the presidency.

For the first year and eight months of the Van Buren administration, no First Lady served in the White House. Van Buren had been a widower for eighteen years and he had no daughters to whom he could assign that role. Following the marriage of his eldest son Abraham to Angelica Singleton, Van Buren designated his new daughter-in-law to assume the hostess role.

Angelica was the daughter of South Carolina planter Richard Singleton and Rebecca Travis Coles Singleton. She was born in Sumter County, South Carolina, on February 13, 1816, and raised there on the family plantation. She attended a prestigious finishing school in Philadelphia.

At a White House dinner with President Van Buren in 1837, she met his eldest son and personal secretary, Captain Abraham Van Buren, a West Point graduate and leader in the Seminole Indian War. Angelica and Abraham married a year later, in November, 1838.

Following their European honeymoon in early 1839, Angelica assumed her White House hostess duties and was widely praised by guests for her grace and hospitality. The president's Whig opponents, however, criticized her for attempting to emulate the royal families of Europe with opulent banquets and plans to decorate the White House while the rest of the country was undergoing its first major economic depression.

Angelica and Abraham had three sons: Singleton, Travis, and Martin III. When the Van Buren administration ended in March, 1841, they alternated residences between Kinderhook and South Carolina. With the outbreak of the Civil War, however, she had divided loyalties. During the war she sent blankets and other supplies to captured Confederate soldiers suffering in prison under deplorable conditions. Angelica died in New York City on December 28, 1878.

Dean M. Shapiro

red and gray hair. Giving further feature to his countenance were big blue penetrating eyes and the ever-present trace of a smile, suggesting benign contentment to some and calculating guile to others. It was the face of a man who might be expected, as one contemporary observed, "to row to his object with muffled oars." Others found in it an explanation for his "noncommittalism," that is, his knack of drawing out the views of others without revealing his own. Van Buren often chuckled at this charge and included one outrageous example of it in his autobiography. When asked if he thought the sun rose in the east, he replied, "I presumed the fact was according to the common impression, but, as I invariably slept until after sun-rise, I could not speak from my own knowledge."

Political success for Van Buren ultimately depended on the power of party. By the first quarter of the nineteenth century, two developments—the triumph of egalitarian ideals and the extension of suffrage to all adult white males—rendered increasingly obsolete older patterns of deference and rule by patrician elites. Permanent party organization and techniques of mass appeal were a response to the new democratic realities, providing a means for mobilizing voters, defining issues, and choosing officials. Politics became a profession and "new men" of politics embraced the opportunity to participate in the governing process. As one of the new men, Van Buren played a central role in party organization. During the decade after the War of 1812, he and close associates forged a disciplined party based on spoils, the secret caucus, and an ethos of absolute loyalty to majority rule. With this organization, soon to be known as the Albany Regency, they were able to challenge their patrician adversary, DeWitt Clinton, and lay a solid base for controlling the state. Claiming lineal descent from Jefferson, they also embraced the old republican ideology.

Elected to the United States Senate in 1821, Van Buren went to Washington, D.C., with the aim of reviving party competition at the national level. The demise of the Federalist Party after the War of 1812 ushered in the so-called Era of Good Feelings, hailed by many as a return to the normal state of affairs. Van Buren, however, saw it as an era of bad feelings: The breakdown of party competition across state and sectional lines fragmented political conflict, led to the Missouri controversy, and assured the election of neo-Federalist, John Quincy Adams, in the disputed presidential contest of 1824. He thus sought to resuscitate the old party alliance of Southern planters and the plain republicans of the North on which Jefferson had built the old Republican Party. As a spokesperson for states' rights and strict construction, Van Buren warned of the consolidationist tendencies in the policies Adams proposed. Meanwhile, he took a leading role in the coalition behind Andrew Jackson to foil the bid of Adams for reelection. He was especially anxious to harness Jackson's enormous popularity for party purposes and to make the election of 1828 a rerun of earlier contests between Federalists and Republicans. Van Buren also ran for governor of New York in 1828 to help the national ticket, and the favorable returns confirmed the wisdom of this move.

After a tenure of three months as governor, Van Buren resigned the post in Albany and returned to Washington, D.C., in early 1829 to join the Jackson administration. There he served in turn as secretary of state, minister to England, and vice president in the second term. As a diplomat he succeeded in opening trade with the British West Indies and in initiating the negotiations that led to French payment of past claims. In domestic affairs, Van Buren exerted little influence over specific policies other than Jackson's opposition to internal improvements. His greatest influence came in the role as confidant to the president, as political interpreter of events, and, most of all, through his efforts to shape Jackson's perception of the presidency in party terms. All earlier presidents, however political and partisan, had clung to the old ideal of the president above party, but starting with

Jackson the president began to see himself as the leader of a party as well as the leader of the nation. In the midst of the tumultuous Bank War, out of which the Whig opposition finally formed, Van Buren summarized for Jackson the statesmanship of a politics of conflict. "Their hatred is the best evidence of your orthodoxy," he assured the president, "and the highest compliment that can be paid to your patriotism." Van Buren saw that party competition was both the inescapable product of a free society and the best means to keep it free.

The great influence Van Buren enjoyed in Jackson's administration predictably inspired opponents to charge that the little magician was at it again. How else, they asked, could a suave New York "politician" gain favor with the "border captain" except by management and intrigue? It was true that Van Buren was not unversed in the arts of flattery; solicitude for Jackson in their private correspondence was matched in public statements with praise for the old hero's virtues. Yet there was something in the relationship that did credit to both men. For all his prudence and caution, Van Buren at times expressed genuine admiration for Jackson's boldness and unflinching courage, his intuitive sense of public opinion, and his ability to command the trust of the people. Jackson also derived great benefit from the relationship. With sensitivity and good taste, Van Buren served as friend and comforter to an often ill and lonely old man. Jackson also depended on his counsel in assessing political situations. While Van Buren was in England, Jackson complained that one adviser could never say no and another "knows nothing of mankind." Most of all, Van Buren was loyal, supporting Jackson's decisions once made with "immovable constancy." Though he initially opposed the Bank War, he assured Jackson in the midst of the battle that "I go with you agt. the world." If this sounded like shameless sycophancy, it expressed even more clearly a political ethic of subordinating private judgment to the will of the party. Even before the political fireworks in Washington, D.C., brought about the fall of John C. Calhoun, whom many took to be the heir apparent, Jackson had privately confided to a friend that Van Buren was worthy of the succession.

The Jackson Succession

With Jackson's support, Van Buren was chosen by the Democratic Party convention in 1832 to be the vice presidential running mate, and four years later he was nominated to succeed Jackson as president. While thus treading in Jackson's steps, he was also following some of his own, for he had done much to shape the party that chose him. A number of political circumstances in 1836 also indicated that he would need to take other steps on his own. Many elements contributed to a pervasive sense of restlessness in the nation. The arising incidence of mob action was directly linked by the Whigs to the Caesarian personality of Jackson and his stormy policies. At the same time a new and strident voice of abolitionism arose in the North. Among other things, its petitions to Congress and the distribution of "inflammatory" propaganda through the mails brought tensions in the South to a new level. One response was the storming of the Charleston post office by a mob; another and more fateful one was the emergence of the argument for slavery as a positive good.

The movement of economic forces enhanced the sense of restlessness and lent new urgency to political debate. A cycle of economic expansion after 1830 mounted to a speculative boom by 1835 and then by the middle of the following year, began to give way to the opposing forces of contraction. Whigs pointed a finger at Jackson's war on the national bank, which, in their view, had exerted a stabilizing influence over the state banks and the currency. More serious for Van Buren was a division within his own party over banking and currency. Senator Thomas Hart Benton spoke for the "hard-

An 1837 cartoon lampoons Van Buren's indecisiveness about his Treasury policy and the influence of former president Andrew Jackson. *(Library of Congress)*

money" Democrats who blamed the economic fluctuations on the state banks, a number of which were being used by the Treasury as depositories. He believed that a greatly enlarged circulation of specie would serve to keep bank paper in check and stabilize the economy. Other Democrats, soon to be called Conservatives, defended the state banks, believing that if properly managed by the Treasury they could at once stabilize the currency and sustain a desirable level of economic growth. Personal ambition gave an added dimension to these intraparty differences. Senator William C. Rives of Virginia, one of the leading Conservatives, felt bitter because he had been passed over for the vice presidential nomination, which went instead to a Western hero of sorts, Colonel Richard M. Johnson of Kentucky, the reputed slayer of the American Indian chief Tecumseh.

Whig strategy in 1836 exploited Van Buren's problems. Instead of uniting behind one candidate, Whigs supported three in the hope that the sectional appeal of each—Senator Hugh Lawson White of Tennessee, General William Henry Harrison of Ohio, and Senator Daniel Webster of Massachusetts—might keep Van Buren from winning an electoral majority and thereby throw the choice of president into the House of Representatives. Making a virtue of their diversity, moreover, Whigs invoked old antiparty ideals for the purpose of condemning Van Buren as a spoilsman politician and the handpicked puppet of Caesar. Finally, they spoke a various language in different parts of the country. In the South, they pictured Van Buren as a covert abolitionist; in the West, as a foppish sycophant in contrast to Harrison, who had defeated the Indians at Tippecanoe; and in the

Northeast, as a proslavery champion and a "Loco Foco," that is, a hard-money man scheming to wreck banking and commerce. Happily for Van Buren, his 170 electoral votes, compared with 124 votes for all of his foes, foiled the Whig strategy.

Van Buren as President: A Call for National Repose

Van Buren entered the White House in 1837 determined to give the nation a breathing spell or, as one adviser put it, to "let the troubled waters subside." To the surprise of many, who considered him the prince of spoilsmen, he made no outright removals from office. If sensitive to the spoilsman charge, he also feared that the competition for jobs might deepen intraparty divisions. He likewise decided to retain Jackson's cabinet, which, in any case, he had played a large role in selecting. For the one vacancy, secretary of the War Department, he turned first to Senator Rives, hoping by the appointment to reassure the South and mollify the senator's disappointment. When Rives refused the appointment, Van Buren gave it to Joel R. Poinsett, a Unionist leader in South Carolina during the nullification crisis.

Van Buren's inaugural address can also be read as a call for national repose. Fifty years after the Constitution was written, he observed, the "great experiment" had proved a success. Most of the dangers that the Founding Fathers feared might wreck the Union had been overcome; now it remained only for the sons to "perpetuate a condition of things so singularly happy." The heroic Fathers had won freedom on the battlefield, ordered it by "inestimable institutions," and left to later generations the task of preservation. To dramatize the unheroic role of preservation remaining to the sons, Van Buren pictured himself as a lesser figure of a later age and invited others to share his reverence for the illustrious predecessors "whose superiors it is our happiness to believe are not found on the executive calendar of any coun-

try." If seen as a bow to the conventional pieties of the day, his self-deprecating position must also be taken as a statesmanlike effort to assess the point at which the nation had arrived.

In this light, he saw only one great danger that remained, namely, the disorganizing effect of abolitionist agitation. Addressing the danger, he reaffirmed a campaign pledge to veto any measure of Congress touching slavery in the District of Columbia. John Quincy Adams, back in the House after his term as president, called Van Buren a "northern man with southern feelings." Van Buren, however, saw himself as a northern man with national feelings, driven by the conviction that the federative Union fashioned in a spirit of concession and that compromise was the highest good.

Maintaining sectional harmony was one of the important achievements of Van Buren's presidency. As the leader of a party, he worked for an accommodation between its Northern and Southern members, and the course he charted while vice president continued after he entered the White House. On the one side, he enlisted the support of Northern Democrats against abolitionism. In concert with leaders in New York, he orchestrated protest meetings condemning the new wave of antislavery agitation. While presiding over the Senate, he cast the deciding vote for Calhoun's bill giving postmasters discretionary power in handling "inflammatory" materials. Behind the scenes in the Capitol, he also supported the so-called gag rule, a procedural rule in the House by which abolitionist petitions would be admitted into the chamber but then tabled.

On the other side, Van Buren persuaded party spokespeople from the South to yield for the time their desire for the annexation of slaveholding Texas. Poinsett, a former minister to Mexico, and Secretary of State John Forsyth of Georgia were among those strongly in favor of Texas, but as good party men they recognized the volatility of the issue in the North and the need to harmonize party councils. When the

183

The Vice President
Richard M. Johnson

Richard Mentor Johnson was born on October 17, 1780, in Beargrass, Kentucky (now Louisville). He attended Transylvania University, where he studied law and was admitted to the Kentucky bar in 1802.

After serving with distinction in the Kentucky State Legislature from 1804 to 1806, he went on to represent his state in the United States House of Representatives in 1806. Johnson returned to Kentucky during the War of 1812 and earned the rank of colonel. He was seriously injured at the Battle of Thames, where he allegedly killed the Indian chief Tecumseh. After the war, Johnson returned to his seat in the House of Representatives, and in 1819, he was elected to the United States Senate.

Around this time, Johnson formed a relationship with his mulatto slave, Julia Chinn, who was his mistress and later his common-law wife. The couple had two children. Johnson was elected vice president in 1836 but was refused renomination by the delegates at the Democratic Convention in 1840.

In 1841, Johnson returned to his home in Kentucky, where he operated a tavern, hotel, and resort. He was elected once again to the Kentucky State Legislature in 1850. However, shortly after his election, he died of a stroke on November 19, 1850.

Texas minister formally requested annexation in August of 1837, Secretary Forsyth served as Van Buren's polite but firm voice against it.

Foreign Affairs

Van Buren's efforts for sectional harmony were matched by his efforts for peace with foreign countries. The bad state of relations with Mexico at the end of Jackson's term required immediate attention. Bent on the annexation of Texas, Jackson had mounted pressures on Mexico to pay old claims, threatening reprisals and delivering a final ultimatum from a naval vessel. Van Buren reversed these priorities, dropped the idea of annexation, and sought peace with Mexico. The response of Mexico to his first effort at negotiation in 1837 was not acceptable, but he quickly agreed to a counterproposal made in April, 1838, for submitting the claims issue to an arbitration commission. The president went an extra mile with Mexico, moreover, patiently indulging delays that held up the formation of a commission until August, 1840. The final award of $2 million to the United States came after he left the White House, but peace was for him of greater value.

Two crises with Britain posed a greater threat to peace. One rose out of the rebellion in Canada, which began in the lower provinces and spread by the end of 1837 to the upper part. Sympathy for the rebels among Americans along the border led many to send aid and others to enlist for action. In this context the *Caroline* affair in late December seemed to make war imminent. The *Caroline*, a small craft supplying rebels out of Buffalo, was seized by British forces on the American side of the Niagara River and sunk with the loss of one life. Yet the drums of war in western New York sounded much fainter in Washington, D.C., where two quick decisions by President Van Buren signaled a peaceful intent. He filed a formal demand for explanations from the British minister, Henry Fox, but indicated a willingness to wait for the response from the home government. He then issued a proclamation, warning Americans that any violations of neutrality would forfeit their right to protection by the government.

A second flare-up came in October, 1838, when Americans joined the rebel invasion of Canada in the Detroit area and at Prescott on Lake Ontario. Strong British forces easily repelled the attacks, in the process of which more than two score of Americans were killed and a larger number captured. News of the defeat cooled enthusiasm for the rebels, as did a second and more strongly worded proclamation from the president in November. By the following year, the promise to Canada of more self-government contained in Lord Durham's report substantially ended the rebellion. Van Buren never received an apology for the *Caroline* incident from the British, but the blessings of peace disposed him, as one close acquaintance observed, to "let sleeping dogs lie."

A second and more serious crisis arose in early 1839 over the disputed Maine-New Brunswick boundary. Possessing little geographical knowledge of the area, the treaty makers at Paris in 1783 probably expected the boundary to be fixed by later negotiation. From the 1790's through the Jackson administration, however, a number of efforts brought agreement on only one thing — that the lower part of the St. John, a river that flowed in a southeast direction from the St. Lawrence highlands to the Bay of Fundy, belonged to New Brunswick. With regard to the upper St. John, profound differences emerged. Americans claimed it all — the main Aroostook tributary on the south side closest to the Maine settlements and the Madawaska tributary farther up the St. John on the north side. For diplomatic reasons Britain also claimed it all, but Britain's primary concern was the Madawaska, the control of which was vital for an overland military road from the Bay of Fundy to Quebec during the winter when the St. Lawrence was frozen. Complicating the prospects of compromise was the political situation in Maine, where each party sought to outmatch the other in opposition to any concessions to the British. By the time Van Buren became president, incidents on both sides had raised tensions to a new level. The presence of Maine census takers in the Madawaska alarmed New Brunswick, and timber poachers from New Brunswick in the Aroostook area threatened one of Maine's vital interests.

The crisis came to a head in February, 1839. Without prior consultation with the president, Governor John Fairfield ordered the Maine militia northward to the Aroostook; in response, British forces at the Madawaska went on the alert. Van Buren moved quickly and evenhandedly to regain control of the nation's relations with Britain. While calling on Congress for added means to defend the nation, he sternly warned Maine that the central government would assume no responsibility for the aggressive actions of the state militia. He then worked out the essentials of a truce with the British minister in Washington to keep the peace until the home governments reached a final settlement of the boundary. By its terms, the Madawaska would be considered in the New Brunswick "sphere of influence," while Maine retained control over the Aroostook. To secure the truce Van Buren then sent General Winfield Scott to the troubled area and by the end of March, Scott was able to announce that the governors of Maine and New Brunswick had agreed to the truce. Van Buren thus achieved his goal of "peace with honor." He also paved the way for a final settlement three years later: The terms of his truce defined the basic boundary provisions of the Webster-Ashburton Treaty.

The Indian Question

The question of peace or war was also involved in another matter of concern — the removal of the Southern Indian tribes to Oklahoma. In 1830, Jackson had pushed enabling legislation through Congress for that purpose, and by the end of his term all the tribes had moved or were in motion, except the Cherokees and the Seminoles. The Cherokees were the larger tribe, numbering from fifteen thousand to twenty thousand and scattered over the states of North

Carolina, Georgia, Alabama, and Tennessee. Under the Treaty of New Echota, made in December, 1835, they were to move the following year, but the repudiation of the treaty by many of the chiefs was among the reasons for delay. With a new deadline fixed for May, 1838, Van Buren called on General Scott to supervise the removal. Using some regular army units and a larger number of state militia, he began the process of rounding up the Cherokees from their scattered villages and directing them to three staging areas on the upper Tennessee River. Low water caused by a summer dry spell held up the process until fall, at which time the Cherokees began the long and painful journey over the "Trail of Tears." Van Buren had more personal doubts about removal than Jackson, yet he accepted it as a commitment that had to be honored. Given the anguish and suffering involved, the removal was a relatively peaceful and orderly process for which Scott won Van Buren's praise.

The Seminoles of Florida posed a far different problem. Along with other reasons for resisting removal was the presence of hundreds of blacks, many of them runaways from Georgia and Alabama plantations. Their language skills and knowledge of farming gave them added influence with their hosts, and they used this influence in opposing the government's policy, fearing that the removal of the Seminoles would leave them behind for reenslavement. Tensions, mounting as the December, 1835, deadline neared, finally erupted in violence with the ambush of more than one hundred United States troops in the Tampa area. With an occasional truce, the war dragged on for seven years. Difficult terrain, a wretched climate, and the scattering of the Seminoles made it a "dirty war," marked by search-and-destroy missions, treachery, and truce violations on both sides. One of the most publicized instances was the capture of Chief Osceola under a flag of truce. George Catlin's sympathetic portrait of him languishing in prison surely expressed the ambivalent feelings of many at the time.

The back of the war was broken under General Philip Jesup during the first two years of Van Buren's term. His strategy was to detach the blacks and to stage the Seminoles at Tampa Bay for removal by way of New Orleans. An undetermined number of blacks did fall into the hands of slaveholders, but as many as four hundred accompanied the Seminoles to Oklahoma. Key statistics summarize what Van Buren's last annual message regarded as a sad and distressing affair: In removing 3,500 to 4,000 Indians, the United States suffered 1,500 casualties and expended upward of $30 million in treasure.

The Panic of 1837

Meanwhile, the livelihood of all Americans was being affected by two basic economic events in the Van Buren presidency—the panic of 1837 and, after a brief recovery, the severer downturn two years later. Several forces contributed to a cycle of expansion after 1830 and then a countermovement of contraction. One was the rapid growth of banks—from 330 to 788—and the loose practices many of them followed. In earlier days, banks had extended credit mainly in the form of discounts on short-term commercial paper, and this fairly liquid asset, along with adequate specie held in their vaults, had secured the notes they put in circulation. The spirit of enterprise, however, and a growing hunger for capital began to pressure even sounder banks to make long-term loans and keep less specie in their vaults. A second force at work after 1830 was an inflow of English credit, much of it used for bank capital in the Southwest and elsewhere for state projects of internal improvement. Although supporting new economic growth, this credit also exerted a specifically inflationary effect on the currency. By paying for the excess of imports over exports, it kept specie from flowing abroad and thus removed a powerful check on the banks. Another inflationary force was a surplus in the Treasury, which began to mount rapidly with the retirement of the national debt. Placed on deposit in selected state banks after Jackson cut the Treasury's ties with the national bank, these funds provided the basis for further loans. In a circular fashion, finally, a mania of speculation greatly increased government land sales and added to the surplus.

The power of English credit to stimulate economic expansion was also the power to take away. In the third quarter of 1836, the Bank of England raised the interest rate to strengthen its own specie reserves. The resulting curtailment of credit to Americans ended the pattern of the preceding years and caused specie to start flowing out of the country. Eastern banks were affected first, and two actions by the government increased the pressures on them. One was the specie circular, an order from the Treasury requiring that after December, 1836, only specie would be received in payment for government lands. It had the effect of keeping specie in the West against the otherwise natural tendency of

specie to flow eastward into the channels of trade. At the same time, an act of Congress ordered the Treasury to distribute its mounting surplus among the state governments. This meant that considerable sums would have to be withdrawn from the big Eastern deposit banks, particularly those in the New York area, where about two-thirds of the nation's import duties were collected. Under this pressure, the Eastern banks greatly curtailed their loans and thereby created severe money pressures in the mercantile community.

Political foes placed all the blame on the specie circular and called on the new president to rescind Jackson's order. Politically, however, Van Buren did not feel free to undo the pet measure of his predecessor. He believed, moreover, that specie in the West helped to shore up the deposit banks there. It was probably too late, in any case, to check the forces of contraction that led New York banks on May 10, 1837, to suspend, that is, to cease paying specie on demand

The panic of 1837 recast by a political cartoonist as a new *Macbeth. (Library of Congress)*

to their depositors and the holders of their notes. Within a week, almost all other banks across the country followed the New York example.

Suspension put the federal government in a difficult position. By law, the Treasury could pay and receive only in specie or the notes of specie-paying banks, and it could deposit its funds only in such banks. Except for a small amount of specie at the Mint, however, the only funds available to the Treasury were the notes of the suspended deposit banks. Nor was much specie likely to flow into the Treasury very soon, for many import merchants were already behind in paying their duty bonds. Faced with these problems, President Van Buren called for the new Twenty-fifth Congress to meet in special session on September 4, 1837. When it assembled, Congress quickly passed a number of relief measures proposed by the president. The banks and import merchants were given additional time to make good on their obligations; the further distribution of the surplus revenue was postponed; and an issue of $10 million in Treasury notes was authorized. Used to pay creditors of the government and made receivable at par for import duties, these notes entered quickly into circulation.

Beyond the measures for immediate relief, Van Buren set before the special session, as his basic response to suspension, the proposal to divorce the Treasury from the state banks. He therefore asked Congress to provide permanent facilities for the Treasury to keep and disburse its own funds, and to make the divorce a total one, he further proposed that the Treasury receive and pay only in specie and not in bank notes. The idea of divorce was considered at the time Jackson withdrew government funds from the national bank, but it was rejected as too radical a departure from previous practice. The panic of 1837 created a new political situation, however, and made divorce the next logical step for Van Buren and his party to take. Only by divorce, Democrats now argued, could the

funds of the government be made safe and secure. Whigs answered this part of the new debate with their old cry of Caesarism, warning that an independent Treasury would in fact become a giant government bank which, by uniting purse and sword, would give tyrannical power to the executive.

Of far greater importance in the debate over the divorce proposal, however, was the impact it was expected to have on the currency. All agreed that divorce would be deflationary, but differences arose over the extent and desirability of this effect. Clearly, the funds held by the Treasury would not be available to banks for new loans and discounts. The steady demand for specie to pay government dues would be another constraint. The added specie put in circulation by Treasury disbursements also meant less specie in bank vaults to serve, by some multiple, as the basis for further note issues. In a less tangible way as well, the refusal of the Treasury to receive bank notes took away the credit the government could bestow on them. In sanguine moments, radical hard-money Democrats professed to believe that the withdrawal of government credit from the credit system of banking would wreck it and create at last an exclusively metallic currency. Moderates such as Van Buren hoped that a larger amount of specie in circulation could stabilize the currency.

Opponents of the divorce proposal in the special session invoked the spirit of enterprise and put themselves forward as the champions of the credit system. Exaggerating the deflationary effect of divorce, they damned the president for making war on the banks and leading the nation backward, as one put it, to a primitive economy of "Dorian purity, iron money, and black broth." Unique circumstances and not any basic flaw, according to Senator Rives, had temporarily thrown the state banks "out of gear." Although most Whigs privately favored a national bank, they publicly lent support to Rives and other Conservative Democrats on behalf of

> *Excerpts from Martin Van Buren's response to the Panic of 1837 at a special session of Congress, September 4, 1837:*
>
> Two nations, the most commercial in the world, enjoying but recently the highest degree of apparent prosperity and maintaining with each other the closest relations, are suddenly, in a time of profound peace and without any great national disaster, arrested in their career and plunged into a state of embarrassment and distress. In both countries we have witnessed the same redundancy of paper money and other facilities of credit; the same spirit of speculation; the same partial successes; the same difficulties and reverses; and, at length, nearly the same overwhelming catastrophe. The most material difference between the results in the two countries has only been that with us there has also occurred an extensive derangement in the fiscal affairs of the federal and state governments, occasioned by the suspension of specie payments by the banks. . . .
>
> Those who look to the action of this government for specific aid to the citizen to relieve embarrassments arising from losses by revulsions in commerce and credit, lose sight of the ends for which it was created, and the powers with which it is clothed. It was established to give security to us all. It was not intended to confer special favors on individuals. The less government interferes with private pursuits, the better for the general prosperity.

renewing the connection of the Treasury with the state banks. In mock fashion, Daniel Webster exclaimed that Van Buren's proposal made him feel as if he were on another planet. For him, the power and the interests of the government should be mingled in a benign and nurturing way with the interests of its citizens, particularly on behalf of a well-regulated paper currency. In like fashion, Henry Clay saw Americans as a "paper money people" and a mildly inflationary currency under government patronage as the basic need for economic recovery and growth.

Politically, the divorce issue served to give greater coherence to party lines and to mature what has come to be called the second party system. During the Bank War in 1834, Jackson's assorted foes—including John C. Calhoun's Nullifiers and Clay's Nationals—came together under the new Whig banner on a platform condemning Jackson as a Caesar. Three years later, an important realignment took place as Calhoun left his Whig allies to support the divorce proposal and many Conservatives, led by Rives and Senator Nathaniel P. Tallmadge of New York, broke with Van Buren and moved toward

the Whigs. The combined vote of Conservatives and Whigs defeated the divorce proposal at the special session and held firm against his renewed efforts in the two regular sessions of the Twenty-fifth Congress.

Van Buren nevertheless persisted in his course. The trait of "Dutch stubbornness" some saw in him was rather, a close associate felt, his "firmness of principle." It reflected, in any case, his concept of the presidency as based on party. He took the divorce proposal to be an irreversible commitment of his party, one that was consistent with its past experience and contributed to its evolving creed. If a politician by trade, he was also an ideologue of party, keenly aware that adherence to basic principles gave direction and corporate identity to his party, which, he profoundly believed, spoke the voice of the nation. Having helped to place Jackson's presidency on a party basis, he was resolved to govern the same way. Private convictions about banking and currency also reinforced this sense of party need. Actions taken during his earlier career had consistently come down on the side of restraint: As a state senator for eight years, he voted for only one new bank charter; as governor, he signed into law a measure setting up a safety fund for New York banks and creating a state regulatory commission. The resumption of the state banks by summer, 1838, also strengthened Van Buren's will to persevere. Encouragement from Washington, D.C., and pledges of financial backing in New York contributed to resumption, but the basic cause was recovery in England and a new flow of credit to the United States.

The Independent Treasury: A Second Declaration of Independence

Paradoxically, however, a new round of bank suspensions by the last quarter of 1839 paved the way for passage of Van Buren's central domestic measure, the independent Treasury. With a second and far more austere policy of retrenchment in England, the flow of credit to the United States virtually ceased. On October 9, the old national bank, under a Pennsylvania charter since 1836, suspended specie payment, and before long almost all other banks to the west and south of Philadelphia took the same action. The new suspension, unlike that in 1837, was followed not by a quick recovery but by a profound economic downturn that lasted for four years.

In his message to the new Twenty-sixth Congress in December, 1839, the president renewed his proposal for divorce and skillfully linked it to recent events. The second suspension clearly strengthened his claim that the funds of the government could be safe only if held as specie in the Treasury's own vaults. On the currency side of divorce, he argued that the inherent fluctuations of bank note issues were greatly aggravated by the ebb and flow of English credit. Indeed, the "chain of dependence" forged by that credit ultimately tended to place the freedom and fortunes of the nation in the power of its ancient enemy. With "Spartan firmness," as one admirer noted, Van Buren advised the nation to pay off its old debts and incur no new ones. Freed from the artificial way in which English

credit maintained an imbalance of imports over exports, the nation would be compelled to buy no more than it sold and to make up any yearly imbalance by the export or import of specie. As a complement to the policy of divorce, foreign trade in real goods for real money would exert a salutary and steady check on banks in the United States. These views clearly embodied Van Buren's more general belief that a laissez-faire posture for the government would allow the natural forces of economic equilibrium to work for enterprise at a sound and sober pace. Beyond present distress he looked to a future relatively free of violent fluctuations.

Democrats in Congress applauded Van Buren's message and supplemented its force with debate over two related matters. The first was a proposal for a federal bankruptcy act that would set up machinery for closing any state bank that suspended specie payments. Strong opposition never allowed the measure to come to a vote, but it did reveal the desire to secure a sound bank currency. Democrats succeeded in a second matter, that of defeating the call of the Whigs for the federal government to assume the debts that the states owed to England. Communications from London bankers suggested that a pledge of the federal revenues to pay old debts might soon induce the flow of new English credits to the United States. This, however, was precisely what Democrats did not want, namely, to be linked in the chain of dependence once more. Although Whigs were reconciled to the passage of the independent Treasury bill, their delay tactics in the House held up the final vote until the end of June, 1840. Because of the timing, President Van Buren waited until July 4 to sign the bill, and the party paper in Washington hailed it as the "Second Declaration of Independence."

Unhappily for Van Buren, the second declaration of independence did not assure him a second term in the White House. Deepening depression by summer, 1840, made even more appealing Whig praises for the credit system and the Whigs' promise of increasing the currency. Support in Congress for an insolvency law, in place of the Democrats' bankruptcy bill, also identified Whigs with the spirit of enterprise. By this means a debtor would be able to initiate action with his creditor and gain freedom to start over again. Clearly, the Whig view of government as a benign means for bringing recovery and economic growth contrasted with what they called the Spartan counsels of Van Buren. With cries of "Van, Van, a used up man" and "Martin Van Ruin," they pointed to a central issue in the presidential campaign of 1840.

The Campaign of 1840: "Tippecanoe and Tyler Too"

Enhancing the force of Whig economic views were a new sense of party unity, a popular candidate, and effective appeals to the voters by a "log cabin" campaign. Whig antiparty ideals and three separate candidates in 1836 gave way to a united convention that passed over Clay and Webster in favor of General William Henry Harrison, the hero of Tippecanoe, and John Tyler of Virginia. Although Tyler was not chosen as running mate for euphonious reasons, his name did lend itself nicely to the slogan "Tippecanoe and Tyler Too." Taking shameless liberties with the truth, Whig campaigners pictured Harrison, scion of an old Virginia family, as a simple farmer at North Bend living in a log cabin with the latchstring always out. Van Buren, by contrast, was presented as a foppish dandy luxuriating in the aristocratic trappings of the White House, sipping French wine, eating from golden spoons, and preening like a peacock before mirrors larger than barn doors. Van Buren became so enraged by the exposure of his lifestyle, one editor mischievously observed, that he "actually burst his corset!"

Harrison struck another democratic note by becoming the first candidate ever to campaign openly for the presidency. His presence often sparked a final element of frenzy generated at mass rallies by torchlight parades, the raising of a log cabin, and group singing in the mode of Methodist revivals. Democrats unctuously deplored the humbuggery of it all, forgetting the hickory poles and other devices used earlier on Jackson's behalf. The second party system had clearly come of age. In a moment of exasperated candor, one Democratic editor exclaimed, "We have taught them how to conquer us!"

Conforming to the practice of past presidents, Van Buren took no active role in the campaign. Occasional letters in response to inquiries indicated his willingness to stand on his record and party principles, but by September, he later wrote, he had resigned himself to defeat when he realized that the Whigs would leave no expedient untried in their determination to win. On the face of the returns, he suffered an overwhelming defeat: He won 60 electoral votes from seven states, while Harrison received 234 electoral votes from the remaining nineteen states. Some consolation doubtless came with the knowledge that he received 400,000 more popular votes than in 1836 and that a shift of about 8,000 votes in four large states would have brought him a majority in the electoral college. At last, however, he suffered the fate of most incumbents in time of economic downturn, and the pattern of the vote points to the crucial issue of currency in the campaign. The seven states that supported Van Buren—Missouri, Illinois, New Hampshire, Virginia, South Carolina, Alabama, and Arkansas—were less integrated into the market economy, and they were less imbued with the spirit of enterprise than the other states.

Van Buren accepted defeat in a spirit of good sportsmanship that had always characterized his political career. Visitors at the White House found nothing in his cheerful demeanor to suggest that he was about to relinquish the highest office in the land. When Harrison came to Washington, D.C., in early 1841, Van Buren paid a social call at his hotel, invited him to the White House as guest of honor, and even offered to vacate the executive mansion so Harrison could move in early. Had he been invited,

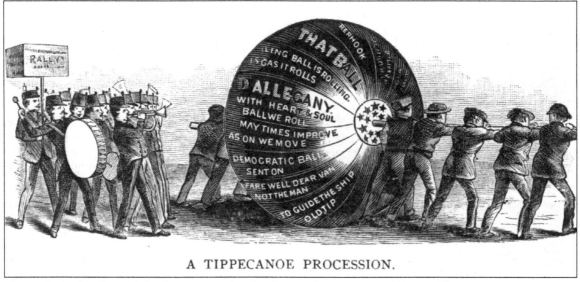

A TIPPECANOE PROCESSION.

The 1840 election featured the first campaigning for the presidency by a candidate, William Henry Harrison ("Old Tippecanoe"). *(Library of Congress)*

he would also have attended Harrison's inaugural ceremonies; only later did it become the custom for the outgoing president of a different party to attend the inauguration of his successor. In any event, Van Buren did not see defeat as fatal either to himself or to his party. Profoundly convinced that there could be only one genuinely popular party, he expected the "sober second thought" of the people to see through the delusions of the log cabin campaign and restore Democrats to their rightful place.

The Achievements of Van Buren's Presidency

Informed with this belief, Van Buren's last message to Congress proudly summarized the achievements of his presidency and reaffirmed its principles. The nation remained at peace and enjoyed relatively secure frontiers. Here, it might be added, Van Buren had resisted the Machiavellian advice of some who would have him divert attention from ills at home by precipitating war abroad. The past obligations of the government had also been met, including the difficult and costly task of Indian removal. In spite of a "formidable" political opposition and

"pecuniary embarrassments," moreover, he had met these obligations without incurring a new debt or raising taxes. Silence on slavery, the only specific issue raised in his inaugural, likewise spoke of success in maintaining sectional harmony. Although recognizing that individuals had experienced derangement in their economic pursuits, he believed that the independent Treasury would contribute to a sound recovery and to stable enterprise. In larger perspective his policy of divorce completed the work of Jackson's presidency in bringing government back to its simple republican tack. As if looking to future elections, finally, he warned that vigilance would be required to preserve these principles: "The choice is an important one, and I sincerely hope that it will be made wisely."

The sequel of events provides a final perspective for assessing Van Buren's presidency. Opposition to the annexation of Texas in 1844 denied Van Buren a third nomination for president by his party. It went instead to James K. Polk on a platform of territorial expansion to the Pacific. War with Mexico in the wake of Texas annexation realized this "manifest destiny," but it also opened in fateful form the sectional controversy over slavery expansion. By the mid-1850's the deepening debate sundered the second party system Van Buren had helped to shape and had used so well to contain sectional tensions, and by the time of his death on July 24, 1862, the sectional conflict had become a civil war that was to transform the federative Union he wanted to save into a consolidated nation. His independent Treasury lasted longer, remaining in operation until the Federal Reserve System was established. Recurring booms and panics in the last half of the nineteenth century belied his hopes that it would bring stability to enterprise. There is no reason to believe, however, that a national bank would have served much better at taming the spirit of enterprise in a rapidly expanding economy. Van Buren began his presidency with the hope of bringing repose to the nation; relative success in achieving this goal constituted a modest but real act of statesmanship.

Major L. Wilson

Suggested Readings

Coles, Donald B. *Martin Van Buren and the American Political System*. Princeton, N.J.: Princeton University Press, 1984. A solid, contextual biography.

Lynch, Denis T. *An Epoch and a Man: Martin Van Buren and His Times*. 1929. Reprint. Port Washington, N.Y.: Kennikat Press, 1971. Although an older volume, it is still useful for examining Van Buren's early career.

Mushkat, Jerome, and Joseph G. Rayback. *Martin Van Buren: Law, Politics, and the Shaping of Republican Ideology*. Dekalb: Northern Illinois University Press, 1997. Examines the importance of Van Buren's law career to his later political success.

Niven, John. *Martin Van Buren: The Romantic Age of American Politics*. New York: Oxford University Press, 1983. A thorough biography.

Remini, Robert V. *Martin Van Buren and the Making of the Democratic Party*. New York: Columbia University Press, 1959. A perspective on Van Buren's great contribution to party development.

Silby, Joel H. *Martin Van Buren and the Emergence of American Popular Politics*. Lanham, Md.: Rowman & Littlefield, 2002. Traces the rise of Van Buren as a politician in an era of great unrest.

Van Buren, Martin. *The Autobiography of Martin Van Buren*. Edited by John C. Fitzpatrick. 1920. Reprint. New York: A. M. Kelley, 1969. Van Buren's life in his own words.

Widmer, Edward L. *Martin Van Buren*. New York: Times Books, 2005. Part of the American President Series, this volume argues that Van Buren created the modern political party system, for which he deserves Americans' "grudging respect."

Wilson, Major L. *The Presidency of Martin Van Buren*. Lawrence: University Press of Kansas, 1984. A biography of Van Buren focused primarily on the presidential years.

William Henry Harrison

9th President, 1841

Born: February 9, 1773
  near Charles City, Virginia
Died: April 4, 1841
  Washington, D.C.

Political Party: Whig
Vice President: John Tyler

Cabinet Members
Secretary of State: Daniel Webster
Secretary of the Treasury: Thomas Ewing
Secretary of War: John Bell
Secretary of the Navy: George E. Badger
Attorney General: John J. Crittenden
Postmaster General: Francis Granger

William Henry Harrison was the oldest man to serve in the presidency until the inauguration of Ronald Reagan in 1981. Sixty-eight years old at the time of his inauguration, in 1841, Harrison served only one month before he died from pneumonia. His early death made Harrison's presidency the shortest in the history of the United States and provided the final irony in a life full of color and controversy.

The son of a signer of the Declaration of Independence, Harrison was born in 1773 at his family's famous Berkeley Plantation in Virginia. He attended Hampden-Sydney College, and briefly undertook the study of medicine under the noted physician Benjamin Rush.

Indian Fighter, Legislator, Diplomat
In 1791, Harrison entered the army serving in the campaigns against American Indians in the Northwest Territory and eventually becoming a lieutenant and aide-de-camp to the commander, General Anthony Wayne. With the conclusion of peace, he remained on garrison duty in the vicinity of Cincinnati. Harrison resigned from the army in 1798 and accepted an appointment as secretary of the Northwest Territory, from which he was elected first delegate to Congress in 1799. With the division of the Northwest Territory into the territories of Ohio and Indiana, Harrison was appointed governor of the Indiana Territory.

Harrison was given a nearly impossible mission: to win the friendship and trust of Ameri-

Portrait of William Henry Harrison. *(Whitehouse.gov)*

can Indians and to protect them from the rapaciousness of white settlers, yet to acquire for the government as much land as he could secure from the Western tribes. Apparently, Harrison had a genuine concern for the plight of American Indians, ordering a campaign of inoculation to protect them from the scourge of smallpox and banning the sale of liquor to them. He actively pursued the acquisition of Indian lands, however, and in 1809, he negotiated a treaty with Indian leaders that transferred some 2.9 million acres in the vicinity of the White and Wabash Rivers to the United States. This cession exacerbated the tensions between Indians and white men in the Northwest and triggered the activities on which Harrison's fame and later career were founded.

Given the uneasy relationship between the United States and Great Britain, many Americans assumed that the "Indian troubles" of the interior were encouraged and fomented by the British. In reality, the growing hostility of the Western tribes was largely an indigenous reaction to the constant encroachments on their lands by white settlers. The Indians' frustrations were finally focused through the leadership of two Shawnee half brothers, the chief Tecumseh and a one-eyed medicine man called The Prophet. Tecumseh developed the concept of a great Indian confederation, arguing that American Indian lands were held in common by all the tribes and could not be bargained away without their unanimous consent. The Prophet promoted a puritanical religious philosophy, and as his following grew, religion and politics gradually merged.

Harrison developed a healthy respect for the brothers' abilities, and he hoped at first that they could be placated. Finally, however, in what must be considered an aggressive move, Harrison marched a force of about one thousand men north from his capital at Vincennes toward Indian lands in northwestern Indiana. On November 7, 1811, Harrison's encampment near an Indian settlement called Prophetstown, near the confluence of the Tippecanoe and Wabash Rivers, suffered an early morning surprise attack. Tecumseh was in the South organizing the tribes of that area, so the Indians who attacked Harrison were led, or at least inspired, by The Prophet. Harrison's forces beat back the attackers and later burned the Indian settlement.

Almost immediately, controversy arose concerning the particulars of the Battle of Tippecanoe and Harrison's performance. Were his troops prepared for the Indian attack? Why had they camped in a vulnerable position? Had Harrison or his companion officers actually commanded the defenses? Were Harrison's men outnumbered? What, in fact, was the size of the attacking Indian force? In the face of such critical questions, Harrison, who was not a paragon of modesty, and his supporters immediately began to construct the legend of a "Washington of the West" who represented the bravery and ambitions of Western Americans.

During the War of 1812 with Great Britain,

(Library of Congress)

The First Lady
Anna Harrison

Anna Symmes was born in Wolpack Township, Sussex County, New Jersey, on July 25, 1775. Soon after she was born, the family of John Cleaves Symmes moved to Flatbrook, New Jersey, near Morristown. Her frail mother died one year later on Anna's first birthday. Anna had only one sibling, Maria, who was fourteen years older.

Because of the Revolutionary War, John Symmes took his baby daughter to her maternal grandparents, who became the greatest influence in her life. Anna was very well educated, and her life was one of security, luxury, and loving care. Along with these blessings, she added an attribute of beauty: She was dainty with unblemished fair skin, large brown eyes, and black hair.

After the Revolutionary War, John Symmes was appointed a judge of New York City. He then accepted the offer of government land agent between the Little Miami River and the Miami River just north of the Ohio River. He brought his nineteen-year-old daughter Anna with him to help maintain a home.

Lieutenant William Harrison was on leave from Fort Washington at Lexington, Kentucky. There he met Anna while she was visiting her sister Maria. The two fell in love and soon eloped over the objections of Judge Symmes.

Much of Anna Harrison's married life was spent rearing their children and using her earlier background of education and religion to school them. She bore ten children and also managed the farmland. Nine children preceded her in death. Only John Scott Harrison, father of future president Benjamin Harrison, survived her. William Henry Harrison and Anna Symmes Harrison are the only president and First Lady to have a grandchild become president.

When William Henry Harrison won the presidency, Anna was too ill to join him in Washington, D.C. Four weeks later, packed and ready to move, Anna was notified that her husband had died.

Anna Harrison defied most preconceptions. She was one of the earliest pioneer women to live in the Ohio and Indiana Territories. Though she spent her entire adult life as a pioneer wife on the edge of rough and dangerous wilderness, the roughness never become part of her manner.

She was born during the Revolutionary War in 1775, and she died at the close of the Civil War in 1864. During her lifetime, she witnessed both the formation and preservation of the Union.

Mary Jane Child Queen

Harrison served in several military positions and eventually became supreme commander of the Army of the Northwest. He broke the power of the British and the Indians in the Northwest and in southern Canada, with the culminating victory in early October, 1813, at the Battle of the Thames. Again controversy followed Harrison's military performance, although his reputation among the general public was apparently enhanced. In May, 1814, he resigned from the army and took up residence on a farm at North Bend, Ohio, on the bank of the Ohio River near Cincinnati.

At North Bend, Harrison engaged in farming and several unsuccessful commercial ventures, and the foundation for another aspect of his public image was established. Harrison's home at North Bend was a commodious dwelling of sixteen rooms, but it was built around the nucleus of a log cabin and became one of the misrepresented symbols of "Old Tip's" 1840 presidential campaign. In 1816, Harrison was elected to the United States House of Representatives, serving until 1819 with no real distinc-

The Vice President
John Tyler

Born to an aristocratic family on March 29, 1790, John Tyler would be the first person to assume the office of the presidency as a result of the death of a president. A graduate of William and Mary College, Tyler was elected to the Virginia Legislature while only in his early twenties. On March 29, 1813, he married Letitia Christian, and together they would have seven children.

Shortly after marrying, Tyler was recruited to serve in the War of 1812. His brief military career ended with the conclusion of the war, and he was subsequently elected to the United States House of Representatives in 1816. After serving three terms in Congress, Tyler resigned, believing his efforts in the nation's capital were put to poor use. Upon returning to Virginia, he was elected governor in 1825, where he oversaw improvements in public transportation. Tyler again had a change of mind and resigned the office in 1826 to serve as a United States senator, a position he would hold for ten years. After his Senate career, Tyler returned to Virginia to serve in the state legislature and was elected Speaker of the House of that body in 1839.

In 1840, Tyler was named the vice presidential nominee for the Whig Party. After the successful election, Tyler was sworn into office on March 4, 1841; however, with the sudden death of President William Harrison one month later, Tyler was thrust into the presidency. As president, he vetoed a bill to recharter the Bank of the United States and suffered a storm of criticism. While in office on September 10, 1842, his beloved wife died after a protracted illness. Tyler met the socialite and former debutante Julia Gardner at a White House reception shortly before his wife's death, and the two began courting in January, 1843, and were married on June 26, 1844. Tyler's children expressed disappointment at their father's quick decision to marry a woman only twenty-four years old.

Upon retiring from political life after serving one term as president, Tyler returned to his 1,200-acre plantation in Virginia with his new bride and had seven more children. During the Civil War, Tyler would leave retirement to serve in the newly established Confederate House of Representatives; however, he was unable to take his seat, for he died on January 18, 1862.

Robert P. Watson and Richard Yon

tion. In 1825, he was elected to the United States Senate by the Ohio legislature. He became chair of the Military Affairs Committee but resigned in 1828 to accept an appointment as United States minister to Colombia. His career as a diplomat was not particularly successful, but when he was recalled after about a year by President Andrew Jackson, it was largely for political reasons.

Following his return from Colombia, Harrison experienced a continuing series of financial and family misfortunes and supplemented his resources by serving as clerk of the Cincinnati Court of Common Pleas. He was observed at this time by a French traveler who described him as "a man of about medium height, stout and muscular, and of about the age of sixty years yet with the active step and lively air of youth." A visitor to the "log cabin," on the other hand, considered Harrison "a small and rather sallow-looking man, who does not exactly meet the associations that connect themselves with the name of general."

The Election of 1840: "Tippecanoe and Tyler Too"

During the height of Jacksonian democracy, many displayed a growing concern about the alleged pretensions of "King Andrew" Jackson, which contributed to the emergence of the

Whig Party. Old National Republicans, former Anti-Masons, and various others who reacted strongly against the president or his policies began to work together, and in 1836 the Whigs made their first run for the presidency against Jackson's chosen successor, Martin Van Buren. William Henry Harrison ran as the candidate of Western Whigs, showed promise as a vote getter, and thus became a leading contender for the nomination in 1840.

By now widely known as "Old Tippecanoe," Harrison the military hero presented an obvious opportunity for the Whigs to borrow the tactics of the Democrats who had exploited "Old Hickory," Andrew Jackson, to great success. Harrison's position on key issues of the day—banking policy, internal improvements, the tariff, abolition—was almost irrelevant, for the old general was to be nominated as a symbol of military glory and the development of the West. The Whigs wanted a candidate who would appeal to a broad range of voters and who was not too closely identified with the issues of the Jacksonian era. They did not offer a real platform, only a pledge to "correct the abuses" of the current administration. If the campaign were successful, the real decisions in a Harrison administration would be made by Whig leaders in Congress.

Harrison's age and health became immediate issues in the campaign, and he traveled from Ohio to Virginia so that he could be seen and "counteract the opinion, which has been industriously circulated, that *I was an old broken-down feeble man*." One observer who met the candidate described him as "about 5 feet 9 inches in hight [*sic*], very slender and thin in flesh, with a noble and benignant expression—a penetrating eye, expansive fore-

head and Roman nose. He is not bald but gray, and walks about very quick, and seems to be as active as a man of 45." During a later trip that Harrison made through New Jersey, a newspaper reported that "his appearance is that of a hale, hearty Ohio Farmer, of about fifty years of age."

The tone and lasting fame of the campaign were established during the battle for the nomination when a partisan of one of his Whig rivals suggested that Harrison should be allowed to enjoy his log cabin and hard cider in peace. An opposition party paper then picked up the idea and said, "Give him a barrel of hard cider and a pension of two thousand a year . . . he will sit the remainder of his days in a log cabin . . . and study moral philosophy." Whig strategists knew a good thing when they read it, and they created a winning campaign around the portrayal of Harrison as a man of the people, a wise yet simple hero whose log cabin and hard cider were highly preferable to the haughty attitude

A souvenir from the first modern presidential campaign. *(Smithsonian Institution)*

The chorus to the 1840 campaign song "Tippecanoe and Tyler Too":

For Tippecanoe and Tyler too—Tippecanoe and Tyler too,
And with them we'll beat little Van, Van, Van.
Like the rushing of mighty waters, waters, waters,
On it will go,
And in its course will clear the way
For Tippecanoe and Tyler too—Tippecanoe and Tyler too.
See the loco standard tottering, tottering, tottering,
Down it must go,
And in its place we'll rear the flag
Of Tippecanoe and Tyler too—Tippecanoe and Tyler too.
Don't you hear from every quarter, quarter, quarter,
Good news and true,
That swift the ball is rolling on
For Tippecanoe and Tyler too—Tippecanoe and Tyler too.
The Buckeye boys turned out in thousands, thousands, thousands,
Not long ago,
And at Columbus set their seals,
To Tippecanoe Tyler too—Tippecanoe and Tyler too.

and trickery of "Old Kinderhook" Martin Van Buren. In the process, the Whigs waged the first modern presidential campaign as they sold souvenirs, published and widely distributed campaign materials, flooded the country with speakers, and employed songs, slogans, and verses, the most famous being their cry of "Tippecanoe and Tyler Too."

A One-Month Presidency and Its Lasting Consequences

Harrison's presidency was anticlimactic. He traveled to Washington, D.C., before his inauguration and was well received both by his former opponent, President Van Buren, and by members of Congress. His inaugural address was widely praised, even though it lasted more than two hours, but it had unexpected results. The day was cold and rainy, and the new president caught a cold, which continued to nag him. Harrison was besieged by people who wanted favors and offices, and he attempted to escape from this pressure by immersing himself in minor details. He visited various government of-

fices to see if they were operating efficiently, and he even concerned himself with the routine matters of running and purchasing supplies for the White House. The development of a legislative program was left to Whig leaders in Congress, and settlement of the *Caroline* affair with Great Britain, growing out of American involvement in an abortive Canadian rebellion in 1837, the only major problem of his brief tenure, was entrusted to the hands of Secretary of State Daniel Webster.

On a cold March morning, the president ventured out to purchase vegetables for the White House. He suffered a chill, which aggravated the cold he had contracted on inauguration day. The cold developed into pneumonia, and on April 4, 1841, Harrison died in the White House. His body was returned to North Bend for burial. Old Tippecanoe had virtually no direct impact on the office of the presidency itself, yet the method of his election and the circumstances of his death were of lasting importance. The 1840 campaign had established a new style of presidential campaigning, and Harrison's death forced the nation for the first time to experience the elevation of a vice president to the Oval Office, an event that established a landmark constitutional precedent.

James E. Fickle

Suggested Readings

Cleaves, Freeman. *Old Tippecanoe: William Henry Harrison and His Times*. 1939. Reprint. Port Washington, N.Y.: Kennikat Press, 1969. An older but solid biography.

Goebel, Dorothy B. *William Henry Harrison: A Political Biography*. 1926. Reprint. Philadelphia: Porcupine Press, 1974. Part of the Perspectives in American History series, the volume is a standard biography.

Green, James A. *William Henry Harrison, His Life and Times*. Richmond, Va.: Garret and Massie, 1941. A laudatory and popular account of Harrison.

Gunderson, Robert G. *The Log-Cabin Campaign*. 1957. Reprint. Westport, Conn.: Greenwood Press, 1977. The classic work that details the election of 1840.

Harrison, William Henry. *Messages and Letters of William Henry Harrison*. Edited by Logan Esarey. 1922. Reprint. New York: Arno Press, 1975. Primary documents taken from the period when Harrison was governor.

Peterson, Norma L. *The Presidencies of William Henry Harrison and John Tyler*. Lawrence: University Press of Kansas, 1989. Provides a thorough examination of Harrison's presidency.

Stevens, Kenneth R. *William Henry Harrison: A Bibliography*. Westport, Conn.: Greenwood Press, 1998. Provides a comprehensive listing of primary and secondary sources on the life and presidency of Harrison.

John Tyler

10th President, 1841-1845

Born: March 29, 1790
     Greenway, Charles City
     County, Virginia
Died: January 18, 1862
     Richmond, Virginia

Political Party: Whig
Vice President: none

Cabinet Members

Secretary of State: Daniel Webster, Hugh S.
    Legaré, Abel P. Upshur, John C. Calhoun
Secretary of the Treasury: Thomas Ewing,
    Walter Forward, John C. Spencer,
    George M. Bibb
Secretary of War: John Bell, John C. Spencer,
    James M. Porter, William Wilkins
Secretary of the Navy: George E. Badger, Abel P.
    Upshur, David Henshaw, Thomas Gilmer,
    John Y. Mason
Attorney General: John J. Crittenden, Hugh S.
    Legaré, John Nelson
Postmaster General: Francis Granger, Charles A.
    Wickliffe

John Tyler is one of the least-known yet most controversial presidents in American history. The first vice president to succeed to the presidency upon the death of a chief executive, Tyler established the precedent that in such circumstances the new president holds the office both in fact and in name. Public and political opinion about Tyler was badly divided in his own time, and later historians have continued to debate his motives, ability, and performance. President Theodore Roosevelt said, "Tyler has been called a mediocre man, but this is un-warranted flattery. He was a politician of monumental littleness." He is often portrayed as a stubborn, vain, and inconsistent leader who was one of the worst presidents. Other writers portray him as a president with strong principles and great integrity who remained true to his beliefs despite tremendous political pressure. They say that even though Tyler was the first president threatened with impeachment and the only one to be formally expelled from his own political party, he deserves recognition as a competent and courageous chief executive.

Portrait of John Tyler. *(Whitehouse.gov)*

A Singular Political Course

Tyler was born March 29, 1790, in tidewater Virginia near Richmond, the son of a distinguished Virginian who served as governor, as speaker of the Virginia House of Delegates, and as a judge. His father was a strict constructionist Jeffersonian Republican. John absorbed and remained deeply imbued with this philosophy throughout his life. He was reared in an atmosphere of aristocratic privilege and refinement, becoming something of a stereotypical representative of the tidewater aristocracy in his beliefs and values.

Upon his graduation from the College of William and Mary, where he had been an excellent student with a growing interest in political theory and practice, Tyler at the age of seventeen began to read law under his father. He was admitted to the Virginia bar in 1809. At the age of twenty-one he was elected to the Virginia House of Delegates. After brief military service in the War of 1812, he returned to politics and was elected to the United States House of Representatives in 1816. As a congressman, Tyler stood for strict interpretation of the Constitution and limitation of the powers of the federal government. He resisted national internal improvements because they might extend the power of the federal government, and he opposed the first Bank of the United States for the same reason, as well as on constitutional and other grounds. He did not favor the slave trade, but he voted against the Missouri Compromise, believing that time and the social climate would eventually doom the "peculiar institution." Defeated in an election for the United States Senate at the age of thirty-one, Tyler served briefly as chancellor of William and Mary, and then as governor of Virginia. He was finally elected to the Senate in 1827 and began to achieve a degree of national prominence.

Remaining true to his constitutional principles, Tyler found himself in an ambiguous political situation. As a Republican, he supported William H. Crawford for the presidency in 1824 and was elected to the Senate as an anti-Jacksonian. He was repelled both by Old Hickory's authoritarianism and by the rising influence of Jacksonian democracy. Tyler was very cordial and effective when dealing with members of his own class, but common folk and their heroes made him uncomfortable. "The barking of newspapers and the brawling of demagogues can never drive me from my course," said Tyler. "If I am to go into retirement, I will at least take care to do so with a pure and unsullied conscience." Nevertheless, in 1828 Tyler supported Jackson and agreed with his opposition to the rechartering of the Bank of the United States. Tyler's principles, however, led him to split with Jackson and the Democratic Party.

Although Tyler favored the positions the president took on certain key issues, he considered Jackson's methods unacceptable, particularly in the nullification crisis and in dealing with the bank. Nullification became an issue during Jackson's presidency because of the linkage of two developments affecting the South. First was the tariff. In 1828, Congress passed a high protective tariff, which Southern planters, dependent on an export economy, strongly opposed. They called it the Tariff of Abominations, and Tyler was among the senators who spoke and voted against it. Second was the fact that with the increasing political integration of the Northwest and Northeast, Southerners were coming to constitute only a minority in national politics. Some Southerners were beginning to talk about separation from the Union in order to escape from the tyranny of the majority. Vice President John C. Calhoun of South Carolina understood Southern frustration, yet he wanted to preserve the Union, and therefore developed the theory of nullification as a permanent protection for minority sections within the Union.

Nullification and the tariff were linked when South Carolina threatened to declare the Tariff of Abominations null and void within its borders if it were not repealed by Congress. De-

The First Lady
Letitia Tyler

Letitia Christian was born into a family of wealthy planters on November 12, 1790, at Cedar Grove Plantation, about twenty miles east of Richmond, Virginia. She received a minimal education similar to that of other young women from a well-to-do family of that time. Letitia met the young John Tyler in 1808 when both were eighteen, and she married him on his twenty-third birthday in 1813.

The couple had eight children. The children were, in order of birth: Mary, Robert, John, Letitia, Elizabeth, Anne, Alice, and Tazewell. Letitia tended to avoid social functions and devote herself to her family. In 1839, while John was a U.S. senator, she suffered a paralytic stroke.

She unexpectedly became First Lady in April, 1841, when John became president following William Henry Harrison's death. However, her fragile health made her unable to host White House social functions. Her daughter-in-law, Priscilla Cooper Tyler, handled that role in her place. Priscilla described her as "the most entirely unselfish person you can imagine . . . Notwithstanding her very delicate health, mother attends to and regulates all the household affairs and all so quietly that you can't tell when she does it."

Letitia's only public appearance in the White House was at the wedding of her daughter Elizabeth in January, 1842. She died on September 10, 1842, about seventeen months after her husband became president. She was the first First Lady to enter the White House following the death of her husband's predecessor, and she became the first First Lady to die while her husband was in office. She was taken to Virginia for burial at the plantation of her birth. John Tyler remarried in 1844.

Dean M. Shapiro

---

spite passage of a new compromise tariff, South Carolina began the nullification process. President Jackson issued an extremely strong proclamation rejecting South Carolina's position, and Congress passed the Force Act, authorizing the president to use force to make sure that federal laws were obeyed. Even though South Carolina eventually backed down and the crisis passed, Tyler found himself in a troubling situation. He shared the general Southern opposition to high tariffs, but he did not agree with the theory of nullification. Still, he believed that Jackson's nullification proclamation was a violation of the Constitution, and he was the only senator to vote against the Force Act. Further, he was repelled by the vehemence of Jackson's reaction to South Carolina's challenge.

The bank question raised similar contradictions for Tyler. Like Jackson, he opposed the attempt to recharter the Bank of the United States, on constitutional as well as on other grounds. Yet, when Jackson attempted to destroy the bank before its charter expired by removing the federal government's deposits from its vaults, Tyler supported resolutions in the Senate condemning the president's action. When the Virginia legislature ordered him to vote for a motion to expunge the resolutions, Tyler resigned from the Senate and left the Democratic Party.

Tyler was now in strange political territory. He had left Andrew Jackson's party and had begun drifting along with other Southern expatriates into the ranks of the emerging Whig Party, which was coalescing in opposition to the executive tyranny of "King Andrew." Yet Tyler had not departed from his constitutional or political principles, and these were not consistent with those of many Whig leaders. The Whig Party was a loose coalition of diverse groups, however, and seemed at first to accommodate considerable philosophical latitude. Defeated in a Senate election in 1839, Tyler was nominated for the vice presidency on the ticket with William Henry Harrison, "Old Tippecanoe," the following year, in an obvious effort by the Whigs to attract Southern states' rights advocates.

Succession to the Presidency: A Historic Precedent

The Virginia politician whose name became part of the most famous campaign slogan in American political history—Tippecanoe and Tyler Too—had matured into a dignified and appealing figure. Although remaining distant from the masses, Tyler was a polished and effective orator. He was patient, considerate, good-humored, and friendly. Even his political enemies found it difficult to dislike him. Tyler was scrupulously honest and had no major vices. He drank, but always in moderation, and he used profanity, but only of the mildest sort. Physically striking, he was 6 feet tall and slender. He was very fair, with a high forehead and aquiline nose, brilliant eyes, and a ready smile. Observers said he reminded them of a Roman statesman or of Cicero. Some said he was vain, but he did have some justification for vanity.

The Harrison and Tyler ticket won the election easily, but within a month of his inauguration "Old Tippecanoe" was dead. Supposedly, his dying words, intended for the vice president, were "Sir—I wish you to understand the true principles of Government. I wish them carried out. I ask nothing more."

Were William Henry Harrison's principles shared by Tyler? Despite the Virginian's long political career and philosophical and constitutional consistency, contemporary observers professed not to know. Tyler had scarcely known Harrison and had not particularly liked what he knew of him. Tyler was a close friend of Henry Clay, and many, probably including Clay, believed that he would support the programs, including plans for a new central bank,

that the Kentuckian planned to introduce in Congress. Tyler's oratory in the campaign had been sufficiently vague to offer some justification for such a belief. Yet within a short period of time Clay would be a political enemy, attacking Tyler as a traitor to the Whig Party.

The first question was fundamental. What was Tyler's status upon Harrison's death? The Constitution is vague, saying that "in case of the removal of the President from office, or of his death, resignation, or inability to discharge the powers and duties of the said office, the same shall devolve on the Vice President. . . . " Does this mean the office itself, or simply the duties of the office? No precedents existed, and in this important crisis Tyler, the strict constructionist, interpreted the Constitution very broadly and claimed all the rights and privileges of the presidency. Although there was some criticism of his interpretation, it has been accepted and followed since that time.

Tyler kept the Harrison cabinet members, reinforcing the Whig perception that little would change. Almost immediately, Clay submitted a legislative program calling for a new Bank of the United States and a higher tariff. Clay quickly discovered that he had badly misread the situation. When Congress enacted legislation creating the new bank and a higher tariff, the president vetoed both, in language reminiscent of Andrew Jackson. Some charged that this was treachery; others held that Tyler was jealous of Clay's assumption of leadership. In fact, Tyler was simply being consistent with the strict constructionist, Southern agrarian views that he had held all along. He stood firm despite recriminations from Clay, tremendous pressure from majoritarian Whigs, and outcries from the public, including a rock-throwing mob that attacked the White House.

Conflicts with Congress: A President Without a Party

Tyler argued that the proposed bank violated constitutional principles and also posed the

The First Lady
Julia Tyler

Julia Gardiner was born on Gardiner's Island, New York, on May 4, 1820, to Senator David Gardiner and Juliana McLachlan Gardiner. A debutante at fifteen, she was the belle of the ball, and the society pages quickly dubbed her the "Rose of Long Island."

Late in 1841, she and her family visited Washington for the winter social season. Soon afterward, through arrangements made by Dolley Madison, she met President John Tyler, a recent widower. Beautiful and flirtatious, Julia received proposals from two congressmen and a Supreme Court justice, but Tyler was the one who took the greatest interest in her. They began a correspondence that evolved into a courtship.

In 1844, Tyler invited Senator Gardiner and his family back to Washington, and he arranged a tour for them of the Navy's newest ship. However, while onboard observing a demonstration of the ship's guns, one of them backfired, and Julia's father was killed in the explosion.

Tyler offered his condolences and comfort to Julia and soon gained her consent to become engaged. They were married in New York on June 26, 1844. He was the first president to marry while in office. Julia served as First Lady for the last eight months of his term. It was she who introduced "Hail to the Chief," the official presidential anthem, to the White House.

The Tylers retired to Richmond, Virginia, where they remained until his death in 1862. They had seven children: David Gardiner (1846-1927), John Alexander (1848-1883), Julia Gardiner (1849-1871), Lachlan (1851-1902), Lyon Gardiner (1853-1935), Robert Fitzwalter (1856-1927), and Pearl (1860-1947). Julia also helped raise Tyler's eight children from his previous marriage.

At the outbreak of the Civil War, Julia collected the family papers and took them to a Richmond bank vault for safe keeping. Later in the war, the bank was destroyed, and the papers were lost along with letters and photos.

As the war raged, Julia fled to New York, where she worked secretly and voluntarily for the Confederacy. The defeat of the South left her without money or means of support. In 1880, Congress voted her a $1,200-per-year pension, and the following year it increased to $5,000.

With her pension, she was able to live comfortably and spent her last years in Richmond, where she died on July 10, 1889, and was buried beside her husband.

Dean M. Shapiro

threat of an economic monopoly. He suggested a modified "exchequer system" as a compromise, but the Whigs in Congress forged ahead with another attempt to create a bank, thinly disguised as a "fiscal corporation." Tyler vetoed that too, and the situation rapidly deteriorated into open warfare between the Whig president and his colleagues in Congress. After Tyler, using the veto as actively as Jackson, struck down Clay's distribution program and other legislation, the Kentuckian resigned from the Senate in frustration. There were public demonstrations against the president, he was burned in effigy, and the entire cabinet, with the exception of Secretary of State Daniel Webster, who was involved in sensitive negotiations with Great Britain, resigned. They were replaced by men like Tyler himself, former Democrats who shared his views. In January, 1843, the Whigs brought impeachment charges against the man they now called "His Accidency." They failed, but proceeded formally to expel Tyler from the Whig Party, which was in shambles.

The president, now a man without a party,

continued to perform the duties of his office, loyal to his principles and in apparent good humor. He actually managed to achieve some successes and even considered an attempt to retain the presidency in the 1844 campaign as an independent candidate. In 1841, he approved the Preemption Act, which made land more accessible to settlers rather than to speculators and stimulated the development of the Northwestern states of Iowa, Illinois, Wisconsin, and Minnesota. He helped to end the Seminole War in 1842. The same year, the dispute with Great Britain over the boundary between the United States and Canada in the Northeast was resolved through the Webster-Ashburton Treaty, and in 1844 the United States signed a treaty with China opening that country to American commerce for the first time. Although Tyler did not occupy the limelight in these diplomatic matters, he wielded considerable influence behind the scenes.

The president built his hopes for election in 1844 on the Texas annexation question. Originally a province of Mexico largely populated by slaveholding American settlers, Texas successfully rebelled in 1836 and hoped for annexation to the United States. The issue was troublesome because of the growing sectional controversy over slavery, and so for several years Texas remained an independent republic. Tyler genuinely believed that the annexation of Texas would be good for the United States, and he was hopeful that advocacy of such an action would generate support for his candidacy in the Southern slave states. He correctly anticipated the developing expansionist impulse in the country, but his personal ambitions were ill founded. When significant support failed to materialize, Tyler withdrew and endorsed Democrat James K. Polk, who ran on an expansionist platform and won. Following the election, Congress passed and Tyler signed a joint resolution of an-

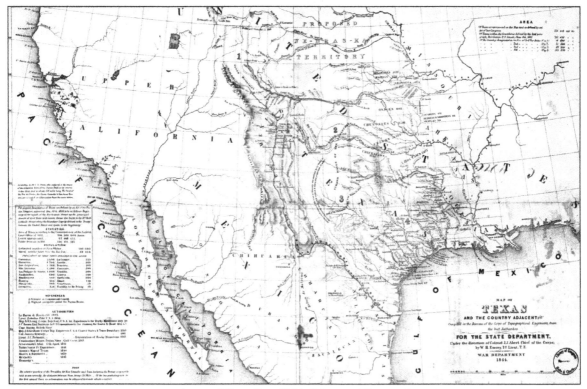

A map of Texas from 1844. *(Library of Congress)*

nexation for Texas. Two days later, during his last full day in office, the Virginian signed a bill admitting Florida to the Union.

Tyler then retired to his plantation home on Virginia's James River. He was coolly received by his neighbors, many of whom were Whigs, but his graciousness, character, and obvious goodwill gradually won them over. The former president became an honored citizen, and as the passions of sectional turmoil built in the 1850's, he was an influential sectional leader. Loyal to the Union, he attempted to promote compromise but finally voted in favor of secession as a delegate to the Virginia secession convention. He served in the provisional Congress of the Confederacy and was elected to the Confederate House of Representatives, but he died on January 18, 1862, before taking his seat. He was buried in Richmond.

Tyler's Achievements: A Reassessment

The first vice president to inherit the presidency upon the death of a president, the first chief executive to face impeachment charges, and the only one to be officially expelled from his party, John Tyler has been remembered primarily as a historical footnote. He deserves better. Although one can disagree with his reasoning on the issues, it is difficult to conclude that he acted out of malice or political expediency. Tyler remained true to his constitutional and political principles, displaying a consistency and courage rare in political leaders. He achieved some positive accomplishments despite the turmoil of his presidency, and he significantly shaped the theory of vice presidential succession under the United States Constitution.

James E. Fickle

Suggested Readings

Chitwood, Oliver Perry. *John Tyler, Champion of the Old South.* 1939. Reprint. New York: Russell and Russell, 1964. A standard biography.

Gunderson, Robert G. *The Log-Cabin Campaign.* 1957. Reprint. Westport, Conn.: Greenwood Press, 1977. Discusses Tyler's role in the 1840 presidential campaign.

Havelin, Kate. *John Tyler.* Minneapolis: Lerner, 2005. A biography written for young adults.

Howe, Daniel Walker. *The Political Culture of the American Whigs.* Chicago: University of Chicago Press, 1979. Analyzes the anti-Jackson movement and Tyler's role within it.

Monroe, Dan. *Republican Vision of John Tyler.* College Station: Texas A&M University Press, 2003. Explores Tyler's ambivalent relationships with the Democrats and the Whigs and how it shaped key events during his political career.

Morgan, Robert J. *A Whig Embattled: The Presidency Under John Tyler.* Lincoln: University of Nebraska Press, 1954. A narrative that focuses particularly on the period of Tyler's presidency.

Moser, Harold D., and Carole B. Moser. *John Tyler: A Bibliography.* Westport, Conn.: Greenwood Press, 2001. Brings together references to primary and secondary resources for further research.

Peterson, Norma L. *The Presidencies of William Henry Harrison and John Tyler.* Lawrence: University Press of Kansas, 1989. Provides a thorough examination of Tyler's presidency.

Schlesinger, Arthur M., Fred L. Israel, and David J. Frent, eds. *Election of 1840 and the Harrison/Tyler Administrations.* Broomall, Pa.: Mason Crest, 2002. Uses primary sources to chronicle the election of 1840.

Seager, Robert, II. *And Tyler Too.* New York: McGraw-Hill, 1963. A joint biography of Tyler and his second wife, Julia Gardiner Tyler.

Walker, Jane C. *John Tyler: President of Many Firsts.* Blacksburg, Va.: McDonald & Woodward, 2001. Details Tyler's presidency with an emphasis on his lasting effects on the geography and foreign relations of the United States.

James K. Polk

11th President, 1845-1849

Born: November 2, 1795
      Mecklenburg County, North
        Carolina
Died: June 15, 1849
      Nashville, Tennessee

Political Party: Democratic
Vice President: George M. Dallas

Cabinet Members

Secretary of State: James Buchanan
Secretary of the Treasury: Robert J. Walker
Secretary of War: William L. Marcy
Secretary of the Navy: George Bancroft, John Y. Mason
Attorney General: John Y. Mason, Nathan Clifford, Isaac Toucey
Postmaster General: Cave Johnson

James Knox Polk was elected in November, 1844, and held office for one term, from March 4, 1845, to March 3, 1849, at age forty-nine the youngest president until that time. He declined to be considered for reelection. Although he was not widely known at the time of his election, he had served fourteen years in the House of Representatives (four of them as speaker) and one term as governor of his home state of Tennessee. As a protégé of Andrew Jackson (he was often called Young Hickory), Polk had represented the interests of the Jackson administration in the lower house of Congress and was recognized as the floor leader in securing Jacksonian legislation. His presidency was the strongest and most vigorous of those between Jackson and Abraham Lincoln. Besides being a loyal Jacksonian Democrat in matters of domestic policy, Polk shared the expansionist fervor of his generation and as president presided over the nation's most dramatic period of territorial expansion. In the brief space of three years, Texas was annexed, the Oregon Country was acquired, and a half-million square miles of

Portrait of James K. Polk. *(Whitehouse.gov)*

Mexican territory was ceded to the United States as a result of the Mexican War. As America's first wartime president since James Madison, Polk did much to define the role of the president as commander in chief. The Mexican War dominated his administration and has influenced his reputation ever since. In spite of the controversy that has often been aroused over Polk's involvement in the war, he has fared well in presidential evaluations, as historians consistently place him among the top ten or twelve presidents of the United States.

Early Life

James K. Polk was born on November 2, 1795, in Mecklenburg County, North Carolina. His family, of sturdy Scotch-Irish stock and staunchly Presbyterian, had been in the United States since the seventeenth century, settling first in Maryland, moving to Pennsylvania, and from there sweeping southwestward with the great migration of Scotch-Irish to up-country North Carolina. Fiercely independent, the Polks resented British rule and were among the earliest to support separation from the mother country. Many of them served in the Continental Army. By the late eighteenth century, the family was among the most prominent in the region.

James K. Polk was the eldest of the ten children of Samuel and Jane Knox Polk. His father was a well-to-do farmer and, like the rest of the family, strongly Jeffersonian in politics. His mother, said to be descended from the Scottish religious leader John Knox, was a tenacious Presbyterian whose life revolved around the Bible and the teachings of the church. Nurtured on tales of America's War of Independence, Polk derived from his parents a strong patriotism, a keen interest in politics, and deep religious convictions.

Like so many North Carolinians following the Revolutionary War, members of Polk's family invested heavily in land in the state's western district, later the state of Tennessee. In 1806,

when Polk was eleven years old, his parents moved to a farm in the Duck River Valley, near Columbia in Maury County, Tennessee. His father expanded his interests from farming to mercantile activity and continued to engage in land speculation during the economic boom that followed the War of 1812.

Because of his frail health, Polk began his formal education later than most youths of his generation. After preparation in Presbyterian academies in Tennessee, he entered the University of North Carolina in Chapel Hill in 1815 as a sophomore, where he studied the classics and mathematics, two subjects he believed would best discipline his mind. He was graduated first in his class in 1818. The following year, he took up the study of law in the office of Felix Grundy, a successful Nashville lawyer and former congressman, and in 1820 was admitted to the bar. Polk established his practice in his hometown of Columbia and prospered almost immediately, thanks to the business his family placed in his charge.

It was not the law, however, but politics that stirred Polk's interest. The times were filled with opportunity for an aspiring politician. The panic of 1819 awakened the American people, jolting them out of their indifference and ushering in a period of change and uncertainty that would lead to new political alignments. In Tennessee, as elsewhere, the economic distress aroused demands that the government be more responsive to the needs of the people. A "new politics" (however vaguely defined) was called for. Symbolizing the rising dissatisfaction with the existing system was Andrew Jackson, the hero of New Orleans.

In 1819, Polk assumed his first political post, that of clerk of the state senate, and four years later he was elected to the lower house of the Tennessee legislature. His academic background, readiness in debate, and persistent application quickly marked him as a promising young leader in Tennessee politics. He supported legislation that would relieve the banking crisis in the state and bring order to its tangled land problems, and in 1823 he voted for Jackson for United States senator. Around the same time, he married Sarah Childress, daughter of a well-to-do farmer and Murfreesboro businessman, a well-educated, refined, and cultured woman who would be an important asset to his career. She would become one of the most respected First Ladies to occupy the White House.

Polk's success as a legislator led him to seek election to Congress. The presidential election of 1824 promised to be one of the most important in years. Jackson had been nominated by the Tennessee legislature two years before, and his election to the Senate further boosted his candidacy. Although his triumph seemed sure, the results of the contest indicated otherwise. Jackson received more electoral and popular votes than any other candidate, but none of the four contenders—Jackson, William H. Crawford, John Quincy Adams, and Henry Clay—received the required majority. The election was placed before the House of Representatives, where in February, 1825, Adams was elected. The cry of "bargain and corruption" was immediately raised by the outraged Jacksonians. Polk shared the belief not only that Jackson had lost because of a nefarious plot involving Adams and Clay but also that his defeat had robbed the people of their choice. The outcome of the election gave new meaning to Polk's campaign for Congress; in August, 1825, he was easily elected from his four-county district in south central Tennessee.

Jacksonian Congressman

Although Polk proved extraordinarily successful in his appeals for the votes of his constituents—he served in the House of Representatives for seven successive terms, fourteen years—he lacked the charismatic quality that brought so many Americans to the side of Jackson. Of somewhat less than middle height, unprepossessing in demeanor, he often gave the

appearance of dullness. He had but few intimate friends. Formal and stiff in his bearing, he was always concerned to maintain his dignity. When he presided over the House of Representatives as speaker during the last four years of his service, it was said that he appeared "in the chair as if he were at a dinner party." Thoughtful and reserved, his speaking style reflected his personality. His political statements lacked the ornamental flourishes common to early nineteenth century political rhetoric; instead, they were plain, sincere, and convincing, demonstrating a command of facts and principles and exhibiting a practical common sense.

John Quincy Adams once characterized Polk's speaking ability as having "no wit, no literature, no point of argument, no gracefulness of delivery, no elegance of language, no philosophy, no pathos, no felicitous impromptus; nothing that can constitute an orator, but confidence, fluency, and labor." Adams spoke as an opponent; others were more charitable.

The charge that Polk had no philosophy was unfair. The aftermath of the panic and the outcome of the presidential election brought his views into sharper focus. The Jeffersonian convictions he had absorbed from his family and the intellectual discipline he had derived from the Presbyterian influence formed the basis on which he built his political outlook. His exposure to moral philosophy at Chapel Hill gave him a well-defined sense of republican virtue and of the obligations that rested on citizens of a republic. The troubled atmosphere of the 1820's, however, revealed the need for something more. Polk found the missing ingredient in the new democratic currents of his time.

Polk prized individual freedom, the rights of the states against the centralizing tendencies of the national government, and a strict interpretation of the Constitution. The sovereignty of the people, he believed, was unquestioned and absolute. In one of his first pronouncements as a congressman, Polk declared his faith in the popular will. "That this is a Government based upon the will of the People," he stated, "that all power emanates from them; and that a majority should rule; are, as I conceive, vital principles in this Government, never to be sacrificed or abandoned, under any circumstances." He would return America's republican government to its beginnings: "I would bring the Government back to what it was intended to be—a plain economical Government."

Polk entered Congress in December, 1825,

determined to vindicate Jackson from his defeat by the Adams-Clay combination. One of his first actions was to support the effort to amend the Constitution to prevent future presidential contests from being decided in the House of Representatives. He proposed that the selection of presidential electors be made uniform throughout the country and argued that election by districts was the fairest, most democratic mode. He agreed with some that the electoral

The First Lady
Sarah Polk

Sarah Childress Polk was the wife of James K. Polk, eleventh president of the United States. Born September 4, 1803, in Rutherford County, Tennessee, to plantation owners, Sarah was a refined and well-bred beauty. She was well-educated by tutors and at Bradley Academy and Abercrombie's Boarding School in Tennessee and the Moravian Female Academy in Salem, North Carolina. Sarah grew up near Murfreesboro, Tennessee, where she was introduced to political figures like Andrew Jackson. Upon her father's death in 1819, she inherited wealth and managed her own resources with skills used later in managing the Tennessee governor's mansion and the White House.

Sarah Childress married James K. Polk, an aspiring lawyer-politician, on January 1, 1824, and they settled in Columbia, Tennessee, while James worked as clerk of the state senate. Sarah campaigned for her husband who ran successfully for election to the U.S. House of Representatives in 1825. He was dubbed "Young Hickory" after 1828 because of his political similarities and friendship with President Andrew Jackson, who was called "Old Hickory." Sarah devoted herself to James's political career as he served as Speaker of the House from 1835 to 1839 and served as Tennessee's governor from 1839 to 1841. The Polks politically rebuilt the Democratic Party in Tennessee, and because their state was a swing state, they cultivated loyal supporters from both Democrats and Whigs using bipartisan policies.

When James K. Polk was elected president of the United States in 1844, Sarah conveyed her husband's views publicly with diplomacy, charm, and grace. She read widely and left newspaper clippings and articles she wished James to read on his desk, thus furthering her agenda to aid women and children. She wrote letters and speeches, engaged in public philanthropy, and became James's most significant political confidante in the White House. As President Polk's most trusted adviser, Sarah supported the annexation of the Oregon Country, the Mexican War and expansionist policies of Manifest Destiny, and improved relations within the Western Hemisphere. She was perhaps the earliest First Lady to develop a working political partnership with her husband. Sarah was careful to maintain her image as a moral exemplar, serving no hard liquor in the White House and prohibiting dancing at presidential functions, believing the United States would be best served by serious attention to matters of state. Widowed for forty-two years following James's presidential term and early death, she remained a Southern icon, well respected during the Civil War and its aftermath until her death on August 14, 1891. Sarah and James K. Polk are buried at the state capitol in Nashville.

Barbara Bennett Peterson

college should be abandoned altogether in favor of a direct vote for president but realized the futility of proposing such a radical change.

Although the movement to amend the Constitution did not succeed, it enabled Polk to express his views on the nature of the presidential office. The president, he believed, was the chief executive of all the people, the only federal officer to be elected by all the people, and the only elected official whose constituency was the entire nation. More than any other officer, the president best reflected the popular will; therefore, he was responsible only to the people.

Polk's course in the House of Representatives established him as a loyal, orthodox Jacksonian. When Jackson defeated Adams in 1828, Polk felt that the people had been vindicated. The election was fought, he wrote, "between the virtue and rights of the people on the one hand and the power and patronage of their rules on the other."

Before long, Polk was recognized as the voice of the Jackson administration in the House of Representatives. He remained in close correspondence with the president, and Jackson frequently sent him directives and thinly veiled suggestions as to the course the House should pursue. Polk proved a trustworthy lieutenant. He waged continual war on Henry Clay's American System ("falsely called," said Polk) and warned against the "splendid Government, differing . . . only in name from a consolidated empire" that Clay's program would create. He fought efforts to fund internal improvement projects with federal money, and when the celebrated bill providing for a road from Maysville to Lexington, Kentucky, came before the House, he was assigned the task of leading the administration forces against it. The bill passed but was struck down in the first of Jackson's important vetoes. On the question of the protective tariff, Polk supported the reduction of duties without ever totally rejecting the principle of protection. When the nullification crisis pitted South Carolina against Jackson and the federal government, Polk was quick to side with the president. He assisted in drafting a compromise tariff that he hoped would placate South Carolina, but when his effort was superseded by Clay's compromise bill, he gave the Kentuckian his full support. Polk was consistent in his stand on behalf of the Union, even though some have found in his support of Jackson's position a contradiction of his Old Republican views.

Polk's appointment to the House Ways and Means Committee and his subsequent designation as its chair placed him in an advantageous position to defend Jackson's assault against the Second Bank of the United States. In early 1833, Polk took exception to the committee's report declaring the bank's soundness and prepared a minority report in which he detailed the weakness and irresponsibility of the institution. A year later, as chair of the committee, he issued a report sanctioning Jackson's removal of deposits from the bank; its adoption by the House of Representatives was a deathblow to the probank forces. In one of his most powerful speeches as a congressman, Polk inveighed against the "despotism of money" and warned that, if not checked, the power of money would soon "control your election of President, of your Senators, and of your Representatives." To Polk, the forces of money and privilege constituted the gravest threat to America's republican system of government.

Polk's election as speaker of the House of Representatives during his last two terms in Congress, from 1835 to 1839, was a tribute to his leadership, his party loyalty, and his administrative ability. As speaker, Polk demonstrated the same relentless devotion to the responsibilities of the post that he exhibited in other offices he had held. During Martin Van Buren's troubled administration, he tried desperately (and not always with success) to hold the Jacksonian coalition together. He wielded a tight and virtually absolute control over the deliberations of the House, for which he was frequently criticized by his opponents. When he left the speakership, he boasted, without exaggeration, that he had decided more difficult and complex questions of parliamentary law and order than had been decided by all of his predecessors.

Polk preferred to remain in the House of Representatives and could easily have been re-elected in 1839. Instead, he was persuaded to run for governor of Tennessee, a move his associates believed would redeem the state from Whig control, weaken the opposition, and influence the 1840 presidential election. Polk was elected, but his term of office (two years) was anticlimactic and uneventful. It was not a good time for Democrats, as much of the public's attention was focused on the effects of the panic of 1837. The party's position in the state was not strengthened. Polk was defeated for reelection in 1841, and two years later he was defeated again. The magic of the Jacksonian appeal was gone, the voters had turned away from the party of their hero, and Polk suddenly seemed an anachronism. At the age of forty-eight, after almost twenty years of public activity and service to his state and nation, his political career appeared to be over.

An Unexpected Candidate

Nine months after his second defeat for the governorship of Tennessee, in an incredible turn-around of his political fortunes, Polk was nominated for president of the United States by the Democratic Party. "Who is James K. Polk?" asked startled Whigs. Historians, taking this cue, have explained the unexpectedness of Polk's nomination by insisting that he was the nation's first "dark horse" candidate. In fact, Polk was not unknown (the Whigs knew very well who he was), nor was he so dark a horse.

When the delegates gathered at the Democratic National Convention in Baltimore in May, 1844, the name of James K. Polk was hardly mentioned. To be sure, Polk's ambitions for a place in the nation's executive branch had been aroused, but it was for the vice presidency, not the presidency. Four years before, as the

parties maneuvered for the 1840 election, his name was paired with that of Van Buren. The Tennessee legislature nominated a Van Buren-Polk ticket, friends worked for his nomination among party leaders in Washington, D.C., and Andrew Jackson gave it his endorsement. Polk's place on the ticket, it was thought, would offset Van Buren's lack of popularity among Southerners. Polk, however, was not nominated, giving way to Kentucky's Richard M. Johnson, and Van Buren lost the election. Both men set their sights on 1844.

Van Buren was the leading contender for the nomination in 1844, long before the convention met. His nomination seemed a foregone conclusion. His delegate strength mounted as state conventions pledged their support (although often without enthusiasm). The presidential race, as everyone seemed to expect, would be run between Van Buren and Clay. Whigs were confident that they would be able to repeat their triumph of four years before.

As Van Buren's candidacy became more and more certain, Polk revived his quest for the vice presidential nomination. Someone acceptable to both the West and the South, he thought, would be sought, and who better to fill the need than himself? Once again, the aid of his friends, including the aged and ailing Andrew Jackson, was enlisted. Polk's record in the House of Representatives as a steadfast and "unterrified" defender of Jacksonian democracy was publicized. His supporters doubled their efforts to advance Van Buren's candidacy for the presidential nomination under the assumption that Polk would get the second position. By the spring of 1844, it appeared that the efforts on Polk's behalf would fall short, as they had four years before, and that Richard M. Johnson would likely be the candidate a second time.

Then on April 27, a bombshell was tossed into the campaign. On that day, Washington newspapers carried letters from both Clay and Van Buren announcing their opposition to the immediate annexation of Texas to the United

States, on the ground that such a move would constitute aggression against Mexico. Van Buren's statement threw his party into confusion, desertions from his ranks began, and his opponents were handed an issue with which to defeat his nomination. The hopes of Van Buren's rivals were raised, and some sent out feelers to Polk seeking the latter's endorsement in return for the vice presidency. To Polk and his supporters, however, Van Buren's downfall suggested a different strategy.

From one of his closest friends, Polk received the suggestion that "if Van Buren is to be thrown over . . . we must have an entirely new man." There was no doubt who that new man should be. Jackson, both disappointed and angered at Van Buren's statement, insisted that the presidential candidate "should be an annexation man and reside in the Southwest" and suggested that Polk would be the "most available." Of one thing Polk was sure: If Van Buren's name were withdrawn, the balance of power in the convention would be held by his supporters; they would be able to control the nominations. "I have never aspired so high," Polk assured his friends, but while he reiterated his ambition for "the 2nd office," he made it clear that they could use his name in any way they thought fit.

Polk's credentials as a Jacksonian were impeccable, as his record in the House of Representatives attested. That he also shared Jackson's strong desire to see Texas annexed to the United States was without question. Ever since Texas's break with Mexico during the last year of his presidency, Jackson had favored annexation, although he declined to make any move in that direction because of the dangers it might create for the Union. By the early 1840's, however, the question could no longer be repressed. "It is the greatest question of the *Age*," declared one political leader, as Americans in the West and South gathered in rallies and demonstrations to demand government action. With an eye on the 1844 election, President John Tyler

promoted annexation, and Democratic leaders carried the demand into Congress. Even before Van Buren's fateful statement, Texas annexationists in the West had been looking for another candidate.

Jackson joined the cry with a letter to one of Polk's close friends in which he urged immediate annexation. Although the letter was not made public until a year later, his position was well-known to Polk. A few days before Van Buren's letter was published, Polk made his views known in response to an inquiry from a committee of Ohio Democrats. Like Jackson, he strongly favored the immediate annexation of Texas, arguing that Texas had been a part of the United States before John Quincy Adams had given it up to Spain in the Adams-Onís Treaty of 1819. He feared, as did many Western Democrats, the rise of British influence in Texas and placed his argument in the broader context of hemispheric security. Unlike Jackson, Polk linked his demand for Texas with the demand that the authority and laws of the United States be also extended to the Oregon Country.

Democratic delegates gathered in Baltimore amid fears that the party would be seriously divided over the Texas issue and Van Buren's candidacy. Although commanding the support of a majority of the delegates, Van Buren faced a growing opposition from the West and South, and when his opponents succeeded in reaffirming the rule requiring a two-thirds majority for the nomination, his chances diminished rapidly. After several inconclusive ballots, on the convention's third day Polk's name was formally presented to the body as a candidate for the presidential nomination, and before the day ended, he had received the necessary two-thirds vote.

Polk's nomination was a compromise between the opposing camps. It was acceptable to the Van Buren forces (one of Van Buren's most trusted lieutenants declared Polk to be his second choice), in part because his nomination denied the prize as well to Van Buren's rivals. The steadfastness with which Polk himself stuck to his support of Van Buren (hoping to get the vice presidential nomination) was impressive. It was New England, notably Massachusetts delegate George Bancroft, which first put his name before the convention. Polk's nomination, however, upset many rank-and-file Van Buren supporters; because it was unexpected, stories of intrigue and chicanery were circulated. Charges that his nomination had been hatched in the Hermitage were made, and the Whigs were quick to exploit them. With Polk's nomination, however, the Democratic Party acquired a candidate whose orthodoxy was above reproach—"a pure, whole-hogged democrat," as one delegate put it. Polk was also an unequivocal proponent of Texas annexation, and in 1844, that is what counted most.

The remainder of the convention was anticlimactic. For vice president, the delegates' first choice was New York's Silas Wright, but Wright refused the nomination. The weary delegates then turned to George M. Dallas of Pennsylvania. With the nominations completed, the platform was adopted almost as an afterthought. To a traditional statement of Jacksonian principles—strict construction, states' rights, opposition to a national bank, a high tariff, and federally funded internal improvements—the convention added one new plank. The title of the United States to "the whole of the Territory of Oregon" was "clear and unquestionable"; "the reoccupation of Oregon and the reannexation of Texas, at the earliest practicable period, are great American measures, which this convention recommends to the cordial support of the democracy of the Union."

The Whigs, who had already nominated Henry Clay, were startled at the turn taken by the Democrats, unbelieving and joyous that their opponents had made such a "ridiculous" nomination. Clay, in a fit of arrogant self-confidence, regretted that a person "more worthy of a contest" had not been chosen.

Clay need not have worried, for the campaign of 1844 was a hard-fought and bitter contest. The parties were evenly matched, a sign that the party system had reached a stage of maturity. Clay was moved to acts of desperation, which in the end cost him dearly. At the last minute, he experienced a sudden change of heart on the Texas question and joined the annexationists, and his efforts to dissociate himself from Northern abolitionists drove their support away, especially in New York. There, the Liberty Party candidate, James G. Birney, took enough voters away from the Whig column to give the state to Polk; it was Polk's victory in New York, in turn, that gave the Democrats their electoral majority.

Polk won the presidency with 170 electoral votes to Clay's 105. His popular vote exceeded that of Clay by only 38,000 out of a total of almost 2,700,000 votes cast. Polk's nomination and election, following so quickly after his failures to win the governorship of Tennessee, has been judged well-nigh miraculous. Although many unique circumstances involving issues, partisanship, and power contributed to his success, Charles Sellers, Polk's biographer, gives the larger share of credit to "the behavior of a remarkably audacious, self-controlled, and prescient politician" who shaped his course "with impressive skill and coolness."

A Continental Vision

Polk's inaugural address was in sharp contrast to the gloomy, rainy weather in Washington on March 4, 1845. It was a message of hope and confidence for a youthful nation from a president who was younger than any of his predecessors. A paean to America's republican system, it exhibited the ardor that many people felt toward the nation's future. The United States, "this Heaven-favored land," he declared, enjoyed the "most admirable and wisest system of well-regulated self-government among men ever devised by human minds." It was the "noblest structure of human wisdom," wherein burned the fire of liberty, warming and ani-

The Vice President
George M. Dallas

George Mifflin Dallas, the son of a lawyer and politician, was born on July 10, 1792, in Philadelphia, Pennsylvania. A graduate of Princeton University in 1807, Dallas studied law with his father in preparation for the bar exam. Losing interest in law, he joined the Pennsylvania militia in 1813; however, his father ordered him to return home.

A exciting opportunity then presented itself to the young man, and Dallas accepted the position of private secretary to Albert Gallatin on a diplomatic mission to Russia in order to settle differences between the United States and Great Britain resulting from the War of 1812. Returning to the United States to present a preliminary peace treaty for President James Madison's approval, Dallas met and immediately fell in love with Sophia Chew Nicklin, the daughter of a prominent businessman. While courting Nicklin, Dallas reestablished his interest in law, and he was admitted to the bar in 1815. On May 23, 1816, George and Sophia were married, and together they had eight children.

Dallas's subsequent career included serving as deputy attorney general of Pennsylvania, United States senator, and foreign minister to Russia. He returned to his home in Pennsylvania in 1839 and resumed his law practice. However, Dallas once again found himself called back to public service when he joined James K. Polk as the vice presidential nominee in 1844. After completing one term as vice president, Dallas returned home to his flourishing law practice.

In 1856, President Franklin Pierce sent Dallas to England on a diplomatic mission, where he would remain for four years. Upon returning home in June, 1861, he accepted the position of president of the Atlantic and Great Western Railroad. Although appearing to be in excellent health, George Mifflin Dallas died unexpectedly from a heart attack on December 31, 1864.

Robert P. Watson and Richard Yon

mating "the hearts of happy millions" and inviting "all the nations of the earth to imitate our example." Under the benign influence of their government, the American people were "free to improve their condition by the legitimate exercise of all their mental and physical powers."

The sheet anchor of American republicanism was the Union; to protect and preserve the Union was the sacred duty of every American. Warning against the forces of sectionalism that would disturb and destroy the Union, Polk struck out at those "misguided persons" whose object was the "destruction of domestic institutions existing in other sections," a reference to the abolitionists. The consequences of their agitation could only be the dissolution of the Union and the "destruction of our happy form of government." Preserved and protected, the Union was the guarantee that the "blessings of civil and religious liberty" would be transmitted to "distant generations." "Who shall assign limits to the achievements of free minds and free hands under the protection of this glorious Union?" he asked.

In a confession of his Jacksonian faith, Polk called for a strict adherence to the Constitution and a scrupulous respect for the rights of the states, each sovereign "within the sphere of its reserved powers." The government must be returned to the "plain and frugal" system intended by its founders. There was no need for national banks "or other extraneous institutions"; in levying tariff duties, revenue must be the object and protection only incidental.

More than a third of his address was devoted to the new spirit of continental expansion.

He rejected the pessimistic view of some Americans that the nation's system of government could not be successfully applied to a large extent of territory. On the contrary, Polk insisted, the "federative system" was well adapted to territorial expansion, and as the nation's boundaries were enlarged, it acquired "additional strength and security." The annexation of Texas, "once a part of our country" that was "unwisely ceded away," was of first importance, and Polk lauded Congress for taking the initial steps to effect the reunion of Texas with the United States. To the settlement of the Oregon question, he stated, he was no less dedicated. America's title to the region was "clear and unquestionable." Thousands of Americans, moreover, were establishing their homes in this far-flung corner, and the extension of the jurisdiction and benefits of the country's republican institutions to the area was an inescapable duty.

Whereas the inaugural address provided the general direction of the course that President Polk had charted for himself, a statement made to the historian George Bancroft supplied the specifics. He intended, he told Bancroft at the time of his inauguration, to accomplish four great measures during his administration. Two of them related to his vision of continental expansion: the settlement of the Oregon boundary question with Great Britain and the acquisition of California. (It is interesting to note that aside from a general concern over the fate of California and the impulsive capture and brief occupation of Monterey by American naval forces in 1842, California had not been seriously mentioned as a target for American expansion.) The third was the reduction of the tariff to a revenue level, and the last was the establishment of the independent Treasury system, the Democrats' alternative to a third national bank. The independent Treasury had been created by Congress in the waning days of the Van Buren administration, only to be repealed by the Whigs in 1841.

It was a large order for the new president, the more so since he had pledged to serve only a single term. Following his nomination, Polk made the promise in order to secure the support of Van Buren's leading rivals, men such as Lewis Cass, James Buchanan, and John C. Calhoun, whose hopes would be dashed if they had to wait eight more years to pursue their presidential ambitions. Concerned lest he appear to be favoring one or another for the succession, Polk refused to select any presidential aspirant for his cabinet. His appointees were to be men devoted to him and not to their own, or someone else's, advancement. He later regretted that he had taken at face value the disclaimer of Buchanan, whom he appointed secretary of state. Polk would thread his way carefully through the cliques and factions of the party, determined to maintain his independence. "I intend to be myself President of the U.S.," he wrote a friend.

Missing from Polk's list of intended achievements was the annexation of Texas, for by the time he was inaugurated, the annexation had already been set in motion. As president-elect, Polk played an important part in the movement. His election in November, 1844, was viewed as a mandate for annexation, and steps were immediately taken in the short session of Congress that followed. Polk himself favored a settlement of the issue before he should be inaugurated. The only question to be resolved was which plan to effect annexation would be adopted — a House resolution to annex simply by a joint resolution of Congress or a Senate bill that called for the appointment of commissioners to negotiate an agreement with Texas. Although he favored the former, Polk sought to avoid an impasse by proposing a compromise, whereby the two modes would be combined as alternatives, with the president empowered to choose between them. The assumption was that the decision would be made by the new president, Polk, rather than by John Tyler, the outgoing president. The measure passed Congress in the last days of the session and was signed by Tyler on March 1. To Congress's surprise, however, it was Tyler who acted quickly to exercise the option; he dispatched a messenger to Texas with the offer of annexation.

It remained only for Polk to complete the process following his inauguration. He could have reversed Tyler's decision (and some senators expected him to do so), but Polk let it stand. In the face of mounting public excitement for annexation in both the United States and Texas, the Texas government assented, but only after the American emissaries (and Polk) agreed to recognize Texas's claim to the Rio Grande boundary and to provide military protection to Texas as soon as annexation had been accepted. On July 4, a Texas convention voted to accept annexation and proceeded to draw up

a state constitution; later in December, Congress admitted Texas to the Union as a state. Polk's role in the annexation of Texas has been closely scrutinized by historians, and some have argued that his insistence on the Rio Grande boundary and his dispatch of troops into Texas were part of a deliberate scheme to provoke Mexico to war and thus open the way for the acquisition of California. Certainly, relations between the United States and Mexico, which had been deteriorating for years, worsened, as the Mexican government charged the United States with an act of aggression against Mexico and recalled its minister from Washington.

With the Texas issue moving toward a resolution, Polk turned his attention to the Oregon boundary question. Although the Democratic

A political cartoon from 1846 examines the Oregon boundary dispute with Great Britain. Polk and the hawkish "General Bunkum" (on the right) negotiate with Queen Victoria, Prince Albert, and the duke of Wellington (on the left), while Irish leader Daniel O'Connell, Russian czar Nicholas I, and French king Louis Philippe look on. *(Library of Congress)*

Immigrants walk the Oregon Trail. *(Library of Congress)*

platform and Polk's inaugural statements brought the question to a head, the dispute with Great Britain had been of long duration. Unable to settle their conflicting claims to the region, the two countries had negotiated a joint occupation agreement in 1818, at the time the boundary between the United States and British North America east of the Rocky Mountains was drawn along the forty-ninth parallel. The agreement, originally to run for ten years, was renewed for an indefinite period in 1827, with the proviso that either country might terminate the agreement by giving the other country one year's notice. Repeated efforts were made to resolve the dispute, the United States offering to extend the forty-ninth parallel to the Pacific and the British insisting on the Columbia River as the boundary. Neither side was willing to give in to the other.

British fur-trading interests were active in the Oregon Country during the early years of the century, but no attempts to settle it permanently were undertaken. Little was done by the United States to challenge the British presence,

even though sentiment favored the ultimate extension of American sovereignty to the region. The situation changed in the 1830's when American missionaries arrived in Oregon; their reports were widely publicized and did much to arouse public feeling in support of an American occupation of the far Northwest. Indeed, the missionary efforts were responsible for the first movement of permanent settlers to Oregon's western valleys. The distress experienced by Western farmers in the aftermath of the panic of 1837 turned further attention to Oregon's rich soil and salubrious climate. Before long, an "Oregon Fever" raged, especially in the Mississippi Valley; people gathered in meetings and demonstrations to sing the praises of the new land and to voice their demands that the United States act quickly to extend its laws and institutions to Oregon's growing population.

Each year, large numbers of families gathered in their wagons in Independence, Missouri (the jumping-off point), and prepared to make the long trek over the Oregon Trail to the Pacific Northwest. As the population of Oregon grew, the settlers became increasingly impatient with the apparent reluctance of the United States government to recognize their needs. Beginning in 1841, they took steps to establish a provisional government of their own that would at least provide a semblance of law and order, but their uppermost desire was to be reunited with their country. The expansionist fervor of Western Democrats, fueled by the movement of Americans to Oregon, found expression in the repudiation of Martin Van Buren's candidacy and in the election of Polk to the presidency.

Following the 1844 election, the Oregon question became a heated national issue, as its supporters moved to the more radical demand that all of Oregon be acquired, meaning all that territory from the forty-second parallel north to 54 degrees 40 minutes. "Fifty-four Forty or Fight" became a new rallying cry. Polk seemed to endorse this new extreme in his inaugural address, although privately he still believed that the extension of the forty-ninth parallel, America's traditional position, was the most feasible solution. The British government became alarmed at the bellicose tone of the American demands and feared that war might break out between the two countries.

Polk had no more intention than the British of fighting a war over the Oregon Country, but he was not above using the more radical demands to strengthen his efforts to settle the boundary dispute. As in the case of the Texas issue, the Tyler administration had taken steps to settle the question, and Polk's first actions were based on those of his predecessor. In July, he offered once again to draw the line along the forty-ninth parallel, without at the same time surrendering the American claim to the whole of Oregon. The offer was categorically rejected by the British minister in Washington without transmitting it to his government in London. Polk was both shocked and furious. He had made the offer, he said, out of deference to his predecessors; the offer was withdrawn, and the claim to all of Oregon was reasserted. The ball

was now in the British court.

Polk was playing a dangerous game. Amid fears that his unyielding attitude would involve the United States in a war with Great Britain, Polk refused to back down. "The only way to treat John Bull," he confided to his diary, "was to look him straight in the eye." At the same time, the issue assumed an added urgency. Relations with Mexico were approaching a crisis, and Polk's attention was divided between the two situations. As with his Texas policy, there were hints that California was in his mind. The settlement of the Oregon question might deter Great Britain from acquiring California (perceived as a real threat in 1845), leaving the way open for an American acquisition through negotiations with Mexico.

Polk's course was bold and daring; at the same time, he was convinced that it was a peaceful one. In his first message to Congress, in December, 1845, he asked Congress to provide the one year's notice that the United States was terminating the joint occupation agreement with Great Britain. Furthermore, he asked that jurisdiction be extended over the Americans living in Oregon and that steps be taken to provide military protection to emigrants along the route to Oregon. Finally, he restated the Monroe Doctrine against any further colonization of North America by a European power, a reference to the British designs on California. Congress responded but not until the spring of 1846, when the one year's notice resolution was finally approved.

As Polk had expected, the passage of the resolution spurred the British government to make a new offer to the United States. It was tantamount to a surrender to the traditional American position. An extension of the boundary along the forty-ninth parallel was proposed, with the provision that British settlers south of that line could retain title to their lands and that the great fur-trading organization, the Hudson's Bay Company, would be allowed the free navigation of the Columbia River. The latter stipulation was not crucial, for by 1846 the company had moved its operations to Vancouver Island in anticipation of the boundary settlement. Polk stood firm but offered to seek the advice of the Senate. When the Senate advised the president by an overwhelming vote to accept the terms, Polk relented, and on June 15, 1846, a treaty was signed by the two powers that brought an end to the boundary dispute.

The settlement of the Oregon boundary has often been seen as a compromise between the United States and Great Britain. Insofar as the United States receded from its extreme demand for all of Oregon, it perhaps was. In the perspective of the long history of negotiations, however, the treaty was clearly a diplomatic victory for the United States—and that is how Polk viewed it. He had secured all that he initially sought; his firm stance had paid off. Western expansionist Democrats saw the result as neither a victory nor a compromise; to them, it was an abject surrender of an unquestioned American claim. Some of them never forgave Polk.

Within fifteen months of his inauguration, Polk had presided over the addition of two immense regions to the United States, Texas and Oregon, not only fulfilling the pledge in the Democratic platform on which he was elected but also bringing his dream of continental expansion closer to reality. There still remained the acquisition of California. That too had been set in motion; one month before the Oregon treaty was signed, Polk announced to Congress that war between the United States and Mexico had begun.

Relations with Mexico

In both Texas and Oregon, Polk carried to fruition problems that he had inherited from a previous administration to the ultimate advantage of the United States. The same was true with the deteriorated state of U.S.-Mexico relations. Ever since Mexico had won its independence from Spain in the early 1820's, relations between the two countries had been on a downward slide. The initial enthusiasm expressed by Americans over the organization of a sister republic waned as Mexico became a country wracked by revolution and plagued by instability. The perception of Mexican irresponsibility (an attitude fomented among Europeans perhaps to a greater extent than among Americans) and of Mexico's inability to provide a sound and efficient republican system grew, and it was easy for critics to explain the situation in racial terms.

Two issues brought relations between the two countries to a crisis in the Polk administration: the claims issue and the issue of Texas annexation. With independence from Spain, Mexico freed itself from the restrictive policies of Spanish mercantilism and opened its borders to foreign commercial activity. The frequency of revolution, exacerbated by an inability by foreigners to appreciate cultural differences, often resulted in the loss of property (and sometimes lives) by foreign nationals. Claims for compensation were lodged against the Mexican government; when it became obvious that Mexico was unable to pay, the claimants appealed to their governments—principally Great Britain, France, and the United States—for support. That the claims were often exaggerated did not lessen the determination of the governments to intervene on behalf of their aggrieved citizens.

The British and French solution was to exact payment by force. The French landed soldiers at Vera Cruz and fought a brief engagement (known as the Pastry War) with Mexican troops; Great Britain followed with a blockade of the Mexican coastline. Both Great Britain and France, with Spanish support, concluded that only the establishment of a monarchy in Mexico, headed by a European prince, could stabilize Mexico. The prospect horrified Americans.

Although Jackson had once threatened war against Mexico over the claims issue, the course of the United States had been a peaceful one.

The Oregon Treaty

Signed June 15, 1846

Her Majesty the Queen of the United Kingdom of Great Britain and Ireland, and the United States of America, deeming it to be desirable for the future welfare of both countries, that the state of doubt and uncertainty which has hitherto prevailed respecting the sovereignty and government of the territory on the Northwest Coast of America, lying westward of the Rocky or Stony Mountains, should be finally terminated by an amicable compromise of the rights mutually asserted by the two parties over the said territory . . . [and] having communicated to each other their respective full powers found in good and due form, have agreed upon and concluded the following Articles:

ARTICLE I. From the point of the forty-ninth parallel of north latitude, where the boundary laid down in existing treaties and conventions between the United States and Great Britain terminates, the line of boundary between the territories of the United States and those of her Britannic Majesty shall be continued westward along the said forty-ninth parallel of north latitude to the middle of the channel which separates the continent from Vancouver's Island, and thence southerly through the middle of the said channel, and of Fuca's Straits, to the Pacific Ocean: Provided, however, That the navigation of the whole of the said channel and straits, south of the forty-ninth parallel of north latitude, remain free and open to both parties.

ARTICLE II. From the point at which the forty-ninth parallel of north latitude shall be found to intersect the great northern branch of the Columbia River, the navigation of the said branch shall be free and open to the Hudson's Bay Company, and to all British subjects trading with the same, to the point where the said branch meets the main stream of the Columbia, and thence down the said main stream to the ocean, with free access into and through the said river or rivers, it being understood that all the usual portages along the line thus described shall, in like manner, be free and open. In navigating the said river or rivers, British subjects, with their goods and produce, shall be treated on the same footing as citizens of the United States; it being, however, always understood that nothing in this article shall be construed as preventing, or intended to prevent, the government of the United States from making any regulations respecting the navigation of the said river or rivers not inconsistent with the present treaty.

ARTICLE III. In the future appropriation of the territory south of the forty-ninth parallel of north latitude, as provided in the first article of this treaty, the possessory rights of the Hudson's Bay Company, and of all British subjects who may be already in the occupation of land or other property lawfully acquired within the said territory, shall be respected.

ARTICLE IV. The farms, lands, and other property of every description, belonging to the Puget's Sound Agricultural Company, on the north side of the Columbia River, shall be confirmed to the said company. In case, however, the situation of those farms and lands should be considered by the United States to be of public and political importance, and the United States government should signify a desire to obtain possession of the whole, or of any part thereof, the property so required shall be transferred to the said government, at a proper valuation, to be agreed upon between the parties.

The issue was submitted to arbitration, the size of the claim was scaled down by two-thirds, and Mexico agreed to make payments to the United States. After only a few installments, Mexico defaulted. The claims issue continued to fester. By 1845, when Polk was inaugurated, it had become a major source of contention between the two countries. Fears, fed by rumors, that California would be either ceded to or seized by the British in payment for the Mexican debt became magnified. To many Americans, California seemed suitable payment for Mexico's unpaid debt to the United States, especially since large numbers of emigrants were now crossing the plains and mountains to settle in California's interior valleys.

It was the annexation of Texas, however, that had a more immediate impact on American relations with Mexico. Ever since Texas had won its independence in 1836, Mexico had nurtured plans for regaining the region. When Texas gave up its independence to accept integration into the American Union, such plans suffered a major setback. The issue became involved in Mexico's domestic politics, and no Mexican leader could ignore the rising anti-American sentiment in the country. Although the hard-line government of Antonio López de Santa Anna had been ousted by a coup in 1844 and replaced with the more liberal administration of José Joaquín Herrera, Mexico could ill afford to recognize the loss of Texas. On the contrary, the passage of the annexation resolution early in March, 1845, was viewed as equivalent to "a declaration of war against the Mexican Republic" and "sufficient for the immediate proclamation of war" on Mexico's part. The Mexican minister to Washington was recalled, and diplomatic relations between the two nations were broken off.

A political cartoon favoring the annexation of Texas. *(Library of Congress)*

The volatility of the claims and Texas issues had never been so great as when Polk assumed office. His initial actions regarding Texas, the recognition of the Rio Grande boundary and the promise of military protection to the Texans, only aggravated the situation. United States Army troops, commanded by Zachary Taylor, entered Texas and took up positions at Corpus Christi, on the south bank of the Nueces River. Mexico responded by ordering an increase in the size of the Mexican army and threatened war against the United States as soon as the annexation process should be completed.

In the face of the heightened tension, Polk sent a personal representative, William S. Parrott (probably a poor choice inasmuch as Parrott was one of the largest claimants against the Mexican government), to probe the possibility of reopening diplomatic relations. When Parrott reported that the Herrera government would receive a qualified commissioner to negotiate the differences between the two countries, Polk moved to the next step. He chose John Slidell, congressman from Louisiana, to go to Mexico with instructions to secure Mexican recognition of the Rio Grande boundary in exchange for the cancellation of the claims and to offer to purchase California and New Mexico for an undetermined sum of money. The threat of British seizure of California seemed real: Parrott had emphasized it in his report from Mexico City, and Polk was determined to frustrate it.

Slidell went to Mexico, however, not only as a commissioner to negotiate a settlement of the disputes but also as a fully accredited minister, an effort on Polk's part to reopen diplomatic relations but one that would place Herrera in jeopardy if accepted. Slidell's arrival in Mexico was greeted by an outburst of anti-American activity as reports spread that Slidell intended to secure for the United States not only Texas but also the northern Mexican borderlands. Under the circumstances, the Herrera government could not receive Slidell; the rebuff, however, did not save it. A revolution forced Herrera out of office, and his place was taken by General Mariano Paredes, a monarchist who almost immediately contacted European powers with the intention of establishing a monarchy in Mexico as the only way the country could be saved from the United States.

Texas was admitted to the Union as a state in December, 1845, and shortly afterward, Taylor's army was ordered to new positions along the Rio Grande; by the end of March, 1846, he had arrived opposite the Mexican town of Matamoros. In the meantime, Slidell applied for recognition to Paredes, but with no different result. If Slidell should be rejected a second time, Secretary of State Buchanan had written, "the cup of forbearance will then have been exhausted." Nothing remained, he stated, "but to take the redress of the injuries to our citizens and the insults to our Government into our hands."

In rejecting Slidell, the Paredes government reiterated the position that the annexation of Texas was a cause for war between the two countries. Paredes followed with an order to mobilize Mexico's armed forces and to reinforce Mexican troops on the south bank of the Rio Grande. Taylor had been told to regard any Mexican attempt to cross the Rio Grande as an act of war, whereas the Mexican commander viewed Taylor's refusal to pull back as an act of war. Paredes further emphasized the Mexican position by declaring a "defensive war" against the United States in April. There matters between the two countries stood in the spring of 1846. Sentiment for war was on the increase in both countries. With European encouragement, Mexico was led to believe that a conflict with the United States would result in easy victory, and Americans, gripped by an expansionist fervor, resentful of supposed insults to their sovereignty and threats against their republican system, were equally persuaded that a war against Mexico would be quick and smooth.

With the arrival of news in Washington,

D.C., that Slidell's mission had failed, Polk was prepared to adopt "strong measures towards Mexico" but delayed until the Oregon question, then reaching its climax, should be settled. When Slidell returned to the capital and reported to the president, Polk agreed that action against Mexico must be taken. After securing cabinet approval, he decided to recommend a declaration of war to Congress. That night, he received a dispatch from General Taylor. Mexican forces had crossed the Rio Grande and had engaged American troops, resulting in some loss of life. To Polk, there no longer was any question as to what policy should be followed.

On May 11, 1846, Polk sent his war message to Congress. "The grievous wrongs perpetrated by Mexico upon our citizens," he declared, "remain unredressed, and solemn treaties pledging [Mexico's] public faith for this redress have been disregarded." The United States, he continued, in what some regarded as an exaggeration, had "tried every effort at reconciliation" but to no avail.

> The cup of forbearance had been exhausted even before the recent information from the frontier of the Del Norte [Rio Grande]. But now, after reiterated menaces, Mexico has passed the boundary of the United States, has invaded our territory and shed American blood upon the American soil. . . . As war exists, and, notwithstanding all our efforts to avoid it, exists by the act of Mexico herself, we are called upon by every consideration of duty and patriotism to vindicate with decision the honor, the rights, and the interests of our country.

Two days later, Congress, by a decisive vote, recognized a state of war between the United States and Mexico, empowered the president to use the army and navy against Mexico, appropriated $10 million for military purposes, and authorized the enlistment of fifty thousand volunteer troops. A short time later, Polk told his cabinet that "in making peace with our adversary, we shall acquire California, New Mexico,

and other further territory, as an indemnity for this war, if we can."

The War with Mexico

The war with Mexico was a short war, as wars go, yet it was an extremely important conflict for the United States. Stung by the taunts of European powers that republics were ill equipped to fight wars and, because they eschewed professional standing armies, helpless to defend themselves, Americans saw in the war an opportunity to strengthen republicanism, both at home and abroad. Those who were uncomfortable with a conflict between two republics were also aware that Mexico's republican institutions had never been allowed to work, that repeated revolution and turmoil had destroyed their effectiveness, and that, in fact, the nation, through much of its life, had been ruled as a military dictatorship. Thus the war for many assumed an idealistic character.

At the same time, it was clear that the United States would benefit greatly by a victory over Mexico. Polk's continental vision would become a reality and his dream of adding California to the nation would be fulfilled. The war was a natural outgrowth of the expansionist feeling of the 1840's, a feeling that Polk shared. Although he denied that it was being fought for conquest, the circumstances of its origin suggested otherwise. As a result, Polk's role has been a controversial one in American historiography, as some historians have insisted that he deliberately provoked an unjust war in order to satisfy his lust for more territory.

Following the call for volunteers, a wave of war excitement passed over the country. Men flocked to the colors, many more than could be handled, and the quotas assigned some of the states were oversubscribed. The war, fought in a distant exotic land, held a romantic appeal for those who volunteered, an appeal that soon faded as the fighting began. The response to the volunteer calls, however, confirmed the belief that the republic could rely on its citizen-soldiers during times of crisis.

The problems faced by the Polk administration in fighting the war were enormous; that they were met and for the most part solved was a tribute to the president's administrative ability. For the first time, the country was compelled to raise large numbers of troops in a short time, to train, equip, and move them quickly to distant points. Knowledge of Mexico was sketchy and the means for gathering intelligence either nonexistent or crude. War material had to be produced on an unprecedented scale, and quartermaster stores (everything necessary to support an army in the field) had to be provided without delay. Ships were built, purchased, or chartered to carry the men to the battle areas. The need to coordinate naval and land operations and to direct the movement of troops in enemy territory placed a premium on military skill and ingenuity.

Military operations were mounted in three areas. General Zachary Taylor crossed the Rio Grande and moved into northern Mexico, fighting a desperate and costly battle for Monterrey in September, 1846, and achieving one of the greatest victories of the war at the Battle of Buena Vista in February, 1847. A second army, commanded by General Stephen Watts Kearny, moved west from Missouri over the Santa Fe Trail, occupying New Mexico and, in conjunction with naval forces, taking possession of California. A third front was opened in the spring of 1847 when General Winfield Scott, in the greatest amphibious operation to that time, landed twelve thousand soldiers at Vera Cruz. Marching inland along the route of Hernán Cortés's sixteenth century invasion, Scott's army fought several sharp engagements, including a series of battles in the vicinity of Mexico City, before occupying the Mexican capital in September, 1847. With the occupation of Mexico City, the fighting came to an end, except for sporadic guerrilla activity along the lines of supply.

In his administration of the war, Polk contributed significantly to a definition of the president's role as commander in chief, and his exercise of military power became a model for future presidents. He assumed full responsibility for the conduct of the war, taking the initiative in securing war legislation and finance, deciding on military strategy, appointing generals and drafting their instructions, directing the supply efforts, and coordinating the work of the various bureaus and cabinet departments. He insisted on being informed of every decision that was made by his cabinet officers. Polk was, as one author has written, "the center on which all else depended."

There were problems, however, on which Polk faltered. He was bothered by the fact that the two senior officers in the army, Winfield Scott and Zachary Taylor, were both Whigs. He had no choice but to rely on them, in spite of the uncomfortable prospect that their exploits would advance their prestige and lead to presidential ambitions. To allay his doubts, he made a clumsy effort to persuade Congress to revive the rank of lieutenant general so that he might appoint a Democrat to this highranking post. Congress refused. His dislike for Scott was deep seated, culminating in Polk's unfair treatment of the general at the end of the war when Scott was relieved of his command and recalled to face a military inquiry. At the same time, Polk made some disastrous appointments of civilians to military commands, the most notorious being that of his former law partner, Gideon Pillow. On balance, however, Polk's conduct of the war was good. There were limits to even his endurance, and the long hours he devoted to his task and his intense application of energy eventually undermined his health.

When Polk delivered his war message to Congress, he anticipated a short conflict. Indeed, he expected Mexico to sue for peace in the very first weeks and months of the war, but the Mexican government, in spite of an unbroken series of military defeats, refused to give up. Almost as soon as the war began, Polk was seeking ways to end it. He made overtures to the Paredes government in the summer of 1846, but without success. At the same time, he entered into discussions with Santa Anna, exiled in Havana, offering to help restore the former Mexican leader to power in return for a peaceful settlement of the conflict. Santa Anna gave his assurances, and Polk foolishly believed him. Following his return to Mexico, Santa Anna assumed personal command of the army, increased its size, and took the field against the Americans.

With the failure of his peace efforts, Polk decided to open an offensive against Mexico City from Vera Cruz and reluctantly placed Scott in charge. Confident that this operation would bring the war to an end, he appointed Nicholas Trist, chief clerk of the State Department, to accompany Scott and granted him authority to suspend hostilities and enter into peace negotiations whenever Mexico might appear receptive. His instructions called for the cession of Upper and Lower California and New Mexico, the cancellation of the claims, and the payment of $15 million to Mexico.

Trist's task was not an easy one. He became involved in bitter personal quarrels with Scott, who resented the encroachment on his own authority, although relations between the two men later improved. Mexico was still unwilling to end the war, and Trist's efforts to lure Mexican representatives to the peace table, including an abortive plan to bribe Santa Anna, proved futile. It was not until the end of the summer, with Scott's army in the environs of Mexico City, that Santa Anna finally appointed commissioners to deal with Trist. Still, there was no meeting of the minds. Polk's impatience mounted. Extreme expansionists in the United States were demanding all of Mexico, and Polk himself apparently concluded that more territory should be taken from Mexico. Finally, in October, 1847, frustrated and at the end of his patience, Polk recalled Trist.

Trist, however, was determined to conclude a peace treaty with Mexico. He disregarded Polk's order and remained in touch with his Mexican counterparts, confident that no one else Polk might send could do better than he. The discussions continued, Polk became exasperated at Trist's arrogance, and Scott began making preparations to resume military operations. British diplomats urged the Mexican government to make peace; the country was rapidly falling into disarray. Santa Anna finally relented at the end of January, 1848.

The Treaty of Guadalupe Hidalgo, named after the town in which the document was signed, followed Trist's original instructions (except for the cession of Lower California). Mexico agreed to recognize the Rio Grande as the boundary of Texas and to cede New Mexico and Upper California to the United States; the United States assumed all the claims against Mexico and agreed to pay Mexico $15 million. Although Trist negotiated and signed the settlement without diplomatic authority, Polk accepted it and in late February transmitted the treaty to the Senate for ratification. By the end of May, the treaty was ratified by Mexico. Dispatched by special messenger to Washington, D.C., the document was delivered to Polk on July 4, when he proclaimed an end to the war amid the festivities celebrating America's independence.

When Polk submitted his fourth and last annual message to Congress in December, 1848, he pointed proudly to the fulfillment of America's expansionist destiny. The acquisition of California and New Mexico, the settlement of the Oregon boundary, and the annexation of Texas, he declared, "are the results which . . . will add more to the strength and wealth of the nation than any which have preceded them since the adoption of the Constitution." Within less than four years, almost 1,200,000 square miles of territory had been added to the United States, an area half as large as the nation before the acquisition. The geographic configuration of the country had undergone a profound change, for "the Mississippi, so lately the frontier of our country, is now only its center."

The war with Mexico, he continued, belied the assertions of Europeans that the United States was a weak and ineffective power. The United States had demonstrated "the capacity of republican governments to prosecute successfully a just and necessary foreign war with all the vigor usually attributed to more arbitrary forms of government." There could no longer be any doubt that a "popular representative government" was equal to any emergency likely to arise. The war had increased American prestige abroad, and even at that moment, Polk declared, European countries were struggling to erect republican governments on the American model.

"Peace, plenty, and contentment reign throughout our borders, and our beloved country presents a sublime moral spectacle to the world.... We are the most favored people on the face of the earth."

Slavery

With the advantage of hindsight, one can now wonder at Polk's optimistic faith in the future of his country, for although the Mexican War resulted in the addition of vast new regions to the republic, it also raised an issue that would rock the nation to its foundations.

It was inevitable that the question of territorial expansion would become involved with that of slavery. The first warning had in fact been sounded in 1819 when Missouri applied for admission to the Union as a slave state. The Missouri Compromise of 1820 resolved the issue, but few Americans believed it to be finally settled. The emergence of a militant abolition movement in sections of the North was a clear indication that the problem would only become more acute. Northern antislavery and abolitionist elements, a small but growing minority, strenuously opposed the annexation of Texas on the ground that it would strengthen the institution of slavery. Later, they took a

The landing of U.S. troops at Vera Cruz during the Mexican War. *(Library of Congress)*

strong stand against the Mexican War, in the mistaken belief that the war was a grand plot of the slave power to extend the institution to new areas, and they vented their spleen against Polk as one of the leading conspirators. Although their cries were drowned out in the enthusiasm that followed the opening of the war, they constituted a formidable political force.

It was not an abolitionist, however, but a disgruntled Pennsylvania Democratic congressman who first interjected the slavery issue into the deliberations on the war. David Wilmot, who believed that the Western territories should be reserved for free white settlers but who also had clashed with President Polk over the latter's tariff and internal improvements policies, introduced a resolution in August, 1846, that would bar slavery forever from all territory taken from Mexico. The so-called Wilmot Proviso, attached to an appropriation bill, became a rallying point for antislavery people and a focus for opposition to the war itself.

Although Polk was a slaveholder with plantations in Tennessee and Mississippi, he had never actively defended the institution. As a member of Congress, he had deplored the persistent agitation of the issue and believed that it only hampered the deliberation of more important questions. He had supported the gag rule, by which antislavery petitions were automatically tabled without being read, and as speaker of the House of Representatives he had enforced it. At the same time, he viewed slavery as an evil that affected not only the South but the entire nation as well, insisting that slaves were a species of property with a difference, inasmuch as they were also rational human beings. Although abolitionists believed otherwise, Polk had never linked his continental vision with a desire to extend slavery throughout the West.

Polk was shocked and dismayed by Wilmot's move, calling the resolution a "mischievous & foolish amendment." He feared that it would only entangle and frustrate his efforts to make peace with Mexico. "What connection

slavery has with making peace with Mexico," he confided, "it is difficult to conceive." Still, the issue would not go away. Although it was never adopted by both houses of Congress, the Wilmot Proviso was raised in the following years, gathering momentum and strengthening the antislavery forces that were opposed to the war. Discussions in Congress became more heated, and Polk worried lest they sidetrack needed war legislation and jeopardize the acquisition of California and New Mexico. The question, he argued, was an abstract one, for not only had Mexico abolished slavery in the territory in question, but also slavery could never exist there. He blamed the "ultra" Northerners and the "ultra" Southerners for placing the Union in danger by their demands. "There is no patriotism on either side," he wrote, "it is a most wicked agitation that can end in no good and must produce infinite mischief."

With the end of the war and the ratification of the Treaty of Guadalupe Hidalgo, the discussion shifted to the question of providing territorial governments for the new lands. In August, 1848, Congress, after much debate, finally agreed on a bill organizing a territorial government for Oregon, with slavery prohibited in keeping with the wishes of the population, and Polk signed it into law, pointing out that the territory lay wholly north of the Missouri Compromise line.

Governments for California and New Mexico were not so easily established. Polk would have been happy to see the Missouri Compromise line extended to the Pacific, but Northern antislavery elements had already defeated that proposal. He was strongly opposed to the Wilmot Proviso's prohibition of slavery in the area because he believed that it would divide the nation, not because he was anxious to see slavery spread. At the same time, he tried to point out that the slavery question involved much more than a matter of property rights to the people in the South. The question "ascends far higher, and involves the domestic peace and security of every family." By the time Congress was able to agree on the organization of governments for California and New Mexico, Polk had not only left office but had also died.

Young Hickory

Although Polk's administration was dominated by territorial expansion and the war with Mexico, other matters on his agenda also demanded his attention. As a lifelong disciple of Andrew Jackson, he was determined to reinstate the Jacksonian program that had suffered erosion under the Whigs following the election of 1840. The modification of the tariff and the establishment of the independent treasury system, both mentioned to Bancroft, formed the core of his domestic program. Equally important was his determination to enforce Jacksonian scruples against the passage of internal improvements legislation by Congress. His program constituted a full-scale attack on Henry Clay's American System.

He succeeded in all three areas. Following the guidelines Polk set forth in his first message to Congress in December, 1845, new tariff legislation was introduced that would reduce the rates established by the Whigs in 1842 and place them on an ad valorem basis. In keeping with Jacksonian orthodoxy, the tariff was designed for revenue only, with protection merely incidental. Polk kept a close eye on the bill's progress, exerted pressure on wavering congressmen, and held numerous conferences with Democratic leaders. In August, 1846, the bill passed and was signed. Almost simultaneously, legislation restoring the independent Treasury system, or constitutional Treasury, as Polk called it, became law. The system, Polk hoped, would end all connection between the government and banks, whether state or national. Henceforth, the government would be the custodian of its own funds, depositing revenues in treasury vaults and disbursing them as the government's business might require. Polk placed great emphasis on these achievements,

commenting that "the public good, as well as my own power and the glory of my administration" depended upon their success.

The question of internal improvements had long been a source of contention between the parties. For the Whigs, it served as an important element in their platform, alongside the protective tariff and the Bank of the United States. Although Andrew Jackson had not always been consistent in the matter, he made opposition to internal improvements projects that were essentially local in nature a primary characteristic of Democratic Party ideology. Polk shared Jackson's conviction that internal improvements bills were violations of constitutional authority.

In 1846, the same year in which the tariff and independent Treasury bills passed Congress, a comprehensive river and harbors bill, to which scores of internal improvement projects had been added, was enacted. Polk promptly vetoed it in one of the most important actions of his administration. The legislation, he insisted, was not authorized by the Constitution. "The whole frame of the Federal Constitution," he wrote, "proves that the Government which it creates was intended to be one of limited and specified powers." An interpretation of the Constitution as broad as that argued by the bill's supporters, he warned, would head "imperceptibly to a consolidation of power in a Government intended by the framers to be thus limited in its authority."

Polk's veto aroused a fierce opposition among many Democrats, especially in the Western sections of the country where internal improvements were deemed essential to economic development, but Polk was unmoved by their protests. The principle behind the question of internal improvements struck at his concept of limited national government and strong states' rights. "I am thoroughly convinced," he wrote, "that I am right on this subject."

Polk stood by his pledge to serve only one term as president and, in spite of the appeals of many of his friends, refused to allow his name to be presented to the Democratic convention in

1848. He also declined to express a preference for his party's nominee. The conflict over the extension of slavery to the Mexican cession continued to worry him, and as it became clear that the party was seriously divided on the question, concern gave way to depression. All that he had worked to achieve seemed threatened by an issue that he had not foreseen. The pressures of the presidential office began to take their toll on his health. When Zachary Taylor won election as president, Polk confided his deep regret to his diary. Taylor, he feared, had no opinions of his own; he would be wholly controlled by the leaders of the Whig Party. "The country," he was sure, "will be the loser by his election." On March 5, 1849, Taylor assumed the reins of government (March 4 had fallen on a Sunday), and that evening Polk and his wife began their journey home.

Polk returned to Tennessee physically exhausted and in ill health. On June 15, 1849, barely three months after he left office, he died unexpectedly. He was fifty-four years old.

Although lacking in charisma and judged by many of his contemporaries to be dull and colorless, Polk brought to the presidency a dynamic quality that few occupants of the office have had. He devoted his full energy to his duties, working tirelessly to achieve his goals. He put in long hours; twelve-hour days were not uncommon. "I am the hardest working man in this country," he once remarked. Polk seldom left the national capital and during his four years as president took only one brief vacation. "No President," he insisted, "who performs his duty faithfully and conscientiously can have any leisure." He maintained a constant surveillance over the departments of the government and kept in constant touch with the leadership in Congress. Polk was his own man, made his own decisions, and seldom allowed them to be changed. Even Jackson found that he could not influence Polk.

Polk left behind a monument to his energy and his dogged determination. Seldom has a president carried out such an ambitious and far-reaching program as did Polk in the brief space of four years. To George Bancroft, one of Polk's devoted supporters and friends, he was "one of the very foremost of our public men and one of the very best and most honest and most successful Presidents the country ever had." To another, a political leader who had tangled with Polk on more than one occasion, he was "the partisan of a principle — of a system of measures and policy which he believed to be essential to the purity and perpetuity of our republican institutions . . . [who] consecrated his life to the cause, and staked his fortunes on the result."

Robert W. Johannsen

Suggested Readings

Bergeron, Paul H. *The Presidency of James K. Polk*. Lawrence: University Press of Kansas, 1987. A thorough examination of Polk's presidential years.

Dusinberre, William. *Slavemaster President: The Double Career of James Polk*. New York: Oxford University Press, 2003. Focuses on Polk's management of his slaves and his public positions on slavery and related issues.

Haynes, Sam W. *James K. Polk and the Expansionist Impulse*. Edited by Oscar Handlin. 2d ed. New York: Longman, 2002. Considers Polk's views on territorial expansion.

James K. Polk Ancestral Home. http://www.jameskpolk.com/new/. The Web site of Polk's only surviving residence, which displays personal belongings and papers of Polk and his family.

Jones, Howard, and Donald A. Rakestraw. *Prologue to Manifest Destiny: Anglo-American Relations in the 1840's*. Wilmington, Del.: SR Books, 1997. Provides context to the Polk years by examining the tense British-American relationship during the 1840's and the two agreements reached regarding land in the Northeast and the Northwest.

Leonard, Thomas M. *James K. Polk: A Clear and Unquestionable Destiny*. Wilmington, Del.: SR

Books, 2001. Explores the complex reasons behind the rapid pace of territorial expansion during Polk's presidency.

McCormac, Eugene I. *James K. Polk: A Political Biography*. 1922. Reprint. Newton, Conn.: American Political Biography Press, 1995. An early but solid biography.

Polk, James K. *Correspondence of James K. Polk*. Edited by Herbert Weaver, et al. 9 vols. Nashville: Vanderbilt University Press, 1969-1996. A documentary examination on Polk's life and presidency.

_____. *The Diary of James K. Polk During His Presidency, 1845 to 1849*. Edited by Milo Milton Quaife. 4 vols. 1910. Reprint. New York: Kraus, 1970. The diary that Polk maintained during his administration.

Sellers, Charles G., Jr. *James K. Polk*. 2 vols. Princeton, N.J.: Princeton University Press, 1957-1966. Considered by many to be the definitive biography of Polk.

Tibbetts, Alison Davis. *James K. Polk*. Berkeley Heights, N.J.: Enslow, 1999. A biography aimed at middle- and high-school readers.

Zachary Taylor

12th President, 1849-1850

Born: November 24, 1784
　　Orange County, Virginia
Died: July 9, 1850
　　Washington, D.C.

Political Party: Whig
Vice President: Millard Fillmore

Cabinet Members
Secretary of State: John M. Clayton
Secretary of the Treasury: William M. Meredith
Secretary of War: George W. Crawford
Secretary of the Navy: William B. Preston
Attorney General: Reverdy Johnson
Postmaster General: Jacob Collamer
Secretary of the Interior: Thomas Ewing

Zachary Taylor entered the White House as a former professional soldier who had never voted in an election or run for public office before the presidential election of 1848. Although he died before completing even half of his term, he exhibited strong leadership during a dangerous period of domestic crisis.

A Military Heritage

Born at Montebello, Orange County, Virginia, on November 24, 1784, Taylor could claim descent from distinguished forebears. One ancestor arrived in North America on the *Mayflower*, and James Madison was the Taylors' second cousin. The family also counted Robert E. Lee as a distant relative. One of seven children born to Revolutionary War veteran Lieutenant Colonel Richard Taylor and his wife, Sarah Dabney Strother Taylor, young Zachary was still an infant when the family moved to Jefferson County, Kentucky. He grew up on a farm near Louisville with the benefit of little formal schooling.

In 1808, Taylor was commissioned a lieutenant of infantry and won promotion to captain two years later in the minuscule regular army of the United States. During the War of 1812, he repeatedly distinguished himself in action. In September, 1812, his determined defense of Fort Harrison in the Indiana Territory won for

Portrait of Zachary Taylor. *(Whitehouse.gov)*

him a brevet promotion to major. In 1814, he led troops against a superior force of British soldiers and American Indians at Credit Island on the Mississippi, attacking aggressively before being forced to withdraw in the face of overwhelming enemy strength. It was the first and last time that Taylor retreated during his military career.

In 1832, Colonel Taylor again served in combat during the brief and tragic Black Hawk's War, which he regarded as a needless waste of lives and resources in a dubious cause. The conquered Chief Black Hawk later recalled Taylor's kind treatment of his people with great gratitude. From 1837 through 1840, he battled the Seminoles in Florida Territory. An ill-managed conflict fought under appalling conditions, the war brought Taylor brevet promotion to brigadier general as the result of his victory over the Seminoles at Lake Okeechobee in 1837. He finished his tour of duty in Florida as commander of all the troops in the territory, having won a reputation for resourcefulness and dogged determination.

In 1810, Taylor married Margaret Mackall Smith, the daughter of a prominent Maryland family. She gave birth to five daughters and one son between 1811 and 1826 before becoming an invalid. In 1835, one of their daughters, Sara Knox Taylor, married Mississippian Jefferson Davis against her father's wishes. Three months later, she died of malaria and Taylor remained embittered against Davis for more than a decade. Taylor's son, Richard, grew up to become one of the most prominent generals in the Confederate army. A second daughter, Mary Elizabeth, served as official hostess of the White House during Taylor's presidency. Despite his frequent absences on campaign or frontier service, Taylor remained a devoted husband to his ailing wife and an affectionate father to his children.

The Mexican War

In 1845, the sixty-year-old Taylor was well known in the army but still little known in the nation as a whole despite his victories in two wars. He was placed in command of the American troops stationed at Corpus Christi, Texas, that year and instructed to guard against Mexican incursions into the newly annexed state. Early in 1846, his "Army of Observation" marched south to the disputed territory between the Rio Grande and the Nueces River and encamped on the eastern bank of the Rio Grande across from Matamoras, Mexico. Fighting erupted in April, 1846, when Mexican troops ambushed an American patrol on the north bank of the Rio Grande. On May 8 and 9, Taylor met and defeated a Mexican army in pitched battles at Palo Alto and Resaca de la Palma. The enemy fled across the Rio Grande, leaving Taylor a new national hero in the United States while giving open justification to President James K. Polk's call for a declaration of war against Mexico.

An aggressive commander, Taylor chose to maintain the momentum of his success by pursuing the beaten Mexicans across the Rio Grande and driving south against the city of Monterrey, a key city in the northern portion of the country. It fell to his troops after fierce fighting raged through the suburbs and streets from September 21 to 23. The defeated defenders were allowed to withdraw their forces under a truce granted by Taylor. This act of chivalry angered President Polk, who desired the swiftest possible conclusion to the war while fearing Taylor's potential rise as a political rival to candidates of his own Democratic Party.

Polk's concerns led him to choose General Winfield Scott rather than Taylor to lead the main American offensive aimed at the conquest of Mexico City. A large portion of Taylor's command was taken from him and assigned to reinforce Scott's expeditionary force as it prepared to drive inland to the west after making an amphibious landing at Vera Cruz on the Gulf coast. Taylor was left to secure control of northern Mexico with a badly depleted army.

From February 21 to 23, 1847, General Anto-

The First Lady
Margaret Taylor

Margaret Taylor was born on September 21, 1788, in Calvert County, Maryland, to a wealthy, influential family. In 1809, while visiting her sister in Kentucky, she met Zachary Taylor, an army officer. They married a year later on June 21, 1810, and settled on a farm in Kentucky, where she bore her first child.

Thereafter their early life together was one of constant moving from command to command on the far western frontier. A genteel and delicate woman, Margaret withstood the hardships and was committed to making a home for her family and educating her children. They had five daughters and one son. In 1820, a bilious fever took two daughters and left Margaret weakened. The three surviving daughters eventually married into the military, and her son became an officer in the Confederate army.

Margaret was a private person who viewed her primary responsibility as serving her family and God. Horrified that Zachary was running for the presidency, she was fearful for his safety and that she would be deprived of his companionship. She vowed that though she would accompany Zachary to Washington, she would not enter into society nor fulfill the First Lady role of hostess. Zachary's opponents unfairly painted her as an uneducated, vulgar, pipe-smoking woman. When Zachary became president, Margaret relegated the official hostess duties to her youngest daughter, Mary Elizabeth, who had married President Taylor's aide, Colonel William W. S. Bliss. Margaret spent most of her time in her family quarters entertaining friends and family. Her only public outings were to attend St. John's Episcopal Church. Though Margaret was devoted to her husband, she did not actively support his presidency.

When Zachary died suddenly in 1850, Margaret was grief-stricken. She vacated the White House immediately and went to live at the Bliss plantation in Mississippi. She died two years later on August 14, 1852, at the age of sixty-three.

Barbara C. Beattie

nio López de Santa Anna learned of the enemy forces' division and decided to strike north to destroy Taylor before turning to face Scott's thrust from the coast. Santa Anna attacked Taylor at Buena Vista, a stretch of rugged, hilly terrain south of Saltillo. Although some of the American volunteers panicked under fire, Taylor masterfully held his line together and bloodily repulsed the enemy assaults with musketry and skillfully handled artillery. The five thousand Americans inflicted heavy casualties on the twenty thousand Mexicans and forced Santa Anna to withdraw in frustration. Buena Vista was the most spectacular victory of Taylor's military career, and it had more to do with his subsequent election to the presidency than any single factor.

Scott successfully captured Mexico City at the climax of his offensive, and a peace treaty was signed at Guadalupe Hidalgo early in 1848. The United States had won vast new southwestern territories extending from the Rio Grande to the Pacific, and Taylor returned home a hero despite Polk's attempts to belittle his fame.

Taylor as President: Free States and Threats of Secession

The Whig Party had last won the White House in 1840 with William Henry Harrison, a part-time soldier with enduring political aspirations. In June, 1848, the Whigs eagerly nominated

Zachary Taylor, an even more glamorous military figure, as their presidential candidate. "Old Rough and Ready," as his soldiers called him, was the perfect candidate for the times. His earthy, unassuming personality and reputation for courage and decisiveness were complemented by an obscure record on the prevailing political issues. His ancestry and ownership of slaves and a cotton plantation made him attractive to Southern voters, while his lack of prior political involvement meant that he had said or done nothing to offend groups in other parts of the country.

The Democrats countered with Lewis Cass of Michigan, a colorless party figure. Cass joined Taylor in conducting a campaign that was purposely vague on the pressing issues of the day: slavery and the future of the new Western territories. Even before the war had ended, debate had raged in Congress over whether slavery should be permitted in the new

territories won from Mexico. Many Northern abolitionists demanded a permanent prohibition against slavery in the new lands, whereas moderates favored the concept of popular or "squatter" sovereignty, which would allow the residents of those territories to make independent decisions on the issue. Neither Taylor nor Cass openly committed himself to either side of the debate, a prudent attempt to win votes by not antagonizing any group in the electorate.

The campaign was complicated by the appearance of the Free-Soil Party. Its candidate, Martin Van Buren, continually agitated against the expansion of slavery westward and attempted to goad his opponents into confronting the issue in a decisive manner. Taylor won a narrow victory, with 1,360,967 popular votes to 1,222,342 for Cass and only 291,253 for Van Buren. In the electoral college, Taylor received 163 votes to 127 for Cass and none for Van

Taylor leads U.S. troops to victory in the Battle of Buena Vista. *(Library of Congress)*

Buren. It is probable, however, that Van Buren deflected enough Democratic votes from Cass in New York to throw the contest to Taylor.

Taylor was the first man to enter the White House with no previous political experience or training. He was also the first professional soldier to hold the office. Although a Southerner and a slaveholder on his Louisiana plantation, he had acquired a national outlook from his military service and was no friend to sectional extremists of any stripe.

Congress had failed to provide any form of civil government for the new territories before Taylor's election, and he disliked the prospect of administration by military governors. The new president wanted both California and New Mexico brought promptly into the Union. Once they had achieved statehood they could dispose of the slavery issue as their citizens desired.

California, where the Gold Rush had resulted in a rapid rise in population and demands for statehood, quickly adopted a constitution that prohibited slavery. When Congress convened in December, 1849, Taylor urged California's admission while calling for popular sovereignty in New Mexico—that is, allowing the people, acting through their legislature, to decide whether the territory should permit slavery. His recommendations were ignored by the bitterly divided Congress. Southern legislators feared that the admission of California would weaken their position in the Senate, and numerous other sectional issues began to be joined with that of what to do about slavery in California and New Mexico.

Determined abolitionists wanted slavery barred from the District of Columbia. Southerners countered that only the state of Maryland could authorize such a measure, for it had donated the land from which the district was organized. Even if Maryland consented to the prohibition, the South could not countenance an act that would place a national stigma on its "peculiar institution."

Southerners were also nettled by Northern sympathy and aid extended to runaway bondsmen. Northern state laws—personal liberty laws—that barred courts and law enforcement agencies from assisting Southerners in finding and returning runaways led them to agitate for a strictly enforced national law that would require Northern assistance in such efforts. This proposal, seen as an attempt to force complicity in slavery, deeply angered abolitionists.

Another sensitive issue arose over Texas's claim to the eastern part of New Mexico Territory. Texans fought what they considered an attempt to annex a portion of their domain to another state and asked the national government to assume their share of the debt that they had incurred in fighting the Mexican War. Antislavery Northerners opposed their claims in an effort to reduce the size of at least one slave state.

The South as a whole was angered and alarmed by the possibility of a new bloc of free states entering the Union. In 1849, the number of free and slave states was equally balanced at fifteen. Only in the Senate did the South retain numerical equality in representation. Moreover, Southerners resented the affront to their honor implied by the enactment of any national law prohibiting slavery in the territories. Many talked of secession, and members of Congress appeared armed in its chambers and corridors. President Taylor faced a major crisis of the Union as 1850 began.

Taylor chose nation over section in his response to the crisis. Supported by most of his fellow Whigs on the issues, he took a firm stand in dealing with the volatile mixture of Democrats and Free-Soilers in Congress. Speaking for the South, John C. Calhoun demanded full rights for the slaveholders in the West and protection for their property in the East. Abolitionists, such as William H. Seward and Salmon P. Chase, decried any compromise with slavery, talked of a higher law than the Constitution—

The Vice President
Millard Fillmore

Millard Fillmore was born on January 7, 1800, in New York. Fillmore enrolled in an academy in New Hope, New York, where he met his future wife, Abigail Powers, who was one of the instructors. In 1819, he became a law clerk for county judge Walter Wood. Disappointed with the progress he was making in his legal career, Fillmore decided to return home and work on the family farm. However, his dreams of being a lawyer were realized when he received a job at the Rice and Clary law firm in 1822. By the following year, he was admitted to the bar.

After setting up a law practice in Aurora, New York, Fillmore finally married his longtime companion Abigail on February 5, 1826. Within a few years he was elected to the New York Legislature and would go on to the United States House of Representatives in 1832. Fillmore did not seek reelection for his House seat in 1842; instead he ran unsuccessfully for governor of New York in 1844. However, four years later, Fillmore was elected vice president, serving in the administration of Zachary Taylor.

With the sudden death of President Taylor on July 9, 1850, Millard Fillmore became president. He chose not to seek reelection in 1852 because of the tensions that existed between Northern and Southern factions. Millard and Abigail Fillmore prepared to return to Buffalo, New York, after attending the inauguration of incoming president Franklin Pierce. Sadly, as a result of inclement weather, Abigail developed pneumonia at the event and three weeks later, on March 30, 1853, she died. One year later, Fillmore would lose his daughter, Mary Abigail, to cholera.

Suffering from severe depression, he consoled himself by traveling extensively through the United States and Europe. In the election of 1856, he made an unsuccessful attempt to win the presidency against James Buchanan. On February 10, 1858, Fillmore married the wealthy widow Caroline Carmichael McIntosh. His latter years were spent in civic affairs, and he was instrumental in the founding of the University of Buffalo, where he served as chancellor. Fillmore suffered three strokes leading up to his death on March 8, 1874.

Robert P. Watson and Richard Yon

the law of God, which slavery contravened — and demanded that slavery be prohibited in all the territories. Henry Clay, meanwhile, joined by Daniel Webster and Stephen A. Douglas, led moderate Northerners in seeking a compromise.

Clay's compromise proposals met with continued Southern opposition, but President Taylor persisted in his insistence that California be admitted to the Union before other issues were considered. He made it clear that Southern recourse to secession would be met with force, and that he was willing personally to lead troops against his native section if it should become necessary to preserve the Union. The stalemate

in Congress persisted, but Taylor's blunt response had effectively called the South's bluff on the threat to secede.

As Congress remained deadlocked, Taylor was suddenly stricken with a violent stomach disorder following an attack of heat prostration. He died on July 9, 1850, and was succeeded by Vice President Millard Fillmore. Taylor's death may have sobered the sectional and antislavery zealots in the government, for an amended version of Clay's original "omnibus bill" was eventually agreed upon by Congress and enacted by mid-September. Passed as five separate measures, the Compromise of 1850 provided for: the admission of California as a free state, the creation of New Mexico Territory without reference to slavery and the payment of $10 million to Texas for relinquishing to New Mexico its claim to the disputed area east of the Rio Grande, the formation of the Territory of Utah without reference to slavery, a strong fugitive slave act, and the abolition of the slave trade in the District of Columbia. With the achievement of this compromise, the survival of the Union was assured for another troubled decade.

In contrast to strife and turmoil on the domestic scene, foreign affairs during Taylor's brief administration were calm and uneventful. The only happening of significance was the signing of the Clayton-Bulwer Treaty with Great Britain. By its terms the two nations agreed to join in promoting a canal across Central America that neither nation should ever fortify or put under its exclusive control. Furthermore, neither party was ever to occupy or claim sovereignty over any part of Central America.

Taylor's Legacy

Zachary Taylor was an able and dedicated soldier. His intelligence, ingenuity, and aggressiveness served the United States well from the War of 1812 through the Mexican conflict. Although he cannot be rated as one of the truly great captains cast in the mold of Robert E. Lee, Ulysses Grant, or Dwight D. Eisenhower, his skillful handling of a greatly outnumbered American force at Buena Vista averted what could have been a costly defeat and a serious setback to the achievement of national aims in the Mexican War. At a time when many Americans suspected the officer corps of harboring aristocratic pretensions, Taylor's simple dignity and lack of pomp won the popular confidence in both his person and his profession.

As president, Taylor left no great body of legislation behind him. He coined no ringing slogans and led the nation on no great crusades. His major contribution as president was his

firm and resolute adherence to the old Union. A slaveholder himself, he had no desire to interfere with the practice where it already existed, but he was determined that it be permitted neither to expand nor to imperil the Union. A Southerner, but also a son of the Western frontier and a staunch nationalist, he displayed great moral courage in defending the Constitution against domestic as well as foreign enemies.

Wayne R. Austerman

Suggested Readings

Bauer, K. Jack. *The Mexican War, 1846-1848.* Lincoln: University of Nebraska Press, 1993. Explores the military phase of Taylor's career.

_____. *Zachary Taylor: Soldier, Planter, Statesman of the Old Southwest.* Baton Rouge: Louisiana State University Press, 1985. A biography that rethinks Taylor's enigmatic role as president and military commander.

Dilworth, Rankin. *The March to Monterrey: The Diary of Lieutenant Rankin Dilworth, U.S. Army.* Edited by Lawrence R. Clayton and Joseph E. Chance. El Paso: Texas Western Press, 1996. As the subtitle reads, this work provides "a narrative of troop movements and observations on daily life with General Zachary Taylor's Army during the invasion of Mexico."

Dyer, Brainerd. *Zachary Taylor.* New York: 1946. Reprint Barnes and Noble, 1967. Although older, still a good biography of Taylor.

Holman, Hamilton. *Prologue to Conflict.* Lexington: University of Kentucky Press, 1964. Deals with the events surrounding the Compromise of 1850 and Taylor's impact on the sectional crisis.

_____. *The Three Kentucky Presidents: Lincoln, Taylor, Davis.* 2d ed. Lexington: University of Kentucky Press, 2003. Argues that the three leaders were shaped by their experiences in the Commonwealth and that their connections to Kentucky influenced their lives politically and personally.

_____. *Zachary Taylor*. 2 vols. Indianapolis: Bobbs-Merrill, 1941-1951. Many historians continue to view this older work as the classic biography of Taylor.

Roberts, Jeremy. *Zachary Taylor*. Minneapolis: Lerner, 2005. A biography written for young adults.

Smith, Elbert B. *The Presidencies of Zachary Taylor and Millard Fillmore*. Lawrence: University Press of Kansas, 1988. An analysis of the presidency of Taylor and his successor.

Millard Fillmore

13th President, 1850-1853

Born: January 7, 1800
    Summerhill, New York
Died: March 8, 1874
    Buffalo, New York

Political Party: Whig
Vice President: none

Cabinet Members

Secretary of State: Daniel Webster, Edward
    Everett
Secretary of the Treasury: Thomas Corwin
Secretary of War: Charles M. Conrad
Secretary of the Navy: William A. Graham,
    John P. Kennedy
Attorney General: John J. Crittenden
Postmaster General: Nathan K. Hall, Sam D.
    Hubbard
Secretary of the Interior: Thomas McKennan,
    A. H. H. Stuart

Millard Fillmore has been characterized as a "handsome, dignified man of no great abilities." Although perhaps harsh, this comment underscores the truth that Fillmore was a man of unrealized expectations. He became president by a tragic fluke of fate, and although possessing some genuine administrative ability, he never displayed the leadership qualities of his predecessor, Zachary Taylor.

An Education in Practical Politics

Fillmore was one of the few prominent nineteenth century American politicians who could truthfully boast of having been born in a log cabin. The second of six children born to a poverty-stricken family in Cayuga County, New York, Fillmore entered the world on the bitter winter day of January 7, 1800. His father apprenticed him in boyhood to a cloth-dressing and carding business in the hope that he would learn a useful trade.

Young Fillmore felt the stirrings of higher ambition and purchased a release from his apprenticeship to pursue an education. While still working at the textile mill, he had already enrolled as a part-time student at an academy in New Hope, New York. In 1819, his father ob-

Portrait of Millard Fillmore. *(Whitehouse.gov)*

tained for him a clerkship in the office of Judge Walter Wood in Montville, New York. Fillmore clerked for Wood's firm and for another firm in Buffalo, New York, for several years. He also supplemented his meager income by teaching school. In 1823, he was admitted to the state bar and began his own practice in East Aurora, New York. As his business prospered, he hired a student clerk, Nathan K. Hall, who would subsequently become his law partner, political associate, and presidential cabinet member. In 1826, Fillmore married Abigail Powers, the daughter of a Stillwater, New York, clergyman and the sister of a local judge. They had a son in 1828 and a dusghter in 1832. The marriage endured until her death in 1853. Fillmore remained a widower until 1858, when he married a wealthy widow from Albany, Caroline Carmichael McIntosh. Her income allowed the Fillmores to live fashionably in a handsome mansion on Niagara Square in Buffalo.

In 1826, Fillmore joined the Anti-Masonic Party. This, the first organized third party in American history, originated in the 1820's in western New York in opposition to the Society of Freemasons and other secret, exclusive, and presumably undemocratic organizations. Fillmore soon became closely linked to the movement's leaders, William H. Seward, Thurlow Weed, and Francis Granger. Marked as a rising figure in local politics, Fillmore rode the Anti-Masonic fervor to win three terms in the state assembly. An amiable legislator, he gained some distinction by sponsoring a bill to abolish imprisonment for debt.

In 1830, Fillmore moved to Buffalo and became a prominent member of the Unitarian Church while continuing to enjoy a thriving legal partnership with Hall. A popular figure in Erie County, he won a seat in Congress in 1832, still upholding the Anti-Masonic banner. By 1834, he was following Weed's leadership as a newly converted Whig but declined the party's congressional nomination for fear of alienating his Anti-Masonic supporters at home. He as-

tutely strengthened his political base by securing the editorship of the *Buffalo Commercial Advertiser* for a close associate.

Reelected to Congress in 1836 as a Whig, he enjoyed three consecutive terms before declining to run again in 1842. Fillmore was a convinced protectionist and used his position as chair of the Ways and Means Committee to secure passage of the 1842 tariff bill through the House of Representatives.

Spurred by his increasing ambition, Fillmore began to chafe at Weed's continued dominance of the New York Whigs. He supported Granger, Weed's rival, for the state governorship in 1838, only to see him lose the nomination to Seward, a Weed ally. Fillmore subsequently declined Seward's offer of a post with the state but secured for Granger the office of postmaster general in the Harrison administration.

Although Fillmore was a liberal Whig and leader of the party's antislavery faction, he opposed interference with the institution where it already existed, even as he staunchly opposed its expansion elsewhere. Like many New Yorkers, Fillmore was preoccupied by the perceived threat of massive foreign immigration, and he led the nativist opposition against fellow Whigs such as Seward and Weed, who saw the influx of foreigners as a way to forge new alliances and win added support for the party.

The Taylor-Fillmore Ticket
Accepting the gubernatorial nomination in 1844, Fillmore lost to his Democratic opponent. He blamed his defeat on "abolitionists and foreign Catholics" and accused Seward and Weed of having placed him in a doomed contest. Serving as state comptroller in 1847, Fillmore sponsored internal reforms in the office and designed a currency system that later served as a model for the National Banking Act of 1863. The following year he returned to the national stage as Zachary Taylor's vice presidential running mate. It was a purely pragmatic move by the Whigs, for Taylor's nomination had antago-

The First Lady
Abigail Fillmore

Abigail Powers Fillmore, the first wife of thirteenth U.S. president Millard Fillmore, was the first president's wife to earn a living before and after marriage. Born on March 13, 1798, in Stillwater, New York, Abigail was the daughter of the Reverend Lemuel Powers and Abigail Newland Powers. During her childhood, her father died, and the family relocated to Sempronius in central New York. In the 1810's, Abigail became a schoolteacher and continued her education at an academy, where she studied with her future husband. She became a governess in Lisle, New York, and from 1824 to 1825, she operated a select school there.

Abigail married Millard in Moravia, New York, on February 5, 1826. She taught classes in the cottage he had built in East Aurora, New York. In 1828, she gave birth to their first child, Millard Powers. In 1830, the family moved to Buffalo, New York, where her husband maintained a thriving law practice, and they became prominent citizens. Their second child, Mary Abigail, was born in 1832. Beginning in 1837, with her husband's second term in the U.S. House of Representatives, Abigail often joined Millard in Washington, D.C., while Congress was in session. She called upon government officials and carried out other duties. She lived with Millard in Albany when he served as state comptroller of New York from 1848 to 1849.

Millard became vice president in 1849 and president in 1850 upon the death of Zachary Taylor. Abigail, a friend of Buffalo's leading abolitionist, reportedly advised her husband not to sign the Fugitive Slave Act. Her interests in literature and music led to the establishment of the White House library, which also functioned as a music room. Guests of the Fillmores included such cultural celebrities as singer Jenny Lind, impresario P. T. Barnum, and authors Washington Irving and William Makepeace Thackeray. Abigail died in Washington of pneumonia on March 30, 1853, within a month of leaving the White House.

Elizabeth Lorelei Thacker-Estrada

---

nized Henry Clay's supporters and antislavery partisans. Fillmore was viewed as a healing agent and assured winner for the ticket in New York State.

The 1848 election gave the Whigs a slim victory in a climate of rising sectional tension as debate flared over the westward expansion of slavery. Fillmore mistakenly believed that the Whigs' victory had ended "all ideas of disunion." The Taylor-Fillmore administration was instead witness to the greatest domestic political crisis the nation had faced since that over the admission of Missouri to the Union as a slave state in 1820. In addition, Fillmore's experience with the traditional frustrations associated with the vice presidency was made even more bitter by internal bickering within the Whig Party. A patronage struggle between Fillmore and Seward ended with Taylor supporting Seward's rival and awarding him control of all patronage appointments in the state of New York. It was typical of Fillmore that he should be personally involved in such minor matters as the nation began to divide ever more deeply along sectional lines.

The long-simmering dispute over slavery threatened to boil over in the wake of the Mexican War. The Wilmot Proviso of 1846 had never become law, but its proposed ban on the importation of slaves into the territories won from

Mexico was still a popular rallying point for antislavery Northerners in Congress. Southern demands for a stringent fugitive slave law, Northern attacks on the existence of slavery in the District of Columbia, and a Texas claim on portions of New Mexico created a sharply divided body when Congress convened in December, 1849.

The House of Representatives numbered 112 Democrats, 105 Whigs, 12 Free-Soilers, and 1 Native American. Sectional rivalry prevented any party from forming a stable majority, and a deadlock resulted whenever an attempt was made to determine the status of the new territories or their eventual acceptance into the Union as slave or free states. Frustrated Southerners spoke openly of convening a secession convention the following June.

The nation's political leadership offered a variety of proposals to defuse the crisis. President Taylor pressed for the immediate admission of California as a free state, while warning that any attempt at secession would be suppressed with the full force of the government. John C. Calhoun led the South in demanding equal rights for slaveholders in the West and blanket protection for the institution where it already existed. Henry Clay of Kentucky joined Daniel Webster of Massachusetts and Stephen A. Douglas of Illinois in sponsoring a compromise settlement. Fillmore joined Taylor in opposing any extension of slavery and hoped to avoid an open breach in the Union. He was disturbed by Seward's adamant refusal to support any compromise with slaveholders.

In May, 1850, Clay's "omnibus bill" presented the compromise package to a restive Congress. Clay proposed that California be admitted as a free state; that in the rest of the Mexican cession, territorial governments be formed without restrictions on slavery; that Texas yield its land claims in New Mexico in exchange for compensation; that the slave trade, but not slavery itself, be abolished in the District of Columbia; and that a strict fugitive slave law be passed.

Earlier versions of this compromise had sparked violent debates in Congress, and sectional suspicions still made agreement over Clay's simplified version difficult.

Inheriting the Presidency: The Compromise of 1850

President Taylor's death in July, 1850, thrust the burden of leadership upon Fillmore, and although he lacked the blunt forcefulness of his predecessor, the unqualified support he and his cabinet gave to Clay's efforts proved decisive. Fillmore's choice of John J. Crittenden as attorney general and Webster as secretary of state, both moderates, was open indication of his desire for a compromise. His August message to Congress called for indemnification of Texas in exchange for that state surrendering its claim to New Mexico Territory. Understanding the importance of give and take, however, Fillmore also sought to placate the South by including an affirmation of states' rights in his first annual message. Such gestures helped to win passage and acceptance for the Compromise of 1850 while soothing the inflamed feelings of the South.

The Compromise of 1850 can rightfully be called the apogee of Fillmore's presidency and public career. In other matters, his administration emphasized national economic development by fostering internal improvements and the growth of overseas trade. Commodore Matthew C. Perry used diplomacy and the implicit threat of his warships to secure open commerce with Japan, which enhanced American interest in Asia and the Pacific. The patronage issue remained a domestic irritant, causing further conflict with Seward and his allies in the party as Postmaster General Hall used his influence to weaken their hold on the system in New York State so that more conservative Whigs could gain posts.

A Career in Decline

In 1852, Fillmore enjoyed strong support from Southern and Northern conservative Whigs for the presidential nomination, but Webster's bid also gained conservative and moderate strength, dividing the party. General Winfield Scott claimed the nomination as the antislavery faction's candidate. Denied renomination by his own party, a disappointed Fillmore went home to Buffalo in 1853 after the inauguration of his successor, Franklin Pierce, and became the chief spokesperson for the rapidly growing nativist Know-Nothing Party.

The rise of the avowedly sectionalist Republican Party concerned him, but his 1856 candidacy for the Know-Nothings saw him finish far behind James Buchanan of the Democrats,

the victor, and John C. Frémont of the Republicans.

Realizing that his national political career was over, Fillmore watched the nation drift toward disunion with mounting alarm. He deplored Abraham Lincoln's election in 1860 and saw little hope of averting a violent Southern response. Although Fillmore remained loyal to the national government during the Civil War, he blamed the Republicans for what he considered a needless tragedy. In 1864, he supported Democrat George B. McClellan against Lincoln. After the war, when the Radical Republicans attacked Andrew Johnson, he sympathized with the embattled president.

Domestic and local affairs also occupied much of Fillmore's attention after leaving the

A parade in San Francisco celebrates California's admission as the thirty-first state in 1850. *(Library of Congress)*

White House. He was the first chancellor of the University of Buffalo, serving from 1846 until his death. He also helped to establish Buffalo General Hospital and was a patron and first president of the Buffalo Historical Society. His second wife became a chronic invalid during the 1860's, which made further demands on Fillmore's time, but their marriage remained stable and happy. Fillmore remained the well-spoken and kindly retired politico until he suffered a paralytic stroke in February, 1874. A second stroke followed, and Fillmore died on March 8, 1874.

Fillmore was a skilled and insightful practical politician. He understood the psychology of his own New York electorate and grasped how issues and personalities could be molded to reach effective compromises in the flow of politics.

Well-read and surprisingly devoid of the overweening egotism that afflicted many of his fellow politicians, Fillmore was essentially a good man of limited perceptions and talents. He was generous and public-spirited among his native New Yorkers, but he feared the influx of foreigners and joined in the persecution of the Masons. Animated by both moral and pragmatic sentiments in his opposition to slavery, he sought accommodation and not confrontation in dealing with Southern threats of secession over the issue.

Sadly shortsighted on the major issues of his day, Fillmore was at least skilled and fortunate enough to delay the Union's dissolution by a decade while avoiding a genuine confrontation with the ills that beset it. Unlike Zachary Taylor, he habitually chose the path of least resistance.

Wayne R. Austerman

Suggested Readings

Billington, Ray Allen. *The Protestant Crusade, 1800-1860*. 1938. Reprint. New York: Rinehart, 1952. Treats Fillmore's involvement with the Know-Nothings in an evenhanded manner.

Craven, Avery O. *The Growth of Southern Nationalism, 1848-1861*. Baton Rouge: Louisiana State University Press, 1953. Provides useful context of the period.

Crawford, John E. *Millard Fillmore: A Bibliography*. Westport, Conn.: Greenwood Press, 2002. Provides a comprehensive list of primary and secondary sources.

Dix, Dorothea L. *The Lady and the President: The Letters of Dorothea Dix and Millard Fillmore*. Edited by Charles M. Synder. Lexington: University Press of Kentucky, 1975. A collection of correspondence between the president and an advocate of reform.

Farrell, J. J., ed. *Zachary Taylor, 1784-1850, [and] Millard Fillmore, 1800-1874: Chronology, Documents, Bibliographical Aids*. Dobbs Ferry, N.Y.: Oceana, 1971. A good aid for primary sources and key biographical information.

Grayson, Benson L. *The Unknown President: The Administration of Millard Fillmore*. Washington, D.C.: University Press of America, 1981. Offers a detailed account of Fillmore's presidency.

Hamilton, Holman. *Prologue to Conflict*. Lexington: University Press of Kentucky, 1964. An invaluable aid to understanding the skein of issues, people, and events surrounding the Compromise of 1850.

Joseph, Paul. *Millard Fillmore*. Minneapolis: ABDO, 2000. A biography written for young adults.

Rayback, Robert J. *Millard Fillmore, Biography of a President*. Publications of the Buffalo Historical Society 40. Buffalo, N.Y.: Buffalo Historical Society, 1959. An older but respected biography.

Scarry, Robert J. J. *Millard Fillmore*. Jefferson, N.C.: McFarland, 2001. A solid biography that is based on family papers that emerged after being lost for decades.

Silbey, Joel, ed. *The American Party Battle — Election Campaign Pamphlets, 1828-1876*. Cambridge, Mass.: Harvard University Press, 1999. Offers a fascinating insight into nineteenth century party politics, campaign efforts, and issues that stirred the interests of the American public.

Smith, Elbert B. *The Presidency of Zachary Taylor and Millard Fillmore*. Lawrence: University Press of Kansas, 1988. Draws parallels and distinctions between the administrations of Taylor and Fillmore.

Franklin Pierce

14th President, 1853-1857

Born: November 23, 1804
    Hillsborough, New Hampshire
Died: October 8, 1869
    Concord, New Hampshire

Political Party: Democratic
Vice President: William R. D. King

Cabinet Members

Secretary of State: William L. Marcy
Secretary of the Treasury: James Guthrie
Secretary of War: Jefferson Davis
Secretary of the Navy: James C. Dobbin
Attorney General: Caleb Cushing
Postmaster General: James Campbell
Secretary of the Interior: Robert McClelland

Franklin Pierce was probably the most obscure man ever elected president. Although he had served in both the House and the Senate, he had been out of national politics for a decade when he was nominated in 1852 and was barely known outside his native state of New Hampshire. Indicative of his lack of national stature, the president-elect stopped in New York City on his way to Washington, D.C., for the inauguration and strolled down a crowded Broadway without once being recognized.

Pierce's unexpected nomination grew out of the deep divisions within the Democratic Party. Factionalism, personal rivalries, and divisions over a number of issues including the expansion of slavery and the Compromise of 1850 increasingly plagued the party. As a result, the 1852 Democratic convention deadlocked, with none of the leading contenders able to secure the necessary two-thirds vote for nomination.

In this situation a number of dark horse possibilities were brought forward, and on the forty-ninth ballot the delegates in a stampede named the little-known Concord lawyer. Lacking any knowledge of Pierce or his principles, most delegates blindly accepted assurances that he was sound on the Compromise of 1850 and would be evenhanded in distributing patronage.

Born in 1804, the Democratic nominee was the son of General Benjamin Pierce, a prominent

Portrait of Franklin Pierce. *(Whitehouse.gov)*

248

New Hampshire politician. In 1824, he was graduated from Bowdoin College, where he formed a lifelong friendship with Nathaniel Hawthorne. Five years later, aided by his name (which the family pronounced "purse"), Pierce entered the state legislature. He subsequently served three terms in the House of Representatives, where he was a strong supporter of Andrew Jackson, and was elected senator in 1836. The youngest member of the Senate, he was a dogged party man, hardworking but unimaginative. Pierce resigned in 1842 before the end of his term. His decision to leave national politics stemmed in part from his wife's dislike of political life and his inability to resist the temptations of Washington society. Genial and well-liked, Pierce was fond of liquor, for which he had a low tolerance and which earned for him a certain notoriety. He became a temperance advocate in the 1840's and struggled the rest of his life with varying success to forgo stimulants. Indeed, his wife, remembering his earlier behavior, collapsed when news arrived of his nomination for president.

Following his retirement from the Senate, Pierce resumed his career as a lawyer, but he reentered public life during the Mexican War as a brigadier general in the army. His military career was also undistinguished, its most notable aspect being his fainting after his horse fell during the Battle of Contreras. On his return home, he resumed his place as a leader of the state Democratic Party but did not hold public office again until his election as president.

An Ill-Starred Administration

Pierce scored a clear victory in the 1852 election. Carrying every state but four, he won a majority of the popular votes, which was increasingly an unusual feat. Pierce's triumph was soon scarred by tragedy, however, as his only surviving child, Benjamin, was gruesomely killed in January, 1853, in a train wreck before his horrified parents' eyes. Plagued for years by religious self-doubt, Pierce was haunted by guilt over his son's death, which he feared was punishment for his own religious shortcomings. A pall of tragedy hung over the entire gloomy Pierce presidency, with the First Lady in mourning and social life held to a cheerless minimum. The accident undermined Pierce's none-too-large self-confidence at the crucial beginning of his ill-starred term in the White House.

When he assumed office, Pierce was forty-eight, the youngest chief executive the country had ever elected. His program to reunite the Democratic Party was twofold. First, he planned to use the federal patronage to heal the rifts in the party. He announced that the past would be forgotten and all factions recognized in appointments. In particular, the president intended to welcome back into the party's good graces the Van Burenite barnburners, who had bolted in 1848 and helped defeat Lewis Cass, the party's presidential candidate, and the radical states' rights men in the South, who had advocated secession following passage of the Compromise of 1850.

His second policy was territorial expansion, which he believed was generally popular and would especially appeal to Democrats. Ignoring the deep divisions that the territorial question had recently produced, Pierce confidently announced in his inaugural address, "My administration will not be controlled by any timid forebodings of evil from expansion." His major goal was to acquire Cuba, long an object of desire for American expansionists and proslavery men. He also hoped to gain more territory southward, especially from Mexico. That slavery would be suitable in most if not all of this territory seemed to Pierce, who had long denounced abolitionists and believed the slavery issue had no place in national politics, an unimportant consideration.

Physically unimposing, Pierce was only 5 feet, 9 inches tall and of wiry build, but he was a genuinely handsome man, with pale coloring, thin features, and a full head of hair. Graceful and well-mannered, he exuded a boyish charm

The First Lady
Jane Pierce

Jane Means Appleton Pierce, known as "The Shadow in the White House," was the wife of the fourteenth president of the United States, Franklin Pierce. She was born on March 12, 1806, in Hampton, New Hampshire, to the Reverend Jesse Appleton and Elizabeth Means Appleton. Her father, the president of Bowdoin College in Brunswick, Maine, died in 1819, and the family moved to Amherst, New Hampshire. During the 1820's, Jane attended Catharine Fiske's Young Ladies' Seminary in Keene, New Hampshire.

Jane married Congressman Franklin Pierce on November 19, 1834, in Amherst. Frail Jane spent some congressional sessions living with her husband in Washington, D.C., boardinghouses and part of the year in New Hampshire. In 1836, she gave birth to her husband's namesake, who died three days later. Franklin became a U.S. senator in 1837. Two more sons were born: Frank Robert in 1839 and Benjamin in 1841.

Franklin resigned from the Senate in 1842 and lived with his family in Concord, New Hampshire, where he practiced law. Son Frank died in 1843. In 1846, Franklin declined the office of United States attorney general, citing his wife's delicate health while living in Washington.

In 1852, Franklin was nominated as a "dark horse" candidate for president and won the election. The Pierces saw their last surviving son, Benjamin, killed in a railroad accident in January, 1853, just two months before Franklin became president.

Jane went into deep mourning. A pious woman, Jane urged White House staff to attend religious services. Relatives and friends, including author Nathaniel Hawthorne, visited. Although Jane attended private dinners, she initially avoided public receptions, and her widowed aunt, Abigail Kent Means, acted as hostess. Jane interceded with her husband to free the imprisoned leader of antislavery settlers in Kansas.

After leaving the White House in 1857, the Pierces traveled to the island of Madeira and toured Europe. They later visited the Bahamas. Jane died of tuberculosis on December 2, 1863, in Andover, Massachusetts.

Elizabeth Lorelei Thacker-Estrada

mingled with a good dose of vanity. For all of his personal attractiveness, however, his flawed character was inadequate to meet the challenge before him. Known as Frank to his intimates, he was a weak and indecisive person, without intellectual depth and excessively optimistic, who when challenged took refuge in stubborn inflexibility. The new president knew few Democratic power brokers when he took office, and the party's real leaders, especially in the Senate, were unwilling to defer to one they considered a nonentity. Social and affable, Pierce desperately wanted to be liked, and rather than confront those he disagreed with, he preferred to seem to endorse whatever policy was recommended to him regardless of whether he agreed with it. Men who left believing that Pierce concurred with them only to see him ultimately adopt a different course naturally accused him of disingenuousness and came to distrust him thoroughly.

Pierce's inexperience and ineptitude came to the fore immediately. He wanted an old friend, John A. Dix of New York, a barnburner who had reluctantly bolted the Democratic Party in 1848, to head his cabinet as secretary of state, and he offered Dix the post. When Southerners and anti-Van Burenites objected, rather than insisting on his right to name his cabinet and on the necessity for all party members to accept his policy of reconciliation, Pierce backed down and withdrew the tendered appointment. Keen-sighted politicians saw that Pierce lacked the inner strength to command acceptance of his policies and could be intimidated.

As finally constituted, Pierce's cabinet was not without talent. Its leading members were Secretary of State William L. Marcy; Secretary of the Treasury James Guthrie, a leading advocate of accepting the barnburners back into the regular party organization; Secretary of War Jefferson Davis, who represented the anti-Compromise Southern wing of the party; and Attorney General Caleb Cushing, a man of distinguished intellectual ability but without any firm political principles. Pierce intended that Marcy, the most politically experienced and capable of the group, be the premier, but the New Yorker was quickly shunted aside in the administration's councils by Davis and Cushing. This development was one pregnant with potential disaster, especially under a weak and vacillating leader such as Pierce. Davis and Cushing were efficient subordinates, but they were too extreme to be given any important say in policy. More and more, they directed the administration along a pro-Southern, proslavery course that badly weakened the party in the North. Pierce's diplomatic appointments were equally unfortunate; they included a gang of romantic adventurers, bumptious representatives of the proexpansion Young America movement, whose antics brought ridicule on the administration, involved the country in a series of unnecessary imbroglios, and helped undermine the president's foreign policy. Compounding Pierce's problems was his failure to put

the administration organ, the *Washington Union*, in loyal hands. Of its two editors, A. O. P. Nicholson, a Cass man, feuded with several members of the cabinet, whereas the talented John W. Forney was personally loyal to James Buchanan and deserted Pierce in 1856.

Repeal of the Missouri Compromise: The Kansas Crisis

Problems were not long in developing. The administration's patronage policies satisfied no one. Not enough jobs existed to buy off every faction, and in any event men resented recogni-

A flyer in 1855 announces a meeting for antislavery "Free-Soilers" in Kansas. *(Library of Congress)*

tion of their rivals. Such problems plagued the party in virtually every state, although the situation in New York was the most intractable and ominous for the party's future. There dissident Democrats refused to accede to the administration's appointment of former Free-Soilers and ran a separate state ticket in 1853, thereby handing control of the nation's leading state back to the Whigs.

Such was the condition of the Democratic Party, with its ranks in complete disarray and the party seemingly rudderless, when Congress assembled in December, 1853. Some men, such as Stephen A. Douglas of Illinois, believed that without vigorous new leadership the party would soon fall apart, whereas a number of powerful Southern senators saw in the existing political chaos a chance to impose new policies and erect a new test of party orthodoxy for Pierce's despised Free-Soil nominees, who had to be confirmed in the upcoming session. The Missouri Compromise of 1820 had forever prohibited slavery in the remaining portion of the Louisiana Purchase, but Southerners now demanded that the principle of popular sovereignty—that the residents of the territory (at some unspecified time) decide whether they wanted slavery—be applied to this region. To be confirmed, Pierce's barnburner nominees would be required to endorse this policy, a bitter pill since they had earlier favored the Wilmot Proviso, which sought to bar slavery from all the territory acquired from Mexico.

Under pressure, Douglas, who was preparing a bill to organize the Kansas and Nebraska territories, agreed to repeal the time-honored Missouri Compromise, but the Illinois senator wanted the administration's endorsement before proceeding with such a controversial move. In a rare Sunday interview at the White House on January 22, 1854, Douglas and a group of Southern leaders induced Pierce to accept the proposed repeal of the 1820 compromise as the unspoken price to get his appointments through the Senate. Knowing the president's unreliability, Douglas insisted that Pierce put his support in writing. In taking this step, Pierce ignored Marcy's advice and was influenced instead by Davis and Cushing, the latter of whom convinced him that the Missouri Compromise was unconstitutional anyway; he was also eager to repel the damaging accusation that his administration was Free-Soil in its sympathies. Pierce's acceptance of the repeal of the Missouri Compromise was the most fateful day of his presidency. It not only made a mockery of the 1852 platform's pledge not to reopen the sectional controversy but also precipitated a series of problems that ultimately drove Pierce from office.

Once committed, Pierce threw the power of the administration behind the Kansas-Nebraska bill. No record remains of the specific means used to secure support for the bill, but aided by these efforts the bill finally passed the House in early May by a vote of 113-100, with Northern Democrats evenly divided. Hailing it as the first great measure of his administration, Pierce signed the bill on May 30. Compounding this error, the *Washington Union* officially announced in another serious blunder that support of the law was a test of party regularity. A number of Northern Democrats refused to support the law and bolted in the fall elections; before long, many of these dissidents would join the new Republican Party, which the Kansas-Nebraska Act spawned. The Nebraska issue contributed to the Democratic Party's crushing defeat in the 1854 elections; the party lost sixty-six Northern seats and control of the House of Representatives, dooming Pierce's legislative program.

Trouble soon erupted in the Territory of Kansas. Southerners believed that an unspoken agreement existed that Kansas would be a slave state and Nebraska free, and Pierce certainly acted as if this were the case. Northerners opposed to the repeal of the Missouri Compromise, however, had no intention of conceding Kansas to slavery. Almost immediately a race developed between pro- and antislavery ele-

The Vice President
William R. D. King

William Rufus Devane King was born in Sampson County, North Carolina, on April 7, 1786. He attended the University of North Carolina at Chapel Hill but left in 1804 before finishing his degree. King was admitted to the North Carolina bar after studying under William Duffy of Fayetteville and, by 1806, opened his own law practice in Clinton. Between 1808 and 1810, he was elected to the North Carolina House of Commons and the United States House of Representatives. In 1816, he was named to serve as secretary of a legation that traveled to Europe.

After returning to the United States in 1817, King bought a plantation in the Alabama Territory and helped organize a new state government. In 1819, King was elected as a senator from Alabama, and he was reelected four times. In 1844, President John Tyler named him United States minister plenipotentiary to France. Upon his return, he was elected to a vacant Senate seat where he served until 1852. King was elected vice president in the election of 1852 with Franklin Pierce as president. Because he was ill and unable to return from Cuba for the inauguration, he was enabled by a special congressional authorization to take the oath of office in Havana, Cuba, on March 4, 1853. As a result, he is the only vice president to be sworn into office on foreign soil.

Upon returning to Alabama on April 18, 1853, he died the next day from tuberculosis, having never presided over the United States Senate.

Robert P. Watson and Richard Yon

---

ments to settle the region, and elections in the territory were marred by massive illegal voting by Missourians. When Pierce upheld the fraudulently elected proslavery territorial legislature, which expelled the legally elected free-state members, enacted a thoroughly unfair election law, and passed a harsh legal code to protect slavery and silence critics, free-state supporters organized their own "state" government, defied the territorial authorities, and petitioned Congress for admission as a free state. With two governments in existence, fighting soon erupted and flared off and on for the next two years.

What would have been a disorganized situation anyway was made worse by Pierce's unfortunate territorial appointments, headed by the volatile Samuel Lecompte, an aggressively proslavery Southerner, as chief justice, and Andrew Reeder, a local Democratic politician from Pennsylvania of no significance and without administrative experience, as governor. Tact-

less and erratic, Reeder was soon at odds with the legislature, and in response to heavy Southern pressure, Pierce finally replaced him with former governor Wilson Shannon of Ohio, an even worse choice. Shannon was incompetent and a tool of the proslavery interests in the territory. In 1856, with the territory ablaze, he resigned and fled in panic. That more capable governors could have completely forestalled the violence in the territory is perhaps doubtful, but poor leadership unquestionably made the situation worse.

Pierce's one-sided response to the Kansas crisis greatly contributed to the welling anger in the North as well. In his discussions of territorial affairs, Pierce took the Southern side and blamed all the troubles on Northern efforts to colonize the territory and on the illegal free-state movement. These criticisms were not completely misdirected, but to overlook or excuse the illegal voting by Missourians, the unconstitutional laws passed by the territorial legisla-

Senator Charles Sumner, who was assaulted by Congressman Preston Brooks for delivering an antislavery speech on Kansas in 1856. *(Library of Congress)*

ture, and the acts of violence by Southerners destroyed whatever influence Pierce might have exercised. Events reached a climax in May, 1856, with the caning of Senator Charles Sumner by the fiery-tempered Preston Brooks, a member of Congress from South Carolina, for a speech Sumner delivered on affairs in Kansas and the raid on Lawrence, Kansas, headquarters of the free-state movement, by a proslavery band. These two events dealt the final blow to Pierce's fading chances for renomination.

Democratic leaders recognized that Kansas could not continue to bleed until the 1856 presidential election. They exerted pressure to force the administration to retreat from its plan to try free-state leaders for treason. More important, Pierce finally selected in John W. Geary a man

capable of handling the duties of territorial governor. Energetically governing in an even-handed manner, Geary brought some semblance of law and order to the territory for the first time. By then, however, Pierce's political career had been irreparably destroyed. More than anything else, bleeding Kansas sank Pierce and almost sent the Democratic Party with him.

In domestic matters, Pierce adhered to the limited government philosophy of the Democratic Party. He vetoed several internal improvement bills, as well as a proposal to dedicate part of the proceeds from public land sales to care for the insane. Pierce's unwillingness to use government power to encourage economic development alienated many business interests, especially in the North. The president and his advisers displayed a positive genius for needlessly making enemies and letting chances to gain friends slip through their fingers.

The Decline of Manifest Destiny

Pierce's foreign policy was equally controversial. Cuba remained the main object of desire. Initially, the administration quietly encouraged the schemes of the proslavery filibusterer John Quitman of Mississippi, who endlessly planned to invade the island, but suddenly in 1854, Pierce shifted to a policy of acquiring Cuba through diplomacy. His program ran athwart his foreign appointments. Prodded by Pierce, three American ministers, led by the theatrical Pierre Soulé, in 1854 drafted the Ostend Manifesto, which urged that the United States offer up to $120 million for Cuba and, if Spain refused to sell, seize the island by force. The memo was intended to be secret, but its contents soon became public, and in the ensuing outcry the administration felt compelled to repudiate it. A public relations disaster, the manifesto discredited the doctrine of manifest destiny in the eyes of many Americans by linking it to naked aggression, and it exposed the administration as a group of bumbling incompetents. At the same time, it reinforced the idea of an aggressive slave power bent on using any means to strengthen slavery and expand the institution's domain. The renewal of sectional agitation rendered any effort to obtain Cuba futile for the remainder of the decade.

More successful were his efforts to secure additional territory from Mexico. Pierce's negotiator, James A. Gadsden, a South Carolina railroad promoter, was unable to gain Lower California or a port on the Gulf of California as Pierce desired, but he did obtain territory south of the Gila River, which afforded the best route for a Pacific railroad from New Orleans. Critics charged that the administration bought the land to facilitate selection of a southern rather than a central or northern route, but as with

other programs, the growing sectional conflict blocked all efforts to construct a transcontinental railroad. The Senate ratified the Gadsden Treaty only after reducing the amount of territory annexed.

It is clear in retrospect that these efforts marked the decline of manifest destiny until after the Civil War. A growing number of Northerners opposed expansion, since it would inevitably be to the south and thus would strengthen slavery. Although the seeming endorsement of the use of force alienated a minority of antebellum Americans, it was the fear of slavery expansion rekindled by the Kansas-Nebraska Act that doomed the administration's program of territorial acquisition. Pierce's failure to recognize this consequence when confronted with the de-

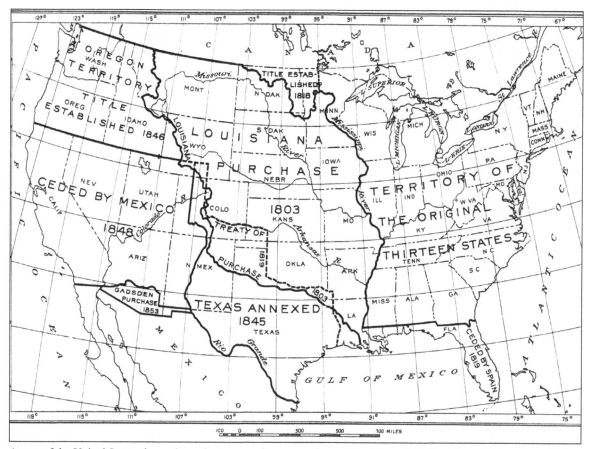

A map of the United States shows the nation's expansion across the continent through territorial acquisitions from 1803 to 1853. *(Library of Congress)*

mand for the repeal of the Missouri Compromise is testimony to his lack of political acumen.

The High Cost of Pierce's Presidency

Pierce actively sought renomination in 1856, but party leaders realized that a new choice was necessary for the party to beat back the challenge of the suddenly powerful Republican Party. At the Cincinnati convention, Pierce had some support among Southern delegations, but his strength soon melted away, and in the end the party nominated James Buchanan. So unpopular had Pierce become in the North that had he been renominated, he almost certainly would have been defeated. Few presidents have squandered so much goodwill at the beginning of their term in such a short time. Pierce became the first elected president not to be renominated by his party.

Pierce did not play an active role in politics after he left the White House. When war broke out in 1861, he tepidly backed the Union cause, but he became a strident critic of the Emancipation Proclamation and the Lincoln administration's regulation of civil liberties. He died in 1869, largely a forgotten man without influence.

Although Pierce's impact on the office of president was negligible, his role in American history was crucial. Taking office at a time when the slavery issue was declining in force, he recklessly reopened the sectional conflict, and his ill-advised policies made the crisis steadily worse. By such actions, he significantly contributed to the events that led to civil war. Pierce should be ranked a failure as president.

William E. Gienapp

Suggested Readings

Bisson, Wilfred J. *Franklin Pierce: A Bibliography*. Westport, Conn.: Greenwood Press, 1993. An annotated list of manuscripts, archival resources, articles, biographies, Pierce's published writings, and commentary on his life and times.

Blue, Rose J. *Formative Years: Jackson to Pierce, 1829-1857*. London: Heinemann, 1997. Part of the Who's Who in the White House series for teens, this volume examines the lives and political careers of presidents from Andrew Jackson through Franklin Pierce.

Gara, Larry. *The Presidency of Franklin Pierce*. Lawrence: University Press of Kansas, 1991. Explores Pierce's rise from obscurity and evaluates his presidency.

Nevins, Allan. *Ordeal of the Union*. 2 vols. New York: Scribner, 1947. This history of the impending Civil War devotes considerable attention to Pierce's term in office in the second volume.

Nichols, Roy F. *Franklin Pierce: Young Hickory of the Granite Hills*. 1931. 2d rev. ed. Philadelphia: University of Pennsylvania Press, 1958. A full-length biography based on a wide knowledge of the sources and displaying a sure grasp of the intricacies of Democratic politics.

_____. "The Kansas-Nebraska Act: A Century of Historiography." *Mississippi Valley Historical Review* 53 (September, 1956): 187-212. A thorough discussion of the origins of the repeal of the Missouri Compromise.

Potter, David M. *The Impending Crisis, 1848-1861*. Completed and edited by Don E. Fehrenbacher. New York: Harper & Row, 1976. Gives good context of the pre-Civil War era and Pierce's presidency.

Silbey, Joel, ed. *The American Party Battle— Election Campaign Pamphlets, 1828-1876*. Cambridge, Mass.: Harvard University Press, 1999. Provides context to the era of Pierce's presidency and the issues that stirred the interests of the American public.

Welsbacher, Anne. *Franklin Pierce*. Minneapolis: ABDO, 2002. An accessible biography intended for young adults.

James Buchanan

15th President, 1857-1861

Born: April 23, 1791
    Cove Gap, near Mercersburg,
    Pennsylvania
Died: June 1, 1868
    Lancaster, Pennsylvania

Political Party: Democratic
Vice President: John C. Breckinridge

Cabinet Members

Secretary of State: Lewis Cass, Jeremiah S. Black
Secretary of the Treasury: Howell Cobb, Philip F. Thomas, John A. Dix
Secretary of War: John Floyd, Joseph Holt
Secretary of the Navy: Isaac Toucey
Attorney General: Jeremiah S. Black, Edwin M. Stanton
Postmaster General: Aaron V. Brown, Joseph Holt, Horatio King
Secretary of the Interior: Jacob Thompson

Few men have entered the presidency with as much political experience as James Buchanan. A veteran of more than forty years of public service, the Pennsylvania leader had served in the state legislature, in both houses of Congress, as secretary of state in the Polk administration, and most recently as minister to Great Britain under Franklin Pierce. With legislative, administrative, and diplomatic experience, Buchanan seemed eminently qualified to be president.

He had been born in 1791 of Scotch-Irish ancestry, the son of a Pennsylvania farmer and merchant. Hardworking and ambitious, he compiled an excellent record at Dickinson College and then trained for a career in the law. He was a successful lawyer and through diligence,

thrift, and shrewd investments amassed a fortune of some $300,000 during his lifetime. In 1819, his life was forever altered, however, when his fiancé, who had broken off their engagement after a quarrel, suddenly died. In reaction, Buchanan vowed that he would never marry; he became the first bachelor president in American history.

Buchanan commenced his political career as a Federalist, but he eventually became a loyal

Portrait of James Buchanan. *(Whitehouse.gov)*

follower of Andrew Jackson and steadily rose in the ranks of the Democratic Party. A loyal party man, he shrank from controversy and built up a large personal following through a voluminous correspondence. After several unsuccessful attempts to gain the party's presidential nomination, he finally secured the prize in 1856, in large measure because he had the good fortune to be out of the country in 1854 and 1855 and was not identified with either the repeal of the Missouri Compromise or the troubles in Kansas. Party managers turned to Buchanan, who seemed a safe, experienced, conservative choice.

Buchanan and the Forces of Sectionalism

To Buchanan, the main issue of the 1856 contest was the Union. The Democratic standard-bearer viewed the Republican Party as a fanatical organization and predicted that if the party carried the election, disunion "will be immediate and inevitable." Aided by the division of the opposition, Buchanan was elected despite winning only a plurality (45 percent) of the popular vote, but the Union had had a narrow escape. In its first national campaign, the sectional Republican Party had come very close to electing a president, and in the aftermath of his victory, Buchanan indicated that his major goal as president would be to defuse the territorial crisis and "destroy" the Republican Party, which was the main threat to the Union.

Tall and heavyset, with a large head, snow-white hair, and a ruddy complexion, the fifteenth president was a gentleman of the old school. He dressed impeccably but in an old-fashioned style, cultivated courtly manners, and had a well-developed taste for fine liquor and cigars. Because of a vision defect, he tilted his head forward and sideways in conversation, which reinforced the impression of great courteousness. He was rather fussy and vain — those in Washington, D.C., dubbed him "Miss Nancy" — and was extremely sensitive to criticism or personal slights. Lonely and never completely adjusted emotionally, he was stiff and

formal and allowed little familiarity; he had few close friends and rarely revealed his feelings on controversial matters to anyone. He had a peculiar relationship with Senator William R. King of Alabama, with whom he lived for many years when in Washington, that led one Tennessee congressman to refer to them as "Buchanan and *his wife*." Ill at ease with confrontation, he was timid and indecisive and often relied on stronger men, yet in spite of his conciliatory nature, he could be petty and vindictive when attacked. Like many insecure men, Buchanan was unable to admit that he had been wrong, and once he made up his mind, he tenaciously held to his position.

Buchanan's greatest handicap was not his irresolute character but his lack of understanding of the conflict between the North and the South. Although he termed slavery a wrong in his memoirs, he felt no great moral indignation over the institution, harbored a deep hatred of abolitionists, and had long contended that Northern agitation of the slavery question was solely responsible for the sectional crisis. Few Northern politicians were so pro-Southern in their policies and feelings, and for many years his closest friends had been Southerners. Willing to see slavery expand, he had wanted to annex more territory from Mexico in 1848 while secretary of state, and he had signed the infamous Ostend Manifesto in 1854, which advocated that the United States acquire Cuba by force if necessary. He had not witnessed at first hand the Northern protest over the Kansas-Nebraska Act and had no appreciation of how much Northern public opinion had changed in a few years. Devoid of any real comprehension of the Republican Party or the reasons for its success, he was intellectually and emotionally unsuited to deal with the forces of sectionalism in American politics.

Less than two months shy of his sixty-sixth birthday when he took the presidential oath, Buchanan, who was uncomfortable around men of intellectual distinction, surrounded himself

The First Lady
Harriet Lane

Harriet Rebecca Lane, the niece of bachelor president James Buchanan, served as First Lady from 1857 to 1861. She was born in Mercersburg, Pennsylvania, on May 9, 1830, to a prosperous merchant family. When Harriet was orphaned at age eleven, her uncle James Buchanan became her surrogate father and legal guardian. She moved into his home in Lancaster, Pennsylvania, and Buchanan sent her to day school and later to boarding school. Harriet finished her education at the highly regarded Georgetown Visitation Convent in 1848. She was cheerful, generous, and popular for both her looks and her good spirits. By the time she was twenty-two, she was an accomplished hostess.

In 1854, Harriet joined Buchanan in London during his service as American minister to Great Britain. In Europe, she acquired a lifelong love for art. She also took up an interest in Native American art and became an advocate for Native Americans, earning the name "Great Mother of the Indians" from the Chippewa.

Upon his election as president, Buchanan asked his niece to serve as official hostess. Her tenure as First Lady was marked by parties, music, and beauty. She was very popular with Americans, and dances, songs, and ships were named for her.

She loyally defended Buchanan against all criticism. Although it appears she privately opposed slavery and secession, publicly she remained silent on the issue of slavery and worried what secession might do to the country.

After her White House years, Harriet married her longtime friend and romantic interest Henry Elliot Johnston on January 11, 1864. They had two children, although both died before adulthood. Her legacies include advocating for Native Americans, starting the Harriet Lane Home for Invalid Children (later part of The Johns Hopkins University), and working for a national art gallery. She donated her art collection to the Smithsonian Institution, which eventually became the nucleus of the National Gallery of Art. She died on January 13, 1903, at the age of seventy-two in Narragansett, Rhode Island.

Robert Flatley

with an undistinguished cabinet. The only member of national stature was Secretary of State Lewis Cass, who was indolent and no longer mentally alert; Buchanan intended to direct foreign policy himself. A few of the other members had some experience in national politics, but they were all men of limited vision and talent. The strongest personalities in the cabinet were Secretary of the Treasury Howell Cobb of Georgia, Secretary of the Interior Jacob Thompson of Mississippi, and Jeremiah S. Black, an old political associate from Pennsylvania who was attorney general. Cobb and Thompson were strongly proslavery, and Black, although no advocate of the institution, usually sided with them on narrowly legalistic grounds. Together they dominated the cabinet and with it the president, who normally followed the collective will of his advisers, although the idea that they constituted a "directory" and ran the government virtually without consulting him is exaggerated. The president's closest adviser outside the cabinet was Senator John Slidell of Louisiana, who despite his New York origins was an ardent Southerner, ready with Cobb and Thompson to push extreme measures to protect the South. None was a very astute judge of Northern public opinion or of the political consequences of their policies, and unfortunately Buchanan lacked the ability to compensate for their shortcomings.

The Dred Scott Decision

Most presidents have a period of time to get their administration organized before dealing with major problems. Buchanan enjoyed no such luxury; his term began in controversy. Two days after his inauguration, the Supreme Court handed down its decision in the famous Dred Scott case. The Court majority (five Southerners joined by one Northerner) ruled that blacks could not be citizens of the United States, that Congress had no power to prohibit slavery from the territories, and that the Missouri Compromise of 1820, which had banned slavery from most of the Louisiana Purchase territory and which had been repealed by the Kansas-Nebraska Act, was unconstitutional. Republicans were incensed, for not only did the Court ignore countless past precedents in propounding this ruling, but the opinion also negated the party's platform.

Buchanan, in fact, had played an important and highly improper role in the decision. Secretly informed of the Court's deliberations, he urged a Northern justice who was undecided to support the majority point of view. Then, knowing that the decision would be favorable to slavery, he announced in his inaugural address with seeming innocence that the Court was about to rule on the question of slavery in the territories and lectured that all good Americans would cheerfully acquiesce in the decision "whatever it may be." In the ensuing outcry, Republicans bitterly denounced the Court and its decision, and, although not informed of his intervention in its deliberations, accused Buchanan of conspiring to extend slavery. Contrary to Buchanan's naïve expectations, the decision did nothing to quiet agitation over slavery or heal sectional animosities. That he thought the decision would have such an effect revealed how little he understood the nature and causes of the sectional conflict.

A second event in 1857 that weakened the administration was the onset in August of a depression. The economic downturn severely reduced government revenues and produced a growing clamor in the North to raise the tariff duties, both as a means to stimulate American manufacturing and to increase government revenues to meet expenditures. Pennsylvania, long a center of protariff sentiment because of its coal and iron industries, was especially prominent in demanding greater protection. Democratic leaders recognized that loss of the state, which Buchanan had carried in 1856, would be a devastating blow. In a rare display of political acumen, Buchanan favored revising tariff duties upward to what they had been under the 1846 Walker tariff, both to increase government revenue and to cool discontent in his home state. His Southern advisers, however, headed by Cobb in the Treasury, were inflexibly opposed to any increase. In their messages to Congress in December, 1857, Buchanan and his secretary assumed opposite positions on the question, prompting Cobb's famous remark, often cited as evidence of Buchanan's weakness, that "Old Buck is opposing the Administration." Unwilling to impose his views on his subordinates, the president failed to muster the resources of his administration behind revision of the tariff, and all efforts at tariff reform failed during his term. Failure to increase the tariff alienated certain groups, especially in the business community, that up to this time had largely opposed the Republican Party.

The Kansas Controversy: A Disastrous Decision

The greatest problem that bedeviled Buchanan in his first year in office, however, was the continuing turmoil in Kansas. Buchanan was determined to bring Kansas into the Union and end the bitter controversy over the status of slavery in that territory. To accomplish this task he selected Robert J. Walker, his colleague in the Polk cabinet and one of the most talented politicians of his generation, to be territorial governor. Knowing Buchanan's tendency to waffle on disputed questions, Walker got the president to pledge in advance support for the policy of submitting the state constitution, which a convention was about to draft, to a fair vote of the territory's residents.

Once he took up his new post, the diminutive governor soon found himself enmeshed in a host of difficulties. Meeting in Lecompton, the constitutional convention, which had a pro-slavery majority because the free-state men refused to vote despite Walker's pleas, drafted a constitution that protected slavery. Then, contrary to Walker's announced policy, the delegates submitted only the slavery clause, rather than the entire constitution, for popular ratification. Residents could vote for the constitution with more slavery or for the constitution with only the slaves already in the territory, but they could not vote against the entire constitution, nor could they vote to abolish slavery. Denouncing the convention's action, Walker hurried to Washington and warned Buchanan that the Lecompton constitution was a fraud and represented the wishes of only a small minority of the residents of Kansas.

Buchanan was now caught in a dilemma. Reaffirming his earlier pledge to Walker, he had written the governor in July that he was willing to stand or fall "on the question of submitting the constitution to the bona fide residents of Kansas." Now he confronted a growing demand from the South and from his Southern advisers that Walker be removed. Their anger increased when the governor threw out obviously fraudulent returns in the legislative election, thereby handing control of the legislature to free-state supporters for the first time in the territory's existence. Through a series of procedures that were outwardly legal, Southern Democrats had the opportunity to make Kansas a slave state, and they desperately grabbed at this chance. Walker, however, gained a powerful ally in Senator Stephen A. Douglas, who insisted that the Lecompton constitution made a mockery of popular sovereignty and demanded a full and fair vote on the constitution.

Dred Scott. *(Library of Congress)*

In a stormy interview, Douglas warned Buchanan that endorsement of the Lecompton constitution would destroy the Democratic party in the North. Nursing a cordial hatred for the aggressive Illinois senator and badly overestimating his power to enforce party discipline, Buchanan affirmed his support for the constitution and warned Douglas, who considered the president a political pygmy, that he would be crushed if he opposed it.

Buchanan, the Democratic Party, and the nation now stood at the crossroads on the road to civil war. The president was about to make the most disastrous decision of his presidency. Warned by his governor that a large majority of the residents of the territory opposed the Lecompton constitution and wanted Kansas to be a free state, and warned by the most popular Northern Democratic leader that the party could not carry the burden of the fraudulent Lecompton constitution in the free states, Buchanan nevertheless plunged ahead, swayed by his Southern sympathies and his obtuse advisers. Abandoned by the president, a dis-

---

Excerpt from James Buchanan's inaugural address regarding statehood for Kansas, March 4, 1857:

We have recently passed through a Presidential contest in which the passions of our fellow-citizens were excited to the highest degree by questions of deep and vital importance; but when the people proclaimed their will the tempest at once subsided and all was calm. The voice of the majority, speaking in the manner prescribed by the Constitution, was heard, and instant submission followed. Our own country could alone have exhibited so grand and striking a spectacle of the capacity of man for self-government. What a happy conception, then, was it for Congress to apply this simple rule, that the will of the majority shall govern, to the settlement of the question of domestic slavery in the Territories. Congress is neither "to legislate slavery into any Territory or State nor to exclude it therefrom, but to leave the people thereof perfectly free to form and regulate their domestic institutions in their own way, subject only to the Constitution of the United States."

As a natural consequence, Congress has also prescribed that when the Territory of Kansas shall be admitted as a State it shall be received into the Union with or without slavery, as their constitution may prescribe at the time of their admission. A difference of opinion has arisen in regard to the point of time when the people of a Territory shall decide this question for themselves.

This is, happily, a matter of but little practical importance. Besides, it is a judicial question, which legitimately belongs to the Supreme Court of the United States, before whom it is now pending, and will, it is understood, be speedily and finally settled. To their decision, in common with all good citizens, I shall cheerfully submit, whatever it may be, though it has ever been my individual opinion that under the Nebraska-Kansas act the appropriate period will be when the number of actual residents in the Territory shall justify the formation of a constitution with a view to its admission as a State into the Union.

---

gusted Walker soon resigned. The referendum called by the constitutional convention produced a large majority in favor of the Lecompton constitution and slavery, but a separate vote a few weeks later scheduled by the antislavery legislature demonstrated quite clearly that a majority of the people of Kansas opposed the constitution. Nevertheless, in a special message in February, Buchanan urged Congress to admit Kansas under the Lecompton constitution.

The stage was now set for a titanic struggle in Congress in which Douglas openly opposed the administration. In this fight, Buchanan showed none of his customary indecisiveness. He bent every power to force the Lecompton constitution "naked through the House," as he phrased it, discharging opponents of Lecompton from federal offices, extending patronage to wavering congressmen, and even offering outright cash to secure the necessary votes. Northern representatives were more sensitive to pub-

lic opinion, and in the end, enough Northern Democrats defected to defeat Lecompton in the House by a tally of 120-112. At this point, the administration agreed to a face-saving compromise, which provided for the residents of the territory to vote on whether they would accept admission under the Lecompton constitution with a reduced land grant. On August 2, 1858, with the free-state supporters participating, the voters of Kansas rejected the land grant, and with it the Lecompton constitution, by a vote of 11,812 to 1,926. The struggle over Kansas was at an end. Slavery was doomed there, and it was only a matter of time until the territory would have sufficient population to enter the Union as a free state (as it did in January, 1861).

Buchanan insisted that the immediate admission of Kansas under the Lecompton constitution would end the territorial controversy and destroy the appeal of the Republican Party. In reality, Buchanan's ill-advised policy had precisely the opposite effect: It strengthened the Northern belief in the slave power and linked the president directly to an alleged conspiracy to force slavery on the unwilling people of Kansas. It broadened the Republicans' appeal by allowing them to pose as the defenders of cherished democratic principles and procedures. Finally, it badly divided the Democratic Party, with Douglas the symbol of this division. The Democratic Party paid this heavy price needlessly, for even Buchanan realized that the South would not have seceded over this question.

The fall elections were a debacle for the administration and the Democratic Party. Republicans scored gains in a number of key Northern states, and Northern congressmen who had supported the Lecompton constitution went down to defeat in droves, while those who had stood with Douglas generally won reelection. The new House had an anti-Democratic majority. More ominous was the loss of Pennsylvania,

which foreshadowed an impending Republican victory in 1860 unless there was a radical change in policy. To all of this Buchanan remained oblivious. His advisers dismissed the losses as the result of temporary causes rather than the administration's pro-Southern policies, and the president, unwilling to confront the harsh political truth, eagerly embraced this explanation.

Desperately needing to shore up the Democratic Party's support in the North, Buchanan instead alienated additional Northern groups by adhering to his outmoded Jacksonian economic principles. As he grew older, Buchanan became increasingly inflexible on economic matters, and during his presidency he consistently opposed using the federal government to promote economic growth. Southerners blocked all attempts to revise the tariff, and Buchanan vetoed several internal improvement bills that got through Congress, which angered popular opinion, especially in the Northwest. He also

Buchanan and his cabinet. *(Library of Congress)*

vetoed a homestead bill designed to appease Western sentiment. Another bill, which donated public land to states to found agricultural colleges, met a similar fate. These vetoes enabled Republicans to picture him as a tool of Southern interests, who used their stranglehold over the federal government to block Northern progress and development, and his actions further damaged the Democratic cause in the free states.

More successful was his handling of the growing difficulties with the Mormons in the Utah Territory. When not-entirely-accurate reports reached Washington that the Mormons under the leadership of Brigham Young were defying federal authority, Buchanan moved with uncharacteristic firmness. He dispatched twenty-five hundred troops to subdue the rebellious saints, but before they arrived in Utah, his emissary negotiated a peaceful settlement under which the Mormons would not be interfered with in their religion but in temporal matters the federal government would be supreme. The so-called Mormon War thus came to an end without bloodshed and with federal authority intact.

In foreign affairs, Buchanan's primary goals were to expand the national domain and check foreign influence in the New World. He did get the British to abandon some of their territorial aspirations in Central America, and he managed to secure commercial treaties with both China and Japan. His efforts to acquire additional territory, however, were doomed to failure. He was rebuffed by Congress when he requested the power to establish protectorates over the northern provinces of Mexico and when he sought authority to invade Mexico to gain redress for wrongs committed against American citizens. In addition, in 1860, the Senate rejected a treaty the administration negotiated with Mexico that would have given the United States the right of unilateral military intervention. Republican senators believed that the treaty's real purpose was to seize additional territory from Mexico and expand slavery. Buchanan also continued to push for the acquisition of Cuba, and in 1859 he backed a bill to appropriate $30 million for negotiations with Spain. Although it could have passed the Senate if brought to a vote, the bill stood no chance in the House, and its introduction was simply a futile gesture. Thus Buchanan's diplomatic record, while not a total failure, fell far short of the goals he had set when entering office.

Administrative Corruption: Damaging Revelations

More damaging to Buchanan's reputation were the revelations of a House committee chaired by John Covode of Pennsylvania, which was appointed to investigate charges of administrative corruption. Covode and his colleagues ferreted out massive amounts of evidence of wrongdoing. Indeed, when the investigation was completed, it was clear the Buchanan had presided over the most corrupt administration in American history up to that point. Testimony revealed that patronage and even money had been offered to editors and congressmen for their support, that campaign contributors had been rewarded with lucrative federal contracts, and that the huge profits from the public printing had been partially diverted to Democratic candidates. Evidence also came to light that completely discredited Secretary of War John Floyd, who had used his office to reward his friends and was criminally lax in his management of accounts. This was not all. It would later be discovered that Floyd had endorsed bills for army supplies before Congress appropriated the money and that he had continued this illegal practice even after Buchanan ordered him to stop. Moreover, some of these notes had been exchanged for $870,000 worth of bonds stolen from the Interior Department by one of the secretary's kinsmen. Although Floyd's malfeasance brought him into complete disgrace, he defiantly refused to resign when Buchanan, through an intermediary, asked him to do so,

The Vice President
John C. Breckinridge

The son of a politician, John Cabell Breckinridge was born in Lexington, Kentucky, on January 16, 1821. He attended Centre College in Danville, Kentucky, and graduated in 1838. After spending six months in Princeton, New Jersey, taking graduate courses, he returned to Kentucky to study law with Judge William Owsley. Breckinridge enrolled in Transylvania University's law school and subsequently opened a practice in Burlington, Iowa, with his cousin, Thomas Bullock. After his engagement and ensuing marriage to Mary Cyrene Burch on December 12, 1843, he returned to Kentucky and established a law practice with another cousin, Samuel Bullock.

On September 6, 1847, Breckinridge was commissioned a major in the Third Kentucky Volunteers unit and was sent to Mexico to defend soldiers as a lawyer in the Mexican War. Between 1851 and 1856, Breckinridge was elected to the Kentucky State Legislature, the United States House of Representatives, and the vice presidency of the United States in the administration of James Buchanan. Elected to the vice presidency at only the age of thirty-five, he was the youngest yet to serve in that capacity. However, President Buchanan's dislike of Breckinridge was clearly evident, and their relationship was poor. With the conclusion of Buchanan's first term in office, Breckinridge ran for president in 1860 and lost to Abraham Lincoln.

However, Breckinridge was elected to the United States Senate. With the start of the Civil War and with two sons serving in the Confederacy, Breckinridge was accused of being a spy and was forced to flee south, and he was formally expelled from the United States Senate. Commissioned a brigadier general in the Confederate army, he would go on to be named major general after the Battle of Shiloh. By the end of the Civil War, he was serving as secretary of war to Confederate president Jefferson Davis. Fearing he would be imprisoned for his participation in the Confederacy, he traveled to Cuba and then on to Toronto, Canada. After traveling around the world, Breckinridge settled in Niagara on the Canadian side, where he hoped to someday return to Kentucky. In 1869, Breckinridge finally received amnesty and returned with his family to Lexington, where he again opened a law practice. As a result of complications caused by cirrhosis of the liver, John Breckinridge died on May 17, 1875.

Robert P. Watson and Richard Yon

and the president meekly backed down. Buchanan had not profited personally from these activities, but the evidence fully documented his weakness of character and lack of judgment.

Buchanan's performance put the Democratic Party badly on the defensive in 1860, and party unity was essential if the Republican challenge were to be turned back. Motivated by narrow personal considerations, Buchanan refused to make any effort to heal the breach with Douglas. The senator's supporters were proscribed or removed from federal office, and some of his most bitter enemies were appointed in their stead. Buchanan also threw the power of the administra-tion against Douglas's bid to win the 1860 Democratic presidential nomination. Pressure was applied to federal officeholders to get anti-Douglas men elected to the national convention, and some of the president's closest associates went to Charleston for the sole purpose of defeating the Illinois senator. In the end the Democratic Party split, with the Northern wing nominating Douglas and the Southern wing Buchanan's vice president, John C. Breckinridge of Kentucky. Buchanan, who had not sought renomination, endorsed Breckinridge and the Southern platform, which demanded a federal slave code for the territories. With the Democratic Party hopelessly divided, Abraham Lincoln was easily elected the nation's first Republican president in November.

The Secession Crisis

With four months remaining until the end of his term, Buchanan now confronted the most serious crisis of his life. Following Lincoln's election, as the states of the Deep South began making preparations to leave the Union, Buchanan's cabinet, which had been noted for its harmony, became a deeply divided and quarrelsome body. Its Northern members, led by Black, heatedly denounced secession, whereas Southern members defended it and denied that the federal government could coerce a state to remain in the Union. Some members, most notably Cobb and Thompson, were merely waiting for their states to act before leaving the administration. Still attached to these men by feelings of affection, Buchanan could not bring himself to dismiss them and reorganize his administration on a pro-Union basis. Instead, he presented to the world the folly of maintaining in office men who now openly advocated disunion. Buchanan rationalized that their dismissal would strengthen secession sentiment in the South, but more revealing was his refusal to break with his personal organ, the *Constitution*, edited by William E. Browne, who was an outspoken secessionist. Not until January, 1861, did Buchanan cut off the paper's official patronage. He even gave his blessing for Thompson, who was still in the cabinet, to go to North Carolina as the representative of the seceded state of Mississippi. Never was his weakness more forcefully demonstrated.

This division in his official family badly paralyzed Buchanan, under whom decisions had usually been a joint effort. Never the most decisive of men, he was now a lame duck, and the recent election had deprived him of most of his political influence. The president immediately grasped the seriousness of the situation. He recognized that the South's fundamental grievance was the continuing agitation over slavery, and the main problem was its accompanying threat of insurrection. He had, however, no constructive ideas on how to deal with this crisis. He considered issuing a proclamation announcing his intention to enforce the laws in the South but backed off from this idea because of the split in his cabinet. In his annual message of December 3, 1860, he again entirely blamed the North for the crisis and recommended that Congress call a constitutional convention to deal with Southern complaints. Embracing the most extreme Southern demands, he urged passage of amendments to secure the return of fugitive slaves and to protect slavery in the states and territories. The recent election had thoroughly repudiated this last idea, and Congress ignored his suggestions.

On the constitutional question of secession, the president's message was hopelessly inadequate. Devoted to Andrew Jackson's concept of a perpetual Union, Buchanan argued that secession was unconstitutional, but he went on to declare that he had no power to prevent it. The federal government, he asserted, could not coerce a state, but he mitigated the force of this statement by reaffirming his sworn duty to enforce the laws. Buchanan's message produced a chorus of indignation in the North. His constitutional argument was specious, since the federal government did not have to coerce states at all but could direct its authority against individuals. Although Buchanan vainly hoped that Congress would devise some sectional settlement, the day of compromise had passed. Neither secessionists nor Republicans were interested in compromise, and although Buchanan might have been more vigorous in promoting a solution, in the end his efforts would not have made any difference. Buchanan's policy was simply to hang on until his term was over without legally recognizing secession or starting a civil war.

Of fundamental importance in Buchanan's eventual response to the secession crisis was the reorganization of his cabinet. In little more than one month, beginning in early December, the secessionists in the cabinet resigned and were replaced by staunch Union men. Black, who took over the State Department, now emerged as the guiding force of the administration; he gained powerful allies in Edwin M. Stanton, who assumed Black's old post as attorney general, and Postmaster General (and subsequently Secretary of War) Joseph Holt. Together these men stiffened Buchanan's resolve not to surrender federal property or to forswear the use of force.

The major point of conflict ultimately was Fort Sumter, in the middle of Charleston Harbor, with its small federal garrison under the command of Major Robert Anderson. Influenced by Black, Stanton, and Holt, Buchanan resisted intense Southern pressure to abandon the fort, and on December 31 he authorized sending a relief expedition. The relief ship was driven off by batteries on the South Carolina shore, but the president was now fully committed to the doctrine, which he outlined in his special message to Congress on January 8, that he had the right to use military force defensively to protect federal property and enforce the laws. South Carolina officials now undertook to starve out the garrison, and Buchanan decided not to send any further supplies or reinforcements until Anderson requested aid. The stalemate that had developed in Charleston continued for the remainder of Buchanan's term. Up until Buchanan's last day in office, Anderson reported that he did not need any supplies or reinforcements.

On March 4, a relieved Buchanan turned the reins of government over to Lincoln. He had managed to leave office without compromising his successor by legally recognizing disunion or precipitating a war. "If you are as happy in entering the White House as I shall feel on returning [home]," he confessed to Lincoln, "you are a happy man indeed."

The Judgment of History
Buchanan retired to his estate, Wheatland. He came under heavy attack by partisan journalists during the war, but he publicly supported the war effort and opposed the peace plank in the 1864 Democratic platform. He was largely out of the public limelight, however, and he spent his retirement writing his memoirs. Published in 1866, they presented a full-scale defense of his actions as president. Finally, on June 1, 1868, death came to the former president at the age of seventy-seven. The day before he died, he told a friend, "I have always felt and still feel that I discharged every public duty imposed on me conscientiously. I have no regret for any public act of my life, and history will vindicate my memory."

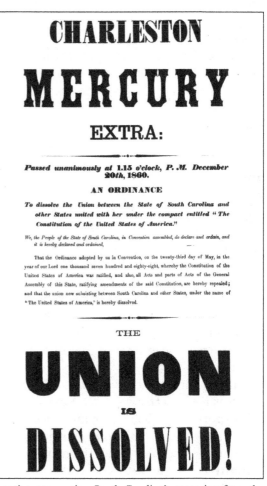

A notice announcing South Carolina's secession from the Union on December 20, 1860. *(Library of Congress)*

Historians have not been as charitable as Buchanan prophesied. Few administrations present such an unbroken record of misjudgments, shortsightedness, sordid corruption, and blundering. Ill-equipped to handle the sectional conflict and blind to the realities of Northern public opinion, Buchanan pursued a course that drove the sections further apart, ruptured his own party, and made a Republican victory all but inevitable in 1860. His incredible belief that the Supreme Court's Dred Scott decision would solve the crisis, his endorsement of the fraudulent Lecompton constitution, his destructive vendetta against Douglas, his zeal to add slave territory to the United States, and his obstruction of much desired economic legislation all aided the Republican Party to varying degrees. Desirous of healing the sectional breach, Buchanan instead promoted policies that escalated the crisis to the point where no compromise was possible. His failure as president had unprecedented tragic consequences for the nation.

William E. Gienapp

Suggested Readings

Binder, Frederick M. *James Buchanan and the American Empire*. Selinsgrove, Pa.: Susquehanna University Press, 1994. Explores foreign relations during the Buchanan presidency.

Birkner, Michael J., ed. *James Buchanan and the Political Crisis of the 1850's*. Selinsgrove, Pa.: Susquehanna University Press, 1996. A compilation of essays that evaluate Buchanan's presidency and examine the political climate of the 1850's.

Buchanan, James. *Mr. Buchanan's Administration on the Eve of the Rebellion*. 1866. Reprint. Freeport, N.Y.: Books for Libraries Press, 1970. Buchanan's memoirs prove essential for understanding his point of view and limited insight into the crisis he confronted.

_____. *The Works of James Buchanan*. 12 vols. Edited by John Bassett Moore. Philadelphia: J. B. Lippincott, 1908-1911. A valuable selection of Buchanan's speeches, state papers, and private correspondence.

Cahalan, Sally S. *James Buchanan and His Family at Wheatland*. Lancaster, Pa.: James Buchanan Foundation, 1988. Details Buchanan's family life in Pennsylvania.

Klein, Philip S. *President James Buchanan: A Biography*. University Park: Pennsylvania State University Press, 1962. Considered by some historians to be among the best biographies of Buchanan.

Meerse, David E. "Buchanan, Corruption, and the Election of 1860." *Civil War History* 12 (June, 1966): 116-131. Discusses the Covode investigation and the scandals of Buchanan's administration.

_____. "Presidential Leadership, Suffrage Qualifications, and Kansas: 1857." *Civil War History* 24 (December, 1978): 293-313. Challenges the view that Buchanan changed his mind on submitting the Lecompton constitution to the voters of Kansas.

Nevins, Allan. *The Emergence of Lincoln*. 2 vols. New York: Charles Scribner, 1950. Contains a full treatment of Buchanan's crucial four-year administration.

Nichols, Roy F. *The Disruption of American Democracy*. 1948. Reprint. New York: Collier, 1962. A thorough examination of the politics of the Buchanan administration. Nichols provides one of the best analyses of the impact of the Lecompton issue on the Democratic Party.

Potter, David M. *The Impending Crisis, 1848-1861*. Completed and edited by Don E. Fehrenbacher. New York: Harper & Row, 1976. The last half of this volume is a superb analysis of the political developments of this period.

Smith, Elbert B. *The Presidency of James Buchanan*. Lawrence: University Press of Kansas, 1975. A brief, balanced treatment of Buchanan's presidential years.

Wheatland: The Lancaster Estate of President James Buchanan. http://www.wheatland .org/. The official Web site of Buchanan's family residence, which offers guided tours and features museum shops and an exhibition on Buchanan's life and times

Abraham Lincoln

16th President, 1861-1865

Born: February 12, 1809
near Hodgenville, Kentucky
Died: April 15, 1865
Washington, D.C.

Political Party: Republican
Vice Presidents: Hannibal Hamlin,
Andrew Johnson

Cabinet Members

Secretary of State: William H. Seward
Secretary of the Treasury: Salmon P. Chase,
William P. Fessenden, Hugh McCulloch
Secretary of War: Simon Cameron, Edwin M.
Stanton
Secretary of the Navy: Gideon Welles
Attorney General: Edward Bates, James Speed
Postmaster General: Horatio King,
Montgomery Blair, William Dennison
Secretary of the Interior: Caleb Smith, John P.
Usher

Popular consensus and polls taken of American historians have named Abraham Lincoln as the country's greatest president, yet at the time of his election, he was not well known to the American people. Only after 1858 was his name recognized beyond the borders of his state, and even then he was known primarily as the challenger of one of the nation's leading political figures. A politician of some local reputation, he had held national office only once, a single term in the House of Representatives, and had never occupied an administrative office (unless one counts his brief stint as postmaster of New Salem, Illinois). Compared with his predecessors in the presidency, Lincoln may well have been the least prepared president in the history of the republic.

Early Life

Lincoln was a product of the frontier, born near Hodgenville, Kentucky, on February 12, 1809. The grandson of a settler who was murdered by American Indians as he worked in his fields and son of an uneducated laborer and farmer, Lincoln epitomized the struggle between civilization and wilderness that has so often been eulogized by American romantics. Lincoln himself found little romance in his early life and was al-

Portrait of Abraham Lincoln. *(Whitehouse.gov)*

ways reluctant to speak of it. To one of his early biographers, he summed up his childhood with a line from Thomas Gray's popular "Elegy Written in a Country Churchyard": "The short and simple annals of the poor."

At the age of two, Lincoln was taken to a hardscrabble farm on nearby Knob Creek, which his father later purchased. The circumstances of Lincoln's early years were not as poor as he had people believe. His father owned three farms, totaling in excess of six hundred acres, and he augmented his farm income with work as a skilled carpenter. Although he never learned to read and could barely sign his name, Thomas Lincoln instilled in his son an appreciation for the value of education. He was a responsible citizen, serving on juries and on the county slave patrol, supervising road construction, and guarding prisoners, and he provided for his family in a manner that placed them among the better-off members of the community. Lincoln's relationship with his father has long puzzled historians. In later years he preferred not to speak of him and rarely mentioned him in anything he wrote; although the distance was not great, Lincoln never visited him, even when his father lay dying.

In 1816, the Lincolns left Kentucky and moved across the Ohio River to southern Indiana. Although Lincoln later recalled that the move was made in part because of Thomas's dislike of slavery, a series of damaging lawsuits over defects in his land titles was probably more important. It was in Indiana, on a farm that had to be hacked out of the woods on Little Pigeon Creek near Gentryville, that Lincoln spent his adolescent years. It was there also that his mother, Nancy Hanks, died two years after the family moved. Although books seem to have been available to the young Lincoln, the opportunities for a more formal education were meager. There was nothing in that frontier environment, he later wrote, "to excite ambition for education." His attendance in school was sporadic, probably amounting to no more than a year in the aggregate. What learning he acquired, he secured through his own exertions. "The little advance I now have upon this store of education," he recalled proudly, "I have picked up from time to time under the pressure of necessity."

After living fourteen years in Indiana, during which time Thomas remarried, the Lincolns were on the move again, lured to Illinois by glowing reports of the state's fertility. Stopping first on the Sangamon River a few miles west of Decatur, the family moved in

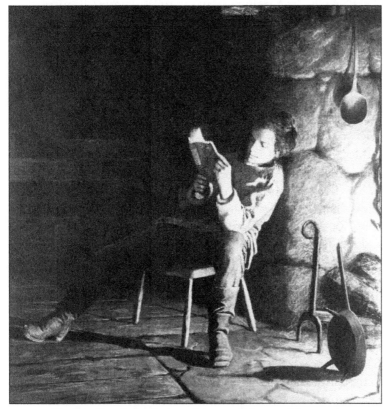

The Boy Lincoln, by Eastman Johnson. *(Library of Congress)*

271

> ## The First Lady
> # Mary Lincoln
>
> Born to prominent parents in Lexington, Kentucky, on December 13, 1818, Mary Todd was an excellent student who spent an unusual twelve years in school. In 1837, she moved to Springfield, Illinois, where she lived with her married sister Elizabeth Edwards. It was in the flourishing capital of Illinois that she met her future husband, Abraham Lincoln. Drawn together by a mutual interest in politics, the couple married on November 4, 1842. In nearly twenty years of married life in Springfield, Mary and Abraham Lincoln raised four children — Robert, who was born in 1843; Edward Baker, who was born in 1846 and died of tuberculosis in 1850; William Wallace, who was born in 1850; and finally Thomas or "Tad," who was born in 1853.
>
> After Lincoln's election to the presidency in 1860, Mary Lincoln took on the role of First Lady enthusiastically and energetically. Even by twentieth century standards, she was an activist First Lady. Despite the threat of Confederate attack, she redecorated the shabby White House. She oversaw the reupholstering of the furniture, and she chose new rugs and wallpaper. Although she overspent the budget granted by Congress to the commissioner of public buildings for the repairs to the White House, even her detractors agreed that the rejuvenated rooms of the president's house were elegant. So too were her parties. To Mary Lincoln, the atmosphere of the White House was critical as a symbol to foreign diplomats of the authority of the Union Government.
>
> However, her years as First Lady brought tragedy to a woman who valued her family above all. Her son Willie died of typhoid fever in 1862, and she was sitting next to her husband when he was assassinated in April, 1865.
>
> Her years as a widow brought further tragedy when her son Tad died in 1871. Four years later, her son Robert orchestrated her unnecessary incarceration in an insane asylum, where she stayed only four months. After a self-imposed exile in France, she died in Springfield in 1882.
>
> *Jean Baker*

1831 to a farm in Coles County, near Charleston, this time without Abraham. Twenty-two years old, ambitious, and eager to leave the hard frontier life behind him, Lincoln struck out on his own.

In 1828, Lincoln made a trip to New Orleans, traveling down the Ohio and Mississippi Rivers on a flatboat loaded with farm produce, and three years later, in the spring of 1831, he made a second trip to New Orleans for an Illinois merchant who offered him employment in his store in the village of New Salem. In each instance, Lincoln returned in style by steamboat. The trips opened his eyes; for the first time he was brought into contact with a life and culture he had hardly imagined back home on the farm.

Lincoln's decision to settle in New Salem, located on the Sangamon River not far from Springfield, marked his transition from rural to urban America and opened a new and significant period in his life. The town was growing and, with the anticipation of a river trade, seemed to have a bright future. Its people were congenial because, like Lincoln, most of them had migrated from the border South. His thoughts and plans now found new directions, as he distanced himself from his background and placed his feet on the pathway upward to social and economic success.

Whig Politician

Lincoln was drawn almost immediately to the pursuit of politics, which to him was the means not only for bringing civilization to the frontier but also for achieving the prestige he so eagerly sought. Seven months after his arrival in the village, he announced his candidacy for the Illinois state legislature. From this moment on, with only rare exceptions, his life was dominated by a quest for office. His decision to follow a political career not surprisingly carried with it a determination to study and practice law. The role of the lawyer was an important one in developing societies, and Lincoln was quick to sense its advantage to an aspiring politician. Lawyers traveled, sometimes extensively, and were able to establish contacts beyond the limits of their own communities. Clients, moreover, and members of juries all voted; if they could be won over by legal arguments, political support would not be far behind. Receiving encouragement from other lawyer-politicians, Lincoln borrowed law books, and he applied himself diligently to their study. In 1836, he was licensed to practice without having passed an examination, an unusual circumstance even in the informal atmosphere of the time, and in the following year, he entered his first partnership. Although he knew very little law, was not inclined to read further once he had received his license, and later conceded that he was "not an accomplished lawyer," Lincoln developed a highly successful and lucrative practice by the 1850's.

Lincoln's first political platform was derived from his own experience. Partisan alignments had not yet hardened in Illinois, but it was clear that the popular figure of Andrew Jackson (then seeking reelection to the presidency) had little appeal for Lincoln. Rather, his Kentucky beginnings drew him to the side of Henry Clay, his "beau ideal of a statesman," and when Clay formed the Whig Party, Lincoln joined the ranks. To Lincoln, the political issues of the 1830's were essentially economic issues. He found in Clay's American System—internal improvements, a protective tariff, and a sound financial structure—the route to national strength and to the material progress that was essential to the development of his region.

Whigs believed that the national government was the proper instrument for the promotion of the national welfare and that all interests would be harmonized by a vigorous use of national power to advance the material well-being of the country. Especially appealing to Lincoln was the Whig insistence that progress could be realized only through an orderly and rational development. In one of his later platform statements, he affirmed the "stake in society" principle, insisting that only those who shared the burdens of government, that is, those who owned property and paid taxes, should share in its governance. He rejected the romantic democracy of Andrew Jackson, embraced by most of his fellow Illinoisans, and like many Whigs accepted the principle of universal suffrage only reluctantly.

Lincoln's first bid for the state legislature ended in defeat, but he ran again in 1834 and was elected. From that time on, he never lost a legislative race, serving four terms altogether. In the legislature, he supported internal improvement bills, defended the state's banking system, and voiced his fears for the security of persons and property against the "mobocratic spirit" he associated with Jacksonian democracy. One of his most important early political statements and his clearest exposition of conservative Whig philosophy was his address before the Springfield Lyceum, "The Perpetuation of Our Political Institutions," in January, 1838. In a vigorous call for law and order, Lincoln warned that the gravest threat to the republic lay in the "wild and furious passions" of the mob that tore at the foundations of government and made it easy for a man "of the loftiest genius" to subvert republican government (he had Andrew Jackson in mind). It was the government's responsibility, Lincoln urged, to protect its "good men" (those who loved tranquillity and obeyed the law) by securing the ordered, regulated society that was essential to economic and social progress. The republic would be saved, he declared, only by a reverence for the Constitution and the laws, and the subordination of passion to "cold, calculating, unimpassioned reason." Let this become, he concluded, the "*political religion* of the nation."

Illinois was a heavily Democratic state, which limited the opportunities for Whigs such as Lincoln. Within the state's Whig organization, however, Lincoln achieved a position of leadership; by the 1840's, he was recognized as a member of the "Springfield Junto," the small group in the state capital that pulled the party strings. In 1846, by prearrangement with other leading Whigs, Lincoln was nominated and elected to Congress from the Springfield district, the only sure Whig congressional district in the state, and seventeen months later, in December, 1847, he took his seat in the Thirtieth Congress.

Lincoln's single term in the House of Representatives is remembered mostly for his stand against the Mexican War, an opposition he hoped would bring him distinction within the party. Lincoln's response to the war, however, suffered from the same ambiguity that plagued Whigs generally. When the war was declared in 1846, he voiced no opposition to it; on the contrary, he urged prompt and united action against Mexico. He had been indifferent to the annexation of Texas, yet later argued that the United States must, under "a sort of necessity," take territory from Mexico. As a congressman, he voted supplies to the army and expressed his pride in the victories that the volunteers had won in Mexico. It was not until he took his seat in the House of Representatives, when the war was won and only awaited the signing of the treaty, that Lincoln expressed his opposition to it, insisting that it had been unconstitutionally begun by President James K. Polk and that Polk had deceived the American people in his war message two years before. Lincoln's speech merely echoed arguments Whigs had been making since the war had begun and did not bring him the prominence he had hoped to achieve.

It was as an Illinois Whig that Lincoln first formed his views on the nature of the presidency and of presidential power. Molded in the turbulent politics of the Jacksonian era, his position was antithetical to Jackson's belief that the president, as the only direct representative of all the people, must be a strong and powerful figure. Lincoln's warning against the rise of a "lofty genius" who would use his popular support to undermine the institutions of republican government was echoed in later statements. He once likened the Jacksonian presidency to a "great volcano . . . belching forth the lava of political corruption." Whigs—and Lincoln—argued instead for a weak executive and a strong legislative branch. The "legitimately expressed will of the people," he believed, must be filtered through their congressional representatives, who, mindful of the need for order and stability, would temper their wishes according to the best interests of the nation.

The presidential veto power, so dramatically employed by Jackson, threatened the separation of powers and, as Lincoln believed, clothed the chief executive with a legislative function that properly belonged to Congress. Lincoln contended that the nation's legislation should rest exclusively with Congress, "uninfluenced by the executive in its origin or progress, and undisturbed by the veto unless in very special and clear cases." That Lincoln believed such cases would be rare was obvious. The notion that the president can "know the wants of the people, as well as three hundred other men, coming from all the various localities of the nation" was "a pernicious abstraction."

As a member of the Whig Party's central committee in Illinois, Lincoln took an active part in the presidential campaigns, organizing the party, planning the strategy, and issuing platform statements. Although Whigs had staunchly opposed the organization of political parties as obstructions to good government, they came to realize by 1840 that only by adopt-

The Vice President
Hannibal Hamlin

The son of a doctor, Hannibal Hamlin was born on August 27, 1809, in Paris Hill, Maine. Subsequent illnesses and deaths in the family impeded Hamlin's attempts at receiving an education beyond local village schools and preparatory academies. While working on the family farm, he did, however, study law at the law firm of Fessenden and Dubois. In 1833, he was admitted to the bar and married Sarah Jane Emery on December 10. The couple moved to Hampden, Maine, where Hamlin opened a law practice.

Elected as a state representative in Maine, Hamlin would go on to be elected to the United States House of Representatives, and then to the Senate, where he established himself as a vocal abolitionist. His wife developed a persistent cough in July, 1854, and succumbed to her bout with tuberculosis on April 17, 1855. That same year, supporters had simultaneously drafted him for the gubernatorial and senatorial elections of Maine. As a result, he won both elections and decided to resign after serving one month as governor in favor of the United States Senate.

On September 25, 1856, he married his wife's half sister, Ellen Vista Emery, who was twenty-five years his junior. In 1859, Hamlin was approached by Republicans to run for president. Confident that he was unable to garner enough votes, he suggested that they nominate another candidate. Abraham Lincoln was nominated with Hamlin as his running mate. Shortly after they were sworn into office, the Civil War began, and Lincoln sent Hamlin to New York City to draft plans to defend the Union. The strain of war had weakened the two men's relationship, and he wrote to his wife, "I am not consulted at all, nor do I think there is any disposition to regard any counsel I may give." He was not renominated for vice president in 1864 and was saddened to find out that Lincoln had orchestrated the replacement. Depressed by both his removal by Lincoln and his unsuccessful bid for the United States Senate, he went back to farming in Maine until he was given the post of port collector in Boston. In 1868, Hamlin gained his goal of serving in the United States Senate, where he held a seat until resigning to become minister to Spain in 1881.

Upon retiring from political life in 1883, Hamlin was still actively working his farm at the age of eighty. He died on July 4, 1891, while playing cards with friends.

Robert P. Watson and Richard Yon

ing the party structure of the Jacksonians could they hope to achieve success. Lincoln was no exception, although he came later than most to an acceptance of the party system. He developed an organizational framework for the party in Illinois that extended to the precinct level and campaigned vigorously that year for William Henry Harrison, the very model of the Whig weak executive. Later he urged the adoption of the convention system, first initiated by the Democrats, while still expressing doubts about its validity. In an 1843 address to the party, he suggested that "while our opponents use it, it is madness in us not to defend ourselves with it."

In 1844, Lincoln had the opportunity to support his idol, Henry Clay, for election to the presidency. Once again, as a leading Whig in Illinois, he urged that limitations be placed on the power of the presidential office. The veto power, he declared, should be restricted "so that it may not be wielded to the centralization of all power in the hands of a corrupt and despotic Executive." Furthermore, he proposed that presidents be limited to a single term, that all executive officers refrain from interfering in local and state elections, and that the president's power of appointment be significantly reduced.

Clay was not elected in 1844. The victor, James K. Polk, a Democrat and protégé of Jackson, became a target for Lincoln's attack on unchecked presidential power. He denounced Polk's "high-handed and despotic" exercise of the veto power as reflecting an "utter disregard of the will of the people." Polk's refusal to approve measures passed by Congress "for the good and prosperity of the country," principally Congress's bills for extensive river and harbor improvements, constituted in Lincoln's view an abuse of presidential authority.

As a Whig member of Congress, Lincoln was most disturbed by Polk's role in the coming of the Mexican War. In his maiden speech in January, 1848, he placed full blame for the war squarely at Polk's feet, charging the president with deception and falsehood in his effort to justify the conflict. In an emotional outburst that revealed the depth of Lincoln's feeling, he likened Polk's arguments to the "half insane mumbling of a fever dream" and charged that the blood of the war would cry out to heaven against him.

More important, Lincoln was convinced that Polk had exceeded his constitutional authority in forcing the war upon the country. He lashed out at the view, held by many of the war's supporters, that the president may "without violation of the Constitution, . . . *invade* the territory of another country" if he thought it necessary to the national defense. To allow the president that power, he warned, was to "allow him to make war at pleasure."

The Constitution clearly gave the war-making power to Congress, not the president. Polk's actions, Lincoln stated, were contrary to the principles of republican government, for they placed "our President where kings have always stood."

Lincoln's stand against the extension of presidential prerogative was carried into the 1848 campaign, when the Whigs sensed an opportunity to oust the Democrats from the executive branch. He abandoned Henry Clay in favor of Zachary Taylor, the hero of the Mexican War, apparently for no other reason than that Taylor had the better chance of winning. It was an ironic twist, for it may have cost Lincoln an appointment to a federal office following Taylor's election. Lincoln campaigned strenuously for Taylor, both within and outside the state of Illinois, urging a return to a Whig presidency, a reassertion of congressional supremacy, and the enactment of the party's economic program. Following the election, he fully expected to be rewarded with a federal appointment but was disappointed when Taylor, eager to mend relations with Clay, gave the office Lincoln sought to an Illinoisan who had remained faithful to the Kentuckian.

Lincoln's adherence to Whig Party doctrine is extremely important to an understanding of his later political positions, for his outlook continued to be flavored by his Whig approach to the nation's problems. Yet Lincoln was no doctrinaire. His thinking always contained a strong streak of pragmatism and expediency, reflected in an ability to shift and modify his stands according to changing circumstances. In this sense, he was a typical Western politician of the early nineteenth century. It was this flexibility and the balance between pragmatism and principle on which it rested that provided strength to his efforts to meet the great crisis of civil war in later years. Lincoln revealed, in these early years, many of those traits that would enable him to carry the nation through its most troubled time—an understanding of human behavior and an ability to use that understanding to achieve his ends, a shrewdness of judgment that made him a master at manipulation and maneuver. An opportunist in the best sense of the word, he was able to seize the moment and bend it to his own purposes. In 1849, however, the full demonstration of these traits lay yet in the future.

The Politics of Slavery

Following his term in Congress, Lincoln re-

The Vice President
Andrew Johnson

Andrew Johnson was born to inn workers in Raleigh, North Carolina, on December 29, 1808. Johnson and his brother were apprenticed to a tailor when Andrew was fourteen. In search of work, Johnson and his entire family moved in 1826 to Greeneville, Tennessee, where he opened a tailor shop. His shop became a gathering place for political discussions, which precipitated his interest in politics and debate. As a result, he joined a debating club and became an active debater. Shortly after arriving in Greeneville, Johnson met his future wife, Eliza McCardle. The two were married on May 17, 1827, and had five children.

By 1829, Johnson's political career was under way. He was elected as alderman, mayor, state representative, and state senator, and by 1843 he was elected to the United States House of Representatives. In 1853, Johnson was elected governor of Tennessee; he was reelected in 1855. In 1857, Johnson was elected to represent the state of Tennessee in the United States Senate.

After the start of the Civil War, President Abraham Lincoln named Johnson brigadier general in the Union army and military governor of Tennessee in 1862. Seeking a Southern moderate to join the national ticket, Lincoln chose Johnson as his running mate in the election of 1864. With the assassination of Lincoln in 1865, in which Johnson was also a target, he was sworn in as president and began the daunting task of unifying the country after the end of the Civil War. Feeling he was consistently undermined by Secretary of War Edwin Stanton, Johnson fired Stanton in 1868. As a result of his actions, Johnson became the first president to be impeached by the United States House of Representatives; however, the Senate found him not guilty. That same year, he was denied the nomination of his party for reelection.

After retiring to Greeneville, Johnson made two failed attempts at a seat in the House of Representatives and the Senate but was victorious on the third attempt, gaining election to the Senate in 1875. After suffering two strokes, Johnson died on July 31, 1875, while visiting the home of his daughter in Carter County, Tennessee.

Robert P. Watson and Richard Yon

turned to Illinois. Rebuffed by the Taylor administration and unable to seek reelection, he saw his political prospects dim. For the next five years, he devoted himself to his law practice while continuing to keep his hand in Whig Party affairs.

The passage by Congress of Stephen A. Douglas's Kansas-Nebraska Act in 1854 abruptly ended Lincoln's "retirement." The organization of two new territories in the nation's heartland on the basis of popular sovereignty (allowing the local population to decide for or against slavery), thereby repealing the Missouri Compromise, so aroused and angered Lincoln that it altered the direction of his life. Douglas's act provoked a storm of protest from antislavery and abolitionist elements and provided the opportunity for Lincoln's return to the political arena.

Lincoln was not a new convert to an antislavery position. He had always opposed slavery on principle but admitted that until 1854 it had been only a "minor question" for him. Confident that the institution had been contained by the Missouri Compromise, he apparently felt little need to argue against it. Furthermore, he had always opposed militant abolitionism as a threat to law and order. The Kansas-Nebraska Act shattered this confidence when it opened a vast new territory to the expansion of slavery. No longer on the defensive, as Lincoln had assumed, slavery had moved to the offense. From 1854 on, his thinking and the direction of his career were dominated by the slavery issue.

Lincoln's opposition to slavery, as it evolved in the 1850's, rested on a foundation of moral principle. If slavery was not wrong, he once said, then nothing was wrong. In his public statements following the passage of Douglas's act, he defined his opposition. He hated the institution because of its injustice and because it negated the promise of the Declaration of Independence, violated the free-labor underpinnings of his political thought, and rendered America's republican example a mockery. To allow the expansion of slavery would be to derail America's mission, to convert progress into "degeneracy," and to make hypocrites of all Americans who proclaimed themselves the "friends of Human Freedom." He called upon his countrymen to put the nation back on track by returning it to the ideals that had given it birth. "Our republican robe is soiled, and trailed in the dust," he declared. "Let us repurify it . . . in the spirit, if not the blood of the Revolution. . . . If we do this, we shall not only have saved the Union; but we shall have so saved it, as to make, and to keep it, forever worthy of the saving."

Lincoln's declarations, however, were balanced by a keen sense of pragmatism. He recognized the complexity of the slavery problem and did not fault Southerners for failing to do what he himself would not know how to do. He was aware of the legal protections that slavery enjoyed and of the practical difficulties involved in any effort to deal with it. What could be done? Like Clay, he leaned toward colonization as the ideal solution but conceded that this was impractical. Free the slaves and treat them as "underlings"? That, he believed, would not improve their condition. Free them and treat them as political and social equals? This too he rejected, for "my own feelings will not admit of

Confederate president Jefferson Davis. *(Library of Congress)*

this; and if mine would, we well know that those of the great mass of white people will not." Lincoln's solution—the only practical course—was to prevent slavery from expanding. By restriction of slavery to the states where it already existed, he believed the institution would be placed in a condition of "ultimate extinction." Rejecting the immediacy of abolition, he favored a vague and indeterminate gradualism. Even so, he knew that the question was so fraught with danger to the Union that he was uncertain which was the greater evil—disunion or slavery. "Much as I hate slavery," he conceded, "I would consent to the extension of it rather than see the Union dissolved, just as I would consent to any GREAT evil, to avoid a GREATER one."

In the years following 1854, Lincoln's voice mingled with the protests of others. Their impact on the party system proved fatal. Whigs became split beyond recovery, Democrats tried vainly to maintain national unity, and a new sectional party with an unabashed anti-Southern and antislavery platform emerged. Lincoln, hoping at first that the Whig Party could be refashioned into an antislavery force, gradually identified himself with the new party and its slavery-restriction demands; by 1856, he was calling himself a Republican. The thrust of the slavery question in politics gave new incentive to his political ambitions. He was elected to the Illinois legislature in 1854 but resigned soon afterward to run for a seat in the United States Senate, only to be defeated by an anti-Nebraska Democrat. Although deeply disappointed, he lost no time in building his candidacy for the Senate in 1858, when Douglas himself would seek reelection.

Lincoln's arguments against slavery became less equivocal and ambiguous as he became more active politically. His views were not only refined but also considerably sharpened in his vigorous campaign against Douglas in 1858. Meeting Douglas in seven joint debates, he sought to discredit the Illinois senator in the eyes of Southern Democrats while at the same time emphasizing his own credentials as a spokesman for the Northern antislavery position. His language assumed a stronger moral tone as he portrayed Douglas as a man without moral scruples. "The real issue in this controversy," Lincoln concluded in the final debate, "is the sentiment on the part of one class that looks upon the institution of slavery *as a wrong*, and of another class that *does not* look upon it as a wrong."

Douglas won the election, but in losing, Lincoln finally gained what had eluded him before—national prominence and visibility. Republicans in other states sought his assistance in their local campaigns, whereas his frequent mention as a candidate for the presidency in 1860 kindled his ambition for the nation's highest office. By the time the election year began, Lincoln's prospects for the Republican nomination were amazingly good for someone whose name was barely known outside his own state only two years before.

If Lincoln's prospects were good, those for the Union were not. The sectional conflict over slavery had reached formidable proportions. Several Southern states had made thinly veiled secession threats, John Brown's trial and execution were fresh in the South's memory, a long and frustrating speakership contest in the House of Representatives threatened a breakdown in Congress, and Jefferson Davis's demand for federal protection of slavery in the territories was matched by new extremes of invective from the abolitionists.

Lincoln himself contributed to the tension of the election year when he delivered his address at Cooper Institute in New York City, warning Republicans against seeking a middle ground between right and wrong and urging them to stand fast in their moral opposition to slavery.

The Presidency, Secession, and War

When the Republicans gathered in their nominating convention in Chicago in May, 1860, Lincoln was ready to do battle against his rivals. New York's distinguished Senator William H. Seward had the greatest support among the delegates, and he might have won the nomination had it not seemed likely that Douglas would receive the Democratic nomination. Seward's position on slavery smacked too much of radicalism. Republican strategy dictated the selection of someone whose views were perceived as moderate, someone who could woo Northern voters away from Douglas and at the same time appeal to the old Whig element in the party. Lincoln was the logical choice. He won the nomination after only three ballots. To satisfy those Republicans with Democratic antecedents and to balance the ticket geographically, the convention nominated Hannibal Hamlin of Maine for vice president.

The presidential election of 1860 was the most critical in the history of the United States. It marked the final breakdown of the existing party system, as the Democratic Party (the only remaining national party) split and presented two candidates: Stephen A. Douglas and John C. Breckinridge. A fourth candidate, John Bell, was presented by the Constitutional Union Party, a collection of old Whigs and former Know-Nothings. The campaign belied the election's importance in its relative calm. By September, it was clear that Lincoln would win. The Republicans had carefully calculated their chances and knew they could elect their candidate without carrying a single Southern vote. Lincoln won in November by a decisive majority in the electoral college, but he carried only 39 percent of the popular vote.

With Lincoln's election, only the executive branch of the government was won by the Republicans. The Democrats would have majorities in Congress (although the party was badly split), and the Supreme Court was firmly controlled by a Democratic proslave majority. All arguments, however, that the South would have nothing to fear from Lincoln were to no avail. On the contrary, Southerners had reason to fear the worst from Lincoln's election; nothing could stay their course toward secession.

Republicans, Lincoln included, did not fully appreciate the depth of Southern feeling. They saw no need to meet or even to understand Southern grievances. Lincoln steadfastly refused to believe that secession was popular, and he blamed disunion on a slave-power conspiracy. He refused to sanction compromise as a means for saving the Union and urged all Republicans in Congress to reject any proposals that would inhibit the party's platform. "The tug has to come," he wrote, "and better now than later." It is obvious that he had no idea that such a stand might result in a war between the sections.

Lincoln assumed the responsibilities of the presidency under the most inauspicious circumstances. Between December 20 and February 1, seven states of the Union seceded, the entire Deep South from South Carolina to Texas.

On February 4, their delegates met at Montgomery, Alabama, to organize a new nation—the Confederate States of America. Hopeful that Lincoln's silence meant that they would be allowed to remain at peace, they were anxious to have the new government organized and functioning by the time Lincoln was inaugurated.

On inauguration day, March 4, Washington, D.C., had the appearance of an armed camp. Rumors that Lincoln would be assassinated, that the South would never allow the president to be sworn in, and that a Southern-led coup would overturn the government had been circulating for days. The air was thick with tension. Soldiers were everywhere in evidence, in the streets, along the route of the inaugural procession, on the Capitol grounds, and in the windows of the Capitol overlooking the gathering crowd. A battery of artillery was drawn up on the grass. The military character of the scene on the day Lincoln began his term of office forecast the character of his administration. It would be dominated, from the first day to the last, by war, with all its horror and bloodshed. Lincoln would never know what it was like to preside over a country at peace.

To say that Lincoln was unprepared to cope with the crisis would be an understatement, although he sensed the magnitude of the difficulties that lay in his path. "No one, not in my situation," Lincoln told Springfield's citizens when he bade them good-bye on February 11, "can appreciate my feelings of sadness at this parting." With an almost eerie prescience, he continued, "I now leave, not knowing when, or whether ever, I may return, with a task before me greater than that which rested upon Washington." Following his election there had been little time to contemplate the crisis, let alone develop a response to it. Republican office seekers, rejoicing in their first presidential victory, descended on Lincoln, eager to share the rewards of his success.

Lincoln's first concern was to shape a cabinet that would reflect the diversity of the Re-

Excerpts from Abraham Lincoln's first inaugural address, March 4, 1861:

That there are persons in one section or another who seek to destroy the Union at all events and are glad of any pretext to do it I will neither affirm nor deny; but if there be such, I need address no word to them. To those, however, who really love the Union may I not speak?

Before entering upon so grave a matter as the destruction of our national fabric, with all its benefits, its memories, and its hopes, would it not be wise to ascertain precisely why we do it? Will you hazard so desperate a step while there is any possibility that any portion of the ills you fly from have no real existence? Will you, while the certain ills you fly to are greater than all the real ones you fly from, will you risk the commission of so fearful a mistake? . . .

My countrymen, one and all, think calmly and well upon this whole subject. Nothing valuable can be lost by taking time. If there be an object to hurry any of you in hot haste to a step which you would never take deliberately, that object will be frustrated by taking time; but no good object can be frustrated by it. Such of you as are now dissatisfied still have the old Constitution unimpaired, and, on the sensitive point, the laws of your own framing under it; while the new Administration will have no immediate power, if it would, to change either. If it were admitted that you who are dissatisfied hold the right side in the dispute, there still is no single good reason for precipitate action. Intelligence, patriotism, Christianity, and a firm reliance on Him who has never yet forsaken this favored land are still competent to adjust in the best way all our present difficulty.

In *your* hands, my dissatisfied fellow-countrymen, and not in *mine*, is the momentous issue of civil war. The Government will not assail you. You can have no conflict without being yourselves the aggressors. You have no oath registered in heaven to destroy the Government, while I shall have the most solemn one to "preserve, protect, and defend it."

I am loath to close. We are not enemies, but friends. We must not be enemies. Though passion may have strained it must not break our bonds of affection. The mystic chords of memory, stretching from every battlefield and patriot grave to every living heart and hearthstone all over this broad land, will yet swell the chorus of the Union, when again touched, as surely they will be, by the better angels of our nature.

publican Party while satisfying the party's leaders. It was a task that demanded a tactful and careful balancing act. To William H. Seward of New York, his principal rival for the party's nomination, Lincoln assigned the State Department. Another presidential aspirant, Salmon P. Chase of Ohio, representing the radical antislavery element in the party, was appointed to the patronage-rich Treasury Department. For attorney general, Lincoln chose Edward Bates, an old Whig from the border slave state of Missouri, and to replace Horatio King as postmaster general he selected Montgomery Blair of Maryland, a member of the influential Jacksonian family of Francis Preston Blair. Gideon Welles of Connecticut represented both New England and the Democratic element in the party as secretary of the navy. Two cabinet members—Simon Cameron of Pennsylvania and Indiana's Caleb Smith—were appointed (secretaries of war and the interior, respectively) to honor deals Lincoln's managers had made at the Chicago convention.

Lincoln continued to grapple with patronage problems during the early stages of his presidency, a distraction from the pressing questions of disunion and war that should have held his full attention. "There is a throng here of countless spoilsmen who desire place," complained one member of Congress. Thousands of office seekers were "fiddling around the Administration for loaves and fishes, while the

The bombardment of Fort Sumter in 1861. *(Library of Congress)*

Government is being destroyed."

As the crisis deepened during the winter of 1860-1861, Lincoln's Whig belief in a weak president began to wane. Although he confessed that his "political education" strongly inclined him against the "free use" of presidential power, he had in fact begun to move toward the Jacksonian conviction of strong presidential leadership. The seeds for Lincoln's shift were sown as early as 1849, when he had proposed that Zachary Taylor avoid the appearance of a "mere man of straw" and adopt some of Jackson's characteristics. "We dare not disregard the lessons of experience," Lincoln warned.

As the slavery issue grew more explosive during the 1850's, Lincoln saw Jackson in a new light, praising his "decision of character" in dealing with South Carolina's defiance of federal authority in 1832. With slavery threatening the nation's moral fiber as well as the Union, Lincoln's early suggestion that the people, through Congress, should "do as they please" now seemed dangerously out of place. It was precisely the weakness of the presidents— Franklin Pierce and James Buchanan—and the near breakdown of order in a Congress dominated by the South that encouraged the aggressions of the slave power.

Following the presidential election, Americans were assured that Lincoln, of whom so many people knew so little, was endowed with the same "sagacity, honesty, and firmness" that characterized Andrew Jackson; printmakers even made Lincoln look like Jackson. Jacksonian phrases crept into Lincoln's rhetoric, and many supporters urged Lincoln to follow Jackson's example in dealing with the South. Lincoln was sustained during the dark days of the "secession winter" at least in part by the spirit of Old Hickory.

Lincoln's inaugural address on March 4, 1861, was eagerly awaited by Americans in both the North and the South, for it would be the new president's first public response to the secession of the seven lower South states and the creation of the Confederate States. No one knew for sure what he would say. Southern leaders had already made it clear that nothing Lincoln could say would induce their states to return to the Union; many Northerners, however, were hopeful that he would propose some policy that would mend the rift in the Union peaceably.

Although he held out assurances to the Southerners that they need have no fears for their peace, property, and personal security under his administration, Lincoln was firm in his rejection of secession. He offered little hope for a peaceful solution to the crisis and indeed recognized a war between the sections as a possibility. "The Union of these states is perpetual," he declared. No state on its own motion can lawfully withdraw from the Union; therefore the "Union is unbroken." Echoing Jackson's statements (and those of Buchanan just two months before), he asserted his strong resolve to see the laws of the nation enforced in all the states, including those that had seceded, and he warned the South that he would use his power to "hold, occupy, and possess" the property of the United States within those states. Once again, he placed the differences between North and South on a moral foundation; the only point of dispute, he said, was the question of slavery's rightness or wrongness. He believed that the people in their intelligence, patriotism, and devotion to God would surely find a way out of the "present difficulty," but he gave no hints on how this might be accomplished. Lincoln ended with both a challenge to the South and an expression of hope that all might yet be put right. "In *your* hands, my dissatisfied fellow-countrymen, and not in *mine*, is the momentous issue of civil war. . . . You can have no conflict, without being your-

selves the aggressors." Reasserting his faith that reason must ultimately prevail over passion, he hoped that the "mystic chords of memory" that united all Americans would "yet swell the chorus of the Union, when again touched, as surely they will be, by the better angels of our nature."

Some elements of conciliation could be found in Lincoln's statement, but they did nothing to allay the crisis. He recognized that many "worthy, and patriotic citizens" sought to save the Union by amending the Constitution, and he favored giving the people an opportunity to act on their proposals, without committing himself to any one of them. Men such as Douglas, who still thought compromise possible, took heart, but neither Lincoln nor his party followed up the suggestion. Southerners reacted to the address with predictable outrage, viewing it as tantamount to a declaration of war against the South.

Of the fifteen slave states in the Union, seven withdrew from the Union in response to Lincoln's election. To the people in the remaining eight, the election of a Republican to the presidency by itself was not sufficient cause for disunion. In turning down secession, however, some of the states issued clear warnings that future action would depend on Lincoln's policy toward the seven. If, as some expected, Lincoln attempted to coerce those states back into the Union against their will, others would have no alternative but to leave the Union as well. Their decision was not long in coming.

Immediately following his inauguration, Lincoln confronted the problem of retaining two small pieces of land in the South that still remained in federal hands: Fort Pickens, near Pensacola, Florida, and Fort Sumter, in the harbor of Charleston, South Carolina. Of the two, Fort Sumter was the more sensitive, largely because of its location. To South Carolinians, the continued federal occupation of Fort Sumter was more than merely insulting to their new nation; it was regarded as a continuing act of hostility against the South. To people in the North, the fort became a symbol of United States authority in the seceded states; evacuation would be a humiliating retreat. Informed only hours after his inauguration that provisions were running low at Fort Sumter and that the garrison could not hold out longer than a few more weeks, Lincoln was forced to make one of the most important decisions of his administration. Consistent with the policy suggested in his inaugural address, he decided to send provisions to the beleaguered fort, but only after some vacillation and confusion resulting from contradictory advice and mixed-up orders. Unwilling to allow this symbol of United States authority to continue to be maintained, Confederate leaders ordered the batteries in Charleston harbor to open fire on the fort early on April 12. Thirty-three hours later the federal garrison capitulated. The Civil War had begun.

The bombardment and surrender of Fort Sumter produced an intense war excitement in both North and South. The tensions and uncertainties of the preceding months were swept away. The air was cleared, and there no longer seemed any doubt as to the course every American should take. In the North, an impressive show of unity gave Lincoln the strength to mobilize the nation against the rebellion. On April 15, the day after the surrender, he issued his first wartime executive proclamation. Seventy-five thousand militia troops, to serve ninety days, were summoned to suppress the resistance to federal authority. At the same time, Lincoln called Congress into special session to meet on July 4 "to consider and determine, such measures, as, in their wisdom, the public safety, and interest may seem to demand." It was Lincoln's hope (shared by many in the North) that the emergency would be short-lived and that Southern resistance would be successfully quelled by the time Congress should meet.

Lincoln's call for troops was the signal for which the other slave states had been waiting. In response to what they maintained was a deliberate policy of coercion against the seceded states, four more states—Virginia, Tennessee, Arkansas, and North Carolina—withdrew from the Union, swelling the size, population, and resources of the Confederate States. The Southern nation now comprised eleven of the fifteen slave states, one-third of the total number of states in the Union. The loyalty of the four border slave states—Delaware, Maryland, Kentucky, and Missouri—was of continuing concern to Lincoln, and his determination to retain their loyalty strongly influenced the direction of his wartime policies.

War and the Power of the Presidency

The months following the surrender of Fort Sumter revealed the firmness with which Lincoln would meet the crisis of civil war, as he embarked on policies that contrasted sharply with his earlier Whig views on the nature of presidential power. The period has been labeled the "Presidential War" and Lincoln's role that of a "constitutional dictator" as he single-handedly placed the nation on a wartime footing, acting wholly without congressional sanction. The situation was desperate. Washington, D.C., during those first weeks was virtually isolated from the rest of the country. Telegraph lines were cut, railroad bridges were destroyed, and a section of the rail line to the West had fallen into rebel hands. Some of the first troops to arrive in the capital had been attacked as they marched through Baltimore. Desperate measures were called for to meet the crisis; by postponing the meeting of Congress for three months, Lincoln indicated that he did not want his action to be inhibited by an endless debate over "constitutional niceties."

In defining the nature of the conflict, Lincoln adopted a deliberate ambiguity, giving flexibility to his policy making. Regarded as an insurrection for some purposes, the conflict became a war between belligerent powers for others. Two proclamations were quickly issued establishing a naval blockade of the Southern coastline, an action that normally followed a congressional

The Emancipation Proclamation

By the President of the United States of America:

A Proclamation.

Whereas on the 22d day of September, a.d. 1862, a proclamation was issued by the President of the United States, containing, among other things, the following, to wit:

"That on the 1st day of January, a.d. 1863, all persons held as slaves within any State or designated part of a State the people whereof shall then be in rebellion against the United States shall be then, thenceforward, and forever free; and the executive government of the United States, including the military and naval authority thereof, will recognize and maintain the freedom of such persons and will do no act or acts to repress such persons, or any of them, in any efforts they may make for their actual freedom.

"That the executive will on the 1st day of January aforesaid, by proclamation, designate the States and parts of States, if any, in which the people thereof, respectively, shall then be in rebellion against the United States; and the fact that any State or the people thereof shall on that day be in good faith represented in the Congress of the United States by members chosen thereto at elections wherein a majority of the qualified voters of such States shall have participated shall, in the absence of strong countervailing testimony, be deemed conclusive evidence that such State and the people thereof are not then in rebellion against the United States."

Now, therefore, I, Abraham Lincoln, President of the United States, by virtue of the power in me vested as Commander-in-Chief of the Army and Navy of the United States in time of actual armed rebellion against the authority and government of the United States, and as a fit and necessary war measure for supressing said rebellion, do, on this 1st day of January, a.d. 1863, and in accordance with my purpose so to do, publicly proclaimed for the full period of one hundred days from the first day above mentioned, order and designate as the States and parts of States wherein the people thereof, respectively, are this day in rebellion against the United States the following, to wit:

Arkansas, Texas, Louisiana (except the parishes of St. Bernard, Palquemines, Jefferson, St. John, St. Charles, St. James, Ascension, Assumption, Terrebonne, Lafourche, St. Mary, St. Martin, and Orleans, including the city of New Orleans), Mississippi, Alabama, Florida, Georgia, South Carolina, North Carolina, and Virginia (except the forty-eight counties designated as West Virginia, and also the counties of Berkeley, Accomac, Northhampton, Elizabeth City, York, Princess Anne, and Norfolk, including the cities of Norfolk and Portsmouth), and which excepted parts are for the present left precisely as if this proclamation were not issued.

And by virtue of the power and for the purpose aforesaid, I do order and declare that all persons held as slaves within said designated States and parts of States are, and henceforward shall be, free; and that the Executive Government of the United States, including the military and naval authorities thereof, will recognize and maintain the freedom of said persons.

And I hereby enjoin upon the people so declared to be free to abstain from all violence, unless in necessary self-defense; and I recommend to them that, in all case when allowed, they labor faithfully for reasonable wages.

And I further declare and make known that such persons of suitable condition will be received into the armed service of the United States to garrison forts, positions, stations, and other places, and to man vessels of all sorts in said service.

And upon this act, sincerely believed to be an act of justice, warranted by the Constitution upon military necessity, I invoke the considerate judgment of mankind and the gracious favor of Almighty God.

declaration of war in a conflict between the powers of equal status. The legality of these actions was later upheld by the Supreme Court by the narrowest of margins. Four justices, including the chief justice, argued that Lincoln had exceeded his constitutional authority, that the president's power to deal with insurrection was not equivalent to a war power, and that only Congress was authorized to declare or recognize a state of war. Perhaps to meet such constitutional objections, Congress in mid-July did recognize a state of war between the United States and the Confederate States but by doing so contradicted Lincoln's assertion that the conflict was a domestic insurrection.

Early in May, 1861, Lincoln issued a call for forty-two thousand volunteer troops (the first of a number of such calls) and at the same time ordered an increase in the strength of the regular army and navy, actions that were regarded as congressional rather than executive powers (although Congress later sanctioned Lincoln's moves as if they had been made under congressional authority). He authorized the requisition and arming of ships "for purposes of public defence" and made arrangements for the transportation of men and supplies, in each instance working through private individuals rather than the appropriate government agencies. To meet the military expenses, Lincoln ordered the payment of funds out of the national treasury, even though the Constitution forbade the disbursement of money without a congressional appropriation.

Finally, in one of his most drastic steps, Lincoln authorized the suspension of the privilege of the writ of habeas corpus in all instances in which resistance to federal authority was suspected, an action that left a wide area of interpretation to military officers. Initially limited to specific locations, the suspension was expanded in September, 1862, to encompass all persons who discouraged enlistments, resisted the draft, or were guilty of disloyal practice, wherever found. The chief justice of the United States ruled in May, 1861, that Lincoln had overstepped the constitutional bounds of his office in suspending the writ, but Lincoln brushed his objections aside. In the spring of 1863, Congress ended all constitutional doubts by sanctioning Lincoln's practice.

The constitutional limits of presidential power were a source of constant concern, both to Lincoln and to his critics. He was sensitive to the objections raised against his actions and uneasy in his own mind about the constitutional question. He was aware that some of his actions were of doubtful legality, but he always believed that the seriousness of the crisis justified them. The Constitution, Lincoln argued, authorized the president to determine the existence of an insurrection and to take steps to suppress it, no matter how extreme. "It became necessary for me," he explained, "to choose whether, using only the existing means, agencies, and processes which Congress has provided, I should let the government fall at once into ruin, or whether, availing myself of the broader powers conferred by the Constitution in cases of insurrection, I would make an effort to save it with all its blessings for the present age and for posterity." If his actions sometimes exceeded even those "broader powers," he pointed out, they were taken because the preservation of the government demanded them.

Lincoln's task was made easier by his knowledge that the people supported him. What he did, he did "under what appeared to be a popular demand, and a public necessity." Like Jackson, he justified his actions by linking them to the popular will. The constitutional power of the president, he believed, was variable, dependent on circumstances. Certain actions, he wrote, "are constitutional when, in cases of rebellion or Invasion, the public Safety requires them, which would not be constitutional when, in the absence of rebellion or invasion, the public Safety does not require them."

Lincoln insisted, as Jackson did before him, that his oath of office allowed him to exercise power that under ordinary circumstances would not be legitimate. In his inaugural address, he reminded the South that he had taken a "most solemn" oath to preserve, protect, and defend the Constitution. This oath, "registered in Heaven," became a source of power in itself, independent of the Constitution. Must the government be allowed to fall, he asked, lest he be charged with violating its laws? Would not his oath be broken "if the government should be overthrown, when it was believed that disregarding the single law, would tend to preserve it?" Lincoln clarified his position in 1864: "My oath to preserve the Constitution imposed on me the duty of preserving by every indispensable means that government, that nation, of which the Constitution was the organic law. Was it possible to lose the nation and yet preserve the Constitution? . . . I felt that measures, otherwise constitutional, might become lawful by becoming indispensable to the preservation of the Constitution through the preservation of the nation." The Constitution must, under some circumstances, be violated in order to preserve it.

Furthermore, Lincoln maintained that he could exercise power that constitutionally belonged only to Congress on the grounds that Congress could always ratify his action after the fact. "It is believed," he stated in reference to his decrees in the spring of 1861, "that nothing has been done beyond the constitutional competency of Congress." Thus, in the crisis, with Congress out of session, the president held legislative as well as executive power. As the war continued, Lincoln moved even beyond this position when he declared that his function as commander in chief enabled him to do things that were constitutionally denied to both Congress and the president. His power, he came to feel, was virtually unlimited, as long as it was wielded in defense of the Constitution and the Union. "As Commander-in-Chief," he stated, "I suppose I have a right to take any measure which may best subdue the enemy." He held the authority to "do things on military ground"

This photograph by Mathew Brady was made in October, 1862, as Lincoln visited General George B. McClellan at his headquarters in Antietam, Maryland. *(Library of Congress)*

that could not be done constitutionally any other way, and indeed this was precisely the justification he offered for his Emancipation Proclamation.

No president brought the executive's war power to so careful and reasoned a definition. That he should grasp the nature of presidential power in a time of crisis so quickly and so astutely was nothing short of remarkable, considering his lack of experience in office. Critics during the war exaggerated his use of power when they denounced him as a dictator and a despot. He exercised the authority of his office with considerable restraint, cautiously weighing the alternatives and consequences, and never losing sight of his larger values. Although he carried presidential power to unprecedented heights, he did so only after he was persuaded that his ends could be accomplished in no other way. Lincoln himself suggested that whereas he may have used extraordinary and unconstitutional means, he had never misused the assumed power. The power, he stressed, was coterminous with the war and would expire with the conflict.

Lincoln's relations with Congress were surprisingly tranquil throughout the war, and on only a few occasions did they reach open disagreement and confrontation (and then, ironically, Lincoln faced the hostility of members of his own party). He made almost no use of the veto power, although he was not hesitant to threaten its use when it suited his purposes. Ever since the tumultuous sessions of the late 1850's, Congress's reputation for calm and efficient deliberation had suffered, and Lincoln shared the distrust that many Americans felt toward the legislative branch. During his administration, Congress served as an arena in which his critics did not hesitate to work their mischief. A standing investigation of the administration and of Lincoln's prosecution of the war by the Joint Committee on the Conduct of the War bordered at times on downright harassment, while a well-orchestrated effort by Senate Republicans to seize power from the president in late 1862 failed only because of Lincoln's skill at maneuver and manipulation. When Lincoln confronted Congress in 1864 on the question of Reconstruction, he had to endure some of the most vicious attacks ever hurled at a chief executive by members of his own party. It is not surprising that Lincoln was happiest when Congress was in recess. When Congress was in session, he followed an independent course without much heed to congressional reaction. No president, historian James G. Randall has concluded, carried the "power of presidential edict and executive order," independently of Congress, as far as Lincoln did.

War Aims: Union and Emancipation

For Lincoln the Civil War held a significance that extended beyond the preservation of the nation. His scrupulous use of his war power was always conditioned by that broader significance; he was determined that nothing he might do should compromise the meaning that America had for the rest of the world. On the contrary, he felt a deep responsibility to preserve America's mission and to find in the war the means for advancing it.

The romantic attachment that early nineteenth century Americans felt toward their revolutionary beginnings touched Lincoln as well. The meaning of the American Revolution first emerged for Lincoln from the pages of Parson Weem's popular biography of George Washington, which he read as a youth. It took shape in his 1838 Lyceum address, but it was not until he joined the antislavery crusade that Lincoln brought to full flower his dedication to the principles of the Revolution. From then on, the American Revolution and the Declaration of Independence it inspired formed the bedrock of his ideas. The Revolution, he believed, provided the "germ" from which the "universal liberty of mankind" would find nurture. The United States alone of all the nations represented the "advancement, prosperity and glory, of human liberty, human right and human nature." He spoke movingly of the spirit of America that was embedded in the country's charter of freedom. The Declaration of Independence was that "electric cord . . . that links the hearts of patriotic and liberty-loving men together, that will link those patriotic hearts as long as the love of freedom exists in the minds of men throughout the world."

Lincoln's faith in America was reflected in his inaugural address, but it was not until later that he fully articulated the relationship between the war and the American mission. The issue, he told Congress in his message on July 4, 1861, "embraces more than the fate of these United States." The war was a test, before "the whole family of man," whether a constitutional

A painting commemorating the Emancipation Proclamation of 1862. *(Library of Congress)*

republic, or democracy, "a government of the people, by the same people," could maintain itself "against its own domestic foes." The fate of democratic government everywhere depended on the outcome of the conflict. "Is there," he asked, "in all republics, this inherent, and fatal weakness? Must a government, of necessity, be too *strong* for the liberties of its own people, or too *weak* to maintain its own existence?" Popular government, he stated, was yet an experiment. Americans had successfully demonstrated that they could establish and administer it; now they were being asked to show the world that they could also maintain it "against a formidable attempt to overthrow it."

The war, Lincoln declared, was a "People's contest." Its goal was to maintain in the world "that form, and substance of government, whose leading object is, to elevate the condition of men — to lift artificial weights from all shoulders — to clear the paths of laudable pursuit for all — to afford all, an unfettered start, and a fair chance, in the race of life." The ideas were not new to the mid-nineteenth century, but few Americans expressed them so well.

To Lincoln, then, the war was being fought to preserve the Union and, by extension, the Union's world mission. In his inaugural address, he disclaimed any intention of interfering with the institution of slavery in the states where it existed, and in his first wartime message he assured the South that his mind had not changed. Looking ahead to the course the government would follow after the rebellion was suppressed, he promised that he would be guided simply by the Constitution and the laws. His understanding of the relations between the states and the nation, he added, would not differ from the sentiments expressed in his inaugural address.

Little more than two weeks later, on July 21, Union and Confederate armies fought their first major engagement at Bull Run, about twenty-five miles from Washington, D.C. The result was a defeat and disorderly retreat for the Un-

Company E of the Fourth U.S. Colored Troops in 1865. *(Library of Congress)*

ion army, a shock to Northerners who had expected a quick and easy triumph. On the following day, Congress, sobered by the defeat, authorized the enlistment of five hundred thousand volunteers for a period of three years. At the same time, it issued the first formal declaration of war aims, the Crittenden Resolution, echoing Lincoln's earlier assurances to the South. The war, according to the statement, was not being waged for conquest or subjugation or to overthrow or interfere with the established institutions of the state; rather, it was being fought simply "to defend and maintain the *supremacy* of the Constitution, and to preserve the Union with all the . . . rights of the several States unimpaired." Congress thus joined the president in disavowing any intention to interfere with slavery in the states where it existed.

Yet the slavery question could not be put aside. Many antislavery Americans believed that the war was the long-awaited opportunity to rid the nation of the hated institution and that with his war power Lincoln had the authority to

emancipate the slaves. Convinced (as was Lincoln himself) that the slavery issue had precipitated the crisis, they believed it the height of folly to fight for the preservation of the Union with slavery left intact.

Lincoln found it increasingly difficult to counter these arguments, but counter them he felt he must. Although he was willing to bend the Constitution and expand his war power in other areas, he was insistent that all the constitutional and legal guarantees be observed when it came to slavery. Four slave states remained in the Union, and he was determined to retain their loyalty, almost at any cost. Any action taken against slavery, he was persuaded, would drive some or all of them into the waiting arms of the Confederate States, rendering a Union victory more difficult if not impossible. Furthermore, he believed that action against slavery would alienate a large segment of Northern opinion, represented in the Democratic Party and among the more conservative members of the Republican Party. His purpose was to draw these elements to his side in support of the war, not to drive them into an opposition to the war. Finally, Lincoln realized what many antislavery people apparently did not, that nothing could ever be done to emancipate the slaves unless the Union were preserved first. The war must be won before slavery could be dealt with; to win the war required the support of all political constituencies. Lincoln's hatred of slavery was well known, his desire to see the institution eliminated deeply felt. Pragmatic considerations, however, outweighed his convictions.

Despite his well-founded intentions, the question of slavery demanded his attention from the moment the war began. Not only was Lincoln's position challenged by a growing number of Americans, but events also revealed the ambiguity of his stand. The Fugitive Slave Act was still in force (it would not be repealed until 1864), necessary legislation to the loyal slave states but ridiculous when applied to the seceded states. The result was that Union field commanders were frequently forced to deal with the practical problems of slavery in the absence of direction from the president. Lincoln's dilemma only worsened.

The issue was confronted early in the war when General Benjamin F. Butler, commander at Fort Monroe in Virginia, refused to return to their owners slaves who came into the Union lines. Instead, he declared them "contraband of war," in effect treating them as captured enemy property. Other field officers, such as Ulysses S. Grant in the West, gathered escaped slaves in camps where they could be cared for and in some instances organized for paramilitary labor. Their status was uncertain, for they were no longer slaves yet neither were they free. The situation was only partially clarified in August, 1861, when Congress enacted its first (or "halfway") confiscation act, providing for the seizure of enemy property, including slaves, that was used for hostile purposes. It was not until the spring of 1862 that military personnel were prohibited from returning escaped slaves to their owners.

Lincoln's policy met its first test in August, 1861, when General John C. Frémont declared martial law in Missouri, ordered the confiscation of the property of persons who supported resistance to the government, and freed their slaves. Frémont's action, aimed at slaveholders in a loyal state, raised an immediate storm of protest in the North. Lincoln, fearing the defection of neighboring Kentucky, was appalled. "I think to lose Kentucky is nearly the same as to lose the whole game," he confided to a friend. Lincoln directed Frémont to change his order to bring it into conformity with the terms of the confiscation act, thus revoking the general's attempt to emancipate the slaves, and later removed him from his command. Where would constitutional government be, he asked, if a "General, or a President" should be allowed to "make permanent rules of property by proclamation"? Abolitionists who rejoiced at Frémont's edict turned their anger on Lincoln.

Lincoln was compelled to act a second time in May, 1862, when General David Hunter, commanding Union-occupied bits of Georgia, Florida, and South Carolina coastline, declared all the slaves in his department to be free. Lincoln intervened once again, countermanding the order lest it damage support for the war. This time he made it clear that military emancipation could not justifiably be left to the decision of field commanders; rather, it was a responsibility he reserved to himself. Lincoln had already begun to move, if ever so slightly, toward the exercise of presidential authority over slavery.

Republicans in Congress, however, were not willing to wait. They began chipping away at slavery, believing not only that the institution must be a casualty of the war but also that action taken against it would weaken the South and hasten Union victory. In April, 1862, slavery was abolished in the District of Columbia with compensation to the slaveholders, and in June it was abolished in the nation's territories without compensation (and in defiance of the Supreme Court's decision in the Dred Scott case). The following month, Congress took the next logical step when it passed the second confiscation act, one of the most important and far-reaching legislative enactments of the war. All property held by persons who supported the rebellion (by definition encompassing all the people in the eleven seceded states) was declared forfeit and subject to confiscation. To make the intent of the act clear, Congress explicitly declared that "all slaves of persons who shall hereafter be engaged in rebellion against the Government of the United States, or who shall in any way give aid thereto...shall be forever free." One year after the passage of the Crittenden Resolution, Congress had reversed itself; slavery was no longer to remain untouched by Union victory.

Lincoln could not ignore the growing sentiment in favor of emancipation. Pressure to take presidential action increased following the failure of General George B. McClellan's spring campaign against Richmond. More drastic measures against the South were demanded. The foreign situation, moreover, was deteriorating. Great Britain and France were providing aid to the Confederacy and seemed to be moving closer to a recognition of Confederate independence. Only an unequivocal emancipation policy, it was thought, could halt this trend. More and more people in the North came to believe that Lincoln's hesitancy stemmed from a lack of understanding of the crisis, and they began to question his competence as president. Lincoln, anguished by military defeat and the growing strength of the Confederacy abroad, searched for a course of action that would meet the objections of his critics and at the same time hold the support of all Northern elements. It was not an easy task.

Still clinging to his constitutional scruples, Lincoln recognized only two means for ridding the nation of slavery: by individual state action or by a constitutional amendment. With one-third of the states out of the Union, the latter was a remote possibility. In a special message to Congress in March, 1862, he revealed his solution to the slavery issue. Abolition, he suggested, must be by state action, it should be gradual rather than sudden (which he believed "is better for all"), and it should be accompanied by compensation "for the inconveniences public and private, produced by such a change of system." The cost to the federal government, he pointed out, would be less than the cost of continuing the war. He hoped to persuade the loyal border states to abolish slavery under his plan, and he even drafted sample legislation that would achieve that goal. The end of the war, he was convinced, would follow soon thereafter.

Lincoln met with border-state representatives and later called them to a conference in the White House in the hope that he might interest them in his proposal. He pleaded with them to carry it to their respective states and to work for its adoption. Lincoln's desperation was apparent. "The pressure," he told them, "is still upon me, and is increasing." He appealed to their patriotism and statesmanship to help save the government "to the world" and vindicate its "beloved history." To make their decision easier, he argued strongly for the colonization of the freed slaves outside the United States, and he later tried to sell the idea to a delegation of blacks. Lincoln's pleas, however, were unavailing. His proposal was rejected by the border states.

The demands of the abolitionists became more intense, and it was obvious that Lincoln would not be able to resist them much longer. To a group of visiting churchmen, he expressed doubts that a presidential proclamation emancipating the slaves could be effective. The world would recognize it as "inoperative," in a class with the "Pope's bull against the comet." He urged once again that the preservation of the Union must be the first priority. When Horace Greeley, the outspoken antislavery editor of the

New York Tribune, denounced Lincoln's recalcitrance and pointed out the inconsistency of putting down the rebellion while upholding its cause, Lincoln replied publicly in one of his best efforts to link the slavery question with the cause of the Union:

> My paramount object in this struggle *is* to save the Union, and is *not* either to save or destroy slavery. If I could save the Union without freeing *any* slave I would do it, and if I could save it by freeing *all* the slaves I would do it; and if I could save it by freeing some and leaving others alone I would also do that. What I do about slavery and the colored race, I do because I believe it helps to save the Union; and what I forbear, I forbear because I do *not* believe it would help save the Union.

The statement was of great import, for it was the first time that Lincoln conceded publicly that he might free either all or some of the slaves. Any emancipation policy he might adopt, he was saying, would rest on expediency and would be tied to the greater good of the Union.

Without the knowledge of Greeley and the visiting churchmen, Lincoln had already decided on just such an expedient policy, a decision known only to members of his cabinet. On July 22, five days after Congress's passage of the second confiscation act, Lincoln placed before his cabinet a document he had prepared that would emancipate all the slaves in the rebellious states. The border states had rejected his pleas for state emancipation; whatever damage might be done to their loyalty by a presidential proclamation had already been done by Congress's action. The proclamation was the last option open to him. On Seward's advice, however, he set the document aside. To issue it on the heels of military defeat, Seward argued, would be to deprive the policy of its sincerity in the eyes of the world. He proposed that Lincoln hold it until the military situation should improve.

Attack on Fredericksburg, December, 1862, by Alonzo Chappel. *(Library of Congress)*

Following McClellan's failure to take Richmond in the spring of 1862, Confederate forces commanded by Robert E. Lee advanced northward toward the Potomac. To stop them, Lincoln turned to John Pope, who had enjoyed some small successes in the Western campaigns. It was an unfortunate choice. The two armies clashed on the last days of August in the Second Battle of Bull Run, another defeat and disorderly retreat for the Union army. Emboldened by his success, Lee decided to carry the war into the Union, hoping that an invasion would liberate Maryland, capitalize on Northern war weariness, and influence the coming congressional elections, thus forcing the Lincoln administration to negotiate an end to the war. On September 5, Lee's forces crossed the Potomac and moved into central Maryland. In desperation, Lincoln restored McClellan to his command and charged him with stopping Lee's advance. The result was the Battle of Antietam on September 17, the bloodiest single day of fighting in the entire war. Lee's invasion was halted and his forces withdrew into Virginia, but McClellan failed to follow up his advantage. It was, however, the best that Lincoln could hope for. Five days later, he issued his preliminary Emancipation Proclamation.

Lincoln's move was a masterstroke, perhaps the most important turning point in the war. He preserved his priorities and left his constitutional scruples undamaged, quieted the opposition from his own party, and at the same time fulfilled a long-held desire. He reiterated his conviction that the purpose of the war was the restoration of the Union and repeated his proposal for financial aid to any slave state that might adopt a plan for gradual abolition. Lincoln, however, now believed that military emancipation was necessary for the preservation of the Union. All slaves living in areas that would still be in rebellion on January 1, 1863, he declared, were "then, thenceforward, and forever free." On that day he issued the final Emancipation Proclamation, listing those areas still in rebellion in which the slaves were freed.

Lincoln rested his action on his power as commander in chief. It was, he said, "a fit and necessary war measure" for suppressing the rebellion, an act of justice "warranted by the Constitution, upon military necessity." The proclamation could have no force beyond the termination of the war. Limited in duration, it was also limited in scope. Slaves living in the four loyal slave states and in those areas occupied by Union forces were excluded; the United States was not at war with those areas and therefore Lincoln's war power could not apply. Indeed, it has been suggested that Lincoln's Emancipation Proclamation fell short of Congress's emancipation in the second confiscation act and that Lincoln acted as if in ignorance of all the actions that Congress had taken earlier. At the same time, the congressional legislation was ineffective without the cooperation of the president. Thus it was Lincoln's proclamation that altered the nation's war aims and changed the course of the war; it was Lincoln's action that committed the American people to the abolition of slavery. With the proclamation, in the words of Allan Nevins, the war became a revolution.

The significance of the Emancipation Proclamation can hardly be exaggerated. Much of Lincoln's historical reputation and the perception of Lincoln as a folk hero rests on his role as the "Great Emancipator." Was he, however, a reluctant liberator, as some have maintained? When viewed from the perspective of his convictions and of his responsibilities as a war leader, it is clear that he was not. The proclamation did not weaken the will of the Southerners to continue their fight for independence, and the war would drag on for another two and a half years. From the point of view of one Confederate general, however, it was not only a great political triumph for Lincoln but also the greatest victory yet for the North.

That Lincoln did not regard his proclamation as the final solution to the vexing question of slavery became evident even before it went into effect. A president had no more power than a general, he had written, to make permanent rules of property by proclamation. In his message to Congress on December 1, 1862, a month before the final Emancipation Proclamation, he returned to the plan he had urged many times before. He proposed that Congress consider a constitutional amendment that would provide federal aid to those states that would adopt a gradual abolition of slavery. Gradual (until 1900, he suggested), compensated emancipation by state action still remained his favored course of action.

As the war continued, however, Lincoln came to recognize the necessity of a constitutional amendment that would simply abolish slavery wherever it existed in the United States. The patchwork manner in which the question was treated — by congressional acts, including the important second confiscation act, and by presidential proclamation — and the limited and confusing policies that declared some slaves free but not others were unsatisfactory. Doubts concerning the effectiveness, as well as the legality, of the Emancipation Proclamation (shared by Lincoln himself) demanded more uniform and unambiguous action. After one unsuccessful attempt to pass a constitutional amendment abolishing slavery (without gradualism and compensation), Congress finally approved the Thirteenth Amendment to the Constitution in January, 1865. Although it was not the amendment he had preferred, Lincoln pushed strongly for its passage, especially after his reelection to the presidency in November, 1864, arguing again that the abolition of slavery was "among the means" to secure the "maintenance of the Union." The amendment was not finally ratified until after Lincoln's death.

The Emancipation Proclamation added a new dimension to the meaning that the Civil War held for Lincoln. He appealed to Americans to overcome their qualms and to accept the commitment to freedom for the slaves. "The dogmas of the quiet past," he urged, "are inadequate to the stormy present." The times called for new thoughts and actions. "We must disenthrall ourselves, and then we shall save our country." In granting freedom to the slave, he declared, "we *assure* freedom to the *free*," thus saving "the last best, hope of earth." Lincoln returned to this theme a year later, in November, 1863, when he dedicated the military cemetery on the field of the great Battle of Gettysburg. The war, he said on that occasion, was a test of whether a nation "conceived in liberty, and dedicated to the proposition that all men are created equal" could "long endure." He urged all Americans to join in resolving "that this nation, under God, shall have a new birth of freedom — and that government of the people, by the people, for the people, shall not perish from the earth." Few Americans ever defined the nation's mission so effectively.

Political Opposition

Lincoln's Emancipation Proclamation eased the pressure from members of his own party, but it did not subdue Republican opposition to his prosecution of the war. Since the opening days of the conflict, when Lincoln deliberately postponed calling Congress into special session, members of that body had been attacking his policies. His proclamation removed one of the areas of contention for a time but left untouched the growing feeling among many in his party that he was incompetent to deal with the immense task that lay before him. Indeed, one of the darkest moments in the war for Lincoln came in December, 1862, between his preliminary and his final Emancipation Proclamation, when Republican opposition was exacerbated by another serious defeat for the Union army.

Lincoln had no military experience when he assumed the presidency (one can hardly count his brief experience in Black Hawk's War), nor had he ever shown any interest in military history. The Mexican War had been of little concern to him, except as a vehicle for registering his opposition to Polk's use of presidential power. Yet his administration was dominated from the day he took office until its end by a bloody war, and he was required, to an unusual degree, to make military decisions that would have taxed even the most experienced of leaders. In the absence of trustworthy commanders, he had to develop military strategy and plan military movements on a large scale with little information and skill. Furthermore, Lincoln's policy of recognizing Democrats as well as Republicans in his military appointments angered members of his own party and made him the object of continuing attack.

The initial defeat of the Army of the Potomac, commanded by General Irvin McDowell, at the First Battle of Bull Run in July, 1861, forecast a long and costly war. In the first of a series of command changes over the next three years, Lincoln replaced McDowell with George B. McClellan, an officer of Democratic antecedents who would cause Lincoln more moments of anxiety than any other general. In November, Lincoln further advanced McClellan to the office of general in chief, in place of the aged and infirm Winfield Scott. Hopes that McClellan would make a successful advance against the enemy, however, faded as it became apparent that the general lacked confidence, was overly cautious, and seemed reluctant to commit his men to battle. To make matters worse, McClellan did not hide his scorn for Lincoln or his impatience at being subject to a commander in chief whom he hardly trusted. He made a habit, moreover, of advising Lincoln on matters of policy, including the question of slavery.

As the nation chafed at McClellan's delay and the pressure on Lincoln to mount an offensive against the enemy increased, Union troops suffered another costly setback at the Battle of Ball's Bluff in October, only a few miles up the Potomac River from Washington. The defeat, in which a prominent Republican senator and close friend of Lincoln was killed, spurred Congress to action. A congressional committee, including members of both houses, was formed "to inquire into the conduct of the present war." Dominated by radical antislavery Republicans, the Joint Committee on the Conduct of the War maintained a continuing surveillance of Lin-

The Gettysburg Address

November 19, 1863

Fourscore and seven years ago our fathers brought forth on this continent a new nation, conceived in liberty and dedicated to the proposition that all men are created equal.

Now we are engaged in a great civil war, testing whether that nation or any nation so conceived and so dedicated can long endure. We are met on a great battlefield of that war. We have come to dedicate a portion of it as a final resting place for those who died here that the nation might live. This we may, in all propriety do.

But in a larger sense, we cannot dedicate, we cannot consecrate, we cannot hallow this ground. The brave men, living and dead who struggled here have hallowed it far above our poor power to add or detract. The world will little note nor long remember what we say here, but it can never forget what they did here. It is rather for us the living, we here be dedicated to the great task remaining before us — that from these honored dead we take increased devotion to that cause for which they here gave the last full measure of devotion — that we here highly resolve that these dead shall not have died in vain, that this nation shall have a new birth of freedom, and that government of the people, by the people, for the people shall not perish from the earth.

coln's administration, often interfering in his military appointments and engaging in investigative practices that bordered on harassment of both the president and the military.

McClellan quickly became a principal point of opposition between Lincoln and congressional Republicans. Responding to their pressure, Lincoln ordered McClellan to open his long-awaited offensive in late February, 1862, but it was not until the following month that McClellan's army began to move. At the same time, Lincoln replaced McClellan as general in chief with Henry Wager Halleck, a former West Point professor whom Lincoln once characterized as a "first-class clerk." After an excruciatingly slow advance up the peninsula between the York and James Rivers, McClellan's army was turned back in a series of bloody encounters known as the Seven Days' Battles. Following

McClellan's failure to take Richmond, relations between the two men deteriorated as attacks against both mounted in intensity. Lincoln had no choice but to reduce McClellan's authority and to bring in another general, in this case the arrogant and inept John Pope, whose appointment had been urged by the joint committee.

Following Pope's defeat at the Second Battle of Bull Run and Lee's invasion of Maryland, Lincoln turned in desperation to McClellan once again. Republicans were furious. Combined with their increasing indignation over Lincoln's apparent reluctance to take action against slavery and the frustration of military defeat, the restoration of the Democrat McClellan seemed the last straw. The governors of Massachusetts and Pennsylvania called a conference of Northern loyal governors to discuss Lincoln's prosecution of the war, fearful that the

An 1864 broadside contrasting Republican candidate Lincoln's advocacy of antislavery with Democratic candidate George B. McClellan's alleged support of the Southern slave system. *(Library of Congress)*

country would soon come to ruin if something were not done. The Battle of Antietam and Lincoln's subsequent Emancipation Proclamation, followed by his final dismissal of McClellan early in November, temporarily eased the situation, and the conference ended on a positive note.

Lincoln's reprieve did not last long. His choice to succeed McClellan, General Ambrose E. Burnside (whose lack of self-confidence was widely known), proved no more able to defeat Lee than had his predecessors. His ill-advised attack on Lee's army at Fredericksburg in December resulted in needless casualties, created open dissension among the officers in the army, and plunged Northern morale to new depths of despair. "We are going to destruction as fast as imbecility, corruption, and the wheels of time, can carry us," moaned one Republican senator. Lincoln was attacked more bitterly than before, as his critics blamed the military disasters on his "utter incompetence." Impressive Democratic victories at the polls in the congressional and state elections the month before underscored the need for drastic changes in Lincoln's administration. *The New York Times* blamed the crisis on Lincoln's inefficiency and concluded that the president was temperamentally unfit to deal with the "stern requirements of deadly war." The influential *Chicago Tribune* wondered if the rebels could ever be beaten with Lincoln at the helm.

Three days after the Battle of Fredericksburg, Senate Republicans met in caucus and voted to force Lincoln to reorganize his cabinet, presumably a first step toward asserting congressional control over the executive branch. Their target was Secretary of State Seward, whom they believed to be the "evil genius" behind Lincoln's decisions, and in seeking his removal they had the support of Lincoln's Treasury secretary, Salmon P. Chase. Rumors swept the capital that the entire cabinet would resign, and some thought that Lincoln himself would give up his office. For Lincoln it was a crisis of the first mag-

nitude. If the Republican senators should succeed, he would lose control of his administration. "What do these men want?" he asked a friend. "They wish to get rid of me, and I am sometimes half disposed to gratify them. . . . We are now on the brink of destruction. It appears to me the Almighty is against us, and I can hardly see a ray of hope."

There was hope, however, and it lay in Lincoln's political acumen and his masterful ability to manipulate his adversaries. Through a series of deft maneuvers, he was able to thwart the senators' attack, and by assuming the initiative he forced them to back off. Having received Seward's resignation, Lincoln so embarrassed Chase that he too offered his resignation. Lincoln emerged the winner when the senators, chagrined and frustrated, decided that Chase's loss from the cabinet was too great a price for Seward's removal. The crisis ended, and the integrity of the executive branch was preserved. The Republican leadership in Congress, however, was not mollified and continued to harbor feelings of rancor and bitterness toward Lincoln.

Lincoln's troubles were far from over. While he was warding off the opposition from his own party, he faced an increasing opposition from the Democratic Party. Only a month after his encounter with the Senate Republicans, he told a visitor to the White House that he feared "the fire in the rear," meaning the Democratic opposition, more than he did the Union army's chances.

The coming of the war had had a disastrous impact on the Democratic Party. With the secession of eleven Southern states, Democratic strength in Congress was reduced, leaving the Republican Party with comfortable majorities in both chambers. The death of Stephen A. Douglas in June, 1861, left the party leaderless, creating a vacuum at the top that was never filled. Lacking effective leadership, the party never became a responsible opposition party to the Lincoln administration. The stresses of se-

The surrender of Robert E. Lee and his army at Appomattox Courthouse to General Ulysses S. Grant on April 9, 1865. *(Library of Congress)*

cession and war also left its ranks divided. Some Democrats moved into the Republican Party; others supported Lincoln's prosecution of the war while trying to maintain an opposition to the administration on the traditional party issues. These were the War Democrats, and it was from their ranks that Lincoln made many of his appointments. Still others—the Peace Democrats, or more derisively, the copperheads—not only opposed Lincoln's handling of the war but also opposed the war itself. By early 1863, their opposition had developed into a full-fledged peace movement.

Democratic opposition rested initially on traditional conservative grounds: a defense of states' rights against the consolidation of power on the national level implied in the Whig-Republican position, and of laissez-faire economics against those elements of the old Whig platform that seemed to favor business and industrial interests over those of the rest of the population. Of more importance, however, were Lincoln's moves to extend presidential prerogative into those gray areas where constitutionality was in doubt.

Lincoln's proclamation of martial law and his suspension of the writ of habeas corpus following the fall of Fort Sumter, although limited in scope and obviously supported by most Americans, were challenged by those who believed only Congress had that power. The belief was confirmed by Chief Justice Roger B. Taney's ruling that Lincoln had violated the Constitution. That Lincoln was undeterred by the decision became evident when he expanded the suspension in September, 1862, a week after the Battle of Antietam, to cover the entire United States. To a growing number of Democrats, Lincoln appeared to be launching a full-scale attack on constitutional civil liberty, using the exigencies of the war as an excuse. When Congress sought to remove all constitutional doubts by ratifying Lincoln's moves in the Habeas Corpus Act of March, 1863, Democratic fears were hardly allayed. Thousands of individuals (the number is uncertain) suffered arbitrary arrest, and some Democratic newspapers were suspended.

The Emancipation Proclamation, issued only a few days before Lincoln's extension of the suspension of the writ of habeas corpus, brought Democratic opposition to a peak. The proclamation, it was charged, was further evidence of Lincoln's disregard of the Constitution. Furthermore, it violated the Republican Party's 1860 platform and Lincoln's often repeated pledges never to interfere with slavery in the states where it existed. By enlarging the war aims, Lincoln, critics maintained, had altered the nature of the war. The charges became entangled with deep-seated antiblack prejudices in many parts of the North as Lincoln's opponents pointed out that while he was impairing the civil rights of whites, he was enhancing the rights of blacks.

Lincoln succeeded in doing with the Emancipation Proclamation what Robert E. Lee had failed to do with his invasion of Maryland, that is, to arouse a political opposition to the Republican administration of the war. The seriousness of the opposition was revealed in the results of the November elections. Although the Republicans retained their control in the House of Representatives, Democratic strength almost doubled. In addition, Democrats made substantial gains in states that the Republicans had carried just two years before, including Lincoln's own state of Illinois. To one leading Republican paper, the election results constituted a vote of no confidence in Lincoln's leadership.

The Battle of Fredericksburg, which had stimulated Republican opposition to Lincoln, also pushed Democrats to a more extreme stand. A congressman from Ohio, Clement L. Vallandigham, emerged as the leader of a peace movement that demanded an end to the useless slaughter of young men. From his seat in the House of Representatives, he denounced the war as cruel and wicked, and he charged Lincoln with attempting to erect a Republican despotism on the ruins of slavery. He attacked the Emancipation Proclamation as illegal, unconstitutional, and even immoral and urged resistance to Lincoln's broadening of the war aims. Vallandigham's condemnation of Lincoln's actions invited the action of the military. In May, 1863, he was arrested, tried by a military commission, and sentenced to imprisonment for the duration of the war. Lincoln was appalled at the arrest, for it gave Vallandigham the martyrdom he sought; in June, Lincoln commuted Vallandigham's sentence to removal beyond the Union lines.

Vallandigham's protests encouraged others to speak out against the war. The passage of the Habeas Corpus Act and of the nation's first Conscription Act in the spring of 1863, along with another Union army defeat at the Battle of Chancellorsville, gave force to the Democratic charges. In the Midwest (including Illinois), legislators called for the cessation of hostilities, the withdrawal of the Emancipation Proclamation, and a negotiated peace with the Confederacy. New York's Governor Horatio Seymour attacked the Conscription Act as a violation of civil liberty in a speech that contributed to the celebrated draft riots in New York City in early July.

Lincoln's distress at the opposition from both Republicans and Democrats was suddenly relieved in midsummer. Military events came to his rescue when two simultaneous and decisive Union victories were won at Gettysburg and Vicksburg. A turning point in the war had been reached. Military success, together with an economic recovery that soon became an unprecedented boom, gave Lincoln the strength to press the war to ultimate victory. With a Union victory at the Battle of Chattanooga in November, the Union's soldiers stood poised on the threshold of the Confederacy's heartland. A new general emerged who demonstrated an

The assassination of Lincoln. *(Library of Congress)*

ability to win. When Ulysses S. Grant was brought to the East and placed in command of all the military forces of the United States, it seemed only a matter of time before the war would end.

The Election of 1864: The Issue of Reconstruction

With the Union army victories in 1863 marking a turn in the military fortunes of the North, the attacks on Lincoln from both Republicans and Democrats subsided. Lincoln's Gettysburg Address in November revealed a new confidence in the eventual triumph of the Union cause. In March, 1864, Ulysses S. Grant was promoted to the rank of lieutenant general (held by only two officers before him, George Washington and Winfield Scott) and was appointed general in chief of all Union armies, an office that Lincoln himself had filled in practice ever since the Bat-

tle of Antietam. As Grant began laying plans for a spring campaign against Lee's army, Lincoln believed that he had at last found his general. All the signs pointed to a quick end to the war.

At the same time, the nation gained the economic strength necessary to push the war to victory. The economic dislocation of the first two years of the conflict, brought on by the disruption of secession and war, had been overcome. With Lincoln's support, the government became an active partner in promoting an economic growth and development that by 1863 seemed unprecedented in its dimensions. Congress passed a series of tariff bills, raising protective duties higher and higher in response to the needs and demands of an expanding industrial establishment. A new national banking system to stabilize and strengthen the country's financial order was created by Congress, a move that, with the issuance of more than $400 million worth of unbacked paper money, made it possible to finance the war. A railroad was begun that would link the Pacific coast with the rest of the nation, the construction to be aided by large-scale government largesse, and a second transcontinental railroad was planned in 1864. Agricultural expansion was boosted with the passage in 1862 of the Homestead Act and of the Morrill Land Grant Act, providing free land to America's farmers and enabling the states to promote agricultural education and research. Never before had the United States government played so active a role in the nation's economic affairs.

The new prosperity and the turn in military fortunes strengthened Lincoln's hand and gave him the power and prestige he needed to save the Union. Toward the end of 1863, poet Walt Whitman spoke for many Americans when he confessed that "I have finally got for good, I think, into the feeling that our triumph is assured" and that the president "has done as good as a human man could do." Lincoln began the critical presidential election year of 1864 with optimism and hope; his reelection hardly seemed in doubt.

Lincoln's opponents, however, were simply biding their time. Some Republicans still questioned Lincoln's competence to see the struggle through to its conclusion, and the Democrats, disturbed by the infringement on civil liberty and shocked by the horrendous loss of life that accompanied Grant's Virginia offensive, still believed that the bloodshed could be halted and the Union preserved by peaceful negotiation. Both sides looked to the presidential election as the opportunity to achieve their ends legally and constitutionally.

As early as the fall of 1863, a number of Radical Republicans, convinced that Lincoln's administration was a failure, promoted the candidacy of Treasury Secretary Salmon P. Chase. Support for Chase, never strong, collapsed in the following spring, when the secretary himself tried to assure Lincoln that he was not in-

volved in the movement. Later, an effort was made to advance the candidacy of John C. Frémont, but it proved to be a small affair (although Frémont took it seriously).

Lincoln had little reason for concern. The Republican convention, in an effort to expand its appeal to the War Democrats by calling itself the Union Party, easily nominated Lincoln for reelection to the presidency and selected Tennessee Democrat Andrew Johnson as his running mate. The platform endorsed Lincoln's wartime policies, urged that the war be pressed to its ultimate military conclusion, and called for the passage of a constitutional amendment that would abolish slavery.

Events that followed in the summer of 1864, however, gave encouragement to Lincoln's critics and raised the hope that even yet he might be removed from the presidency. In the first place, the military situation took a turn for the worse. After pushing southward in Virginia, maintaining a relentless pressure on the depleted manpower resources of the Confederacy, Grant was stopped by Lee's army at Petersburg, a few miles south of Richmond. By mid-June he had settled down to a long and frustrating siege that would extend into the early months of 1865. In the meantime, Confederate General Jubal Early swept out of the Shenandoah Valley and reached the outskirts of Washington, D.C., threatening the capital and apparently demonstrating the weakness of the Union command. In the West, General William Tecumseh Sherman's advance into Georgia was stopped by Confederate forces at Atlanta. The promise of victory, so evident at the beginning of the year, had given way to stalemate, and by the late summer the North was plunged into another abyss of defeatism and despair.

More critical to Lincoln's relationship with his party was the discord that burst into the open over Reconstruction policy. Lincoln began thinking early in the war about the terms that would govern the return of the seceded states to the Union, and as the Union army occupied larger portions of the Confederacy the need for a policy became more urgent. Before December, 1863, Lincoln groped for a workable plan that could be applied to the occupied areas. In approaches to both Tennessee and Louisiana, he proposed certain vague steps toward the organization of new governments but seemed uncertain about how to reconcile the Emancipation Proclamation with a desire "to have peace again upon the old terms under the Constitution." When Congress met in December, 1863, with Union victory on the horizon, Lincoln issued his program for the restoration of the states to the Union in a Proclamation of Amnesty and Reconstruction.

Lincoln based his plan on two assumptions: first, that since secession was not recognized either in law or in the Constitution, the states had not left the Union; and second, that it was the responsibility of the president and not of Congress to devise and oversee the steps by which the states would resume their former places in the Union. The seceded states, he believed, were simply out of their practical relation with the other states. His plan looked to a speedy, easy resumption of that practical relation. Concerned primarily with the status of the states in the Union, Lincoln was more concerned with their restoration than he was with their reconstruction. Any internal changes would follow once the states had been restored to their former positions; furthermore, Lincoln appeared ready to allow Southerners a role in the formulation of these changes.

Lincoln was insistent that the authority to restore the states to the Union was his by virtue of his war power as commander in chief and of his constitutional authority to grant pardons. In his exercise of this authority, he argued for flexibility, expediency, and a forward-looking practicality. He had little patience for delay.

In his proclamation, Lincoln promised pardon to all in the seceded states who would take an oath to support, protect, and defend the Constitution and Union and to support all the actions of Congress and the president relating to slavery. Barred from the oath-taking were several categories of high-ranking Confederate civil and military officials. When 10 percent of the eligible voters in any state should have taken the oath and received the pardon, they could establish a new state government. Lincoln urged but did not require the new states to declare permanent the freedom of those who had been slaves. Once the states had fulfilled his conditions, they would presumably be restored to their former relations with the other states, although Lincoln conceded that Congress would have the final determination whether their representatives should be seated in the legislative body.

Lincoln's 10-percent plan was implemented in Arkansas and Louisiana in the spring of 1864 and in Tennessee later in the year, but not without confusion and uncertainty. Republicans in Congress, especially the radicals, responded bitterly to Lincoln's initiative. Not only did they believe that the terms of his plan were far too liberal, but also they resented Lincoln's contention that Reconstruction was the president's responsibility. After months of debate, they passed the Wade-Davis bill, in which their own Reconstruction program was outlined. Congressional intentions became clearer when the elected representatives from Louisiana and Arkansas were denied seats, in effect destroying Lincoln's plan.

The Wade-Davis bill replaced Lincoln's terms with harsher and more stringent provisions. An alternative oath was prescribed that gave assurance of the oath taker's past loyalty, and the 10 percent figure was raised to 50 percent. The new states were required to abolish slavery and to repudiate their Confederate debt. The bill, designed to postpone Reconstruction until after the war by making it virtually impossible for the Southern states to comply with its terms, revealed the gulf that existed between the president and Congress.

The confrontation widened when Lincoln

expressed his opposition to the bill by exercising the seldom-used pocket veto. In a curious move, however, he issued a proclamation detailing his objections (no message is required for a pocket veto) that only incensed Congress the more. He was, he wrote, unwilling to be "inflexibly committed to any single plan of restoration," suggesting that he was not fully committed to his own plan. Furthermore, he was unwilling both to set aside the governments that had already been established in Louisiana and Arkansas and to concede to Congress the power to abolish slavery in the states. Having registered his objections, Lincoln then declared that he was "fully satisfied" with the bill as representing "one very proper plan." Finally, he offered the seceded states a choice between his plan and that of Congress, a meaningless gesture inasmuch as the latter had been pocket vetoed.

If Lincoln's proclamation was an effort to unify support for his reelection, it fell wide of the mark. Instead, it solidified Republican dissatisfaction with his leadership. Outraged and puzzled by his statements, the authors of the bill issued a fierce diatribe against his action—the Wade-Davis Manifesto. Arguably no president has had to endure such vilification from his own party. Lincoln's action was denounced as a political attack on the friends of the government, a "grave Executive usurpation," and a "studied outrage on the legislative authority of the people." He was charged with subverting the Constitution in the interest of his personal ambition. The manifesto concluded with a thinly veiled warning against Lincoln's use of presidential power. "The authority of Congress," Lincoln was reminded, "is paramount"; the president must "confine himself to his executive duties—to obey and execute, not make the laws."

The confrontation between Lincoln and the Republicans in Congress, with the defeatism that swept the North following the military stalemate, revived demands among some leading Republican spokespeople that Lincoln be replaced. Lincoln, declared one prominent editor, could no longer be reelected. Only another ticket (Grant or Sherman was suggested) could save the country "from utter overthrow." Plans were made for another Republican convention to find a new candidate "who commands the confidence of the country."

The furor had a dispiriting effect on Lincoln, and he began to doubt his own chances for reelection. The military impasse on top of the army's heavy losses encouraged the Peace Democrats, and once again demands were made for an end to the war through peace negotiations with the South. Lincoln's call for an additional five hundred thousand volunteers intensified the protests against the further needless sacrifice of lives. Even some Republicans, such as Horace Greeley, urged the president to explore every possible avenue toward a peaceful end to the conflict. Lincoln, by late August convinced that he would be beaten, exacted a pledge from his cabinet that they would cooperate with the president-elect to save the Union between the election and the inauguration, for it could not possibly be saved afterward. A week later, the Democratic convention nominated George B. McClellan for the presidency and placed him on a platform that demanded that hostilities cease immediately and that peace be restored "on the basis of the Federal Union."

Within days, however, the entire picture suddenly changed. Admiral David Glasgow Farragut forced his way into Mobile Bay and sealed off one of the last Southern ports open to the outside world. On September 2, General Sherman's army marched into Atlanta on the heels of the retreating Confederate force, and later General Philip Sheridan ended Confederate resistance in the Shenandoah Valley, freeing the national capital of any further threat from the enemy. Northerners, with victory once more in sight, rallied to the side of Abraham Lincoln. A nervous John C. Frémont withdrew his candidacy, and the plans for a Republican convention were abandoned. Mclellan strongly endorsed the prosecution of the war to ultimate Union victory. Lincoln was rescued by military events, and on election day in November he coasted to an easy victory in both the popular vote and the electoral college.

The End of the War and Assassination

Lincoln's reelection ended all doubts that the war would continue until the nation's goals were achieved. The Republicans not only won the presidency but also swept the congressional elections, increasing their majority in the lower house of Congress and maintaining their strong lead in the Senate. With their triumph as a mandate, they succeeded in passing the Thirteenth Amendment to the Constitution, abolishing slavery throughout the United States. General Sherman's army moved out of Atlanta and began its march across Georgia; by Christmas it had reached the sea at Savannah and, turning northward, began its movement into the Carolinas.

In the Confederacy, the desire for peace reached a peak. Jefferson Davis, partly to mollify his critics, agreed to meet with Northern representatives to negotiate a peaceful end to the bloodshed. Lincoln also agreed to take part, although, like Davis, he had no faith that such an endeavor could succeed. The conference was doomed before it started; Davis wrote of a meeting "to secure peace to the two countries," whereas Lincoln indicated a readiness to bring "peace to the people of our one common country." A Southern delegation headed by Vice President Alexander H. Stephens met with Lincoln and Seward aboard a Union transport vessel in Hampton Roads, off Norfolk, Virginia, on February 3, 1865. Lincoln presented his terms for an end to the war: the restoration of the Union, the abolition of slavery, and the disbanding of all military forces hostile to the United States. It took only four hours for the Southerners to realize that they were not going to dissuade Lincoln from his position.

One month later, Lincoln delivered his second inaugural address. In a brief, sensitive statement, he reiterated his belief in the sanctity of the Union and the necessity for its preservation and attributed to God's will the end of slavery through "this mighty scourge of war." He ended on a note of forgiveness and goodwill, as he looked ahead to the war's conclusion:

> With malice toward none; with charity for all; with firmness in the right, as God gives us to see the right, let us strive on to finish the work we are in; to bind up the nation's wounds; to care for him who shall have borne the battle, and for his widow, and his orphan—to do all which may achieve and cherish a just, and a lasting peace, among ourselves, and with all nations.

The end now came swiftly. In the latter part of March, Lincoln met with Generals Grant and Sherman to plan the final campaign. He expressed his desire for a quick end to the bloodshed and urged each general to offer generous terms of surrender to the Southern troops. As Sherman's force advanced through the Carolinas, Grant broke the siege of Petersburg with a swift flanking movement.

Petersburg fell, and on April 3 Grant's army entered Richmond. The Confederate government was in flight. Within a few days Lee asked Grant for his surrender terms, and on Sunday, April 9, at the Appomattox Courthouse, the conditions were agreed on by the two commanders. With Lee's surrender, the Civil War, for all practical purposes, was at an end.

While the nation rejoiced, Lincoln's attention was focused on the question of Reconstruction as he sought some way out of the tangle into which his plans had fallen. Earlier, in February, he had revealed that he still preferred a form of compensated emancipation, even in the face of the Thirteenth Amendment, when he proposed to his cabinet that the government pay $400 million to the Southern states in proportion to their slave populations, a kind of recompense for the loss of slavery but also a form of federal aid to their economic reconstruction. The cabinet was not enthusiastic, and the matter was dropped. Governments established under Lincoln's 10-percent plan were functioning in three of the states, but they were feeble and shaky, owing their existence to Union occupation troops. Lincoln had hoped that some limited form of black suffrage might be adopted and urged the states to provide for the education of the freedmen.

Two days after Lee's surrender, on April 11, Lincoln was serenaded at the White House by a crowd of jubilant citizens. He defended his Reconstruction policy and alluded in some detail to its operation in Louisiana, which he regarded as the showcase of his program. He emphasized that the "sole object" of the government should be the restoration of the states to their "proper practical relation" with the Union. The question whether the states were in the Union or out of it he believed to be nothing more than a "pernicious abstraction." "Finding themselves safely at home," he declared, "it would be utterly immaterial whether they had ever been abroad." Lincoln urged again that flexibility be maintained. This situation was "so new and unprecedented" that "no exclusive, and inflexible plan can safely be prescribed." That his own views were still evolving became apparent. "It may be my duty," he told his audience, "to make some new announcement to the people of the South. I am considering, and shall not fail to act, when satisfied that action will be proper."

What that "new announcement" was to be, whether he intended to ease the confrontation with Congress or exacerbate it, will never be known. Three days after his address, feeling relaxed for the first time in years, Lincoln decided to spend an evening at the theater with his wife.

Abraham Lincoln's assassination at the hand of John Wilkes Booth as he sat in the presidential box at Ford's Theater on the night of April 14, 1865, struck the North like a thunderbolt. All the rumors of impending attacks on the president that had swept through Washington, D.C., from the day of his first inauguration had hardly prepared the public mind for the actual deed. The murder of the president seemed inconceivable, and Americans had difficulty comprehending the horror of the act. Reports circulated wildly that the assassination had been planned in Richmond and that Jefferson Davis himself had been involved in its execution.

Booth and the cluster of characters he had gathered about him acted out of an obsessive and irrational hostility toward Lincoln's wartime politics. A strong and devoted supporter of Southern independence and slavery, Booth had denounced Lincoln as an oppressor and a tyrant, charging the president with subverting liberty and justice and trying to uplift blacks at the expense of whites. The plot evolved from a bizarre scheme to kidnap Lincoln and hold him hostage, but the war's end dashed Booth's hope that the plan could help the Confederacy win its independence. The decision to murder Lincoln rather than kidnap him was apparently made on the spur of the moment; some of Booth's conspirators demurred, whereas others took part in only a halfhearted manner.

The significance of the assassination to the course of Reconstruction cannot be minimized. Coming only five days after Lee's surrender at Appomattox, Lincoln's murder had a profound effect on the Northern psyche. The great wave of rejoicing and jubilation that had followed the news of the surrender was turned abruptly into deep sorrow and grief. The assassination was widely viewed as the last, crowning act of treachery by the South against the Union. It called out for vengeance. There was no more conclusive proof, declared one Northern intellectual, that the Union's cause had been the cause of humanity against barbarism. Any story of Southern wickedness now became believable.

To many Americans, the assassination was a sign of God's intervention, but why, they asked, had God intervened? Ministers sought to explain God's action from their pulpits for weeks and months following the deed. Lincoln, it was said, had failed to appreciate the real evil of the South and of slavery; he had spoken of leniency and charity when sterner, harsher measures were necessary. Lincoln had served as God's instrument for the preservation of the Union; that task was accomplished. God removed Lincoln so that abler, firmer hands could take over the task of Reconstruction. The tragedy was God's way of arousing the North from its complacency, of reminding the people that the struggle against the South was not over yet. God had snatched up Lincoln in the moment of his glory and had made him a martyr, a "citizen of the ages." The apotheosis had begun.

When George Bancroft, America's first great historian, delivered his memorial address on Abraham Lincoln less than a year after the assassination, the dimensions of the demigod and folk hero were already taking shape. Lincoln, he pointed out, had been God's agent in carrying out his will that the United States should live. Guided by God's light and obeying the eternal truths of liberty, he had brought the nation through its peril to safety. Through his faith in the perpetuity of the Union and the righteousness of its mission, he had renovated the nation's moral purpose and unity.

Lincoln was called to this task, Bancroft continued, because he was the very embodiment of America. His humble origins, his identification with the frontier, and his self-education and intuitive wisdom were "altogether American." Lincoln "lived the life of the American people, walked in its light, reasoned with its reason, thought with its power of thought, felt the beatings of its mighty heart, and so was in every way a child of nature, a child of the West, a child of America."

One need not indulge in the rhetoric of mid-nineteenth century America to concede Lincoln's greatness. Few today challenge the judgment of the nation's scholars that Lincoln was America's greatest president. That he was able to surmount the obstacles placed in his path and to carry to triumphant conclusion the goals he

had set for himself and for his country must certainly point to qualities of greatness, although he was also at times the beneficiary of fortuitous military and economic events. Lincoln's faith in himself, in human beings generally, and in his country ran deep; it never wavered, even during the darkest days of the war. His grasp of America's meaning to the world, of its moral destiny, and of the quality of its mission was firm and unequivocal.

Robert W. Johannsen

Suggested Readings

Abraham Lincoln Presidential Library and Museum. http://www.alplm.org/. The official Web site of the state-of-the-art library and museum that opened in the fall of 2004.

Basler, Roy P., et al., eds. *The Collected Works of Abraham Lincoln*. 9 vols. New Brunswick, N.J.: Rutgers University Press, 1953-1955; supplements, 1974, 1990. A comprehensive collection of Lincoln's writings.

DiLorenzo, Thomas. *The Real Lincoln: A New Look at Abraham Lincoln, His Agenda, and an Unnecessary War*. Roseville, Calif.: Forum, 2002. Argues that Lincoln's real agenda in the Civil War was more about furthering the centralization of government in an economically interventionist state rather than the liberation of slaves.

Donald, David Herbert. *Lincoln*. New York: Simon & Schuster, 1995. A prize-winning biography of Lincoln that draws on personal papers and those of his contemporaries, as well as the voluminous records of Lincoln's legal practice that were discovered in the late twentieth century.

_____. *Lincoln at Home: Two Glimpses of Abraham Lincoln's Family Life*. New York: Simon & Schuster, 2000. Includes all the known letters exchanged by Lincoln, Mary Todd Lincoln, and Robert Todd Lincoln.

Donald, David Herbert, Jean H. Baker, and Michael F. Holt. *The Civil War and Reconstruction*. New York: Norton, 2001. Provides excellent social, political, and historical context to Lincoln's presidency.

Einhorn, Lois J. *Abraham Lincoln, the Orator: Penetrating the Lincoln Legend*. Westport, Conn.: Greenwood Press, 1992. A rhetorical analysis of Lincoln's speaking skills, including a collection of his major speeches and an extensive primary and secondary bibliography.

Harris, William C. *With Charity for All: Lincoln and the Restoration of the Union*. Lexington: University Press of Kentucky, 1997. Maintains that Lincoln's efforts to restore the Southern states to the Union began long before the end of the war and Reconstruction.

Kauffman, Michael W. *American Brutus: John Wilkes Booth and the Lincoln Conspiracies*. New York: Random House, 2004. Kauffman, one of the foremost Lincoln assassination historians, uses archival sources and recent research to shed new light on the Lincoln murder conspiracies.

Kunhardt, Philip B., Jr., Philip B. Kunhardt III, and Peter W. Kunhardt. *Lincoln: An Illustrated Biography*. New York: Knopf, 1992. An engaging pictorial biography.

Neely, Mark E., Jr. *The Abraham Lincoln Encyclopedia*. New York: McGraw-Hill, 1982. An indispensable guide to all aspects of Lincoln's life.

_____. *The Last Best Hope of Earth: Abraham Lincoln and the Promise of America*. Cambridge, Mass.: Harvard University Press, 1993. A solid biography.

Oates, Stephen B. *With Malice Toward None: The Life of Abraham Lincoln*. New York: Harper & Row, 1977. Many historians consider this volume one of the best biographies on Lincoln.

Time 166, no. 1 (July 4, 2005). This special issue of *Time* magazine, titled "Uncovering the Real Abraham Lincoln," brings together several articles that reassess Lincoln's presidency and examines issues such as his views on race, his relationship with Mary Todd, and his struggles with depression.

White, Ronald C. *The Eloquent President: A Portrait of Lincoln Through His Words*. New York: Random House, 2005. Critical essays trace the development of Lincoln's political rhetoric.

Wills, Gary. *Lincoln at Gettysburg: The Words That Remade America*. New York: Simon & Schuster, 1992. An extensive analysis of the circumstances and impact of Lincoln's historic speech.

Andrew Johnson

17th President, 1865-1869

Born: December 29, 1808
　　　Raleigh, North Carolina
Died: July 31, 1875
　　　near Carter Station, Tennessee

Political Party: Republican
Vice President: none

Cabinet Members

Secretary of State: William H. Seward
Secretary of the Treasury: Hugh McCulloch
Secretary of War: Edwin M. Stanton, Ulysses S. Grant, John M. Schofield
Secretary of the Navy: Gideon Welles
Attorney General: James Speed, Henry Stanbery, William M. Evarts
Postmaster General: William Dennison, Alexander Randall
Secretary of the Interior: John P. Usher, James Harlan, O. H. Browning

Born on December 29, 1808, in Raleigh, North Carolina, Andrew Johnson was the third child of Jacob and Mary Johnson, illiterate tavern servants. Jacob Johnson died when Andrew was three, leaving his wife to eke out a living by sewing and taking in laundry. This hardscrabble existence and an unwise second marriage forced Mary Johnson to apprentice Andrew and his older brother William to a Raleigh tailor. Johnson was an able and diligent worker but also headstrong and possessed with a burning passion for education and self-improvement. By listening to the reading of famous American speeches in the tailor shop, Johnson was encouraged to learn to read. For reasons now obscure, in 1825 Andrew and William ran away

from their apprenticeship. They drifted into South Carolina, failed in business, grew homesick, and returned to Raleigh but could not pacify their irate employer.

At the age of seventeen, Johnson fled from his background of poverty and from the aristocratic pretensions of Raleigh society to begin a new life on the Tennessee frontier. He settled in the small town of Greeneville and there became a successful tailor. After his marriage to Eliza McCardle in 1827, both Johnson's personal and business life prospered. The Johnsons had five

Portrait of Andrew Johnson. *(Whitehouse.gov)*

children, three sons and two daughters. Johnson read avidly, learned to write with his wife's help, and was a stalwart participant in a local debating society.

From Tailor's Shop to Congressional Chambers

Andrew Johnson used his connections made in the tailor shop and his natural speaking ability to enter politics. Elected alderman in 1829 and mayor of Greeneville in 1831, by 1835 he had moved on to the state legislature. At 5 feet, 10 inches and 175 pounds, the dark-haired, dark-eyed Johnson was already an impressive stump orator. An admirer of Andrew Jackson, Johnson early displayed a dogged commitment to strict constitutional construction regardless of political consequences. Although his own East Tennessee constituents were clamoring for improved transportation, the new legislator opposed state aid to railroads, thereby paving the way for his own defeat at the next election. After that, Johnson returned to Nashville in 1839, having modified his opposition to state-supported internal improvements. By this time, he had become an avid advocate of hard money and a stridently partisan Democrat, ready on all occasions to lash out at Whig policies and candidates.

Elected to Congress in 1842, Johnson served five consecutive terms in the House of Representatives. Reflecting his impoverished background, he quickly elevated public parsimony into the highest of virtues. The Smithsonian Institution and both military service academies became for him symbols of government extravagance and aristocratic privilege. Johnson loyally supported the expansionist and war policies of Democratic president James K. Polk, but he never got along well with the presidents during his congressional service because of dissatisfaction with their patronage policies. Johnson saw himself as a special defender of the common people's interest and long pushed for the abolition of the electoral college in favor of direct popular election of the president. Most politicians, in his view, were selfish timeservers, and he made few friends of any kind in Washington, D.C. He especially resented the arrogance of certain Southern politicians such as Mississippian Jefferson Davis, who in Johnson's mind represented "an illegitimate, swaggering, bastard, scrub aristocracy." Despite this largely negative philosophy, Johnson was a strong supporter of one forward-looking measure—a homestead bill. He saw this as a way to serve the real people—the small farmers—and to prevent the growth of concentrated economic power based on the ownership of land and slaves. Johnson's unsuccessful fight for 160-acre homesteads during the early 1850's gave him his first taste of national prominence.

As a Southerner in the midst of growing sectional conflict, Johnson occupied an anomalous position. Although an orthodox defender of slavery and himself a small slaveholder, the Tennessee congressman was no fire-eater. Like his hero Andrew Jackson, Johnson was a staunch Union man and saw sectional agitation as both dangerous and unnecessary. He voted for all the provisions of the Compromise of 1850, except for the bill that abolished the slave trade in the District of Columbia.

Successful as a spokesperson for small farmers and sectional peace, Johnson suddenly encountered the realities of politics in a state that neither party effectively controlled. In 1852, the Whig-dominated legislature gerrymandered him out of his congressional seat. This proved to be a temporary and perhaps fortunate setback because Johnson won election as governor of Tennessee in 1853. In that office, he successfully pushed for a tax to support education, but for the most part he quarreled with a legislature that contained enough Whigs to stymie any gubernatorial initiatives. Frustrated by the time spent on administrative detail, he nevertheless successfully ran for reelection in 1855, braving the Know-Nothing tide then sweeping across the nation.

The First Lady
Eliza Johnson

Born October 4, 1810, Eliza McCardle married the future president, Andrew Johnson, on May 17, 1827. Eliza and eighteen-year-old Andrew married at younger ages than any presidential couple. Eliza, daughter of Sarah Phillips and innkeeper-cobbler John McCardle, had received a basic education at a private academy. She and Andrew, a tailor, moved into a tiny building in Greeneville; one room housed his shop and the other the family. Eliza bore daughter Martha in 1828 and son Charles in 1830. Later children included Mary (1832), Robert (1834), and Andrew, Jr. (1852). As Johnson's business and political career prospered, the family moved to a large brick house and eventually owned nine slaves.

Andrew Johnson was first elected to local office in 1829, and he became a state representative in 1837. He later served as U.S. congressman, Tennessee governor, and U.S. senator. Johnson was away from home much of the year, and Eliza managed the household, tailor shop, real estate holdings, and a farm in his absence. By the 1850's, she showed increasing signs of tuberculosis. Nevertheless, when the Civil War separated the staunch Unionist couple, Eliza persevered in Confederate-occupied Greeneville even as her husband became Tennessee's military governor. When the Rebels gave her thirty-six hours to leave Greeneville in 1863, Eliza valiantly found her way through enemy lines to join Johnson. The family moved to Washington in 1864 when he became U.S. vice president.

Lincoln's assassination in April, 1865, propelled Johnson into the White House, and Eliza lived there throughout his term of office. Johnson credited Eliza with teaching him to read and used her as his most trusted adviser on public policy. Eliza's illness kept her confined to a room on the second floor of the White House, and she attended only four social functions as First Lady. She told a visitor that she never had a happy moment in Washington; her husband's impeachment was painful to her although she said she always knew he would be acquitted.

Eliza longed for a peaceful life in Greeneville after leaving the White House, while Johnson returned to his political life. He was again elected U.S. senator in 1874 but died in July, 1875. Eliza was too weak to attend the funeral, but she administered his estate. She passed away on January 15, 1876.

Ann Toplovich

Johnson in the Senate: The Secession Crisis

By 1857, Democrats had regained control of the legislature and awarded Johnson the prize he coveted most, a seat in the United States Senate. Johnson the senator was little different in outlook or approach from Johnson the young member of the House. He seemed less willing to compromise on sectional questions than he had been in 1850, but he was hardly a Southern radical. He bitterly accused Northern Republicans of incendiary agitation during the debates over John Brown's raid at Harpers Ferry, but in 1860, Johnson still saw himself as a possible compromise presidential candidate for a badly divided Democratic Party. Yet he was curiously passive, and although the Tennessee delegation supported his candidacy for thirty-six ballots at the tumultuous Charleston convention, Johnson refused to instruct them on a possible political truce with Northern Democratic leader Stephen A. Douglas. The disruption of the Democratic Party, opposition from Southern Democrats to his beloved homestead bill, and the more and more strident sectional rhetoric of politicians such as Jefferson Davis made Johnson increasingly uncomfortable. He belatedly agreed to stump for John C. Breckinridge, the presidential candidate of the Southern Democrats, but considered preserving the Union more important than winning an election.

The secession crisis marked the final break between Johnson and the Southern Democratic leadership. In blistering rhetoric on the Senate floor, he condemned disunionists as traitors, accused them of wishing to destroy not only the Union but also political democracy, and even called for their swift and condign punishment. For his efforts, Johnson received warm denunciations from many Tennessee Democrats but equally fervent applause from the state's Whigs and from Northern Republicans. Despite threats against his life, in April, 1861, Johnson returned to Greeneville to take part in a last desperate round of speechmaking in an effort to hold Tennessee in the Union.

When his state seceded in June, however, Johnson returned to Washington, D.C., and defended the policies of the new Republican president, Abraham Lincoln. Johnson had always been a committed Unionist; still, when Lincoln put Johnson in charge of distributing patronage for the administration in East Tennessee, he could weld political principle to long-standing personal ambition. When the Confederate defense of Tennessee collapsed in 1862, Lincoln appointed Johnson military governor of the state. In this post, Johnson found it difficult to remain patient with plodding Union generals in Tennessee and was continually frustrated by the lingering spirit of disunion there. Johnson treated the Confederates in his jurisdiction harshly and put great store in administering loyalty oaths to would-be penitents.

Considering Johnson's strongly Unionist record and the Republican desire to build bipartisan support for Lincoln's war policies, party leaders asked Johnson, a lifelong Democrat and former slaveholder, to become the vice presidential nominee in 1864 on the "Union" ticket. By the end of this grueling campaign, Johnson was exhausted and ill. On Inauguration Day, he drank some whiskey to fortify himself for the occasion and as a consequence delivered a rambling and incoherent address filled with boastful references to his "plebeian" origins. Although Lincoln stood by him, many Republicans began to doubt Johnson's fitness for high office. Also, Johnson never seemed to realize that he owed his position not only to his own courage in standing up to the secessionists but also to the Republican Party. When Lincoln was assassinated on April 14, 1865, this great symbol of Southern Unionism who breathed fire against Confederates and who would now be the nation's chief executive was unknown to many Americans and an enigma to politicians, North and South.

Johnson as President: An Enigma in the White House

Johnson's long experience in the rough-and-tumble of Tennessee politics had ill prepared him to be president during a period of revolutionary upheaval. Johnson shared Lincoln's belief in the primary responsibility of the president for reconstructing the Union. Indeed, he pledged to carry out the martyred president's policies, but these were hardly clear at the time, and historians are still debating what Lincoln would have done after the war. Some Radical Republicans believed that Johnson's harsh wartime statements about punishing traitors meant that he would support their plans for a thoroughgoing reconstruction of the South. Yet Republicans of all stripes and Democrats as well courted the new president and sought to shape the course of his administration.

Initially, Johnson was greatly influenced by Secretary of War Edwin Stanton, especially in dealing with Lincoln's murderers. Both men believed that leading Confederates, including Jefferson Davis, were behind the actions of John Wilkes Booth and the other conspirators. The assassination undoubtedly presented Johnson with an opportunity to punish traitors as he had often promised to do, and he issued a proclamation offering a reward for the capture of Davis and other supposed rebel conspirators. Johnson signed the execution orders for those convicted by the military commission established to try the case, but, apparently, he did not see the recommendation of mercy for Mary Surratt, mother of conspirator John Surratt. Johnson was probably following the advice of Stanton and Judge Advocate General Joseph Holt when he approved her execution, but historians remain divided over whether Stanton and Holt intentionally kept him from seeing documents that might have saved Mrs. Surratt's life.

The influence of Stanton, who favored black suffrage, was less evident when Johnson began to outline his plans for reconstructing the South than for punishing the alleged assassins of Lincoln. In a series of proclamations in the spring of 1865, Johnson demanded neither black suffrage nor any other dramatic change in the Southern political order. The president announced that he would appoint provisional governors for each of the Southern states, who in turn would call for constitutional conventions to set up new state governments. Johnson promised amnesty and therefore the right to vote in these proceedings to Southerners who would take a prescribed oath. He did exclude from this general amnesty high civil and military officials of the Confederacy and — reflecting his continued hostility toward Southern aristocrats — rebels who held more than $20,000 in property. Even these men, though, could take an oath, petition for special pardon, and, if it were granted, regain the franchise. Johnson's approach thereby put more emphasis on loyalty oaths, as if the very act of swearing allegiance could blot out past sins, than on efforts to remold Southern institutions.

Johnson was apparently pleased at having old political enemies assume the attitude of supplicants, and he spent an inordinate amount of time — sometimes almost all of his working day — poring over pardon applications. The pardon policy also affected the government's attitude toward the recently freed slaves, be-

cause a presidential pardon meant the restoration of confiscated property to former Confederates. This brought an end to the wartime experiment of dividing up confiscated plantations among the freedmen. Although all of this seemed to indicate a conservative policy, the several proclamations that the president issued were general enough to gain support from various factions, and their meaning would clearly depend on how they were administered and interpreted. Radicals such as Congressman Thaddeus Stevens and Senator Charles Sumner were worried about the direction of Johnson's policies, but most Republicans in the summer of 1865 were prepared to be very patient with the new president.

In dealing with the provisional governors he had appointed to carry out his policies in the "states lately in rebellion," the president made it clear that the constitutional conventions meeting in them would have to ratify the Thirteenth Amendment to the United States Constitution, declare their ordinances of secession null and void, and repudiate the Confederate debt. Johnson suggested that the states might enact a qualified form of black suffrage but did not insist on it. Indeed, his failure to press the new state governments in the South to protect the civil rights of the recently freed slaves proved to be a fatal weakness in this conciliatory approach to the problems of Reconstruction. Southern politicians took advantage of Johnson's liberality and made as few concessions as possible to Northern opinion.

Johnson highly valued constitutional consistency, and his policy reflected an unbending belief that secession had never taken place. In his view, individuals, but not states, could commit treason. The president alone could deal with these individuals; Johnson saw only a secondary role for Congress in restoring the Southern states to their full constitutional relations. Thus, he could be stern with individuals while being very lenient with states — not recognizing that the restoration of loyalty was an institutional as well as an individual problem. Ironically, Johnson maintained the fiction of state sovereignty while at the same time attempting to reshape the state governments in the South.

In his first annual message to Congress in December, 1865, the president claimed that his policy was working well and that full restoration of the South to the Union was nearly complete. He based these assertions on fragmentary evidence gathered by several Northern emissaries, including General Ulysses S. Grant, who had recently visited the Southern states, but he ignored reports of other travelers who had found many signs of continuing rebellion in the South. Congressional Republicans remained skeptical, particularly after elections in several Southern states revealed a clear voter preference for selecting former Confederates to important offices, and refused to seat representatives and senators from the South.

Reconstruction

Republican leaders, unhappy with Johnson's efforts, decided to try their own hand at Reconstruction and formed the Joint Committee on Reconstruction to investigate conditions in the former Confederate states. Johnson believed that the critics of his policy constituted a radical minority who could be isolated if met with executive firmness. Yet in vetoing a bill extending and expanding the Freedmen's Bureau, he outraged moderate Republicans and actually strengthened rather than isolated the radicals. The president claimed preeminent authority over Reconstruction policy and objected to the bureau as unconstitutional and discriminatory to whites. He mistakenly believed that the Joint Committee on Reconstruction constituted a radical "cabal" bent on undermining administration policy. Johnson and his critics began to show signs of paranoia—both sides seeing in the actions of their opponents vile conspiracies against freedom and the public good. Addressing a crowd of Washington serenaders on February 22, 1866, Johnson claimed the radicals

were as much a threat to the Union as the secessionists and denounced Charles Sumner, Thaddeus Stevens, and Wendell Phillips by name. In a speech filled with personal references and pathetic appeals for public sympathy, Johnson portrayed himself as the popular defender of constitutional principles against unscrupulous conspirators.

Johnson quickly followed this remarkable performance with a veto of a civil rights bill that would have extended citizenship and legal protection to the freed slaves. This veto all but made inevitable a final break between Johnson and the Republican majority in Congress. Moderate Republicans could not accept Johnson's states' rights version of the Constitution and increasingly considered him a major, if not dangerous, obstacle to restoring loyalty in the Southern states. For Johnson, Congress (he drew no distinction between moderate and Radical Republicans) was the enemy. He ignored the advice of some cabinet members and other supporters to be more accommodating to Congress and instead established a totally inflexible position based on what he thought to be sacred constitutional principles and the popular will.

It came as no surprise, therefore, when Johnson publicly denounced the proposed Fourteenth Amendment, which would have made blacks citizens, forbade the states from denying to any citizen "due process" or "equal protection" of the laws, reduced representation for states not adopting universal manhood suffrage, and barred leading former Confederates from holding public office. For the president, this marked the culmination of a scheme by congressional Republicans to control the government by destroying the sovereignty of the states. Any amendment at this time was inappropriate, Johnson claimed, because the Southern states remained without representation. If this all sounded like the rhetoric of a Northern Democrat, there was little doubt that Johnson was steadily moving back toward his old party allegiance. He could never admit it, but his course had thrown the moderate and Radical Republicans together; by the summer of 1866, only the most conservative members of the party stood with the president.

The more Southerners and copperheads found to praise in Johnson's policies, the more unpopular the administration became in the North. When a bloody race riot broke out in New Orleans in July, 1866, Republicans blamed the president for not using military force to protect the lives of Southern Union men and blacks and thought the violence the logical result of the president's stubborn and mistaken course.

Johnson sought to rally his supporters behind a National Union Party, which would serve as a campaign vehicle against congressional Republicans in the fall election campaign. From the first, this jerry-built coalition of Southerners, conservative Republicans, and Northern Democrats showed both weakness and division. Republicans denounced the meeting of these desperate elements in Philadelphia as a conclave of copperheads and rebels, and several cabinet members were decidedly unenthusiastic about the National Union movement. Johnson, on the other hand, hyperbolically described the National Union meeting as the most important convention in the United States since 1787 and remained oblivious to his increasingly precarious political position.

Democrats supported Johnson to promote their own party interests but would do little more; moderate Republicans resented the seeming Democratic control of the National Union movement and were even more embittered when the president began wholesale removals of Republican officials — offices then handed over to ungrateful Democrats. Although some historians have suggested that Johnson would have been better advised to divide his opposition by broadening his campaign to include the currency and tariff questions, there is little evidence to suggest that including these complex and badly understood issues could have salvaged the situation.

With his political coalition about to collapse, Johnson turned to what had always worked for him before — the stump speech. He took his case to the people on a "swing around the circle" from New York to Missouri. In Cleveland, Ohio, he delivered a series of ill-considered impromptu remarks to a rowdy crowd. Johnson accused Congress of plotting to break up the government and, losing all sense of presidential dignity, exchanged crude remarks with hecklers. In several speeches, he bragged of his plebeian origins, compared his pardon policy with the forgiveness of Jesus Christ, and portrayed himself as a martyr to constitutional principles. Johnson appeared foolish (several Republican newspapers charged that he was drunk during the trip) and probably lost more support for his policy than he won.

As Northern voters prepared to cast their ballots, Johnson sought to move against Stanton, the cabinet member who appeared to be most sympathetic to his political enemies. In a complex maneuver, the president sought to send General of the Army Grant on a diplomatic mission to Mexico and bring General William Tecumseh Sherman to Washington, D.C., to become the new secretary of war. Grant, however, refused to go, and Sherman was averse to becoming mixed up in Washington politics.

The fall elections spelled disaster for the administration. The Northern voters undoubtedly shared Johnson's desire for a speedy restoration of the Union but also sought to keep the former rebels from resuming political power while providing minimal rights for the freedmen. The Republicans gained two-thirds majorities in both houses — what amounted to a veto-proof Congress — and could thank the political blunders of Andrew Johnson for their success. Yet the president ignored his advisers' suggestions for a conciliatory approach to Congress and still expected Northern opinion to turn against the radicals. In his annual message to Congress in December, 1866, Johnson called for the readmission of the Southern states to representation and made no concessions to his opponents. He did not even mention the proposed Fourteenth Amendment.

There was some talk of a possible compromise between Congress and the president based on Southern ratification of a modified version of the Fourteenth Amendment, but Johnson ended it when he encouraged the Southern states to reject the amendment. His intervention both demonstrated his longtime commitment to states' rights and testified to his firm belief in white supremacy and belligerent opposition to black suffrage. Johnson, the enemy of the large slaveholders, had never been the friend of the slave. In a passionate wartime speech, he had promised Tennessee blacks to be their Moses, but this signified little beyond a general commitment to Lincoln's emancipation policy. He considered moderate black leader Frederick Douglass to be a dangerous incendiary. Johnson never overcame the prejudices of his background and class and failed to recognize the revolutionary changes in race relations wrought by the Civil War.

Congress Rebels: The Tenure in Office Act
When the lame duck session of the Thirty-ninth Congress assembled in December, 1866, most Republicans were at last ready to build a more thoroughgoing Reconstruction policy based on abolishing the Southern state governments and establishing black suffrage. Outraged by the president's intransigence, Southern foot dragging, and growing violence against blacks and Union men in the South, on March 2, 1867, Congress passed the first Reconstruction Act, which placed the South under military rule until "loyal" state governments could be established. As expected, Johnson vetoed the bill, warning of its dangerous and revolutionary character. He also appealed to racial fears by unfavorably contrasting the bill's enfranchisement of blacks to its disfranchisement of whites.

While putting forward a new Reconstruction plan, the Republicans in Congress also sought to limit the president's ability to subvert their policy. Still stinging from Johnson's use of patronage against loyal Republicans, the congressional majority pushed through the Tenure of Office Act. This measure prohibited the president from removing officials whose appointment had been confirmed by the Senate unless that body approved the removal. Unable to agree on whether the act should cover cabinet members, the Republicans included an ambiguous clause, which stated that cabinet officers "shall hold their offices... during the term of the President by whom they may have been appointed, and for one month thereafter, subject to removal by and with the advice and consent of the Senate." Some observers thought this provision was meant to protect Stanton, and during a cabinet discussion, Johnson cleverly induced his secretary of war to denounce the bill as unconstitutional. Congress also attached a rider to the Army Appropriations Act, forcing the president to issue military orders through the general of the army, Grant, and forbidding him to remove the general's headquarters from Washington, D.C.

These laws demonstrated the ironic fact that the success of congressional Reconstruction depended on executive cooperation. Johnson allowed Grant to select the commanders of the military districts established by the Reconstruction Act and seemed unwilling to risk a confrontation with Congress by failing to enforce the law. Although politically weakened, Johnson still possessed the power of his office. Indeed, the Republicans had given the president an opportunity to influence Reconstruction by their slipshod and hasty drafting of the Reconstruction Act (defects only partly remedied by a second Reconstruction Act, which was passed by the new Fortieth Congress on March 23, 1867).

Johnson might have recouped some of his lost power and prestige by turning the nation's attention to matters other than the condition of the South. Despite his own firm belief in paying off the national debt quickly and reducing government expenditures, however, his administration failed to devise a financial policy that could please both Western interests, who demanded currency inflation, and Easterners, who favored protective tariffs and hard money. Traditionally, presidents have recouped political prestige by diplomatic triumphs, and Secretary of State William H. Seward was as skillful and loyal in serving Johnson as he had been in serving Lincoln. When Seward managed to purchase Alaska from Russia at a bargain price, even rabid enemies of Johnson, such as Charles Sumner and Thaddeus Stevens, approved. Johnson failed to make the most of these accomplishments.

The Southern question would simply not go away. The Reconstruction Acts had only vaguely defined the qualifications for voting, and the powers of district commanders in the South were also poorly delineated. Attorney General Henry Stanbery issued opinions in May denying the power of the district commanders in the Southern states to remove civil officials and also limiting their power to disfranchise voters. Although Grant instructed the district commanders that the attorney general's opinion was not an official order and Johnson refused to press the matter further, Congress drafted a bill for yet a third Reconstruction Act in July, 1867, which closed up the loopholes Stanbery had found in the first two acts. Both Grant and Stanton worked with the more radical district commanders, particularly General Philip Sheridan, to administer the Reconstruction Acts in the South with a broad and liberal view of congressional intent.

The Stanton Affair

Johnson was furious at Sheridan, military governor of Louisiana, for his many attempts to remove Democratic civil officials in Louisiana and his apparent willingness to defy presidential orders. The president also received new reports supporting a long-held suspicion that Stanton was in frequent consultation with congressional radicals. Johnson therefore decided to remove Sheridan, suspend Stanton, and make Grant secretary of war ad interim. The cabinet had been cool to the idea of removing Sheridan, and so Johnson decided not to consult it on the Stanton matter. Stanton had earlier refused a direct presidential request to resign and now only yielded to what he pointedly described as "superior force." Stanton undoubtedly believed that he had remained in office to protect the interests of the army and the loyal citizens of the United States. Yet he had often acted disingenuously, if not deceptively, toward Johnson, especially in cabinet meetings. Andrew Johnson, however, for all his tenacity on fine points of constitutional law, could be very indecisive. Evidence of Stanton's "disloyalty" to the administration had been accumulating for more than a year, but the president had failed to replace Stanton earlier when he could have removed him without a serious confrontation with Congress.

Grant at first protested Sheridan's removal but finally acquiesced. Johnson also moved swiftly to remove the radical General Daniel Sickles from command in the Carolinas. Increasingly, Grant saw Johnson as an obstruction, not only to Reconstruction in the South but also to his own political future; the general feared that Johnson would continue to interfere in the operations of the army or might attempt to use him in a battle with Congress. Newspaper speculation arose during the fall about additional cabinet changes, including the replacement of Seward and Secretary of the Treasury Hugh McCulloch, but Johnson refused to dismiss these faithful cabinet officers.

Indeed, the president's prospects brightened considerably when the Democrats did well throughout the North in the 1867 state elections. Johnson interpreted that success as vindication and perhaps envisioned the Democrats making him their nominee in 1868. Still, he feared the radicals might grow desperate as their political prospects dimmed and might attempt to impeach him.

The prospects of impeachment, however, had faded, at least for the moment. As early as December, 1866, radical congressman James Ashley of Ohio had introduced an impeachment resolution, accusing the president of abusing his patronage powers and delivering the country back into the hands of the rebels. Ashley and Benjamin F. Butler of Massachusetts even believed that Johnson had been involved in the conspiracy to assassinate Abraham Lincoln and apparently attempted to suborn perjury to prove this wild charge. During the spring and summer of 1867, the House Judiciary Committee called several witnesses, collected Johnson's public speeches, and even examined the president's bank accounts, but the committee could not discover any "high crimes or misdemeanors." All of this simply roused Johnson's seldom dormant persecution complex, and he continued to press Grant over whether the general would cooperate with Congress in placing him under arrest during an impeachment trial.

When the Judiciary Committee in December, 1867, suddenly voted articles of impeachment, the cabinet advised Johnson to resist any attempt to place him under arrest during a Senate trial. In his annual message to Congress, Johnson issued another blast against the "unconstitutional" Reconstruction Acts and ominously warned that a situation might occur in which the president would have to stand firm against any congressional attempts to encroach on the constitutional prerogatives of his office. Despite the president's inflammatory document, Republican moderates helped handily defeat an impeachment resolution in the House.

Although the performance of Sheridan's successor in Louisiana, the conservative general Winfield Scott Hancock, and the removal of General John Pope from command in Georgia, Alabama, and Florida caused some irritation in Congress, the attempt to remove Stanton remained the outstanding source of conflict between the executive and legislative branches. In a carefully prepared message in December, 1867, Johnson outlined in detail Stanton's duplicitous behavior. He asserted his authority as president to remove a cabinet official but studiously ignored the Tenure of Office Act, despite the fact that he had, to that point, followed its provisions in the Stanton case. On January 13, 1868, the Senate voted overwhelmingly not to concur in Johnson's suspension of Stanton.

This decision left Grant in a most uncomfortable position. Johnson expected Grant to hold onto his office in defiance of Congress or at least turn the office back to the president in time to prevent Stanton from resuming his position. He believed that Grant shared his understanding, but there had apparently been no firm agreement. As it happened, Grant handed the key to the office back to the acting adjutant general, who in turn gave it to Stanton. A series of meetings and, finally, a lengthy and public exchange of letters followed, in which Grant and Johnson in essence called each other liars. To some extent, Grant had deceived Johnson, and certainly the president had shown a lack of firmness and direction throughout his troubles with Stanton. Grant succeeded brilliantly in protecting himself from being caught between the president and Stanton while at the same time promoting his own political interests. The radicals now applauded Grant, and Johnson once again emerged as a bumbling and hesitant leader.

Impeachment

With Stanton back in the cabinet, Johnson searched desperately for someone else to replace his wily secretary of war. Sherman was clearly his first choice, but Sherman hated Washington, D.C., despised politics, and adroitly avoided being trapped in the War Department morass. Johnson at last settled on the garrulous, occasionally besotted, and increasingly senile adjutant general, Lorenzo Thomas. On February 21, the president sent a message to the Senate, which announced the removal of Stanton and the appointment of Thomas as secretary of war ad interim. Thomas tried to assume the post, but Stanton refused to yield it. To moderate Republicans, the entire Reconstruction program seemed to be in danger; the House hastily and overwhelming voted to impeach the president.

Both sides feared a possible civil war. Stanton stayed in the War Department and posted armed men in the basement. Johnson believed that Congress might attempt to place him under arrest during the trial in the Senate. Radicals heard rumors that Johnson had ordered the blowup of the Capitol with nitroglycerin and that the old rebel cavalry chieftain John Mosby was about to descend on Washington, D.C. Stanton arranged to have Thomas arrested for violating the Tenure of Office Act but quickly had the charges dropped, perhaps fearing that he had inadvertently provided the judicial test of the law's constitutionality that Johnson apparently wanted.

On February 24, the day the House voted on his impeachment, Johnson sent a message to the Senate nominating Hugh Ewing, Sr., to be secretary of war. Thomas continued in his bumbling way to try to take the war office from Stanton, but even the president paid little attention to him. Johnson had blundered through the Stanton affair, first acting too slowly, then indecisively, and in the end too hastily and without consulting his cabinet. Whether he had been guilty of "high crimes and misdemeanors" remained for the Senate to decide, but he had clearly shown political ineptitude on a colossal scale.

The House appointed Thaddeus Stevens, Benjamin F. Butler, and five other Republicans to present the case for Johnson's removal to the Senate. The first eight articles of impeachment set forth detailed charges against the president for violating the Tenure of Office Act in attempting to remove Stanton and appoint Thomas in his place. A ninth article charged that Johnson had attempted to induce General William H. Emory to carry out orders that had not been properly sent through Grant. Butler added an article about Johnson's various speeches questioning the authority of Congress, and Stevens drafted a general article summing up the other ones and, for good measure, accusing the president of failing to execute faithfully the Reconstruction Acts. Ironically, it is this clause, added almost as an afterthought, which some historians have argued was the strongest and most serious charge against the president.

With Chief Justice Salmon P. Chase presiding, the Senate eventually allowed Johnson sixteen days to prepare his case. After weighing the possibility, Johnson fortunately decided not to appear before the Senate in person to defend himself. He hired five attorneys, including Henry Stanbery and prominent Republican William M. Evarts of New York. They had a difficult client—one inclined to speak too freely with reporters and to question the advice of his own lawyers. Stanbery and Evarts skillfully prevented the president from destroying their carefully planned defense strategy with some final public blunder.

Johnson fully believed that he would be vindicated and even expected the Supreme Court to declare the Reconstruction Acts unconstitutional; indeed, he saw impeachment as the final effort by his enemies in Congress to destroy the Constitution. Johnson's attorneys, however, concentrated on getting their client acquitted rather than proving the wisdom of his Reconstruction policies. By focusing on relatively narrow legal questions, they tried to defuse, at least partially, the political dynamite inherent in the trial.

Stanbery and Evarts carefully dissected the issues surrounding the attempted removal of Stanton and the appointment of Thomas. They argued that the Tenure of Office Act was unconstitutional and surpassed the House managers in piling up legal precedents to buttress their point. More important, however, they showed that regardless of whether the tenure law was constitutional, it did not protect Stanton. The

Excerpts from Andrew Johnson's veto of the first Reconstruction Act, March 2, 1867:

I have examined the bill "to provide for the more efficient government of the rebel States" with the care and the anxiety which its transcendent importance is calculated to awaken. I am unable to give it my assent for reasons so grave that I hope a statement of them may have some influence on the minds of the patriotic and enlightened men with whom the decision must ultimately rest.

The bill places all the people of the ten States therein named under the absolute domination of military rulers; and the preamble undertakes to give the reason upon which the measure is based and the ground upon which it is justified. It declares that there exists in those States no legal governments and no adequate protection for life or property, and asserts the necessity of enforcing peace and good order within their limits. Is this true as matter of fact? . . .

The bill . . . would seem to show upon its face that the establishment of peace and good order is not its real object. The fifth section declares that the preceding sections shall cease to operate in any State where certain events shall have happened. . . . All these conditions must be fulfilled before the people of any of these States can be relieved from the bondage of military domination; but when they are fulfilled, then immediately the pains and penalties of the bill are to cease, no matter whether there be peace and order or not, and without any reference to the security of life or property. The excuse given for the bill in the preamble is admitted by the bill itself not to be real. The military rule which it establishes is plainly to be used, not for any purpose of order or for the prevention of crime, but solely as a means of coercing the people into the adoption of principles and measures to which it is known that they are opposed, and upon which they have an undeniable right to exercise their own judgment.

I submit to Congress whether this measure is not in its whole character, scope, and object without precedent and without authority, in palpable conflict with the plainest provisions of the Constitution, and utterly destructive to those great principles of liberty and humanity for which our ancestors on both sides of the Atlantic have shed so much blood and expended so much treasure.

cabinet proviso of the act specified that cabinet members should hold offices during the term of the president who had appointed them. Since Stanton had been appointed by Lincoln, he could be removed by Johnson. Although the managers quibbled about the meaning of the word "term" in the law, Johnson's attorneys had discovered and vigorously exploited the weakest point in the prosecution's case.

The other defense arguments were not as strong. The contention that Johnson had not violated the law because Stanton remained in office could not stand close scrutiny. The assertion that Johnson had only removed Stanton so that the constitutionality of the tenure law could be tested in the courts could hardly excuse the chief executive from faithfully executing the law. In describing impeachment as a judicial rather than a political process, the president's attorneys entered a constitutional thicket. In the opinion of some scholars, the Constitution's "high crimes and misdemeanors" are not confined to indictable criminal offenses. By its very nature, impeachment is a political process conducted by politicians. Chief Justice Chase's attempts to run the impeachment trial as a judicial proceeding angered many Republicans, who believed that he biased the process in Johnson's favor.

Both sides turned the contest into an oratorical marathon. The president's lawyers called witnesses to prove that Stanton himself had declared the tenure law unconstitutional and that Johnson simply intended to bring the matter to a judicial test. Moreover, they cited statements from Republican senators made in February and March, 1867, which declared that the tenure law did not protect Stanton. The House managers and a majority of Republican senators decided to exclude some of this defense evidence, especially testimony from General Sherman and Secretary of the Navy Gideon Welles. To some moderates, this seemed patently unfair, as did Butler's badgering of old General Thomas on the witness stand.

Acquittal

During the trial, the president uncharacteristically acted with discretion, allowing his attorneys to carry the rhetorical burden of proof. Their appeal was clearly to the Republican Party center. If they could convince seven Republican senators of Johnson's innocence, the president would escape removal from office. If Johnson were removed, the president pro tempore of the Senate, Benjamin F. Wade of Ohio, would become president. Moderate senators, such as William Pitt Fessenden of Maine and Lyman Trumbull of Illinois, detested Wade and had been skeptical about impeachment from the beginning. The president sought to assuage

Republican fears by promising to nominate moderate general John M. Schofield to be the new secretary of war. He also dropped some careful hints that he would do nothing to undermine the course of Reconstruction if he were acquitted. Johnson grew more confident of acquittal, especially as news of dissension among the Republicans spread through the capital. In the end, only two impeachment articles came to a vote, and Johnson escaped conviction by one vote on each of the articles. For once, Johnson's mercurial temper was not in evidence, and he received the news with equanimity but undoubted relief.

Most historians have argued that Johnson's acquittal was justified because the president, whatever his political ineptitude, had committed no impeachable offenses. Although some scholars have argued that Johnson's removal would have set a dangerous precedent, the circumstances of Reconstruction were extraordinary and the weight of such a precedent doubtful. The impeachment illustrated the deadly

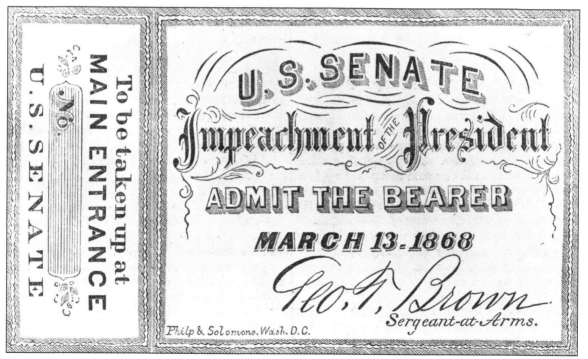

A ticket to Johnson's impeachment trial in the Senate. *(Library of Congress)*

An engraving that depicts the Senate serving as a court of impeachment for the trial of Andrew Johnson. *(Library of Congress)*

serious nature of the debate over Reconstruction policy, the revolutionary nature of the era, and the tendency of both the president and the Radical Republicans to color opponents in the darkest possible hues.

The Radicals lashed out at the seven "recusant" Republicans who had voted "not guilty," and Butler made wild charges of bribery against them, but most Republicans simply wanted to forget impeachment as quickly as possible. The nomination of Grant as the party's presidential candidate, coupled with the president's fulfillment of his promise not to use the army to interfere with the Reconstruction process, pacified the country. Yet Johnson had abandoned his opposition to congressional Reconstruction; he vetoed bills readmitting seven Southern states under the terms provided by the Reconstruction Acts.

The president's hope for popular vindication lay in capturing the Democratic presidential nomination. Although he claimed not to be "ambitious of further service," he hoped for a popular groundswell in his favor and believed that he could defeat Grant in November. He timed a general amnesty proclamation to coincide with the opening of the Democratic National Convention in July, 1868. Johnson's friends opened negotiations with New York Democrats whose prime interest was in federal patronage. The president considered currying Democratic favor by removing McCullough, but the secretary's hard money policies were popular with many conservative Democrats. Johnson likewise refused to get rid of Seward. He could never understand why the Democrats would not readily hand him the nomination if they approved of his presidency as much as they claimed that they did. The continuing attacks of the Radical Republicans should, in Johnson's view, have made him even more deserving of the prize. Despite some Southern support on the early ballots, the Democrats did not think Johnson was either astute or trustworthy enough to run under their banner. Instead, they nominated former governor Horatio Seymour of New York.

The remainder of the Johnson presidency was surprisingly busy. Seward worked on completing arrangements for the purchase of Alaska, and the president personally received a delegation from China at the White House. Congressional hostility to Johnson had occasionally spilled over into the conduct of foreign policy, and key Republican leaders blocked Seward's plans for additional territorial acquisitions in the Caribbean.

Johnson paid only passing attention to these diplomatic developments; he was much more interested in the election campaign and what he hoped would be Grant's defeat. He begrudgingly recognized the ratification of the Fourteenth Amendment and appointed conservative generals to command the troops in the recently readmitted Southern states. As the early state elections pointed to a Republican victory, the president grew discouraged, his only comfort being a steady faith in the eventual triumph of his political principles.

In his last annual message to Congress, Andrew Johnson condemned the Reconstruction Acts yet again. He also criticized selfish bondholders and proposed scaling down the interest on the national debt. Ever the democrat, he called for the direct popular election of the president, the vice president, and United States

ELEVATION--At the White House.   DEPRESSION--At the Tribune Office.

EFFECT OF THE VOTE ON THE ELEVENTH ARTICLE OF IMPEACHMENT.

One cartoonist's depiction of the reaction to Johnson's acquittal. *(Library of Congress)*

senators. The president and Congress continued to squabble over minor matters for the rest of his term. Johnson moved his family out of the White House before Grant's inauguration, stayed at the capital signing bills on Inauguration Day, and rode off in a carriage without even speaking to the new president.

When Johnson left Washington, D.C., for East Tennessee, he did not abandon politics; he still yearned for vindication and refused to fade away into retirement. He campaigned for conservative candidates in the summer of 1869 and was nearly elected to the United States Senate by the legislature. Although Johnson remained popular in Tennessee, many former Confederates as well as Republicans could not forgive his past. In 1872, he entered an at-large congressional contest by running as an independent but finished third behind a former Confederate general and the victorious Republican candidate. His political career seemed over. Friends reported that Johnson drank heavily, and he was stricken by cholera in 1873. He recovered, however, in both body and spirit by working hard to get back his old Senate seat. In 1875, he won a close fight in the legislature and prepared to return to Washington. Attending a special session of the Senate in March, he was at last able to get a measure of revenge against Grant. In his last public speech, Johnson denounced the president for using troops to support the carpetbag government of Louisiana, emphasizing his favorite themes of "military despotism" and constitutional government. He returned to Tennessee apparently with political plans laid, but at his daughter's farm, he collapsed with a paralytic stroke and died two days later, on July 31, 1875.

Johnson's Presidency in Perspective

Johnson's historical reputation has fluctuated dramatically ever since. It remained low until a flood of works after World War I elevated him to the status of a courageous patriot who fought against the Radical Republicans to preserve sacred constitutional principles. In the 1950's, Reconstruction scholars began to reexamine critically Johnson's presidency. These historians pointed to the obvious defects in Johnson's character: his stubbornness, indecisiveness, and lack of good judgment. Other historians portrayed Johnson as a racist who attempted to subvert needed constitutional reforms and to return the Southern states to conservative control.

Johnson's honesty and reverence for the Constitution (at least as he defined it) are unquestioned. Certainly, he worked as hard as any president since Polk. Johnson, however, could never transcend his background in the frontier politics of Tennessee. Unlike Abraham Lincoln, who showed enormous capacity for growth during his presidency, Johnson attempted to apply the same crude style of stump-speaking politics to Washington, D.C., that he had used so often back home. More important, he failed to see that the problems of Reconstruction demanded flexibility of both means and ends. Like many of his opponents, he was far too quick to equate opposition with evil intent and therefore wasted several opportunities to work with moderate Republicans to build a national consensus on Reconstruction. Even his friends conceded that Johnson's political judgments were often defective, and he failed to see that the war had wrought enormous changes in race relations and in the power of the national government. In the end, Johnson largely failed. His presidency was characterized by lost opportunities but also by perpetual conflict with Congress and, eventually, constitutional crisis. When Johnson returned to Tennessee in 1869, he left behind a presidency much weaker than the office he had inherited from Abraham Lincoln.

George C. Rable

Suggested Readings

Benedict, Michael L. *The Impeachment and Trial of Andrew Johnson.* New York: Norton, 1973. Provides good detail about the impeachment.

Brabson, Fay W. *Andrew Johnson: A Life in Pursuit of the Right Course, 1801-1875.* Durham, N.C.: Seeman Printery, 1972. A good biography.

Castel, Albert. *The Presidency of Andrew Johnson.* Lawrence: Regents Press of Kansas, 1979. A solid synthesis of modern-day scholarship on Johnson's presidency.

Johnson, Andrew. *The Papers of Andrew Johnson.* 16 vols. Edited by Leroy P. Graf and Ralph W. Haskins. Knoxville: University of Tennessee Press, 1967-2000. Years of correspondence offer important insights into Johnson's career and character.

McCaslin, Richard B., comp. *Andrew Johnson: A Bibliography.* Westport, Conn.: Greenwood Press, 1992. Lists more than two thousand primary and secondary sources and includes an extensive chronology of Johnson's life.

McKitrick, Eric L. *Andrew Johnson and Reconstruction.* Chicago: University of Chicago Press, 1960. A perceptive, interpretive account of the Johnson presidency.

Mantell, Martin E. *Johnson, Grant, and the Politics of Reconstruction.* New York: Columbia University Press, 1973. A good contextual study.

Milton, George F. *The Age of Hate: Andrew Johnson and the Radicals.* 1930. Reprint. Hamden, Conn.: Archon Books, 1965. An older work that is nonetheless valuable for its enormous quantity of information.

Nash, Howard P. *Andrew Johnson: Congress and Reconstruction.* Rutherford, N.J.: Fairleigh Dickinson University Press, 1972. A look at the relationship and tensions between the U.S. Congress and Johnson.

Rehnquist, William H. *Grand Inquests: The Historic Impeachments of Justice Samuel Chase and President Andrew Johnson.* New York: William Morrow, 1992. A dramatic account of two of the most important legal decisions ever rendered, giving valuable insight into the impeachment process.

Schroeder-Lein, Glenna, and Richard Zuczek. *Andrew Johnson: A Biographical Companion.* Santa Barbara, Calif.: ABC-Clio, 2001. An encyclopedic examination of Johnson's career which includes more than 180 articles, historical documents, a chronology, and a bibliography.

Sefton, James E. *Andrew Johnson and the Uses of Constitutional Power.* Boston: Little, Brown, 1980. A brief but sound modern biography.

Trefousse, Hans L. *Andrew Johnson: A Biography.* New York: Norton, 1989. A solid biography.

_____. *Impeachment of a President: Andrew Johnson, the Blacks, and Reconstruction.* 1975. Rev. ed. New York: Fordham University Press, 1999. Examines the reasons behind Johnson's acquittal and the links between the impeachment and the failure of Reconstruction.

Welsbacher, Anne. *Andrew Johnson.* Minneapolis: ABDO, 1999. An accessible biography intended for young adults.

Ulysses S. Grant

18th President, 1869-1877

Born: April 27, 1822
    Point Pleasant, Ohio
Died: July 23, 1885
    Mount McGregor, New York

Political Party: Republican
Vice Presidents: Schuyler Colfax, Henry
    Wilson

Cabinet Members

Secretary of State: Elihu B. Washburne,
    Hamilton Fish
Secretary of the Treasury: George S. Boutwell,
    William A. Richardson, Benjamin H.
    Bristow, Lot M. Morrill
Secretary of War: John A. Rawlins, William
    Tecumseh Sherman, W. W. Belknap,
    Alphonso Taft, James D. Cameron
Secretary of the Navy: Adolph E. Borie,
    George M. Robeson
Attorney General: Ebenezer R. Hoar, Amos T.
    Akerman, G. H. Williams, Edwards
    Pierrepont, Alphonso Taft
Postmaster General: John A. J. Creswell,
    James W. Marshall, Marshall Jewell,
    James N. Tyner
Secretary of the Interior: Jacob D. Cox,
    Columbus Delano, Zachariah Chandler

Cold fog enveloped the city in the gray morning. Shivering in the damp were army units: Marchers from Irish, German, and other clubs; the firemen; veterans' groups; the Boys in Blue; Lincoln Zouaves; and other Republican clubs tried to organize their formations along Pennsylvania Avenue, beyond the White House toward Georgetown. Carriages carrying the justices of the Supreme Court, the judges of the court of claims, foreign ambassadors, presidential electors, and other dignitaries searched for their places, found them, and milled about, their drivers huddled miserably against the chill rain. Tens of thousands of visitors slogged through the mist, lining the route General Ulysses S. Grant and the rest of the procession would take down Pennsylvania Avenue to the Capitol, where he would be inaugurated the eighteenth president of the United States.

Portrait of Ulysses S. Grant. *(Whitehouse.gov)*

At 10:45 a.m., Grant emerged from his headquarters and the parade lurched toward its destination. At the Capitol, Grant and Vice President-elect Schuyler Colfax went to the Senate chamber, where Colfax was sworn in and delivered his short inaugural speech. Then Grant, Colfax, the senators, the members of the House of Representatives, and other dignitaries marched to the special platform erected on the east front of the Capitol. Chief Justice Salmon P. Chase stepped forward, turned to Grant, and administered the oath of office. The artillery boomed and bells began to ring all over Washington, D.C. An immense cheer went up from the crowd, and the sun broke through the clouds.

Ulysses S. Grant entered the White House on March 4, 1869, at the age of forty-six the youngest man elected to the presidency to that time. A veteran of the Mexican War and, more recently, the Civil War, Grant was known as the hero of the Union: It was to Grant that the Confederate general Robert E. Lee had surrendered at Appomattox Courthouse on April 9, 1865. Grant subsequently was appointed to the new post of general of the armies of the United States. Admired by a nation just beginning to recover from the ravages of war, Grant inspired the confidence of the nation.

This Silent Man

Ulysses Grant has been an enigma to biographers. An apparent failure before the Civil War, in that great struggle he demonstrated a com-

---

The First Lady
Julia Grant

Julia Dent Grant was born into a wealthy plantation family on January 26, 1826, in St. Louis, Missouri. She was well-educated. She met Lieutenant Ulysses S. Grant in 1844 but held off marriage until after the Mexican War. They married on August 22, 1848.

Their early years together reflected the hardships of army life. Julia learned how to cook and keep house and to deal with separation. She bore three boys and a girl. When the Civil War began, Julia's cheerful personality had a positive influence on Ulysses, and when it was safe she often joined him to support him and buoy his spirits.

Julia reveled in Ulysses' war hero fame and was ecstatic when he was elected president. She refurbished the White House, creating an opulent but warm atmosphere. Elaborate multiple-course meals were served regularly. Her china remains one of the handsomest sets. She began Tuesday afternoon receptions and made a point of welcoming blacks to the White House.

Serving a full eight years as First Lady, Julia successfully reestablished the White House as a social center. She loved her position. When Ulysses did not seek reelection for a third term, she wept openly. Julia's legacy is as a warm, humorous, and supportive companion to her husband; however, she held no political influence with him. Ulysses disregarded her opinions on political issues and preferred that she devote herself to domestic matters.

Unwise speculation soon left the Grants in financial ruin. When Ulysses was diagnosed with throat cancer, he wrote his memoirs as a way of supporting Julia after his death. They were a huge success, and a bereft Julia eventually returned to Washington, D.C., to live as a "grand dame," enjoying friendships with other high-profile political wives. She also supported Susan B. Anthony's suffragist movement. She was the first First Lady to dictate her own memoirs. Julia died on December 14, 1902, at the age of seventy-six, and was buried beside her husband.

Barbara C. Beattie

mand of tactics and strategy, a talent for organization, and an ability to inspire confidence that enabled him to succeed where all others had failed. He rode an avalanche of popularity and respect into the presidency, but most historians have considered his administration a disaster. A later Pulitzer Prize-winning biographer decided that the secret to Grant was that there was no secret—he was a completely ordinary man thrown by accident into a situation where his few real talents and some of his characteristics proved of crucial value.

Such a judgment surely would have surprised most of Grant's contemporaries. It parallels that of the small group of reformers who blasted away at Grant for most of his presidential career and afterward. From the time he became commander of the Union armies, however, most Americans perceived greatness in him. Many came to detest him; many more continued to idolize him; none questioned his stature.

By the nature of things, the journalists, litterateurs, and scholars who have written about Grant have been part of an intellectual community that has shared a set of expectations about how men of conscious intellect behave. When a man makes a great public reputation, one expects him to demonstrate an interest in public events, to leave a record of his views and explanations of his actions.

Grant disappoints such expectations. His leading characteristic was his taciturnity. Future president James A. Garfield, college professor-soldier-politician, who delivered speeches all over the United States and who left books and diaries and a huge correspondence filled with his views, marveled that "no man . . . carried greater fame out of the White House than this silent man." That silence could be disconcerting. "He has a wonderful capacity of letting you talk, without moving a muscle and then saying nothing himself," a young lion of Boston's intellectual society recorded in his journal after meeting him.

The last photograph of General Grant taken in the field by Mathew Brady, August, 1864. *(Library of Congress)*

Others, in contrast, found him genial. Another future president, Rutherford B. Hayes, noted that "after he warms up he is . . . cheerful, chatty, and good natured. . . . I feel just as much at ease with him as I do with intimate friends." The great black leader Frederick Douglass likewise remembered, "Many who approached him told me he was a silent man. To me, he was one of the best conversationalists I have ever met."

The simple fact was that Grant felt no compulsion to talk. He did not break into conversations, and if a visitor out of nervousness or egotism felt obliged to carry the conversation, Grant would let him, silently listening until the speaker felt positively foolish.

This pattern carried over into the way Grant made decisions. He encouraged his subordinates to discuss matters before him or to present him with clear statements of the case and proposed courses of action. "[T]he suggestions of others were presented simply, and either accepted or rejected as his judgment dictated," one of his aides remembered. He barely explained his reasons, and woe to the man who argued. "He was never persuaded."

That stolidity frustrated those whose suggestions he rejected. Among that number was the most reform-minded member of Grant's early cabinet, Jacob D. Cox, who watched his influence being undermined by men of far lesser intellect. "A certain class of public men adopted the practice of getting an audience and making speeches before him, urging their plans . . .," he recalled. "They would then leave him without asking for any reply, and trust to the effect they had produced." Cox wanted to know Grant's objections to his proposals; he wanted to explain why those objections were mistaken. He wanted to persuade. He never had a chance.

Grant was no more forthcoming in public. His public speeches would not fill a pamphlet. His messages to Congress were brief requests to consider a course of action, with almost no effort to persuade. His call for legislation to suppress violence in the South in 1871, a major reversal of policy raising difficult constitutional issues, consisted of four short paragraphs, taking up about one-third of a page in James D. Richardson's *Messages and Papers of the Presidents* (1896-1899). His veto of the inflationary Currency Act of 1874, the most controversial of his presidency, on an issue of utmost importance to the public, ran about two and a half pages.

No volume of public speeches and addresses of President Grant exists. The collections of correspondence between him and his family and friends attend hardly at all to public matters. When Grant did write *Personal Memoirs of U. S. Grant* (1885-1886), the book consisted almost entirely of his descriptions of tactics and battles. It is a classic of the genre, but it contains almost nothing about his political career or the reasons that motivated his actions; nor is his private correspondence more enlightening.

From West Point to Appomattox

Grant simply did not care much about abstractions. He retained facts easily. Naturally, he grew bored with the mere recitation that made up most teaching in the early nineteenth century, but he disliked debate and argument, in which young scholars honed their critical abilities. Romantic novels and travel fired his enthusiasm. He was born Hiram Ulysses Grant in Ohio on April 27, 1822. He devoured books and was surely the best-traveled boy in his small Ohio town, taking every excuse to replace his father on business trips, despite his inexperience. Still, even he was fooled by his disinterest in formal schoolwork into thinking that he was stupid. His father perceived Grant's potential better than young Ulysses himself. He finagled an appointment to West Point for his son, who was convinced that he would embarrass himself and his family by failing the entrance examinations. Instead, he passed without trouble. (His name change occurred as the result of an error during the application process.) In fact, he found academics at West Point easy, never reviewing his texts once he had read them, and he finished in the upper quarter of his class. His ambition was to teach mathematics for a while at West Point and then spend the rest of his life as a college professor.

These plans did not materialize. After Grant served a short tour of duty near St. Louis, where he became engaged to (and later married) Julia Dent, the sister of a West Point classmate, the United States precipitated war with Mexico. To his surprise, Grant found that he enjoyed war and that he had a talent both for command and for organization. At the same time, the war gave him another opportunity to travel. Mexico was the most exotic place he had ever visited, and he etched his experiences with photographic precision in his memory.

Unlike the majority of West Point graduates, Grant delayed leaving the army at war's end. He was plainly unwilling to turn to his own or his wife's family for support, although both were in comfortable, if not plush, circumstances. Assigned to remote frontier outposts in the Northeast and in California, he looked for business opportunities that would permit him to support his wife on the level to which she was accustomed. He rose to captain, a high rank in the peacetime army of the 1850's, but finally resigned in 1853 without achieving his goal. Forced to turn to his family after all, Grant tried farming his father-in-law's land in Missouri, went into business as a debt collector in St. Louis, and finally moved up the Mississippi River to Galena, Illinois, to join two brothers in a leather and harness business set up by his enterprising father.

Living throughout the trying years from 1853 to 1861 in better circumstances than most Americans, Grant and his wife still surely were dismayed at their reverses. Writing Julia just as he left the army, he described "the *downs* of all I have done. (Before this I had never met with a down.)" In Galena, he slowly established himself as a respected member of the community, living in a brick house (a mark of gentility) near other rising men. When Southerners fired on Fort Sumter, beginning the Civil War, the townspeople called on him, as a nonpartisan newcomer, to preside at a mass meeting to reaffirm their loyalty to the Union.

The war made it possible for Grant to return to the field in which he felt most confident and in which it slowly became clear that he excelled. In battle, Grant eschewed the theories that dominated strategic and tactical thinking at the time. Clockwork field maneuver and polished dress and drill meant little to him. Battles were won by securing the best ground, bringing to bear a stronger force than that of the enemy, and then using it to kill until the opposing army broke. Such an approach took a fearful toll of both enemy and friendly forces; it required superior organization so that one could move immense numbers of men and amounts of material quickly. Most of all, such generalship required an iron serenity, an ability to ignore the frightful possibility that one's opponent had acquired a stronger force or had put into effect some brilliant plan of attack. General after general on the Union side failed this test, paralyzed into inaction at crucial moments, until President Abraham Lincoln found Grant.

As one of his aides described it, after Grant made a decision, he "settle[d] in." "He had done what he could, and he gave himself no anxiety about the judgment or the decision." Grant himself told an interviewer, "I never get excited, and I have made it a rule through life never to borrow trouble or anticipate it. I wait until it

---

Excerpts from Ulysses S. Grant's first inaugural address, March 4, 1869:

The country having just emerged from a great rebellion, many questions will come before it for settlement in the next four years which preceding Administrations have never had to deal with. In meeting these it is desirable that they should be approached calmly, without prejudice, hate, or sectional pride, remembering that the greatest good to the greatest number is the object to be attained.

This requires security of person, property, and free religious and political opinion in every part of our common country, without regard to local prejudice. All laws to secure these ends will receive my best efforts for their enforcement. . . .

It will be my endeavor to execute all laws in good faith, to collect all revenues assessed, and to have them properly accounted for and economically disbursed. I will to the best of my ability appoint to office those only who will carry out this design. . . .

In conclusion I ask patient forbearance one toward another throughout the land, and a determined effort on the part of every citizen to do his share toward cementing a happy union; and I ask the prayers of the nation to Almighty God in behalf of this consummation.

Grant and his cabinet in 1869. *(Library of Congress)*

reaches me." The aide explained, "This confidence engendered composure. . . . This was the secret of his courage and of the steadiness which held him to his purpose." Others thought that Grant's incredible stolidity suggested lack of imagination. Meeting him at a particularly trying time during his presidential administration, Garfield noted in his diary, "His imperturbability is amazing. I am in doubt whether to call it greatness or stupidity." It was Grant's peculiar greatness. His calm in crisis inspired all around him, especially during the Civil War, when the nation's existence lay in the balance. He was a rock in a sea of uncertainty, and that was the source of the hold he had on those who served with him.

The Election of 1868

At the war's end, Grant was commanding general of all the Union armies, at the pinnacle of his military career. After Abraham Lincoln, he was the most popular man in the victorious North. As customary in nineteenth century America, Grant eschewed political ambition. Offices were supposed to seek the man, not the man the office; even the most blatantly ambitious politicians honored this ritual. During the Reconstruction crisis, both the Democrats and the Republicans wooed him, and Grant carefully kept his options open and his opinions to himself — an easy accomplishment for a man who disliked argument.

In the Reconstruction controversy, he found himself in closest sympathy with the moderate Republican leaders in Congress. Intensely practical, he was not moved by the devotion of President Andrew Johnson and his Democratic supporters to the principle of states' rights — certainly not when the practical consequence was to revive the power of the old leaders of the Confederacy. Furthermore, he was no more receptive to Radical Republican commitment to the abstract principle of racial justice. Such enthusiasm led men into impracticalities and interfered with the business of administering a government (or an army). Like other conservative Republicans, he finally endorsed equal suffrage as the best way out of the Reconstruction muddle. He came to see it as a practical solution to the problem of how to guarantee civil rights to the freedmen: Let them protect their own rights through their influence as voters.

By 1868, Grant had broken with Johnson and was the favorite of the Republican conservatives for their party's presidential nomination. Moreover, he had the support of leading intellectuals, who insisted that the war had settled the slavery issue. What the country now needed was stable, expert leadership to reform the financial and civil service systems, precisely the sort of leadership one could expect from this most practical and stable man. Radical Republicans, however, were suspicious of him.

As the popularity of the Republican Party waned in 1867-1868, Radical Republican hostility to Grant's nomination collapsed. Without Grant as its candidate, the Republican Party would risk defeat. "Let us have peace," he wrote in his terse letter of acceptance. After twenty years of conflict over slavery, it was what most Americans wanted to hear. To the audience at his inauguration, the transition from Johnson's administration to Grant's was as cheering as the burst of sunlight that accompanied it.

As Grant entered the White House, Americans faced public problems in a variety of areas. First was what most Americans expected to be the winding up of Reconstruction. Virginia, Texas, and Mississippi had not yet complied with the conditions that Congress had set for restoration to the Union—ratification of the Fourteenth Amendment and new state constitutions guaranteeing civil and political equality between the races. In each state, radicals had tried to impose further conditions that more

conservative Republicans and Conservatives (former Democrats and Whigs who opposed the Republicans) resisted. Moreover, the Georgia state legislature had expelled its black members, disrupting Reconstruction there. Finally, in several of the restored states, so much anti-black and anti-Republican violence remained that the more radical Republicans were demanding some national action to stop it.

In the area of foreign affairs, the most important task was to settle the bitter dispute between Great Britain and the United States over tacit British support of the Confederacy. Americans were demanding reparations for destruction of American shipping wreaked by Confederate ships built in Great Britain and permitted to use British ports during the war. The Johnson administration had negotiated a settlement of these so-called *Alabama* claims (named after a Confederate cruiser built by a British shipyard), but in the first months of his administration, Grant and Congress rejected it as too conciliatory. Bellicose Republicans, such as Nathaniel Banks and Benjamin F. Butler, spoke of war, and even more moderate Republicans hankered after Canada as a suitable compensation.

Beyond that, many Americans were demanding that Spain give up control of Cuba, where it maintained a slaveholding regime against perennial Cuban insurrection. In general, many Americans continued to believe that it was the nation's "manifest destiny" to become the dominant power in the Caribbean basin.

The Currency Crisis

Most Northerners probably thought that the linked questions of funding the national debt, controlling the amount of currency in circulation, taxation, and banking were the most important matters facing the country. They directly affected the economic vitality of the nation. To finance the war, Republicans had dramatically increased both internal taxes and tariffs on imports. They had issued paper money, or "greenbacks," which they made legal tender for the payment of all debts, even though they were not redeemable in gold or silver. Congress had borrowed an immense amount of money by selling bonds bearing high rates of interest and, to help their sale, had exempted them from state or national taxation. It also created a national banking system, forcing new and preexisting banks to secure national banking charters and making such charters conditional on banks buying government bonds. National banks were authorized to issue banknotes, which would be legal tender, in proportion to their holdings of government bonds. Soon all the bonds earmarked for banks were sold. Naturally, people hoarded gold (not much

silver was available), and the value of both greenbacks and banknotes fell below that of specie. As a consequence, the Civil War was a time of inflation in prices and, to a lesser degree, wages.

With the end of the war, powerful interests demanded a return to the "specie standard" — that is, a system where all paper money could be converted into gold or silver. Backed by most theoretical economists, they insisted that only specie had real value and that it was impossible to plan business properly if the value of currency were unstable. Most Republicans agreed, and in 1866 they authorized the secretary of the treasury to withdraw greenbacks from circulation at his discretion by exchanging them for government bonds. The practical effects of this,

---

The Vice President
Schuyler Colfax

Schuyler Colfax was born on March 23, 1823, in New York. As a young boy he attended public schools, but because of his family's financial hardships, he was forced to end his schooling. Colfax's father died before he was born, and his mother married a second time to George W. Matthews. The family moved to New Carlisle, Indiana, in 1836. At his family's urging, Colfax began studying law but grew disinterested and instead decided to write articles on politics for local newspapers. On October 10, 1844, Colfax married Evelyn Clark, and the couple set up home in South Bend, Indiana.

In 1845, Colfax joined a partnership with Albert W. West to buy a local newspaper, which they renamed the *St. Joseph Valley Register*. Colfax served as the influential newspaper's editor for eighteen years, during which time he cultivated a political career. In 1854, Colfax won election to the United States House of Representatives as a member of the Whig Party. In 1863, while in Congress, his beloved wife died and was buried in South Bend. The couple had no children.

Colfax was elected as Speaker of the House the same year of his wife's passing and served in the office for three terms. In 1868, on the same ticket with Ulysses Grant, Colfax won the vice presidency. Shortly after the election, he married Nellie Wade, and the two had one child. Disinterested in being renominated to the vice presidency, Colfax retired from political life. Scandal, which was a prominent feature of the Grant presidency, did not escape the vice president and most likely was a determining factor in his decision to end his political career. Colfax was accused of accepting stock shares at reduced prices while vice president from a company seeking to avoid a federal investigation. He fervently denied the charges and received the support of President Grant.

While in retirement, Colfax became a public speaker and earned a handsome living. On January 13, 1885, while taking a train trip to a speaking engagement in Iowa, Colfax died from a massive heart attack.

Robert P. Watson and Richard Yon

however, aroused strong opposition. By contracting the amount of currency in circulation, the government raised the value of that remaining, forcing prices down and interest rates up. Republicans were forced to repeal the contraction program.

By the time Grant became president, Americans were completely divided on the currency, tax, and banking questions. Most of the national banks were in the Northeast, and thus most of the banknotes were issued there. With plentiful money, Northeasterners did not feel the effects of contraction so severely. Other regions, particularly the West (Indiana to California) and the South, had few banks and therefore fewer banknotes in circulation. Moreover, banks themselves in these areas had to borrow money in the Northeast to secure money to lend, raising interest rates far above those in the more favored region. Also, as contraction caused prices to fall, it became harder to make enough money to pay one's debts.

Worse, from the standpoint of Westerners and Southerners, they bore an unfair burden in paying for the system. Since Northeasterners were richer than other Americans, they had bought more bonds, which were exempt from taxation. Moreover, tariffs enabled American manufacturers, mostly based in the Northeast, to raise prices without fear of foreign competition.

To remedy the inequity and promote economic growth, most Westerners and Southerners called for increasing the number of greenbacks in circulation. They demanded the elimination of the national banking system, or the establishment of "free banking," whereby the Treasury Department would be obligated to sell bonds to any newly organized bank. Many Westerners demanded that the interest and principal on government bonds be repaid in greenbacks rather than gold, reducing the taxes it would take to pay them off and increasing the amount of currency in circulation. They called for reduction of tariffs. Finally, many Western-

ers insisted that the "bloated bondholders" pay taxes on their bonds. Northeasterners generally opposed all these proposals and demanded contraction of the currency and a return to specie payments. Although the dominant division was sectional, Western and Southern Republicans tended to be more moderate in their demands for contraction, and some even favored taxation of government bonds.

The reform-oriented intellectuals in the Republican Party took extreme positions on these issues, based on what they thought were fundamental principles. They demanded the quickest possible return to "hard money" — that is, gold. A paper money system permitted the government to manipulate the money supply and therefore enabled political majorities to affect the value of the dollar. The complaints of Westerners and Southerners, these intellectuals contended, were simply those of people who did not want to pay their debts at full value. Refusal to redeem government bonds in gold or silver would be dishonest and immoral. They agreed, however, with Westerners and Southerners on the tariff. Tariffs artificially redistributed wealth by forcing consumers to pay more for goods so that owners and workers in a protected industry could make more money. Seeing the issues as ones of principle, they viewed compromise on them as immoral.

These reformers were the supporters of civil service reform. They worried that an active government — one that promoted economic development through manipulation of the currency, protective tariffs, subsidies for transportation, and similar legislation — invited corruption. Those seeking such help inevitably would try to secure it through their influence with the government, not by mere persuasion. Already Washington, D.C., and the state capitals were full of "logrolling lobbyists," exercising improper influence and even bribing government officials. Politicians tolerated this because all they were interested in was gaining office. Political parties were more and more turning into "machines," which secured votes not on issues, but through strong organizations cemented by "patronage"—that is, government offices given in exchange for service to the party rather than on the bsis of merit. A reform of the civil service, making appointment to office dependent on ability rather than politics, would end corruption and also remove the main pillar sustaining machine politicians. This would enable the reformer intellectuals—the "best men"—to wield more influence in politics.

Finally, the reformers wanted a quick end to Reconstruction. Eliminate the radical proposals in Virginia, Texas, and Mississippi that were delaying these states' readmission to the Union, force Georgians to readmit black state legislators, and then turn to other matters, they insisted. Black Southerners, protected by their right to vote, would have to work out their own relationship with their former masters. This would enable the government to turn to the more important matters of finances, tariff reduction, and civil service reform. Moreover, it would weaken the hold of Republican machine politicians, who kept the support of Republican voters by stressing the dead Reconstruction issue.

Grant's Conception of the Presidency

Although Grant had been so reticent, or perhaps because he had been so reticent, many thought that they knew where he stood on some of the issues. On Reconstruction, they presumed that he shared the views of his strongest supporters, the moderate and conservative Republicans. Reformers happily took his slogan "Let us have peace" to mean that he, too, regarded Reconstruction as settled. In foreign affairs, they expected a hard line on the *Alabama* question from the former chief of the Union forces, and his rejection of the proposed settlement seemed to confirm their expectations. Grant's financial views were less certain, but most of his conservative and reform Republican allies were committed to following his lead.

Finally, reformers expected Grant to take the lead in breaking the power of Republican politicos. One of his greatest strengths as a military leader was his ability to identify capable commanders, such as William Tecumseh Sherman and Philip Sheridan, and his willingness to remove incompetent ones, even if politically powerful, such as Benjamin F. Butler. Organization and administration were his strong points. Surely he would demand skilled government officers, selected on merit.

These expectations assumed an active president, committed to establishing policies that he favored, but in fact, as he entered the presidency, Grant did not see his role that way. Grant was succeeding three presidents—James Buchanan, Lincoln, and Johnson—who not only had sought to push their programs through Congress but also had used all the powers of the presidency to overcome opposition. By 1869, all Northerners perceived Lincoln's greatness, but he had exercised his leadership in a time of crisis, when constitutional niceties and traditional divisions of power were at discount. Buchanan's and Johnson's peacetime efforts had proved disastrous. Buchanan's attempt to impose a Southern solution on the question of slavery in the territories had disrupted his party and precipitated the Civil War. Johnson had paralyzed the government, been impeached, and escaped removal by one vote. In his inaugural address, Grant assured his audience that "on all leading questions agitating the public mind I will always express my views to Congress and urge them according to my judgment." Final decisions would rest with Congress. "I shall on all subjects have a policy to recommend, but none to enforce against the will of the people." As to appointments, reformers were cheered. "The office has come to me unsought," he reminded the crowd. "I commence its duties untrammeled." He owed nothing to the party on whose ticket he had been elected; he had no debts to pay with offices.

In fact, Grant did seem to perceive himself as

a man above parties. He chose his cabinet from among the least partisan and most conservative of Republicans, so much so that Republicans in Congress rebelled. He made the mistake of nominating for secretary of the treasury Alexander T. Stewart, a leading importer and former ally, asking Congress to repeal a law prohibiting appointment of anyone doing business subject to departmental oversight. Republicans refused, at the same time making plain their unhappiness with Grant's cabinet choices. He smoothed things over by appointing the influential Massachusetts Republican politico George S. Boutwell to the Treasury position. At the same time, senate Republicans blocked repeal of the Tenure of Office Act, passed to limit Andrew Johnson's control over government appointments. This meant that Grant would not be able to remove government officers permanently unless the Senate confirmed their successors. Refusals to confirm would restore the old officers, giving senators a crucial vote in the distribution of patronage.

As a consequence of the brief, sharp struggle, Grant essentially withdrew from patronage matters. He insisted that a few government positions go to personal friends and relations. (His father was appointed postmaster in Covington, Kentucky, for example.) For the rest, he delegated the job of selection of government officers to his cabinet. Some, like Boutwell and Postmaster John A. J. Creswell, another traditional politician, followed customary practices in distributing offices. They consulted the Republican congressional delegations about appointments in their states and generally accepted their recommendations. Others, like Cox, repudiated the traditional pattern and sought to establish one based on merit rather than partisanship.

In like manner, despite the promise of his inaugural address, Grant did little in the way of devising and pressing policies on Congress. The division in the cabinet over the criteria for appointments was one example. Reformers expected Grant to require all cabinet members to reform the process, to introduce merit as the main criterion. They were dismayed when he failed to force Boutwell and Creswell into line.

Reconstruction provided another example. In April, 1869, after Congress deadlocked on the question, Grant acted on Reconstruction. Over the objections of radicals and Conservatives, he issued a proclamation that permitted the people of Virginia, Mississippi, and Texas to vote separately on the provisions of their proposed state constitutions. With the administration evidently taking a conciliatory approach to former Confederates, Republicans in those states and in Tennessee divided, some joining Conservatives to support conservative Republicans against regular Republican nominees for state offices.

Grant refused to take a position. He permitted some cabinet members to sustain the regular Republican nominees and others to remain neutral. Without guidance from the administration, Republican newspapers and officeholders in the affected states felt free to bolt the Republican ticket, while Northern Republican newspapers were divided in their sympathies. As a consequence, the bolters and Conservatives won control of the governments in Virginia and Tennessee, and dissident Republicans in other Southern and border states, especially Georgia, Missouri, and West Virginia, were encouraged to fashion similar alliances with Conservatives.

In Georgia, too, the administration failed to take a clear stand, as a few influential Republicans joined Conservatives to oppose the Republican governor, claiming that they better reflected the administration's conciliatory position than did the party regulars. The result was a bitter struggle both in Georgia and in Congress over how to deal with the expulsion of the black legislators, as a consequence of which the divided Republicans lost control of the state.

Rather than promoting programs, Grant concentrated on administration, something at which everyone thought he excelled. As he had in the army, he proceeded by finding capable

An ambush by the Ku Klux Klan, c. 1869. *(Smithsonian Institution)*

subordinates and then advising without instructing them. In fact, with the exception of the soon-replaced secretary of the navy, all the cabinet members whom he appointed in the first month of his presidency were excellent administrators. All observers recognized the improvement.

The Taint of Corruption: Currency Reform and Black Friday

The Treasury Department earned the highest praise. As high tariffs brought in more gold than the government needed to pay its expenses (in fact, most government spending was in greenbacks), Boutwell creatively interpreted existing laws to permit him to sell gold for greenbacks. He then used the greenbacks to buy outstanding government bonds, reducing the national debt. In the first four months of the new administration, Boutwell proudly reported, the debt had been reduced by $50 million.

At the same time, by withdrawing some of the greenbacks from circulation and replacing them with gold, Boutwell brought the value of the two currencies closer together, an essential step in restoring specie payments without totally disrupting the economy. It had the effect of lowering prices somewhat within the country and raising the cost of American exports. This slowed the economy, especially in the South and West, whose farmers depended on exporting their crops and where money was in shorter supply.

In the spring of 1869, two aggressive, young speculators, Jay Gould and Jim Fisk, joined with Grant's brother-in-law and the assistant treasurer in New York, in charge of selling gold for greenbacks, to try to take advantage of the system. Through the brother-in-law, Gould lobbied to convince Grant that the value of greenbacks and banknotes should be lowered to enable the farmers to get better prices for their crops and at the same time make them cheaper on the international market. To accomplish this, all that was necessary was for the government temporarily to stop withdrawing greenbacks from circulation through its gold sales. Thinking they had convinced Grant, Gould and Fisk then bought up gold futures, driving the price of gold ever higher and "cornering" the outstanding gold. People who had agreed to sell them gold at low prices would have to pay them high prices to get it, or default on their contracts. As the price of gold soared on "Black Friday," September 24, 1869, hundreds of brokers and financial institutions faced bankruptcy and begged Grant and Boutwell to have the government sell gold to lower its price. Finally, Grant and Boutwell did so, breaking the conspiracy as the price of gold plummeted.

Although Grant plainly had no part in the conspiracy, his brother-in-law and a key government appointee were proved corrupt, and even Julia came under suspicion. Boutwell's continued reduction of the national debt, through purchases of outstanding bonds and exchange of old, high-interest bonds for new, lower-interest ones, continued to earn praise, but Black Friday was the first of many instances where Grant's administration would be tarnished by corruption near the top.

While Boutwell worked assiduously to reduce the national debt, the administration took no position on the tariff issue and played no active role in the fight over free banking, expansion or contraction of the currency, or efforts to

---

The Vice President
Henry Wilson

Henry Wilson was born with the name Jeremiah Jones Colbath on February 16, 1812, in Farmington, New Hampshire. His family was destitute, and his father was an alcoholic. From the ages of sixteen to twenty-one, Colbath served as an indentured servant to a farmer. In June, 1833, Colbath petitioned the state government to legally change his name to Henry Wilson for some unknown reason. That same year, Wilson learned the trade of a cobbler and opened his own shop. After saving his money, he attended two different academies between 1836 and 1837 but returned to making shoes when more gainful employment could not be found.

Eventually, Wilson's business grew—he had eighteen employees and realized a considerable profit. He proved himself to be quite adept at debating and used those skills to win election to the General Court of Massachusetts. On October 20, 1840, he married Harriet Malvina Howe, who was only sixteen years old. Serving as a representative in the state legislature, Wilson ran for the state senate and lost. He joined the Massachusetts Volunteer Militia and was commissioned a captain. In 1844, he returned to politics and won a seat in the Massachusetts Senate. In June, 1846, Wilson was promoted to colonel and then brigadier general. Growing increasingly dissatisfied with the Whig Party, he helped found the Free Soil Party in 1848. Wilson made an unsuccessful bid for governor of Massachusetts in 1853, but within two years, he was elected to the United States Senate, where he served for eighteen years.

With the start of the Civil War, Wilson worked tirelessly to make sure Union soldiers were provided with necessary supplies and resources. Approached by the Republican Party to run for vice president in 1868, he declined because of the failing health of his wife, who was suffering from cancer. She died the following year. On June 10, 1872, Wilson was nominated as vice president with the incumbent, President Ulysses Grant. Within three months of taking office however, Vice President Wilson suffered a stroke while presiding over the Senate. He died on November 22, 1875.

Robert P. Watson and Richard Yon

redistribute currency to the South and West. This inaction dismayed reformers and regular Republicans alike.

Foreign Affairs: The Santo Domingo Initiative

Under the Constitution, the president has primary responsibility for foreign affairs, so it is natural that the Grant administration most actively promoted particular policies in that area. The Cuban issue caused the most trouble, because Grant's advisers were divided. His close friend John A. Rawlins, secretary of war, endorsed the groundswell of public support for tough action against Spain. His respected secretary of state, Hamilton Fish, backed by Charles Sumner, the chair of the influential Senate Foreign Relations Committee, urged moderation. They succeeded in preventing hasty action, and after Rawlins died in September, 1869, Fish was able to turn Grant into a bulwark against reckless attacks on the Spanish holdings in the Caribbean.

Allies on the Cuban question, Sumner and Fish differed widely on relations with Great Britain, and Grant backed Fish. Sumner tried to persuade the administration to claim such large damages from Great Britain for its conduct during the war that cession of Canada would be an appropriate setoff. That policy risked war, and many Americans would have welcomed it, despite the damage the British were likely to inflict on foreign trade. When Fish and Grant rejected such a risky course, Sumner tried to impose his own foreign policy through his authority in the Senate, which would have to ratify any settlement, and his influence with the American ambassador to Great Britain, John Lothrop Motley, who owed Sumner his appointment. Motley violated the instructions that he received from Fish, who was forced to try to take away from him the primary responsibility for dealing with the British on the issue.

At the same time, Grant enthusiastically endorsed efforts by his close friend and private secretary, Colonel Orville E. Babcock, and several American and Dominican speculators to annex the Dominican Republic, which the Americans called Santo Domingo, as a new state in the Union. Without much enthusiasm, Fish cooperated. Sumner promised Grant personally to give the matter his deepest consideration, affirming that he was "an administration man" and sympathetic to its desires. When the annexation treaty came before the Senate early in 1870, however, Sumner attacked it bitterly, violating what Grant had interpreted as a promise of support. Opinion became divided all over the country, and the treaty stalled.

By 1870, it was clear that neither the Grant administration nor the Republican Congress had any firm policies to offer the people. While Grant's Santo Domingo initiative sputtered, Republicans divided over the currency question,

---

Ulysses S. Grant's veto of the Currency Act of 1874, April 22, 1874:

Among the evils growing out of the rebellion, and not yet referred to, is that of an irredeemable currency. It is an evil which I hope will receive your most earnest attention. It is a duty, and one of the highest duties, of Government to secure to the citizen a medium of exchange of fixed, unvarying value. This implies a return to a specie basis, and no substitute for it can be devised. It should be commenced now and reached at the earliest practicable moment consistent with a fair regard for the interests of the debtor class. . . . Fluctuation, however, in the paper value of the measure of all values (gold) is detrimental to the interests of trade. It makes the man of business an involuntary gambler, for in all sales where the future payment is to be made both parties speculate as to what will be the value of the currency to be paid and received.

tariff reform, and civil service reform. Southern Republicans reported that organized bands, generally known as the Ku Klux Klan, were waging campaigns of increasing violence against them, but the administration and Republican leaders in Congress, afraid to reopen an issue that was "settled," rejected all proposals to intervene. Republicans seemed adrift, and the reformers openly urged voters to defeat Republicans who stood in the way of tariff reduction, contraction of the currency, and civil service reform. Their sympathizers in the cabinet, especially Cox, urged Grant to unify his administration on the reform side.

Matters came to a crisis in the summer of 1870. In Missouri and West Virginia, dissident Republicans bolted the party nominations and joined Conservatives to put forward Liberal Republican tickets for state offices. They called for the reenfranchisement of former rebels to finally settle the Civil War issues. Seeking the support of reform elements in the Republican Party, they also called for tariff and civil service reform. Reformers declared the Missouri election a test of strength for control of the Republican Party and demanded that Grant's administration stay neutral, as it had in similar conflicts of 1869.

Grant's inability to secure Republican support for his Santo Domingo treaty finally convinced him that something had to be done to unify party ranks. Regular Republicans, cleverly supporting the Santo Domingo annexation, warned him that the party faced disaster in 1872 if it did not rally around some popular issue and discipline bolters. To begin to unify the cabinet, he nominated Attorney General Ebenezer R. Hoar to the Supreme Court. When senators rejected the nomination to punish Hoar for his refusal to agree to follow their patronage recommendations, Grant accepted his resignation from the cabinet. When Cox tried to force Grant's hand by refusing to honor the custom of assessing campaign contributions from employees in the Interior Department and refusing to give them leave to return to vote, Grant forced him out. In state after state, the administration began to remove federal government employees accused of being lax or inept partisans. None of this could save Missouri or West Virginia, which elected the Liberal Republican tickets, but it committed Grant to fulfilling his responsibility as party leader. In response, most Republican leaders, who had been critical of him, now came to support his renomination in 1872. To allay suspicions that he had completely abandoned civil service reform, Grant named a civil service commission, led by a respected reformer, to suggest changes in the system.

Grant hoped to rally Republicans around his proposal to annex Santo Domingo. To show that he meant business, he replaced Sumner's friend Motley as minister to Great Britain. Then, when Sumner bitterly attacked Grant in the Senate and refused to associate with Secretary of State Fish, Senate Republican leaders stripped Sumner of his chairmanship of the Foreign Relations Committee.

All of this alienated the reformers, and Sumner's removal so shocked Republican voters that it became impossible to pass the Santo Domingo treaty. His and Motley's removals, however, did facilitate settlement of the *Alabama* claims dispute with Great Britain. In May, 1871, the British and Americans agreed to establish a tribunal to arbitrate all claims.

This did not, however, revive Republican fortunes. Still unable to unite on the tariff and currency questions, and afraid that civil service reform would destroy the party machinery, the divided Republicans seemed to be careening toward disaster despite Grant's efforts to unify the party. They were saved by the issue that had created their party—the issue of North versus South.

The Ku Klux Klan Act

Committed to revitalizing their party, Republican leaders could no longer ignore the efforts of such organizations as the Ku Klux Klan to terrorize it out of existence in the South. Prepared to let the reformers leave the party rather than continue to disrupt it, the leadership no longer feared to alienate them by reopening Civil War issues. In the spring and summer of 1871, urged on by a brief message from Grant, Republicans passed an act to enforce the Fourteenth and Fifteenth Amendments, popularly dubbed the Ku Klux Klan Act, which authorized Grant to impose martial law in Southern counties where violence had overawed state authorities.

As Republicans documented the atrocities the Klan had committed in the South, the effect was electric. Reformers lamented the sacrifice of "real" issues, such as tariff and civil service reform,

One political cartoonist's view of the corruption in the Grant administration: Hawaiian king Kalakaua tattoos a list of scandals on Grant. *(Library of Congress)*

to the "dead" one symbolized by the "bloody shirt" that outraged Congressman Benjamin F. Butler brought to the floor of the House to illustrate Klan cruelty. Throughout the North, however, Republicans rallied to protect the fruits of Northern victory in the Civil War. Democrats denounced the imposition of martial law in scattered counties of South Carolina and the use of federal troops elsewhere as gross violations of civil liberty, but they were also forced at last to give up their open hostility to equal rights and black suffrage. Announcing a "new departure," they promised to accept the finality of the Thirteenth, Fourteenth, and Fifteenth Amendments.

The new departure enabled Democrats, reform Republicans, and some Republican politicians who had lost power in their party to unite against Grant's reelection. Calling themselves Liberal Republicans, the dissident Republicans

met in Cincinnati in June, 1872, to frame a platform and name a candidate whom the Democrats would endorse. The nominee, newspaper editor Horace Greeley, was, however, more the candidate of dissatisfied politicians than of the reformers. Incredibly, he was an advocate of high tariffs and only shakily committed to civil service reform. Worse, he was an outspoken advocate of temperance legislation. That made him anathema to German Americans, whom Liberals had counted on for political support. All of his life, Greeley had been a trenchant critic of the Democratic Party; it would be hard to persuade rank-and-file Democrats to vote for him.

Greeley agreed with the reformers and Democrats primarily on the need to lay the Civil War issues to rest. Ironically, this difference between Republicans and Liberals on war issues became the main focus of the campaign. The war issues united the Republicans, whereas

Greeley's position on the tariff and temperance divided the Liberals and Democrats. Grant swept to reelection in an immense victory.

Grant's Second Term: A False Spring

At the inauguration of his second term in 1873, Grant was at the high point of his career. The savior of his country in war, he was hailed for his accomplishments in peace. He had settled its dangerous dispute with Great Britain. He had been forceful in suppressing violence in the South, yet all knew that he bore no malice toward the brave people whom he defeated in the field.

Grant seemed equally successful in his economic policies. The Treasury Department's steady hand had made a significant dent in the national debt and fostered economic recovery from the depression of 1867 to 1869. Grant instituted a few measures of civil service reform, appointing a commission to make recommendations, and the civil service seemed more efficient than it had been under Johnson and prewar Democrats. Nevertheless, such disasters lay ahead that most historians still count Grant among America's least successful presidents.

The Panic of 1873

Six months into Grant's second term, panic struck the stock market. Prices, especially of railroad stocks, collapsed. Leading financial institutions that had invested in them were forced to close. Although the Treasury Department immediately began to add small amounts of currency to the circulation by buying bonds, it was not enough to reverse the economic slide. Desperately, businessmen pressed Grant to stimulate the economy by increasing the amount of money in circulation. Others, especially the doctrinaire reformers and academic economists, insisted that the economic depression was the natural consequence of the artificial prosperity induced by the already inflated currency. The only way to secure stable prosperity, they insisted, was to return to the gold standard as quickly as possible. Unable to decide between the two extremes, Grant seemed paralyzed.

Without administration leadership, Congress was left to try to deal with the depression itself. Both parties were divided on the issue, with Easterners still tending to favor contracting the currency and Southerners and Westerners calling for inflation and free banking. Farmer and labor organizations demanded that government take responsibility for restoring prosperity and joined the call for inflation. After their initial panic, most businessmen turned against the movement, fearing the growing militancy of farmers and workers. Reformers and businessmen joined in great rallies protesting inflation proposals, but in April, 1874, Congress nevertheless passed legislation adding $64 million to the circulation.

Reformers and businessmen lobbied Grant to veto the bill. Hit from all sides, Grant continued to vacillate; finally, he came down on the side of the contractionists, vetoing the bill. Now he at last articulated a firm policy. He urged the repeal of the Legal Tender Act, which had created the greenbacks; he wanted a law requiring that all contracts made in the future be payable in coin; he wanted all greenbacks of under ten dollars withdrawn from circulation; and he wanted Congress to authorize the Treasury to exchange government bonds for all the greenbacks still in circulation. Western and Southern Republicans were stunned by Grant's course. As Democrats in those regions swung firmly behind inflation, Republicans faced political disaster.

Fraud and Corruption

At the same time, Republicans were plagued by renewed charges of corruption. The most important scandal was the exposure of the Crédit Mobilier fraud. Investigation showed that during the 1860's the men whom Congress had authorized to build the Western Union Railroad had subcontracted the work at inflated prices to a company they themselves had organized, the Crédit Mobilier. To prevent any embarrassing questions, their representative, Congressman Oakes Ames, had spread stock in the company among important members of the House of Representatives. As the shock spread, congressmen voted themselves a retroactive $7,500 raise in salary.

None of this directly involved the administration, but there was a Republican majority in the offending Congress; the "salary grab" was managed in the house by Grant's ally, Massachusetts's congressman Benjamin F. Butler; and the episodes reminded the people of Black Friday and allegations of corruption in the civil service. The perception was strengthened when Grant nominated Alexander H. Shepherd to be governor of the territorial government that administered Washington, D.C. As building commissioner, Shepherd had undertaken a massive building campaign in the city, beginning its transformation from a sleepy Southern town to a monumental capital. He had financed the change by borrowing, issuing bonds authorized in referenda in which poor black citizens far outvoted wealthier, taxpaying whites. In the opinion of many Americans, this paralleled the activities of New York's corrupt Tammany Hall, and Shepherd's promotion raised a tremendous outcry.

Reformers seized on the concern to renew their challenge to the machine politicians, calling again for civil service reform and insisting that corruption was the natural consequence of the present patronage system. Grant, however, was now firmly allied with the regular politicians in his own party. They depended on their patronage-disciplined organizations, and he depended on them. Grant ignored the recommendations presented by his civil service commission, and when key members resigned in the spring of 1873, advocates of change attacked him as the main obstacle to reform. In early 1874, yet another scandal broke, this time cen-

tering on F. B. Sanborn, an ally of Butler, the reformers' favorite target.

Despite mounting criticism, Grant began to think about an unprecedented third presidential term. He had given up his military commission, had never been successful in private business, and must have wondered how he would support his family if he left the White House. At the same time, the regular Republican politicians faced a serious challenge from the reform elements of the party. With Grant as president, they could maintain their patronage-based organizations. Besides, who knew who might succeed him? If a new president allied with the reformers, cutting off the regulars' patronage, they would be in serious trouble.

Grant's veto of the inflation bill may have been aimed at securing support of the business community for a third term and reducing reformer hostility. He also tried to restore the good feeling that had existed between him and former Confederates when he had first entered the White House. He had the Justice Department drop prosecution of arrested Klan members. He refused to intervene on behalf of Texas and Arkansas Republicans, who claimed that they had been defeated only by fraud and violence in the 1872 elections.

The Justice Department worked out a compromise between rival Democratic and Republican claims for control of the Alabama state legislature. He openly dickered with Virginia and South Carolina Conservatives. As violence flared anew in Alabama and Mississippi, he ignored the calls of their Republican governors for United States troops. Only in Louisiana, where his brother-in-law was a leading Republican, did Grant seem to side actively with Republicans in a dispute over who had won the 1872 state elections. Even there he urged Congress to relieve him of the responsibility by passing legislation to deal with the matter.

In the summer of 1874, however, Conservative Southerners forced Grant's hand. Emboldened by his inaction, they formed "White

Leagues" in Alabama, Louisiana, and Mississippi. In each of the states, they terrorized their Republican opponents. In rural Louisiana and Mississippi, they violently overthrew Republican city and county governments. In the course of the confrontations, numerous black and some white Republicans were murdered. Still, Grant resisted calls for troops until after violence had broken out. Finally, in September, 1874, the Conservatives of New Orleans rose against the Republican state government, defeated the state police in a pitched battle, and replaced Republican state officials with Conservatives. A coup d'état of this magnitude was too much even for the most sympathetic of reformers, and Grant intervened forcefully to restore the Louisiana Republicans to power. Southern Conservatives attacked him violently for doing so, and in the countryside, Conservatives continued to wrest power from Republicans by force.

By the summer and fall of 1874, as most states held congressional and local elections, the Grant administration and the Republican Party were completely on the defensive. In the North, Democrats blamed them for the depression and stressed corruption and the salary grab. In the South, Conservatives blasted Grant's support for local Republicans and his intervention in local affairs. They warned that Republicans in Congress were preparing a new civil rights bill, which would guarantee blacks equal access to schools, churches, hotels, streetcars, and other public facilities. Reformers determined to prove their power by urging their supporters to back Democratic candidates or to refrain from voting at all. In many states, Democrats and reformers made the question of a third term for Grant a key issue of the campaign. Elect

Republicans, they warned, and it would be taken as a sign of Grant's popularity and make his renomination certain.

The results were disastrous for the Republicans. They were routed nearly everywhere. The Republicans lost ninety seats in the House of Representatives; the Democrats gained eighty, with the rest going to fourteen independent inflationists. In New York, where the Democrats ran almost entirely on the issue of a third term for Grant, Samuel J. Tilden defeated the popular Republican incumbent by thirty thousand votes, a shift of eighty thousand since 1872.

The Democratic landslide of 1874 not only demolished Grant's hopes for renomination but also discredited him with much of the party. Republican vice president Henry Wilson lamented, "Grant is now more unpopular than Andrew Johnson in his darkest days." He was a "millstone around the neck of our party that would sink it out of sight."

Charges of corruption persisted throughout Grant's second term of office. To restore confidence in the administration's financial policy and to add a Southerner to his cabinet, Grant

Grant's tomb. *(Library of Congress)*

named Benjamin H. Bristow secretary of the treasury, with a mandate to clean house. Immediately, Bristow and his subordinates began to investigate the "Whiskey Ring," which involved Treasury employees who had taken bribes to permit whiskey to go untaxed. When the trail led to personal friends whom he had appointed to government positions in St. Louis, Grant backed away from his commitment to reform. When Bristow and his investigators told him that his close friend and personal secretary, Babcock, was involved in the ring, Grant could not believe it. As reformers began to groom Bristow for the 1876 Republican presidential nomination, Grant decided that the investigations were designed merely to discredit his administration, and he began to undermine Bristow's efforts. By careful maneuvering and dogged resistance, Grant managed to prevent Babcock's conviction on fraud charges and then forced Bristow's resignation. His reputation for rectitude was now in shambles. When investigators learned that Secretary of War W. W. Belknap had accepted kickbacks from contractors, his impeachment in 1876 merely confirmed the popular perception of a generally crooked administration.

Grant was not much more fortunate in his economic policies. For a brief moment, he considered pressing for a program of government works to ease unemployment, but that notion was far too radical for his advisers and the dominant molders of public opinion. Instead, Grant adhered to the idea that restoration of the gold standard would somehow revive business confidence. He took no strong role in the bitter fight over financial policy that wracked Congress in the 1874-1875 winter session. To restore party unity on the divisive issue, congressional Republicans finally compromised on a resolution calling for the resumption of specie payments by 1879, but it was to be done not by contracting the amount of money in circulation but by building up the government's reserve of gold. As a result of the compromise, the Republicans clearly became the party of hard money; the Democrats remained badly divided. The benefits became clear in the fall of 1875 when Republicans used the money issue to defeat squabbling Democrats in key Northern state elections. Grant, however, could claim little credit for the accomplishment.

Reconstruction: A Continuing Struggle

The most intractable problem that Grant faced remained Reconstruction. By 1875, Northern sympathy for Southern Republicans had largely dissipated. Southern Republicans had undertaken expensive projects designed to improve public facilities and promote economic growth. Moreover, they had responded to their mostly black constituency by opening schools and other state institutions to them. Like Shepherd in Washington, D.C., they had paid for the programs by issuing bonds, greatly increasing their state debt and tax rates. Southern Conservatives complained that propertyless blacks sustained these policies over the objections of white taxpayers. They charged that Republicans stole much of the money or spent it on expensive "jobs" put up by corrupt political supporters. Many Northern Republicans came to believe that their Southern allies were no better than Tammany Hall. Grant himself had little use for them and had tried to distance his administration from them in 1873-1874.

As president, however, Grant could not permit their overthrow by violence. Having prevented one such coup d'état in Louisiana in September, 1874, he faced another a few months later. Both Republicans and Conservatives in Louisiana claimed to have elected a majority of the state legislature in 1874. When the legislature met in January, 1875, the Conservatives took control by force, seating conservative claimants from disputed districts and ousting Republicans. Acting on their own initiative but under Grant's general orders, United States troops entered the legislature and purged the offending Conservatives, restoring the preexisting balance of parties.

Throughout the North, Democrats and reform Republicans organized meetings to protest the purge. It had been undertaken without any judicial authorization, by presidential fiat, they complained. It suggested military despotism; it destroyed states' rights. Republicans were stunned at the depth of the feeling. When the military authorities in Louisiana formally reported the circumstances, however, a favorable reaction set in among Republicans. Grant urged Congress to pass legislation authorizing him to protect voters in the South from violence and to reverse Conservative victories in Arkansas and Louisiana based on intimidation, but such bold steps were too risky for the Republicans in the wake of the shattering defeat of 1874. Lame duck Republicans in Congress passed a new civil rights bill, but they allowed a new Force Act to die.

Such caution encouraged Southern Conservatives to continue their campaign of violence. In 1875, Mississippi Conservatives incorporated violence as an integral part of their election strategy. Grant vacillated as the Republican governor pleaded for troops to protect Republican voters. Northern Republicans lobbied Grant to reject the request, fearing to raise the military interference issue during the election season in the North. Grant agreed and told his attorney general to reject the request for protection. Exaggerating Grant's sentiments in order to win reform support in the North, the attorney general wrote cruelly, "The whole public are tired out with these annual autumnal outbreaks in the South, and the great majority are now ready to condemn any interference on the part of the government," as if the fault lay with the victims rather than the perpetrators of the violence.

The Election of 1876

By 1876, Grant's administration had been generally discredited. The only chance most Republicans believed they had to win the presidential election of 1876 was to nominate a candidate not identified with Grant and to hope that Northerners remained unwilling to trust pro-Southern Democrats. Reformers took advantage of Republican doubts to push Bristow as the Republican most identified with reform. Former House speaker James G. Blaine cleverly distanced himself from Grant and sought the nomination as a hard-money reformer. Other candidates closer to the administration found little support outside their states and a few pockets of the South. Finally, the Republicans turned to Rutherford B. Hayes, who had won the gubernatorial election of 1875 in Ohio by stressing the hard-money issue and who had diligently cultivated good relations with leading Republican reformers.

The nomination was a repudiation of Grant, although Hayes wisely remained silent on exactly how far he would go in changing administration policy. Hayes's victory would do little more to vindicate Grant's administration than his defeat. Grant did little to help Hayes, perhaps because Republicans thought his vocal support would do more harm than good.

Yet Grant did not work to subvert Hayes's campaign, as some Republican reformers feared that he would. In fact, regular Republicans went all out to secure victory. Grant permitted the campaign managers a strong say in matters of patronage and did his best to harmonize feuding party factions. During the campaign, Republicans began cautiously to point to the accomplishments of his administration. Stressing Democratic untrustworthiness and instability, they contrasted these qualities to Grant's steadiness. By the end of the canvass, many Republican critics were once more speaking of Grant almost with affection. "Unpopular as the later years of his administration have been," wrote one of the bitterest, "he will go out of office amid general good will."

Grant played a critical role during the crisis that followed the election. Neither Hayes nor the Democratic candidate, Samuel J. Tilden, had a clear majority of the electoral votes, with those of three Southern states claimed by both. As each side warned of the danger of violence, Grant calmly maintained order in the capital and in the disputed Southern states. Grant's firmness played an important role in convincing Democrats that they could not simply have the House of Representatives name Tilden president, as they insisted it had the right to do. At the same time, Grant pressured Hayes's supporters to compromise with Democrats, hinting that he would not sustain their claim with military force if it came to that. By the time the electoral commission created by the compromise ruled in favor of Hayes, all had come once more to appreciate Grant's steadiness in times of crisis.

Grant in Retirement

On leaving the presidency, Grant decided to satisfy his lifelong love of travel. Two months after stepping down, he and Julia launched themselves on a world tour. Everywhere he went—from Great Britain to the Continent to the Orient—he was feted as the representative type of the self-made American man. As correspondents reported triumph after triumph, Grant's popularity in the United States climbed to the same level that he had enjoyed after Appomattox. By 1879, his allies in the Republican Party determined to make him president for a third term and thus to recover their own positions of party leadership. Reform Republicans bitterly resisted, aided by Hayes's allies in the party. At the 1880 Republican National Convention, slightly more than three hundred delegates—some seventy short of the required majority—stood by Grant through thirty-five ballots, until his enemies combined to defeat him.

His political career at an end, Grant cast about for an occupation. Always a plunger in business, seeking quick riches, Grant put all of his money into a banking and financial partnership with his son and his son's friend, Ferdinand Ward. Ward, however, was a charla-

tan, inflating his business with borrowed money, and when the pyramid collapsed, Grant lost everything he had. Refusing to accept gifts, Grant scrimped along on small loans from personal friends.

To recoup his fortune, Grant accepted a long-standing invitation to write his memoirs. Harnessing his remarkable memory, he recalled his days as a young lieutenant in the war with Mexico. In straightforward style, he limned his Civil War battles, modestly disavowing his talent as a tactician or strategist and demonstrating surprising deftness in characterizing friends and foes. As he wrote, he began to suffer from terrible pain in his jaw. Doctors diagnosed cancer, and with grim determination Grant labored to provide for his destitute family by finishing his work before he died. His biographers have described the agonizing effort as the greatest personal accomplishment of his life—equal in its way to his great wartime triumphs. He completed *Personal Memoirs* on May 23, 1885; he died on July 23, once again a great American hero, beloved by the nation.

Assessing Grant's Presidency: The Need for Balance

Historians and political scientists have generally considered Grant's administration of the presidency to be a failure. He has consistently been ranked among the country's worst presidents. Scholars have felt revulsion for the corruption that surrounded Grant as president; they have perceived his economic policies to be unfairly favorable to big business; and until recently, they have considered him unwise in trying to protect black rights in the South.

This assessment, however, is probably too extreme. A considerable amount of corruption actually occurred in Grant's administration, and Grant did not take a strong interest in rooting it out, but much of what scholars have called corruption was merely the dominant mode of choosing government officials through the patronage system. Scholars have tended to accept the judgment of the anti-Grant reformers that this system was inherently corrupt, but that is a very questionable conclusion, and reformers had ulterior, political motives for making the charge.

Once one gets beyond the corruption issue, Grant's administration emerges in a better light. With the exception of the controversial Santo Domingo treaty, his foreign policy was one of recognized achievement. His economic policies certainly did not challenge the dominant economic wisdom of his time, but he can hardly be blamed for that; in fact, he carried them out so efficiently that by the end of his term it was possible to set a definite date for the return to a specie-based currency, a significant achievement in the opinion of most contemporaries.

Grant's effort to protect the rights of black and white Republicans in the South did fail, not because it was misguided, but because of the recalcitrance of Southern whites and waning support in the North. Most analysts now consider Grant correct in making the attempt and wonder whether he manifested enough commitment to it. There can be no doubt that Grant wavered in the face of mounting political opposition to intervention in the South. Nevertheless, Grant remained committed to protecting civil and political rights in the South after most Republican leaders had given up. Given the capacities of the national government at that time and considering the degree of suppression of normal civil and political liberties that a firmer policy would have required, it is doubtful that any president could have succeeded where Grant failed.

Overall, Grant's administration was neither an abject failure nor a great success. A great general, he made an adequate president. Intending to play only a modest role in the making of policy, he seems a pale figure compared with such giants as Andrew Jackson, Lincoln, or the Roosevelts. Still, he dominated his era, a stronger president than most have recognized.

Michael Les Benedict

Suggested Readings

Arnold, James R. *Grant Wins the War: Decision at Vicksburg*. New York: John Wiley, 1997. Focuses on Grant's strategy in the decisive siege of the Civil War.

Badeau, Adam. *Grant in Peace: From Appomattox to Mount McGregor, A Personal Memoir*. 1897. Reprint. Freeport, N.Y.: Books for Libraries Press, 1971. Many of Grant's associates wrote biographies of him or described their association with him. Of these, Badeau's is the most informative, furnishing insight into Grant's character as seen by an associate and friend.

Bunting, Josiah. *Ulysses S. Grant*. New York: Henry Holt, 2004. Reexamines Grant's infamous presidency in a more positive light and attempts to debunk several myths about the man.

Gillette, William. *Retreat from Reconstruction, 1869-1879*. Baton Rouge: Louisiana State University Press, 1979. Concentrates on the Grant administration's Reconstruction policy.

Grant, Ulysses S. *Personal Memoirs of U. S. Grant*. 1885-1886. Reprint. New York: AMS Press, 1972. Offers insight into Grant's character but attends only slightly to his presidential years.

Korda, Michael. *Ulysses S. Grant: Unlikely Hero*. New York: Atlas Books/HarperCollins, 2004. Although Grant's two terms were fraught with political and financial scandals, this biography argues that he managed to exert a calming influence on a country bruised by war.

McFeely, William S. *Grant: A Biography*. New York: Norton, 1981. An excellent, well-written biography with updated information.

Nevins, Allan. *Hamilton Fish: The Inner History of the Grant Administration*. 1936. Rev. ed. New York: F. Ungar, 1957. An account based largely on the diaries of Grant's conservative secretary of state.

Perret, Geoffrey. *Ulysses S. Grant: Soldier and President*. New York: Random House, 1997.

Details Grant's military and political careers.

Perry, James M. *Touched with Fire: Five Presidents and the Civil War Battles That Made Them.* New York: PublicAffairs, 2005. Uses diaries, letters, and other firsthand accounts to bring life to the war battles that formed the character and political drive of presidents Grant, Hayes, Garfield, Harrison, and McKinley.

Scaturro, Frank J. *President Grant Reconsidered.* Lanham, Md.: University Press of America, 1998. Argues for a positive reassessment of Grant's presidency as one of strength, achievement, and principle.

Simpson, Brooks D. *Let Us Have Peace: Ulysses S. Grant and the Politics of War and Reconstruction.* Chapel Hill: University of North Carolina Press, 1991. Concentrates on the Grant administration's Reconstruction policy.

Smith, Jean Edward. *Grant.* New York: Simon & Schuster, 2002. A biography that recognizes Grant's failures but also emphasizes the value of his character.

Rutherford B. Hayes

19th President, 1877-1881

Born: October 4, 1822
    Delaware, Ohio
Died: January 17, 1893
    Fremont, Ohio

Political Party: Republican
Vice President: William A. Wheeler

Cabinet Members
Secretary of State: William M. Evarts
Secretary of the Treasury: John Sherman
Secretary of War: George M. McCrary,
    Alexander Ramsey
Secretary of the Navy: Richard W. Thompson,
    Nathan Goff, Jr.
Attorney General: Charles A. Devens
Postmaster General: David M. Key, Horace
    Maynard
Secretary of the Interior: Carl Schurz

Rutherford Birchard Hayes was born five years after his parents, Rutherford and Sophie Birchard Hayes, moved from Vermont to the central Ohio community of Delaware and less than three months after the death of his father. He was left in the care of his mother, a strong-willed and protective woman, and her bachelor brother, Sardis Birchard, who became the dominant male influence in his life. A bright but frail child, "Ruddy" grew up in a sheltered world, his early years marked by a close attachment to his sister Fanny, the only other sibling to survive childhood.

With financial help from Birchard, an established businessman in Lower Sandusky (later Fremont), Rutherford attended private grammar schools and a college preparatory school in

Connecticut before enrolling at Kenyon College in Gambier, Ohio. Studious and intense, he gained a reputation as a mediator of campus disputes, began to dabble in Whig politics, and was graduated first in the class of 1842. A bachelor of law degree from Harvard in January, 1845, capped a good formal education for the young Hayes.

After a less than satisfying law practice of four years in Lower Sandusky, late in 1849 Hayes moved south to the bustling river city of

Portrait of Rutherford B. Hayes. *(Whitehouse.gov)*

The First Lady
Lucy Hayes

Lucy Ware Webb was born on August 28, 1831, in Chilicothe, Ohio, the youngest child and only daughter of Doctor James Webb and his wife, Maria Cook Webb, both of whom were early temperance people. Her father's death when Lucy was two left the family in dire straits, but Mrs. Webb took in laundry and boarders to make ends meet. The Webb family moved to Delaware, Ohio, where Lucy first met Rutherford B. Hayes, who was nine years older. Lucy entered the Wesleyan Female College in Cincinnati, where she graduated in June, 1850. Lucy and Hayes were married on December 30, 1852, in Cincinnati. The couple had eight children although three died. Lucy's views in the 1850's were decidedly more radical than they would be during her White House years. She attended several suffrage meetings with her sister-in-law Fanny Hayes Platt, but Fanny's early death ended Lucy's interest in suffrage. She later believed that education for women should come before the right to vote. As the wife of Ohio's governor for several terms, Lucy Hayes visited the state asylums and schools, an interest she maintained all of her life. A charmingly approachable figure, Lucy had a unique ability to win over friends and enemies alike. She smiled easily and, in an age where people often looked grim in their photographs, she appeared happy and relaxed. From the moment she entered the White House, Lucy was seen as the "New Woman" because of her college degree, her interest in social causes such as insane asylums and orphanages, and her charity for the homeless. She took an active interest in the history of the White House and added portraits of the presidents who were missing from the collection, and she had an Ohio artist paint a full-length portrait of Martha Washington to hang opposite the Gilbert Stuart portrait of George Washington. She and her husband were the first White House couple to cross the country while in office (in 1880), and she accompanied Hayes on his trip to the Deep South, where she met former First Lady Sarah Polk.

Upon leaving the White House, the couple returned to their home in Fremont, Ohio. Lucy Hayes took up her duties as president of the Women's Christian Missionary Society of her Methodist Church. She had a stroke on June 22, 1889, and with her husband by her side, died on June 25, 1889.

Craig Schermer

Cincinnati. As he quickly rose to become one of the city's leading barristers, he courted Lucy Ware Webb, and they were married late in 1852. From their union would come eight children — of whom four boys and one girl would survive childhood. Bright, well-educated, gregarious, and an excellent hostess, Lucy became her husband's faithful confidante and companion in the political trials and triumphs that lay ahead.

As the sectional crisis broke up the Whig Party during the mid-1850's, Hayes moved into the new Republican coalition. Never radically antislavery, he worked quietly in the party as his interest in local politics grew. In 1858, the city council appointed him city solicitor — a post

to which he was elected the following year. He worked at the local level for the election of Abraham Lincoln in 1860 but admitted that he could not "get up much interest in the contest." His seeming indifference to the ensuing secession crisis disappeared with the firing on Fort Sumter in April, 1861, and early in June he readily accepted a commission as major in the Twenty-third Ohio Volunteer Infantry.

The Twenty-third spent most of the next four years in West Virginia, one of the more rugged minor theaters of the Civil War. Holding the area, as historian T. Harry Williams put it, involved "small and nasty work — fighting in pygmy battles, chasing guerrillas, patrolling lonely mountain roads, repressing civilian sympathizers of the South." On only two occasions did the Twenty-third take part in the major battles of the East—at Antietam in 1862 and with General Philip Sheridan in his Shenandoah Valley campaign of 1864. A regimental and brigade commander, Hayes compiled a good record and steadily advanced in rank to brigadier general of volunteers by 1864. He adapted easily to army life; combat brought out his leadership qualities, and the experience made him more assured and ambitious.

Hayes's war record helped launch his postwar political career. Through the influence of a prominent Cincinnati editor, Hayes was nominated for Congress in 1864. Rather than take a furlough to campaign, he remained at the front and in October easily overwhelmed his Democratic opponent. Seated in December, 1865, and reelected the following year, Hayes served during the critical period when Congress rejected President Andrew Johnson's conservative Reconstruction policy and formulated its own.

Although some historians classify Hayes as a moderate "Centrist" in the Republican-dominated House, his voting record on most Reconstruction issues was similar to that of Radical leaders. He privately expressed reservations about harsh treatment for the former Confederate states, but he quietly supported congressional efforts to wrestle control over Reconstruction from Johnson. He voted for the Fourteenth Amendment and the final congressional plan of Reconstruction, and toward the end, he sided with those calling for Johnson's impeachment.

By the time Johnson was brought to trial, Hayes was serving the first of three terms as governor of Ohio. Nominated for the position in June, 1867, he resigned from the House the following month and won a narrow victory over Allen G. Thurman, Ohio's popular chief justice. He enhanced his reputation as a vote getter two years later when he took the "sound" money ground and won reelection over George H. Pendleton, a prominent proponent of the "Ohio Idea" to pay off the Union war debt in depreciated greenbacks.

Hayes's first two gubernatorial administrations (1868-1872) were clean and untroubled, and demonstrated his commitment to reform. He helped secure Ohio's ratification of the Fifteenth Amendment, called for a state civil service system and state regulation of railroads, and won the enactment of a coal-mining safety code. He also recommended upgrading the state's prisons and mental hospitals, and he convinced the legislature to establish a new agricultural college, which became Ohio State University in 1878.

Hayes declined to run for a third term and refused entreaties to become a candidate for fellow Republican John Sherman's seat in the U.S. Senate. Also, when several close political friends joined the Liberal Republican revolt against President Ulysses S. Grant in 1872, Hayes stayed with the regular Republican organization even though he was troubled by the Grant administration's record. In that year, Hayes reluctantly but dutifully accepted an unwanted nomination for Congress, only to suffer defeat by a narrow margin.

Out of public life for the first time since 1858, Hayes moved his family to Fremont in 1873, and early in the following year Sardis Birchard died, leaving the bulk of his estate including his fine home, Spiegel Grove, to Hayes. At fifty-two years of age in 1874, Hayes looked the part of a settled, successful man. Of medium height, with his 180 pounds distributed over a stocky frame, Hayes had dark blue eyes, a ruddy complexion, and a once reddish full beard that was now touched with gray. Of moderate tastes and conciliatory by nature, Hayes had a dignified yet open and friendly manner. Always close to his family, he enjoyed traveling, reading history, and tracing his genealogy. Hayes had done well with his own investments and, with the property inherited from Birchard, he would leave an estate of nearly a million dollars at his death.

On his return to Fremont, Hayes avowed that his public career was over. It proved to be an opportune time to be retired from Republican politics. Much troubled by corruption, a failing policy of Reconstruction, and economic depression following the panic of 1873, the Republican Party lost heavily in the elections of 1874. Still, when Republican leaders asked him to enter the gubernatorial race against incumbent Democrat William Allen in 1875, Hayes assented and conducted a vigorous campaign on the issues of sound money and free schools.

The Election of 1876: Disputed Returns

Hayes's close victory over Allen in October, 1875, and his attractive record as a moderate reformer catapulted him into the national spotlight as a possible presidential contender in 1876. As his friends began to organize in his behalf, Hayes shrewdly maintained a pose of public silence and detachment, while privately he conceded his availability and carefully avoided alliances with any of the more prominent candidates for the nomination.

The leading contender, James G. Blaine of Maine, was the three-time speaker of the House of Representatives and leader of the so-called Half-Breed faction, which at least gave lip service to reform. Grant supposedly favored New York Senator Roscoe Conkling, an avowed enemy of Blaine and the recognized leader of the Stalwart faction of machine politicians and spoilsmen. Another, somewhat milder Stalwart aspirant, Senator Oliver P. Morton of Indiana, was a favorite of Southern Republicans because of his continuing advocacy of Reconstruction. A third faction in the party, the Liberal Republican element which had bolted the party in 1872, favored reformer Benjamin H. Bristow of Kentucky.

At the national convention in June, Hayes's supporters worked quietly and effectively to make him the second choice of delegates favoring other candidates. As the front runner, Blaine became the target for all other contenders and

failed to receive a first-ballot nomination. On that ballot Hayes ran a weak fifth, but he moved up steadily. When Morton, Bristow, and Conkling were withdrawn on the seventh ballot, Hayes was the primary beneficiary and won the needed majority to defeat Blaine. To balance the ticket, the convention turned to New York Representative William A. Wheeler.

Two weeks later, the Democrats chose reform governor Samuel J. Tilden of New York as their standard-bearer with Thomas A. Hendricks of Indiana as his running mate, and what would turn out to be a long and bitter struggle for the presidency began. As was traditional, neither Tilden nor Hayes made public speeches in the canvass, although Hayes did help bring Liberal Republicans fully back into the party with a call for civil service reform in his letter accepting the nomination. Despite the clean images and reform postures of both Hayes and Tilden, however, the campaign was intensely partisan, and as the returns came in on the evening of November 7, Hayes's chances looked dim. Tilden had won the popular vote by about 250,000, and he had 184 electoral votes—just one shy of the 185 needed for victory. In addition, Democrats felt assured of victory in South Carolina, Florida, and Louisiana—the last three Southern states with Republican regimes at the time of the election. With a certain claim to only 166 electoral votes, Hayes returned late in the evening believing that he had lost the election.

In reality, however, the contest had just entered a new phase—thanks to a sudden aggressiveness at Republican campaign headquarters in New York. Party leaders, seeing the critical importance to Hayes of the three Southern states with their 19 electoral votes, asked prominent Republicans in each state if they could hold their states in the Republican column. When the positive replies came in, party chair Zach Chandler released his famous statement, "Hayes has 185 electoral votes and is elected."

Representatives of both national parties hastened South to secure the disputed states in

The Vice President
William A. Wheeler

The son of a lawyer, William Wheeler was born on June 30, 1819, in Malone, New York. As a result of an eye ailment and a lack of money, he was able to attend the University of Vermont for only one year. However, he studied law under Asa Hascell back in his hometown of Malone and was admitted to the New York bar in 1845. That same year, on September 17, he married Mary King.

Wheeler's political career began in 1846, when he held the office of district attorney of Franklin County, New York. From there, Wheeler served in the New York State Assembly from 1850 to 1851 and then in the New York Senate in 1855. In 1861, Wheeler won election to the United States House of Representatives and served just one term. However, he returned to the U.S. Congress in 1869 and was later named chairman of the Pacific Railroads Committee.

Accompanied by six other congressmen, Wheeler was sent by President Ulysses Grant to Louisiana to ease political tensions resulting from a disputed election under Reconstruction. Wheeler received acclaim for having successfully reached a compromise with the Louisiana state government. Shortly after returning from his mission, on March 3, 1876, his wife, Mary, died. The couple had no children. That same year, he was elected vice president and served with President Rutherford B. Hayes. However, still grieving the death of his wife and suffering from ill health, Wheeler retired to his home after serving one term.

Wheeler died on June 4, 1887. President Hayes eulogized his vice president by stating, "He was one of the few Vice Presidents who was on cordial terms, intimate and friendly with the President. Our family was heartily fond of him."

Robert P. Watson and Richard Yon

their interest. Republicans, certainly the more active, collected affidavits charging Democrats with intimidation, and the Republican-controlled state returning boards threw out returns from counties or parishes where it was apparent that Democrats had "bulldozed" Republican voters. By early December, the returning boards ruled that Hayes had carried the disputed states. The Democrats immediately charged the returning boards with partisanship and fraud and submitted a second set of returns signed by the minority (Democratic) members of the boards proclaiming victory for Tilden. In addition, the Democrats challenged one of Oregon's three Republican electors on the grounds that he had been a federal employee at the time of the election.

The Republican Senate and Democratic House quickly deadlocked on procedure for determining which set of returns should be accepted, and the impasse was not broken until January 29, 1877, when Congress, much to the displeasure of Hayes, agreed to form an electoral commission as a mechanism for resolving the dispute. To be composed of five members from each house of Congress and five from the Supreme Court, the commission was to hear arguments and decide which sets of returns were valid. As anticipated, the House chose three Democrats and two Republicans to sit on the commission; the Senate, three Republicans and two Democrats; and the supposedly nonpartisan Court, two known Democrats and two known Republicans. The final Court seat on the commission was to go to David Davis of Illinois, thought to be an independent, but Davis was disqualified when the Illinois legislature selected him for the Senate. With Davis eliminated, the justices chose Joseph P. Bradley, a Republican appointee, as their fifth member, and although all fifteen members were to act impartially, Hayes's chances suddenly improved.

In the interim there were some Democratic threats of insurrection if Tilden were not chosen, almost constant behind-the-scenes dealing among party partisans, and rampant speculation and rumors. For his part Hayes avoided any public statements but kept in close communication with Republicans in Washington, D.C., especially Ohioans Stanley Matthews, James A. Garfield, and John Sherman. In comparison with the Republicans, Tilden and his managers appeared ill organized and inactive—much to the distress of Southern Democrats, who feared that Southern Republican regimes might be reinforced if Tilden lost. With that eventuality in mind, some Southern Democrats conducted a useful flirtation with a handful of Northern Republicans throughout the crisis. A few Southerners, amply assisted by lobbyists for Thomas A. Scott's Texas and Pacific Railroad,

wanted pledges that Hayes, if elected, would favor further subsidies for the completion of Scott's Southern transcontinental railroad. Still others wanted Southern representation in the Hayes cabinet, and there was some loose talk of Southern Democrats allowing Republicans to organize the next House with Garfield as speaker. The parties to these talks were few, however, and overall these side issues were of little consequence in helping to resolve the dispute. Of paramount importance to the South were Republican guarantees to withdraw federal support from Republican regimes in South Carolina and Louisiana—the last two Southern states in which Republicans were still contending for control, Florida having peacefully inaugurated a Democratic administration in January.

Against this backdrop the electoral commission began work on the first of February with hearings and deliberations on Florida. Within a

The arrival of freedmen and their families in Baltimore. *(Library of Congress)*

week, the commission decided by a partisan 8-7 vote to accept the returning board's decision to award the state to Hayes. The 8-7 margin soon became familiar, with the commission awarding Louisiana, the disputed Oregon vote, and finally, on February 28, South Carolina to Hayes.

Although only one house of Congress had to accept the commission's decisions for them to take effect, the Democratic majority in the House frequently held up the count throughout February with dilatory motions and filibustering. Yet Southern Democrats could not maintain the delaying tactics alone, and the Northeastern Democratic leadership, under pressure from settlement-minded businessmen, haunted by their overwhelming endorsement of the electoral commission idea, and sensing the futility and danger of resisting its decisions, were noticeably reluctant to promote a filibuster. It was in this atmosphere that Southern Democrats sought final assurances from Northern Republicans that Hayes, once inaugurated, would agree to "home rule" for South Carolina and Louisiana.

Those assurances came in meetings between a handful of Southern Democrats and several of Hayes's close friends, and with the acquiescence of Northern Democrats, the filibustering efforts ended on March 1. The count proceeded; at 4:10 a.m. the next day, Congress declared Hayes elected with 185 electoral votes to 184 for Tilden. Hayes learned of the decision on his way to Washington, D.C., and on the evening of March 3, he privately took the oath of office in the presence of the chief justice and Grant.

Hayes in Office: Efforts Toward Reconciliation

On a cool and overcast March 5, Hayes became the nineteenth president of the United States, amid some concern for his safety. He calmly delivered a short inaugural address that stressed the "supreme importance" of settling the Southern question, repeated his call for "thorough, radical, and complete" civil service re-

form, and promised to work for specie resumption—making all currency redeemable in gold or silver—to hasten the return of prosperous times. Overall, the address was a quiet, nationalistic appeal to lay aside partisan differences and unite once again for the common good. The president, he said, should "be always mindful of the fact that he serves his party best who serves the country best."

As he noted in his diary during the electoral crisis, Hayes wanted a cabinet with no holdovers from the Grant administration, no "presidential candidates," and no appointments to "take care" of anybody. Although he did not live up to these criteria fully, the nominations he sent to the Senate reflected his interest in reform and his independence from the Stalwart faction of the party. The three key nominees were William M. Evarts of New York, a distinguished lawyer and a longtime opponent of Conkling, as secretary of state; Senate Finance Committee Chairman and close friend John Sherman as secretary of the treasury; and reformer Carl Schurz of Missouri, who had led the Liberal Republican revolt against Grant in 1872, as secretary of the interior. Of less import were Charles A. Devens, a Massachusetts Supreme Court judge, as attorney general, Congressman George M. McCrary of Iowa as secretary of war, and Richard W. Thompson of Indiana, a protégé of Senator Oliver P. Morton, as secretary of the navy. Finally, as a concession to the South, Hayes chose Senator David M. Key of Tennessee, a Democrat and former Confederate, as postmaster general.

The nominees, particularly Schurz, Evarts, and Key, quickly aroused the ire of leading Senate Stalwarts, who had been denied any voice in the selection process. There was talk of blocking approval of the whole cabinet, with Zach Chandler raging that Hayes had "passed the Republican party to its worst enemies," but reform-minded Republicans and independents supported the nominees and Hayes won the first of many clashes with con-

---

Excerpt from Rutherford B. Hayes's inaugural address, March 5, 1877:

I ask the attention of the public to the paramount necessity of reform in our civil service — a reform not merely as to certain abuses and practices of so-called official patronage which have come to have the sanction of usage in the several Departments of our Government, but a change in the system of appointment itself; a reform that shall be thorough, radical, and complete; a return to the principles and practices of the founders of the Government. They neither expected nor desired from public officers any partisan service. They meant that public officers should owe their whole service to the Government and to the people. They meant that the officer should be secure in his tenure as long as his personal character remained untarnished and the performance of his duties satisfactory. They held that appointments to office were not to be made nor expected merely as rewards for partisan services, nor merely on the nomination of members of Congress, as being entitled in any respect to the control of such appointments.

The fact that both the great political parties of the country, in declaring their principles prior to the election, gave a prominent place to the subject of reform of our civil service, recognizing and strongly urging its necessity, in terms almost identical in their specific import with those I have here employed, must be accepted as a conclusive argument in behalf of these measures. It must be regarded as the expression of the united voice and will of the whole country upon this subject, and both political parties are virtually pledged to give it their unreserved support.

The President of the United States of necessity owes his election to office to the suffrage and zealous labors of a political party, the members of which cherish with ardor and regard as of essential importance the principles of their party organization; but he should strive to be always mindful of the fact that he serves his party best who serves the country best.

---

gressional Stalwarts.

The most immediate problem facing the new administration was what to do about rival claimants for power in Louisiana and South Carolina. In Louisiana both Republican Stephen B. Packard and Democrat Frances T. Nicholls claimed to be duly elected, and a similar standoff existed in South Carolina between Republican Daniel Chamberlain and Democrat Wade Hampton. De facto authority, however, lay with the Democrats — the Republicans controlled little beyond their respective state houses, which were protected by small contingents of federal troops under orders to maintain the status quo.

Like most Northerners, Hayes had become increasingly disillusioned with the use of military force to prop up Southern Republican regimes. "There is to be an end to all that," he had written Carl Schurz in February; still, he had to move slowly. Southern Republicans beseeched

him not to abandon them; congressional Stalwarts, already irked because of his cabinet appointments, urged him to support Packard and Chamberlain; and old Northern Radicals and abolitionists readily joined the chorus. After several weeks of delay, Hayes extracted pledges from Hampton to safeguard the rights of all South Carolina citizens, and when he removed the soldiers from the state house on April 10, Chamberlain reluctantly relinquished the governor's office to Hampton. Ten days later, after securing promises from Nicholls in Louisiana that blacks and other Republicans would be protected in their rights and not prosecuted "for past political conduct," Hayes withdrew the troops from the Packard-held state house, and Reconstruction was over — much to the relief of Southern conservatives and most Northerners.

Removal of the troops was only the first part of Hayes's broader Southern strategy to attract former Whigs and "respectable" Democrats to the Republican standard through a conciliatory posture and a nonpartisan patronage policy. Working with Key and other advisers, Hayes went out of his way to appoint Democrats to federal positions in the South—one-third of his Southern appointments during the first five months went to conservatives. To demonstrate further his good will, in September, 1877, Hayes and a large party toured several Southern states—accompanied most of the way by Governor Hampton of South Carolina. The entourage received enthusiastic receptions and Hayes returned much encouraged.

Other signs, however, were not as positive. Democrats who had accepted patronage positions remained Democrats and sometimes turned even more vehemently on Republicans in their areas. When the new Forty-fifth Congress met in October, 1877, no Southern Democrats voted to help Republicans organize the House—allegedly violating a promise given during the electoral crisis. (Shortly after this, Hayes came out directly against further federal subsidies for the Texas and Pacific Railroad, and another frail compromise agreement fell by the wayside.) Moreover, in local elections in November, the South went heavily Democratic.

Criticism of Hayes's policy from within the party steadily increased as prominent leaders charged him with destroying what remained of the Southern Republican Party and abandoning the freedmen to the care of brutal Redeemers. By early 1878, party support for his Southern policy had evaporated, and in the November elections fraud, violence, and widespread intimidation of black voters created as solidly a Democratic South as the nation had yet seen. Only four Republicans remained in the sixty-three-man Southern delegation to the House, and Democrats won control of the Senate for the first time since before the war.

In an interview after the election, Hayes lamented the Southerners' failure to live up to their promises to protect black voters and reluctantly admitted "that the experiment was a failure." In fact, his Southern strategy was a pipe dream that showed no understanding of the depth of racial prejudice and the degree to which party loyalty had become an article of faith among white Southerners. True to his Whiggish background and lifelong desire for harmony, Hayes had tried conciliation to ease out of Reconstruction, but his naïve and misplaced faith in Southern conservatives led to failure. In his defense, his alternatives were perhaps nonexistent—given the failure of coercion, the pervasiveness of Southern racism, and the absence of continued Northern commitment to safeguarding the rights of Southern blacks.

Forced after the elections of 1878 to take a harder line against the South, Hayes called for larger appropriations to enforce the election laws, but the lame duck Congress failed to take action. When the new Congress met in 1879, the Democrats, now in control of both Houses, attached riders repealing federal election laws to appropriation bills, but they were stopped by five separate Hayes vetoes—much to the pleasure of congressional Republicans and the party press. As a result, Southern repression of the freedmen, made all the more evident by the plight of black "Exodusters" leaving the South, served to reunite the various Northern Republican factions in the campaign of 1880 against a solidly Democratic South—the reverse of what Hayes had initially intended.

An Unfortunate Precedent: Federal Troops and the Railroad Strike of 1877

Whereas Hayes declined to use federal force in the South, he believed that he had to use it in the railroad strike of 1877. Railroad labor had, with good cause, been restive for some time. The ongoing depression had trimmed railroad revenues, less available work meant increased idle time with no pay for many employees, and several lines had cut the wages of their already hard-pressed labor force.

The crisis began on July 16, when a 10-

percent wage cut was to go into effect on the Baltimore and Ohio Railroad. Workers walked off their jobs and began stopping trains in Maryland and West Virginia. Strikes against other lines, marked by a considerable amount of looting, violence, and loss of life, soon followed. Some fourteen midwestern and northeastern states were affected, and at one point strikes closed all five major trunk lines from the East to the Midwest. Local police forces and state militia often proved incapable of controlling the situation; in a period of eight days the administration received requests for aid from nine governors. After cabinet debate, Hayes issued warnings against further disorder, sending federal troops to four states. The soldiers restored order without further bloodshed, and the crisis was over in a few weeks.

Although Hayes had avoided declaring martial law and sent troops only when the governors had convinced him that the situation was beyond their control, his actions set an unfortunate precedent for the use of the federal military to break strikes. As he confided to his diary, he knew that the workers' grievances deserved attention, but he made no recommendations for new work laws, and Congress showed little interest in legislation to ease the workers' plight.

The Currency Question

In part, the railroad strikes resulted from a troubled economy and a set of monetary problems that had plagued the government since the end of the Civil War. Forced off the gold standard in late 1861, the Union had resorted to nonspecie-backed currency (the "greenbacks"), which had quickly depreciated. Fiscal conservatives such as Hayes believed a gradual contraction of the currency necessary to return it to par with gold, but a banking panic in September, 1873, thrust the nation into an economic depression which spawned inflationist sentiment in both parties. In an effort to restore Republican Party unity on the money question, John Sherman and other hard-money advocates pushed through the Resumption Act in early 1875. The act provided for gradual contraction of the greenbacks and directed the secretary of the treasury to build a gold reserve in preparation for the resumption of specie payments on January 1, 1879.

Hayes had advocated hard money and specie resumption in his gubernatorial campaigns, and his choice of Sherman to head the Treasury Department was a signal to businessmen and creditors that his administration would work to achieve resumption. Quite clearly, the contraction of the greenback circulation in preparation for resumption hurt the debt-ridden farmers in the South and West, and there were sound arguments that the nation needed a greater volume of currency. Hayes, however, believed that the nation's paper currency must be redeemable in gold: He considered resumption critical to restoring confidence in the economy and ending the depression. Through Sherman's diligent stockpiling of gold and shrewd management of bond issues, greenbacks reached par with gold late in 1878, and on January 2, 1879, greenbacks were favored over gold in New York markets. Most of the plaudits by financial and commercial interests went to Sherman, but his success was at least partially the result of Hayes's backing and persistence.

Meanwhile, many of those demanding an expansion of the monetary circulation had turned to silver as a new panacea for the nation's economic problems. Silver had originally circulated with gold (in a set 16-1 ratio in value) as legal tender, but owing to its increasing scarcity before the war, silver began commanding a premium in gold and generally disappeared from circulation. In 1873, Congress had quietly discontinued coinage of the silver dollar and restricted the legal tender power of silver to amounts not exceeding five dollars. This action, which later gained notoriety as the "Crime of '73," effectively demonetized silver. In late 1876, after considerable agitation by inflationists and silver-mining interests, the House passed Democrat Richard P. Bland's bill to renew coinage of the silver dollar and restore its legal tender status, but the Senate, in the midst of the electoral crisis, failed to take action.

When the new Congress convened in late 1877, the House repassed the Bland bill and sent it to the Senate, where Finance Committee Chair William Boyd Allison reported it with an amendment limiting government purchases of silver for coinage to between $2 million and $4 million a month. In the meantime, both houses had passed a concurrent resolution declaring that the principal and interest on the public debt might be paid in silver dollars. The chambers agreed to the Bland bill as modified by Allison's amendment and sent it to Hayes for his signature.

In the firm belief that gold should be the sole standard of value, Hayes vetoed the Bland-Allison bill, declaring that it would be "justly regarded as a grave breach of the public faith" to pay the public debt in silver coin. Both chambers quickly overrode the veto (the only successful override among Hayes's thirteen vetoes), and to the president's disappointment the nation went back to a limited extent on the bimetallic standard.

Fraud and Favoritism: Charges and Countercharges

As Hayes confided to his diary after Congress overrode his veto of the silver bill, "I am not much liked as a president by the politicians in office, in the press or in Congress." In addition to encountering opposition to his monetary and Southern policies, Hayes had just lost a round in his efforts to reform the New York Customhouse. To add to his troubles, later that spring House Democrats began to investigate new allegations that in 1876 Republicans had used fraud to secure a Hayes victory in Florida and Louisiana. Although Hayes was not directly implicated, the reputation of the men who

The Sixth Maryland militia opens fire on railroad strikers on July 20, 1877, killing twelve. *(Library of Congress)*

served as his managers during the electoral dispute were damaged by the revelations of the investigating committee headed by Clarkson N. Potter. Sherman suffered the most. Although he denied ever promising to "take care" of members of the Louisiana returning board as alleged, an inordinate number of tainted Louisiana Republicans later secured jobs in the Hayes administration—particularly in Sherman's Treasury Department.

It was an ordeal for Hayes, but his fortunes improved in October when the Republican *New York Tribune* decoded and published a series of secret telegrams sent by Democrats during the electoral crisis which implicated Democrats, including some close to Tilden, in corrupt dealings with the Florida and South Carolina returning boards. Much to the embarrassment of Democrats, House Republicans forced the Potter Committee to look into the "cipher dispatches." In the end, the involvement of Democrats in wrongdoing took much of the pressure off the Republicans, and Hayes himself later counted the Potter investigation as one of the "most fortunate" episodes in his administration. Still, the ongoing dispute over his title to the office haunted his presidency. The stinging epithets of "Rutherfraud" and "His Fraudulency" were favorites of a particularly abusive Democratic press, and many Republican editors, piqued over his appointments, Southern policy, antisilver stance, prohibition policy at White House functions, and the like, were often less than cordial until late in his term. Hayes endured the abuse and deprecation silently, rarely responding in public and taking solace in gatherings of family and friends and a wide range of White House activities and visitors.

Civil Service Reform: A Mixed Record

In his inaugural address, Hayes had stressed the pressing need for civil service reform—a plea repeated in his annual messages to Congress. Although Congress remained singularly unresponsive, Hayes took some significant steps on his own to start cleaning up the spoils system. His first executive order instructed officers in all departments of the government not "to take part in the management of political organizations, caucuses, conventions, or election campaigns" and prohibited the common practice of assessing officers and subordinates for political contributions. Enforcement of the order varied from department to department, and later "voluntary" contributions were permitted, but it was an important step toward reform. Believing that satisfactory officeholders should have security, Hayes removed fewer government employees than had most previous presidents. He also encouraged the use of competitive merit examinations for subordinate jobs, made extensive nonpartisan appointments, and resolutely avoided nepotism.

His own high-level appointments tended to be solid, able, and occasionally outstanding men—his placing of John Marshall Harlan of Kentucky on the Supreme Court is a prime example. He also won the applause of civil service reformers for appointing Schurz to the cabinet and allowing him an influential voice. Schurz effectively applied civil service standards in a four-year effort to clean up the Department of the Interior and was especially active in reforming the Indian Bureau, both in personnel and with new sets of regulations. Although American Indians suffered their last major defeats at the hands of the military during the Hayes years, Schurz's reforms lessened the bitterness and helped launch a new era in American Indian relations.

Still, Hayes's appointment record was a mix of reform impulses and partisan and personal considerations that often frustrated civil service reformers outside the administration. His appointment of Southern Democrats to federal offices was done in a spirit of reconciliation and nonpartisanship, but it also represented an effort to build the Republican Party in the South. Similarly, his choice of black leader Frederick Douglass as marshal for the District of Columbia was at least partially intended to disarm critics who claimed that he was abandoning the freedmen. He rewarded key people who had worked for his nomination and election and served his interests during the electoral crisis, and he received a substantial amount of criticism late in his term for nominating Stanley Matthews to the Supreme Court. The press saw the nomination, admittedly personal, as a reward for Matthews's work during the electoral crisis, and the Senate rejected the nomination. Finally, despite hints of wrongdoing, neither Hayes, Key, nor Horace Maynard, who became postmaster general late in the administration, probed deeply enough to uncover the ongoing corruption in the postal service inherited from the Grant administration. The problem, which erupted as the notorious Star Route frauds after Hayes had left office, became the only major blot on his administrative record.

Hayes's mixed motives, his caution as a re-

former, and his battle to win back some control over federal appointments from entrenched Stalwart senators were evident in his celebrated effort to reform the New York Customhouse. Most of the more than one thousand customhouse employees owed their positions to the patronage of Senator Roscoe Conkling's Stalwart faction of the New York Republican Party, and there was ample evidence of favoritism to New York merchants, bribery, fraud, and inefficiency.

Hayes decided early to make the customhouse a showcase for civil service reform, but it also presented an opportunity to strike at Conkling's machine while perhaps elevating the opposing faction to which Secretary of State Evarts belonged. After an investigation detailed customhouse "irregularities" in late May, 1877, Hayes asked for the resignation of Collector Chester A. Arthur and Naval Officer Alonzo B. Cornell. Both refused, and Cornell openly de-

Hayes welcomes Chun Lan Pin, the first Chinese minister to the United States, in 1878. *(Library of Congress)*

fied Hayes's executive order forbidding political activity. Rather than removing them forthwith as reformers wished, Hayes waited until Congress returned in October to recommend anti-Conkling replacements. Conkling quickly lined up Senate opposition on the grounds that Hayes was trampling over the "right" of senators to control patronage, and all but six Republicans voted with the majority to reject the nominees.

After Congress adjourned for the summer of 1878, Hayes struck back and replaced Arthur with Surveyor Edwin A. Merritt and Cornell with Deputy Naval Officer Silas W. Burt, long a favorite of reformers. Although the new appointments were less obnoxious to the Stalwart faction, Conkling renewed the fight when Congress reconvened in December. A majority of Republican senators still voted against the appointments, but Hayes finally won approval for them in February, 1879, after a two-year struggle—thanks to Democratic support, the switch of a few more Republican votes, and some astute lobbying by Sherman. Most important, Merritt and especially Burt took seriously Hayes's instructions to organize the customhouse in a more efficient and businesslike manner. Although problems remained with political activity, the operation of the customhouse under Merritt and Burt pleased reformers and showed that civil service reform would work.

Foreign Relations

In contrast to the troubles at home, foreign relations were relatively peaceful during the Hayes years. The major ongoing problem involved Mexico, where Porfirio Díaz had overthrown the established government in 1876. Because counterrevolutionary activity kept Díaz from preventing Mexican and Indian raids on U.S. soil, Hayes withheld diplomatic recognition and, in June, 1877, authorized army commanders in Texas to pursue the raiders back across the border. Although Hayes finally extended diplomatic recognition in April, 1878, the "hot pursuit" policy remained in effect until Díaz was able to suppress the raids to Secretary of State Evarts's satisfaction early in 1880.

In another area, violent anti-Chinese demonstrations in San Francisco during the summer of 1877 prompted Congress to pass a bill restricting Chinese immigration in early 1879. Hayes personally favored restriction, but he feared that the congressional bill, which revoked part of the Burlington Treaty with China, might lead the Chinese to abrogate the entire treaty. Rather than risking the loss of the commercially favorable treaty and possibly creating a situation endangering Americans in China, Hayes vetoed the bill and quickly sent a commission to China to negotiate a new treaty. The Chinese agreed to a new commercial agreement and another treaty, approved in early 1881, to regulate immigration as the United States desired.

A final diplomatic problem emerged in 1879 when Ferdinand de Lesseps, the French engineer who had built the Suez Canal, unveiled a plan to construct a canal across the Panama isthmus. While trying to secure French support, de Lesseps also offered construction company stock to Americans. In a strong message to the Senate, Hayes declared that the United States would not surrender control of the canal project to foreign powers, nor would it support a private building company backed largely by foreign capital. With neither French nor American backing, de Lesseps began the project in the early 1880's, but his company collapsed later in the decade. In the meantime, Hayes had helped shape American policy for eventual control of the isthmian canal.

When he accepted the Republican nomination in 1876, Hayes had expressed his "inflexible purpose" to retire after only one term. As the election year of 1880 approached, he was tired of the office—yet perhaps disappointed that no party leader encouraged a draft movement that he could then decline. He took no part in the

363

process of selecting a Republican candidate and made no endorsements. Garfield's nomination pleased him, but instead of campaigning he left the White House in late August for an extensive tour of the Far West and did not return until the day before the election. Garfield's victory and the return of both houses of Congress to Republican control, which Hayes viewed as a vindication of his policies, brightened his last months in office. He relished the final White House functions and the tributes paid his administration by friends and former opponents, but as he noted in his diary, he looked forward to "retiring from this conspicuous scene to the freedom, independence and safety of our obscure and happy home in the pleasant grove at Fremont."

After Garfield's inauguration the Hayes family returned to Fremont, where Hayes immersed himself in community organizations, worked to improve his Spiegel Grove estate, and traveled extensively with Lucy and his family. He seldom missed the annual reunions of Civil War veterans. In the belief that education offered the best hope for resolving the South's racial problem, he served as a trustee of the Peabody Educational Fund for the South and as president of the Slater Fund for black education.

Although he maintained a private interest in politics, he removed himself completely from the public political scene and had little association with those still active in the party. With the exception of appearing at funerals for Garfield, Grant, Arthur, and others, he disappeared, largely forgotten, from the public eye. What is most interesting, his political philosophy changed in his later years. Strongly influenced by the social criticism of Henry George, Mark Twain, and William Dean Howells, he worried about the emergence of monopolies, the decline of fair competition, the deteriorating condition of labor, and the general corrupting influence that "vast accumulations of wealth" had on society.

As he lamented the course the country was taking, Lucy suffered a stroke in June, 1889, and died a few days later. Although the shock of her passing affected him deeply, he busied himself with a heavy regime of travel and work. While in Cleveland on business in January, 1893, he suffered a sharp chest pain and his son hurried him back to Fremont. Bedridden, he talked of plans to travel, yet knew that he was "going where Lucy is." He died late in the evening of January 17.

Hayes's Presidency in Retrospect

Despite the political turbulence that marked his years in office, historians have tended to view the Hayes administration as something of a calming, transitional regime during which the nation withdrew from the turmoil of Reconstruction and settled down after the Grant years. Reconstruction was ended — with bitterness and acrimony in some quarters, with relief in others. After five years of depression the economy revived and stabilized, perhaps aided, as Hayes believed, by specie resumption. The nation continued its emergence as an industrial power, with all the attendant problems of business concentration, labor unrest, and market expansion.

In their periodic evaluations of presidential performance, historians and other commentators have consistently ranked that of Hayes toward the top and more recently in the middle of the "average" category. Hayes might well have been satisfied with this ranking given the difficulties he faced. Handicapped from the beginning by his disputed title, Hayes entered the office of the presidency in the midst of economic depression and would have to preside over the bitter end of Reconstruction. With the exception of a Republican Senate during the first two years of his administration, he had to work with a hostile Democratic Congress, and he often faced considerable congressional opposition from within his own party. Some of his problems, however, were of his own making. Hayes proved far more adept at seeking the office than in occupying it effectively. Once in the presidency, he was often too independent and high-minded for his own good, too much the nonpartisan nationalist and too little the pragmatic party politician. At times he appeared to lack the drive and a good sense of the best means of achieving his often laudatory goals. In the case of civil service reform, he seemed content to do what he could on his own and to make general recommendations to Congress, but he never pushed vigorously, working and lobbying with Congress, for specific reform legislation. At other times, as in the case of his Southern policy, he was too abrupt in choosing his course and then too resolute in adhering to it. Often he would have been better served if he had listened to others than his cabinet advisers and worked with party leaders to make adjustments in his programs and policies. In an age of close party divisions in Congress, he also needed to establish a working relationship with powerful factions in the party, but on the whole he failed to do so.

These factors and others clearly limited his performance. His two primary goals when he entered the office—to promote sectional reconciliation and civil service reform—were achieved only to a limited extent. Some recent historians have been particularly harsh in evaluating his Southern policy—especially his misplaced trust in southern conservatives to treat African Americans fairly. Yet even in retrospect viable alternatives are not apparent given the overriding racial problems. Although Congress ignored his pleas for civil service reform and he often failed to live up to his own standards in appointments, he did lay some important groundwork for later reform efforts. With his attempts to win greater control over appointments from Congress and his vetoes of the Democratic riders, he also restored some of the independence and power to the executive branch that had been lost beginning with the presidency of Andrew Johnson. Finally, Hayes worked diligently to restore respectability and a measure of dignity to the office. This was per-haps his chief legacy when he left the presidency in 1881.

Terry L. Seip

Suggested Readings

Barnard, Harry. *Rutherford B. Hayes and His America*. 1954. Reprint. New York: Russell and Russell, 1967. Considered by many to be the standard biography of Hayes.

Benedict, Michael L. "Southern Democrats in the Crisis of 1876-1877: A Reconsideration of Reunion and Reaction." *Journal of Southern History* 46 (November, 1980): 489-524. Argues for a reconsideration of the events during the crisis.

Davidson, Kenneth E. *The Presidency of Rutherford B. Hayes*. Westport, Conn.: Greenwood Press, 1972. A thorough coverage of the White House years.

De Santis, Vincent P. *Republicans Face the Southern Question: The New Departure Years, 1877-1897*. Baltimore: Johns Hopkins University Press, 1959. Chronicles the development of Hayes's Southern policy.

Gillette, William. *Retreat from Reconstruction, 1869-1879*. Baton Rouge: Louisiana State University Press, 1979. A critical view of the Hayes presidency and his policy toward the South.

Hayes, Rutherford B. *Hayes: The Diary of a President, 1875-1881*. Edited by T. Harry Williams. New York: D. McKay, 1964. A consistent diary keeper, Hayes left a valuable record of his administration.

Hayes Presidential Center. *Hayes Historical Journal: A Journal of the Gilded Age*. In semiannual publication since 1976, the journal features scholarly articles on Hayes and his times.

Hirshson, Stanley P. *Farewell to the Bloody Shirt: Northern Republicans and the Southern Negro, 1877-1893*. Bloomington: Indiana University Press, 1962. Covers Hayes's Southern policy.

Hoogenboom, Ari A. *The Presidency of Rutherford B. Hayes*. Lawrence: University Press of Kansas, 1988. A good overview of

Hayes's presidency.

_____. *Rutherford B. Hayes: Warrior and President.* Lawrence: University Press of Kansas, 1995. A biography that was released nearly fifty years after the last significant one, this volume has received praise by critics for being revisionist, comprehensive, and relevant.

Morris, Roy. *Fraud of the Century: Rutherford B. Hayes, Samuel Tilden, and the Stolen Election of 1876.* New York: Simon & Schuster, 2003. Details the politics and personalities involved in the contested 1876 election.

Perry, James M. *Touched with Fire: Five Presidents and the Civil War Battles That Made Them.* New York: PublicAffairs, 2005. Uses diaries, letters, and other firsthand accounts to bring life to the war battles that formed the character and political drive of presidents Grant, Hayes, Garfield, Harrison, and McKinley.

Polakoff, Keith I. *The Politics of Inertia: The Election of 1876 and the End of Reconstruction.* Baton Rouge: Louisiana State University Press, 1973. Examines the electoral crisis and the resulting tensions and forged political relationships.

Rutherford B. Hayes Presidential Center. http://www.rbhayes.org/hayes/. The official Web site of Hayes's former home, now a library and museum.

Williams, T. Harry. *Hayes of the Twenty-third: The Civil War Volunteer Officer.* New York: Knopf, 1965. A perceptive treatment of Hayes's wartime experiences.

Woodward, C. Vann. *Reunion and Reaction: The Compromise of 1877 and the End of Reconstruction.* Boston: Little, Brown, 1951. Details the complex, behind-the-scenes negotiations during the electoral dispute.

James A. Garfield

20th President, 1881

Born: November 19, 1831
      Orange Township, Ohio
Died: September 19, 1881
      Elberon, New Jersey

Political Party: Republican
Vice President: Chester A. Arthur

Cabinet Members

Secretary of State: James G. Blaine
Secretary of the Treasury: William Windom
Secretary of War: Robert Todd Lincoln
Secretary of the Navy: William Hunt
Attorney General: Wayne MacVeagh
Postmaster General: Thomas James
Secretary of the Interior: S. J. Kirkwood

It was hardly a coincidence that one of James Abram Garfield's campaign biographies was written by Horatio Alger. The last president to have been born in a log cabin, Garfield seemed to have stepped out of the pages of one of Alger's novels. Born in Orange Township near Cleveland, Ohio, on November 19, 1831, left fatherless as an infant, reared in rural poverty by his plucky mother, canal boy, carpenter, student (at what would later be Hiram College and then at Williams College in Massachusetts), preacher in the Disciples of Christ denomination, professor of ancient languages, Civil War hero, and eight-term congressman, he combined in one career the politically potent themes of home, mother, school, church, and country. Above all, he seemed to embody the American dream of upward mobility. As Rutherford B. Hayes put it, "The boy on the tow path has become in truth the scholar and the gentleman by

his own unaided work. He is the ideal candidate because he is the ideal self-made man."

The real James A. Garfield was more complex than this caricature. A scholarly, introspective man, lacking in self-confidence, he projected an aura of amiability that misled some into dismissing him as a shallow backslapper. Actually, he was a misplaced intellectual cast into the world of action. Gifted with a prodi-

Portrait of James A. Garfield. *(Whitehouse.gov)*

The First Lady
Lucretia Garfield

Lucretia Randolph Garfield served as First Lady for only six months. Born on April 19, 1832, in Garrettsville, Ohio, her parents were well-to-do farmers who believed in the education of women. Lucretia (known as "Crete") completed both grade school and college and became a teacher. Independent and strong willed, Lucretia was initially uncertain of marriage. She informed her future husband, "My heart is not yet schooled to an entire submission to that destiny which will make me the wife of one who marries me."

After a long courtship, she married Garfield, a schoolmate, on November 11, 1858. The marriage started out poorly but developed into a very close partnership. They had a total of seven children, with five living to adulthood.

In 1869, as James's political career prospered as a congressman from Ohio, the Garfields moved to Washington, D.C., and settled down for the first time in his career. She transformed the house into the model of Victorian domesticity, and this period was a happy time. As her children grew up, Lucretia began to take more of an interest in her husband's career.

She was a great help to her husband. Her pragmatism naturally tempered his idealism and made him a more effective politician. However, her usefulness to him as president was short lived—he was shot on July 2, 1881, by an assassin. Although she heroically nursed Garfield for two months, he died on September 19, 1881.

She became the first presidential widow to organize her husband's memorial service. She spent the rest of her life arranging her husband's papers for posterity, writing letters, and basking in the success of her children. In her later years, she moved to California and stayed active. In a show of her independent streak, she supported Democrat Woodrow Wilson in 1916. Two years later, on March 14, 1918, Lucretia died at the age of eighty-five in Pasadena, California.

Robert Flatley

gious memory and a fanatic capacity for sustained intellectual effort, he seemed more at home in the classroom or library than in the rough-and-tumble of the political arena. Yet he never lost an election in his life, and in a political environment characterized by blood feuds and bitter personal vendettas, he stood out as a man virtually without enemies.

It was this quality of accommodation as much as anything else that led to his surprise nomination for president in 1880. Garfield had come to the Republican National Convention in Chicago as the floor manager for Ohio's John Sherman. The leading candidate was Ulysses S. Grant, whose third-term bid was led by New York's haughty and imperious boss, Roscoe Conkling. A great hater, Conkling was not even on speaking terms with James G. Blaine, Grant's leading competitor for the nomination, nor had he ever forgiven Sherman for his role in firing Conkling's protégé, Chester A. Arthur, from his post as collector of the port of New York. Riven by such deep personal and factional fissures, the convention deadlocked, with neither the friends of Grant (the so-called Stalwarts) nor his opponents willing to yield to the other. On the thirty-sixth ballot, the convention spontaneously and dramatically turned to Garfield, who was not an avowed candidate but who was the one man acceptable to all elements of the party. Arthur was chosen as his running mate as a sop to the Stalwarts.

The Republican presidential nominee had all the makings of an attractive candidate: muscular, 6 feet tall, with a full beard (though balding) and a golden voice. He would have been an eloquent, persuasive campaigner had not nineteenth century convention dictated that presidential candidates should pretend not to electioneer on their own behalf as did candidates for lesser office. Garfield ingeniously evaded this restriction by inventing what would later be called the front porch campaign: staying at home in Mentor and greeting visiting delegations with noncampaigning campaign speeches.

His victory in November was the closest on record: only a 7,368 vote plurality over the Democratic candidate, Winfield Scott Hancock, less than one-tenth of 1 percent of the total vote cast. This narrow margin dramatized the necessity for party unity. Had any Republican other than Garfield been nominated, he very likely would have lost the votes of some members of the rival faction and thereby lost the election. The culti-

vation of Republican unity, therefore, became Garfield's first order of business as president.

An Aborted Presidency

The new president tried his best, but the gap between Republican factions was too wide to be bridged by good intentions. The first signs of trouble appeared even before the inauguration with the construction of the cabinet. When the choice post of secretary of state was offered to Blaine, Conkling demanded the right to choose the equally prestigious secretary of the treasury. His choice was unacceptable to Garfield. Rather than compromise, Conkling attempted to force his followers to boycott the ungrateful administration. With remarkable patience, the president persisted in his attempts to placate Conkling and his friends by offering them other offices.

Now it was Blaine's turn to be alarmed. He induced Garfield to appoint William H. Robert-

---

The Vice President
Chester A. Arthur

Chester Arthur was born on October 5, 1829, in Fairfield, Vermont. He graduated from Union College and went to work at the law firm of Culver and Parker in New York City. Within a few months, he was admitted to the bar and became a partner in the firm. On October 25, 1859, Arthur married Ellen Lewis Herndon, and the couple had two children.

With the start of the Civil War, he was named assistant quartermaster general of the New York militia and was promoted to quartermaster general after the post was vacated because of retirement. After the Civil War ended, Arthur was hired as an attorney for the New York City Tax Commission. For seven years, beginning in 1871, he worked as the collector of fees of the port of New York City. After being dismissed from the position in 1878 by President Rutherford B. Hayes for soliciting money from employees for the Republican Party, he returned to his law practice. Two years later, Arthur was devastated by the untimely death of his wife as a result of pneumonia. That same year he was elected vice president on the ticket with President James Garfield. However, only four months after taking office, President Garfield was shot by an assassin; he died from his injuries ten weeks later.

Arthur took the oath of office as president on September 20, 1881. As president, he signed into law a bill creating the Federal Civil Service system, which ended the spoils system, and he redecorated the White House in late Victorian style. Unable to secure the nomination as president in his own right, he returned to his law firm in New York City to resume practice. Not as active as he once was as a result of failing health, he had a stroke on November 18, 1886, and died two days later.

Robert P. Watson and Richard Yon

The assassination of Garfield. *(Library of Congress)*

son's appointment by invoking the hallowed principle of "senatorial courtesy," the struggle took on the aspect of a constitutional crisis. Garfield's stand could now be portrayed as a struggle for presidential independence from congressional dictation. Ever since the Civil War, the power of the presidential office had been in decline. The impeachment trial of Andrew Johnson represented the low point of that decline. The passive presidential style of Grant and the clouded title of Hayes had not appreciably strengthened the office. Now, by accepting the challenge of a powerful senator, Garfield was making a dramatic test of the potential power residing in the White House.

His victory was complete. Not only was the Robertson appointment confirmed, but also Conkling and his fellow New York senator, Thomas Platt, resigned their seats in protest. By destroying Conkling, Garfield had dramatically enhanced the power of his office and set the presidency on the road to the twentieth century.

Although the struggle against senatorial courtesy overshadowed all else, there were other significant activities in the early days of the Garfield administration. Since the House of Representatives was not in session, no legislation could be introduced, but the executive departments were off to a strong start. Postmaster General Thomas James was considering a plan to reform the patronage abuses of the postal system. Discovery of an earlier abuse of the so-called Star Route postal service spurred Attorney General Wayne MacVeagh to launch an investigation, even though the suspects were highly placed Republicans. Secretary of Treasury William Windom triumphantly refunded the national debt, and Secretary of the Navy William Hunt took the first significant steps

son as collector of the port of New York. Since Robertson was a Conkling foe, it was hardly surprising that the New York senator strongly opposed the appointment. Realizing that he was being whipsawed between the rival factions of his party, Garfield attempted to reach an understanding with Conkling, but the arrogant senator rejected any compromise and declared war on his own party's leader. This drove Garfield firmly back into Blaine's camp, where his inclinations probably would have led him in any event.

What had begun as a petty patronage squabble now escalated into a struggle for the soul of the Republican Party. Conkling represented machine politics in its most narrow and retrogressive form; Blaine and Garfield were groping for a more modern national organization capable of promoting industrial growth and an aggressive foreign policy.

When Conkling undertook to block Robert-

since the Civil War to rebuild the decaying United States Navy. The most vigorous activity came from the State Department, where Blaine was attempting to reorient American foreign policy rom its traditional emphasis on Europe to a greater concern with what today would be called the Third World, especially Latin America.

The president's energies were largely consumed by patronage matters. With more than a hundred thousand government offices needing to be filled, with office seekers hovering around him as eager as "vultures for a wounded bison," he had time for little else. "My services ought to be worth more to the government than to be thus spent," he wearily concluded, and he began to consider schemes for general civil service reform. He was also considering a fresh approach to the perennial Southern problem, which would feature federal aid to education as the solution for black economic and political handicaps.

Nothing came of any of these initiatives. On July 2, 1881, after only 120 days in office, Garfield was cut down by a crazed religious fanatic, Charles Julius Guiteau. The president lingered for another eighty days amid the glare of morbid public curiosity and died on September 19.

What sort of president Garfield might have become had he been spared can never be determined with certainty. John Hay, Abraham Lincoln's private secretary, thought that Garfield had entered office with better training and greater intellectual endowments than any president for more than half a century. After a shaky beginning, his administration was beginning to live up to that glowing assessment, until Guiteau's bullets brought it to an abrupt end, leaving it to enter history only as a question mark.

Allan Peskin

Suggested Readings

Ackerman, Kenneth D. *Dark Horse: The Surprise Election and Political Murder of President James A. Garfield*. New York: Carroll & Graf, 2003. An engaging read about Gilded Age political culture, Garfield's campaign for presidency, and the public's reaction to his win.

Bates, Richard O. *The Gentleman from Ohio: An Introduction to Garfield*. Durham, N.C.: Moore, 1973. An accessible biography.

Booraem, Hendrik. *The Road to Respectability: James A. Garfield and His World, 1844-1852*. Lewisburg, Pa.: Bucknell University Press, 1988. Traces the political rise of Garfield.

Clark, James C. *The Murder of James A. Garfield: The President's Last Days and the Trial and Execution of His Assassin*. Jefferson, N.C.: McFarland, 1993. Recounts Garfield's death.

Doenecke, Justus D. *The Presidencies of James A. Garfield and Chester A. Arthur*. Lawrence: Regents Press of America, 1981. Draws parallels and distinctions between Garfield and Arthur.

Garfield, James A. *The Diary of James A. Garfield*. Edited by Harry James Brown and Frederick D. Williams. East Lansing: Michigan State University Press, 1967-1981. Garfield's inner life is presented with remarkable candor. The fourth (and final) volume deals with the presidency.

Hoogenboom, Ari. *Outlawing the Spoils: A History of the Civil Service Reform Movement, 1865-1883*. Urbana: University of Illinois Press, 1961. Clarifies Garfield's split with Conkling.

Leech, Margaret P., and Harry James Brown. *The Garfield Orbit*. New York: Harper & Row, 1978. A solid discussion of Garfield's life and times.

Marcus, Robert D. *Grand Old Party: Political Structure in the Gilded Age*. New York: Oxford University Press, 1971. Traces the growth of party organization during Garfield's era.

Morgan, H. Wayne. *From Hayes to McKinley: National Party Politics, 1877-1896*. Syracuse, N.Y.: Syracuse University Press, 1969. A highly readable survey of the politics of the Gilded Age.

Perry, James M. *Touched with Fire: Five Presi-

dents and the Civil War Battles That Made Them. New York: PublicAffairs, 2005. Uses diaries, letters, and other firsthand accounts to bring life to the war battles that formed the character and political drive of presidents Grant, Hayes, Garfield, Harrison, and McKinley.

Rupp, Robert O. *James A. Garfield: A Bibliography.* Westport, Conn.: Greenwood Press, 1997. A detailed annotated list of primary and secondary resources.

Shaw, John, ed. *Crete and James: Personal Letters of Lucretia and James Garfield.* East Lansing: Michigan State University Press, 1994. Gives excellent insight into Garfield's courtship and marriage as well as details of his daily life between 1853 and 1881.

Smith, Theodore C. *The Life and Letters of James Abram Garfield.* New Haven, Conn.: Yale University Press, 1925. After a spate of campaign and memorial biographies in 1880 and 1881, Garfield was neglected until this monumental publication.

Chester A. Arthur

21st President, 1881-1885

Born: October 5, 1829
    Fairfield, Vermont
Died: November 18, 1886
    New York, New York

Political Party: Republican
Vice President: none

Cabinet Members

Secretary of State: Frederick T. Frelinghuysen
Secretary of the Treasury: Charles J. Folger,
    Walter Q. Gresham, Hugh McCulloch
Secretary of War: Robert Todd Lincoln
Secretary of the Navy: William E. Chandler
Attorney General: Benjamin J. Brewster
Postmaster General: Thomas James,
    Timothy O. Howe, Walter Q. Gresham,
    Frank Hatton
Secretary of the Interior: Henry M. Teller

In American political folklore, the career of Chester Alan Arthur reads something like Hans Christian Andersen's tale of the Ugly Duckling. In this fable, Chet Arthur, a faintly corrupt, highly partisan politician, is magically transformed into a competent, dignified, mildly reformist president, much to everyone's delight and astonishment. As a contemporary put it, "No man ever entered the Presidency so profoundly and widely distrusted as Chester Alan Arthur, and no one ever retired from the highest civil trust of the world more generally respected, alike by political friend and foe."

A Victorian Gentleman

In truth, however, this alleged transformation was not as startling as it has been portrayed. The prepresidential Chet Arthur was not the ugly spoilsperson that many believed him to be, nor was President Arthur quite as successful as some have painted him. Instead of the two Arthurs of folklore, there was only one: an exceedingly competent, intellectually limited Victorian gentleman, ponderous and self-centered but loyal to the code of whatever station he found himself called upon to occupy.

Chester Alan (rhymes with salon) Arthur was born on October 5, 1829, in a remote corner of Vermont, close enough to the Canadian border to give rise to later charges that he was actually born on the wrong side. He was the fifth

Portrait Chester A. Arthur. *(Whitehouse.gov)*

child and the first son of William Arthur, a college-educated Baptist minister with abolitionist leanings who had emigrated from Ulster almost a decade earlier.

Young Chester dutifully pursued a traditional course of study at Schenectady's Union College, taught school briefly, and then studied law. A mildly successful attorney who occasionally defended runaway slaves, he naturally gravitated to the infant Republican Party. Latching onto the coattails of New York's governor, Edwin D. Morgan, Arthur joined his staff and on the outbreak of the Civil War was appointed quartermaster general of the state, a position that enabled him to use the politically potent title of general in later years.

Energetic and efficient, Arthur made himself useful to the state and to his party, fitting himself so smoothly into the New York Republican machinery that when the imperious Roscoe Conkling assumed its control after the war, he inherited Arthur along with the party organization. By this time, Arthur had become a family man, with two children from his marriage to Ellen Herndon, the musically gifted daughter of a naval captain who had heroically gone down with his ship.

Family and private life, however, took a back seat to politics. Arthur was the perfect organization man, loyally working his way up to the powerful and lucrative position of collector of the port of New York. Arthur himself was impeccably honest. "If I had misappropriated five cents," he once said, "and on walking downtown saw two men talking on the street together, I would imagine they were talking of my dishonesty, and the very thought would drive me mad."

The post over which he presided, however, was such a foul nest of corruption and blatant partisanship that when Arthur was fired by President Rutherford B. Hayes, it could be portrayed as a blow for honest government. Conkling and his friends did not see it that way, and Arthur's dismissal only widened the

breach between these so-called Stalwarts and the rest of the Republican Party.

Garfield's Assassination

Arthur's surprise nomination as vice president in 1880 did not heal that breach. Conkling soon turned his wrath upon the new president, James A. Garfield. Arthur loyally stood by his old friend as they tried to bring down the administration of which Arthur was vice president. Conkling and Arthur roomed together and plotted together and were associated in the public mind. When Garfield was shot, in July of 1881, that association almost destroyed Arthur's reputation. It did not help matters that the crazed assassin, Charles J. Guiteau, exulted, "I am a Stalwart! Arthur is now president!"

Had Garfield died instantly, it is unlikely that the public would have accepted Arthur, but during the eighty days in which the wounded president clung to life, Arthur displayed such tact and dignity that his star began to rise. In fact, the low esteem in which Arthur had been held may actually have worked in his favor. After such initial low expectations, any sign of competence on his part would be greeted with pleased surprise.

The new president was far from incompetent, and he well realized the delicacy of his situation. Like William Shakespeare's Prince Hal, once he assumed power, he abandoned the disreputable companions of his youth. When Conkling pressed him to continue the feud with Garfield's followers, Arthur repudiated his former benefactor, which earned for him a place on Conkling's lengthy list of enemies. To balance the score, Arthur also removed from the cabinet Conkling's prime enemy, Secretary of State James G. Blaine, along with all the other holdovers from Garfield's cabinet, except for Secretary of War Robert Todd Lincoln. This posture may have been intended to demonstrate manly independence, but its practical result was to alienate Arthur from all the factions that constituted the Republican Party. Arthur had assumed not only the presidency but also the leadership of a bitterly divided party. Rather than healing those divisions, his policies only exacerbated them.

Such a course might seem strange in a man whose whole life had been devoted to politics, but as historian H. Wayne Morgan perceptively notes, "Arthur was less a politician than an organizer and administrator." Essentially a technician, he was incapable of building a personal following or generating grassroots appeal. A languid, urbane, intensely private man, Arthur lacked the common touch.

Under his supervision, the White House attained an elegance that it had not known for generations. The mansion itself was refurbished in high Victorian style under the direction of Louis Tiffany. The president, a portly six-footer with well-combed sideburns, made a striking host. Because of the death of his wife early in 1880, the president's sister, Mrs. John McElroy, served as official hostess, planning the twelve-course meals that her gourmet brother enjoyed. For the first time since the Grant administration, wine flowed freely at the White House. When a temperance spokeswoman urged him to continue the abstinence policy of "Lemonade Lucy" Hayes, Arthur frostily replied, "Madame, I may be President of the United States but my private life is nobody's damned business" — a remark that fairly summed up his attitude toward the office he held.

A Passive Conception of the Presidency

Presidents in the nineteenth century were not

The First Lady
Ellen Arthur

Ellen Lewis Herndon died on January 12, 1880, before her husband, Chester A. Arthur, became president in 1881. She was born on August 30, 1837, in Culpeper, Virginia, the only child of William Lewis Herndon and Elizabeth Hansbrough. She was raised in a distinguished, upper-class Virginia family that had descended from royalty in England. Little is known about her education other than that she was a talented singer and loved music.

She was introduced to Arthur on a visit to New York City by a cousin in 1856. They became engaged in 1857, although their marriage was delayed until 1859 because of her father's tragic death at sea. The couple had three children. Their first son died when he was only two. A second son was born in 1865 and a daughter in 1871. The two children were treated to the best of everything, as Arthur's career flourished as a successful New York City lawyer. Ellen would often give opera recitals to raise money for charities. Some evidence exists, however, that she was unhappy with the long hours Arthur spent away from home and even considered a separation.

Their world turned upside down in 1880 when Ellen died suddenly on January 12 from a cold that turned into pneumonia. She was only forty-two. Her death greatly affected Arthur, and it was a shock from which he never recovered. None of his achievements consoled him. Upon being elected vice president in 1880, he said "Honors to me now are not what they once were." He kept his wife's room in their New York home just as she had left it.

Although Ellen never served as First Lady, her presence was felt in the White House. Arthur never had anyone assume her role, although his sister, Mary McElroy, did take care of some of the social duties of First Lady. Arthur placed fresh flowers next to her portrait every day and donated a stained-glass window to St. John's Church that he could see from the White House.

Robert Flatley

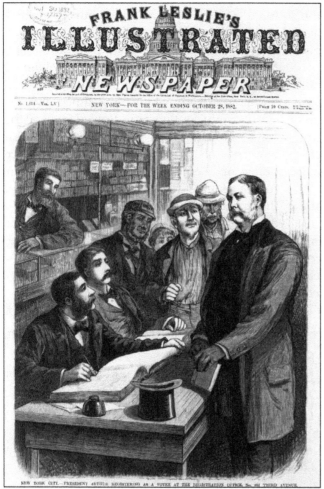

A drawing on the cover of *Frank Leslie's Illustrated Newspaper* shows Arthur registering to vote in New York City in October, 1882. *(Library of Congress)*

supposed to be bold or innovative statesmen. Except during wartime, they were expected merely to staff and administer the executive departments, enforce the laws, and generally follow the lead of Congress. This passive conception of the presidency was congenial to Arthur's temperament as well as to his political philosophy. Consequently, it is hardly surprising that his list of domestic accomplishments (including his chief pride—lowering the cost of first-class postage from three to two cents) seems meager by present-day standards.

Arthur was not devoid of ideas, but he sel-

dom pursued them vigorously. He advocated government control of the railroads, but he was content to make the suggestion and then let the matter drop. He flirted with tariff reform and even appointed a commission to study the matter. It recommended a general reduction of duties, but Congress was otherwise inclined. It passed the Mongrel Tariff of 1883, which increased the duty level for most goods. The president passively signed the bill into law. On two occasions, Arthur did bestir himself to veto significant bills but then failed to follow through. When Congress passed a Chinese exclusion act, contradictory to the spirit of existing treaties, Arthur interposed his veto. The revised legislation made only minor changes, but the president professed himself to be satisfied and allowed the bill to become law. A pork-barrel rivers and harbors appropriation bill also proved unpalatable to the president. This time, Congress contemptuously overrode his veto. Content with having made a gesture, Arthur pulled no strings to ensure that his veto would be sustained.

Constitutionally, presidents have more leeway in foreign affairs than in domestic matters, so it is hardly surprising that more activity was displayed by the State Department than by many other branches of the executive arm. Yet, even here, the activity was essentially negative—to undo the innovations inaugurated by Blaine.

Protected by its oceans, preoccupied with its internal development, the United States had stood aloof from the rest of the world ever since the end of the War of 1812. The State Department made do with only a few dozen permanent employees, and the secretaryship was often a refuge for influential, gentlemanly politicians. According to Hayes's secretary of state, William M. Evarts, "There are just two rules at

A political cartoon shows a crowd of corrupt politicians protesting Arthur's attempts at civil service reform. *(Library of Congress)*

the State Department: one, that no business is ever done out of business hours; and the other is, that no business is ever done *in* business hours."

Garfield's secretary of state, the dynamic, ambitious James G. Blaine, could hardly be expected to conform to this leisurely pace. He busied himself especially with Latin America, injecting American influence into the many and various quarrels that were then upsetting the continent's peace. Dissatisfied with these piecemeal adjustments—"patching up a peace treaty between two countries today, securing a truce between two others tomorrow"—he determined to institute a more comprehensive continental policy to be inaugurated at a grand panAmericanAmerican conference. Plans for the conference were under way when Garfield was shot. Blaine attempted to secure Arthur's approval for the project, but when no satisfactory answer was forthcoming, he resigned from the cabinet. He

was succeeded by Frederick T. Frelinghuysen, a cautious New Jersey aristocrat who promptly repudiated all of Blaine's flamboyant initiatives and set American foreign policy back on its traditional unenterprising course.

The activities of most of the other executive departments were equally lackluster. At the Justice Department, Attorney General Benjamin J. Brewster botched the prosecution of the Star Route case, a scandalous post office fraud dating from the Hayes administration that involved some of Arthur's former cronies. The other cabinet posts were managed with routine competence, with the most notable flashes of energy coming from the Navy Department where New Hampshire's William E. Chandler vigorously laid the foundation for the new navy. It was badly needed. In the early 1880's, the American war fleet was so weak, obsolete, and impotent that some officials feared even a fourth-rate power such as Chile could sweep it from the seas. By the 1890's, the seeds Chandler had planted would blossom into the fleet that would win for the United States an empire from Spain.

Chandler was equally active in politics, having been given the task of rebuilding the shattered Republican organizations in the Southern states. In this assignment, success eluded him, but not for want of trying. With the abandonment of Reconstruction in the mid-1870's, the Bourbon Democrats were everywhere resurgent, creating the "Solid South." Southern blacks, the backbone of the Republican Party in the region, were intimidated, demoralized, and disfranchised. Seeing no hope for success from that quarter, Chandler bypassed the largely black, regular Republican Southern organizations and relied instead on alliances with dissident Southern whites. There was no consistency in his program other than "Anything to beat the Bourbons!" He tried alliances with readjusters, greenbackers, maverick Democrats, and independents. He came tantalizingly close to success in some states, but nowhere was he able to break the grip of the white Democrats. The Solid South remained solid.

Political problems dogged the Arthur administration in the North and the West as well as in the South. The midterm elections of 1882 produced some of the worst Republican setbacks of the decade. Aided by a faltering economy and a rudderless opposition, the Democrats not only recaptured the House of Representatives but also enjoyed a comfortable margin of more than eighty seats. The New York canvass was an especially bitter defeat for the president. He had personally intervened in the gubernatorial contest, pulling all the administration's strings to secure the nomination of his crony Charles J. Folger and so alienated his party in the process that Folger was inundated by a margin of more than two hundred thousand votes. This result was not only a personal repudiation of Arthur's leadership, but it also gave a boost to the meteoric rise of the victorious Democratic governor, Grover Cleveland.

The Pendleton Act: The Death of the Spoils System

After these reversals, the lame duck Republican Congress was receptive to new issues that might win back its disaffected electorate. Reform of the civil service held attractive political potential. The cause had steadily been gaining popular support ever since the Grant administration, and after the assassination of Garfield by a crazed job seeker, it even had a sanctified martyr. If the Republicans could get credit for enacting the reform, independent voters might turn to the party out of gratitude; if, despite all, the Democrats should win the 1884 election, then civil service reform would lock thousands

of Republican officeholders into their jobs, safe from Democratic dismissal. Democrats, not surprisingly, sniffed at civil service reform as poisoned bait, even though one of their own, Ohio's Democratic senator George Pendleton, had given his name to the measure. Enough of them voted for it, however, to enable it to pass Congress and be sent to the president for his signature.

Signing the Pendleton Act is generally regarded as the greatest accomplishment of the Arthur presidency, and some have found a delicious irony in the fact that a once-notorious spoilsman presided over the death of the spoils system. Actually, the bill was not the sort of civil service reform that Arthur had in mind when he had earlier recommended "discreet reform." Like all presidents, Arthur was anxious to support any measure that would relieve him of the frightful pressure exerted by hopeful office seekers, but like all politicians, he was distrustful of competitive examinations and lifetime tenure. He supported the Pendleton Act with misgivings; a man with his past to live down could hardly afford to oppose it.

Personal ambition played no part in Arthur's action. In 1882, he learned that he was suffering from Bright's disease and had at best only a few years to live. He kept his fatal condition secret from the world and even went through the motions of seeking renomination. Even had he been in perfect health, it is unlikely that he would have been nominated by the Republican Party, all of whose factions he had managed to alienate. Instead, the party turned to his chief rival and longtime foe, James G. Blaine. Arthur became only the third incumbent president, after Millard Fillmore and Franklin Pierce, to be so humiliated by his own party. He sat out the rest of the election on the sidelines, taking grim satisfaction in Blaine's narrow defeat.

Arthur's last official act as president was signing the bill that restored pension rights to his dying predecessor, Ulysses S. Grant. Arthur soon followed Grant to the grave, dying on November 18, 1886, only twenty months after the conclusion of his own competent but undistinguished presidency.

Allan Peskin

Suggested Readings

De Santis, Vincent P. *Republicans Face the Southern Question: The New Departure Years, 1877-1897*. Baltimore: Johns Hopkins University Press, 1959. Chronicles the development of the Southern policy.

Doenecke, Justus D. *The Presidencies of James A. Garfield and Chester A. Arthur*, 1981. Lawrence: Regents Press of America, 1981. Draws parallels and distinctions between Garfield and Arthur.

Hoogenboom, Ari. *Outlawing the Spoils: A History of the Civil Service Reform Movement, 1865-1883*. Urbana: University of Illinois Press, 1961. Provides political context for Arthur's era.

Howe, George F. *Chester A. Arthur: A Quarter-Century of Machine Politics*. 1935. Reprint. New York: F. Ungar, 1966. A good contextual examination of the political culture that gave rise to Arthur's presidency.

Joseph, Paul. *Chester Arthur*. Minneapolis: ABDO, 1999. A biography written for young adults.

Karabel, Zachary. *Chester Alan Arthur*. New York: Times Books, 2004. Chronicles the life and times of Arthur and details his successes and failures as president.

Morgan, H. Wayne. *From Hayes to McKinley: National Party Politics, 1877-1896*. Syracuse, N.Y.: Syracuse University Press, 1969. A highly readable survey of the politics of the Gilded Age.

Pletcher, David M. *The Awkward Years: American Foreign Relations Under Garfield and Arthur*. Columbia: University of Missouri Press, 1962. Covers foreign policy developments during the era.

Reeves, Thomas C. *Gentleman Boss: The Life of Chester Alan Arthur*. New York: Knopf, 1975. A good biography of Arthur.

Sturgis, Amy H., comp. *Presidents from Hayes Through McKinley, 1877-1901: Debating the Issues in Pro and Con Primary Documents*. Westport, Conn.: Greenwood Press, 2003. A collection of primary documents and commentary is used to debate a range of issues that were pertinent during the tenure of all presidents serving between 1877 and 1901.

Grover Cleveland

22d President, 1885-1889
24th President, 1893-1897

Born: March 18, 1837
    Caldwell, New Jersey
Died: June 24, 1908
    Princeton, New Jersey

Political Party: Democratic
Vice Presidents: Thomas A. Hendricks,
    Adlai E. Stevenson

Cabinet Members (1st Administration)
Secretary of State: Thomas F. Bayard
Secretary of the Treasury: Daniel Manning,
    Charles S. Fairchild
Secretary of War: William C. Endicott
Secretary of the Navy: William C. Whitney
Attorney General: A. H. Garland
Postmaster General: William F. Vilas, Don M.
    Dickinson
Secretary of the Interior: L. Q. R. Lamar,
    William F. Vilas
Secretary of Agriculture: Norman J. Colman

Cabinet Members (2d Administration)
Secretary of State: Walter Q. Gresham, Richard
    Olney
Secretary of the Treasury: John G. Carlisle
Secretary of War: Daniel S. Lamont
Secretary of the Navy: Hilary A. Herbert
Attorney General: Richard Olney, Judson
    Harmon
Postmaster General: Wilson S. Bissel, William L.
    Wilson
Secretary of the Interior: Hoke Smith, David R.
    Francis
Secretary of Agriculture: J. Sterling Morton

Stephen Grover Cleveland was a notably confident man during an age when confidence came naturally to prosperous men. An observer could read Cleveland's personal and political philosophy in his body and face. He was a big man and grossly overweight. He moved slowly, cautiously, and often with great effort. Sitting behind a desk, however, he was tireless, capable of working continuously for twenty-four hours or more at exacting mental labor. His face was stoic and phlegmatic. A walrus mustache and several chins hid his lower face from the world. Only his eyes, surprisingly innocent

Portrait of Grover Cleveland. *(Whitehouse.gov)*

and kind, gave a hint at the man inside. In public he seldom spoke, but when he did, it was with confidence and conviction. He had faith in his beliefs, and he never doubted—indeed, he may never have questioned—that he was right.

A Man of Definite Convictions

Faith and confidence were his at birth. Richard Cleveland, his father, was a Yale-educated preacher. Born in Caldwell, New Jersey, on March 18, 1837, Grover, the fifth of nine children, inherited his father's strong and unquestioning Presbyterian faith. Richard Cleveland was a kind, gentle man, but not a prosperous one. He died when Grover was sixteen, and he left his son little more than the fruits of conscientious rearing.

Financial pressures forced Grover Cleveland to find a job. For a year he lived in New York City and taught at the New York Institute of the Blind, a task he found as unrewarding mentally as financially. Like many men of his

---

The First Lady
Frances Cleveland

Frances Cleveland became the youngest First Lady on June 2, 1886, when, at the age of twenty-one, she married Grover Cleveland, who had become president the year before. She was only the second woman to marry a sitting president and the first to marry one in a ceremony at the White House. In President Cleveland's second term, she also became the first presidential spouse to bear children in the White House: Her second and third children, Esther and Marion, were born there in 1893 and 1895. Her first child, Ruth, was born in 1891, between President Cleveland's two terms in office.

Born Frances Folsom on July 21, 1864, she was the daughter of Oscar Folsom, a lawyer in Buffalo, New York, who was a close friend of Grover Cleveland. She later added "Clara" as a middle name and was also known as "Frank" or "Frankie." Her father died in a horse-and-buggy accident in 1875, at which time Grover Cleveland became executor of Oscar Folsom's estate and an unofficial guardian of eleven-year-old Frances. She used to refer to him as "Uncle Cleve."

Frances was educated at schools in Buffalo and in Medina, New York, and then attended Wells College in Aurora, New York. While at college, she corresponded with Cleveland, and he proposed to her by letter. Once in the White House, Frances won praise for her charm, beauty, and poise. She also was credited with rejuvenating the president and making him less gruff and more polite.

She did not involve herself in politics or policy making, declining to associate herself with any causes. She did, however, go on tours with the president, and when rumors spread that he had mistreated her, she released a strongly worded letter denying them.

She was known for hosting a great many receptions, luncheons, and teas and made a point of having some on Saturdays so that working women could attend them. She also became involved in charity work, helping found the Washington Home for Friendless Colored Girls.

After Cleveland's second term as president, the Clevelands moved to Princeton, where Frances gave birth to two sons, Richard and Francis, in 1897 and 1903. Her oldest daughter, Ruth, died of diphtheria in 1904. Grover Cleveland died in 1908, and in 1913, Frances married Thomas J. Preston, Jr., a professor of art and archaeology at Wells College. During World War I, as the head of the National Security League's speakers' bureau, she arranged public meetings and patriotic rallies. She also sat on the board of Wells College and worked to encourage the creation of educational opportunities for women. She died on October 29, 1947.

Sheldon Goldfarb

"The Mugwump Party" and Cleveland, by G. Y. Coffin, 1884. *(Library of Congress)*

generation, he then decided that his fortune and future waited in the West. His western trek ended abruptly, however, in Buffalo, New York, where his wealthy uncle, Lewis P. Allen, who exerted considerable influence in the Buffalo area, soon found Cleveland a job as a clerk in a solid and respectable local law firm. After four years of study, Cleveland, in 1859, was admitted to the bar. For the next twenty-three years, he practiced law in virtual public anonymity. Never a showman, he disliked appearing in the courtroom and instead tried whenever possible to settle a case before it went to court. Hardworking, fair, and possessing absolute integrity, Cleveland aptly and conscientiously mastered the details of each case and plodded his way toward a just settlement.

Life in Buffalo suited him. He had his work and his friends, and he seldom expressed much interest in the world around him. Even the Civil War failed to excite him greatly. He was unsympathetic with the crusade against slavery, although he believed the Union should be preserved. He did not, however, feel impelled to take up arms to save the Union. He had a mother and several sisters to support; these were concrete duties in his mind. Thus while two of his brothers enlisted, Grover hired a substitute for $150.

Cleveland never expressed regret over his decision not to enlist. Nor did he ever lament his relatively uneventful years in Buffalo. He enjoyed an unimaginative social and intellectual life. Work and duty compelled him to study law; simple curiosity never pushed him much further. Outside of the poetry of Alfred, Lord Tennyson, he had no love for literature and was strikingly uneducated in the classics. He was similarly uninterested in attending church or working his way into Buffalo's genteel society.

A bachelor until late in life, Cleveland enjoyed the company of other men. Although not a heavy drinker, he was drawn to the nightlife offered at cozy street-corner saloons. A plate of pickled herring, Swiss cheese, and chops suited his appetite. A quart of beer quenched his thirst. A day of hunting or night of card playing satisfied his entertainment needs. There were women in his life, but they were not the kind he thought of marrying. With one, a widow named Maria Halpin, Cleveland may have fathered a son. Although Cleveland doubted that he was the father, he did accept financial responsibility for the child.

The Veto Mayor
However unimaginative and dull Cleveland seemed, something nevertheless burned inside him. Perhaps it was personal ambition, perhaps it was a desire to make Buffalo a better place.

Probably it was a combination of the two. Whatever it was, it pushed him into politics. In 1863 he was elected a ward supervisor and then assistant district attorney of Erie County. Seven years later, at the age of thirty-two, he was elected sheriff of Buffalo County. The job paid well, and Cleveland performed well. As sheriff he showed the strengths on which he would later base his political career. He worked hard and he strove to make his post a model of honesty and efficiency. Nor did he balk at difficult tasks. When he had to press the lever to hang two convicts, he did so. In 1873, when his three-year term as sheriff ended, he went back to his law office.

He returned to politics in a much larger role in 1881. In that year the Democratic Party nominated him to run for mayor of Buffalo. Wealthy, influential Democrats turned to Cleveland because they wanted to rid their city of inefficiency and corruption. Cleveland, who had an unassailable reputation for honesty and hard work, certainly spoke their language. "We believe," he said, "in the principle of economy of the people's money, and that when a man in office lays out a dollar in extravagance, he acts immorally by the people." With the Tweed Ring still a haunting memory, Cleveland's words also struck a soothing chord with the voters, and he was elected mayor. As always, Cleveland proved to be a man of his word. He was quick to veto all inappropriate or corrupt appropriations. Overly legalistic, he never exceeded delegated authority, but he did provide Buffalo with efficient and honest leadership. He even made small gains in the area of public health by expanding Buffalo's inadequate sewer system.

Cleveland's political ambitions and fortunes rose fast. Less than one-half year after becoming mayor of Buffalo, he was seeking support for a bid at the governorship of New York. Again backed by the wealthy Democratic business community and favored by incredible luck, Cleveland moved forward. When the Republicans nominated machine-controlled Charles J. Folger for governor, the Democrats saw their chance. Popular sentiment was against urban machines, the corruption and inefficiency of which were well publicized. Clearly, Cleveland was free of machine ties and as honest as Boss Tweed was corrupt. He was the right man at the right time in the right place. The powerful and wealthy New York Democratic organizer William C. Whitney realized this. As he told Democratic state chairman Daniel Manning, "The man who can defeat the Republicans worst is that buxom Buffalonian, Grover Cleveland. You up-State Democrats want to unite with the New York Democracy on Cleveland, and we'll not only elect him Governor this fall but President a little later."

The two Democratic groups united, and in the fall Cleveland was swept into office in a landslide. Both Democrats and reform-minded Republicans voted for the largely unknown candidate. They wanted honest government, efficient government. This—and little more—Cleveland was prepared to give them.

Cleveland took office on January 3, 1883. Before his inauguration he penned a telling and worried letter to his brother, the Reverend William N. Cleveland. He wrote that he wanted "to do some good to the people of the state. I know there is room for it, and I know that I am honest and sincere in that desire to do well, but the question is whether I know enough to accomplish what I desire." His concern was well founded. As governor his honesty and ignorance led him to political triumphs and social failures.

In the governor's office, as he had in the mayor's office, Cleveland used his veto power freely. Poorly drafted bills and bills of questionable constitutionality Cleveland quickly sent back to the legislature. His faith was in the letter of the law, not the spirit, and he used this strict interpretation of the Constitution to veto a wide range of socially progressive bills. He vetoed the popular five-cent fare bill, a measure aimed at reducing the cost of riding on the New York City elevated railroad, and he vetoed another bill that attempted to establish maximum hours for the conductors and drivers of horse-drawn streetcars. As a lawyer for corporations, he believed in an individual's freedom of contract. As governor he continued to act on those beliefs to block any regulation of working hours or wages.

The poor and the manual laborers were little served by Cleveland. Business leaders, however, found much to applaud. Cleveland did bring order, economy, and efficiency—"good government"—to the state. His appointments were made to improve government, not to satisfy the desires of political machines. This position brought Cleveland into conflict with Tammany Hall, New York's most powerful machine. It also split the Democratic Party in New York. The short-term results of Cleveland's actions, however, pleased wealthy reformers. They had found their champion in the honest and conservative politician from Buffalo.

The Campaign of 1884: Bourbon Democrats and Mugwumps

By late 1883, Cleveland certainly had his eyes on the White House. His future in New York State politics was problematic at best. By alienating Tammany Hall, he had badly hurt the state Democracy, and it is doubtful if he could have restored it to health. It was better and easier for Cleveland to move up the political ladder. Again fortune was on his side, for national Democratic leaders were looking for a candidate of Cleveland's beliefs and abilities. For most of the last third of the nineteenth century, Bourbon Democrats controlled the party. They spoke for the businessmen and railroad men, extolling the virtues of free enterprise and laissez-faire economics and fighting the demands of urban wage earners and farmers. They believed that government should be efficient and honest, but most of all they thought it should be inexpensive. This entailed restricting such government giveaways as the Civil War pensions and reducing such special favors as the high protective tariff. For the Bourbons, Cleveland's record as governor, and his conservative nature, were irresistible.

Cleveland's stock rose further after the Republicans chose James G. Blaine to carry their banner in 1884. In most ways an admirable and effective politician, Blaine's reputation still suffered from railroad scandals in which he had been involved during the 1870's. His nomination split the Republican Party. A group of "good government" reformers known as mugwumps vowed to vote for an honest Democrat rather than Blaine. Sensing their opportunity, Bourbon Democrats pushed through the nomination of Cleveland.

The 1884 campaign was notable for its circuslike atmosphere and mudslinging. Dem-

"Another Voice for Cleveland"—a reference to his alleged illegitimate child. *(Library of Congress)*

ocrats and mugwumps reminded the voters of Blaine's dishonest past, harping on his unethical dealings with the Little Rock and Fort Smith Railroad and his duplicitous attempt to escape condemnation. In turn, Republicans unearthed Cleveland's indiscretions before he became mayor of Buffalo. Although no political or financial scandals clouded Cleveland's past, there was his illicit affair with Maria Halpin. "Ma, Ma, Where's My Pa?" became the Republican chant.

In truth, the campaign focused on personalities largely because of the parties' unwillingness to take stands on the major issues of the day. Neither Democratic nor Republican Party leaders wanted to alienate voters by talking too much about tariffs, monopolies, or the money question. In an age when presidential elections were always very close, a strong stand on a major issue could lead to defeat at the polls. It was easier instead to focus on Blaine's financial dealings and Cleveland's sexual life. As far as the Democrats were concerned, a mugwump summarized the campaign and the issues most clearly:

> We are told that Mr. Blaine has been delinquent in office but blameless in public life, while Mr. Cleveland has been a model of official integrity but culpable in his personal relations. We should therefore elect Mr. Cleveland to the public office which he is so well qualified to fill, and remand Mr. Blaine to the private station which he is admirably fitted to adorn.

In the end, the election may have been decided by several unwise political decisions Blaine made during the closing days of the campaign. On the morning of October 29, 1884, an exhausted Blaine met with a group of clergymen, whose spokesperson told the Republican candidate that the Democratic Party was one of "Rum, Romanism, and Rebellion." Democrats seized on this remark, which Blaine did not challenge, to drive a wedge between Blaine and his Irish supporters. That night Blaine committed another mistake. He attended a fundraising dinner at Delmonico's that was attended by two hundred of the wealthiest men in the United States. Dubbing it the "prosperity dinner," newspaper editorialists and cartoonists used it to emphasize Blaine's support for the monied interests in America. A *New York World* cartoon showed "Belshazzar Blaine" eating terrapin and canvasback duck and sipping champagne while a starving family begged for crumbs.

Less than a week later, Cleveland won a narrow victory. The election was particularly close in New York, which Cleveland carried by a plurality of only 1,149 votes. Mugwump support, Bourbon politics, and Blaine's own mistakes had carried a Democrat into the White House, the first to make his home there in twenty-four years.

First Administration: Pensions, Tariffs, and the Nation's Currency

Cleveland was forty-eight when he took office. Short but weighing more than 250 pounds, he was clean-shaven, except for a mustache, during an age when most politicians wore beards. Close friends found him a boon companion on hunting and fishing trips, but in public he was cold and distant. Intellectually, he was much the same man that the citizens of Buffalo had elected mayor in 1881. His goals still included governmental efficiency and economy, and he was more than ever the friend of business. His cabinet reflected his leanings. Although it contained Bourbon Democrats from every section of the country, it contained no voice for farmers, wage earners, or blacks. For Cleveland and his cabinet, there would be no conflicts between "good government" and good business.

Cleveland never forgot his promise. He strived mightily to bring order, efficiency, and economy to every office under his control. Although he used his patronage power to reward Democrats, he appointed only well-qualified persons, and his cabinet members achieved

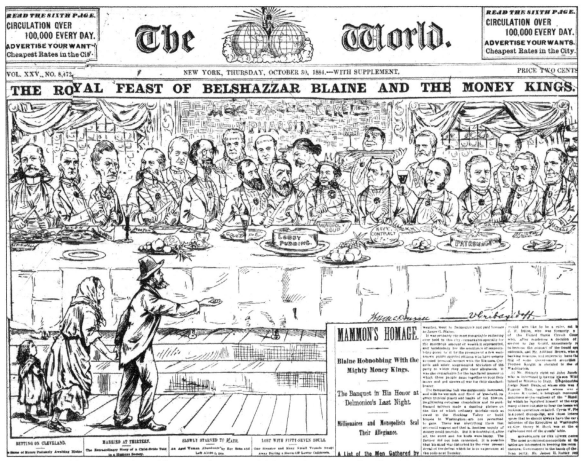

The *New York World*'s view of James G. Blaine at the "prosperity dinner." *(Library of Congress)*

commendable successes. Friend, adviser, and supporter William C. Whitney, who became Cleveland's secretary of the navy, proved particularly able. He worked closely with Cleveland and the leaders of American steel companies to construct a modern steel navy.

Nor were his business ties severed. He did not use his office to enrich his business friends, but his approach to most problems implicitly demonstrated a probusiness mentality. The Dawes Act of 1887, which Cleveland supported, aptly illustrates this. In a sincere attempt to integrate American Indians into American life, the act encouraged them to own land as individuals rather than as tribes. Of course, as free agents in a free country, they were then free to lease their land to loggers and real estate

agents. Cleveland was not unethical or Machiavellian, but his policy soon proved disastrous for the tribal system.

Even Cleveland's approach to reform was influenced by his probusiness mentality. In his inaugural address, he had promised "reform in the administration of government, and the application of business principles to public affairs." This was not idle rhetoric. Cleveland saw no reason why government should not be run like a profitable business. Trim the fat and streamline the process—if it worked for the giant meatpackers in Chicago, Cleveland reasoned, it should work for the government in Washington, D.C.

Given the Republican tradition of high protective tariffs, liberal land grants and subsidy payments to railroads, and generous pension plans for veterans, Cleveland discovered plenty of fat to trim. He moved first against pension waste. Since the end of the Civil War, Grand Army of the Republic supporters in Congress had pushed through more than half a million pension bills, many involving cases of questionable merit. Cleveland was determined to stop this raid on the public treasury. Unlike presidents Grant and Hayes, he read carefully all the private pension bills that Congress passed and sent on for his signature. What he read sickened him. About a fourth of the bills were based on fraudulent claims. Some of the more flagrant examples were cited by Allan Nevins:

> One claimant explained that he had been registered "at home" and had set out on horseback *intending* to complete his enlistment, that on the way his horse had fallen on his left ankle, and that he was thus entitled to a cripple's pension. A widow whose husband had been killed by a fall from a ladder in 1881 traced this to a slight flesh-wound in the calf of 1865! . . . One gallant private claimed that a disease of the eyes had resulted from army diarrhea.

These and more than two hundred like claims Cleveland unhesitatingly rejected, although he also signed nearly fifteen hundred private pension bills.

Cleveland moved beyond private pension bills in early 1887. In January of that year Congress passed a piece of legislation dubbed the "pauper's bill." It "offered pensions to all disabled veterans who had served honorably for at least ninety days and were dependent upon their own efforts for support." A veteran's disability did not have to be the result of his wartime activities; old age disabilities and nonmilitary injuries also qualified a veteran for a pension. Cleveland predictably vetoed the bill. Government, he implied, was not in the charity business.

Pension corruption was not the only pressing financial problem that Cleveland confronted. Currency and tariff issues proved to be

---

The Vice President
Thomas A. Hendricks

The son of a farmer, Thomas Hendricks was born near Zanesville, Ohio, on September 7, 1819. He graduated from Hanover College in Madison, Indiana, in 1841 and then studied law for eight months in Chambersburg, Pennsylvania. In 1843, Hendricks was admitted to the Indiana Bar and opened a law practice in Shelbyville. On September 26, 1845, Hendricks married Eliza C. Morgan, and they had one son.

Leaving his law practice, Hendricks was elected to the Indiana House of Representatives in 1848 and then went on to the United States House of Representatives in 1852. After serving two terms, he accepted a position as commissioner of the General Land Office in President Franklin Pierce's administration. Resigning the post in 1859, Hendricks returned to Shelbyville and opened another successful law practice. In 1863, Hendricks was elected to the United States Senate and, in 1872, was elected governor of Indiana. Four years later, he was nominated as vice president on a ticket with Samuel J. Tilden, but they lost to Rutherford B. Hayes.

Eight years later, however, Hendricks won election to the vice presidency in 1884, serving with Grover Cleveland. One year later, he died in Indianapolis at the age of sixty-six after suffering a stroke.

Robert P. Watson and Richard Yon

more vexing and complex—and more important problems. Although in early 1885 some politicians feared that the Treasury's gold reserve was falling too low, by 1886 it had a surplus. Indeed, by 1888 the surplus amounted to $255 million, or $125 million in excess of what was needed to support the currency in circulation. The effect of this surplus was to depress the economy, and unless the government did something to reduce it, financial experts predicted there would be a depression.

Opportunities for disposing of the surplus abounded. Veterans and their supporters certainly wanted more and higher pensions. Other special interest groups also were anxious to get on the government's payroll. Some politicians wanted the government to purchase the telegraph business. Others sought to spend more money on harbors, internal improvements, and education. Still others wanted to reduce the excise taxes on whiskey and tobacco.

Cleveland rejected all these proposals. He and his advisers decided that the best way to reduce the surplus was to lower the tariff, thereby reducing the government's income. High protective tariffs, he maintained, taxed consumers for the benefit of protected industrialists and other producers. Lower tariffs would help rid America of specially privileged groups and enhance economic egalitarianism; it would force American producers to act in an economically efficient manner and reduce the cost of goods to consumers.

In 1887, Cleveland devoted his annual message to Congress exclusively to the need for tariff reform. This was the first time in history that a president's annual message concerned only one issue. He called for reductions on major consumer items and on the raw materials used to produce those items. In a moderate tone, he explained that laborers would benefit from his proposed reforms and that manufacturers would not be hurt.

Most people applauded Cleveland's speech, but such demonstrations of support did not move Congress. With an election less than a year away, most politicians did not want to run the risk of alienating any of their supporters. Never a strong leader and unpopular with most Democrats in Congress, Cleveland was unable to push through legislation to reform the tariff.

At the end of his first term in office, Cleveland's record was mixed. In an age marked by political manipulation and graft, he had returned a certain dignity to the office of the presidency. Honest and hardworking, he had tried with some success to impose those qualities on his administration. As a politician, however, he often had been tactless and closed-minded. He had lectured Congress rather than led it, and he had paid little attention to the urgent cries of hard-pressed farmers and laborers. Too often he had seen only Bourbon solutions to problems and had been impatient with even honest opposition.

The greatest event in Cleveland's personal life during his first term was his marriage. On June 2, 1886, the forty-nine-year-old president wed Frances Folsom, an attractive and well-educated woman twenty-seven years his junior. Frances was the daughter of Oscar Folsom, Cleveland's friend and law partner, who died in 1875. The marriage was destined to be a happy one and one that helped to enhance Cleveland's social graces. Unfortunately, it did not seem to improve his skill as a politician.

The Campaign of 1888: Defeat Despite Victory in the Popular Vote

The Democratic Party renominated Cleveland at its 1888 convention. It could hardly do less. But while doing so, the party and its nominee did attempt to soften the president's earlier antiprotectionist position on the tariff. The Republicans, however, nominated as their candidate an ultraprotectionist, Benjamin Harrison of Indiana, and forced the tariff issue into the forefront of the campaign. Republican propagandists portrayed Cleveland's tariff stand as

---

The Vice President
Adlai E. Stevenson

Adlai Stevenson, the founder of a political dynasty, was born on October 23, 1835, in Christian County, Kentucky. In 1854, he entered Centre College in Danville, Kentucky, and quickly fell in love with Letitia Green, the daughter of the college president. Stevenson married his sweetheart in December, 1866, and they had three children. Unable to finish his degree because of the death of his father, he began studying law and was admitted to the Illinois bar in 1858.

For ten years, Stevenson practiced law in the general county court in Metamora, Illinois. After serving as district attorney between 1865 and 1869, Stevenson opened a law practice with his cousin, James S. Ewing. In 1874, he entered politics and was elected to the United States House of Representatives, but he was defeated when he ran for reelection. However, in 1878 Stevenson returned to the House, where he served until 1881. President Grover Cleveland named him to be assistant postmaster general in 1885.

In 1889, after the first Cleveland administration, Stevenson returned to his law practice. In 1892, he was elected vice president and served in the second Cleveland administration. After Cleveland's term of office ended, Stevenson returned to his home in Bloomington. President William McKinley appointed Stevenson to the Monetary Commission in 1900. That same year, he ran unsuccessfully for the vice presidential nomination with William Jennings Bryan. In 1908, he also lost his bid for governor of Illinois. Stevenson outlived his wife by six months. He died on June 14, 1914.

Robert P. Watson and Richard Yon

---

one that was overly friendly to free-trade-loving Britain and dangerous to American businessmen, industrialists, farmers, and laborers. They equated high tariffs with high wages and low tariffs with economic disaster. Forced on the defensive, Cleveland's political ineptitude became all the more apparent.

Although the tariff was the major issue, other factors also figured in the campaign. For many Americans, prohibition or Civil War pensions as well as regional, ethnic, or religious prejudices outweighed purely economic concerns. Cleveland's attempt to return captured Confederate flags to the South enraged many Northerners. Of even greater importance, however, was the Murchison letter affair. This letter, released to the press in Los Angeles a few weeks before the election, was a Republican trap. It baited Sir Lionel Sackville-West, the British minister in Washington, D.C., into writing that in effect a vote for Cleveland was a vote for England. Given the anti-English sentiment in the United States, es-

pecially among Irish Americans, the letter's impact was obvious. Cleveland failed to carry New York, and although he won a plurality of the popular vote, he lost the election.

Cleveland did not leave office with a whimper. In his last State of the Union address in December, 1888, he issued some stern warnings to Americans. In many ways it was the most important address Cleveland ever gave. He spoke openly about the growing gulf between rich and poor in America, and he lashed out against the powerful trusts, combinations, and monopolies. With a voice seldom heard before, he sympathized with the plight of farmers and urban laborers. In the end, he condemned all special privileges—especially the tariff. Unfortunately, Cleveland saw the problems in a much clearer focus than the solutions.

The Harrison Administration: Free-Spending Republicans
The period between 1889 and 1892 took more

the form of a hibernation for Cleveland than a retirement. Cleveland returned to New York and resumed the practice of law, although he handled few cases. He maintained his ties with politicians through letters rather than personal meetings. He enjoyed summers in his cottage at Buzzards Bay and winters in New York City. He fished and hunted and attended Broadway plays and exclusive parties. All in all, he followed a pleasant routine. Later, he said that these years were the happiest of his life.

Perhaps with some satisfaction he watched the new administration wrestle with some economic problems that his had faced. The Republicans' answer to the Treasury surplus was to spend it. A substantial portion went to the veterans. The Dependents' Pension Act more than doubled the number of pensioners. Congress also spent money on upgrading coastal defenses, building schools, and improving rivers and harbors. In 1890 the reserve was $190 million; by 1893 it had dropped to $108 million. In addition, Congress passed the McKinley tariff, which raised rates on both farm and industrial products to the highest levels ever. Finally, Congress pushed through the Sherman Silver Purchase Act, which required the Treasury to purchase 4,500,000 ounces of silver each month and angered sound money supporters such as Cleveland.

Unfortunately for the Republicans, their spending and support of various special interests came at a time when the economy began to turn downward. Predictably, they paid the price. Democrats and agrarian independents made remarkable gains in the 1890 elections. More important for Cleveland, the prospects looked bright for a Democratic presidential victory in 1892. Next to the extravagant Republicans, the tightfisted Cleveland took on a certain

A crowd in Buffalo, New York, celebrates Cleveland's nomination for president. *(Library of Congress)*

luster of sagacity. "Good government," tariff reform, and the gold standard were seen by many Americans as the proper cure for the nation's ills.

Cleveland's Second Administration: A Shift in Public Sentiment

Between the 1890 elections and the 1892 Democratic convention, Cleveland regained leadership of the Democratic Party. Although publicly he said he would not campaign actively for the presidency, he worked industriously for it behind the scenes. At the Chicago convention, Cleveland was nominated on the first ballot, and Adlai Stevenson of Illinois was chosen as his running mate. The platform committed the party to tariff and currency reform. After four years of Republican spending, the country was once again ready for Cleveland's frugal policies. In November, Cleveland defeated Harrison by a margin of 132 electoral votes, and the Democrats regained control of both houses of Congress.

Excerpts from Grover Cleveland's last State of the Union address of his first presidential term, December 3, 1888:

As we view the achievements of aggregated capital, we discover the existence of trusts, combinations, and monopolies, while the citizen is struggling far in the rear or is trampled to death beneath an iron heel. Corporations, which should be the carefully restrained creatures of the law and the servants of the people, are fast becoming the people's masters.

Still congratulating ourselves upon the wealth and prosperity of our country and complacently contemplating every incident of change inseparable from these conditions, it is our duty as patriotic citizens to inquire at the present stage of our progress how the bond of the Government made with the people has been kept and performed.

Instead of limiting the tribute drawn from our citizens to the necessities of its economical administration, the Government persists in exacting from the substance of the people millions which, unapplied and useless, lie dormant in its Treasury. This flagrant injustice and this breach of faith and obligation add to extortion the danger attending the diversion of the currency of the country from the legitimate channels of business.

Under the same laws by which these results are produced the Government permits many millions more to be added to the cost of the living of our people and to be taken from our consumers, which unreasonably swell the profits of a small but powerful minority.

The people must still be taxed for the support of the Government under the operation of tariff laws. But to the extent that the mass of our citizens are inordinately burdened beyond any useful public purpose and for the benefit of a favored few, the Government, under pretext of an exercise of its taxing power, enters gratuitously into partnership with these favorites, to their advantage and to the injury of a vast majority of our people.

This is not equality before the law.

The existing situation is injurious to the health of our entire body politic. It stifles in those for whose benefit it is permitted all patriotic love of country, and substitutes in its place selfish greed and grasping avarice. Devotion to American citizenship for its own sake and for what it should accomplish as a motive to our nation's advancement and the happiness of all our people is displaced by the assumption that the Government, instead of being the embodiment of equality, is but an instrumentality through which especial and individual advantages are to be gained.

The arrogance of this assumption is unconcealed. It appears in the sordid disregard of all but personal interests, in the refusal to abate for the benefit of others one iota of selfish advantage, and in combinations to perpetuate such advantages through efforts to control legislation and improperly influence the suffrages of the people. . . .

When to the selfishness of the beneficiaries of unjust discrimination under our laws there shall be added the discontent of those who suffer from such discrimination, we will realize the fact that the beneficent purposes of our Government, dependent upon the patriotism and contentment of our people, are endangered.

TO AMEND BUT NOT DESTROY.

UNCLE SAM. "How much o' that dew ye calkelate ter take off?"
G. C. "The rough edges, merely."

Cleveland's 1887 message to Congress on tariff reform won applause but not votes. *(Library of Congress)*

The victory celebration ended quickly. No sooner had Cleveland taken office than the financial panic of 1893 began. Depression racked the country. Thousands of businesses failed, and hundreds of banks suspended operations. In the cities, unemployment rose and charities were unable to ease the suffering of millions of homeless and hungry Americans. State and federal officials ignored the anguished pleas of the urban and rural poor. The governor of New York spoke for many in government: "In America, the people support the government; it is not the province of the government to support the people."

Cleveland blamed the depression on the Sherman Silver Purchase Act and the McKinley tariff. To deal with it, he concentrated his efforts on repealing the Republican legislation. First he went after the Sherman Silver Purchase Act, which he believed was rapidly draining the Treasury's gold reserves. Essentially, the depression had driven politicians into one of two financial camps. Cleveland, Bourbons, and conservative Republicans called for a return to the gold standard, while Agrarian Democrats and Republicans and Populists demanded the free coinage of silver in order to inflate the currency and raise prices.

It was a time of high drama. On June 30, 1893, Cleveland summoned a special session of Congress to convene on August 7, to repeal the Sherman Silver Purchase Act. About the same time, he noticed a rough spot on the roof of his mouth, which medical experts soon diagnosed as cancer. The very day he called for the special session of Congress, Cleveland boarded a private yacht to undergo surgery. The operation was a success, as was a later one to provide him with an artificial jaw of vulcanized rubber. As biographer Horace Samuel Merrill noted, "Neither his facial appearance nor the quality of his voice was thereby altered. But he seemed less rugged and more irritable, and he weighed less."

The operation was performed under a cloak of secrecy. The public did not learn of the event until twenty-five years later. The battle over the Sherman Silver Purchase Act, however, was waged in the open. Cleveland refused to compromise. Finally, in late October, 1893, he prevailed, and the act was repealed. The gold standard was saved, but Cleveland and the Bourbon Democrats paid dearly for their victory. The issue split the Democratic Party, a division that eventually led to the defeat of the Bourbon element within the party. In addition, the repeal neither ended the financial crisis nor

The first shipment of meat leaves the Chicago stockyards under escort by the U.S. cavalry during the Pullman Strike of 1894. *(Library of Congress)*

restored public confidence.

The Treasury reserve continued to decline. After other efforts to maintain the reserve by selling bonds for gold failed, finally in 1895 the president asked the major New York bankers for help. A banking syndicate headed by J. P. Morgan agreed to buy $65 million in bonds at a special discount and to use its influence to keep the gold from being withdrawn from the Treasury. Although this move helped the situation, it was roundly condemned by the agrarian population of the South and West especially as a crooked deal with Wall Street.

Politically weakened by the fight over the money question, Cleveland found the struggle for tariff reform all the more difficult. The Wilson bill that emerged from the House provided significant reductions, but it was badly mauled in the Senate. The resulting Wilson-Gorman bill was only slightly less protectionist than the McKinley tariff. Cleveland was bitterly disappointed and accused Congress of "party perfidy and party dishonor." The bill became law without his signature.

Unpopular with professional politicians, Cleveland, by 1894, was equally unpopular with the American people. The depression exposed the heartlessness of his economic beliefs. "While the people should patriotically and cheerfully support their Government," he wrote, "its functions do not include the support of the people." He did not believe the government should be in the relief business. It violated every principle he held. It was uneconomical, favored a special interest, and went beyond the scope of the Constitution. Thus when Jacob S.

Coxey led his ragtag army on a march toward Washington. D.C., in an effort to encourage government public works relief legislation, Cleveland showed no sympathy. When the "petitioneers in boots" arrived at the Capitol in 1894, they were rudely dispersed.

Strikers received similar treatment from Cleveland. In the spring of 1894, four thousand workers in the Pullman Company of Chicago went on strike. The American Railway Union, headed by the able Eugene V. Debs, soon supported the strikers and boycotted Pullman cars. Cleveland and his attorney general, Richard Olney, a former railroad lawyer, acted quickly. They used the excuse of protecting the mails to come to the aid of the railroad managers. Over the protest of the governor of Illinois, the government sent two thousand troops to the Chicago area, and a federal court issued a blanket injunction that virtually ordered the union leaders to do nothing to continue the strike. Debs and his associates were convicted of defying the injunction and were imprisoned, and the strike ended. Some industrialists and businessmen cheered Cleveland's and Olney's high-handed methods, but labor was bitter.

While wrestling with intractable economic problems, Cleveland also had to deal with foreign policy matters. A staunch anti-imperialist, he blocked the annexation of Hawaii because he believed American sugar interests on the island had been involved illegally in the request. He also refused to involve the United States in Cuba's war for independence from Spain. Yet, as his first administration's efforts to build a modern steel navy attested, Cleveland still supported an active role for the United States in certain situations. In 1895, he intervened in a long-standing dispute between England and Venezuela over the boundary between British Guiana and Venezuela. When gold was discovered in the disputed territory, Britain pressed its case. Cleveland took the position with the British foreign office that its claim violated the Monroe Doctrine. When Cleveland's offer to arbitrate the dispute was rudely refused by Britain, the president secured authority from Congress to locate the boundary and force the British to recognize it. For a few tense months, war seemed a possibility. Then Britain yielded. The matter was settled by arbitration largely in Britain's favor. Certainly, Cleveland's actions enhanced the Monroe Doctrine and bolstered America's international prestige, but the dispute hardly warranted Cleveland's bellicose actions.

By 1896, Cleveland was a defeated man. Most Americans disagreed with his handling of the depression and even the majority of his own party now rejected his conservative fiscal policies. Silver Democrats, who favored the free and unlimited coinage of silver, wrested control of the party from the Bourbons. Speaking for the new power in the Democratic Party, William Jennings Bryan intoned, "We have petitioned, and our petitions have been scorned; we have entreated, and our entreaties have been disregarded; we have begged, and they have mocked when our calamity came. We beg no longer; we entreat no more; we petition no more. We defy them." At the national convention that summer, Democrats nominated Bryan to carry their banner.

Tired, bitter, and defeated, Cleveland retired from active politics. He bought a modest house in Princeton, New Jersey. He wrote and delivered a few speeches, and he fished and hunted. Even in retirement he lived a full and active life. In time, the bitterness of the mid-1890's died, and the nation's attitude toward him softened. Then on June 24, 1908, in the middle of the convention season, Cleveland died.

Cleveland's Record: Honesty and Inflexibility

As for his performance as the nation's chief executive, Cleveland was honest and courageous, and he gave the American people an honest, efficient, and courageous administration. During an age of shabby political dealings, Cleveland helped to restore prestige to the office of the presidency. He was, however, narrow and inflexible. He could never identify with the suffering farmers in the South and West or the struggling laborers in the growing cities. When the economic situation demanded flexibility and empathy, Cleveland was found wanting. His failure contributed to the people's sufferings in the mid-1890's and led to the permanent decline of the Bourbons in the Democratic Party.

Randy Roberts

Suggested Readings

Brodsky, Alyn. *Grover Cleveland: A Study in Character*. New York: St. Martin's Press, 2000. An admiring and revisionist biography that emphasizes Cleveland's commitment to maintaining personal morality throughout the issues that arose during his presidencies.

Graff, Henry F. *Grover Cleveland*. New York: Times Books, 2002. Graff, a distinguished historian, examines the 1888 election with excellent detail and offers insight into Cleveland's presidencies as a whole.

Jeffers, H. Paul. *An Honest President: The Life and Presidencies of Grover Cleveland*. New York: W. Morrow, 2000. A biography that focuses on Cleveland as a reformer and a man who used honesty and grace as a leader.

Joseph, Paul. *Grover Cleveland*. Minneapolis: ABDO, 1999. A biography written for young adults.

McElroy, Robert. *Grover Cleveland: The Man and the Statesman*. New York: Harper & Brothers, 1923. Although an older title, this remains of interest for the scholar.

Marszalek, John F. *Grover Cleveland: A Bibliography*. Westport, Conn.: Meckler, 1988. A good aid for secondary sources.

Merrill, Horace S. *Bourbon Leader: Grover Cleveland and the Democratic Party*. Boston: Little, Brown, 1957. A critical analysis of Cleveland's party role.

Nevins, Allan. *Grover Cleveland: A Study in Courage*. 1932. Reprint. New York: Dodd, Mead, 1962. A thorough biography.

_____. *Letters of Grover Cleveland, 1850-1908*. Boston: Houghton and Mifflin, 1933. A collection of Cleveland's important writings.

Tugwell, Rexford G. *Grover Cleveland*. New York: Macmillan, 1968. Another good biography.

Vexler, Robert I. *Grover Cleveland, 1837-1908: Chronology, Documents, Bibliographical Aids*. Dobbs Ferry, N.Y.: Oceana, 1968. A thorough collection of useful primary documents.

Welch, Richard E. *The Presidencies of Grover Cleveland*. Lawrence: University Press of Kansas, 1988. Provides an in-depth analysis of Cleveland's terms as president.

Benjamin Harrison

23d President, 1889-1893

Born: August 20, 1833
    North Bend, Ohio
Died: March 13, 1901
    Indianapolis, Indiana

Political Party: Republican
Vice President: Levi P. Morton

Cabinet Members

Secretary of State: James G. Blaine, John W. Foster

Secretary of the Treasury: William Windom, Charles Foster

Secretary of War: Redfield Procter, Stephen B. Elkins

Secretary of the Navy: Benjamin F. Tracy

Attorney General: W. H. H. Miller

Postmaster General: John Wanamaker

Secretary of the Interior: John W. Noble

Secretary of Agriculture: Jeremiah M. Rusk

Benjamin Harrison, the twenty-third president of the United States, became the first grandson of a former president to hold the office. His grandfather, William Henry Harrison, died only one month after his inauguration, and whereas "Little Ben" served a full term, cynics sneered that he had no more impact on the office than "Old Tippecanoe." If this were true, it was not because Harrison lacked motivation or intelligence.

Born August 20, 1833, on his grandfather's famous farm at North Bend on the Ohio River near Cincinnati, Benjamin Harrison was the son of a farmer and two-term congressman who was skeptical about the motivation of the typical political officeholder. Benjamin, a short, stocky boy, was reared in bucolic surroundings. He attended private schools and was graduated from Miami University in Oxford, Ohio. After reading law in a Cincinnati firm, young Harrison was admitted to the bar in 1854 and soon moved to Indianapolis to practice.

"Little Ben": Idealism and Intolerance

Harrison's family lineage was Whig, and its long identification with the political life of the old Northwest gave Benjamin an immediate advantage when he entered local politics in Indianapolis. From the beginning, he exhibited a strong streak of idealism, demonstrating a gen-

Portrait of Benjamin Harrison. *(Whitehouse.gov)*

The First Lady
Caroline Harrison

Caroline Lavinia Scott Harrison was born October 1, 1832, in Oxford, Ohio, where her father was a professor at Miami University. Caroline was well versed in literature, music, and the arts, and she developed a lifelong passion for painting.

Caroline met Benjamin Harrison when the family moved briefly to Cincinnati, where her father opened an all-girls school. When the family relocated the school back to Oxford, Benjamin followed and enrolled in Miami University to be near Caroline. Caroline earned a degree in music, and Benjamin went on to study law.

They married on October 20, 1853, and moved to Indianapolis, where Benjamin worked hard to establish a law practice. During this time, Caroline felt neglected. While serving in the Civil War, Benjamin realized the importance of his wife and children, and he returned as a very attentive husband and father.

Caroline's outgoing personality offset Benjamin's aloofness and was an asset during his presidential campaign. She brought a convivial atmosphere to the White House by introducing dancing to social functions, decorating the first White House Christmas tree, and giving china-painting classes to wives and daughters of White House staff. Caroline was noted for her extensive renovation of the White House, creating roomier accommodations, installing electricity, and filling the greenhouses with orchids and other varieties of plants and flowers. She also organized the china collections used by former First Ladies and made a formal display, which is now a tourist attraction. Caroline was also involved in her church and community work.

Caroline was an open-minded and forward-thinking woman of her time. During her tenure as First Lady, she helped organize the Daughters of the American Revolution and served as its first president-general. She also negotiated the admittance of women to Johns Hopkins Medical School.

Caroline developed tuberculosis and died on October 25, 1892, at age sixty.

Barbara C. Beattie

uine concern for the plight of slaves and identifying with the new Republican Party as it rose during the 1850's. Deeply religious, Harrison became an elder in the Presbyterian Church and a strong supporter of local philanthropies.

After holding local and state office as a Republican, Harrison fought in the Civil War as commander of an Indiana brigade, rising to the rank of brigadier general on merit. His supporters referred to him as General Harrison throughout the remainder of his public life. After the war, he returned to an increasingly lucrative law practice in Indianapolis, substantial activity in philanthropic causes, and a steady rise up the Republican political ladder. An ardent supporter of Radical Republicanism during Re-

construction, he later became known as a member of the party's progressive wing, supporting civil service reform, labor legislation, railroad regulation, the protective tariff, and liberal veterans' pensions. In 1876, Harrison ran unsuccessfully for governor, but four years later he became influential in the national party as chair of the Indiana delegation to the Republican convention. Elected to the United States Senate, he served from 1881 to 1887 and chaired the committee on territories, demonstrating a strong interest in the admission of the Western territories to statehood.

By 1887 Harrison was being pushed for the Republican presidential nomination to run against the incumbent, Grover Cleveland. Although one of his major assets was his name, there was more to Benjamin Harrison than that. He had developed a well-deserved reputation for ability and integrity, and both in his political career and as a Civil War commander, he had demonstrated courage, compassion, and solid judgment. Yet although he had earned respect, he was never the recipient of great affection, even from his political allies and supporters. His nickname, Little Ben, referred to his small stature — he was only about 5 feet, 6 inches tall — but it certainly was not an affectionate sobriquet. Although Republican campaigners sang that "Grandfather's Hat Fits Ben," they were unable to dispel the cold aura the candidate generated.

Despite this image, Benjamin Harrison was a very convincing speaker when addressing large crowds. He spoke in a forceful manner and exuded dignity, presence, and ability. His speeches were characterized by clarity, common sense, and excellent organization. Eschewing rhetorical bombast, Harrison illustrated his addresses with appropriate similes and never talked down to his audiences. Even political skeptics were impressed by the effectiveness of Harrison's public style.

It is ironic that, although a forceful and effective public speaker, Harrison was miserably unsuccessful in dealing with individuals. Both critics and friendly observers agreed that "he could charm a crowd of twenty thousand . . . but he could make them all enemies with a personal handshake." He was called "Mr. Harrison, the man who never laughs." Uncomfortable in social situations, he hated small talk and insincer-

Harrison and his cabinet in 1889. *(Library of Congress)*

ity and was something of a loner. He was a well-known figure in Indianapolis social and legal circles but was not at all outgoing, speaking only when spoken to and certainly not courting familiarity. In part, this attitude was a result of his idealism. He had high standards and expectations and was intolerant of those who failed to measure up. His reputation as a cold individual may have been somewhat unfair. Harrison was comfortable with children and could apparently unwind when away from the pressures of office and public life. A friend once noted, "When he's on a fishing trip, Ben takes his drink of whiskey in the morning, just like anyone else. He chews tobacco from a plug he carries in his hip pocket, spits on his worm for luck, and cusses when the fish gets away." This description would have amazed colleagues and subordinates, who were continually taken aback by Harrison's brusqueness, impatience, and icy manner.

In the 1888 campaign, President Cleveland remained aloof from the fray, believing campaigning to be beneath the dignity of his office. Harrison conducted a "front porch" campaign from his solid and comfortable home on North Delaware Street in Indianapolis. He spoke reasonably and clearly, and although he did not always tell his audiences exactly what they wanted to hear, they respected him. The professional politicians were surprised by the effectiveness of his speeches as he defeated Cleveland in the electoral college, even though he trailed Cleveland by 90,000 in the tally of the popular vote.

The Businessman's Cabinet

In his inaugural address, Harrison promised civil service reform, pensions for veterans, the free ballot for blacks, and continuation of the protective tariff. He immediately got off on the wrong foot with many of the party professionals. Matthew Quay, the Republican boss of Pennsylvania, reportedly reacted to Harrison's remark that he owed his victory to Providence with the comment that "Providence hadn't a damned thing to do with it." He supposedly said that "Harrison would never learn how close a number of men were compelled to approach the gates of the penitentiary to make him president where he could return thanks to the Almighty for his promotion." In any case, no evidence exists that Harrison was personally involved in the corrupt machinations of what was an extremely dirty campaign.

Harrison later recalled, "When I came into power, I found that the party managers had taken it all to themselves. I could not name my own Cabinet. They had sold out every place to pay the election expenses." Torn between the promises of his campaign and his personal integrity on one hand and the pressures of party politics on the other, Harrison pleased no one. He extended the number of jobs under civil service and appointed the formidable Theodore Roosevelt as a civil service commissioner, dismaying the party bosses. He also, however, appointed Philadelphia merchant John Wanamaker as postmaster general in return for Wanamaker's heavy financial contributions to the presidential campaign. Wanamaker used this traditional position for patronage dispensation to carry out one of the largest and most blatant campaigns of spoils-oriented appointments in the nation's history. The members of Harrison's cabinet were generally noted for their status as geographical party bosses rather than for their integrity or suitability for office, and they collectively became known as the Businessman's Cabinet. Even Harrison's extension of the civil service system had a partisan aspect—now newly appointed Republican officeholders would be protected when the Democrats came back into power.

A Presidency of Restricted Scope

Like other presidents of the period, Harrison had a rather limited view of the parameters of his office. He believed that policy initiatives should come primarily from Congress, with the

The Vice President
Levi P. Morton

The son of an ordained minister, Levi Parsons Morton was born on May 16, 1824, in Shoreham, Vermont. As a result of a lack of money, Morton was able to acquire only a limited education. At the age of fourteen, he began work as a store clerk, and by 1843, he was named manager of a general store in Hanover, New Hampshire. At the age of twenty-one, he bought the store from its owner and began to expand its operations. In 1849, Morton was approached to be a partner in a management company; he accepted and quickly established himself as a success. On October 15, 1856, he married Lucy Young Kimball in Long Island, New York. Tragically, on July 11, 1871, Lucy Morton died, leaving her husband in despair. Two years later, he married Anna Livingston Reede Street, and they had six children.

In 1878, Morton was elected to the United States Congress. In 1880, he was invited to accept the vice presidential nomination; however, he turned it down as a result of the advice of a close political adviser, Roscoe Conkling. After the election, President James Garfield named Morton minister to France in 1881. In his new position, Morton formally accepted the Statue of Liberty as a gift from France on July 4, 1884. Upon his return to the United Sates, he made two unsuccessful attempts to win a seat in the Senate. However, in 1888, he was asked to accept the Republican nomination for vice president, serving on the ticket with Benjamin Harrison. Following the defeat of the ticket in 1892 after a single term, Morton returned to New York where he was elected governor in 1894.

Five years after his election as governor, he retired from politics and founded the Morton Trust Company in New York. He lost his wife in 1918, and Morton died on his birthday two years later on May 16, 1920, at the age of ninety-six.

Robert P. Watson and Richard Yon

president responsible for their promulgation and general administration. During the first half of his term, the Republicans controlled Congress, and thus it would seem that Harrison should have had a relatively positive experience. From the beginning, however, he was uncomfortable with the job and with the demands that it placed on his principles and his family.

He cherished privacy and had an essentially adversarial relationship with members of the press; neither did he like the police officers and other officials who were supposed to shield him from the public. The president rose early and often walked in the White House garden, in Lafayette Park, or, if not many people were about, along Pennsylvania Avenue. As in Indianapolis, he was a familiar figure with his Prince Albert coat and umbrella. One historian who has described the period notes that "in a close-fitting Prince Albert, with an erect stance and dead-level look, Harrison resembled a pouter-pigeon on parade in LaFayette Square or Dupont Circle. Returning to the White House, he would nod curtly at the historic columns: 'There is my jail.'" After praying and breakfasting with his family, he undertook what was usually a long day's work.

Harrison immersed himself thoroughly in the most minute administrative details of the government. The White House became a model of bureaucratic efficiency, of which the president was inordinately proud. He based decisions on thorough, factual information, never shirked or avoided the hard questions, and resented those who wasted his time or failed to measure up to his standards of competence. Visitors were seldom invited to take a chair, lest they stay too long, and stories of his brusqueness became legend. Harrison never complained about the burdens of office, taking it for granted that people would understand, and he had little toleration for those who complained. Clearly, his forte was administration, which he greatly preferred to the role of political leader. Just as clearly, Harrison's obsession with minor administrative detail, his inability or unwillingness to delegate authority, and a tendency toward overwork, which compounded his personal intolerance and curtness, combined to undermine the effectiveness of his leadership.

Perhaps in the political climate of the time no president could have completely risen above or taken command of the system, but Harrison failed to make a significant effort. Although later students of his presidency have given him credit for being his own man and trying to influence policy, the fact remains that the accomplishments of the time, even those that the president supported, owed their genesis and achievement to other leaders and forces. Other political figures were on the scene who were far more effective at using the system than was Little Ben. These expert politicians included William McKinley, the congressman from Ohio, later something of a disappointment in the presidency but an effective and powerful force in the Congress; Tom Platt and Matthew Quay, the political bosses from New York and Pennsylvania; and above all, Thomas B. Reed of Maine, the speaker of the House of Representatives. Reed, a large and caustic man, presided over the

In cartoonist Joseph Keppler's 1890 parody of Edgar Allan Poe's *The Raven*, "Grandpa's Hat" overwhelms Little Ben. *(Library of Congress)*

House with an iron hand and became famous as "Czar Reed" became of his arbitrary ruling that members of Congress would be counted in determining a quorum even if they were present but not voting on a particular issue. This ruling limited the ability of the Democratic opposition to stymie the operations of the House, and it increased the power of the Republican majority. These men, and others like them, would have a greater effect in determining national policy than the dour Hoosier in the White House.

Significant Legislation: The Sherman Antitrust Act

Under such leadership, major legislation poured out of the Congress, much of it enacted in 1890. Among the more significant was the Sherman Antitrust Act, sponsored by Senator John Sherman of Ohio. By this time, public pressure was growing for governmental action to curb the power of the trusts, and several states had already attempted to deal with the problem at that level. The act (which outlawed every "contract, combination . . . or conspiracy in restraint of trade or commerce among the several states or with foreign nations") was passed with the support of both parties and the administration. It was the first national effort to deal with the problem of conspiracies in restraint of trade, and both its nature and its effectiveness have been disputed. Some have argued that the law was deliberately written to be vague and unenforceable; others hold that the failure of the law to have any major effect before 1901 was primarily a result of unfavorable interpretations by the Supreme Court. In any case, Harrison signed the bill into law, although it should be noted that, like other conservative chief executives of the period, he made little effort to enforce it.

Congress also moved to deal with the money question by passing the Sherman Silver Purchase Act, which required the Treasury to buy a stipulated amount of silver and pay for it in Treasury notes redeemable "in gold or silver coin." A compromise between those who wanted to increase the monetary supply by the coinage of silver and the hard money faction, which wanted a restricted monetary system and a return to the gold standard, the law had no significant effect and satisfied no one. It was based

on a plan promoted by Secretary of the Treasury William Windom and supported only halfheartedly by the president, and it was designed at least in part to win the support of Western congressmen from silver-mining states for the high tariff duties that were so dear to Republican hearts.

The third legislative accomplishment of 1890 was passage of the McKinley tariff, the highest protective tariff in American history. It was designed primarily to protect United States industry, but to placate farmers, increased duties were also established for agricultural products. Consistent with Harrison's principles, the measure included a reciprocity provision, which he had promoted, that allowed the president to lower duties if other countries did the same. Harrison and Secretary of State James G. Blaine, anxious to increase trade with Latin America, used this provision to begin negotiating reciprocal trade agreements.

In his first message to Congress, Harrison recommended federal protection for black voters, improved conditions for railroad workers, and generous pensions for veterans. The first two recommendations came to naught, but in 1890 Congress passed a liberal Dependents' Pension Act, which broadened coverage to make eligible for pensions all disabled veterans, regardless of whether their disabilities were service-connected, and their dependents, and thereby opened the door to drastically increased governmental pension expenditures. These were accompanied by other government outlays for internal improvements, subsidies to steamship lines, and enlargement of the navy. The last two areas were pet projects of President Harrison, who wanted to build a two-ocean navy and promote the American merchant marine. The cost was enormous. The fifty-first Congress was the first to spend $1 billion in peacetime, but when the critics howled and the Democrats termed it the "Billion Dollar Congress," Speaker Reed simply responded that the United States was a billion-dollar country.

Foreign policy was dominated by Secretary of State Blaine. Long a power, presidential aspirant, and kingmaker in the Republican Party, Blaine was a man of ability who had helped to decide on Harrison's nomination. His stature was such, however, that he would dominate an administration. Harrison knew this and delayed for some time before offering the state portfolio to the "Plumed Knight." Nevertheless, in the final analysis Harrison had no other choice than to bring "the man from Maine" into the cabinet. Blaine would prove a productive secretary of state, although some disagreement exists about whether Blaine, Harrison, or both should receive the credit for his accomplishments.

In 1889, the first Pan-American Congress met in Washington, D.C., and promoted cooperation among hemispheric nations by, among other things, creating the Pan-American Union. Other diplomatic activities included an abortive attempt at the end of the term to annex Hawaii, an agreement to arbitrate the Bering Sea controversy with Great Britain over fur seals in that area, and the establishment of a joint protectorate over the Samoan Islands.

By the middle of Harrison's term, the rising tide of political protest was becoming stronger, and in the 1890 midterm elections the Republicans lost control of Congress. Strong popular reaction against the new McKinley tariff was partially responsible, but it was also true that the administration and Congress seemed to be out of harmony with the popular mood, and Harrison had not demonstrated an ability to lead the public or the legislature toward support of his policies. The emergence of the Populist Party, intervention by the federal government in the bloody strike at the Homestead works of the Carnegie Steel Company, and public concern about the dissipation of a sizable federal Treasury surplus through prodigal expenditures combined to seal Harrison's fate. The election year 1892 saw a replay of the 1888 presidential election, but the results were reversed. Benjamin Harrison was defeated by Grover Cleveland by more than 63,000 popular votes and 132 electoral votes, and he returned to Indianapolis and the practice of law. His last major public endeavor was to represent Venezuela in the arbitration of its boundary dispute with Great Britain in 1897. Little Ben died at his home on March 13, 1901, and was buried in Indianapolis.

An Instinctive Failure

Benjamin Harrison was a prime example of the fact that high marks for integrity, courage, and intellect do not necessarily make a good president. Harrison's inability or unwillingness to function within the glad-handing, give-and-take world of practical politics made it virtually impossible for him to influence legislators or other political constituents and power brokers, and achieve his goals; neither was he able to build a coterie of close personal associates or friends to help him through the political battles. Although recent historians have tended to give him more credit than did their predecessors, Harrison's was essentially a failed presidency. A recent biographer treats him very generously, yet concludes that he "seems to emerge greater as a man than as a president."

James E. Fickle

Suggested Readings

Calhoun, Charles W. *Benjamin Harrison*. New York: Times Books, 2005. Unlike standard biographies of Harrison that depict his presidency as corrupt and inactive, Calhoun dispels the stereotypes in order to emphasize the accomplishments of Harrison.

Faulkner, Harold U. *Politics, Reform, and Expansion: 1890-1900*. New York: Harper, 1959. Examines the political climate of the era in which Harrison served as president.

Josephson, Matthew. *The Politicos: 1865-1896*. 1938. Reprint. New York: Harcourt and Brace, 1966. A biography that tends to be critical of Harrison.

Keller, Morton. *Affairs of State: Public Life in Late*

Nineteenth Century America. Cambridge, Mass.: Harvard University Press, 1977. Provides excellent background for the political and domestic affairs during the Harrison presidency.

Morgan, H. Wayne. *From Hayes to McKinley: National Party Politics, 1877-1896.* Syracuse, N.Y.: Syracuse University Press, 1969. A highly readable survey of the politics of the Gilded Age.

Perry, James M. *Touched with Fire: Five Presidents and the Civil War Battles That Made Them.* New York: PublicAffairs, 2005. Uses diaries, letters, and other firsthand accounts to bring life to the war battles that formed the character and political drive of presidents Grant, Hayes, Garfield, Harrison, and McKinley.

Sievers, Harry J. *Benjamin Harrison.* 3 vols. Chicago: H. Regnery, 1952-1968. A favorable biography.

Socolofsky, Homer E., and Allan B. Spetter. *The Presidency of Benjamin Harrison.* Lawrence: University Press of Kansas, 1988. A good analysis of the Harrison administration.

Sturgis, Amy H., comp. *Presidents from Hayes Through McKinley, 1877-1901: Debating the Issues in Pro and Con Primary Documents.* Westport, Conn.: Greenwood Press, 2003. A collection of primary documents and commentary is used to debate issues that were pertinent during the tenure of presidents serving between 1877 and 1901.

William McKinley
25th President, 1897-1901

Born: January 29, 1843
    Niles, Ohio
Died: September 14, 1901
    Buffalo, New York

Political Party: Republican
Vice Presidents: Garret A. Hobart,
    Theodore Roosevelt

Cabinet Members
Secretary of State: John Sherman, William R. Day, John Hay
Secretary of the Treasury: Lyman J. Gage
Secretary of War: Russell A. Alger, Elihu Root
Secretary of the Navy: John D. Long
Attorney General: Joseph McKenna, John W. Griggs, Philander C. Knox
Postmaster General: Joseph Gary, Charles E. Smith
Secretary of the Interior: Cornelius N. Bliss, E. A. Hitchcock
Secretary of Agriculture: James Wilson

William McKinley was born in Niles, Ohio, on January 29, 1843, and attended Allegheny College before enlisting in the Union army in 1861. He attained the rank of major and was known by that title during his political life. His combat record in the Civil War added to his public appeal in late nineteenth century America. After the war he became a lawyer and served as prosecuting attorney for Stark County, Ohio, from 1869 to 1871. He married Ida Saxton in 1871. Their two children died early in life, and Mrs. McKinley became a perpetual invalid on whom her husband lavished care and affection.

In 1876, McKinley, then a prosperous attorney in Canton, Ohio, was elected to Congress.

He served there until 1891. He became identified with the protective tariff as an expression of the nationalism of the Republican Party, and he helped frame the McKinley tariff of 1890. Defeated for reelection in 1890 in a Democratic year, he ran successfully for governor of Ohio in 1891 and was reelected in 1893. His ability to carry this key Midwestern state and his broad national popularity made him the front-runner for the Republican presidential nomination in 1896. The friendship and support of the Ohio industrialist Marcus A. Hanna helped him secure the nomination, but it was McKinley's appeal to the broad mass of the GOP that made him the

Portrait of William McKinley. *(Whitehouse.gov)*

party's standardbearer.

William Jennings Bryan won the Democratic nomination as the champion of inflationary solutions to the depression of the 1890's. His advocacy of "free silver" at a ratio of sixteen to one with gold and his youthful energy made him a formidable adversary as he stumped the country for the Democrats and the farmer-based People's Party. McKinley campaigned from his front porch in Canton. More than three-quarters of a million people heard his deft speeches that attacked inflation and praised the protective tariff as the Republican cure for hard times. While the candidate reached the electorate in controlled circumstances that conveyed an image of dignity and calm, the Republicans, with Hanna as campaign chairman, sent out 250,000,000 pamphlets and documents that echoed McKinley's themes. The Republicans did not buy the election of 1896 with their ample campaign treasury. They used the money that Hanna raised from wealthy contributors to conduct a "campaign of education." In the end, the voters went decisively for McKinley's pluralist, inclusive doctrine. He received 271 electoral votes to Bryan's 176 and the largest plurality in the popular vote since Ulysses S. Grant in 1872.

McKinley was fifty-four when he came to the presidency. A British journalist who observed him in 1896 noted that he had a "strong cleanshaven face" with "clear eyes, wide nose, full lips—all his features suggest dominant will and energy rather than subtlety of mind or emotion." He was 5 feet, 6 inches, and sought in dress and posture to appear taller than he really was. Because McKinley wrote few personal letters and rarely shared intimate thoughts with friends, he was not an easy man to know. Enemies called him irresolute and cautious. Those who worked with him knew better. "He was a man of great power," said Elihu Root, "because he was absolutely indifferent to credit. His great desire was 'to get it done.' He cared nothing about the credit, but McKinley *always had his way*."

McKinley's First Term: The Power of the Presidency Revitalized

When McKinley took the oath of office on March 4, 1897, the presidency was still weak relative to Congress, and the institution lacked the modern mechanisms that enable a chief executive to govern. Grover Cleveland had asserted presidential prerogatives to deal with the economic crisis of the decade, but his inept handling of Congress, his party, and public opinion had pushed the presidency lower in popular esteem. The nation's first citizen seemed aloof and remote from the average American. During his four and a half years in office, McKinley laid the basis for the modern presidency and revitalized the institution's power. The Spanish-American War accelerated this process, but even before that conflict the new president showed his intention to reassert his authority.

The cabinet that he assembled was a conventional official family. It reflected the geographical balances within the Republican Party in its selection of John D. Long of Massachusetts as secretary of the Navy, Joseph McKenna of California as attorney general, and Joseph Gary of Maryland as postmaster general. Lyman J. Gage, an Illinois banker, went to the Treasury Department, and Cornelius N. Bliss of New York served in the Interior Department. Two weak choices flawed the cabinet. Russell A. Alger of Michigan became secretary of war because of his service to the party and popularity with fellow Civil War veterans. McKinley failed to ask how he might perform in the event of war.

The choice of secretary of state became entangled with the problem of a reward for Mark Hanna. After Hanna declined to be postmaster general, the possibility arose that Senator John Sherman of Ohio might be persuaded to take the State Department and thus make a vacancy to which Hanna could be appointed by the governor of Ohio. Later talk of a deal overlooked that McKinley approached another senator first about the State Department and that Sherman himself wanted the appointment. The problem was that Sherman's mind was failing and he was not up to his new duties. That a friend of the president, William R. Day, would be Sherman's assistant and keep an eye on him did not overcome the basic error of naming Sherman. When Hanna was appointed to the Senate, the whole topic gained unfortunate public attention. Sherman was a poor choice who had to be ignored while in office and eased out once the war with Spain began.

The new administration pursued varied political and diplomatic initiatives in its first year. McKinley called Congress into special session on March 15, 1897, to revise the tariff, and the protectionist Dingley tariff became law on July 24. Although the Dingley law raised customs duties, it also contained language that autho-

rized the president to seek tariff reciprocity treaties with trading partners. McKinley used these provisions to seek a lowering of trade barriers from 1897 onward.

Negotiations with France and Great Britain for an international agreement to promote a wider use of silver in world commerce began with promise but collapsed in October, 1897, over British opposition to any breach in the gold standard. Following that result, McKinley moved toward an endorsement of gold that led eventually to the passage of the Gold Standard Act of 1900.

In foreign affairs, the administration addressed the long-standing disputes with Great Britain and Canada over fur seals, Newfoundland fisheries, and the Alaskan boundary ques-

The First Lady
Ida McKinley

Ida Saxton McKinley was born on June 8, 1847, in Canton, Ohio, to a prominent family of a wealthy banker. She was an educated, independent, and socially active young woman.

While working in her father's bank, Ida met attorney William McKinley. They married on January 25, 1871. Later that year, their first child, Katharine, was born. In early 1873, Ida's mother died. Shortly after, Ida gave birth to her second daughter, but the baby died a few months later. About a year later, in 1875, Katharine also died.

Ida never recovered emotionally from these deaths. She became depressed, developed epilepsy, and suffered from phlebitis and headaches. She was a shadow of her former self, living as an invalid, often medicated, with William tending to her needs while also tending to his political aspirations. Though rumors circulated about Ida's condition and character during his presidential campaign, William was respected by society for his unfaltering devotion to her.

William was elected president in 1896. Ida tried to fulfill her role as First Lady by sporadically serving as hostess and attending social functions, but she always required special accommodations. William broke White House seating protocol in order to sit beside her, enabling him to cover her face with a handkerchief whenever she experienced a seizure.

Ida supported her husband behind the scenes by sharing her political insights and advising him about presidential appointments. She was influential in William's commitment to the temperance movement, and she most likely played a role in his decision to annex the Philippines at the end of the Spanish-American War. Her only personal contribution to society was her knitting of slippers to be sold by charities for fund-raising.

When William was shot in 1901 by an insurgent, Ida showed courage during his injury, death, and funeral. She returned to Canton and lived for six more years. She died on May 26, 1907.

Barbara C. Beattie

The Vice President
Garret A. Hobart

Garret A. Hobart served as the vice president in the first administration of William McKinley. Born on June 3, 1844, in Long Branch, New Jersey, Hobart was educated in local public schools. He graduated from Rutgers College in 1863 and became a schoolteacher in Marlborough, New Jersey. After a short stint as an educator, Hobart studied law under Socrates Tuttle in Patterson, New Jersey, and was admitted to the bar in 1866.

In 1869, Hobart established a law firm in Patterson with his former legal mentor, Tuttle. That same year, he married; he and his wife, Jeannie, had one son and one daughter. Hobart's entry into politics came in 1871, when he was elected to Patterson's city council. In 1872, he was elected to the New Jersey Assembly, and two years later, he rose to the rank of speaker of the assembly for two years. In 1876, Hobart was elected to the New Jersey Senate, where he served until 1882, the last two years as the chamber's president. Despite his success in the state legislature and chairing the state's Republican Committee from 1880 to 1881, he was unsuccessful in his bid for the U.S. Senate in 1883.

After his defeat, Hobart was elected to his party's national committee at the 1884 Republican National Convention. Hobart enjoyed considerable success when he returned to his legal practice, securing clients from prominent railways, banks, and a steamship company. He also served as the director of banks and other enterprises and managed the unsuccessful campaign by John W. Griggs for governor of New Jersey in 1895. The following year, Hobart was nominated as McKinley's vice presidential candidate. The campaign was successful, and Hobart served as vice president until his death on November 21, 1899, at his home in Patterson.

Robert P. Watson and Richard Yon

tion with Canada. A joint high commission began considering these interrelated questions in 1898; these talks were also part of a general improvement in Anglo-American relations that marked the McKinley years.

More difficult was the perennial problem of Hawaiian annexation. Republicans had long favored acquiring the islands, and tension with Japan over Japanese immigration and that nation's ambitions in the Pacific led to the writing of a treaty of annexation. The Senate received the pact at the end of the special session in June, 1897, but a vote could not come until Congress reconvened in December. McKinley exercised presidential persuasion on behalf of the treaty in early 1898, but opposition from Southern Democrats, whose states competed with Hawaiian sugar, stalled the administration short of the two-thirds majority needed. It was decided to pursue the approach of a joint resolution of annexation once the foreign policy crisis with Spain was concluded.

The president also sought to revitalize his office in 1897. The White House, surrounded by sentries and detectives in Cleveland's final years, became easier to visit. McKinley also traveled extensively in a manner that publicized the openness of his administration and gave him a means to influence public opinion. He devoted equal attention to relations with the press. Newsmen were given a table on the second floor where those assigned to the White House had seats. McKinley allowed no formal interviews, and direct quotation of the president was also forbidden. The chief executive was, however, an adept leaker, and he served as a much better news source for the administration than students of his presidency have realized.

McKinley used his staff and cabinet in ways

Excerpts from William McKinley's message to Congress requesting the declaration of war against Spain, April 11, 1898:

The present condition of affairs in Cuba is a constant menace to our peace and entails upon this Government an enormous expense. With such a conflict waged for years in an island so near us and with which our people have such trade and business relations; when the lives and liberty of our citizens are in constant danger and their property destroyed and themselves ruined; where our trading vessels are liable to seizure and are seized at our very door by war ships of a foreign nation; the expeditions of filibustering that we are powerless to prevent altogether, and the irritating questions and entanglements thus arising — all these and others that I need not mention, with the resulting strained relations, are a constant menace to our peace and compel us to keep on a semi war footing with a nation with which we are at peace.

These elements of danger and disorder already pointed out have been strikingly illustrated by a tragic event which has deeply and justly moved the American people. I have already transmitted to Congress the report of the naval court of inquiry on the destruction of the battle ship *Maine* in the harbor of Havana during the night of the 15th of February. The destruction of that noble vessel has filled the national heart with inexpressible horror. Two hundred and fifty-eight brave sailors and Marines and two officers of our Navy, reposing in the fancied security of a friendly harbor, have been hurled to death, grief and want brought to their homes and sorrow to the nation.

The naval court of inquiry, which, it is needless to say, commands the unqualified confidence of the Government, was unanimous in its conclusion that the destruction of the *Maine* was caused by an exterior explosion — that of a submarine mine. It did not assume to place the responsibility. That remains to be fixed.

In any event, the destruction of the *Maine*, by whatever exterior cause, is a patent and impressive proof of a state of things in Cuba that is intolerable. That condition is thus shown to be such that the Spanish Government can not assure safety and security to a vessel of the American Navy in the harbor of Havana on a mission of peace, and rightfully there. . . .

The issue is now with the Congress. It is a solemn responsibility. I have exhausted every effort to relieve the intolerable condition of affairs which is at our doors. Prepared to execute every obligation imposed upon me by the Constitution and the law, I await your action.

---

that anticipated modern practices. The president's secretary, John Addison Porter, and his assistant, George B. Cortelyou, worked out a system to manage the release of official speeches and statements that made the White House a more important center for news. As the efficient Cortelyou supplanted Porter and became more influential, his role in arranging McKinley's tours and supervising the flow of business made him a forerunner of the twentieth century White House staff. McKinley employed his cabinet as a sounding board for policy but left no doubt as to who was in charge.

John Sherman said that the meetings were "not a free exchange of opinions but rather the mandates of a paramount ruler." The quality of the cabinet improved when John Hay joined it as secretary of state in 1898 and Elihu Root became secretary of war in 1899.

At the end of his first year in office, McKinley had made important progress toward a revitalized presidency. He had established good relations with the press, publicized his office through travel, and expanded his influence with Congress. In the government, he had tested his associates and reasserted formal procedures for decision making that brought power back to the presidency. All these accomplishments would be needed as McKinley confronted the foreign policy crisis that would determine the nature of his remaining years in the White House and the way history has depicted him.

The Spanish-American War

The Spanish-American War, which began in April, 1898, is most often characterized as an unnecessary conflict that McKinley did not want but lacked the courage to prevent. It is rarely recognized that real issues separated the United States and Spain in these years. In 1895, a rebellion against Spanish rule broke out in Cuba. The Cuban rebels sought independence from Madrid and refused to contemplate a negotiated settlement of the war. Spain regarded Cuba as part of the Spanish nation, and committed several hundred thousand men to subdue the uprising. The Spanish people would never have tolerated a resolution of the fighting that took the "Ever Faithful Isle" away from Spain without a war. No basis for a compromise existed between these two adversaries.

Grover Cleveland followed a course that allowed Spain the chance to put down the rebellion and preserve its sovereignty over Cuba. The administration hoped that Spain would improve conditions on the island, prevent European intervention, and maintain its hegemony. Cleveland's policies persuaded Madrid that the United States would not impose a deadline and that procrastination on American demands might eventually produce success in Cuba. Because of the unpopularity of Cleveland's approach in Congress and the country at large, the United States had no viable policy toward Cuba when McKinley took office.

The new president decided that Spain must have a chance to end the rebellion, but that military action could not continue indefinitely without result. Moreover, Spain must conduct the war within humane limits and not use "fire and famine to accomplish by uncertain indirection what the military arm seems powerless to directly accomplish." Finally, any settlement must be acceptable to the Cuban rebels. McKinley wanted to convince Spain, by a process of gradual diplomatic pressure, to relinquish Cuba peacefully. Such a decision would, he believed, serve Spain's own interests. The Americans hoped that Spain would yield Cuba; the Spanish vowed never to do so. If both sides stood firm, in the end war was inescapable.

Through the second half of 1897, the McKinley administration believed that its policy of intensifying diplomatic pressure was altering Spanish behavior. In November, the Madrid government ended the practice of moving Cubans into "reconcentration" camps and announced an autonomy plan for the island. The Cubans obtained more home rule, but Spanish sovereignty remained in place. Nevertheless, the direction of Spanish action seemed positive as the year ended. In his annual message to Congress in early December, McKinley called it "a course from which recession with honor is impossible."

Events deteriorated in January, 1898. On January 12, riots against the new autonomy program occurred in Cuba that persuaded McKinley that Spain could not live up to its promises. As the situation worsened, the administration decided to send a warship to Havana harbor, and the battleship *Maine* arrived on January 25. On February 1, the Spanish reiterated their view that their sovereignty over Cuba must be preserved and any foreign intervention resisted. President McKinley received this information on February 9.

That same day American newspapers proclaimed that the Spanish minister to the United States, Enrique Dupuy de Lome, had written a private letter, intercepted and published by the Cubans, that called the president "weak and a bidder for the admiration of the crowd." Such insulting language led to Dupuy le Lome's recall. More significant were his words that indicated that Spain was stalling for time in its negotiations with Washington and not acting in good faith.

Six days later, on February 15, the *Maine* blew up in Havana harbor, killing more than 260 officers and men. Modern research has shown that the explosion had an internal cause, probably spontaneous combustion in a coal bunker. Public opinion at the time believed that the cause was external and that Spain was either responsible or negligent in allowing the explosion to occur. For McKinley, the problem was to retain control of the situation in the face of public excitement and to determine the cause of the tragedy. A naval court of inquiry was set up, and the president knew that when it reported, he would face a deadline for action. While the country awaited the court's verdict in mid-March, 1898, the administration sought to bolster national defense and explored, without success, the idea of buying Cuba from Spain.

Time ran out for McKinley's policy as the month concluded. Senator Redfield Proctor of Vermont told the Senate on March 17 of conditions in Cuba in a speech that moved public attitudes closer to intervention. Two days later, the president learned that the naval board had concluded, based on the physical evidence and scientific knowledge then available, that an external explosion had destroyed the *Maine*. When he submitted the report to Congress four or five days later, pressure for war would mount.

Over the next several weeks, McKinley pressed Spain to grant an armistice or to accept American mediation leading to Cuban independence. In response to the first initiative of the United States, extended in late March, Spain refused to contemplate independence for the island, either at once or through negotiations. Under intense pressure from Congress for war, McKinley tried to buy time to allow Spain to see the wisdom of relinquishing Cuba peacefully. Spain's negative answer to the American proposals, which reached the White House on March 31, 1898, meant that the president had to

lay the matter before Congress. He prepared to send a message to the lawmakers during the first week of April.

McKinley's message went to Capitol Hill on April 11. Many historians believe that Spain had in fact capitulated to American demands by the time the president acted, making war unnecessary. This judgment is incorrect. What Spain did on April 9 was agree, under the prodding of its European allies, to ask for a suspension of hostilities in Cuba. Unlike an armistice, this break in the fighting did not involve a political recognition of the rebels. It would gain time for Spain to defend Cuba against the United States, especially since the length of the pause would be determined by the Spanish military commander in the field. Spain still balked at Cuban independence and, on the key American conditions, had not capitulated at all.

The argument that McKinley's "weakness" prevented a peaceful settlement rests on a false premise. Spain had not yielded, and the president had not missed a chance for a negotiated peace. His message to Congress, read by a clerk, asked for presidential authority to end the hostilities in Cuba through the use of armed force. "The war in Cuba must stop," he concluded. He mentioned Spain's proposed suspension of hostilities at the end but gave it little weight.

Congress spent the next week debating its response. It adopted the Teller Amendment, which disclaimed any goal to control Cuba, but voted down efforts to accord political recognition to the rebels. On April 19, Congress passed a resolution that McKinley could accept, giving him the authority to intervene militarily. The president signed it on April 20. Spain broke diplomatic relations on the same day and declared war on April 24. Congress said on April 25 that a state of war between the two nations had existed since April 21. In the end, the Spanish-American War took place because both countries believed that their cause was just. McKinley had sought a diplomatic solution until that option was clearly impossible, and he conducted the negotiations with Spain with more tenacity and courage than his critics have been willing to recognize.

The Spanish-American War lasted a little more than three months, and it was a decisive military triumph for the United States. For the president, it became a test of his leadership ability as he played a crucial part in directing military operations and shaping diplomatic policy to end the fighting. The most important event in the war's initial stage was the overwhelming victory that Commodore George Dewey and his naval squadron won at Manila Bay in the Philippines on May 1, 1898. The American navy was in the Asian archipelago to further war plans that had been developed since 1895. The celebrated telegram that Assistant Secretary of the Navy Theodore Roosevelt sent Dewey on February 25, 1898, was an element in this large process, not a decisive departure from it.

Acquisition of the Philippines

After Dewey's success, the McKinley administration sent American troops to the Philippines in May, 1898. This military commitment reflected the president's intention to keep a United States option to acquire the islands as a result of the war. In the opening weeks of the conflict, McKinley thought that a port in the islands might be all that the country would need, but he intended to preserve flexibility. "While we are conducting war and until its conclusion we must keep all we get," he wrote privately. "When the war is over we must keep what we want."

The emerging United States policy in the summer of 1898 brought tensions with Filipinos, led by Emilio Aguinaldo, who were in revolt against Spain in pursuit of national independence. McKinley instructed Dewey and the army officers in the islands not to have any formal dealings with the Filipino forces. At the same time, he pushed anew for the annexation of Hawaii and employed presidential influence and lobbying to get an annexation resolution through the House in June and the Senate in July. The Hawaiian Islands would be an important supply link for a military campaign in the Philippines.

The primary focus of the fighting against Spain was Cuba. Proponents of war had argued that taking the island would be easy. In fact, however, raising an army, moving it to Cuba,

The front page of the New York *World* for February 17, 1898, depicts the explosion of the *Maine* in Havana. *(Library of Congress)*

and winning the battles proved to be a task that required McKinley to exercise close presidential supervision and leadership of the war effort. There was no shortage of volunteers to fight in this most popular conflict, and the army, along with Secretary of War Alger, was ill-prepared to cope with the sudden flood of eager recruits. Nearly 280,000 men saw active duty in the war. Many of them complained about shortages of supplies, ammunition, and the quality of the food in their rations. An experiment with canned roast beef produced an inedible meal and a major postwar controversy. By the time the fighting had ended, the War Department and the secretary had resolved most of the logistic problems that marked the early weeks of the fighting. Nevertheless, the impression of confusion and ineptitude lingered in the public mind and made Alger the subject of scathing press criticism.

Initially, the administration expected to fight a naval battle for Cuba. It became clear, however, that troops on the ground would be required to ensure political control of Cuba's fate and forestall any prospect of European intervention. An invasion of Cuba was planned for May. Then the focus of the assault became the harbor and city of Santiago de Cuba, where the Spanish fleet, under Admiral Pascual de Cervera, had been bottled up by June 1. American troops, commanded by General William R. Shafter, got ashore in late June, after a series of delays.

From the War Room in the White House, McKinley followed closely the combat that ensued. A switchboard with twenty telegraph lines, maps, and a staff of clerks gave the president the capacity to communicate with Shafter within twenty minutes, projecting a presidential presence directly to the battlefield. On July 1, American ground forces defeated the Spanish defenders at San Juan Hill; on July 3, the navy destroyed the Spanish fleet outside Santiago harbor. With these victories the focus shifted to securing the surrender of the Span-

iards in Cuba and bringing the war to an end. Over the next two weeks, the president kept the pressure on his commanders to achieve Spanish capitulation, which came on July 17. At the same time, American forces under General Nelson A. Miles captured Puerto Rico. The most significant danger to the United States military in the Caribbean was the prospect of tropical disease, especially malaria and yellow fever.

As Spain's military position collapsed in mid-July, 1898, the Spanish government asked France to approach Washington about peace negotiations. In discussions that began on July 26, McKinley insisted that Spain give up Cuba and Puerto Rico and that the Philippines be the subject for the peace conference that would follow the end of the fighting. The president stood firm even though he knew that the physical condition of his army in Cuba was deteriorating. Word leaked out to the press about sickness in the army in early August, but the news did not have an adverse effect on the American negotiating position. Reluctantly accepting the terms of the United States, Spain agreed to an armistice on August 12, 1898.

In the immediate aftermath of the armistice, the administration arranged for soldiers from the Cuban expedition to come home at once. Sickness in Cuba and the United States killed more than 2,500 soldiers; battle deaths in the war reached a total of 281 officers and men. To meet the public outcry over the condition of the army, McKinley created a commission under Grenville M. Dodge, a Union army veteran and railroad owner, to investigate the War Department and its leadership. This body enabled the president to avoid a congressional investigation and to diffuse the political impact, during an election year, of problems in the conduct of the war. The Dodge Commission also promoted reform in the army through the recommendations for change it made in its report.

Although governing Cuba remained a large task after the fighting ended, the fate of the Philippines was a central concern for McKinley in

413

WHAT WILL HE DO WITH IT?

A cartoon from June, 1898, questions the fate of the Philippines after the Spanish-American War. *(Library of Congress)*

the autumn of 1898. The president had replaced John Sherman as secretary of state with William R. Day when the war began. Now Day was replaced by John Hay, who was to lead the American delegation to the peace talks with Spain in Paris. To that body, McKinley added three senators who would vote on any treaty they negotiated. The president knew that the issue of the Philippines was exacerbated by increasing tension between American troops and the Filipinos. He was also aware of German and Japanese interest in the islands should the United States depart. McKinley had already decided against an independent Philippines under an American protectorate, but the administration did not yet go beyond retaining one island, Luzon, in the archipelago. The prospect that the United

States might take all the Philippines and acquire an overseas empire had aroused opposition from those who styled themselves anti-imperialists, and an important political battle was imminent as the peace negotiations went forward.

To rally support for his foreign policy, President McKinley made a speaking tour of the Midwest in October. Ostensibly nonpolitical, the junket helped Republican candidates in the congressional elections and allowed McKinley to sound themes that prepared the nation for the acquisition of all the Philippines. In Iowa, he said that "we do not want to shirk a single responsibility that has been put upon us by the results of the war." The president used the publicity weapons of his office to set the terms of the debate and to move opinion in the direction he desired.

Later in the month the question of the Philippines became crucial at the Paris talks. The American delegates asked on October 25 for precise instructions, and McKinley responded three days later. He could see "but one plain path of duty—the acceptance of the archipelago." The celebrated anecdote that has McKinley seeking guidance from God through prayer at this pivotal juncture is implausible and represents one of those cases of embroidered reminiscence that attach themselves to presidents who have died in office. The decision to take all the Philippines was a logical outgrowth of the policy McKinley had followed since Dewey's victory in May.

Spain and the United States signed a peace treaty on December 10, 1898, by which the victor gained the Philippines, Puerto Rico, and Guam. Spain relinquished Cuba and received a $20 million payment. McKinley's political task was to secure Senate ratification of the treaty.

Over the next two months, he used the extensive array of methods open to a strong president. In the South, where Democratic senators represented a key bloc of votes, McKinley made public appeals in December. The administration wooed other lawmakers with promises of patronage and exerted pressure on the state legislatures, which in those days elected senators. Support for approval of the pact from William Jennings Bryan and divisions among its opponents also helped McKinley. All these elements helped bring ratification of the Treaty of Paris on February 6, 1899, by a vote of 57 to 27, one more vote than necessary.

On the day of the vote, Americans knew that fighting had begun in the Philippines between United States soliders and Filipino troops under Aguinaldo's command. Relations had been increasingly tense in December and January, as it became evident that the United States intended to exercise political control over the islands and to assert its sovereignty. McKinley sent a commission to the islands in late January, 1899, to establish a civil government. Before that body arrived, the fighting had begun. McKinley asserted that the United States had "no imperial designs" on the Philippines, but intended to carry out the obligations assumed under the peace treaty. Anti-imperialists and Filipinos saw the question differently, and the president faced domestic opposition to the fighting even in its earliest stages.

The Vice President
Theodore Roosevelt

Roosevelt served as vice president in the second McKinley administration. Teddy Roosevelt was born on October 27, 1858, in New York City. Born into wealth and privilege, Roosevelt traveled to Europe several times and attended prestigious private schools until his acute asthma required him to be educated at home by tutors. Roosevelt's health improved, and he was graduated from Harvard University in 1880. That same year, he married Alice Hathaway Lee on his birthday. The couple had one daughter. Roosevelt's entrance into politics came while he was only in his twenties when he was elected to the New York Assembly, where he served in 1881 and was twice reelected.

However, the year 1884 would prove to be a tragic one when both his mother and his wife died on the same day — February 14. To escape his sorrow, Roosevelt traveled the American West, where he hunted, worked on a ranch, and regained his enthusiasm for politics. Roosevelt also started his other successful career, as an author, while in his twenties. Over the course of his life, he would publish a number of books and essays on an impressive array of subjects, from naval warfare to hunting.

After returning to New York from the West, he was unsuccessful in a bid to be mayor of New York City in 1886. On December 2 of that same year, he married his childhood friend Edith Carow in London. The couple had four sons and a daughter. President Benjamin Harrison appointed Roosevelt as U.S. Civil Service commissioner in 1889, and he was selected as New York City's police commissioner in 1895. In both positions he earned a record and reputation as a bold reformer. President William McKinley appointed him as his assistant secretary of the Navy in 1897, but he resigned with the outbreak of the war against Spain, organizing his famous Rough Riders unit. Returning as a war hero, Colonel Roosevelt was elected governor of New York in 1898, then nominated as McKinley's vice president in 1900. His vice presidency was brief, as McKinley was assassinated only months into his term, and Roosevelt rose to the presidency. One of America's most admired and beloved politicians, Roosevelt died on January 6, 1919.

Robert P. Watson and Richard Yon

In the wake of the Spanish-American War, McKinley had an array of foreign policy issues to confront during 1899 and 1900. The struggle in the Philippines was the most urgent. Militarily, the Americans gained an ascendancy over the Filipinos in the spring of 1899 in a series of conventional battles. During the rainy season from May to October, the Philippines Commission tried to establish a civil government within the president's framework that put American sovereignty at the center of any political arrangements. The Filipinos refused to accede to American plans. In the meantime, the anti-imperialists at home criticized the army's policy of censoring news from the islands as well as the way the war was being waged. By the end of the year, the army had defeated the Filipino forces in regular warfare. Aguinaldo now decided to shift to guerrilla tactics. With the combat situation improving, McKinley sent a second Philippines Commission in early 1900 under William Howard Taft, to pursue the goal of civil government.

Critics of McKinley at the time and since have alleged that American soldiers pursued a genocidal policy toward the Philippine natives and were also guilty of war crimes and atrocities in combat. The first charge is not true. The second has a basis in fact. Though official policy neither condoned nor approved the mistreatment or killing of prisoners, American troops did violate the rules of war and army regulations in the Philippine fighting. The nation that had condemned the harsh tactics of Spain in Cuba now found itself using the same techniques in its own colonial war.

American Interests in Central America

The fate of Cuba was of almost equal importance to the McKinley administration in 1899-1900. The president believed that the Teller Amendment had to be respected, but he also wanted to ensure that Cuba remained free from interference by nations—such as Germany—with ambitions in the Caribbean. During 1899, a military government ran the islands. The soldiers improved the economic situation of the war-ravaged country and oversaw the disbanding of the rebel army. Once McKinley selected Elihu Root to be secretary of war in July, 1899, the task of establishing a civil government got under way and went forward throughout 1900. At all times, however, the president made clear that Cuba would have political and military links to the United States.

The outcome of this process was the Platt Amendment of 1901. Attached to an army appropriation bill, the amendment prohibited Cuba, once it became independent, from allying itself with a foreign power. It also gave the United States the right to intervene to preserve a stable government in the island and granted American rights to have naval bases on Cuban soil. The amendment, which McKinley shaped, reflected apprehensions about Germany's intentions in the region at the turn of the century and was designed to prevent a recurrence of the events of 1898. Instead, it became a permanent source of Cuban-American friction until it was abrogated in the 1930's.

President McKinley addressed other issues arising out of the war in these months. To achieve a route for a canal across Central America required an agreement with Great Britain to revise the Clayton-Bulwer Treaty of 1850, which barred both countries from having exclusive control of a canal. That goal in turn required a resolution of the controversy over the boundary between Alaska and Canada. The McKinley administration could not settle the boundary issue, which was left to Theodore Roosevelt to end in 1903. The president and John Hay did negotiate a treaty with Great Britain that allowed the United States to build an unfortified canal that all nations could use even in time of war. Because of these provisions, the first Hay-Pauncefote Treaty encountered strong opposition in the Senate and had to be renegotiated in 1901 before it achieved approval after McKinley's death.

The Rough Riders on San Juan Hill, Cuba. *(Library of Congress)*

American Interests in China: The Open Door Notes

In Asia, the president was aware of European efforts to dominate China through economic and political spheres of influence. Anxious about American trade with China and concerned to preserve that nation's territorial integrity, the administration, through Secretary Hay, issued what were called the Open Door notes in September, 1899. These messages asked the European countries active in China to safeguard trading privileges, local tariffs, and other economic rights that gave the United States a chance to compete for markets. As diplomatic statements, the Open Door notes had less significance at the time they were sent than they later had as an assertion of American interests in China that rationalized involvement in Asia in the twentieth century.

Domestic issues produced less presidential activism than foreign policy had done during McKinley's first term. On the subject of race

relations, the president emphasized sectional reconciliation between North and South ahead of the preservation of black rights. Little was done to offset the impact of segregation and violence on African Americans in those years. The problem of trusts and industrial mergers gained increasing public attention after 1897, but the administration responded slowly to pleas for a greater federal regulatory role. By 1899, McKinley grew more aware of the problem, and he asked Congress for additional action on trusts in his annual message. His record on trusts was cautious in his first term; he expected to do more in his second.

In the area of civil service, McKinley drew back from the reformist position of Cleveland in his second term and expanded, in an order of May 28, 1899, the list of positions to which competitive examinations did not apply. On the whole, however, the administration's record on honesty and efficiency in the federal service was creditable. Criticism in the first half of 1899 also focused on the War Department and the record of Secretary Alger. The hearings of the Dodge Commission produced some public outcries over allegations of "embalmed beef" in the soldiers' rations. The handling of the canned beef that the troops received had been inept, but no corruption or conspiracy was involved. The most constructive result of the hearings was recommendations for changes in the structure of the army and pressure on McKinley to replace Alger. He finally did so in

The assassination of McKinley. *(Library of Congress)*

the summer of 1899 when the secretary endorsed a political opponent of the president in McKinley's home state. Alger's replacement, Elihu Root of New York, was an excellent choice.

In the autumn of 1899, President McKinley made another tour of the Midwest, continuing the public advocacy of his positions that characterized his first term. Republican successes in the off-year elections seemed to forecast a victory for the GOP when McKinley ran again in 1900. Only the death of his vice president, Garret A. Hobart, in November, 1899, complicated the president's political future, and talk quickly arose that Theodore Roosevelt should be his next running mate.

The session of Congress that convened in late 1899 proved more troublesome than McKinley had anticipated. In his annual message, he said it was the nation's "plain duty" to extend free trade to Puerto Rico. This proposal struck at the Republican policy of tariff protection, and opposition arose within the president's party. McKinley shifted his ground, accepted a modest tariff on Puerto Rican goods, and used his influence to push the compromise measure through Congress. He also withstood Senate opposition to the Hay-Pauncefote Treaty

and attacks on tariff reciprocity treaties the administration had negotiated with the nation's trading partners. It was a difficult session, but McKinley emerged with his prestige intact.

The Campaign of 1900: McKinley's Mandate Confirmed

As the Republican national convention neared, the most important political decision for McKinley was the choice of a running mate. The governor of New York, Theodore Roosevelt, was popular with the Republican rank and file. An easterner who was strong in the West, he represented a good balance for the president. The White House would probably have preferred someone less volatile and more conventional than Roosevelt, but no good alternative emerged. When it became clear that the Republican convention was likely to nominate Roosevelt anyway, McKinley stopped efforts of others to thwart the New Yorker's election. As a result, the GOP put forward its strongest possible ticket against William Jennings Bryan, who made his second race for the Democrats.

When McKinley accepted the party's nomination in mid-July, the nation was looking with concern at the fate of Westerners trapped in China by the Boxer Rebellion. Though the

United States was not at war with China and Congress was not in session, the president sent several thousand American soldiers with the China Relief Expedition to Peking. It was another example of McKinley's innovative use of the war power to support the foreign policy of his presidency. He was equally surefooted in seeing that the soldiers left China as soon as possible after the safety of the Westerners was guaranteed.

In 1900, McKinley observed the tradition that prevented incumbent presidents from campaigning for reelection, and he let Roosevelt do most of the actual speaking. The president's speech of acceptance and his letter of acceptance set the tone for the Republicans. With the tide of economic prosperity running their way and the foreign policy successes of the administration, the Republicans easily defeated their opponents. McKinley increased his popular vote margin over 1896, and he won by a margin of 292 to 115 in the electoral college. "I am now the President of the whole people," McKinley said after his victory.

In the congressional session of 1900-1901, the president secured approval from the lawmakers, through the Spooner Amendment, of his authority to govern the Philippines once the insurrection had been quelled. This achievement was additional proof of McKinley's dominance of Capitol Hill. The capture of Emilio Aguinaldo in March, 1901, was another positive sign for the American side, though all resistance did not end for several years after the president's death. During this session, Congress also worked out the Platt Amendment for Cuba. One newspaper said that "no executive in the history of the country" had exercised greater influence on Congress than had McKinley.

McKinley's Assassination: An Anarchist's Bullet

As the second term began on March 4, 1901, William McKinley was very much the strong president. "You are going to see an Emperor in a dress suit," a French visitor was told before he went to the White House. Under Cortelyou's adroit direction, the size of the presidential staff had expanded and the business of the executive office had become more standardized. Relations with the press reflected Cortelyou's desire for order and system in the treatment of newsmen. For McKinley himself, a routine of hard work and diligent attention to policy characterized his approach to the presidency after a full term in office. As one journalist put it, "The power originally vested in the executive alone has increased to an extent of which the framers of the Constitution had no prophetic vision."

In his second term, McKinley intended to travel more widely and even had plans to break precedent by leaving the continental boundaries for a trip to Cuba or Puerto Rico. First he wanted to pursue the program of tariff reciprocity that he had been quietly preparing for several years. His aim was to achieve gradual, controlled reductions in the protective system that would help the United States secure foreign markets. To that end, the administration had pushed for Senate ratification of reciprocity treaties in 1900. With a mandate from the electorate, McKinley now prepared to argue for reciprocity again and challenge the protectionists in his own party in Congress. During the spring of 1901, he prepared to make speeches for the treaties on a western tour, but an illness of Mrs. McKinley cut the trip short. The president decided to resume his campaign when he traveled in September to Buffalo, New York, to see the Pan-American Exposition.

On September 5, 1901, he told his audience that "the period of exclusiveness is past," and contended that "the expansion of our trade and commerce is the pressing problem." The speech signaled the president's intentions for his second term, including a desire to lead his party in a new and more constructive direction. A day later, on September 6, while standing in a receiving line in the Temple of Music, McKinley was shot by Leon Czolgosz, an anarchist. Eight days later, on the morning of September 14, 1901, William McKinley died. Eulogizing him in 1902, John Hay said that the president "showed in his life how a citizen should live, and in his last hour taught us how a gentleman could die."

McKinley and the Modern Presidency: An Important Historical Role

McKinley's historical reputation declined in the 1920's as disillusion over the war with Spain led to charges that he lacked the courage to preserve peace. Perceived as a conservative Republican in the era of the New Deal, he became a byword for reaction and weakness in the presidency. Since the 1960's, however, newer appraisals have given him due credit for his strength and purpose as a foreign policy leader. He was the first modern president, and he laid the foundation on which Theodore Roosevelt and Woodrow Wilson expanded. In his use of the war power, fruitful relations with Congress, deft management of the press, and shrewd handling of public opinion, he acted as would imperial chief executives in the century that followed. William McKinley was an important figure in the history of the presidency, and his historical significance is likely to increase.

Lewis L. Gould

Suggested Readings

Damiani, Brian P. *Advocates of Empire: William McKinley, the Senate, and American Expansion, 1898-1899*. New York: Garland, 1987. Examines the foreign policy of McKinley.

Gould, Lewis L. *The Presidency of William McKinley*. Lawrence.: Regents Press of Kansas, 1980. Details the political climate of the era and discusses the key issues of McKinley's administration.

_____. *The Spanish-American War and President McKinley*. Lawrence: University Press of Kansas, 1982. An examination of McKinley's attitudes on territorial expansion, foreign relations, and the Spanish-American War.

Gould, Lewis L., and Craig H. Roell. *William McKinley: A Bibliography*. Westport, Conn.: Meckler, 1988, Lists primary and secondary sources for further study of McKinley.

Joseph, Paul. *William McKinley*. Minneapolis: ABDO, 1998. A biography for young adults.

Leech, Margaret. *In the Days of McKinley*. New York: Harper, 1959. A thorough and interesting narrative on the president and his wife.

McElroy, Richard L. *William McKinley and Our America: A Pictorial History*. Canton, Ohio: Stark County Historical Society, 1996. An illustrated biography of McKinley.

Morgan, H. Wayne. *William McKinley and His America*. 1963. Rev. ed. Kent, Ohio: Kent State University Press, 2003. One of the best full biographies of McKinley.

Olcott, Charles S. *Life of William McKinley*. 2 vols. Boston: Houghton Mifflin, 1916. An older but nonetheless worthwhile biography based on primary materials.

Perry, James M. *Touched with Fire: Five Presidents and the Civil War Battles That Made Them*. New York: PublicAffairs, 2005. Uses diaries, letters, and other firsthand accounts to bring life to the war battles that formed the character and political drive of presidents Grant, Hayes, Garfield, Harrison, and McKinley.

Phillips, Kevin. *William McKinley*. New York: Henry Holt, 2003. Less a narrative of McKinley's life and more a study of his strategies and successes, the book is an excellent reassessment of McKinley's administration.

Rauchway, Eric. *Murdering McKinley: The Making of Theodore Roosevelt's America*. New York: Hill and Wang, 2003. Explores the political climate that gave rise to McKinley's assassination and details the impact of McKinley's death on the American public.

Sturgis, Amy H., comp. *Presidents from Hayes Through McKinley, 1877-1901: Debating the Issues in Pro and Con Primary Documents*. Westport, Conn.: Greenwood Press, 2003. A collection of primary documents and commentary is used to debate issues that were pertinent during the tenure of presidents serving between 1877 and 1901.

William McKinley Presidential Library and Museum. Http://www.mckinleymuseum .org/. The Web site for the official presidential library for McKinley.

Theodore Roosevelt

26th President, 1901-1909

Born: October 27, 1858
   New York, New York
Died: January 6, 1919
   Oyster Bay, New York

Political Party: Republican
Vice President: Charles W. Fairbanks

Cabinet Members

Secretary of State: John Hay, Elihu Root, Robert Bacon

Secretary of the Treasury: Lyman J. Gage, Leslie M. Shaw, George B. Cortelyou

Secretary of War: Elihu Root, William Howard Taft, Luke E. Wright

Secretary of the Navy: John D. Long, William H. Moody, Paul Morton, Charles J. Bonaparte, Victor H. Metcalf, T. H. Newberry

Attorney General: Philander C. Knox, William H. Moody, Charles J. Bonaparte

Postmaster General: Charles E. Smith, Henry C. Payne, Robert J. Wynne, George B. Cortelyou, George von L. Meyer

Secretary of the Interior: E. A. Hitchcock, James R. Garfield

Secretary of Agriculture: James Wilson

Secretary of Commerce and Labor: George B. Cortelyou, Victor H. Metcalf, Oscar S. Straus

There was something about Theodore Roosevelt that endeared him to his contemporaries and gave him while still living a cult following new in the annals of American political history. He won the presidential election of 1904 by a plurality wider than anyone before had ever achieved, and the succeeding generation of Americans saw fit to enshrine his memory in the granite of Mount Rushmore in the rather exclusive company of George Washington, Thomas Jefferson, and Abraham Lincoln. The reputation of "America's President" is, however, somewhat in eclipse, among both historians and the general public. That can be attributed in part to the fact, so neatly encapsulated by John Morton Blum's decision to entitle his 1954 study *The Republican Roosevelt*, that the name Roosevelt is now more likely to evoke im-

Portrait of Theodore Roosevelt. *(Whitehouse.gov)*

ages and memories of Franklin Delano than of Theodore. There are also other reasons, both more important and more revealing.

As exemplified in Richard Hofstadter's 1948 critical essay "The Conservative as Progressive," historians have had difficulty finding an appropriate political classification for Theodore Roosevelt. He once playfully described himself as a conservative radical, but such a category has little resonance in either American political or intellectual tradition. Although practically all historians recognize that he was a major figure in the evolution of the presidential office and in the structure of the national government and find some of his achievements noteworthy and admirable, few have been inclined to endorse him wholeheartedly. Historians with a conservative political orientation usually praise his foreign policy but are less attracted to his efforts at domestic reform. Their accounts tend to emphasize his personal ambi-

The young Roosevelt as frontiersman. *(Library of Congress)*

tion, his demagoguery, and his attempt to usurp congressional, judicial, and state powers and concentrate all the reins of government in his own hands. Historians with a leftist political orientation usually praise his domestic policies (though most believe that he could have done more, that his progressivism was too limited) but are likely to execrate his foreign policy for its imperialistic and nationalistic overtones and to feel, as Stuart Sherman once put it, that "he can never again greatly inspire the popular liberal movement in America." The point is that Roosevelt does not fit conventional political categories, and hence modern critics are not as comfortable with him as were his contemporaries.

If Roosevelt were to have an opportunity to answer his critics, he would undoubtedly try to explain that his domestic and foreign policies were complementary and that in both realms he operated on the basis of a well-defined philosophy of history and politics. Privately, Roosevelt might even have been willing to acknowledge the basic truth of H. L. Mencken's observation that he believed more in government than he did in democracy. Though not quite *sui generis* in the American political system (he was, after all, the product of a regional class and culture with Federalist antecedents and sympathies), Roosevelt's views are probably more understandable when placed in a European context. His intellectual affinity with members of the British upper classes attracted to social imperialism and with Otto von Bismarck, who looked favorably on reforms that might strengthen the German national state, is marked. Roosevelt not only adhered to and preached an aristocratic value system but also tended toward the European aristocratic view that both capital and labor were to be made subservient to the state.

Distressed by the deepening divisions between capital and labor that threatened the country internally and attuned to the equally fundamental struggle for world power and position, Roosevelt envisioned a new kind of federal executive power to control the complex

423

The First Lady
Edith Roosevelt

Edith Roosevelt, long thought of as "the ideal First Lady" before her niece Eleanor Roosevelt changed the model, never sought the public life. Edith Kermit Carow Roosevelt was born August 6, 1861, in Norwich, Connecticut, to the aristocratic but unstable Carow family. She was a close friend of Theodore Roosevelt from childhood, and though there were no formal plans, it was expected that they would eventually marry. Then, when Roosevelt was a student at Harvard, they had a quarrel, and Roosevelt married the beautiful Boston debutante Alice Hathaway Lee.

Edith, nonetheless, stayed in Roosevelt's life, and after Alice's death in childbirth, they reunited and quietly married. Edith insisted on raising his daughter, Alice, as their own and also bore him five more children. As their family grew, so did Roosevelt's career, and he always considered her opinion when choosing whether to run for each office. As he rose to prominence, Edith struggled to maintain a balance between her public duties as a political wife and her young family's privacy.

When President William McKinley's assassination launched Roosevelt into the White House, Edith's skill as a hostess earned her acclaim as the First Lady "who never made a mistake." She walked a careful tightrope when it came to publicity, providing official photos and press releases, while refusing interviews. Her greatest accomplishments as First Lady included overseeing a renovation of the White House that resulted in restoration of the interior decoration to Federal-era simplicity and a clearer delineation between public and private spaces in the White House. After Roosevelt's presidency, Edith was happy to return to private life but nonetheless missed life in the White House. Later in life, she continued to travel and publicly supported Herbert Hoover in the 1932 election. She died on September 30, 1948, in Oyster Bay, New York.

Susan Roth Breitzer

processes of the modern American industrialized state and at the same time advance the interests of that state in the international arena. Seeing more strength and promise for the American future than danger in the new industrialism, Roosevelt was not wont to advocate reform for the mere sake of reform. His first interest was in increasing the strength and cohesion of the American national state, and reform was often a means to that end, but he never had any intention of destroying or even seriously impairing the kind of corporate system that had brought the United States to the threshold of world power. The interests of the state were paramount, and both capital and labor had to be made to understand that. In a country where both the Left and Right have been historically suspicious of many aspects of governmental power and in a country that, as Georg Wilhelm

Friedrich Hegel once observed, had no tradition of the state and was not yet a "real state," such views were what set Theodore Roosevelt apart from traditional American politics.

A Patrician in Politics

In the absence of a hereditary aristocracy, some historians have made the mistake of describing Theodore Roosevelt's family as upper middle class. Patrician is probably a much more meaningful class description. Only in comparison with the fortunes of the magnates of the new late nineteenth century industrialism could his family have been considered other than a very wealthy one. Roosevelt, the second of four children and the first son, was born on October 27, 1858, in Manhattan (one of the few American presidents to have been born in a large city). He was the product on his father's side of an old, longtime affluent Knickerbocker family and was descended from families that had been established in America by 1764, most of them in the seventeenth century. Though his lineage on his father's side went directly back to Klaes Martenszen Van Rosenvelt, who arrived at New Amsterdam in 1649, it is important to note that Theodore Roosevelt was actually only one-fourth Dutch and that the family had forsaken their traditional Dutch Reformed Church for a more fashionable Presbyterian Church.

His father, Theodore Roosevelt, Sr., was not only a merchant and banker in the family tradition but also a socially prominent philanthropist and reformer. His mother was Martha Bulloch, the daughter of a well-to-do and socially distinguished Georgia planter, a woman who was beautiful and socially adept, who was steeped in the manners and mores of the Old South, but otherwise rather ineffectual. Young Theodore was reared in a family that was self-consciously aristocratic, devoted to values that transcended those of mere money making, but a family nevertheless accustomed to power and influence. Such families, with their traditions of public service and noblesse oblige, had only scorn for upstart industrialists but had begun to discover that power in the United States was gravitating toward those with the great new fortunes, however rude their antecedents. Much of what Theodore Roosevelt did in later life can be seen as an effort to preserve a place in American public life for the patrician virtues with which he was imbued as a child and to neutralize the power of those who did not respect those virtues. It was precisely the peculiar social and political conditions attendant on nineteenth century American industrialization that could turn a conservative into a reformer.

The stories are legion about how young Theodore, a frail, nearsighted, severely asthmatic child, acting on the urging of the father whom he idolized, built up his body to the point where he could endure incredible physical hardship.

The Vice President
Charles W. Fairbanks

Charles Warren Fairbanks served as vice president in the second administration of Theodore Roosevelt. Born on May 11, 1852, in Unionville Center, Ohio, Fairbanks was educated in public schools and graduated from Ohio Wesleyan University in 1872. After college, he worked for the Associated Press in its Pittsburgh and Cleveland offices while attending Cleveland Law School. In 1874, Fairbanks was admitted to the bar and married Cornelia Cole.

That same year, Fairbanks moved to Indianapolis and established a successful law practice that included large railways as clients. He was also named a trustee at his alma mater. Fairbanks began his political career not as a candidate but as a campaign manager and party leader. He managed unsuccessful presidential and senatorial campaigns, as well as served as chair for the Indiana Republican Convention in 1892 and a delegate to the Republican National Convention in 1896. Fairbanks was elected to the U.S. Senate in 1896 and was reelected in 1902. In 1898, President William McKinley sent Fairbanks to Alaska as an envoy to the Alaskan border dispute with Canada.

In 1904, Fairbanks was nominated as Roosevelt's vice president. After a successful term in office, he returned home but remained active in the Republican Party. In 1916, he was nominated vice president on the unsuccessful ticket with Charles Evans Hughes. Fairbanks died on June 4, 1918, in Indianapolis.

Robert P. Watson and Richard Yon

His has become a staple American success story, as much part of American folklore as Lincoln's rail splitting. It is very tempting, and many observers have succumbed to the temptation, to explain not only Roosevelt's devotion to the philosophy of the strenuous life but also the sum total of his political thinking and his conduct of the presidency in terms of his childhood personality development. Though useful, such an approach is not sufficient. It does help to explain certain facets of his personality — his courage, his confidence, his determination, and certainly his hyperactivity, but it is not nearly so compelling when it is used to explain the ends toward which his activity was directed. For that purpose, one must plumb his intellectual development and place him in his social context.

Roosevelt was educated primarily at home by private tutors. Two year-long trips to Europe and the Near East significantly broadened his horizons. He attended Harvard College, where he distinguished himself in natural history, a subject that in the age of Charles Darwin was pregnant with political implications, and his

overall record was good enough to merit election to Phi Beta Kappa. When, in later years, he tended to denigrate his undergraduate educational experience, it was probably because little at Harvard caused him to question the viewpoint of the class from which he came. He tended to judge his fellow students by whether they were gentlemen, and his own antecedents made easy for him the ascent of Harvard's social terraces — the Dicky, the Hasty Pudding Club, and the Porcellian, the last probably America's most exclusive undergraduate social club.

Although it is tempting to think of Roosevelt as unique in personality and viewpoint, his early views were common among his class. Neither the doctrine of the strenuous life nor that of the wisdom of cultivating military virtues was personal to Roosevelt or even of his own devising, but was rather the generational response of a group of patrician intellectuals profoundly influenced by the psychic legacy of the Civil War and at odds with the value system of business America. These men tried to counter the current business ethic with a social ethic of public ser-

TR with members of the Rough Riders in 1898. *(Library of Congress)*

vice and a noncommercial lifestyle. Related to this was an attempt to reinvigorate the Federalist tradition in American history and to knock the Jeffersonian tradition from the pedestal it had so long occupied. Roosevelt's very first book, *The Naval War of 1812*, begun while he was an undergraduate and published when he was only twenty-four, strongly reflects this point of view. Though extremely technical in its discussion of naval maneuvers, it is also strongly anti-Jeffersonian and reflective of a lifelong commitment to preparedness and the necessity for leadership and the cultivation of the military virtues. As Hofstadter put it, Roosevelt began his career as a member of an "American underground of frustrated aristocrats" who constantly complained of the alienation of education, intellect, and family reputation from significant political and economic power.

Though Roosevelt flirted with the idea of becoming a naturalist, as a result of interests he developed as a young child and cultivated all of his life, one suspects that he ultimately decided that such a life was too contemplative and too removed from what his generation regarded as the battle for America's soul. He chose to attend law school (which he never completed) and to pursue what he probably hoped would be a lifetime of public service. What he never contemplated was a career in business. A triggering event may very well have been the Senate's refusal to ratify President Rutherford B. Hayes's appointment of his father as collector of the port of New York. Roosevelt was extremely close to his father, had long since taken him as a model for his own conduct, and was desperately shaken by his father's death while he was still an undergraduate. Equally important may be the fact that on his father's death he inherited about $200,000, certainly sufficient in those days to allow him to do whatever he wanted with his life.

Despite the counsel of his social set, who tended to assume a condescending aloofness toward ordinary politics, Roosevelt quickly joined the local regular Republican organiza-

tion in New York City and before long was a successful candidate for the state assembly. Here personal traits of determination, ambition, and an aggressive hyperactivity may well have been decisive; Roosevelt was constitutionally incapable of sitting on the sidelines. "I intended," he said, "to become one of the governing class"; and if he could not hold his own with the rough and vulgar men who then dominated that class, "I supposed I would have to quit, but I certainly would not quit until I had made the effort and found out whether I was too weak to hold my own in the rough and tumble." Though sometimes dismissed for his dandyism, Roosevelt really had little trouble holding his own, and in the process he did much to recapture political power for the cultivated and to make politics once more an attractive career for well-educated, talented men and women who thought of public service in terms other than personal aggrandizement. He virtually rehabilitated the idea of the patrician in politics; the result was not accidental but consciously intended. As Hofstadter has written, he was "the first reformer to understand how much the stigma of effeminacy and ineffectuality had become a handicap to reformers" and also the first to show others how that stigma might be overcome, to blaze a path by demonstrating and dramatizing the compatibility of education, social status, and reform with energy, vitality, and Americanism.

The energy he poured into sport, scholarship, politics, and even actual physical combat in the next two decades made him something of a national legend long before he became president and early gave him an unusual ability, as his friend Henry Cabot Lodge expressed it, to command the popular imagination. Even if there was no calculation in his early decision to try ranching in the then untamed Dakota territory (and he was not the only aristocrat attracted by adventure in the West), his identification with the West and with the outdoor life in general soon became a part of his political style,

TR refused to shoot a cub during a bear hunt in 1902. Cartoonist Clifford Berryman used this incident to invent the "teddy bear." *(Library of Congress)*

a means of identifying himself with an energetic, manly, and uncorrupted way of life, with the straightforward politics Americans idolize and yet never seem to achieve. Stories about his feats in the West eventually became a part not only of his own personal political capital but also of the American political legend. Roosevelt hunted grizzlies and cougars in the Rockies, matched shooting skills with American Indians, captured armed thieves, and knocked out a tough in a brief barroom brawl. In real life he seemed to demonstrate precisely the frontier virtues he tended to idolize in his historical writing.

Roosevelt's energy was always prodigious. For example, in the twenty years between his graduation from Harvard and his accession to the presidency, he wrote nine books, including two serviceable biographies, *Thomas Hart Benton* (1887) and *Gouverneur Morris* (1888), and, while governor of New York, an extremely self-revelatory study, *Oliver Cromwell* (1900). He also published a major four-volume history of the early trans-Appalachian West, *The Winning of the West* (1889-1896), which was well received by professional historians and, though far from pro-Indian in point of view, demonstrated a considerable interest in and understanding of American Indian culture.

None of this caused him to neglect politics and government service. He served three terms in the New York State legislature, where he developed a reputation as an exposer of corruption and a battler for the public interest. Though conventionally conservative in most respects, he did advocate state regulation of business in a few limited areas, and he early developed an aversion for both the judiciary's narrow devotion to laissez-faire economics and its seeming inability to understand the necessity of according priority to the public interest.

In 1886, he ran unsuccessfully for mayor of New York City in a famous three-cornered race with Abram Hewitt and Henry George, and he was appointed to the United States Civil Service Commission by President Benjamin Harrison in 1889. He was reappointed by Grover Cleveland, a Democrat, four years later and continued to serve in that capacity until appointed head of the New York City Board of Police Commissioners in 1894. On both commissions, he managed to attract national attention and add to his reputation as an active and effective reformer. He proved to be a singularly adept administrator, combining a mastery of detail and careful planning with bold vision. Above all, he was a master at dramatizing the need for reform and using the press skillfully to that end. At the same time, he dramatized himself, and as early as 1895 some of his friends were predicting that he would eventually come to high national office, perhaps even the presidency itself. His political skills were especially apparent in his ability to establish a reputation for principled, nonpartisan administration of the law while keeping his fences within his own party carefully mended.

TR and the Rough Riders: The Spanish-American War

Through the advocacy and mediation of high-placed political friends, Henry Cabot Lodge foremost among them, Roosevelt was next appointed assistant secretary of the navy in 1897 by President William McKinley, for whom he had conducted an extensive speech-making tour of the Northeast and the West. Long an advocate of naval expansion and preparedness, Roosevelt regarded this as a position of considerable substance and challenge. Handicapped by a public opinion and an administration that did not share his priorities, he nevertheless did much to prepare the navy for the struggle with Spain, which he not only foresaw but for which he fervently wished. Owing to Secretary John Davis Long's having taken the day off, Roosevelt found himself in actual control of the United States Navy on February 25, 1898, ten days after the destruction of the battleship *Maine* in Havana Harbor. Acting on his own and with great dispatch, he ordered the Pacific fleet, commanded by Commodore George Dewey, whose appointment Roosevelt had been instrumental in securing, to stand by at Hong Kong prepared for combat with the Spanish fleet in the Philippines to prevent its movement across the Pacific toward the American mainland. He thereby set the stage for the Battle of Manila Bay and eventual American annexation of that large Asian archipelago.

Once the war that Roosevelt so long and vehemently advocated was declared, he, acting against the advice of friends and family, resigned his office and helped to organize a voluntary cavalry unit (under the command of Leonard Wood with Roosevelt as his second) composed of a few hundred cowboys, a good number of Ivy League football players, a few New York City police officers, fifteen American Indians, and assorted other adventurer types. Roosevelt strongly believed in leadership by example (a style not frequently cultivated in the United States): If one advocated a course of national conduct that entailed sacrifices, then one should be foremost in one's willingness to incur those sacrifices. The First Cavalry Regiment, quickly dubbed "The Rough Riders" by the press, with Lieutenant Colonel Theodore Roosevelt as battle commander, saw brutal action in the hills overlooking San-

Roosevelt was a champion of conservation. Here he stands with naturalist John Muir at Glacier Point, above California's Yosemite Valley. *(Library of Congress)*

tiago, Cuba, and suffered extraordinary casualties.

Though undoubtedly brash on the field of battle, Roosevelt proved an excellent leader; he was not only a good motivator but also extremely solicitous of his men's welfare when it came to provisions. He himself was in the forefront of the unit's military engagements, and perhaps the wonder is that he managed to survive. In the parlance of the day, the war was a "splendid little one," and Roosevelt and his Rough Riders were soon returned to Montauk Point on Long Island. While still waiting to be mustered out in August of 1898, Roosevelt began to receive political visitors within a few hours of disembarkation. The year 1898 was thought to be a Democratic one in New York because of the charges of corruption that were rocking the current Republican regime. Roosevelt, owing to his wartime fame, was deemed to be the only Republican with even a chance of success. As a result, the bosses came to Roosevelt, an event unlikely under other circumstances, and Roosevelt became the GOP gubernatorial standard-bearer. He conducted an extremely vigorous canvass, seldom appearing without a vanguard of Rough Riders and never reluctant to talk about his recent military exploits. The result was a narrow victory and a two-year stint for Roosevelt as governor of the nation's most populous state.

Nothing short of the White House could have been a better testing ground for his ideas and abilities than was the governorship of a state such as New York, certainly urban and industrial but otherwise almost as diverse as the nation. Roosevelt's methods were by now familiar: He walked a fine line between consultation with the Republican bosses and the maintenance of his integrity and independence; he held almost daily news conferences and used the press as a means of getting advance reaction to proposals and of putting his own ideas constantly before the people; and he regularly sought the advice of experts in all areas of pro-

jected legislation. He popularized the idea of the neutral state — neutral, that is, between capital and labor but positive in promoting the general welfare. In but two short years, he had boasted a considerable achievement, generally improving the quality of state administration by a series of excellent appointments and getting through a boss-ridden legislature bills extending the civil service system, treating franchises as real estate for tax purposes, increasing the power of factory inspectors, licensing sweatshops more rigorously, and regulating the hours of drug clerks and of employees on state work. Though by no means successful in all of his reform efforts, it is the opinion of the closest student of his governorship that he developed an excellent grasp of the mechanics of political power and had as governor already "worked out a philosophy and a program by which his party could attack the great domestic problems of the day."

Roosevelt certainly wanted at least a second term as governor, but that was not to be. By a congruence of circumstances as unusual as those that made him governor, he was chosen to run with McKinley as the vice presidential nominee in 1900. Thomas C. Platt, boss of New York Republicanism, clearly wanted him out of the state; a reformer so adept at politics was a definite menace to his power. Equally important, Roosevelt already had a strong national following and was particularly popular in the West where William Jennings Bryan, the likely Democratic nominee, had his greatest strength. The powers in the Republican Party regarded Roosevelt, not with affection, but as a considerable asset to the national ticket and so he proved, conducting a campaign exceeded in vigor — miles logged and speeches made — perhaps only by the exertions of Bryan himself. McKinley was reelected by a comfortable margin, and Roosevelt began to settle into a job, the vice presidency, so lacking in power and work to do that he expected to be bored and even contemplated a renewal of his legal studies.

President by an Act of Fate: Restoring the Stature of the Office

Then, less than a year later, in September, 1901, at the Pan-American Exposition in Buffalo, yet another assassin changed the course of American political history by killing President McKinley and putting Theodore Roosevelt, that "damn cowboy" as Mark Hanna called him, in the White House. Roosevelt, not yet quite forty-three, was the youngest man ever to hold the office, and the powers that ruled the Republican Party had certainly never intended him to do so. Yet, he was almost supremely qualified; he had extensive administrative experience and was extremely well read and well traveled. Moreover, he was a serious thinker about major contemporary issues, both domestic and foreign, and he had both the makings of a program and the confidence that he knew what the country needed.

At home and abroad, his task was a formidable one. In domestic affairs, the Republican Party had long since abandoned its Federalist and Whig antecedents and now stood for weak government, especially in the economic arena. The judiciary dominated American policy making on economic matters, and the judiciary in this period was disposed to interpret the Constitution narrowly and reserve for the states all powers not expressly granted to the federal government. The problem was that the states were incapable of regulating the new giant economic concerns that spanned the nation. The revolution in business organization, production, and marketing that had so drastically changed the face of the nation in the last several decades had rendered archaic a constitutional and legal system that still assumed that the trusts were exercising private power in the same manner as had the small entrepreneurs who serviced local communities in earlier eras. Competition was no longer free; a few very large interstate corporations were too powerful to permit that, but they had a vested interest in pretending that conditions were still the same.

The matter was complicated by the fact that Americans had no tradition of the state (even the Constitution was antistatist and restrictive of government power in philosophy) and had historically been susceptible to much antigovernment demagoguery. In addition to these factors, Roosevelt faced a congressional coalition of conservative Republicans. As representatives of the interests of the new mammoth corporations, these conservatives opposed a derogation of power from the judiciary and the states and Southern Democrats, who feared any enlargement of federal power for their own regional and racial reasons. As Roosevelt saw it, his primary task was to reestablish the legitimacy of federal power, even of federal executive power, for neither the courts nor the legislative branch of the federal government was doing the job of protecting the American people from ravages of unrestrained corporate power. If he could not gain widespread popular support for federal restraint of this new great private power, the alternative appeared to be some form of socialism and that, he believed, was likely to inhibit the growth of American economic power and hence interfere with the growing international power of the American nation.

It has become fashionable to denigrate Roosevelt's achievements, especially in legislation, by means of invidious comparison with those of such successors as Woodrow Wilson and Roosevelt's cousin Franklin D. Roosevelt. The opposition to Theodore Roosevelt's plans, however, were formidable and so deeply entrenched that one should probably be more impressed by his actual achievements than by what historians writing in retrospect see as having been left undone. Certainly, he made the presidency once again, for the first time since Abraham Lincoln, a meaningful institution for most Americans, and certainly he not only greatly increased the scope of federal power but also did much to shape the nature of the modern American presidency. Wilson, who as a political scientist had once detailed the workings of what he called congressional government, drastically revised and upgraded his estimate of the power inherent in the presidency as a direct result of witnessing Roosevelt's conduct of the office.

In his efforts to gain popular support for a larger federal role in the economy, Roosevelt was his own best asset; his enormous talent for publicity served him especially well. His was one of the great commanding personalities of American political history. Even his enemies were usually charmed. Moreover, as recent studies have shown, he was assiduous in his cultivation of the press and an absolute master at managing the news and securing headlines when it so served his purposes. As important as his management abilities was the fact that he literally reveled in the presidency. He enjoyed being president, he said; "I like the work and I like to have my hand on the lever." He also considered the White House (he changed the name from the more formal Executive Mansion) a bully pulpit, and he preached from that pulpit with great frequency and with considerable effect. He was one of the great exhorters of American history and was able to rivet the country's attention on Washington, D.C., and, not incidentally, on himself. As George Will has written, "Because politics is 95 percent talk, and the Presidency is 98 percent talk, there's nothing the President can do on his own except move the country, and by moving the country with his rhetoric move Congress, and once Congress is moved, then, but only then, can he govern." No one understood that better than Theodore Roosevelt.

As Roosevelt himself later wrote, apart from his belief in the need for more and better government, he did not enter the presidency with any deliberate planned and far-reaching scheme of social betterment. He offered no panacea or all-encompassing idea; indeed, he had an abiding distrust of those who did. He simply persuaded the voters that he had a conscience, that he would be fair, and that he knew how to lead.

In domestic politics as in international politics, there were no final solutions; politics was only a means of reconciling conflicting interests. He was forever engaged in a delicate balancing act, gathering support by excluding from the national consensus only those at the extreme ends of the American political spectrum. As Hofstadter commented, "The straddle was built, like functional furniture, into his thinking." He despised the idle rich, but he also feared the mob. The abuses of big business aroused his ire, but that did not mean that he was in favor of indiscriminate trust-busting. He favored reform, but that impulse was mitigated by the fact that he disliked the personality and methods of the militant reformers. Roosevelt coined the name "muckraker" and it was not meant to be complimentary, yet there was some truth to House Speaker Joseph G. Cannon's charge that Roosevelt himself was the chief muckraker, a master at arousing the indignation of progressives against the practices they considered antisocial. He never attacked the violent Left on one side but what he also execrated the plutocracy, the "malefactors of great wealth," on the other side. He often deliberately and publicly offended the big businessmen who contributed to his campaign, but at the same time he distanced himself from what he called "the La Follette type of fool radicalism on the left." This made for excellent political strategy under American political conditions, for he was telling the vast American middle class precisely what it wanted to hear. In performing this balancing act Roosevelt was doing two things, suggesting that somewhere was a golden mean and also that he was the one person best equipped to discover it. He had long since convinced himself that only someone of his class and background could stand above the fray, serving as a kind of impartial arbiter devoted to the national good and ensuring that right and justice would always prevail. One can applaud the effort without believing that he or anyone else is that capable of transcending his or her own interests.

Roosevelt visits the construction site for the Panama Canal in 1906. *(Library of Congress)*

Moral Government: High Ideals and Political Realities

For Roosevelt's generation, the key to national consensus was moral government. The moral element always dominated his political rhetoric; he fancied his role as being that of "national moralist," and he once defined progressivism as "the fundamental fight for morality." He often claimed that "we are neither for the rich man, nor the poor man as such, but for the upright man rich or poor." He pushed this insistence on morality so far sometimes that one of his advisers was once tempted to quip, "What I really admire about you, Theodore, is your discovery of the Ten Commandments." In all of this, the similarity with Woodrow Wilson is

readily apparent, but an important distinction needs to be made. Whereas Wilson thought that morality was God-given and that he was chosen to interpret it to the American people, Roosevelt, less the believer though nevertheless religious, usually thought of morality in terms of a cultural consensus—in other words, in political terms. Progressivism for Roosevelt was always little more than a search for standards of justice that all Americans could accept.

What worked well in generality was not necessarily that helpful when it came to concrete legislation. As a result it should not be surprising that both Roosevelt's major political programs, the initial Square Deal and the later New Nationalism, had a certain ambiguity about them.

His attacks on the corporate plutocracy were both vigorous and moderate. In his first annual message to Congress he declared, "There is a widespread conviction in the minds of the American people that trusts are in certain of their features and tendencies hurtful to the general welfare. This is based upon the sincere conviction that combination and concentration should be, not prohibited, but supervised and within reasonable limits controlled; and in my judgment this conviction is right." The following year he informed Congress, "Our aim is not to do away with corporations; on the contrary, these big aggregations are an inevitable development of modern industrialism, and the effort to destroy them would be futile unless accomplished in ways that would work the utmost mischief to the entire body politic. . . . We draw

433

the line against misconduct, not against wealth." He thereby practically invited Finley Peter Dunne's famous burlesque of his remarks, "The trusts says he are heejous monsthers built up be the enlightened interprise iv th' men that have done so much to advance progress in our beloved country, he says. On won hand I wud stamp thim undher fut; on the other hand not so fast." Though gaining a reputation as a trust-buster, Roosevelt, when confronted by the complexities of antitrust, often shifted from one foot to the other, moving to break up an unpopular holding company in the Northern Securities case and permitting United States Steel to take over a competitor in the Tennessee Coal and Iron case.

His attitude toward the labor movement was also rather ambiguous. The federal government had previously intervened in labor disputes, but heretofore as a strikebreaker for the employers. Roosevelt moved to make the government an impartial arbiter instead. His interest was not so much in strengthening the unions per se (though he thought strong unions a necessary countervailing power) as in strengthening the government. As in his dealings with the corporate plutocracy, he wished government to be paramount over the conflicting economic forces and neutral between their struggles. To his way of thinking, strengthening the state was the only way of achieving social responsibility in an increasingly impersonal society. The large corporations had already corrupted (and the unions were on their way to doing the same thing) the old Jeffersonian individualistic ideal, and the result was not only an undemocratic society but also a chaotic and conflict-ridden one. Jeffersonian weak government was no longer sufficient. Democratic ends and national cohesion could now only be accomplished by Hamiltonian means, by more and stronger government.

Roosevelt was always cautious in confronting private power. He did not aim at breaking the trusts but at satisfying public concern about corporate power and hence heading off socialism. His solution from the start was regulation rather than dissolution. As Roosevelt explained in his *Autobiography*, it was the only workable solution:

> One of the main troubles was the fact that the men who saw the evils and who tried to remedy them attempted to work in two wholly different ways, and the great majority of them in a way that offered little promise of real betterment. They tried (by the Sherman-law method) to bolster up an individualism already proved to both futile and mischievous; to remedy by more individualism the concentration that was the inevitable result of the already existing individualism. They saw the evil done by the big combinations, and sought to remedy it by destroying them and restoring the country to the economic conditions of the middle of the nineteenth century. This was a hopeless effort, and those who went into it, although they regarded themselves as radical progressives, really represented a form of sincere rural toryism. . . . On the other hand, a few men recognized that corporations and combinations had become indispensable in the business world, that it was folly to try to prohibit them, but that it was also folly to leave them without thoroughgoing control.

Roosevelt wanted to work out methods of controlling the big corporations without paralyzing the energies of the business community. He feared the politics of big business, not its size. If government could get the upper hand, all would be well. He envisioned a new kind of federal executive power to control the complex processes of an industrialized state. In this, demonstrating considerable vision, he anticipated the methods of the future, the methods for the positive government of an industrialized society that began to emerge in the 1930's under his kinsman Franklin. Roosevelt always saw more strength than danger in the new industrialism and never preached reform for reform's sake alone. His first interest was in increasing the strength and cohesion of the Ameri-

The Panama Canal Act

June 28, 1902

An Act to provide for the construction of a canal connecting the waters of the Atlantic and Pacific oceans.

SECTION 1: Be it enacted, . . . That the President of the United States is hereby authorized to acquire, for and on behalf of the United States, at a cost not exceeding forty millions of dollars, the rights, privileges, franchises, concessions, grants of land, right of way, unfinished work, plants, and other property, real, personal, and mixed, of every name and nature, owned by the New Panama Canal Company, of France, on the Isthmus of Panama, and all its maps, plans, drawings, records on the Isthmus of Panama and in Paris, including all the capital stock, not less, however, than sixty-eight thousand eight hundred and sixty-three shares of the Panama Railroad Company, owned by or held for the use of said canal company, provided a satisfactory title to all of said property can be obtained.

SECTION 2: That the President is hereby authorized to acquire from the Republic of Colombia, for and on behalf of the United States, upon such terms as he may deem reasonable, perpetual control of a strip of land, the territory of the Republic of Colombia, not less than six miles in width, extending from the Caribbean Sea to the Pacific Ocean, and the right to use and dispose of the waters thereon, and to excavate, construct, and to perpetually maintain, operate, and protect thereon a canal, of such depth and capacity as will afford convenient passage of ships of the greatest tonnage and draft now in use, from the Caribbean Sea to the Pacific Ocean, which control shall include the right to perpetually maintain and operate the Panama Railroad, if the ownership thereof, or a controlling interest therein, shall have been acquired by the United States, and also jurisdiction over said strip and the ports at the ends thereof to make such police and sanitary rules and regulations as shall be necessary to preserve order and preserve the public health thereon, and to establish such judicial tribunals as may be agreed upon thereon as may be necessary to enforce such rules and regulations. The President may acquire such additional territory and rights from Colombia as in his judgment will facilitate the general purpose hereof.

SECTION 3: That when the President shall have arranged to secure a satisfactory title to the property of the New Panama Canal Company, as provided in section one hereof, and shall have obtained by treaty control of the necessary territory from the Republic of Colombian as provided in section two hereof, he is authorized to pay for the property of the New Panama Canal Company forty millions of dollars and to the Republic of Colombia such sum as shall have been agreed upon. . . . The President shall then through the Isthmian Canal Commission hereinafter authorized cause to be excavated, constructed, and completed, utilizing to that end as far as practicable the work heretofore done by the New Panama Canal Company, of France, and its predecessor company, a ship canal from the Caribbean Sea to the Pacific Ocean. Such canal shall be of sufficient capacity and depth as shall afford convenient passage for vessels of the largest tonnage and greatest draft now in use, and such as may be reasonably anticipated, and shall be supplied with all necessary locks and other appliances to meet the necessities of vessels passing through the same from ocean to ocean; and he shall also cause to be constructed such safe and commodious harbors at the termini of said canal, and make such provisions for defense as may be necessary for the safety and protection of said canal and harbors. . . .

SECTION 4: That should the President be unable to obtain for the United States a satisfactory title to the property of the New Panama Canal Company and the control of the necessary territory of the

Republic of Colombia and the rights mentioned in sections one and two of this Act, within a reasonable time and upon reasonable terms, then the President, having first obtained for the United States perpetual control by treaty of the necessary territory from Costa Rica and Nicaragua, upon terms which he may consider reasonable, for the construction, perpetual maintenance, operation, and protection of a canal connecting the Caribbean Sea with the Pacific Ocean by what is commonly known as the Nicaragua route, shall through the said Isthmian Canal Commission cause to be excavated and constructed a ship canal and waterway from a point on the shore of the Caribbean Sea near Greytown, by way of Lake Nicaragua, to a point near Brito on the Pacific Ocean.... In the excavation and construction of said canal the San Juan River and Lake Nicaragua, or such parts of each as may be made available, shall be used.

SECTION 5: That the sum of ten million dollars is hereby appropriated, out of any money in the Treasury not otherwise appropriated, toward the project herein contemplated by either route so selected. And the President is hereby authorized to cause to be entered into such contract or contracts as may be deemed necessary for the proper excavation, construction, completion, and defense of said canal, harbors, and defenses, by the route finally determined upon under the provisions of this Act. Appropriations therefor shall from time to time be hereafter made, not to exceed in the aggregate the additional sum of one hundred and thirty five millions of dollars should the Panama route be adopted, or one hundred and eighty millions of dollars should the Nicaragua route be adopted.

SECTION 6: That in any agreement with the Republic of Colombia, or with the States of Nicaragua and Costa Rica, the President is authorized to guarantee to said Republic or to said States the use of said canal and harbors, upon such terms as may be agreed upon, for all vessels owned by said States or by citizens thereof. . . .

can national state, and reform was a means to that end. He never had any intention of destroying the kind of corporate system that had given the United States the economic leadership of the industrialized world.

Roosevelt was a consummate political tactician. A master of the symbolic act, he chose both his issues and his enemies very carefully and always with an eye toward what actions were likely to advance his cause and which were likely to prove detrimental. He began his presidency very cautiously, assuring a worried business community that he not only would retain McKinley's cabinet but also would continue his policies for the peace and prosperity of the country. Before long, however, he had a well-nigh perfect issue on which to distinguish his administration from his predecessor's.

In 1902, J. P. Morgan contrived a massive merger of E. H. Harriman's Union Pacific with James J. Hill's northern railroads in an effort to control rail transport in a vast section of the Middle and Far West. Morgan offered Roosevelt a perfect target, the public having been sensitized to the trust issue by his recent spectacular consolidation of the steel industry. Roosevelt had his attorney general file suit against the Northern Securities Company, the holding company Morgan established to accomplish his ends, for violation of the Sherman Antitrust Act. The suit was successful and was even upheld in a 5-4 decision by the Supreme Court, which had to admit, however reluctantly, that the railroad industry was engaged in interstate commerce and hence subject to federal power. Roosevelt himself viewed this successful Northern Securities prosecution as the most important achievement of his first administration, not because one further consolidation had to be prevented, but because the president had been able to thwart several of the country's leading business tycoons. In putting Morgan in his place, Roosevelt did what no recent president had been able to accomplish and also gave considerable impetus to his plans for making business subordinate to government. When he went after other trusts, such as Standard Oil and the tobacco and meat trusts, he chose his targets well (all were already unpopular) and to the same end.

He had another opportunity to discipline monopolistic business in the summer and fall of 1902 as a result of the intransigence of the country's coal mine operators and their determination to crush the United Mine Workers. This was more than a fight between miners and a few coal operators. Seventy percent of the anthracite mines in the country were owned by six railroad companies, which were themselves controlled by the country's largest financial houses. Public sympathy was generally with the miners, not only because so many homes were heated by coal but also because George Baer, president of the Reading Railroad and spokesperson for the mine owners, had the audacity to declare that "the rights and interests of the laboring man will be cared for, not by the labor union agitators, but by the Christian men to whom God, in his infinite wisdom, had given control of the property interests of the country." Roosevelt had his foil, and he yearned for some means of taking control of the industry in the public interest, the more so as a prolonged strike would most likely damage Republican prospects in the November elections. He even seriously contemplated using federal troops to operate the mines; he realized he had no constitutional authority to do so, but he let it be known that he was prepared to invoke the higher imperatives of government. He may have been bluffing, but J. P. Morgan got the message and twisted the appropriate arms. The result was an agreement on a presidentially appointed commission to arbitrate a settlement, but without any recognition of the mine workers union. The step was a small one; still, never before had there been a similar kind of federal government intervention in industrial life.

By 1903, public unhappiness with the nation's corporate hierarchy had become so great that Roosevelt was able to challenge another right that American business once considered sacred. Against the bitterest conservative opposition, he secured the passage of legislation that established a Department of Commerce and Labor and, within it, a Bureau of Corporations authorized to investigate and publicize suspect corporate dealings. Though the legislation had no real teeth and rested on the idea of inhibition under the threat of adverse publicity, it served to establish a public and governmental right to know as a means of holding private economic power accountable.

The Election of 1904: A Roosevelt Landslide

Roosevelt had to spend a good portion of his first term endeavoring to sidetrack a possible conservative challenge to his renomination. Mark Hanna was the most likely alternative, but the threat evaporated with Hanna's untimely death. Then in the fall of 1904, Roosevelt beat the Democratic nominee Alton Parker by a huge margin of 2.5 million votes, up to that time the largest plurality ever recorded, and he truly became president in his own right. Just when his power appeared to be at its height, he undercut it by announcing that he would under no circumstances be a candidate for reelection to a third term in 1908. Most of his advisers regarded that announcement as his greatest political blunder, and most historians agree. It may, however, have served his purposes rather well. Like strong presidents before him (Andrew Jackson, for example), he was probably more politically vulnerable to the charge of usurpation of power than to any other. In fact, Roosevelt had lived through an era of American history in which images of governmental usurpation had been regularly presented to the public by special interests trying to preserve their immunity from any form of public control. Moreover, as Richard Abrams has suggested, Roosevelt's action may not only have served to blunt such criticism but may also in his own

"The Busy Showman"—TR making peace in Morocco. *(Library of Congress)*

and Drug, and Hepburn Railroad acts demonstrated the president's political adroitness in the management of Congress and considerably advanced his larger purposes. These acts established the federal government as a major power in the direction of the nation's economic life, and taken together they might well be considered as marking the birth of the modern regulatory state. Each served to bring order to the economy by increasing the power of independent regulatory commissions, which alone, in Roosevelt's view, could provide the requisite "continuous disinterested administration." Each established a federal agency with not only investigatory powers but also the authority to fix

mind have freed him morally to stretch the Constitution whenever his own view of the national interest seemed to require it.

By the end of his second term, the conservatives in Congress had fought Roosevelt to a standoff, and he was forced to choose his issues carefully, eschewing tariff reform, for example, as not only divisive for his party but likely to detract from his own priorities as well. Nevertheless, his legislative achievements in the first years of his second term were considerable, even remarkable given the political complexion of the Congress.

Domestic Achievements: Conservation and Progressive Legislation

The year of 1906 was the high-water mark for Roosevelt's brand of progressive legislation. The passage of the Meat Inspection, Pure Food

at least some of the conditions under which goods could be transported and sold across state lines. The federal government's constitutional power to regulate interstate commerce was now stretched to include the supervision of the production of certain merchandise that entered that commerce. In the case of the Hepburn Railroad Act, the passage of which taxed all of Roosevelt's tactical and promotional talents, the Interstate Commerce Commission was even given limited rate-making powers, which meant in reality a form of price control unprecedented for the federal government. In retrospect, it is easy to minimize Roosevelt's achievements, both because only limited segments of the economy were made subject to governmental supervision and because in all three cases he had substantial support from business groups that had been placed at a disadvantage by the chaotic conditions and unfair competition that had previously prevailed, but all three acts established significant precedents and were an integral part of his long-range plans for shifting the nexus of power in American society.

Perhaps Roosevelt's greatest triumphs and most significant achievements lay in the area of the conservation and regulation of the nation's natural resources. Though Presidents Cleveland and McKinley had made some effort to stem the tide, for years private interests, assuming it was their right, had been laying waste the timber, mineral, soil, and water resources of the West, just as they had once done in the older settled regions of the continent. Vast stretches of public land had been allowed to slip into the control of private interests under conditions of considerable corruption and without thought of preventing destructive use, requiring replenishment of renewable resources, or preserving portions for public recreational use. In this, as in so many other areas, Roosevelt sought expert advice. He was strongly influenced by an educated elite of new, self-conscious professionals (engineers, scientists, and public servants), spearheaded by Gifford Pinchot and Frederick Newell, men with the vision to see that the long-term national interest required that the depletion of the nation's natural resources be stopped. The ideas (multiple-purpose irrigation projects for the development of water and land resources, forest replenishment, parks for recreation and the preservation of wildlife) certainly did not originate with Theodore Roosevelt, but without his ability to publicize them and invest them with the kind of moral imperative that captured the popular imagination, the results would probably have been rather meager. No doubt Roosevelt was sometimes demagogic in appealing to the public's antimonopoly sentiments and often simplistic in characterizing the conservation cause as a clear-cut struggle between special interests and the people, but here, too, Roosevelt's purposes were larger than assumed. Conservation was important per se,

but the cause took on added significance because it was an area in which the business ethic and the social ethic were so clearly in conflict. Thus, Roosevelt was provided with a convenient vehicle for convincing the country of the desirability of increased federal power in the name of a higher public ethic.

Much was accomplished by way of legislation. The Newlands Reclamation Act of 1902, which earmarked revenues from the sale of public lands for the construction of irrigation projects, was an important beginning. During Roosevelt's tenure in office, more than thirty such projects, including Roosevelt Dam in Arizona, were launched. Congress also agreed in 1905 to establish the Forest Service with broad powers to manage the country's forest reserves. Roosevelt named Pinchot chief forester and, acting in tandem, they withdrew countless areas of public land from the clutches of private exploiters. In fact, the whole conservation movement depended to a large extent on the president's use of executive orders and other administrative prerogatives. Especially toward the end, Roosevelt was forced to achieve his purposes by some quick-footed maneuvering before Congress's efforts to restrict such orders could take legal effect.

Whereas some historians, their views colored by the legislative achievements of Wilson and Franklin D. Roosevelt, fault Theodore Roosevelt for not having accomplished more as president, others see in his actions the seeds of the abuses of presidential power that came to mark what has been dubbed the imperial presidency. The charges are somewhat contradictory. Roosevelt could be arrogant and arbitrary in his use of power (as in his peremptory discharge of a company of African American soldiers accused of a raid on the "good, white citizens" of Brownsville, Texas), and he certainly took both the Republican Party and a conservative Congress further in a progressive direction than they ever wanted to go. It is very unlikely that under prevailing political circumstances anyone could have done more (as subsequent events confirmed, the conservatives were very deeply entrenched in their control of the Republican Party), and despite all of Roosevelt's efforts and achievements, the power that resided in the presidency when he left office was still remarkably small.

Foreign Policy: Imperialism and Noblesse Oblige

Like all presidents, Roosevelt had more latitude when it came to the conduct of foreign policy, and that aspect of his presidency has been more severely criticized than any other. Not atypical is the comment of John Morton Blum that Roosevelt's

> belief in power and his corollary impatience with any higher law presumed that governors.. . possessed astonishing wisdom, virtue, and self control. As much as anything he did, his direction of foreign policy made that presumption dubious.

Critics, dominating historical discourse, have regularly derided his imperialism and his bellicosity, described by the appellation "Big Stick Diplomacy," and with almost equal vigor have denounced his supposed racist assumptions and the secret understandings he contracted with other powers. Even his manifest accomplishments have been minimized by reducing his own role in them. Such criticism has two wellsprings: Americans have never been able to agree about the basis on which the United States should conduct its foreign policy, and Roosevelt had some clear-cut ideas about how American foreign policy ought to be conducted and, moreover, tried to put them into practice. He probably deserves much better marks in this area than he has received.

By the time the mantle of the presidency descended on Roosevelt's shoulders, the United States, by reason of its great economic resources alone, was already a world power. By no stretch of the imagination, however, could it have been

deemed a responsible world power. Severely hampered by an incompetent foreign service, impeded by a Congress lulled by America's safe position in the world into regarding foreign policy issues as little more than the sources of possible domestic advantage, and faced by a people who clung tenaciously to the isolationist shibboleths of the past rather than face the realities of a complex, interdependent, modern world, Roosevelt was nevertheless determined to make the United States a responsible force in international affairs.

Roosevelt presents historians with special problems; because he is considered a modern president, one tends to expect him to share modern values. He was, however, the product of an age whose values differed markedly. He was, for example, an imperialist, even a rather belligerent one, and no doubt he was also a militarist, in some senses of the word. He found it easy to divide the world into "civilized" and "barbarian" countries, and strongly believed that peace would never prevail "until the civilized nations have expanded in some shape over the barbarous nations." Like Walter Lippmann, he thought in terms of parceling out among the civilized nations stewardships over those who had not yet reached that stage, and he had no qualms about the use of military force to accomplish such ends. The American Civil War had demonstrated for his generation the necessity of sometimes using military force to accomplish moral ends; only northern military superiority had saved the Union and abolished slavery. Moreover, many commentators of his generation and the coming of World War I have emphasized its widespread willingness to risk or accept war as a reasonable solution to a whole range of problems, political, social, and international.

Roosevelt's imperialism was also of a special variety; it was almost naïvely idealistic and was dominated by a strong sense of noblesse oblige. He sincerely believed that the United States should endeavor to take civilization to the rest of the world, much as his father had organized

Bible classes in the slums of New York City. The United States, as a specially advanced and privileged nation, had a moral obligation to play a major role in modernizing the backward peoples of the world. He strongly and publicly eschewed the imperialism of economic exploitation and was determined to make American administration of the Philippines a model, a means of showing the more exploitation-minded Europeans how it really ought to be done.

Though his successes were limited by a Congress intent on protecting local and regional agricultural interests, he expended considerable effort in trying to push through tariff arrangements that would give the Filipinos and the Cubans advantages in the American market likely to encourage their own rapid economic development. Moreover, he regarded imperialism as bound to be beneficial for Americans, not economically but morally. It would divert Americans from their preoccupation with material gain and set up a standard of conduct for a generation of idealistic young Americans who would administer dependent areas in such a selfless way as to remove even the possibility of the charge of American economic exploitation.

It has been fashionable to label Theodore Roosevelt a racist, but modern usage does not do justice to the complexity of Roosevelt's thinking. He was a historian, well attuned to the fact that the world's great civilizations had all eventually succumbed, whether to the vagaries of human nature or to superior military force. Though he proclaimed the superiority of Anglo-Saxon civilization in his world and celebrated its spread across the Earth's surface, he had a strong sense of the fact that such developments were not fixed for all time. His estimate of nations and peoples was always strongly conditioned by considerations of power. Although his attitude toward the Chinese, for example, was always one of condescension bordering on scorn, he was reacting much more to Chinese weakness than to Chinese racial characteristics, though it must be admitted that he sometimes had difficulty maintaining a rigid distinction between the two. Moreover, he never begrudged respect for individuals, regardless of race or ethnic origin, when he thought it warranted by achievement or character. The friendships he cultivated with foreigners and his appointments of African Americans and other minority group members to federal office all attest that fact.

Particularly revealing in this regard was his attitude toward the Japanese. For them he had only great respect, a respect based almost entirely on their rapid economic development and especially on their demonstrated military prowess. In fact, Roosevelt, contrary to the views of most Americans, was quite willing to assign to the Japanese responsibility for civilizing and policing major portions of East Asia, likening Japan's paramount interest in the area surrounding the Yellow Sea to that of the United States in the area of the Caribbean. Not only did he believe that Japan deserved to control Korea but he also thought that it had a world historical role to play in bringing China "forward along the road which Japan trod" toward membership in the exclusive club of great civilized powers.

Much criticism has been directed against Roosevelt's actions in Central America and the Caribbean. Some of the criticism is justified, especially that concerning means (called by some, "Big Stick Diplomacy"), but here as elsewhere it is important to understand that his object was not simply to advance the interests of the United States but to stabilize the region in the interest of peace and world order as well.

The Panama Canal

Roosevelt considered the building of the Panama Canal to be his greatest achievement in office and in later years was once so bold as to claim that he "took" Panama. His actions came under considerable criticism at the time; the Democratic Party took up Roosevelt's treatment of Colombia as a political issue, and the United States Congress later acknowledged its guilt by paying Colombia additional monies, if only after Roosevelt's death and in an effort to pave the way for American oil leases. The whole affair had its immediate cause in the publicity surrounding the ocean-to-ocean dash of the USS *Oregon* around Cape Horn in 1898 in a futile effort to bolster the American fleet before the Spanish-American War ended. The epic underscored the necessity for a canal across the Central American isthmus for security reasons. The idea had gained currency about the middle of the nineteenth century for economic reasons, and its attractiveness had grown as Californians and Westerners chafed under the transportation charges exacted by the great transcontinental railroad companies.

After the eruption of a volcano in Nicaragua lessened the attractiveness of that route, the Isthmus of Panama became the logical choice. A French company had once made an effort in that area and still held a valid charter. Panama had always been an unruly province of Colombia. During the course of the nineteenth century, Colombia had to cope with more than fifty insurgencies there aimed at secession, and at least four times Colombia had called on the United States, under an 1846 treaty in which the United States pledged to help assure safe transit across the isthmus, to assist in repressing Panamanian rebellions.

Colombia was never averse to the construction of a canal across the isthmus (in fact, it initiated negotiations in 1900), but as American interest peaked it was prepared to exact a price. In January, 1903, Roosevelt offered Colombia $10 million plus a quarter of a million a year for a ninety-nine-year lease of a 6-mile-wide canal zone. Congress also authorized a $40 million payment to the French Panama Canal Company to assume the company's rights to the route. The Hay-Herran Treaty embodying these terms was quickly negotiated and as quickly ratified by the U.S. Senate. It was, however,

turned down by the Colombian Senate, acting under instructions from the Colombian dictator, who normally dispensed with his legislature entirely but had summoned it to consider the treaty while permitting it to pursue no other business. Basically, the Colombian dictator wanted to exact more money, which raised Roosevelt's dander and resulted in a flow of expletives directed at the Colombians, "homicidal corruptionists" being among the milder of them. To Roosevelt's way of thinking, such behavior lessened the regard he needed to pay to Colombia's sovereign prerogatives; moreover, he determined not to let legal technicalities stand in the way of the more fundamental moral imperatives wrapped up in the march of civilization.

Although it is true that Roosevelt contemplated a direct seizure of the isthmus, that action proved unnecessary. The Panamanians, with their own interest in the construction of a canal, soon rebelled against Colombian authority. The United States did not make the Panamanian Revolution, nor did it create the conditions that engendered the rebellion against Colombia's authority. The Panamanians, however, had good reason to believe that the United States would smile on their efforts. Roosevelt's instructions to the acting secretary of the navy were "to prevent the landing of any armed force, either Government or insurgent," and although this was technically in accord with the American obligation (under the 1846 treaty) to preserve transit across the isthmus, its effect was to block Colombian military efforts to suppress the new insurgency instead of aiding those efforts as had sometimes happened in the past. Roosevelt hastily recognized the Republic of Panama and quickly negotiated a canal treaty with that new country, the terms of which were even more favorable to the United States than those previously negotiated with Colombia. Years later, in his autobiography, Roosevelt boasted, "I took the Isthmus, started the canal and then left Congress not to debate the canal, but to debate me." Certainly, his methods were somewhat high-handed, but the construction of the canal was a great achievement, and without Roosevelt's actions it might have been long delayed.

The canal (though not completed during Roosevelt's presidency) solved the country's major strategic problem by permitting the quick passage of the American navy from one major ocean to the other. It also occasioned new concerns. The European powers had just completed their division of Africa and were casting longing eyes at Latin America; blocking their encroachment into the Caribbean (into the area that controlled the approaches to the projected vital canal) became a matter of high national priority. The most likely threat was posed by European powers moving into the area in an effort to collect debts owed to European creditors by impecunious countries or their dictators.

The problem was that the United States was having difficulty invoking the Monroe Doctrine against European intervention in the absence of any willingness to assume responsibility itself. The idea that power and responsibility went hand in hand was in fact the principal rationale for the Roosevelt Corollary to the Monroe Doctrine; as Roosevelt told his friend George Otto Trevelyan, "We cannot perpetually assert the Monroe Doctrine on behalf of all American republics, bad or good, without ourselves accepting some responsibility in connection therewith." In taking such an approach (now criticized as paternalistic), Roosevelt was doing little more than meeting the demands of the Europeans, perhaps best expressed in Lord Salisbury's reply to President Cleveland's rather peremptory note during the Venezuelan crisis of 1895. Salisbury's point was that "the Government of the United States is not entitled to affirm as a universal proposition, with reference to a number of independent states for whose conduct it assumes no responsibility, that its interests are necessarily concerned in whatever may befall those states simply because they are situated in the Western Hemisphere."

Chastened by German bombardment of the Venezuelan coast in 1902 (an incident that was contained by the dispatch of an American squadron under Admiral Dewey and a private warning to the kaiser), Roosevelt decided that the only way to prevent such dangerous incidents in the future was for the United States to step in first, so that there would be no pretext for European intervention. In the interest of national security and peace in the region, he told Congress that the United States had to see to it that order prevailed and that just obligations were met. When internal disorders threatened payments on the Dominican Republic's foreign debt, Roosevelt, acting on his authority as commander in chief, took over the Santo Domingo customhouse and soon established that country on a sound financial footing.

Historians have usually assumed that Roosevelt coveted additional territory in Latin America and was widely resented there for assuming the role of hemispheric police officer. In fact, he did not desire the annexation of either Cuba or Santo Domingo (in his ever-colorful language this was expressed as having "about the same desire to annex" another island "as a gorged boa constrictor might have to swallow a porcupine wrong-end-to"). Moreover, American prestige was exceptionally high under Theodore Roosevelt. He was held in great esteem for his role in the war for the liberation of Cuba and even more highly regarded for his honoring of the American pledge to withdraw from Cuba in 1903 and for the limitations that he imposed on subsequent interventions. Roosevelt usually resisted the temptation to preach to Latin Americans, and in turn many of them saw him, not as a Yankee imperialist, but as their protector against European ambitions.

Roosevelt's Diplomacy in Retrospect

Roosevelt was actually one of the United States' premier diplomat presidents, often serving as his own secretary of state while nevertheless

443

making distinguished appointments (John Hay and Elihu Root) to that office. He was the first president in a long time who could be called a cosmopolitan man: He had traveled extensively in Europe as a child and had a wide circle of European friends and correspondents, and a few non-European ones as well. Despite his reputation for brashness and vigorous speech, he was extremely sensitive to the feelings of other countries and to those of their diplomats, several of whom (for example, Jules Jusserand of France, Speck von Sternberg of Germany, and Cecil Spring Rice of Britain) were among his innermost circle of friends. Historians, in their emphasis on the "big stick" aspect of Rooseveltian diplomacy (and in their reference to Roosevelt's thinking that demonstrations of military force and diplomacy went hand in glove), have frequently neglected the other aspect of Roosevelt's aphorism: He always talked of speaking softly, while carrying a big stick, and his most insistent complaint about his fellow countrymen was that they tended to want to "combine the unready hand with the unbridled tongue." Although pursuing a substantial naval building program, he was invariably punctilious in his treatment of the Japanese. Many of his countrymen (including too many of their representatives in Congress), in contrast, sought every occasion to insult the Japanese yet were nevertheless eager to cut naval appropriations.

Not since the early years of the Republic had an American president held such a firm grasp on the geopolitical realities of world politics. Unlike most Americans, Roosevelt recognized the oneness of the early twentieth century world. He once told the U.S. Congress that "the increasing interdependence and complexity of international political and economic relations render it incumbent on all civilized and orderly powers to insist on the proper policing of the world." The United States could no longer shut itself off from the rest of the world. Its security depended on maintaining the balance of power both in Europe and Asia (and Roosevelt was

acutely aware of how closely interrelated the two were). Moreover, Roosevelt believed that as a great power the United States had commensurate international responsibilities and obligations; it was in the interest of the United States to work actively for world peace. This he did most effectively; his work at the Portsmouth Conference, mediating between Russia and Japan to end their recent war, earned for him the Nobel Peace Prize, and he also played a major role behind the scenes in the Algeciras Conference, which smoothed over a potentially volatile Franco-German conflict over Morocco. As Frederick Marks had written, "For the first time, America was taken into account by world leaders, not only in questions affecting the Western Hemisphere, but in all major diplomatic decisions." Even those who like to speak of Roosevelt's "imperial internationalism" have had to admit that his role in world politics was eminently constructive. He took risks and often incurred domestic political disadvantage, but his achievement becomes clear when set against his successors' inactivity during the second Moroccan crisis in 1911 and during the fateful summer of 1914.

Howard Beale contends that Roosevelt had a particularly noteworthy concern with power relationships: "He was intrigued with power, with problems of power, and with rivalries for power." Indeed, Roosevelt himself once confessed that he believed in power, though it is important to note that the full quotation states, "I believe in power, but I believe that responsibility should go with power." Often in American history such thoughts have been sufficient to condemn someone, and just as often they have been used to obscure the truth. Roosevelt understood that idealism was not a self-fulfilling proposition and that what he had done could have been accomplished only from a position of strength. In fact, he was extremely proud of the things he had done to make the United States into a major military power, and he was inclined to put his doubling of the size of the U.S.

Navy at the very top of his list of accomplishments. He wanted to increase the power of the United States in the international arena for many of the same reasons that he sought to increase the power of the federal government and of the presidency in the domestic arena. Only such power, he thought, could establish order both at home and abroad. It was important that this great new power be accumulated in the right hands, but whether in his hands or in those of the United States, Roosevelt did not doubt that either he or the United States was playing a progressive and righteous role.

Thanks to the innovative work, bridging psychology and history, of Kathleen Dalton, who studied the countless letters that Roosevelt received from the proverbial man and woman in the street, historians are coming to understand precisely what it was about Theodore Roosevelt that endeared him to so many Americans and gave him while still living a cult following new in the annals of American history. Dalton argues that Roosevelt understood that the symbolism of harmonious social unity and equality drew the public to him and that he consciously intended to portray himself in his 1899 book *The Rough Riders* "as a leader who could unite an odd assortment of American types — cowboys, polo-players, derelicts, football stars, Indians, and Wall Street lawyers." The question remains whether Roosevelt used his talents simply to secure power for himself or in an effort to reunite a very fragmented society and imbue it with a new sense of purpose. One suspects that in his own mind at least the distinctions between the two were blurred, but it also cannot be denied that by the time he stepped down in 1909, he had established the basic conditions under which the American state would eventually assume its modern responsibilities.

At fifty, he was still a young man when he retired from the presidency. His initial intentions were the best; he went off on a long African safari in order to permit his successor, William Howard Taft, to put his own stamp on the presidency. He found it very difficult, however, to stay out of the political limelight. Upset by some of Taft's policies, particularly in foreign affairs, antitrust enforcement, and conservation, Roosevelt, in 1912, challenged his renomination. When Taft defeated Roosevelt at the Republican convention, Roosevelt bolted the party and sought to rally his followers in a third-party bid for the presidency.

In a race against Taft, the Democrat Woodrow Wilson, and Socialist Eugene V. Debs, Roosevelt campaigned on a platform that accepted the existence of big business but called for federal regulation to prevent abuse of its power and that endorsed federal social welfare legislation such as workers' compensation and child labor laws. Roosevelt finished a strong second to Wilson, who won partly because of the split within Republican ranks. World War I broke out in Europe two years after the election, and Roosevelt became an ardent supporter of preparedness and a vocal critic of Wilson's policy of neutrality. When Wilson finally took the nation into war in 1917, Roosevelt sought but failed to receive Wilson's approval to raise a division and lead it into combat. Roosevelt remained critical of the Wilson administration but nevertheless became a vitriolic supporter of the war effort.

By 1918, he had begun to lay plans for another try at the Republican nomination for president, but he died on January 6, 1919. In his treatment of Taft and harsh attitudes toward those who were not as enthusiastic as he was about aligning the United States with Great Britain during World War I, Roosevelt had often succumbed to his less generous impulses. Nevertheless, it is likely that had he lived, he could not have been denied the Republican presidential nomination in 1920. Had that happened, Republicanism in the 1920's would have had an entirely different tenor, and American history probably would have taken a markedly different course.

William C. Widenor

Suggested Readings

Beale, Howard K. *Theodore Roosevelt and the Rise of America to World Power.* Baltimore: Johns Hopkins University Press, 1956. A comprehensive study of Roosevelt's foreign policy.

Blum, John Morton. *The Republican Roosevelt.* 1954. 2d ed. Cambridge, Mass.: Harvard University Press, 1977. A classic analysis of Roosevelt and his presidency.

Brands, H. W. *T.R.: The Last Romantic.* New York: Basic Books, 1997. An engaging portrait of Roosevelt's life and personality.

Burton, David. *Theodore Roosevelt: Confident Imperialist.* Philadelphia: University of Pennsylvania Press, 1968. A specialized study of Roosevelt's foreign policy.

Cooper, John Milton. *The Warrior and the Priest: Woodrow Wilson and Theodore Roosevelt.* Cambridge, Mass.: Belknap Press of Harvard University Press, 1983. A good comparative biography of Wilson and Roosevelt.

Gould, Lewis L. *The Presidency of Theodore Roosevelt.* Lawrence: University Press of Kansas, 1991. An extensive analysis of Roosevelt's presidency.

Harbaugh, William H. *The Life and Times of Theodore Roosevelt.* 1959. Rev. ed. New York: Oxford University Press, 1975. Among the best single biographies of Roosevelt.

Hart, Albert B., Herbert R. Ferleger, and John A. Gable, eds. *Theodore Roosevelt Encyclopedia.* Rev. 2d ed., 1989. Topics related to Roosevelt and his presidency are arranged in encyclopedia form.

Hofstadter, Richard. *The American Political Tradition and the Men Who Made It.* 1948. Reprint. New York: Viking Books, 1989. A classic book in the field of political science that profiles Roosevelt.

Jeffers, H. Paul. *Colonel Roosevelt: Theodore Roosevelt Goes to War, 1897-1898.* New York: J. Wiley and Sons, 1996. An examination of Roosevelt's military career.

McCullough, David. *Mornings on Horseback.* New York: Simon & Schuster, 1981. Details Roosevelt's youth and contains some intriguing speculation about the effect of Roosevelt's asthma on his personality development.

Marks, Frederick W., III. *Velvet on Iron: The Diplomacy of Theodore Roosevelt.* Lincoln: University of Nebraska Press, 1979. A sympathetic exploration of Roosevelt's conception of the world and his manner of conducting the nation's foreign policy.

Miller, Nathan. *Theodore Roosevelt.* New York: Morrow, 1992. A solid biography.

Morris, Edmund. *The Rise of Theodore Roosevelt.* 1979. Reprint. New York: Modern Library, 2001. Explores the seminal events in Roosevelt's family and professional life that led to his political career.

Putnam, Carleton. *Theodore Roosevelt: A Biography.* New York: Scribner, 1958. Pays particular focus to Roosevelt's childhood.

Renehan, Edward J. *The Lion's Pride: Theodore Roosevelt and His Family in Peace and War.* New York: Oxford University Press, 1998. Explores the bond between Roosevelt and his children and contrasts his heroic war exploits with the tragic experiences of his four sons during World War I.

Roosevelt, Theodore. *The Adventures of Theodore Roosevelt.* Washington, D.C.: National Geographic Society, 2005. A chronological account of Roosevelt's lifetime of outdoor adventures, culled from Roosevelt's own writings. Each selection is introduced with appropriate historical context.

_____. *The Letters of Theodore Roosevelt.* Edited by H. W. Brands. New York: Cooper Square Press, 2001. A collection of letters that spans Roosevelt's entire life.

_____. *Theodore Roosevelt: The Rough Riders and an Autobiography.* Edited by Louis Auchincloss. 1899, 1913. Reprint. New York: Library of America, 2004. Roosevelt's two original autobiographical volumes are combined here for an indispensable read for scholars.

Samuels, Peggy. *Teddy Roosevelt at San Juan: The Making of a President.* College Station:

Texas A&M University Press, 1997. Gives a detailed account of Roosevelt's military career and its legacy on his presidency.

Theodore Roosevelt Association, The. http://www.theodoreroosevelt.org/. The Web site of an association that dates back to 1919 and strives to preserve the ideals and goals of Roosevelt.

William Howard Taft

27th President, 1909-1913

Born: September 15, 1857
    Cincinnati, Ohio
Died: March 8, 1930
    Washington, D.C.

Political Party: Republican
Vice President: James S. Sherman

Cabinet Members

Secretary of State: Philander C. Knox
Secretary of the Treasury: Franklin MacVeagh
Secretary of War: Jacob M. Dickinson, Henry L.
    Stimson
Secretary of the Navy: George von L. Meyer
Attorney General: George W. Wickersham
Postmaster General: Frank H. Hitchcock
Secretary of the Interior: Richard A. Ballinger,
    Walter L. Fisher
Secretary of Agriculture: James Wilson
Secretary of Commerce and Labor: Charles
    Nagel

William Howard Taft, by background, training, and experience, was ideally suited to serve as the twenty-seventh president of the United States. His father, a distinguished lawyer and judge in Cincinnati, served in Ulysses S. Grant's cabinet briefly as secretary of war and as attorney general. Several years later, President Chester A. Arthur appointed him minister to Austria-Hungary and then transferred him to the Russian capital of St. Petersburg. Taft, one of five children, was born September 15, 1857, and was reared in a privileged, urbane, and Republican family. His entering public life, while not inevitable, was certainly assured after he was admitted to the bar in 1880. After attending

public schools in Cincinnati, Taft entered Yale in 1874 and then the Cincinnati Law School. He was an excellent student, first in his class in grade school, salutatorian in his high school class, and second in his class at Yale, where he delivered the class oration. While attending law school he was a part-time court reporter for the *Cincinnati Commercial.*

Taft Before the Presidency

His political rise, if not as meteoric as that of Theodore Roosevelt, his predecessor and mentor, was nevertheless remarkable and distinguished. He achieved the presidency without

Portrait of William Hoawrd Taft. *(Whitehouse.gov)*

The First Lady
Helen Taft

Helen "Nellie" Herron Taft was born on June 2, 1861, in Cincinnati, Ohio. She was reared in an intellectual home immersed in law and politics and received a private-school education. She taught and gave music lessons until her marriage to Taft on June 19, 1886. Robert Alphonso, their child born in 1889, later distinguished himself in the U.S. Senate. Daughter Helen, born in 1891, achieved a successful academic life. Son Charles Phelps II, born in 1897, also pursued a career in law and politics.

During Taft's four-year term as governor general of the Philippine Islands, Nellie enjoyed a near-royal life in a palatial estate with many servants, allowing her to entertain lavishly. She traveled to Japan, China, and several remote Filipino provinces, despite threats of political unrest and tropical disease. The experience instilled in Nellie an appreciation of diverse cultures and Asian artistry.

When Theodore Roosevelt appointed Taft as secretary of war, Nellie's hopes for her husband's presidency swelled. However, when Roosevelt later suggested a Supreme Court seat for Taft, she intervened to preserve her White House ambitions. Though Taft was a reluctant candidate, Nellie was overexcited throughout his campaign and rejoiced at his 1908 election. Unfortunately, a stroke that affected her mobility and speech marred Nellie's first White House year. She withdrew from the public, her husband devotedly guiding her rehabilitation. After resuming active life, Nellie saw Potomac Park as a fitting site for promenade and musical entertainment. She arranged for the now-famous Japanese cherry trees to be planted along the riverbank, along with a bandstand for Marine Band performances.

In 1914, Nellie published her memoirs titled *Recollections of Full Years*. Her influence upon her husband's career waned after his appointment to the Supreme Court, a position in which he possessed self-confidence. Nellie died in Washington, D.C., on May 22, 1943, and is buried next to her husband in Arlington National Cemetery.

Mimi Lynette Bogard

previously being elected to any legislative or executive office. Conservative by background, by training at Yale where he was greatly impressed by the laissez-faire views of William Graham Sumner, and by preference, Taft was president as the progressive reform impulse crested throughout the United States. He much preferred and was more at home in sedate judicial chambers among legal brethren discussing and resolving crucial questions predicated on the logic of the law, uninfluenced by clamorous and noisome public pressures. The fact that when he entered the presidency at the age of fifty-two he was more than 6 feet tall and weighed 332 pounds might also help explain his preference for an ordered, traditional, and precedent-bound approach to both his public and private life. So too might a weakness for procrastination help explain Taft's preference for the law, which was a rather casual mistress for some practitioners. Yet his entire career, aside from his brief stint as a journalist and five years as a practicing lawyer, was devoted to public service, a not unexpected endeavor given his abilities and his father's prominence in the Republican Party.

Shortly after receiving his LL.B degree in 1880 from the Cincinnati Law School, Taft was appointed assistant prosecuting attorney of Hamilton County, Ohio. Then in rapid succession, except for a short stint in the 1880's when he practiced law, Taft was appointed collector of internal revenue in Cincinnati (1882-1883), assistant county solicitor (1885-1887), and superior court judge in Cincinnati (1887-1890). He was appointed to the court by Governor Joseph Foraker to fill an unexpired term. He successfully ran for election to the office but was invited to serve as United States solicitor general by President Benjamin Harrison in 1890 before the conclusion of his judicial term.

In Washington, D.C., Taft first met Theodore Roosevelt, then a young, ambitious civil service commissioner. After two years, Taft returned to Cincinnati as a United States circuit court judge, a post he held until 1900, when President William McKinley recruited him to bring civil order to the newly acquired Philippine Islands. As a federal judge, Taft exhibited surprising sympathy for the concerns of working people, recognizing, for example, their right to organize and to strike and ruling that employers could not plead contributory negligence by workers when statutory safety provisions had been violated. In an important case involving the Sherman Antitrust Act, Taft decided that a combination of cast-iron pipe manufacturers was restraining trade and issued an injunction to curb the practice.

When he accepted the presidency of the Philippines Commission, Taft for the first time became an executive and administrator. His performance did much to enhance his reputation. As president of the Philippines Commission (1900-1901) and as governor general (1901-1904), Taft supervised the establishment of civil government ending military rule on the islands. Encouraging education, pacifying still-rebellious natives, and resolving the troublesome issue of the friars' lands were among the important goals he achieved. In the last instance, Taft in 1902 conferred with Pope Leo XIII in Rome and concluded an agreement in which the United States paid $7.2 million for the friars' lands, which then became available for sale to residents at fair prices. Before his return to the United States in 1904, Taft devoted his energies to improving the economic status of the Philippines and also toward establishing limited self-government.

While in the Philippines, engrossed in his challenging job, Taft twice declined appointment to the Supreme Court. In 1904, satisfied that his work on the islands could be relinquished to another, Taft joined the Roosevelt administration as secretary of war. He quickly became a close adviser, friend, and troubleshooter for the president, Taft's genial conservatism balancing the more impulsive Roosevelt. In 1904, he went to the Canal Zone to launch the actual construction of the Panama Canal. Two years later Roosevelt hurriedly sent Taft aboard a cruiser to Cuba to forestall a threatened revolution. In the end, Taft helped impose a provisional American government under the terms of the Platt Amendment to

Theodore Roosevelt and his successor, Taft. *(Library of Congress)*

the Cuban constitution, which permitted the United States to intervene.

Roosevelt's declaration after his decisive victory in 1904 that he would not run again, plus Taft's increasingly prominent role in government and his growing friendship with the president, brought Taft's name to the fore as a successor to his chief. Few, if any, seemed better qualified than he to follow Theodore Roosevelt as president of the United States. Late in 1907, Roosevelt publicly let it be known that Taft was the person he wished to succeed him. Vigorously campaigning as Roosevelt's man, he was easily victorious in 1908, defeating William Jennings Bryan, who was seeking the presidency for the third time, by more than a million votes (Taft, 7,637,636; Bryan, 6,393,182) and with 321 electoral votes to his opponent's 162. Bryan carried no Northern state and only three (Nebraska, Colorado, and Nevada) in the West. His other votes came from the "Solid South."

Taft in Office: Frustrated Hopes

Much was expected of Taft as president; he would continue the Roosevelt policies and thereby enhance, in the words of the Republican platform, "justice, equality, and fair dealing" among the American people and further the nation's standing as a world power seeking stability and peace in a world where the balance of power was most tenuous. Unfortunately for Taft and his party, however, which had dominated the national government since the defeat of Bryan in 1896, his administration turned out to be an abject failure, paving the way for the election of Woodrow Wilson in 1912. Taft failed because, despite a genial personality and a keen sense of humor, he was unable to project, as his predecessor could, the image of the presidency as an institution that could further the goals and aspirations of the American people. He could not articulate with memorable words or phrases either the goals of his administration or what the people were striving to achieve. Few could identify with him, and very quickly it be-

came evident that he was unable to lead and guide his own party and mobilize public opinion behind his legislative program. As the head of his party, as the chief spokesperson of the American people, and as the chief legislator who outlined a program he wished the Congress to translate into law, Taft's presidency was a failure, notwithstanding the fact that more significant legislation was enacted during his term of office than during any presidency since Abraham Lincoln occupied the White House. At the end of Taft's tenure, he and Roosevelt were hurling barbed epithets at each other. Theirs was a friendship that split the Republican Party.

At the outset, however, few if any observers could foresee these developments. Roosevelt literally had groomed Taft as his successor. He was nominated on the first ballot with almost no opposition. Also, he inherited a most prosperous nation. His party's platform proudly proclaimed, "The United States now owns one-fourth of the world's wealth and makes one-third of all modern manufactured products. In the greatness of civilization, such as coal, the motive power of all activity; iron, the chief basis of all industry; cotton, the staple foundation of all fabrics; wheat, corn, and all agricultural products that feed mankind, America's supremacy is undisputed." So confident was his party in providing "equal opportunities for all" that its platform declared unequivocally for tariff revision by a special session of Congress immediately following the inauguration. Here was a time bomb, one that Roosevelt had avoided, which marked the start of Taft's difficulties. When Taft and Roosevelt rode up Pennsylvania Avenue on March 4, 1909, however, it was the first time since Andrew Jackson and Martin Van Buren had passed that way, more than seventy years before, that a retiring president would not have preferred another seatmate than the one the fortunes of politics had thrust upon him. Owing to a violent snowstorm and wind, the two men rode in a closed carriage, and the ceremony was held in the Senate chamber instead of its customary place on a platform in front of the Capitol. The inaugural parade and other festivities were greatly curtailed. Numerous celebrants were unable to reach Washington, D.C., which was almost cut off from the outside world by the downing of telegraph wires.

Roosevelt soon departed for Africa to hunt game, and Taft assumed the reins of office by summoning a special session of Congress to convene on March 15 to consider tariff revision, a matter he considered of the most pressing importance. Taft said in his inaugural address that the revised tariff should secure an adequate revenue and at the same time adjust duties in such a manner as to afford labor and industry, whether of the farm, factory, or mine, protection equal to the difference between the cost of production abroad and at home. Taft envisioned that such a tariff would "permit the reduction of rates in certain schedules and will require the advancement of few, if any." What he got was almost a six-month debate. The bill was not passed until August 5. It was strenuously opposed, especially in the Senate, by Republicans who asserted that the platform pledge called for greater reduced rates than Taft's bill proposed. These Republicans and their constituents, primarily in the Midwest and the West, saw the tariff as a means of providing a more equitable distribution of wealth by curbing the special privileges protection afforded large corporate interests, popularly called trusts.

Largely overlooked in the debate and the furor that accompanied it was a section in the tariff act that imposed a 1 percent tax on all joint-stock companies enjoying net earnings or profits in excess of five thousand dollars a year. By imposing this tax, Congress assumed the right to ascertain the earnings of corporations and to prescribe the forms of return, a long step toward federal control and supervision of large corporations whose business encompassed more than one state. The rates, however, were higher than Taft had initially envisioned, owing to the efforts in the Senate of Nelson W. Aldrich, an extreme high-tariff advocate. Though at one time during the long-drawn-out debate Taft had considered vetoing the measure, instead he made himself its defender, signed the bill, and in September began a speaking tour lasting two months and covering every state in the Union. He defended and even extolled the Payne-Aldrich Tariff Act while taking on a broad range of issues. On October 15, he defied tradition and crossed the Rio Grande, formally calling on the president of Mexico on Mexican soil. When he returned to Washington, D.C., the contours of his presidency were evident. There was a deep and growing fissure within his own party, and Taft, unlike his predecessor, was aligning himself with the old-guard, standpat wing of the Republican Party, a situation that ran counter to public opinion in many parts of the nation and from which the Democrats, who had not controlled a branch of Congress since 1894, stood to benefit greatly.

By itself, since it came early in Taft's tenure, the political damage done through his handling of the tariff issue might have been repaired. Yet more was to come, and in the course of his managing a conservation issue Taft alienated his mentor, Theodore Roosevelt. On January 7, 1910, the president dismissed Gifford Pinchot, chief forester of the United States, after Senator Jonathan P. Dolliver read a letter from Pinchot on the Senate floor endorsing charges leveled by subordinates against the secretary of the interior, Richard H. Ballinger, of opening for private sale a tract of valuable coal land in Alaska, acreage that Roosevelt previously had withdrawn from the market. Before his appointment to the cabinet, Ballinger had been the attorney for the syndicate seeking the Alaska coal lands. Taft, when the subject was brought to his attention, made public a letter in September, 1909, exonerating Secretary Ballinger and dismissing from office the chief field inspector of the Interior Department for filing misleading information against his superior officer. Thus when Pinchot's letter

"Taking No Sides" in the rift between "regular" and "insurgent" members of the Republican Party—Taft at his desk with a Rooseveltian "teddy bear." *(Library of Congress)*

was made public, the controversy attracted widespread attention and further convinced Congress that an investigation of the charges was necessary. Since Pinchot was a friend of Roosevelt, the controversy opened a breach between the former president and his successor and widened the fissure in the Republican Party, despite the fact that the congressional joint committee later in the year on a closely divided vote exonerated Secretary Ballinger.

Taft was now seen as an enemy of conservation, and public criticism within a year led to Ballinger's resignation and the cancellation of the Alaska coal land claims. Yet Taft's record in withdrawing from public sale water power sites and mineral and forest lands was every bit as impressive as Theodore Roosevelt's. He also endorsed the expenditure of public monies to further reclamation projects in the arid regions. Since he had exacerbated tensions over policy, however, controversies and feuding within various agencies in the Departments of the Interior and Agriculture continued unabated, and their ramifications boded ill for both Taft and his party. Still, an even greater crisis was in the offing.

Rebellion in the Party

On March 17, 1910, a relatively obscure Nebraska congressman, George W. Norris, precipitated a parliamentary revolution by introducing a resolution that successfully challenged the power of the speaker to appoint committee members by removing him from membership on the Rules Committee, which performed this assignment and which the speaker chaired. Since the Rules Committee also determined the order of business in the House of Representatives, depriving the speaker of membership seriously weakened his power. Although Taft was not directly involved in these events, Joseph G. Cannon, the speaker, championed the president's programs, as did the old-guard, stand-pat members of Congress. Norris and the insurgent members had opposed the Payne-Aldrich Tariff and had endorsed Pinchot in the conservation fight. For their refusal to go along, Taft had withdrawn their patronage. In opposing what they considered Speaker Cannon's autocratic use of power in the president's interest, the insurgents further aggravated divisions within the Republican Party and gave the Democrats, who supported the resolution to curb the power of the speaker, a chance to capitalize on Republican dissension and gain control of the House of Representatives in the November elections.

Popular discontent with the Republican leaders was quickly evident in a Massachusetts by-election in which a Democrat was elected by a majority of nearly six thousand votes from a district that had been invariably Republican and where the late member in 1908 had beaten his Democratic opponent by fourteen thousand votes. Shortly after, in a by-election at Rochester, New York, a Republican stronghold, the Democratic candidate won an almost equally striking victory. Equally foreboding to Republican ascendancy was the impending retirement at the close of the existing (Sixty-first) Congress of Senators Nelson Aldrich of Rhode Island and Eugene Hale of Maine, who for many years had controlled the Senate in the interest of Republicanism and extreme protectionism.

Yet despite these developments, so ominous for the prestige of both the president and his beleaguered party, the results of the session seemingly helped restore the Republicans' credit with the American people. More constructive legislation was enacted than at any time since the Civil War. The Interstate Commerce Commission was granted further authority over railroad rates, and telephone as well as telegraph lines were brought within its jurisdiction. A court of commerce was created to allow carriers and shippers seeking judicial review of rates an opportunity for prompt consideration. New Mexico and Arizona were admitted as states of the Union. A system of postal savings banks was established, and the following Congress approved a parcel post system. A bureau of mines was created, and, in an important step toward the conservation of natural resources, the president was granted authority to withdraw public lands from sale, pending a decision by Congress on their use. A commission was established to inquire into the corporate practice of issuing stock in excess of assets, and another investigated the cost of production in the United States compared with that of foreign countries, with a view to readjusting tariff schedules. Also, candidates for Congress were henceforth to be required to publish particulars of their campaign costs. These accomplishments were largely the result of the president's influence—and the result of compromises that did little to resolve the divisions within the Republican Party.

These divisions became evident as campaigning got under way for the fall elections. Theodore Roosevelt, fresh from a triumphal tour of Europe following his successful venture in African big-game hunting, reentered politics. In various speeches he estranged Republican "machine" politicians by commenting, among other things, on industrial and social conditions in the anthracite coal region, advocating the conservation of natural resources, suggesting that social evils might be the result of a wrong system, indirectly attacking the Supreme Court, and formulating his "New Nationalism," which widened the breach with conservative elements in both parties and led many to believe that he was ready to lead the insurgents, now increasingly called Progressives, in an effort to head again the Republican Party. In almost all of his speeches, Roosevelt advocated increased federal control—over corporations, natural resources, wages and hours, and the conditions of rural life. Though he was careful not to criticize the president, and at times he praised Taft and some of his policies, Roosevelt's speeches were generally regarded as widening the breach in the Republican ranks. In three weeks Roosevelt traveled fifty-six hundred miles through fourteen states and had spoken in some twenty cities, besides addressing hordes of people from his railroad car.

Roosevelt's tour was only one indication of the troubles affecting the Republican Party in that election year. Insurgent candidates were successful in party primaries in several states, chiefly in the Midwest. The Vermont elections on September 6 showed a greatly reduced Republican majority; those in Maine, six days later, witnessed the election of a Democratic governor and two congressmen in that traditionally Republican state. Elsewhere tensions within the Republican Party also came to the fore as delegates selected candidates for the November elections.

The result was a great Democratic victory. For the first time since 1894 the Democrats would control the House of Representatives. Key states—New York, Ohio, New Jersey, Massachusetts, and Connecticut—elected Democratic governors, and insurgent or Progressive Republican senators increased their numbers as did the Democrats, drastically reducing the Republican working majority in the Senate. Throughout the country the president and his party suffered severe reverses. Theodore Roosevelt, writing in the *Outlook*, said the fight for progressive popular government had merely begun. It would continue despite roadblocks and the fact that the last two years of Taft's tenure would be marred by intense partisanship, ripping the Republican Party asunder and bringing a Democrat to the White House in 1912. Taft, never a president to exercise strong leadership, was rendered almost impotent during his remaining years in the White House. He was caught up in forces that he no longer could effectively control, but to his credit, he tried. Unfortunately, some of his efforts further contributed to the deteriorating political situation.

Taft's aspirations for an Anglo-American arbitration treaty, expressed at the meeting in Washington, D.C., of the Society for the Judicial Settlement of International Disputes on December 19, 1910, was soon crowned with a measure of success when in June of the following year a joint agreement among Great Britain, Russia, Japan, and the United States was announced that curbed the wanton destruction of the seal rookeries in the Bering Sea. Also, in August, 1911, the president was truly pleased when treaties of arbitration with Great Britain and France were placed before him for his signature. Unfortunately, the Senate refused to ratify them, and Taft again found himself at odds with his party. Earlier, on January 26, Taft had sent a special message to the Senate, making a powerful appeal for Canadian reciprocity. He insisted that the time was ripe "to facilitate commerce between the two countries and thus greatly to increase the natural resources available to our people" and to "further promote good feeling between kindred peoples." In numerous speeches the president warmly supported the project. Yet it seemed likely that the Senate, de-

> *Excerpts from a 1912 paper by William Howard Taft about his policy of Dollar Diplomacy:*
>
> The diplomacy of the present administration has sought to respond to modern ideas of commercial intercourse. This policy has been characterized as substituting dollars for bullets. It is one that appeals alike to idealistic humanitarian sentiments, to the dictates of sound policy and strategy, and to legitimate commercial aims. It is an effort frankly directed to the increase of American trade upon the axiomatic principle that the Government of the United States shall extend all proper support to every legitimate and beneficial American enterprise abroad.
>
> How great have been the results of this diplomacy, coupled with the maximum and minimum provision of the Tariff Law, will be seen by some consideration of the wonderful increase in the export trade of the United States. Because modern diplomacy is commercial, there has been a disposition in some quarters to attribute to it none but materialistic aims. How strikingly erroneous is such an impression may be seen from a study of the results by which the diplomacy of the United States can be judged. . . .
>
> In the past, our diplomacy has often consisted, in normal times, in a mere assertion of the right to international existence. We are now in a larger relation with broader rights of our own and obligations to others than ourselves. A number of great guiding principles were laid down early in the history of this government. The recent task of our diplomacy has been to adjust those principles to the conditions of today, to develop their corollaries, to find practical applications of the old principles expanded to meet new situations. Thus are being evolved bases upon which can rest the superstructure of policies which must grow with the destined progress of this nation.
>
> The successful conduct of our foreign relations demands a broad and a modern view. We cannot meet new questions nor build for the future if we confine ourselves to outworn dogmas of the past and to the perspective appropriate at our emergence from colonial times and conditions. The opening of the Panama Canal will mark a new era in our international life and create new and worldwide conditions which, with their vast correlations and consequences, will obtain for hundreds of years to come. We must not wait for events to overtake us unawares. With continuity of purpose we must deal with the problems of our external relations by a diplomacy modern, resourceful, magnanimous, and fittingly expressive of the high ideals of a great nation.

spite its Republican majority, would not go along because those members from agricultural states, such as Iowa, Minnesota, the Dakotas, and Wisconsin, feared that their staple products might be adversely affected by the proposed free list or by reduced rates on competing Canadian agricultural products.

Rather than trying to achieve Canadian reciprocity through a treaty, which would require a two-thirds vote in the Senate, Taft sought an agreement necessitating majority approval in both chambers of the Congress. In this endeavor he was ultimately successful. During the debate in the House of Representatives, however, the speaker-designate of the next (Sixty-second) Congress, Champ Clark of Missouri, created a sensation when he expressed support for reciprocity because he hoped that Canada would become part of the United States. A Republican member from New York, William S. Bennet, followed by introducing resolutions favoring annexation. Taft was unable to secure congressional support at this time, but he called the new Congress into special session early in April. The Democrats, now controlling the House of Representatives, approved the measure before the month was out, and the Senate, several months later, followed suit. Taft, who had labored long and hard for the agreement, signed it on July 26, 1911. All his efforts came to naught, however, when, in September, the Canadian government of Sir Wilfrid Laurier, the Liberal Party premier, went down to defeat. Laurier had made the consummation of reciprocity the prime issue in his campaign for reelection. The new premier, Robert L. Borden, had depicted Taft as a duplicitous leader seeking Canadian annexation.

To embarrass the president further and to define an issue for the next presidential campaign, the Democrats in the House of Representatives introduced several low-tariff measures: a woolen bill, a cotton bill, and a farmers' freelist bill, which the Progressive Republicans in the Senate also endorsed, allowing these "pop" tariff bills to receive congressional approval. Taft vetoed them as haphazard measures of tariff reduction.

Trust-Busting and Dollar Diplomacy

In his broad view of the trust problem and in a wide-ranging application of the Sherman Antitrust Act, Taft used an approach that truly entitled him, rather than his predecessor, to the title of trust buster. Whereas Theodore Roosevelt invoked the Sherman Act to further his political and national goals in a sparse number of instances, Taft seemed to interpret the law literally, and his attorney general, George W. Wickersham, launched a vigorous attack. The wire trust was compelled to dissolve; the electric trust dissolved itself after an adverse legal decision. Proceedings were also initiated against the lumber trust, the ice trust, the magazine trust, and others for unlawful combination and conspiracy in restraint of trade. The steel trust in October, 1911, announced its intention to cancel its lease of Minnesota iron range ore lands and to reduce the ore rates on its railroads. Nevertheless, the government instituted proceedings against it for violating the Sherman Act by monopolist practices. Earlier in the year the Supreme Court in suits against the Standard Oil and tobacco trusts ordered their dissolution but at the same time reassured business interests that "reasonable" restraint of trade was not ille-

gal.

The suit against the steel trust seemingly violated an agreement Roosevelt had formulated during the panic of 1907 sanctioning the purchase of a controlling interest in the Tennessee Coal and Iron Company by the United States Steel Corporation to prevent the failure of the smaller firm, the largest iron and steel producer in the South, and to help curb the financial panic. Taft's action in this instance further widened the breach with his predecessor. Roosevelt, in opposing Taft's trust policy of initiating court action as a means of securing reasonable and legal competition, advocated legislation for supervision and control of the companies.

In a significant way Taft's major thrust in foreign policy also differed significantly from that of Roosevelt. Although accepting the nation's commitment as a world power, Taft pursued this approach largely through a policy of Dollar Diplomacy, encouraging economic interests in pursuing national interests. He described it as a policy of "substituting dollars for bullets" and sought to persuade American bankers to enter international consortiums to refinance Nicaragua's foreign debt and to support railroad building in China. Taft said that his approach was "frankly directed to the increase of American trade upon the axiomatic principle that the Government of the United States shall extend all proper support to every legitimate and beneficial American enterprise abroad." Although there was nothing new or original about Taft's approach, in the heated political climate of the latter part of his administration it aroused intense debate and controversy involving anti-imperialists, progressives and others critical of the role of large banking firms, and followers of Theodore Roosevelt who viewed national interests in much broader terms. Moreover, before Taft's presidency there had been little American investment in China.

Dollar Diplomacy, in the case of the Caribbean and Central America, would provide the means for helping those countries achieve stability by rehabilitating their finances, establishing sound monetary systems, securing efficient administration of customhouses, and establishing reliable banks. Such policies, Taft envisioned, would curb revolutions, further secure the Panama Canal, and avoid the danger of international complications brought about by foreign creditors. In addition, in 1912 the Senate approved a resolution that in effect extended the Monroe Doctrine to include an Asiatic power and foreign corporations that sought control over potential military or naval sites.

Roosevelt's Challenge: The Race in 1912

The year 1912 marked the disintegration of Taft's presidency, exhibited the acceptance of

A cartoon contrasting the 1912 presidential candidates' confident public personas with the nervousness each candidate privately feels. *(Library of Congress)*

the reform spirit in both major parties, and split the Republican Party asunder in the fifty-eighth year of its existence. By the end of 1911, Senator Robert M. La Follette, creating the Progressive Republican League, announced his intention of seeking his party's presidential nomination. Also, early in the new year a movement in favor of Theodore Roosevelt's nomination was clearly evident, despite his disclaimer in 1904 of ever again seeking the presidency. By the end of February, Roosevelt openly acknowledged that he would challenge Taft for the nomination. The widening breach between these two former friends helped complete the rending of their party. Roosevelt declared Taft's support of the arbitration treaties "an unworthy and, however unconsciously, a hypocritical move against the interests of peace and the honor and interests of the United States and civilization." Taft, for his part, in a speech on Lincoln's birthday described the insurgents and Progressives as "political neurotics" whose proposals threatened to reduce the country to conditions paralleled only in the history of South America or in the French Revolution. Later their barbs became more direct and personal.

In seeking the nomination, Roosevelt endorsed a program of reform that included the recall by popular vote of judicial decisions, the initiative and referendum, presidential primaries, and an amendment calling for the direct election of United States senators. He later included woman suffrage. Taft had reservations about the entire reform program, but along with most conservatives, he was particularly adamant about Roosevelt's endorsement of the recall of judicial decisions. Roosevelt's managers, however, appealed to the public by denouncing the Taft administration as lacking in leadership, destroying the Republican Party, disheartening the country, and bewildering business. Roosevelt himself charged Taft with being an oligarch, the friend of reaction and privileged minorities.

In the few states, fifteen out of forty-eight, with presidential primaries, most of the delegates endorsed Roosevelt. With the Republican convention scheduled to meet in Chicago on June 18, the leading candidates engaged in much reciprocal vituperation, with Taft accusing Roosevelt of deliberately misrepresenting his speeches and actions, of knowingly making false statements about him, of distorting his views, and more. He supported some of his charges by reading from his private correspondence with "My dear Theodore." Roosevelt responded in kind, describing Taft as "biting the hand that fed him" and yielding through feebleness to the "bosses" and the "interests" and at-

tacking him for presenting confidential correspondence without permission.

As the primary results became known, it was evident that Roosevelt had real popular support, although New York decisively and Massachusetts rather uncertainly declared for Taft. Ohio, the president's home state, selected an overwhelming majority of Roosevelt delegates. When Republican delegates headed for Chicago in June, it was estimated that Taft and Roosevelt had secured anywhere from 400 to 450 delegates apiece. The outcome was centered on the contesting delegations, chiefly from the Southern states, consisting mainly of officeholders and African Americans, individuals holding patronage appointments in areas where Republican strength was small or virtually nonexistent. The task of deciding these contests fell to the Republican National Committee, which met in Chicago on June 6. On June 16, the result of its deliberations was announced. Taft was awarded 235 seats; 20 went to Roosevelt

Taft (center) on the Supreme Court in 1921. *(Library of Congress)*

delegates. Taft's renomination was now assured. Roosevelt, charging that the president was a receiver of stolen goods, no better than a thief, called on his followers to bolt the convention and to form a new party dedicated to progressive reform principles and proposals. On August 6, the Progressive Party meeting in Chicago nominated Theodore Roosevelt by acclamation.

Roosevelt's candidacy and that of Woodrow Wilson, selected by the Democrats at their convention in Baltimore, prompted the widely held view that Taft had little chance of reelection. Roosevelt and Wilson both championed the cause of reform. Nevertheless, the platform of the Republican Party contained numerous progressive planks, including regulating by law the working conditions of women and children, workmen's compensation, simplifying judicial procedures, further conservation measures, and a federal trade commission to curb monopoly practices. It was so progressive that several prominent Republicans favorable to reform refused to support Roosevelt and remained loyal to their party.

During the campaign, Taft talked about the integrity of the Constitution and maintaining prosperity through a moderate and scientific tariff. Roosevelt, he intimated, was seeking to aggravate and exploit unrest in his own interest, whereas Wilson was a dangerous idealist who would break up the Constitution. Progressives and Democrats, he charged, were increasing popular dissatisfaction with talk of evils they had trouble defining and appeared incompetent to cure.

When Congress recessed at the end of August, Taft vetoed several tariff and appropriation bills, one of which indirectly abolished the Interstate Court of Commerce. He approved several reform measures, however, adding to the body of significant legislation enacted during his administration. One called for an eight-hour day for all government workers and for employees on the Panama Canal after com-

pletion was approved; another prohibited the manufacture of white phosphorous matches. The third session of the Sixty-second Congress, the last of the Taft administration, would convene in December after the results of the vehement and hardfought presidential campaign were known.

An indication of what was to come was evident after the Vermont election on September 2, usually regarded as a political barometer. The Republicans lost heavily to the Progressives, while the Democrats gained in this traditional Republican state which, nevertheless, was carried by Taft. A week later, Maine, also a traditional Republican state, went for Wilson. In all, Taft carried one additional state, Utah, in the November elections for a total of 8 electoral votes to 88 for Roosevelt and 435 for Wilson. Taft also trailed Wilson and Roosevelt in the popular vote. In addition, the Republicans lost control of the Senate and failed to regain control of enough states, so that the Democratic Party prevailed in a majority of state houses as well. Taft and his party were discredited and repudiated in the election of 1912, a complete reversal of the situation in 1908, when Taft was overwhelmingly approved by the voters as Theodore Roosevelt's successor.

Taft's Achievements

The election results meant that Congress in the last months of Taft's presidency would accomplish little in the way of significant legislation. Both were "lame ducks" waiting for their terms to end. Yet policies launched by the Taft administration continued to be implemented in the early months of 1913, before the inauguration of Woodrow Wilson. The campaign against trusts continued in the courts. Officials of the National Cash Register Company, for example, were fined and some were jailed after being convicted of violations of the Sherman Antitrust Act. In the House of Representatives, a subcommittee reported evidence of the existence of a "money trust," a few great banking firms controlling through interlocking directorships vast enterprises capable of depriving rival or competing concerns of their ability to secure adequate access to capital.

Among the pieces of legislation approved by Congress were several that added to the body of progressive measures during Taft's administration. Included were laws calling for the "physical valuation" of railroads so that rates would reflect the actual properties and not the paper (security) value of the enterprises and for the creation of a department of labor. Before Taft left office, the Sixteenth Amendment to the Constitution, calling for a federal income tax, secured the necessary support of three-fourths of the state legislatures. Soon after, the Seventeenth Amendment, providing for the direct election of United States senators, was ratified. Both were approved by Congress during Taft's presidency.

The Taft administration had been unfortunate in many ways. It had failed to achieve tariff reform; it had been weakened by a dispute over conservation policy and by the traditional association of the Republican Party with big business and organized capital. Countries in Latin America had been alarmed by Dollar Diplomacy, and the consortium designed to take the Manchurian railways out of politics had been ill received. It had also blundered in its reciprocity campaign. Still, Taft had done his best to provide international arbitration, and he had signed into law much useful legislation. The executive branch, moreover, had combated trusts with energy and success. Yet when he left office, his party was in shambles and he had suffered a humiliating defeat, which he accepted with dignity. Though well liked as an individual, his deficiencies as a politician and a leader made his four years in the White House a trial and an ordeal. More than any previous president, he escaped from Washington whenever he possibly could. In four years he traveled a total of 150,000 miles, a record for a president, crisscrossing the country, appealing in effect for a reversal of the popular verdict against his administration. He retired with dignity to a professorship at Yale Law School.

His later career was more suited to his talents and provided infinitely more satisfaction than his presidency. During World War I, he returned to Washington to serve as joint chairman of the National War Labor Board. Then on June 30, 1921, President Warren G. Harding rewarded Taft and gratified his heart's desire by selecting him for the highest official honor ever to be given to a former president, an office that he coveted far more than the presidency itself—the chief justiceship of the United States. Here Taft's abilities as a coordinator and conciliator could function in a more meaningful and harmonious atmosphere. Taft died on March 8, 1930.

Richard Lowitt

Suggested Readings

Anderson, Judith I. *William Howard Taft: An Intimate History*. New York: Norton, 1981. Anderson employs a psychological approach in her biography of Taft.

Burton, David. *William Howard Taft: Confident Peacemaker*. Philadelphia: Saint Joseph's University Press, 2004. Examines Taft's foreign policy initiatives throughout his entire political career.

Butt, Archibald W. *Taft and Roosevelt: The Intimate Letters of Archie Butt, Military Aide*. 1930. Reprint. Port Washington, N.Y.: Kennikat Press, 1971. An older but still valuable biography.

Chace, James. *1912: Wilson, Roosevelt, Taft and Debs—The Election that Changed the Country*. New York: Simon & Schuster, 2004. Chace details the campaign engagingly and argues that it brought forth a conflict between progressive idealism and conservative values that held significant impact for politics throughout the twentieth century.

Coletta, Paolo E. *The Presidency of William Howard Taft*. Lawrence: University Press of

Kansas, 1973. A thorough and sound study of the Taft administration.

_____. *William Howard Taft: A Bibliography*. Westport, Conn.: Meckler, 1989. Provides a comprehensive listing of primary and secondary sources on Taft's life and presidency.

Joseph, Paul. *William Howard Taft*. Minneapolis: ABDO, 2000. A biography of Taft for young adults.

Lowitt, Richard. *George W. Norris: The Making of a Progressive, 1861-1912*. 1963. Reprint. Westport, Conn.: Greenwood Press, 1980. Gives insight into the insurgency movement that plagued Taft's presidency.

Manners, William. *TR and Will: A Friendship That Split the Republican Party*. New York: Harcourt, Brace, and World, 1969. Reviews the relationship between Taft and his predecessor in the White House.

Minger, Ralph E. *William Howard Taft and United States Foreign Policy: The Apprenticeship Years, 1900-1908*. Urbana: University of Illinois Press, 1975. Explores Taft's political career prior to the presidency.

Pringle, Henry F. *The Life and Times of William Howard Taft*. 2 vols. 1939. Reprint. Hamden, Conn.: Archon Books, 1964. An older but nonetheless worthy biography.

Romero, Francine Sanders. *Presidents from Theodore Roosevelt Through Coolidge, 1901-1929: Debating the Issues in Pro and Con Primary Documents*. Westport, Conn.: Greenwood Press, 2002. A collection of primary documents and commentary is used to debate issues that were pertinent during the tenure of presidents serving between 1901-1929.

Scholes, Walter, and Marie V. Scholes. *The Foreign Policies of the Taft Administration*. Columbia: University of Missouri Press, 1970. A careful examination of Dollar Diplomacy and international affairs.

Taft, William Howard. *The Collected Works of William Howard Taft*. Edited by David H. Burton. 8 vols. Athens: Ohio University Press, 2001-2004. A collection of important political writings of Taft.

Woodrow Wilson

28th President, 1913-1921

Born: December 28, 1856
    Staunton, Virginia
Died: February 3, 1924
    Washington, D.C.

Political Party: Democratic
Vice President: Thomas S. Marshall

Cabinet Members

Secretary of State: William Jennings Bryan,
    Robert Lansing, Bainbridge Colby
Secretary of the Treasury: William Gibbs
    McAdoo, Carter Glass, David F. Houston
Secretary of War: Lindley M. Garrison,
    Newton D. Baker
Secretary of the Navy: Josephus Daniels
Attorney General: James C. McReynolds,
    Thomas W. Gregory, A. Mitchell Palmer
Postmaster General: Albert Burleson
Secretary of the Interior: Franklin K. Lane,
    John P. Payne
Secretary of Agriculture: David F. Houston,
    E. T. Meredith
Secretary of Commerce: William C. Redfield,
    J. W. Alexander
Secretary of Labor: William B. Wilson

Thomas Woodrow Wilson was born on December 28, 1856, in Staunton, Virginia. His father, Joseph Ruggles Wilson, a Presbyterian minister, was a powerful influence on his son "Tommy," as Woodrow Wilson's parents called him until he declared one day in his twenty-second year that he wished to be known as T. Woodrow Wilson (the initial quickly disappeared). He, along with his older sisters Annie and Marion and his younger brother Joseph, Jr., was brought up by

a mother and father who nurtured him and shaped his personality and temperament in profoundly significant ways. From his father, Wilson gained a heady sense of confidence and of duty to fulfill his destiny as one of God's elect. He also developed an abiding moral intransigence, a stubborn self-righteousness that dogged him throughout his career.

Intensely ambitious for her son and completely uncritical of his faults, his mother made him feel intellectually and morally superior to his classmates and colleagues. Often ill herself, she helped develop in Wilson a preoccupation with his health. During his life he had a number

Portrait of Woodrow Wilson. *(Whitehouse.gov)*

The First Lady
Ellen Wilson

Ellen Louise Axson was born on May 15, 1860, in Savannah, Georgia, to Edward and Janie Hoyt Axson. One year later, Georgia succeeded from the Union, and her father went off to be chaplain to the First Regiment of the Georgia Infantry. Illness forced him out of the Confederate Army in 1863, and his family moved to Madison, Georgia, where Edward served as pastor of the Madison Presbyterian Church. Ellen's first schooling was at the Madison Male and Female Academy, where her father taught.

When her family moved to Rome, Georgia, Ellen enrolled in the Rome Female College at the age of eleven. She studied philosophy, natural history, and algebra, and she even taught herself trigonometry during one summer. Ellen's mother died on November 4, 1881, leaving Ellen to raise her two small brothers. She attended services at her father's church in Rome on April 8, 1883, and caught the eye of a young lawyer from Atlanta, Woodrow Wilson.

After a two-year courtship, Ellen and Woodrow were married on June 24, 1885, in Savannah. Three daughters were born to the Wilsons: Margaret Woodrow Wilson on April 16, 1886; Jessie Woodrow Wilson on April 28, 1887; and Eleanor Randolph Wilson on October 10, 1889. Upon her husband's election to the presidency in 1912, Ellen immediately became an activist First Lady. She gave him political advice and edited his speeches.

Ellen was encouraged by the National Civic Federation to improve the living conditions of African Americans in Washington, D.C. She was taken on a tour of the slums in which they lived in shacks with no electricity and running water. Ellen urged the Congress to pass the "Alley Bill" that would fund model homes to replace the shacks. The bill was passed just hours before Ellen Wilson died on August 6, 1914, of Bright's disease. Future First Ladies used Ellen's example to speak out and seek action on issues important to them. At the time of her death, she was also working on plans to renovate the area of the White House grounds that is now known as the Rose Garden.

David Murphy

of serious ailments; from the age of thirty-nine until his death in 1924, he suffered from cerebral vascular disease. In 1896 a stroke left him with a marked weakness in his right hand. Another stroke in 1906 weakened his right arm and left him almost blind in his left eye. In addition to periodic stress and related bouts of debilitating headaches and stomach problems, he continued to suffer from carotid artery disease, which caused a massive stroke in October, 1919, completely paralyzing the left side of his body and affecting his mental attitude and personality.

Wilson was also a dyslexic. He was nine before he knew his letters and eleven or so before he could read. Nevertheless, he was a good if not brilliant student. In 1873, he enrolled as a freshman at Davidson College, a tiny Presbyterian school near Charlotte, North Carolina. He stayed for two semesters at Davidson, where he played second base on the freshman baseball team and was active on the campus debating team. After spending the next year with his parents in Wilmington, North Carolina, Wilson entered Princeton in 1875. He had given up any plans he may once have had to enter the ministry and looked ahead to a political or literary career.

Following his graduation from Princeton, Wilson enrolled as a law student at the University of Virginia in the autumn of 1879, but he quickly developed a distaste for legal studies and grew depressed about his career. Wilson left the university after a year, reentered in the autumn of 1880, but then, in December, withdrew again and went home to Wilmington.

He remained at home for some eighteen months. In the fall of 1882, he passed the Georgia state bar examination and set up practice in Atlanta. Yet his heart was not in his work, and he grew increasingly restless. He wanted to become "a master of philosophical discourse, to become capable and apt in instructing as great a number of persons as possible, . . . a speaker and writer of the highest authority on political subjects. This I *may* become in a chair of political science."

In 1883, therefore, Wilson gave up his law practice and gained admission to The Johns Hopkins University in Baltimore, where the "seminary" of Herbert Baxter Adams was the very citadel of political scholarship in the United States.

Soon after his arrival at Johns Hopkins, Wilson began writing his first book, *Congressional Government*. Drawing on earlier essays he had written and borrowing much from the British essayist Walter Bagehot, he finished the work in October, 1884. In it, Wilson described how laws were made, how Congress operated, and how the legislative branch dominated the government. Based on little original research, the book was full of glib generalizations and stylistic infelicities and sorely remiss in its depiction of economic realities in Gilded Age America. Yet in the book Wilson expressed some of the basic principles of political action that he would himself put into practice as president of the United States, and this alone makes *Congressional Gov-*

The First Lady
Edith Wilson

Edith Bolling Wilson was the second wife of the twenty-eighth U.S. president. An intelligent and strong-willed woman, Edith became one of Woodrow Wilson's most trusted advisers.

Born on October 15, 1872, in Wytheville, Virginia, Edith was one of eleven children of circuit court judge William Bolling and Sallie White. Considered part of the southern aristocracy, Edith was educated at home with a few formal years of schooling at two Virginia academies during the late 1880's, Martha Washington College and Powell's School.

She married Norman Galt, owner of a jewelry and furnishings business, in 1896. When Norman died in 1908, Edith ran the jewelry business. She was introduced to President Wilson in March, 1915, and Woodrow courted Edith through eloquent love letters. This disturbed the president's advisers since his wife, Ellen, had died less than a year before. However, Edith and Woodrow were married on December 18, 1915.

During the contentious 1916 election, Edith suffered personal insults as a result of the couple's rapid courtship, but she persevered. When the United States entered World War I in 1917, Edith persuaded American women to conserve resources, but she saw her main role as Woodrow's sounding board. She urged him to travel to Paris to personally negotiate the peace treaty in November, 1918.

When Woodrow had a paralyzing stroke in 1919, Edith served as a shield between him and his work. She handled his dictation and relayed his communication to and from cabinet members and other officials. After his term ended in 1921, they resided in Washington, D.C. She continued caring for her husband until his death in 1924. Afterward, she staunchly protected his image and personal papers and served as a pillar for the Woodrow Wilson Foundation until her death on December 28, 1961.

Lisa A. Wroble

ernment Wilson's most noteworthy book. His *Constitutional Government in the United States* (1908) is a gloss on the earlier book. *The State* (1889) is a mediocre textbook. *Division and Reunion* (1893) is a short and derivative history of the country from 1829 to 1889. *George Washington* (1896) is a potboiler that Wilson, in haste and carelessness, wrote to pay for a new home. *A History of the American People* (1902), in five volumes and profusely illustrated, he also did in a hurry and for money.

By the spring of 1884, nearing the end of his first year at Johns Hopkins, Wilson wanted to leave. He wanted to marry Ellen Axson, the daughter of a minister in Rome, Georgia, whom he had met the year before, but to do so he had to have a job. In January, 1885, he found one: teaching at Bryn Mawr, a new Quaker college in Pennsylvania for women. On June 24, 1885, he and Ellen were married.

During the next twenty-nine years, besides giving birth to three daughters—Eleanor Randolph, Jessie Woodrow, and Margaret Woodrow—Ellen Axson gave Wilson unflagging devotion and constant affection, even tolerating a brief romance that Wilson suddenly developed in 1907-1908 with Mary Allen Hulbert Peck, a vivacious and talented, if vain and frivolous, woman whom he met while he was on vacation (without Ellen) in Bermuda. In 1914, Ellen Axson died. A few months later, at the age of fifty-eight, Wilson fell passionately, boyishly in love with Edith Galt, a forty-two-year-old widow of statuesque beauty and sexual magnetism, and in December, 1915, he married her.

Wilson may never have reached the White House or any height of professional achievement without the women in his life to sustain him. He may also never have reached the presidency without the particular ascent he followed from college teaching to the presidency of Princeton University to the governorship of New Jersey. From 1885 to 1888, Wilson taught at Bryn Mawr College, then at Wesleyan University for two years, and from 1890 to 1902 he was

professor of jurisprudence and political economy at Princeton. In 1902, he became president of Princeton and at once inaugurated some bold changes at the university. He revised the curriculum, established a preceptorial system of guided study, and brought in a number of promising young teachers and scholars. In 1906-1907 he tried—and failed—to abolish undergraduate eating and social clubs. In 1909-1910, he lost a bruising fight over the establishment and control of a graduate college.

Wilson's successes at Princeton brought him to the attention of New Jersey politicians, who asked him to seek the Democratic nomination for governor in 1910. His failures at Princeton, along with his old aspirations for high political office, prompted him to seize the opportunity to move from the halls of ivy to the corridors of political power.

New Jersey in 1910 was controlled by a corrupt alliance of political bosses and railroad and public utilities magnates. Republicans had held the governorship since 1896. Democratic bosses hoped to regain the office by putting forth as gubernatorial candidate a prominent citizen they could control, who would run on a liberal platform they could disregard. Wilson, at the time of his nomination, was a political conservative with little awareness of the great Progressive reform movement sweeping through American (and New Jersey) politics since the turn of the century. Quick to grasp the chance for nomination, Wilson was equally quick to adopt some of this reform program as his own. Repudiating the machine that nominated him, he swept into the governorship by a fifty-thousand-vote majority.

He then openly broke with the state bosses, established his own firm control over the Democratic Party in the state, and pushed through a reform program—a direct primary system, corrupt practices legislation, workers' compensation, strict state control of railroads and public utilities—that soon provoked an intensive campaign by Democratic progressives to make him the party's presidential nominee in 1912.

The 1912 Campaign

Wilson himself thirsted for that nomination, and early in 1911, he began his campaign to gain it. Up and down the country he went, seeking delegates, speaking incessantly. His chief rival for the nomination was James B. "Champ" Clark of Missouri, elected to Congress in 1892 and elected speaker of the House in 1911. When all the 1,088 delegates to the Baltimore convention had been chosen, 436 had pledged to Clark and 248 had pledged to Wilson, with the remaining 400 or so unpledged or pledged to Oscar Underwood of Alabama and other minor candidates. Clark, on the early balloting, held a substantial lead. On the fourteenth ballot, the veteran presidential candidate and powerful voice in the party, William Jennings Bryan, a delegate from Nebraska, spoke out against Clark and voted for Wilson, but his move caused little change in the balloting. After a riotous and bitter fight, the convention finally chose Wilson on the forty-sixth ballot. The progressive wing of the Democratic Party, as demonstrated by Wilson's recently developed progressivism and the support for him by old agrarian reformers such as Bryan, now controlled the party. It remained for Wilson to win the election, a challenging task.

Except for Grover Cleveland's two terms, from 1885 to 1889 and from 1893 to 1897, Republicans had controlled the presidency since Lincoln's election in 1860. In 1912 the Republicans renominated William Howard Taft, who had already served one term. A progressive faction of the Republican Party, rebelling against the Taft nomination, chose Theodore Roosevelt as candidate on the Progressive, or "Bull Moose," ticket. Roosevelt was formidable opposition. During his tenure in the White House, from 1901 to 1909, he had dramatically transformed the office and powers of the presidency, altered the course of American politics, and shaped the Republican Party into an instrument of progressive reform. In 1912, Roosevelt, not the Republican Taft (and not Eugene V. Debs, nominated on the Socialist Party ticket), was Wilson's chief opponent.

Roosevelt's program in 1912 bore the label the New Nationalism. Wilson countered with the New Freedom. The veteran journalist William Allen White once described the difference between the two as that between Tweedledum and Tweedledee. If by this reference to *Alice's Adventures in Wonderland* White meant that there was no difference at all, he was nearly but not quite right. On some issues the two candidates took remarkably similar stands, but they also displayed significant, if subtle, differences. Both men minimized two important issues of 1912—woman suffrage and racial discrimination—since neither man cared about them. Both were white racists, the New Yorker Roosevelt more so than the Southern-born Wilson. Wilson neither supported nor opposed woman suffrage; Roosevelt endorsed nationwide suffrage but only to gain support from reformers such as Jane Addams. Differences between the candidates showed up most clearly in the matter they discussed most: the role of the federal government (and the president) in exercising controls over the economy. Each man advocated federal controls under a strong chief executive. Roosevelt thought concentration of wealth and economic power in commerce and industry inevitable and even desirable, and he would use federal regulation and direction to help rationalize economic growth while seeking social justice for the powerless masses victimized by the system. Wilson talked of using federal power to break up certain economic conglomerates, to restore competition, and to provide the small entrepreneur with a better chance to compete against the existing economic giants. Also, Wilson opposed any kind of special interest legislation.

As he campaigned, Wilson's speeches glowed with phrases about social righteousness and economic justice. Roosevelt, although he ran a strong race, failed to draw progressive Democrats from Wilson and failed to draw Old

The Vice President
Thomas R. Marshall

Born on March 14, 1854, in North Manchester, Massachusetts, Thomas Riley Marshall spent his youth traveling. His father, a doctor, moved the family from Massachusetts to Illinois, Kansas, Missouri, and Indiana. During this time, Marshall was educated at local public schools. He was graduated in 1873 from Wabash College. Marshall continued his education by studying law in Judge Walter Old's office in Fort Wayne, Indiana, and he also earned a master's degree from Wabash in 1876.

Marshall was admitted to the bar in Columbia City, Indiana, in 1875 and set up a law practice with William McNagny. Despite an unsuccessful campaign for prosecuting attorney in 1880, Marshall became a member of the Columbia City school board, and he also taught Sunday school classes at his local Presbyterian church. On October 2, 1895, Marshall married Lois Irene Kimsey. The couple had no children. The following year, he became chair of his local Democratic committee, where he served until 1898.

In 1908, Marshall was elected governor of Indiana, where he earned a reputation as a progressive and a reformer. During the 1912 presidential campaign, Marshall was considered for the highest office but was instead selected as Woodrow Wilson's vice presidential running mate. After two terms in office—the first vice president since John C. Calhoun and Daniel Tompkins to serve two terms—which were among the most active of any vice president, Marshall returned home to Indianapolis. He remained active in politics, serving as a member of the Federal Coal Commission from 1922 to 1923 and as a trustee at Wabash College. Marshall died on June 1, 1925, in Washington, D.C.

Robert P. Watson and Richard Yon

Guard Republicans from Taft. Wilson polled 6,293,019 popular votes; Roosevelt, 4,119,507. Taft received 3,484,956 votes; Debs, 901,873. Wilson received less than half the popular vote, but in the electoral college he won by a landslide—435 votes to 88 for Roosevelt and 8 for Taft. The Democrats also won control of both the House and the Senate.

The Administration

Few if any political figures in American history have made, so late in life, such a meteoric ascent from comparative obscurity to the pinnacle of power that Wilson reached with his inauguration as twenty-eighth president on March 4, 1913. Yet he felt no heady sense of triumph on the occasion. In his inaugural address he declared, "This is not a day of triumph; it is a day of dedication." Two weeks later, he wrote in a private communication,

I am administering a great office, no doubt the greatest in the world, but ... it is not me, and I am not it. I am only a commissioner, in charge of its apparatus, living in its offices and taking upon myself its functions.

Such "impersonality," he said, perhaps robbed the office of intensity, of pride, and even of enjoyment, but it "at least prevents me from becoming a fool, and thinking myself IT."

If Wilson in March, 1913, felt neither pride in having gained the office he occupied nor enjoyment from it, he found abundant joy in the Wilson family that now lived in the White House. Besides his wife and three daughters, who made up his immediate family, there were other women around the house. Wilson's widowed sister, along with several female cousins and honorary cousins, visited often. Wilson once joked that he was "submerged in petticoats." In the intimacy of his family, this trim and slender man, with refined face and aggressive jaw, with penetrating blue-gray eyes that narrowed behind his pince-nez when he talked, this austere public figure with the wintry smile could play the fool, wag his ears, do droll and skillful mimicries, joke and tease, and, on medical advice, sip an occasional Scotch. Except for golf, which he played often ("ten or eleven holes . . . almost every day" was his estimate in August, 1913), Wilson cared little for entertainment and social ceremonies outside his beloved family circle. He dispensed with the traditional inaugural ball. He refused to join the Chevy Chase Country Club, to which presidents before him had belonged as a matter of course. He had no interest in meeting smart or rich or distinguished people. Even for advice and information on affairs of state, he scarcely reached out beyond his own private world. In fact, he cared not for information or advice but for comfort and reassurance, and this he derived largely from the women in his family, but even they played no important part in the political decisions he made.

Wilson's White House entourage consisted of his secretary, Joseph Tumulty, his personal doctor, Admiral Cary T. Grayson, and Colonel Edward M. House, a wealthy Texan with a consuming interest in politics who functioned as a manipulator and emissary behind the scene rather than as a conspicuous occupant of elective office. House became Wilson's intimate friend and one of the most important figures in Wilson's administration. House was one of the few men—perhaps the only man—to whom Wilson ever turned for advice, although it was loyalty and spiritual support more than advice that Wilson wanted from House. Because he understood Wilson and handled him shrewdly, House enjoyed Wilson's confidence and affection from 1912 until 1919, when amid the terrible tensions and perplexities of the postwar peace conference, Wilson abruptly ended their friendship.

As Wilson began to plan the legislative program he would ask Congress to implement, he commissioned House to find candidates for the cabinet. Wilson named William Jennings Bryan secretary of state, a surprising choice in view of Bryan's insularity and inexperience in foreign affairs. Wilson did not remotely anticipate the enormous foreign problems he would face. He remarked just before his inauguration, "It would be the irony of fate if my administration had to deal chiefly with foreign affairs." In 1915, after Wilson had begun to deal much if not chiefly with foreign affairs (although that stage would soon begin), Bryan resigned in protest over Wilson's policies toward Germany. Wilson replaced him with Robert Lansing, who shaped American foreign policy even less than Bryan. That policy, from 1913 to 1921, remained largely in the hands of Woodrow Wilson, who was in essence his own secretary of state.

A Wilson campaign van. *(Library of Congress)*

William Gibbs McAdoo became Wilson's secretary of the treasury in 1913. He also became Wilson's son-in-law in May, 1914, upon marriage to Wilson's daughter Eleanor—a marriage that, to some observers, made McAdoo "Crown Prince." McAdoo was a forceful, loyal, and successful member of the cabinet as well as the director-general of railroads during World War I. In 1920, his relationship to Wilson would hinder rather than help him in his bid for presidential nomination.

For attorney general, Wilson first considered Louis D. Brandeis, a renowned and controversial lawyer from Kentucky by way of Boston, who had been the major source of ideas for Wilson's New Freedom campaign in 1912. Instead, Wilson listened to Colonel House and gave the job to James C. McReynolds, a native Kentuckian practicing law in New York. In 1914, Wilson named the irascible and unlikable McReynolds to the Supreme Court, where in time he became one of the "Fearsome Foursome" who in the 1930's ruled, automatically and absolutely, against the New Deal in cases brought before the Court. Wilson replaced McReynolds in the cabinet with Thomas W. Gregory, a Texan, under whose direction the Justice Department during World War I would do whatever seemed necessary to keep opponents of "Mr. Wilson's War" in line. In 1916, in a courageous move that provoked a grueling fight over confirmation, Wilson named Brandeis to the Supreme Court, the first Jewish appointment ever made to that bench.

For secretary of war, Wilson chose Lindley M. Garrison, a New Jersey chancery court judge. An able and forthright man and a superb administrator, he chose to resign rather than compromise during a battle over preparedness in 1916. Wilson replaced him with Newton D. Baker, who had gained a certain fame as progressive mayor of Cleveland, Ohio. Josephus Daniels, editor of the *Raleigh* (North Carolina) *News and Observer* and Wilson's chief supporter in the state, became secretary of the navy.

Daniels would suffer ridicule for his alleged ignorance of naval affairs and for his attempts, in the name of reform and his version of Methodist morality, to close down red-light districts near naval stations and to eliminate the navy's traditional grog ration. Nevertheless, Daniels and Baker, who also felt the sting of critics for his supposed incompetence, were to be instrumental in the creation of the U.S. Army and Navy that fought in the war that Wilson led the nation into in 1917.

Albert Burleson of Texas, who became postmaster general, used the patronage system to strengthen the Democratic Party in the states. During the war, he banned antiwar literature from the mail and exercised other powers of repression and censorship that were extralegal and arbitrary and that showed no consideration for traditional freedom of speech and press.

The remaining four secretaries left no major mark on Wilson's administration. Franklin K. Lane, a Californian whom Wilson named secretary of the interior, was the chief gossip of the cabinet. David F. Houston, a native North Carolinian who was president of Washington University in St. Louis in 1913, became secretary of agriculture. William B. Wilson, Democratic congressman from Pennsylvania mining country and a veteran union organizer, was an apt choice to head the recently established Labor Department. William C. Redfield became secretary of commerce. A congressman from Brooklyn, Redfield used his office to serve and protect business.

Domestic Program: Enacting the New Freedom—and More

As president, Wilson was in command of the executive branch. He was leader of his party in the Congress and the nation and had in mind a program that he wanted to see enacted and implemented. To do so, however, he had to unite his rather badly divided party behind him. The party was made up of a "Solid South" of conservative white agrarians, strong ethnic coalitions of reformers in the industrialized, urbanized North, and urban and rural Western progressives, all of them hungry for power to achieve reforms, to further their special interests, or to cash in on patronage after years in the political wilderness. Each of these factions and large interest groups had a spokesperson or two in the cabinet, and each had representation in the Congress. It was up to Wilson to work with and unite the discrete Democratic representatives in the Congress, himself initiating and guiding through to passage a legislative program that would gain enactment of his New Freedom program and turn the Democrats into the nation's majority — and progressive — party.

Immediately after his inauguration, Wilson called Congress into special session and on April 8 appeared in person to deliver a message — the first president since John Adams to make such an appearance. The next day, April 9, he went to the Capitol and held the first of many conferences with Democratic leaders. He asked Congress for tariff revision and got it, after heavy lobbying by private interests and a strong and dramatic attack on them by Wilson. The Underwood-Simmons Tariff Act lowered rates to levels not seen since before the Civil War. To make up for the loss of tariff revenue, Congress added to the tariff bill a provision for a graduated income tax, the first such tax under the Sixteenth Amendment, which was ratified on February 25, 1913.

Next, Wilson and Congress took up the major objective of the New Freedom: banking and currency reform. Everyone informed on the subject — bankers, businessmen, economists, leaders of both political parties — agreed that the existing banking system, one first established during the Civil War, needed drastic overhauling. It lacked any effective central control. Banking reserves were inadequate and the money supply too inelastic to allow the system to cope with periodic crises. No public agency had any voice in determining such critical matters as the money supply, the location of banking facilities, and the links that banks had with business corporations. Southern and Western farmers complained that all of the money was locked up in Eastern banks, which charged farmers exorbitant interest rates on loans. Reformers wanted federal control over the money supply. Bankers themselves wanted to increase the money supply and wanted a more centralized (yet private) system, one that could pool reserves and shift them about to meet unusual demand. One Democratic faction, with William Jennings Bryan as spokesperson, wanted to create a centralized, government-owned bank. Another faction, with Congressman Carter Glass of Virginia as spokesperson, wanted a loose association of private banks.

Wilson knew practically nothing about the details of the matter. His primary goal was some form of public supervision over a private banking system. In June, 1913, Wilson went before Congress and called for

President Wilson throws the first pitch on baseball's opening game day in 1916. *(Library of Congress)*

creation of a presidentially appointed Federal Reserve Board to supervise a private banking system. The nation would be divided into twelve Federal Reserve regions, with a Federal Reserve bank—a "bankers' bank," it came to be called—in each region. The Federal Reserve System would issue paper currency, in the form of Federal Reserve notes. Besides shifting currency reserves about the country to meet demands, the board could exercise other controls over the flow and supply of money, primarily by raising or lowering the "rediscount rate" it charged to private member banks when the Reserve banks issued Federal Reserve notes (currency) to these banks in exchange for the commercial and agricultural paper the banks had taken in as security from borrowers.

Late in December, 1913, after six months of debate, Congress passed the Federal Reserve Act, called by one Wilsonian authority the "greatest single piece of constructive legislation of the Wilson era." Constructive it was, radical it was not. Interlocking directorates still existed. Private bankers still largely controlled the supply and availability of money. The Federal Reserve Bank of New York dominated the system. The Federal Reserve Board did not control the nation's bankers, and the board used its influence over discount rates sparingly until after the crash of 1929. A new and flexible currency had been created, and the private banking system had been retained—but under a degree of federal regulation, with potential for more in crises to come.

Late in 1913, as the Federal Reserve bill neared passage, Wilson began to consider one or two antitrust measures he might support. Most Democratic Party leaders wanted simply to amend the Sherman Antitrust Act of 1890 and enumerate and outlaw specific unfair trade practices. A minority of Democrats, however, agreed with Theodore Roosevelt that it would be impossible to draw up such a list. Louis Brandeis and other progressive Democrats wanted to see Wilson establish a powerful, in-

dependent trade commission, one with broad powers to investigate business activities and issue "cease and desist" orders suppressing unfair competition whenever and however it arose. Wilson had to choose between his own proposal of 1912 and that of Theodore Roosevelt. He also had to consider the outcry from Samuel Gompers and his American Federation of Labor, which had supported Wilson in 1912, that the Clayton antitrust bill then before Congress did nothing to exempt labor unions from antitrust prosecution. Wilson agreed to see added to the Clayton bill a few mild—and essentially useless—provisions to protect labor. Congress passed the Clayton bill in June, 1914, and labor unions proclaimed it their "Magna Carta," which, however, it was not.

Wilson, meantime, all but ignored the Clayton Act, even before its passage, and threw his support behind a Federal Trade Commission bill, one drafted partly by Louis Brandeis that came closer to Roosevelt's New Nationalism than to Wilson's New Freedom. The bill that became law on September 10 established the Federal Trade Commission, composed of five members appointed by the president and charged with preventing the growth of new monopolies by seeing to it that businesses competed fairly and openly—although the law did not specify in detail what this meant. Implementation of the commission's powers would depend on the inclinations of the members named to the commission, most of whom in the years to come showed little disposition really to go after business monopolies.

After passage of the Federal Trade Commission bill and the Clayton antitrust bill, Wilson announced that his New Freedom program was completed. He had thus far opposed any special interest legislation—for manufacturers, bankers, laborers, farmers, or children. As much as possible, government should, in the tradition of Democratic Party liberalism, keep hands off, giving favors to no one. Wilson opposed establishment of rural banks that would provide long-term loans at low interest rates to needy farmers. He opposed a bill to abolish child labor, saying that "domestic arrangements" were for states, not Washington, D.C., to supervise. Yet within the Democratic Party, as well as among Roosevelt Republicans of 1912, a great many reformers were demanding even more changes than Wilson's New Freedom legislation had wrought in the system by 1915.

Since the turn of the century, when reformers had first begun to give voice to the proposals, slogans, programs, and aspirations that would collectively be labeled "progressivism" by historians, diverse groups of reformers had called for various reforms: stringent regulation of industry; woman suffrage; child labor legislation; government aid to labor, farmers, and the unemployed; public health programs; prohibition; even laws against profanity. In his first two years in office, Wilson had satisfied some, but by no means all, of these reformers. In the state and congressional elections of 1914, the Democrats lost control of several key states they had carried in 1912 and saw their House majority reduced from seventy-three to twenty-five. Fearful that he and his party would lose control in 1916, Wilson set out to bring all progressives, all reform elements, Democrat or Republican, into the party.

When the new Congress convened in December, 1915, Wilson took command again, and under his leadership Congress enacted a sweeping and progressive program, one that could more easily bear the label New Nationalism than New Freedom. Between December, 1915, and September, 1916, Congress created a tariff commission; established a shipping board to regulate and aid merchant seamen; established the Federal Farm Loan Board, which extended long-term loans to farmers; prohibited child labor in interstate commerce (through the Keating-Owen Act that the Supreme Court would nullify in 1918); provided an eight-hour day for railroad workers (the Adamson Act); sharply increased income and inheritance taxes

on the rich; and even passed a bill providing federal aid for highway construction. One Wilson scholar called 1916 "the year of the new progressive dispensation." Another declared that Wilson took over Roosevelt's New Nationalism "lock, stock, and barrel." Practically every important proposal that Roosevelt or his supporters made in 1912 had now become law—with Wilson's blessings. Although the 1916 measures included no laws comparable in importance to the Federal Reserve Act, and although he had exercised less planning, perseverance, and mediation in 1916 than he had displayed in 1913-1914, Wilson went to the country in 1916 claiming that the Democratic Party was also the progressive party, the party of social justice for all.

The 1916 Campaign

By campaign time, 1916, the war in Europe, which had begun in August, 1914, threatened increasingly to provoke American entry. Since Wilson had struggled for two years to keep the United States out of the war, he could campaign in 1916 as a progressive Democrat and also with a slogan (one he did not coin and did not like, because of the false hopes it seemed to raise): "He kept us out of war." Roosevelt, who had moved back to Republican orthodoxy since his defeat in 1912, was now supporting the regular Republican candidate and attacking Wilson for not having at once gone to war on the British side against "the beastly Hun." Roosevelt's tactic simply increased Wilson's support. Wilson's Republican opponent, the estimable Charles Evans Hughes, entered the campaign enjoying the respect and admiration of many Democratic journals, but his petty criticism and his failure to offer constructive alternatives to Wilson's policies earned for him the nickname Charles "Evasive" Hughes. As Wilson campaigned around the country, he did not mention that he had opposed a national woman suffrage amendment and had done little to abolish or even to restrict Jim Crow practices in his ad-

Pancho Villa. *(Library of Congress)*

ministration, but he did speak of what he had done for labor, farmers, and children. Prominent Progressives who had supported Roosevelt in 1912 came out for Wilson. Thousands of urban, ethnic voters who had preferred Eugene Debs in 1912 also swung to Wilson. The 1916 presidential contest revealed an almost perfect alignment of Democratic progressives versus Republican conservatives. The election was a cliff-hanger. Wilson received only 23 more electoral votes than Hughes (277 to 254). The popular vote was 9,129,606 for Wilson and 8,538,221 for Hughes. Even so, Wilson received nearly three million more votes in 1916 than he did in 1912 and by winning in 1916 became the first Democrat since Andrew Jackson to win reelection for a second consecutive term. If Wilson's first term had been a spectacular success, however, his second term would prove to be a

tragedy.

The nemesis of Wilson's second term was revolution and war. Policies he had formulated in confronting these great cataclysmic forces in his first term led him inexorably toward entrance into World War I in April, 1917, toward intervention in the Russian Revolution in the summer of 1918, and toward a tragic denouement of World War I, the Versailles peace settlement of 1919.

Relations with Mexico

Three years before Wilson took office in March, 1913, revolution erupted in Mexico. Wilson was ignorant of, even indifferent to, the Mexican Revolution and to foreign affairs generally when he became president. Nevertheless, in 1913 and thereafter he held fast to certain provincial and arrogant notions about the world beyond the United States. He assumed the superiority of Anglo-Saxon people and their political and religious institutions. He formulated foreign policies, not in light of the exigent and the expedient, but in light of what were, to him, eternal verities. He could not conceive of a people who did not share his moral principles, who did not want for themselves the kind of government that the United States enjoyed. Again and again, in matters of diplomacy and war, Wilson played missionary, trying to do to and for other people what he thought was right and good and moral—by his definition. Whatever else may have been involved in Wilson's foreign policy—naïveté, protection of American economic interests, imperialistic ambition, military security—Wilson was driven by two principal motives: to advance the cause of international peace, even if, as in 1917, it meant going to war in Europe to end war and achieve peace, and to give other people the blessings of American-style democracy and Protestant Christianity, even if they did not want them. A case in point in Wilson's first term is his policy toward the revolution in Mexico.

The Mexican Revolution of 1910 was like a

volcanic explosion that released decades of pent-up feelings. By 1910, when he abdicated power in Mexico and fled into exile in Paris, Don Porfirio Díaz had ruled the country for thirty-six years. Díaz had imposed law and order for the benefit of the propertied, both Mexican and foreign, making Mexico the best-policed country in the world. Through bribery and force Díaz controlled the state. By paying his officers well and by drafting young malcontents into the enlisted ranks, he controlled and used the army. He made Mexico a virtual colony of foreign capital ("Díaz held Mexico while foreigners raped her"). American, and to only a somewhat lesser degree British, capital developed railroads, sugar and rice and coffee plantations, oil wells, and gold and silver mines. Americans owned millions of acres of good land, and among Mexicans themselves less than three thousand families owned nearly 50 percent of the nation's land. By contrast, in some Mexican states between 95 and 99 percent of the Mexican people owned no land at all. The presidential election of 1910 brought to a head a quarter century of discontent by landless, exploited, oppressed Mexicans.

Francisco Madero, a liberal landowner from the state of Coahuila, ran for the presidency against Díaz in what the latter regarded as a farcical election. Predictably, Díaz won, but then Madero issued a *pronunciamiento*, a manifesto that demanded free and orderly elections. Madero proclaimed himself provisional president and designated November 20, 1910, as the day on which Mexicans should rise up in revolution against the oppressive Díaz regime. When several local leaders in Mexico—among them Francisco "Pancho" Villa, Emiliano Zapata, and Venustiano Carranza—rallied to Madero, Díaz fled into exile, saying, "Madero has unleashed a tiger; let us see if he can control him."

Madero did not, could not, control the tiger of revolution. President William Howard Taft extended Madero diplomatic recognition, but the American ambassador to Mexico, Henry Lane Wilson, entered into a plot with several European ambassadors to oust Madero and replace him with General Victoriano Huerta, a man cut closer to the Díaz model of authoritarian caudillo and one partial to foreigners and their Mexican investments. In February, 1913, Madero was assassinated and Huerta became provisional president. Taft refused to recognize Huerta, but his refusal did not reflect a judgment on Madero's murder. Rather, on the advice of his State Department, Taft planned to use, or anticipated Wilson's using, recognition as a bargaining weapon for settling certain disputes over the rights and property of Americans in Mexico.

As soon as Wilson took office, he came under heavy pressure to recognize Huerta—from Ambassador Henry Lane Wilson in Mexico, from foreign service officials in the State Department, from the American colony in Mexico City, and from powerful financial interests in the United States. Wilson refused. Recognition of Huerta would sanction government by assassination. "I will not recognize a government of butchers," said Wilson. If not Huerta, then, whom should Wilson recognize? Wilson began sending personal agents into Mexico to contact Villa, Carranza, Zapata, and other revolutionaries who had supported Madero and were now opposing Huerta. He hoped to determine which, if any, one of these might be worthy of obtaining American support to oust Huerta and form a "legitimate," a "constitutional," Mexican government.

Wilson's agents gave him conflicting advice, some wanting him to support Carranza, some recommending Villa. All of them denounced Huerta, but not all of them recommended actual military intervention of U.S. troops against him—although it finally came to that. From the State Department itself Counselor John Bassett Moore advised Wilson that European nations, which had promptly recognized Huerta, were correct in recognizing de facto regimes such as

Wilson announces the United States' official break with Germany before Congress in February, 1917. *(NARA)*

his and that such recognition was traditional American policy. Wilson, however, believed that to recognize a government's existence was to approve it as moral.

Wilson was in a quandary. He refused to approve of Huerta, but he was unable to come to terms with any other Mexican leader. He made an incredible proposal to Carranza and his so-called Constitutionalist Army that the United States join Carranza in a war on Huerta if Carranza would confine the revolution to orderly and constructive channels. Wilson felt responsible for the lives and property of American citizens in Mexico caught up in the revolution, which by 1914 had become civil war between Huerta and several other forces, some of them fighting Huerta and some of them fighting one another as well. Wilson even felt pressure from Britain to recognize either Huerta or a successor who would protect Britain's considerable investment in Mexican petroleum, an investment of critical importance to Britain on the eve of war in Europe. One scholar has judged Wilson to have been in a state of "righteous pa-

ralysis," drifting and uttering platitudes.

In April, at Tampico, a chain of events began that led to overt American intervention in the Mexican Revolution, to Huerta's downfall, to Carranza's rise to power—and to still another American armed intervention that ended just short of an American-Mexican war. U.S. Navy ships were stationed in force in Tampico Bay to protect American property in the city and along the coast. On April 10, a colonel in Huerta's army unit holding Tampico arrested the paymaster and several crew members of the USS *Dolphin* when they came ashore to pick up the mail and inadvertently ventured beyond prescribed limits. The Americans were promptly released, and the Huertistas in Tampico at once apologized to Admiral Henry T. Mayo, ranking American officer in the area. Mayo, dissatisfied, demanded a twenty-one-gun salute and court-martial of the colonel who had arrested the Americans. Huerta, when notified of the incident, refused to accede to Mayo's demand. Wilson, when notified, chose to support Mayo. Declaring America's "honor" at stake, Wilson accused Huerta of deliberately insulting the United States and asked Congress for authority to use military force to obtain redress. Armed conflict broke out the next day, but at Vera Cruz, not at Tampico.

Wilson learned that a German steamer loaded with arms consigned to Huerta was about to land at Vera Cruz. Without waiting for congressional response to his earlier request, Wilson ordered the U.S. Navy to occupy Vera Cruz and prevent the German vessel from docking. Nineteen invading Americans and three hundred Mexicans who resisted the invasion died in the landing. The German ship simply docked and unloaded at a port farther down the coast. Appalled at the deaths, Wilson accepted an offer from Argentina, Brazil, and Chile to mediate, although he insisted that he would accept only a settlement that removed Huerta from power. Huerta condemned the American invasion, as did Carranza, who by now was pressing his Constitutionalist Army closer and closer to Mexico City. His funds exhausted and under pressure from the oncoming Constitutionalists, Huerta abdicated in July, 1914. In August, Carranza marched into Mexico City, but the Mexican Revolution—and Wilsonian interference—abated not at all.

Since Carranza spurned his offers of support, Wilson now turned to Pancho Villa, when

---

Excerpts from Woodrow Wilson's war message to Congress, April 2, 1917:

The present German submarine warfare against commerce is a warfare against mankind. It is war against all nations.

American ships have been sunk, American lives taken, in ways which it has stirred us very deeply to learn of, but the ships and people of other neutral and friendly nations have been sunk and overwhelmed in the waters in the same way. There has been no discrimination. The challenge is to all mankind.

Each nation must decide for itself how it will meet it. The choice we make for ourselves must be made with a moderation of counsel and temperateness of judgment befitting our character and our motives as a nation. We must put excited feeling away. Our motive will not be revenge or the victorious assertion of the physical might of the nation, but only the vindication of right, of human right, of which we are only a single champion. . . .

With a profound sense of the solemn and even tragical character of the step I am taking and of the grave responsibilities which it involves, but in unhesitating obedience to what I deem my constitutional duty, I advise that the Congress declare the recent course of the Imperial German Government to be in fact nothing less than war against the government and people of the United States; that it formally accept the status of belligerent which has thus been thrust upon it; and that it take immediate steps not only to put the country in a more thorough state of defense but also to exert all its power and employ all its resources to bring the Government of the German Empire to terms and end the war. . . .

It is a distressing and oppressive duty, Gentlemen of the Congress, which I have performed in thus addressing you. There are, it may be, many months of fiery trial and sacrifice ahead of us. It is a fearful thing to lead this great peaceful people into war, into the most terrible and disastrous of all wars, civilization itself seeming to be in the balance.

But the right is more precious than peace, and we shall fight for the things which we have always carried nearest our hearts, for democracy, for the right of those who submit to authority to have a voice in their own governments, for the rights and liberties of small nations, for a universal dominion of right by such a concert of free peoples as shall bring peace and safety to all nations and make the world at last free.

the great primitive guerrilla bandit revolted against Carranza and sought control over the revolution for himself. For a year or more, Carranza and his gifted military leader Álvaro Obregón fought Villa and Zapata for control of the revolution. Finally, Carranza won. Villa retreated north to his stronghold in Chihuahua. Finally aware that Carranza could be deposed neither by support for his rivals nor by Wilsonian rhetoric, and ever more concerned with the European war, Wilson in October, 1915, extended de facto recognition to Carranza.

Then Villa reentered the picture. Deflated and resentful, he tried to provoke an American intervention that would allow him to pose as hero against the Yankee invaders. In January, 1916, his forces killed sixteen American engineers taken from a train in Sonora. In March, 1916, Villa raided the small border town of Columbus, New Mexico, killed nineteen Americans, and vanished into the Mexican desert. Wilson ordered General John J. Pershing at Fort Bliss in El Paso, Texas, to lead a punitive expedition into Mexico in pursuit of Villa. Carranza agreed to the proposal that a small detachment of Americans cross the border for this purpose, but when Villa, eluding Pershing, raided Glen Springs, Texas, Wilson mobilized the National Guard along the border and the U.S. Army prepared for a full-scale invasion of Mexico. When Pershing's troops moved more than three hundred miles into Mexico, Carranza ordered his generals to resist any further southward movement by the Americans. Neither Carranza nor Wilson wanted war. Carranza was preoccupied with the revolution in Mexico and Wilson with the war in Europe. Also, Wilson had evidence that Germany was trying to stir up trouble between the United States and Mexico along the border and preoccupy Wilson there to discourage him from intervening in the European war against Germany. In January, 1917, Wilson ordered the Pershing expedition to withdraw from Mexico. In March, Wilson extended Carranza de jure recognition.

Wilson in 1913 had set out to rid Mexico of Huerta and teach the Mexicans "to elect good men." The Vera Cruz occupation played a part in Huerta's downfall, but the U.S. Navy's intervention and the U.S. Army's thrust into northern Mexico in 1916 poisoned U.S.-Mexican relations for years to come. Wilson wanted an American-style democracy for Mexico, but Carranza, who finally after years of bloody civil war emerged as victor and obtained Wilson's recognition, was more dictator than democrat, although he and his Constitutionalists were also more bourgeois than revolutionary. They welcomed American trade and investments, and despite the rhetoric of the Mexican constitution they drew up in 1917, they had no intention of ousting American oil companies from Mexico. Some of those oil interests, along with Catholics and professional patriots, had pressured Wilson to intervene far more than he did. Wilson refused to make open war on Mexico, although in the spring of 1916 he came perilously close to doing so. American outrage over Villa's border raids and over combat deep in northern Mexico that saw Americans captured by Mexicans led Wilson on June 27 to begin preparing a war message to Congress. The next day the prisoners were released, and telegrams, ten to one against any form of war, poured into the White House. Wilson had come close to a war he did not want out of a mistaken belief that national sentiment as well as national policy demanded it. Colonel House told Wilson, "The people do not want war with Mexico. They do not want war with anybody." Neither did Wilson. In 1916, he avoided war in Mexico. In 1917, he entered war in Europe.

World War I

When the Central Powers (Germany and its allies) went to war against the Allied Powers (Britain, France, and their allies) in August, 1914, Wilson issued a routine proclamation of neutrality and a few days later made an appeal to Americans not to take sides, to be "neutral in

The Fourteen Points

January 8, 1918

I. Open covenants of peace, openly arrived at, after which there shall be no private international understandings of any kind but diplomacy shall proceed always frankly and in the public view.

II. Absolute freedom of navigation upon the seas, outside territorial waters, alike in peace and in war, except as the seas may be closed in whole or in part by international action for the enforcement of international covenants.

III. The removal, so far as possible, of all economic barriers and the establishment of an equality of trade conditions among all the nations consenting to the peace and associating themselves for its maintenance.

IV. Adequate guarantees given and taken that national armaments will be reduced to the lowest point consistent with domestic safety.

V. A free, open-minded, and absolutely impartial adjustment of all colonial claims, based upon a strict observance of the principle that in determining all such questions of sovereignty the interests of the populations concerned must have equal weight with the equitable claims of the government whose title is to be determined.

VI. The evacuation of all Russian territory and such a settlement of all questions affecting Russia as will secure the best and freest cooperation of the other nations of the world in obtaining for her an unhampered and unembarrassed opportunity for the independent determination of her own political development and national policy and assure her of a sincere welcome into the society of free nations under institutions of her own choosing; and, more than a welcome, assistance also of every kind that she may need and may herself desire. The treatment accorded Russia by her sister nations in the months to come will be the acid test of their good will, of their comprehension of her needs as distinguished from their own interests, and of their intelligent and unselfish sympathy.

VII. Belgium, the whole world will agree, must be evacuated and restored, without any attempt to limit the sovereignty which she enjoys in common with all other free nations. No other single act will serve as this will serve to restore confidence among the nations in the laws which they have themselves set and determined for the government of their relations with one another. Without this healing act the whole structure and validity of international law is forever impaired.

VIII. All French territory should be freed and the invaded portions restored, and the wrong done to France by Prussia in 1871 in the matter of Alsace-Lorraine, which has unsettled the peace of the world for nearly fifty years, should be righted, in order that peace may once more be made secure in the interest of all.

IX. A readjustment of the frontiers of Italy should be effected along clearly recognizable lines of nationality.

X. The peoples of Austria-Hungary, whose place among the nations we wish to see safeguarded and assured, should be accorded the freest opportunity to autonomous development.

XI. Rumania, Serbia, and Montenegro should be evacuated; occupied territories restored; Serbia accorded free and secure access to the sea; and the relations of the several Balkan states to one another determined by friendly counsel along historically established lines of allegiance and nationality; and international guarantees of the political and economic independence and territorial integrity of the several Balkan states should be entered into.

XII. The Turkish portion of the present Ottoman Empire should be assured a secure sovereignty, but the other nationalities which are now under Turkish rule should be assured an undoubted security of life and an absolutely unmolested opportunity of autonomous development, and the Dardanelles should be permanently opened as a free passage to the ships and commerce of all nations under international guarantees.

XIII. An independent Polish state should be erected which should include the territories inhabited by indisputably Polish populations, which should be assured a free and secure access to the sea, and whose political and economic independence and territorial integrity should be guaranteed by international covenant.

XIV. A general association of nations must be formed under specific covenants for the purpose of affording mutual guarantees of political independence and territorial integrity to great and small states alike.

fact as well as in name, impartial in thought as well as in action." To Wilson the outbreak of war in Europe was simply another manifestation of the immorality and power politics of the Old World, to which America stood in shining contrast. He knew little and cared less about the origins or the causes of the war. The conflict, he said, was "like a drunken brawl in a public house," disgusting, although as between the antagonists his sympathies in 1914 lay more with Britain and France than with Germany.

Although calling for neutrality in thought and deed in 1914, Wilson soon began to change his mind. By early 1915, he had begun to plead for "the rights of a neutral," for the "rights" of Americans to continue to trade with and travel to Europe. When that trade and travel (and the British blockade) provoked German submarine attacks on Allied shipping and Americans drowned, Wilson declared America "too proud to fight." In April, 1917, in his war message to Congress, he declared, "Right is more precious than peace." He had decided that America's "moral purposes" should be fulfilled, not by remaining aloof but by going to war. He would go to war not to win it but to end it and, with the moral leverage he gained thereby, write a treaty that would end war forever. A "just and lasting peace," a Wilsonian peace, would follow a war fought to end all wars.

Parallel to this lofty Wilsonian rationale and vision, and working reciprocally with it, ran more mundane day-to-day exigencies: British propaganda that fell on the receptive ears of Anglophile Americans in the Wilson administration, British naval blockades and search-and-seizure episodes, German submarine attacks, American loans to Britain and France made to help the Allies pay for the American trade and commerce that increased from $800 million in 1914 to $3 billion in 1917 (whereas it dropped from $170 million to $1 million with the Central Powers in the same period).

Practical, nagging questions about Wilson's neutrality policy arose at the very beginning of the war: Was true American neutrality possible? Did neutrality mean continued trade with both sides? Britain, however, could not allow American trade with Germany, and to ask the British to stop using their surface blockade of Germany would be like asking Germany to stop using its army. Did neutrality mean prohibiting trade with both sides? Such prohibition would not have maintained true neutrality, since Britain was far more dependent than was Germany on international exchange. A Wilsonian embargo in 1914 on all foreign trade would have harmed Britain and helped Germany. On August 6, 1914, Secretary of State Bryan informed the Allies and the Central Powers that American neutrality did not mean it was unlawful to export goods in the ordinary course of commerce. Neither the British nor the Germans, however, agreed with this policy. The British used their navy to stop shipment of goods to Germany, and the Germans used their submarines to stop shipments to Britain. Wilson, despite some controversies, came to accept the British blockade as legitimate, but German submarines were another matter, since they did not and could not follow the established rules of search and seizure that Britain followed. The Germans torpedoed vessels and drowned passengers; the British ordered vessels into port, searched them, seized contraband, and sometimes but not always even paid compensation for what they seized ("the British were thieves, but the Germans were murderers," was one bitter contemporary distinction).

In May, 1915, off the Irish coast a German submarine fired a single torpedo and sank the *Lusitania*, a British liner carrying 1,257 passengers, 128 of them Americans. In a series of notes Wilson warned the Germans that he would hold them to "strict accountability" for any more such incidents. Germany eased off submarine warfare, but then on August 19, a submarine, without warning, sank the *Arabic*, a large British liner, with two Americans listed among the forty-two casualties. Wilson let it be known that if Germany did not give satisfactory response to the incident he would contemplate a break in diplomatic relations. Germany pledged that "liners will not be sunk by our submarines without warning." On March 24, 1916, a submarine, without warning, torpedoed the British liner *Sussex* and eighty men drowned, among them four Americans. Wilson issued Germany an ultimatum: Unless the German government abandoned "its present practices of submarine warfare," America would sever diplomatic relations altogether. Germany agreed to suspend unrestricted submarine warfare, conditional on American efforts to compel the British to abandon their blockade of Germany. If the British blockade continued, so might the German submarine campaign.

Late in January, 1917, Germany announced that after February 1, German submarines would sink without warning all ships, belligerent and neutral, found in a zone around Britain, France, and the eastern Mediterranean. The Germans knew they were risking war with the United States, but they believed that through loans and trade America was already an ally of Britain and France and an opponent of Germany. Perhaps an intensive all-out submarine campaign could cut off supplies coming to Britain and France and drive them to surrender before the United States declared war — or at least before America, even if it did declare war, could effectively mobilize and train an American army and bring it to the Western Front.

When the Germans announced resumption of submarine warfare, Wilson promptly broke diplomatic relations with them, yet held on to hopes of mediating and bringing the war to an end short of an American entry. He announced to Congress that he wished no conflict with Germany. Then on February 25, he learned that German foreign minister Alfred Zimmerman had instructed the German minister in Mexico City to propose a German-Mexican alliance against the United States if Germany and America went to war. To one New York newspaper, the Zimmerman note was "final proof that the German government has gone stark mad." Wilson, however, still committed to his peculiar interpretation of neutral rights, ordered guns and naval crews placed on board American merchant ships; he also ordered that the crews shoot on sight any submarine observed. On March 18, German submarines sank without warning and with heavy loss of life three American merchant vessels. At mass meetings throughout the country, Americans demonstrated and called for war on Germany, although advocates of peace also held mass rallies and demanded that Americans stay out of the war zone and called for a general strike if war were declared.

As war tensions mounted in the United States, revolution erupted in Russia in February and March, the first of two great Russian revolutions in 1917, this one overthrowing the czarist regime, which, in alliance with Britain and France, had gone to war against Germany in 1914. With the czar replaced now by a constitutional monarchy—and one that pledged to carry on the war against Germany—Americans found it easier than before to believe that the war in Europe was a war between good and evil, between freedom and despotism.

Wilson still agonized over what to do. He learned that the Allies were in desperate straits and that only American intervention could save them. On March 21, he called Congress into special session for April 2, "to receive a communication concerning grave matters of national policy." On March 24, he ordered Secretary of the Navy Josephus Daniels to begin coordination of American naval operations with those of Britain. On March 25 and 26, he called National Guard units into federal reserve. Wilson, seeing no alternative, was clearly moving toward war. He was trapped by his own pronouncements. In 1916 he had said, "I shall do everything in my power to keep the United States out of war. . . . But if the clear rights of American citizens should ever unhappily be abridged or denied [by a warring power], we . . . have in honor no choice as to what our course should be." Wilson could not consent "to any abridgement of the rights of American citizens in any respect. The honor and self-respect of the nation is involved. We covet peace, and shall preserve it at any cost but the loss of honor."

On February 2, 1917, Wilson had told his cabinet that he did not care which side won the war, that both sides were wicked. Only weeks later, driven to find moral justification for what he was about to do, he decided that Germany was not merely wicked but had challenged America's honor as well. He still distrusted the Allies and did not believe they genuinely cared about democracy and self-government as much as he did, but by joining with them in war on Germany, he would save them all. He would save the world. He would enter the war and make it "a war to end all wars," a war that would end in "a just and lasting peace," a war that would "make the world safe for democracy."

On April 2, 1917, Wilson went before a joint session of Congress and asked for a resolution of war. On April 4, the Senate adopted the resolution, 82 to 6. On April 6, the House concurred, 373 to 50, and on April 7, Wilson signed the resolution. A headline in *The New York Times* read, "America in Armageddon."

Wilson had led the country into war, but the country was not yet ready for war. Neither Wilson nor his administrators nor the Congress in April, 1917, was prepared for the great economic mobilization they would finally achieve. Congress, however, quickly gave virtual dictatorial power over the economy to Wilson, who promptly delegated it to administrators he named as directors of new administrative boards he created, such as the War Industries Board, the War Labor Board, the U.S. Food Administration, and the Emergency Fleet Corporation. Wilson launched his crusade for democracy abroad with a push toward autocracy at home. Rationalizing the economy, standardizing parts and production, even in a few cases nationalizing elements of the economy for the duration became Wilsonian tactics and strategy. A network of agencies throughout the country—state and local but mostly federal—produced the greatest concentration of public bureaucratic power Americans had ever experienced, a bureaucracy that oversaw the production of massive supplies of ships, arms, goods, and food for America and America's allies.

When Wilson asked for war and Congress declared it, neither he nor they envisioned mobilizing a great American army to send to Europe to fight, but after six weeks of impassioned debate over how to raise an army, Congress, on May 18, passed the Conscription Act of 1917. Through that act's selective service system and through other more voluntary means, some four million Americans entered the American armed forces. Some entered with reluctance.

At the peace conference in Versailles (left to right): British prime minister David Lloyd George, Italian prime minister Vittorio Emanuele Orlando, French premier Georges Clemenceau, and Wilson. *(Library of Congress)*

Since the Conscription Act offered them little leeway, twenty thousand conscientious objectors underwent actual induction. About sixteen thousand of them changed their minds, or were persuaded to do so, after reaching camp. Four thousand absolutists refused to change their views. Some thirteen hundred of these finally went into noncombat units, about twelve hundred more gained furloughs to do farmwork, and some five hundred suffered courts-martial and imprisonment. Conscientious objectors were a tiny minority when compared with some seventeen thousand draft evaders—"slackers" they were called in 1917—and compared with the millions inducted into the armed forces. With varying degrees of enthusiasm, chauvinism, and romanticism, two million Americans went off to France to fight in the Great War, some imbued with Wilson's own sense of mission, some regarding it all as a "great adventure," and some bewildered and painfully ignorant about the war and what it meant to them and to America. More than fifty thousand

Americans died on the battlefield in France from wounds received there; fifty-six thousand more died from disease. Thousands of those who returned home vowed never to wear a uniform again, and when Wilson lost the peace he sought to achieve after the war, they began to doubt the justification Wilson had made for the war they had fought.

If American military mobilization reflected a spectrum of doughboy experience and outlook ranging from unqualified enthusiasm for "service" (a term stressed by Wilson) to absolute and principled refusal to serve, American civilians at home reflected a comparable range of attitude and behavior. As war began, Wilson said, "It is not an army that we must train for war, but a nation." To carry out that task, to mobilize minds as well as men and matériel, the Wilson administration, assisted by the Congress and by private citizens, turned the nation into a virtual surveillance state. The Committee on Public Information, chaired by Wilson's appointee George Creel, set 150,000 workers to the task of publicizing and propagandizing the virtues of America and its allies and the heinous crimes and cruelties of Germany. Wilson's postmaster general, with the president's approval, banned antiwar literature from the mail. Wilson's attorney general, with the president's approval, prosecuted cases arising under the Espionage Act of 1917 and the Sedition Act of 1918, acts designed to silence, and if necessary to imprison, critics of the war. Eugene V. Debs wound up in Atlanta federal penitentiary, following his arrest and conviction for speaking out in opposition to the war.

When the United States entered the war, Wilson told a friend that war "required illiberalism at home to reinforce the man at the front" and that a "spirit of ruthless brutality" would enter American life. Required or not, illiberalism and brutality came, and the Wilson administration did little to hinder their coming. Alongside the Wilsonians, carrying on their censorship and repression, ran private vigilante groups — the Boy Spies of America, the Sedition Slammers, the Terrible Threateners, the Knights of America — who tarred and feathered and otherwise harassed and sometimes even murdered Americans who seemed pro-German, or who were merely critics of the war, or who refused to buy war bonds, or who refused to stand up when the national anthem was played. While some Americans were ostensibly fighting for democracy abroad, others were undermining it at home. The wartime hysteria over things German turned into hysteria over things Russian in 1919-1920, and Wilson paid no more attention to violations of civil liberties in the Red Scare after the war than he paid to violations during the war.

During Wilson's second term in the White House, progressivism was perverted into suppression. Abroad, however, America's contribution of men and matériel to the Allies on the Western Front was crucial in the last months of the war, and when the war ended on November 11, 1918, Wilson announced from the White House, "Everything for which America fought has been accomplished. It will now be our fortunate duty to assist by example, by sober, friendly counsel and by material aid in the establishment of just democracy throughout the world."

The Peace Settlement

For many weeks Wilson had worked for the armistice now reached. Early in October, the German government had asked Wilson "to take steps necessary for the restoration of peace." Through October and into November, Wilson had maneuvered his fellow Allies and the defeated Germans into accepting an armistice on Wilsonian terms. Both the Allies and the Germans entered the armistice understanding that

Wilson's Fourteen Points of January, 1918, along with his subsequent statements of principles, would provide the basis for peace negotiations soon to begin in Paris.

Months before the war ended, Wilson began to concentrate on formulating the postwar peace settlement. After November, 1918, the task came more and more to possess him until, finally, he all but abdicated leadership at home in desperate pursuit of his diplomatic goals abroad. Between December, 1918, and July, 1919, Wilson spent only ten days in the United States, so preoccupied was he with the peace conference in Paris. He came home for good in July, but in September he suffered a stroke that left him partly paralyzed. For the next seven months, he was bedridden and out of touch with the nation as it stumbled through 1919-1920 toward the "normalcy" of Warren G. Harding. In December, 1919, a veteran newspaperman wrote that in Washington there was "no government, no policies. . . . The Congress is chaotic. There is no leadership worthy of the name." It is far from certain that a more healthy and active Wilson could have prevented the national spiral downward from armistice exhilaration and hopes for postwar reconstruction reforms to the brutal suppressions of the Red Scare of 1919-1920, but clearly Wilson did nothing to halt the country's drift rightward. Yet if Wilson defaulted on leadership at home after the war, he became in international politics a figure of renown.

On November 18, 1918, when Wilson announced that he was going to Paris, debate broke out at once over his decision. Criticism ranged from trivial to telling: His trip was unconstitutional, unprecedented, unseemly; Wilson would be a poor negotiator in Paris, where he would become enmeshed in personal quarrels, but an able one in Washington, where he could remain aloof and yet influential. Many Republicans resented Wilson's presumption that in Paris he would speak for all of America. Wilson had campaigned for a Democratic majority in the recent congressional election and had made the forthcoming peace conference a party issue, only to see his party lose heavily to the Republicans. Out of partisanship if not from conviction, Republicans now declared Wilson repudiated, and they objected to his presence in Paris. Wilson intensified this Republican partisanship—and made all but inevitable the Republican opposition to the treaty that he brought home in July, 1919—when he failed to take Republican advisers with him to Paris, although even had he done so he would have given them scant heed, just as he mostly ignored the Democrats who did accompany him. This was to be, essentially, Woodrow Wilson's great and solitary mission.

On December 4, 1918, Wilson embarked for Europe aboard the *George Washington*. In London and in Paris, he received frenzied and spontaneous acclaim from huge, delirious crowds that pressed about his carriage. Wilson, as John Maynard Keynes expressed it in a famous essay, was "the man of destiny, who, coming from the West, was to bring healing to the wounds of the ancient parent of his civilization and lay for us the foundations of the future." If Wilson had a messiah complex when he arrived in Europe, his reception heightened it. The masses in England and France who adored Wilson, however, also hated the Germans and were set on revenge and recompense, and British prime minister David Lloyd George and French premier Georges Clemenceau, the two men who with Wilson thrashed out the Paris peace treaty, were far more responsible to their own people than to Woodrow Wilson.

Both Clemenceau and Lloyd George found Wilson boring and exasperating, with his prim, missionary manner, his thoughts for the day typed out on his own typewriter and delivered as from a pulpit—his "sermonettes," Clemenceau called them—and above all his points and principles that he brought to every meeting of the peace conference. Clemenceau grumbled that dealing with Wilson was like dealing with Jesus Christ. A more caustic observer saw Wilson, in his dealings with Lloyd George and Clemenceau, behaving like "a long-faced virgin trapped in a bawdy house and calling in violent tones for a glass of lemonade." As one historian has said, more prosaically and accurately, the moment Wilson set foot in the same room with Clemenceau and Lloyd George he was doomed, "overborne by their infinitely nimbler wits, their irresistibly stronger wills, . . . two of the most determined and resourceful politicians in history."

Between January and June, 1919, in the Paris suburb of Versailles, Wilson and the Allied representatives—except for Russians—hammered out the Treaty of Versailles. Russia sent no representative spokesperson to Paris, but Bolshevik Russia hovered like a specter over the Paris proceedings. By January, 1919, when the peace conference opened, Wilson had spent more than a year groping for a policy toward Russia. When the February, 1917, revolution overthrew the czarist government, Wilson promptly recognized the new provisional regime and even dispatched a goodwill mission to Russia in the spring of 1917.

When the Bolsheviks—V. I. Lenin, Leon Trotsky, and company—seized control of Russia in October, 1917, Wilson chose not to extend diplomatic recognition. United States-Russian relations began immediately to deteriorate, so much so that some analysts have located the beginnings of the Cold War of mid-century in this period following the Bolshevik Revolution of 1917.

In the summer of 1918, Wilson ordered American forces into Russia. Some five thousand U.S. troops landed at Archangel on the Baltic, alongside twenty-four hundred British and nine hundred French troops. Nine thousand more Americans moved into Vladivostok on the Pacific coast of Russia, as did seventy-two thousand Japanese troops. Speculation over these landings has been abundant ever since they occurred, with five or six basic interpretations put forward: Wilson intervened to help the anti-Bolshevik forces in Russia regain power and crush the Bolshevik Revolution; he intervened to resume the eastern front war against Germany, since the Brest-Litovsk Treaty of March, 1918, between the Germans and the Bolsheviks had ended war in the east; he intervened in the name of self-determination of peoples, hoping that the American troops in Vladivostok, for example, would help rescue several thousand Czech prisoners of war who had escaped and were trying to get back home and fight the Germans; he intervened in Siberia to keep an eye on the Japanese and to guarantee a continued Open Door policy in Asia at the end of the war; he intervened in Archangel because the British and the French—openly and sharply anti-Bolshevik—wanted him to, and he was anxious to maintain good relations with these Allies as peace talks drew near; he intervened to strike at the Bolsheviks because he believed they were actually German agents.

Wilson and his advisers may never have developed a "policy" toward the Russian Revolution. They may have been confused and uncertain of just what they were doing, as well as why they were doing it. Rather than a deliberate and reasoned scheme, Wilson's Russian diplomacy may have been a day-to-day matter, turning on the contingent and the unforeseen, although perhaps in retrospect moving in one direction more than in another. Whatever the motive or design that had driven Wilson to order troops to Russia, his attitude toward the Bolsheviks was inseparable from his goals and strategies at the peace conference. Wilson's aims and methods at Paris ran head-on into conflict with those of Lenin, who, although not invited to Paris and scornful of its deliberations, was as vital a figure in those deliberations as any one at the conference. Wilson proposed to change Europe, if not the entire world, into an American image (or at least Wilson's image of America), to the advantage of liberal capitalism everywhere. Lenin was trying, by revolutionary violence, to bring about a new social and economic order that in

theory held no place for capitalism, liberal democracy, or nation-states—the very things Wilson came to Paris to sustain and to spread.

Wilson in Paris confronted Lenin in absentia. He confronted Lloyd George and Clemenceau face to face. Although they, too, were perhaps haunted by the specter of bolshevism, they were patently scornful of Wilson's sermonettes and the kind of peace settlement he wanted to make with Germany. Again and again, from January when the conference opened to June when it ended, Wilson found himself forced to compromise one after another of his Fourteen Points. His slogan about the self-determination of peoples, his plea to exact no punitive indemnities from the Germans, his call for "open covenants of peace openly arrived at," his cry for a peace between equals ran up against the hard realities of European history, as read and lived and remembered by Clemenceau and Lloyd George. Wilson also from time to time in his negotiations stumbled into compromise unwittingly, owing to his own ignorance. When he promised Italy the South Tyrol, he did not know its population was Austrian. When he approved the boundaries of the newly created Czechoslovakia, he did not know that two million Germans lived within those boundaries.

Other compromises he knew he was making. Each time he compromised, each time he accepted French occupation of German territory, British and French mandates over former German and Turkish territory, British and French demands for heavy reparations from Germany, or creation of national boundaries in Eastern Europe that did violence to his principle of national self-determination, he fell back in desperate hope on his fourteenth point, a League of Nations. He had envisioned drawing up at Paris a "peace without victory," a term that prompted one pundit to remark that there were three sides at Paris: the winners, the losers, and Wilson. Each compromise he made rendered the peace settlement less just and hence more certain to fail, to lead to war, not peace. A

League of Nations, with the United States as an essential member, became an obsession with him. Owing to the treaty's imperfections, Wilson needed the League of Nations to forestall the wars that the treaty's terms might engender, and without a lasting peace he had no justification for having led his country into war.

Wilson agreed that Britain and France could, by treaty, demand massive reparations from Germany and in the infamous Article 231, the "war guilt" clause of the treaty, assign Germany full responsibility for starting the war. In return for these blatant compromises with his Fourteen Points, Wilson received support for his proposed league. His obsession about the league may have developed not only because of the compromises he had struck with his principles but also because of his sickness of body and mind. On April 3, he suffered an attack of coughing, vomiting, and high fever that may have been caused by a cerebral vascular occlusion, complicated by a viral inflammation of the brain. Whatever his illness, he became a changed man after the attack: He was forgetful. He stumbled. He was paranoid about his French servants. He groped for ideas, worried needlessly about trivial matters, was irascible. He held some of his ideas ever more rigidly, especially about the league. He had compromised enough. On the league he would not budge. The league would be his and the world's salvation.

On June 28, 1919, a German delegation, after waiting for days in a Paris hotel, signed the Treaty of Versailles. Wilson returned to the United States and on July 10, 1919, presented the treaty to the Senate for its consideration. If the Senate ratified it by the necessary two-thirds vote, America's war with Germany would officially end and, more significant, the United States would become a member of the League of Nations. Wilson, by way of a league constitution or "covenant" written into the treaty, had managed to make ratification of the treaty inseparable from American membership in the league. It was this inseparability of treaty and league that led to Wilson's undoing.

While Wilson and the Europeans had entered into their parlays, running from January to June, Americans demobilized, readjusted from war to peace, moved toward the Red Scare, and from time to time talked about the peace conference. Even before the peace conference opened, the league became an acrimonious issue. Republican Senator William E. Borah of Idaho voiced his objections as early as December, 1918. Borah did not propose to surrender to a league "the power to say when war shall be waged," the power to "conscript American boys and take them to Europe to settle differences." Borah was close to the archetypal isolationist. Republican Henry Cabot Lodge of Massachusetts, chair of the Senate Foreign Relations Committee and arch enemy of Woodrow Wilson, was a fervent expansionist, who objected to the league not because it would involve the United States in world affairs but because it would, in his view, restrain American freedom of action in the world.

Neither Lodge nor Borah spoke for the majority of the Senate. When Wilson presented the treaty to that body for consideration, forty-three Democrats and one Republican proposed ratification, without qualification. Fifteen Republicans supported the treaty except for a few "mild reservations." Twenty Republicans expressed "strong reservations" with regard to the treaty's terms, mostly about the league. Twelve Republicans and three Democrats were "irreconcilably" opposed to the treaty in any form, and Borah vowed war to the death on "the unholy thing with the holy name." On September 10, 1919, the Senate voted on the treaty with numerous amendments and reservations attached. Wilsonian Democrats defeated them all. Again in November the Senate voted, again with various reservations attached (Lodge puckishly offered fourteen of them), and again the treaty failed to pass.

Wilson had opposed every reservation

raised. He was convinced of his own rectitude and convinced that the treaty was the best one he could have negotiated in the circumstances. Above all, he regarded ratification and American entry into the league as a matter of his and America's moral salvation. Having failed to gain approval from the Senate, Wilson went to the people. While on a westward tour in the fall of 1919 trying to arouse support for the treaty, he collapsed in Pueblo, Colorado, and was brought home to the White House where he remained, sick and all but shut off, for seven months, from the nation and from the Senate deliberations over the treaty. Suffering from an occlusion of the right middle cerebral artery, he was completely paralyzed on his left side and had lost vision in the left half fields of both eyes. His voice became weak and his speech lost its resonance and fluency. As a result of the stroke, Wilson developed what neurosurgeon Edwin Weinstein, in a recent medical biography, analyzes as anosognosia—literally, "lack of knowledge of disease." Wilson did not deny that he was physically ill, but he did deny that he was unable to continue carrying on his duties.

In November, 1919, the Senate cast its second vote on the treaty, as amended by numerous reservations including the fourteen from Lodge, and following Wilson's directive, the Senate Democrats joined with Republican irreconcilables and rejected it. In March, 1920, for a third time the Senate voted on the treaty with reservations attached; Wilson again ordered his loyal followers to reject and once more the treaty failed to pass. On May 15, 1920, by joint resolution, Congress repealed its war resolution of April, 1917, against the Central Powers and reserved to the United States all rights expressed in the Treaty of Versailles. Wilson vetoed the resolution. The United States did not ratify the Treaty of Versailles and did not enter the League of Nations.

Wilson clung to his belief that the United States should and would enter the league. During the 1920 presidential campaign, he expressed the hope that the election would be a "solemn referendum" on the league, a vote for Democrat James M. Cox registering a vote for the league and a vote for Republican Warren G. Harding a vote against it. Harding drubbed Cox in the election, but it would be a distortion to say that his lopsided victory reflected American opposition to the league. Neither candidate had taken a distinctive position on the league, and a number of prominent Republicans, such as William Howard Taft, were outspoken in support of it. Yet if the election was not the solemn referendum on the league that he had hoped for, it was a cruel referendum on Woodrow Wilson. Some five weeks before Harding's election, Herbert Hoover wrote to a friend, "Since the Armistice, the present administration has made a failure by all the tests that we can apply. . . . The responsibilities of government should now, therefore, be transferred." "The people," wrote one historian, "were tired of star-reaching idealism, bothersome do-goodism, and moral overstrain. . . . Eager to lapse back into 'normalcy,' they were willing to accept a second-rate President—and they got a third-rate one." On March 4, 1921, Wilson and Harding rode down Pennsylvania Avenue to the inauguration of normalcy, the careworn face and wracked condition of the great retiring president in stark contrast to that of his handsome, bumbling, smiling, inept successor.

The Last Years

For four years after his retirement Wilson lived in a house on S Street in Washington, D.C. Although he regained his sense of humor and his interest in language, he turned down offers to write articles and refused all offers to speak. In 1923 his health worsened and he became almost blind. He grew extremely depressed, became upset at any mention of death, and was obsessed with fears of abandonment. Late in January, 1924, he weakened badly. His personal physician, Dr. Cary Grayson, found him in extremis and called in two medical colleagues. As they were about to enter his room, Wilson whispered, "Be careful. Too many cooks spoil the broth." It was his last jest. He died on the morning of February 3, 1924.

The distinguished Wilson scholar Arthur S. Link once wrote, "There is no more tragic and searing story in history and mythology than the ordeal of Woodrow Wilson." Perhaps so. Yet to be placed by historians in the company of Washington, Lincoln, and Roosevelt as one of America's great presidents is success and not failure, victory and not defeat, triumph and not tragedy.

Burl Noggle

Suggested Readings

Blum, John Morton. *Woodrow Wilson and the Politics of Morality*. Boston: Little, Brown, 1956. A succinct biographical essay.

Buckingham, Peter H. *Woodrow Wilson: A Bibliography of His Times and Presidency*. Wilmington, Del.: Scholarly Resources, 1990. A good biography.

Clements, Kendrick A. *The Presidency of Woodrow Wilson*. Lawrence: University Press of Kansas, 1992. A solid overview of the Wilson administration.

Cooper, John Milton. *The Warrior and the Priest: Woodrow Wilson and Theodore Roosevelt*. Cambridge, Mass.: Belknap Press of Harvard University Press, 1983. An engrossing analysis of the contrasts and comparisons in two parallel careers.

Devlin, Patrick. *Too Proud to Fight: Woodrow Wilson's Neutrality*. New York: Oxford University Press, 1974. A definitive and exhaustive study of Wilsonian diplomacy from August, 1914, to April, 1917.

Esposito, David M. *The Legacy of Woodrow Wilson: American War Aims in World War I*. Westport, Conn.: Praeger, 1996. Examines Wilson's foreign policies.

Ferrell, Robert. *Woodrow Wilson and World War I, 1917-1921*. New York: Harper & Row, 1985. A volume in the New American Nation series that serves as a sequel to Arthur Link's volume in that series.

Heater, Derek B. *National Self-determination: Woodrow Wilson and His Legacy*. New York: St. Martin's Press, 1994. A good discussion of diplomatic history during World War I.

Knock, Thomas J. *To End All Wars: Woodrow Wilson and the Quest for a New World Order*. Princeton, N.J.: Princeton University Press, 1992. Explores the approaches that Wilson took toward foreign policy and diplomacy.

Lentin, A. *Lloyd George, Woodrow Wilson, and the Guilt of Germany: An Essay in the Pre-history of Appeasement*. Leicester, England: Leicester University Press, 1984. An excellent essay on an old and troublesome issue.

Link, Arthur S. *Woodrow Wilson and the Progressive Era, 1910-1917*. 1954. Reprint. New York: Harper & Row, 1975. An indispensable volume in the New American Nation series.

_____, ed. *The Papers of Woodrow Wilson*. Princeton, N.J.: Princeton University Press, 1966-1993. Link, considered the Wilson authority for scholars, chronicles Wilson's life using primary documents.

Link, Arthur S., and William M. Lary, Jr., comps. *The Progressive Era and the Great War, 1896-1920*. New York, Appleton-Century-Crofts, 1978. Lists hundreds of books and articles on Wilson and his era.

Mulder, John. *Woodrow Wilson: The Years of Preparation*. Princeton, N.J.: Princeton University Press, 1978. Focuses with sympathy and insight on Wilson's religious and intellectual development to about 1910.

Mulder, John, Ernest M. White, and Ethel S. White, comps. *Woodrow Wilson: A Bibliography*. Westport, Conn.: Greenwood Press, 1997. A comprehensive guide to the secondary literature on Wilson.

Saunders, Robert M. *In Search of Woodrow Wilson: Beliefs and Behavior*. Westport, Conn.: Greenwood Press, 1998. Examines the effectiveness of Wilson's leadership.

Stid, Daniel D. *The President as Statesman: Woodrow Wilson and the Constitution*. Lawrence:

University Press of Kansas, 1998. An analysis of the evolution of Wilson's views on the constitutional separation of powers.

Weinstein, Edwin A. *Woodrow Wilson: A Medical and Psychological Study*. Princeton, N.J.: Princeton University Press, 1981. A fascinating study by a neurosurgeon who brings the discipline of history and the findings of medical science and psychiatry to bear on the life of Wilson.